# STUDIES IN
# INTERNATIONAL
# LAW

BY

F. A. MANN

CLARENDON PRESS · OXFORD

1973

*Oxford University Press, Ely House, London W.1*

GLASGOW NEW YORK TORONTO MELBOURNE WELLINGTON
CAPE TOWN IBADAN NAIROBI DAR ES SALAAM LUSAKA ADDIS ABABA
DELHI BOMBAY CALCUTTA MADRAS KARACHI LAHORE DACCA
KUALA LUMPUR SINGAPORE HONG KONG TOKYO

PRINTED IN GREAT BRITAIN
BY WILLIAM CLOWES & SONS, LIMITED
LONDON, BECCLES AND COLCHESTER

# PREFACE

THIS volume brings together twenty-one essays which, with the exception of the fifth now published for the first time, appeared in the course of three decades and were dispersed over a number of legal works or periodicals. The theme from which the twenty-one variations are derived and which they illustrate is the interrelationship between and, indeed, the interdependence of international and national law, certainly distinct branches of the law, yet branches of the same tree. All the topics, though apparently relating to public international law *stricto sensu*, have benefited from the teachings of municipal law. Conversely, subjects prima facie concerned with municipal law turned out to have some connecting link with public international law.

The predominance of that theme meant that there had to be excluded from the present volume such other work (comprising more than twenty articles, not to mention shorter pieces, case notes, or work in the German language) as was devoted to private law only, that is to say, to the conflict of laws, to comparative law, to expropriation and its history, and to the law of arbitration. Contributions to monetary law were omitted, because they have, and ought to retain, another home of their own. Three articles on trading with the enemy and the fate of enemy property at present seem to lack actuality to such an extent as to render resurrection inappropriate.

The friends who suggested the publication of these collected (and selected) papers will judge for themselves whether they should regret the advice they gave. The author who accepted it will, he hopes, on this special occasion be allowed a word of personal lament.

In the first place, just as no painter could ever paint exactly the same picture again because his vision continuously changes, or just as the very same musical development would not a second time be written by a composer, so no writer would express himself in exactly the same way if he were to propound the same thought at a later date. Someone, not now identifiable, employed much more attractive language to state the stark fact that, however humble the process of creation may be, the product invariably bears the stamp of the moment of creation. It follows that, in reading lines written years ago, one is very conscious of the inadequacy of formulation, the need for better, clearer, shorter expression, the more polished version which then failed to present itself, but now seems to be so ready at hand. The printed word is cruel. There is no escape from it. Furthermore, the editor of essays is faced with innumerable editorial problems. They can only be solved by strict adherence to the original text, warts and all. As soon as one attempts the correction of errors other than mere misprints one runs into insurmountable difficulties: a case has been overruled; new cases have been decided and filled gaps that previously existed; new material may have appeared; Dicey has become Dicey and Morris and, what is worse, has in the course of time changed his views, so that criticism put forward years ago may no longer have any basis. Or material, existing at the time of the original publication, was then very regrettably overlooked and cannot now be added. Indeed, real mistakes of substance may have been made, or views which earlier appeared correct may no longer be maintainable. Yet such and similar circumstances had to be disregarded. The process of rewriting or overhauling, once started, would be endless. In fact it would be so impossible to draw a line that no start could be made. And as regards howlers, there is no alternative but to abide by Einstein's consolation that 'death alone can save one'.[1] Nor was it practicable to add postscripta. In many cases they would have reached almost the size of a new essay. Even if they had been confined to references to new material, these would frequently not have been helpful without extensive remarks of an explanatory or, occasionally, critical character. In short the printed word had to be left as it is. It will be for the reader to say whether its reappearance in unadulterated form is justified and approximates Goethe's test laid down, for a loftier species

---

[1] *The Born–Einstein Letters* (translated by Irene Born, London, 1971), Letter 42.

of writing, on 17 February 1831 in conversation with Ecker-mann[1]:

When a writer leaves monuments on the different steps of his life, it is chiefly important that he should have an innate foundation and goodwill, that he should, at each step, have seen and felt clearly, and that, without any secondary aims, he should have said distinctly and truly what has passed in his mind. Then will his writings, if they were right at the step where they originated, remain always right, however the writer may develop or alter himself in after times.

An author who had to spend most of his life outside the intellectual testing ground which academic institutions provide is particularly grateful to the Delegates to the Clarendon Press who, by accepting this work for publication, gave much encouragement to what is still felt to be a hazardous and perhaps presumptuous enterprise. He is also greatly indebted to the Curatorium of the Hague Academy of International Law and the editors of the *British Year Book of International Law*, the *International and Comparative Law Quarterly*, the *Law Quarterly Review*, the *Modern Law Review*, the *Transactions of the Grotius Society*, the *American Journal of International Law*, and the *Virginia Law Review*, who kindly agreed to the republication of contributions previously published by them. Finally thanks are due to Miss Christine Fellner, B.A., B.C.L., who prepared the Index and the tables of Statutes and Cases and assisted in reading proofs.

*London*, 12 October 1972

F. A. M.

---

1 Translation by John Oxenford, 1850.

# CONTENTS

# TABLE OF STATUTES

# TABLE OF ENGLISH CASES

# TABLE OF SCOTTISH AND COMMON-WEALTH CASES

# TABLE OF CASES DECIDED BY
# COURTS OF THE UNITED STATES
# OF AMERICA

# TABLE OF DECISIONS OF INTERNATIONAL TRIBUNALS

# I

# THE DOCTRINE OF JURISDICTION
# IN INTERNATIONAL LAW*

## CONTENTS

* From *Recueil des Cours* 111 (1964 i) 1.

# 1. THE DEFINITION OF JURISDICTION

## I

WHEN public international lawyers pose the problem of jurisdiction, they have in mind the State's right under international law to regulate conduct in matters not exclusively of domestic concern.

Some elements of this definition require further elaboration.

(1) The problem of international jurisdiction relates to the activities of a *State*, though it can arise also in the case of an international organization which, by the treaty creating it, usually is empowered to act within a limited sphere and which, by exceeding it, would be acting ultra vires. But jurisdiction in international law has nothing to do with the question of municipal law whether certain State organs have jurisdiction

in a given case, whether, for instance, a Court has jurisdiction to entertain certain proceedings, or whether an Inspector of Taxes has jurisdiction to set aside an assessment. These are matters of internal organization in which international law does not ordinarily have any interest.

(2) Jurisdiction involves a State's *right* to exercise certain of its powers. It is a problem, accordingly, that is entirely distinct from that of internal power or constitutional capacity or, indeed, sovereignty. There is, of course, no doubt that, as a matter of internal law, a State is free to legislate in whatever manner and for whatever purpose it chooses. But like all other attributes of sovereignty this liberty is subject to the overriding question of entitlement. The existence in fact or in municipal law of the State's power to do a particular act does not by any means imply its international right to do so. The American Law Institute's proposed Official Draft of the Foreign Relations Law of the United States of May 1962—hereinafter referred to as Draft Restatement 1962—speaks of 'the capacity of a State', when defining jurisdiction.[1] Others use the word 'power'[2] or 'pouvoir'[3] or 'authority'.[4] None of these terms is satisfactory. Although in a particular context they may be unambiguous, they should be avoided.

Jurisdiction is by no means concerned only with the problem of ascertaining the State which, in a given case, has the sole right of regulation. There are many sets of circumstances which, by their nature, more than one State may be entitled to regulate. To a large extent legislative jurisdiction is concurrent rather than exclusive.[5] Thus if A in Holland shoots at B in Belgium and if in consequence of the injury B dies in France, three States may have international jurisdiction. If two of them were to be deprived of the right to impose criminal liability, this could at present only be achieved by treaty. In the field of taxation numerous such treaties have been concluded and in due course they will perhaps lead to the acceptance of a rule of

---

[1] p. 25.
[2] For instance Beale, *The Conflict of Laws* (1935), i. 274.
[3] For instance, Cavaré, *Le Droit International Public Positif* (1951), i. 164: 'pouvoir légal d'exercer une activité juridique'.
[4] Holmes J., below p. 6, n. 3.
[5] Cf. Verdross, *Völkerrecht* (4th ed., 1959), p. 248; Franz Kahn, *Abhandlungen zum Internationalen Privatrecht*, i. 282.

customary international law establishing exclusivity of tax jurisdiction. But such a development lies in the future. It is no doubt evidence of the rudimentary state of international law and a matter for regret that international jurisdiction is almost always concurrent. But international lawyers may console themselves by the thought that not even the most highly developed federations have succeeded in evolving what has been called a rule of immunity, for instance, from taxation by more than one State.[1]

(3) The existence of the State's right to exercise jurisdiction is exclusively determined by *public international law*. Moreover, it will be necessary to turn to public international law to ascertain the consequences of the wrongful exercise of jurisdiction. Joseph Beale made this very clear, when he stated that 'the sovereign cannot confer jurisdiction on his courts or his legislature when he has no such jurisdiction according to the principles of international law'.[2] It was an unexplained and an inexplicably retrograde change of heart which ten years later led Beale to suggest the very opposite: jurisdiction 'is with us a question of our own common law, and not of a generally accepted doctrine of the law of nations', and is 'fixed by the common law'.[3]

Thus, to take an example which in a different context and in a more limited field has led to some discussion in Britain, a statute of the United Kingdom may provide that a marriage between persons either of whom is under the age of sixteen years shall be void.[4] It may even make it a criminal offence for a person below the age of sixteen to go through a form of marriage. Let it be assumed, further, that the statute is intended to apply irrespectively of the parties' nationality, domicile, or residence and irrespectively of the place of celebration of the marriage.

---

[1] In the United States of America many decisions of the Supreme Court had developed and proclaimed such a principle of immunity; they are discussed and summarized in *Burnet* v. *Brooks*, 288 U. S. 378 (1933). But in 1942 a majority of the Court overruled these cases and held that the Constitution did not include any guarantee against subjection to the tax jurisdiction of more than one state of the Union: *State Tax Commission* v. *Aldrich*, 316 U. S. 174 (1942).

[2] 36 *Harv. L.R.* (1922–3), 241, 243.

[3] Conflict of Laws, i.274, 275.

[4] See the Age of Marriage Act, 1929, and its interpretation in *Pugh* v. *Pugh* (1951) P. 482; Morris, 62 *L.Q.R.* (1946), 170 and Dicey, p. 260. The Act does not impose criminal liability. See further below, p. 58.

Such legislation doubtless constitutes an excess of jurisdiction; at what point the excess occurs and how it is to be confined and avoided is a question concerning the solution of the problem of jurisdiction rather than its definition which alone arises at present.

The consequences of an excess of jurisdiction are twofold.

In the first place, a State measure which is not supported by international law may involve an international delinquency, so that the State whose national has been injured by it may be entitled not only to protest but also to espouse an international claim for damages. This would be the appropriate remedy, for instance, if Britain were to enforce her hypothetical legislation by criminal proceedings against persons below the age of sixteen who marry somewhere in the world, who later happen to enter British territory but who have no other connection with Britain at all.[1]

Secondly, however, if Britain lacks jurisdiction to control the age at which marriage may be contracted in the rest of the world, outside Britain the attempt to exercise such control may be ignored or treated as invalid. This is so both in an international and in a municipal court. It does not matter whether the latter court reaches its decision by applying *ordre public* or, more simply and much more attractively, by giving direct effect to public international law,[2] for the result cannot be in doubt. It is supported by a remarkable English decision[3] arising out of a statute enacted in Malta and making void all marriages of Roman Catholic Maltese contracted otherwise than by canon law. The argument that the marriage contracted by Roman Catholic Maltese in an English register office was void was rejected, for, as Sir Jocelyn Simon said,[4] it would be 'an intolerable injustice that a system of law should seek to impose extraterritorially, as the condition of the validity of a marriage, that it should take place according to the tenets of a particular faith'. The Maltese attempt to exercise extraterritorial juris-

---

[1] Thus damages were claimed by France from Turkey in the *Case of the S.S. Lotus*, P.C.I.J., Series A, No. 10.

[2] The importance of this question which to some extent depends on constitutional law should not be overrated. See, generally, 'International Delinquencies before Municipal Courts', below p. 366.

[3] *Lepre* v. *Lepre*, [1965] P. 52.

[4] at p. 744.

diction was, therefore, ineffective and led to international invalidity.[1]

It is necessary to emphasize this, because the Draft Restatement 1962 suggests[2] that lack of jurisdiction should give to the State adversely affected only 'a claim that may be adjudicated in an appropriate forum'. Such a view is far too narrow and irreconcilable with the realities of international practice and the demands of justice.

(4) Jurisdiction is concerned with the State's right of *regulation* or, in the incomparably pithy language of Mr. Justice Holmes, with the right 'to apply the law to the acts of men'.[3]

It does not matter whether it is exercised by legislative, executive or judicial measures, though for the sake of convenience one frequently speaks simply of legislative jurisdiction.

Legislation is, of course, the most striking assertion of jurisdiction, but there is no reason why common law rules based on judicial decisions should not likewise be tested by the standards of international law. It is in evidence that on many occasions these standards have, in fact, guided judges in reaching their decisions.

Whatever form it takes, regulation may occur either by prescribing or by enforcing legal rules and one thus speaks of prescriptive or, more attractively, of legislative jurisdiction which designates a State's international right to make legal rules, and of enforcement or prerogative jurisdiction involving the right of a State to give effect to its legal rules in a given case. The distinction is strongly emphasized by the Draft Restatement 1962[4] and is indispensable to explain several aspects of the problem of jurisdiction.[5] Failure to observe it has led to much misunderstanding.

---

[1] Cf. *St. Louis* v. *The Ferry Co.*, 11 Wall. 423, 430 (1870): 'If the legislator of a State should enact that the citizens or property of another State or country should be taxed in the same manner as the persons and property within its own limits and subject to its authority, or in any other manner whatsoever, such a law would be as much a nullity as if in conflict with the most explicit constitutional inhibition. *Jurisdiction is as necessary to valid legislation as to valid judicial action.*' (Italics supplied.)

[2] § 8, p. 29.

[3] *Wedding* v. *Meyler*, 192 U. S. 573, 584 (1904); *Central Railroad* v. *Jersey City*, 209 U. S. 473, 479 (1908).

[4] § 7, p. 26.

[5] On the distinction see Johnson, *Bases of International Jurisdiction*, Report of the International Law Conference, 1962 (The David Davies Memorial Institute of

Thus it is obvious that a State, though entitled to exercise its prescriptive jurisdiction, is not by any means necessarily entitled to enforce it: a State may subject its nationals to military service, but is precluded from sending its officers into neighbouring States to bring its nationals within its boundaries. Moreover, the mere exercise of prescriptive jurisdiction, without any attempt at enforcement, will not normally have to pass the test of international law, for so long as a State merely introduces a legal rule without taking or threatening steps to enforce it, foreign States and their nationals are not necessarily affected. But this depends on the facts, and it is not difficult to visualize circumstances in which the exercise of legislative jurisdiction so plainly implies the likelihood of enforcement that foreign States are entitled to challenge its presence on the statute book.

(5) The problem of jurisdiction only arises *in matters not exclusively of domestic concern.*

If there occurs in a State a certain set of facts (such as the celebration of a marriage) which involves only persons who are nationals of, and domiciled and resident in, that State, and if these facts have to be considered by a tribunal sitting within that State, if, in other words, the case is entirely and exclusively domestic in character, there is no room for any problem of international jurisdiction, just as there is no room for any problem of the conflict of laws. No one doubts that, except possibly in the case of the infringement of fundamental human rights, the scope of a State's jurisdiction within its own territory and over its own subjects is unlimited. No theory of jurisdiction is needed to establish this proposition, just as there is no occasion to raise the question what law should govern. It is only when there is some foreign element, when the State purports to affect or reach persons of foreign nationality, domicile or residence or facts which happen abroad that the problem of international law, whether public or private and, in particular, the problem of international jurisdiction makes its appearance.

On the other hand this may happen even where the foreign

International Studies), pp. 33–5, who is perhaps too pessimistic about its value. It is accepted, for instance, by Bourquin, 35 *Recueil* (1931 i), 5, 100 sqq. who in the course of a valuable discussion contrasts 'attribution des compétences' and 'exercice des compétences'. For another helpful statement see Salmond, *Jurisprudence* (11th ed., 1957, by Glanville Williams), p. 75 who distinguishes between the territoriality of law enforcement and the territoriality of law.

element is no more than a contingency. For it is one of the most significant characteristics of the problem of jurisdiction that the international aspects giving rise to it may occur only indirectly or incidentally and may emerge, therefore, in any connection. If, for instance, a marriage between persons either of whom is under the age of sixteen years is void and a criminal offence and if the scope of such a statute were unlimited, it would, in effect, purport to regulate the conduct of foreigners abroad. As persons affected by such a statute may at some time set foot on British territory and thus come under the sway of British legislation, they cannot disregard it entirely. This is even clearer in cases where the legislation concerns trading relationships. People all over the world would have to take account of and obey such legislation merely because they or their property may become subject to it. Yet no State is entitled to impose its legislation upon other States. Here, then, is a source of serious conflict which the doctrine of jurisdiction must overcome. If it is said that almost all legislation may have such international implications and would be brought within the ambit of the doctrine so as to extend it extraordinarily, the comment would be justified. But it would also be in line with modern experience that almost all questions which are believed to be primarily domestic are liable to become the concern of international law.

Jurisdiction, it thus appears, is concerned with what has been described as one of the fundamental functions of public international law, viz. the function of regulating and delimiting the respective competences of States, 'de conférer, de repartir et de réglementer des compétences'.[1] The same idea is expressed, when in German reference is made to the 'Geltungsbereich' of laws,[2] or the 'Gesetzgebungsgewalt' of States.

---

[1] Rousseau, 93 *Recueil* (1958 i), 373, 395 who gives a long list of authors who have expressed the idea in similar terms. See also Batiffol, *Traité élémentaire de droit international* (3rd ed., 1959), p. 310, and Guggenheim, i.334.

[2] Verdross, p. 247 and *passim*; Dahm, *Völkerrecht* (1958–61), i.224 sqq. uses the less usual expression 'staatliche Jurisdiktion'. The conception of 'Geltungsbereich' has led to much discussion of a highly academic character on the Continent, but its significance is by no means obvious. See Zitelmann, *Internationales Privatrecht* (1897), i.40 sqq.; *Festschrift für Bergbohm* (1919), pp. 207 sqq.; Gutzwiller, *Festgabe für U. Lampert* (Fribourg, 1925); *Geltungsbereich der Währungsvorschriften* (1950), pp. 10 sqq. with further references p. 22.

## II

Legislative jurisdiction should be clearly distinguished from sovereignty.

The doctrine of legislative jurisdiction answers the question whether and in what circumstances a State has the right of regulation. If, and insofar as, the right exists, it is exercised by the State in virtue of its sovereignty. The distinction is, therefore, pronounced. It is the same as that between public international law and municipal law in general; the former is the higher law which decides upon the rightful existence of a power, the latter is the subordinate instrument whereby the State as sovereign gives effect to the power allowed to it.

It may be that, when one comes to define the content of jurisdiction and to say whether, in given circumstances, jurisdiction does or does not exist, it will be found to be determined by the conception of sovereignty. Thus it may be that, as a matter of international law, the jurisdiction of a State extends to the limits of the State, that jurisdiction is co-extensive with sovereignty, that it reaches as far as, but no further, than sovereignty. Whether or no this is so is the substantive problem which will have to be clarified.[1] If the answer were in the affirmative, jurisdiction would, in effect, be no more than a specific aspect or a concomitant of sovereignty, but even on that basis the two conceptions would not lose their inherent unlikeness.[2]

There are some who include in the heading of jurisdiction all questions of a State's territorial and personal limits. It is, of course, possible and, as only a point of terminology is involved, it may be innocuous to discuss, within the framework of jurisdiction, such questions as the right of States over their territory, the sea and air, over bays, islands or the continental shelf and so forth. Nor is it in any way objectionable to treat personal sovereignty as a feature of jurisdiction and, therefore, to comprehend in it problems of nationality, the rights over corporations, ships or armies, as well as such exceptions as arise from sovereign or diplomatic immunity. But the intrinsic or substantive right of regulation would seem to be a problem which is

---

[1] Below, p. 22.
[2] Probably Schwarzenberger, *International Law* (3rd ed., 1957), i.184 would disagree, for he regards sovereignty and jurisdiction as 'complementary terms'.

fundamentally different from the physical extent of territorial rights or the range of a State's rights over persons and which requires separate treatment. At this point there will be some who, not for the only or last time, will invoke the doctrine of sovereignty in order to ask whether it is not inherent in the notion of a sovereign State that its rights are absolute and unqualified and whether, accordingly, there is need or even room for the discussion of a right which every State must necessarily possess and which cannot be curtailed. It is, however, much too late to put forward a view of sovereignty which involves the assertion that it is a matter for each State's discretion whether or no it has a certain right. Wherever its international implications are concerned, 'jurisdiction which, in principle, belongs solely to the State, is limited by rules of international law'.[1] No theory of sovereignty can displace them. Although the contrary has occasionally been asserted,[2] a holding to the effect that a State is without jurisdiction is, of course, far removed from an attack on such State's sovereignty. Were this not so, it would be possible, in the name of sovereignty, to impose measures which are outside the State's jurisdiction. This would be an intolerable result.

III

If it is the function of jurisdiction to allocate legislative competence to States, it becomes necessary to establish its relationship with the conflict of laws, for this, too, has been said to be concerned with the delimitation of the competence of States. Von Bar, for instance, put this view forward towards the end of the nineteenth century[3] and numerous scholars have since made the same point,[4] among them Gutzwiller[5] who describes private

---

[1] Cf. P.C.I.J. in *Nationality Decrees in Tunis and Morocco* (1921), Series B, No. 4, pp. 23–4. For a valuable statement in the sense of the text see Cavaré (above p. 3, note 3), p. 167.

[2] Particularly in connection with the doctrine of the foreign Act of State. Thus a Florida Court said that to declare invalid a Cuban act of expropriation 'would be a denial of the sovereignty of a foreign State': *National Institute of Agrarian Reform* v. *Terry Kane*, 153 So. 2d 40 (1963).

[3] *Lehrbuch des Internationalen Privatrechts* (1892), p. 2.

[4] Some of them are collected by Gutzwiller, *Internationalprivatrecht* (1931), p. 1537, n. 5, or by Balogh, *Mélanges Streit*, i.71.

[5] ibid.

international law as a body of 'Zuständigkeitsbestimmungen' the object of which 'consists exclusively in the most appropriate distribution of the ambit of the various systems of private law'. Nothing different was meant when others spoke of a 'juste partage de souveraineté'.[1] In employing such and similar phrases scholars invariably visualize private international law in the strict sense as opposed to the conflict of laws which has, or should have, a wider meaning and comprises a large body of law usually, though somewhat illogically, banned from the field of private international law; international criminal, administrative and tax law are the principal examples.[2]

Such descriptions are accurate, enlightening and helpful, but they cannot, or at least should not, be used to support any conclusions or decisions in an actual case. Nor are they apt to form the basis of sound legal theory, though there are writers who have read more and, indeed, much too much into what is merely a phrase of elementary explanation.[3]

Rather it is worthy of emphasis that those descriptions, emanating from private international lawyers, are identical with the phrases which, as has been shown, are used by public international lawyers to throw light upon the doctrine of jurisdiction. So remarkable and striking a coincidence is likely to be the symptom of a deep-rooted doctrinal link. In the course of

---

[1] Pillet, *Principes de Droit International Privé*, pp. 55, 64.

[2] For a vigorous defence of the view that such branches of the law should be ignored by private international law see Batiffol, sections 245–7. This view, which is widely held and practised and about which Anglo-American writers seem to have so little doubt that most of them do not even discuss it, is, however, not free from doubt. Batiffol argues that in connection with international criminal law the French judge merely asks whether the facts constitute a crime in France. If not, he does not continue to ask whether any foreign law is applicable, and therefore one cannot say 'qu'il résout un conflit de lois'. But this happens also in private international law. The French judge who holds that a person cannot be adopted in France does not necessarily have to decide whether he can be adopted elsewhere. In any event, it would seem that the point in essence depends only on a matter of formulation.

[3] It may be sufficient to mention two. Maury, 57 *Recueil* (1936 iii), p. 364, in discussing the object and function of the conflict rule, speaks of and analyses two different solutions, 'la thèse de la délimitation des souverainetés législatives' and 'la thèse de la réglementation des situations ou rapports à éléments extranationaux'; Niederer, *Einführung in die allgemeinen Lehren des Internationalen Privatrechts* (1954), pp. 125 seq. distinguishes between the theory of competence and the theory of incorporation (by which he means, in effect, the American local-law theory and its Italian counterpart). One must express grave doubts about the value as well as the justification of such distinctions.

later discussions jurisdiction will in fact be seen to be much influenced by the history and teachings of private international law.[1] In the present context a preliminary question arises. Is there a special connection between international jurisdiction and private international law? Are jurisdiction and private international law perhaps the same thing, or are they at least fruits from the same tree? Or, on the contrary, have they nothing at all to do with each other?

The answer is that conflict rules are a product of municipal law, which has to stand the test of the international doctrine of jurisdiction. In other words, it is the function of jurisdiction to define the international scope which the municipal legislator is entitled to give to his enactments. The conflict rule implements and gives effect to the requirements of public international law. If jurisdiction provides the frame or limit, the conflict rule fills it in. If jurisdiction directs that in given circumstances a person, thing or act may be made subject to the law of a given State, whether it be private, criminal, fiscal or any other law, it is the municipal law of that State and possibly of other States that makes the person, thing or act so subject. If the doctrine of jurisdiction defines the States enjoying, in given circumstances, the international right of regulation, private international law decides which of several laws enacted in the exercise of such right shall prevail in a given country. However, public international law does not contain detailed rules regulating the application of this or that legal system. It merely provides the principles which limit the freedom or competence of States in enacting the conflict rule. In this sense the international rule of jurisdiction and the municipal rule are complementary. To illustrate the point: The statute prohibiting, and imposing criminal liability in respect of, a marriage between persons under the age of sixteen is, of course, municipal in character and origin. International law is indifferent towards it so long as it has no possible international implications. But if, for instance, it were to be so construed as to apply to marriages celebrated in foreign countries between foreigners, then the question would arise whether the legislator has complied with the standards of international law, whether he has acted within the limits of international jurisdiction.

[1] Below, pp. 16, 17 and 87.

It is implied in this approach that the conflict rule is a rule of municipal law. The almost daily legislative practice of States permits no other conclusion. It is, indeed, so obvious that no reference to examples or authority is needed to establish it.[1]

It also follows, to look at the other side of the picture, that the conflict rule cannot be said to be the same as, or to be derived from, or to be an aspect or an emanation of, public international law. With the exception of some provisions in treaties and a few principles which have become generally recognized by civilized nations public international law includes no conflict rules. It is perhaps open to some doubt whether even the 'internationalist' or 'universalist' school which has had many adherents, particularly on the Continent, ever intended to assert the contrary,[2] for none of them seems to have gone so far as to make the following type of submission: when, for instance, it is a question of determining the legal system which governs the validity of a marriage between persons under the age of sixteen, public international law demands the application of this or that law. Only if this is said and meant, would it be possible to speak of a theory of integral internationalism which treats the conflict of laws as a branch or part of public international law.

What has been said since the days of Story and Savigny and even of Huber, what is the true kernel of the 'internationalist' school and a doctrine of great force and persuasiveness is something entirely different: public international law contains certain rules bearing upon the conflict of laws; among them the rules relating to jurisdiction take pride of place; they must be complied with by a municipal legislator who exercises his right of regulation; they are, therefore, the standard by which the municipal conflict rule is measured.

---

[1] As to England see, however, *Dynamit A. G.* v. *Rio Tinto*, [1918] A. C. 292, 302 per Lord Parker.

[2] Not even Zitelmann, *Internationales Privatrecht* (1897), i.71 sqq. did so. His view was that public international law requires the municipal legislator to enact conflict rules conforming to certain principles of public international law. If he enacted a conflict rule of a different type, a judge sitting in the same country was bound by it. But where it was open to the judge to find the appropriate conflict rule himself, he had to apply the rules required by public international law as a (subsidiary) source. There is a vast difference between the suggestion that the conflict rule is a rule of public international law, and the statement that the conflict rule should be so shaped as to conform to certain principles of public international law. Whether such principles exist is, of course, another question, on which see below, p. 45.

The subjection of private international law, as of all other municipal law, to the doctrine of jurisdiction has frequently been denied. Thus an American scholar[1] believed he could safely make the following generalization: Where A in State X sets a force in motion which injures B in State Y and B goes to and as a result of the injury dies in State Z, either X, Y or Z, if it can get its hands on A, can apply its own criminal law to the case. What each will do will depend *solely* upon its own positive law, common or statutory, and not upon any inherent principles of 'jurisdiction' limiting its powers. Its choice, therefore, will have to be *purely* pragmatic—as to what, all things considered, it is *desirable* to do.

Another American scholar, speaking of the international effects of anti-trust legislation, states that 'there is no binding external authority to which the United States has submitted these questions' and that therefore 'the decision to restrict jurisdiction is a matter of national policy'.[2] Even Dr. Cheshire[3] has remarked that, while it is the function of the conflict rule to indicate the application of laws in space, 'a sovereign is free to provide, if he chooses, that the area over which a rule of substantive law, whether domestic or foreign, is to prevail, shall be wider than the territorial jurisdiction in which it originated'. Such approaches have serious and unfortunate consequences, but they also proceed from a misconception of the relationship between public international and municipal law, which is one of subordination of the latter to the former. Looked at from another point of view, they are based on a misconception of sovereignty; that neither the King nor the State *legibus solutus est*, that the dogma *lex supra regem* applies to both, is today fundamental to our ideas of constitutional as well as international order.

This, it is hoped, is an interpretation[4] of the relationship

---

[1] W. W. Cook, *The Logical and Legal Bases of the Conflict of Laws* (1949), pp. 13, 14 (italics supplied).

[2] Brewster, *Anti-Trust and American Business Abroad* (1958), pp. 286, 287.

[3] *Private International Law* (6th ed., 1961), p. 6.

[4] It claims no originality at all. It is merely a synthesis of elementary teachings of public international law and the conflict of laws—a synthesis which has for long been obvious to those representatives of both branches of the law who have some knowledge of each other's method of approach. It should, perhaps, be made clear that is it not intended to give support to Georges Scelle's 'law of functional duplication', another of those wholly unprofitable theories with which the conflict of laws abounds—the local-law theory mentioned above, p. 11, n. 3, and wisely discussed by Cheshire, p. 35, is a further example—and which has gained nothing from a singularly barren analysis by Wiebringhaus, *Das Gesetz der funktionellen Verdoppelung* (1955).

between jurisdiction (or public international law as a whole) and the conflict of laws, which is likely to prove its worth in practice and avoids the abstract and almost wholly sterile discussions of the subject which have filled so large a part of the literature on the conflict of laws, particularly on the Continent. It is an interpretation that is in line with the most persuasive teaching about the *raison d'être* and, indeed, the necessity for a system of the conflict of laws. For this is, as Savigny put it, the idea of the community of the family of nations, based on public international law. And although this has so frequently been misunderstood, it is the same when Anglo-American writers speak of the demands of the comity of nations[1] or, as a Swiss author recently said, the function of the conflict rule is international, though its origin is municipal.[2]

## 2. THE DOCTRINE OF LEGISLATIVE JURISDICTION (GENERAL PART)

THE doctrine of jurisdiction, as appears from the preceding discussion, is one of those subjects which touch upon both public international law and the conflict of laws. It stands somewhere on the borderline between international and municipal law and cannot be treated in isolation from either. This situation is emphasized by the history of the doctrine which has two different, yet convergent strands, and by its sources which are spread over a large and varied field. It may be that it is this multiplicity of tributaries that accounts for the surprising dearth of studies aiming at a comprehensive and penetrating review of legislative jurisdiction in international law. Although there exists abundant

---

[1] The language of the nineteenth century was in many ways different from that of the present day. Those writers who developed the idea of comity were not merely thinking of the State's duty to be courteous. They were thinking in terms of an obligation, of what today one would designate as public international law, This can at present only be stated or suggested, but cannot be proved without much closer analysis. See, however, H. Lauterpacht, *Cambridge L.J.*, 1947, 331. On comity, in the legal sense, see the telling remarks of Gray J. in *Hilton* v. *Guyot*, 159 U. S. 113, 163 (1895) and, generally, Oppenheim, p. 34, n. 1.

[2] Niederer, pp. 143, 145, 146. See also p. 78. The learned author is one of the few modern authors who attractively explain the 'dual character' of the conflict rule.

material on specific aspects of jurisdiction, not a single monograph seems to have been devoted to the doctrine as a whole.
Professor Rousseau's statement,[1] made in 1953, that 'aucun au-
teur n'a présenté jusqu'ici une théorie générale des compétences
en droit international', remains true today. There are even
established textbooks on the law of nations, which treat it with
a marked degree of indifference.[2] That those interested in
municipal law, including the conflict of laws, almost invariably
ignore it,[3] is perhaps less surprising if their deeply regrettable,
yet general, *insouciance* about public international law is remembered. The following contribution cannot attempt more
than a summary of an introductory kind.

## I

For centuries public international law (insofar as it existed at
all) and the conflict of laws were hardly thought of as distinct
branches of the law. Hence the suggestion that the origin of the
international doctrine of jurisdiction lies in the conflict of laws
would not have caused surprise in earlier days. Its correctness is
even today unlikely to be questioned, for a fruitful and effective
history of public international law starts some four centuries
later than the history of the conflict of laws.

It would be inappropriate (and probably unnecessary) to aim
at a detailed account of the history of the doctrine of jurisdiction;
such an undertaking would require a different context and an
author trained as a historian. It must suffice to point to a few
highlights in the history of legal thought. They are, perhaps,
almost arbitrarily selected, but have a special bearing upon the
doctrine that began to emerge in the seventeenth and took its
final shape in the nineteenth century. The thread which runs
through a period of about seven centuries is sovereignty and its
territorial character or, in other words, the territorially and
personally limited scope of the *statutum*, of legislation. To
discern and recognize that thread is important, because, when

---

[1] *Droit International Public* (1953), section 247, n. 1.

[2] In Oppenheim, for instance, the problem receives very little attention. See,
on the other hand Hyde, *International Law* (2nd ed., 1945), i.726, or more recently,
Dahm, i.254, where a fairly full discussion will be found.

[3] Beale, i. ch. 3, p. 273, is a notable exception.

one comes to assess the authority of the present theory of juris-diction, the depth of its historical foundation cannot be dis-regarded. The Roman law did not contain any rule bearing upon the scope of legislative jurisdiction. In later centuries, it is true, D. 2. 1. 20 was frequently invoked by publicists: *Extra territorium jus dicenti impune non paretur. Idem est et si supra jurisdictionem suam velit jus dicere.* But these passages contemplate the power of the judi-ciary, they deal with civil jurisdiction and it is only by analogy that they can be and, indeed, were relied upon for purposes of jurisdiction in the sense of these lectures.[1] It was as late as about 1200 that, apparently for the first time, it was said in Italy[2] that *statutum non ligat nisi subditos.* This rule, accepted by all later authors, was intended to deny the absolute and sole control of the *lex fori*: The legislation of the forum applies only to subjects, but does not necessarily bind aliens, for *statutum non ligat forensem.*[3] Such an approach, as Meijers has pointed out,[4] 'est partie d'une idée de la souveraineté de l'Etat'. Here one finds the first hint of the distinction between the domestic and the extraterritorial effect of legislation—a distinction which was more clearly developed when a century later Bartolus (1314–57) formulated the two guiding questions as follows: *Primo, utrum statutum porrigatur intra*[5] *territorium ad non subditos? Secundo, utrum effectus statuti porrigatur extra territorium statuentium?* These are the questions which to this day have not been finally solved. It is true that it is not now doubtful that within a legislator's territory legislation applies or may apply to all, subjects and

---

[1] In particular by Huber, *De Conflictu Legum*, par. 2; Story, p. 8, and Lord Halsbury L.C. in *Macleod* v. *Attorney General for New South Wales*, [1891] A. C. 455; see also Lord Selborne in *Gordyal Singh* v. *Rajah of Farikdote*, [1894] A. C. 670.

[2] By Karolus de Tocco. See Meijers, *L'Histoire des Principes Fondamentaux du Droit International Privé*, 49 *Recueil* (1934 iii), 547, 594; Gamillscheg, *Der Einfluss Dumoulins auf die Entwicklung des Kollisionsrechts* (1955), p. 80.

[3] See Gutzwiller, *Le Développement Historique du Droit International Privé*, 29 *Recueil* (1929 iv) 291, 317.

[4] op. cit., p. 629.

[5] Most writers print '*extra*' and Beale, *Bartolus on the Conflict of Laws* (1914), p. 17, even translates: 'first, whether a statute extends beyond its territory to those not subject; second, whether the effect of a statute extends beyond the territory of the legislator'. But this makes no sense, because it expresses the same thought twice and fails to bring out the contrast which is obviously intended. Gamillscheg, op. cit., p. 54, n. 2 has convincingly shown that '*extra*' is a copying error and that the original text must have included '*intra*'.

aliens alike. But the extent to which legislation has extraterritorial effect is, of course, still a fundamental problem. The themes formulated by Bartolus led to numerous and often somewhat unoriginal variations by later scholars. The kernel of a theory of State sovereignty, its internal strength and its external limitations, was at the back of their minds, though it was not fully developed before the second half of the sixteenth century, when Bodin (1530–96) wrote. Eight years after the publication of his principal work in 1576 his contemporary Bertrand d'Argentré (1519–90) seems to have been the first to develop the connection between *potestas* and *jurisdictio*: *omnis enim potestas extra fines potestatis attributae aut propriae privata est persona, et finitae potestatis finita jurisdictio et cognitio; ideo et statuta extra territoria sua sine usu sunt.* All State power, whether granted or original, has outside its boundaries only the quality of a private person, and where State power ends jurisdiction and judication also end; therefore legislation is without force outside its territory. This was the heyday of the statute theory with its distinction between *statuta realia, statuta personalia* and *statuta mixta* and d'Argentré's remark was primarily directed to defining the ambit of the real statute and the *lex situs*.[1] It was left to the Dutch school of the following century to put the final gloss upon his ideas 'by bringing in the conception of sovereignty'.[2] It was, in particular, Ulricus Huber (1636–94) whose short tract *De conflictu legum diversarum in diversis imperiis*,[3] published in 1684, was destined to have lasting and far-reaching influence. For him the conflict of laws is 'part of the jus gentium, a kind of secondary public international law',[4] as appears from his 'trois illustres axiomes'.[5] Translated into English, they read as follows:

(1) The laws of every sovereign authority have force within the boundaries of its state and bind all subject to it, but not beyond.

---

[1] Gamillscheg, op. cit., p. 69 and see pp. 101–3.

[2] M. Wolff, *Private International Law* (2nd ed., 1950), section 24.

[3] The text with an English translation was conveniently made available by D. J. Llewelyn Davies, *British Year Book of International Law* 1937, 49, 64, whose translation will be used in the text. For a summary of the maxims see also Cheshire, *Private International Law* (6th ed., 1961), p. 27.

[4] Gamillscheg, op. cit., p. 176, quoting Kollewijn, *Geschiedenis van de nederlandse wetenschap van het internationaal privatrecht tot* 1880 (1937), 134, f.

[5] Gutzwiller, op. cit., p. 327.

(2) Those are held to be subject to a sovereign authority who are found within its boundaries, whether they be there permanently or temporarily.

(3) Those who exercise sovereign authority so act from comity that the laws of each nation, having been applied within its own boundaries, should retain their effect everywhere so far as they do not prejudice the power or rights of another state or its subjects.

Of the first maxim Gutzwiller has said that it is deduced *ex summo jure et ratione naturali*.[1] The second was described by Huber himself as *certissimam esse, cum natura reipublicae et mos subigendi imperio cunctos in civitate repertos* (as 'absolutely certain, for it is in accordance both with the nature of the state and the practice of subjecting all persons found therein to its authority'). As to the third, it is again Huber who states that it is derived *ex commodis et tacito populorum consensu*,[2] from the convenience and tacit consent of nations, or as he says elsewhere,[3] *mutuae populorum utilitatis respectu, quod est fundamentum omnis hujus doctrinae*, from the mutual convenience of nations, which is the basis of the whole of this subject. Foreign law is applied, although *leges alterius populi apud alium directe valere non possunt* (although the laws of one country cannot have any direct force in another)[4] or, not by virtue of the immediate force of a foreign law (*vi legis alienae immediata*), but *accedente consensu Potestatis summae in altera Civitate*,[5] in consequence of the consent of the supreme power in the other state.

Huber said of the conflict of laws that 'the subject itself pertains more to the law of nations than to the civil law, since that which different nations should observe among themselves clearly pertains to the law of nations' (*ipsa quaestio magis ad jus Gentium quam ad jus Civile pertineat, quatenus quid diversi populi inter se servare debeant, ad juris Gentium rationes pertinere manifestum est*). If to this day Huber's principles, properly understood,[6] dominate and, perhaps, put the seal to any discussion of the nature of the conflict of laws, it is their effect, and in particular the effect of the first and the second principles upon the infinitely more important problem of international jurisdiction that gives them their peculiar weight and authority. It would seem that they were

---

[1] op. cit., pp. 327, 328.
[2] This and the preceding quotation are to be found in para. 2.
[3] Para. 9. Llewelyn Davies's translation of *utilitatis* by 'convenience' is open to doubt.
[4] para. 2.  [5] para. 9.  [6] See above, p. 15, n. 1.

immediately and fully accepted in the course of the eighteenth century.[1] This is not surprising, seeing that they were based on a long historical development, that they appealed to reason and experience and dovetailed to contemporary thought about State and sovereignty. Their essence was, though without reference to them, judicially approved when, speaking on behalf of the Supreme Court of the United States, Mr. Justice Story said in 1824[2]: 'The laws of no nation can justly extend beyond its own territories, except so far as regards its own citizens. They can have no force to control the sovereignty or rights of any other nation within its own jurisdiction'. And it was Joseph Story, the Dane Professor of Law in Harvard University, who restated them in the first edition of his seminal work on the Conflict of Laws, curiously enough without referring to what ten years earlier he had said in his judicial capacity.[3] Significantly, he called them 'general maxims of international jurisprudence', and, omitting the third which relates to private international law *stricto sensu*, one may summarize them as follows[4]:

(1) As every nation possesses an exclusive sovereignty and jurisdiction within its own territory, the laws of every State affect and bind directly all property, whether real or personal, within its territory; and all persons who are resident within it, whether natural-born subjects or aliens; and also all contracts made and acts done within it.

(2) No State can, by its laws, directly affect or bind property out of its own territory or bind persons not resident therein, except that every nation has a right to bind its own subjects by its own laws in every other place.

This, then, is what has become known as the territorial theory of jurisdiction. The expression is not entirely correct in that the extension of jurisdiction to non-resident nationals introduces an element which lacks territorial character. But, as Story himself points out, the jurisdiction of a State over its non-resident nationals can be enforced only within the State's own territory, not within the country of the national's residence. It retains, therefore, an aspect of territoriality.

---

[1] Some of the material is quoted by Story, *Conflict of Laws*, p. 18, n. 1, and see Professor Llewelyn Davies' article above, p. 18, n. 3.

[2] *The Apollon*, 9 Wheat. 362, 370 (1824). See already Chief Justice Marshall in *Rose* v. *Himely*, (1808) 4 Cranch, 241, 279, though his words may be understood to apply mainly to enforcement jurisdiction.

[3] He relied on other American cases: p. 20, n. 5.

[4] Sections 18–22.

## II

Story's general maxims were immediately and universally accepted and to this day dominate the doctrine of international jurisdiction. When in 1843 Foelix published in France his *Traité de Droit International Privé*, he defined his starting point by expressly relying upon and adopting Story.[1] Savigny in 1849 stated that he was not only prepared to grant the truth of the Huber–Storyan maxims, but would accept their greatest possible extension, though, with his usual perception, he did not think that they would greatly assist in developing rules of the conflict of laws.[2] And in 1855 Henry Wheaton, the public international lawyer, relying curiously enough not on Story, but on Foelix, reformulated the principle in words[3] which still appear in the sixth English edition published in 1929[4]:

Every independent State is entitled to the exclusive power of legislation, in respect to the personal rights and civil state and condition of its citizens and in respect to all real and personal property situated within its territory, whether belonging to citizens or aliens.

Since then almost all scholars in all countries of the world have expressly or impliedly proceeded from Huber and Story. In the British Commonwealth of Nations and in the United States of America the principle that 'all legislation is prima facie territorial', has been judicially approved[5] and the Supreme Court of Israel has described it as 'the cornerstone of the Anglo-American system'.[6] But it is hardly open to doubt that it is also recognized by the courts of other countries; thus the German Supreme Court had no hesitation in stating[7] that 'a German law is a priori to be considered as enacted only for German territory'. This is not the context in which it would be appropriate to multiply quotations. Much further material will have

---

[1] Sections 9–11.    [2] *System des Römischen Rechts*, viii.24, 25.
[3] pp. 122 sqq.    [4] By Keith: i.204 sqq.
[5] In particular by Brett L.J. in *Ex parte Blain*, (1879) 12 Ch. D. 522, 528, and the Supreme Court of the United States in *American Banana Co.* v. *United Fruit Co.* 213 U. S. 347, 357 (1909), per Mr. Justice Holmes on behalf of the Court.
[6] *Amsterdam and others* v. *Minister of Finance*, Int. L.R. 1952, 229 at p. 231 per Agranat J. on behalf of the Court.
[7] 18 April 1921, *Fontes Juris Gentium*, Series A, Section II Volume 1, p. 69. The decision which is not reported elsewhere gave a negative answer to the question whether a German Maximum Price Order was intended to apply to sales by foreigners of goods destined for Germany. See Enneccerus–Nipperdey, quoted below, p. 52, n. 2.

to be considered, when specific instances illustrating the application of the principle will be discussed.[1]

For the purposes of the present inquiry of a general character it is, however, necessary at this point to explain the foundation of the territorial theory of jurisdiction. Jurisdiction is an aspect of sovereignty,[2] it is coextensive with and, indeed, incidental to, but also limited by, the State's sovereignty. As Lord Macmillan said,[3] 'it is an essential attribute of the sovereignty of this realm, as of all sovereign independent States, that it should possess jurisdiction over all persons and things within its territorial limits and in all cases, civil and criminal, arising within these limits'. If a State assumed jurisdiction outside the limits of its sovereignty, it would come into conflict with other States which need not suffer any encroachment upon their own sovereignty. The territorial theory, therefore, expresses the idea of universality and mutuality; what the one State may or may not do any other State may or may not do, and the assertion that State A is entitled to take a particular step which may affect State B means that State B is entitled to take the same step and thus affect State A. Such a system seems to establish a satisfactory regime for the whole world. It divides the world into compartments within each of which a sovereign State has jurisdiction. Moreover, the connection between jurisdiction and sovereignty is, up to a point, obvious, inevitable and almost platitudinous, for to the extent of its sovereignty a State necessarily has jurisdiction.

Considerations such as these not only form the basis of the territorial doctrine, but also go far to account for its immediate and continuing success, for they are simple, cogent and seemingly accurate. Whether they overcome the real difficulty, i.e. the problem of the extent or delimitation of jurisdiction, is a matter which only the complex conditions of recent times have brought to the forefront and which will have to be analysed. It has been suggested, it is true, that the basis of the territorial doctrine is geographical[4]: The Anglo-American

---

[1] Below, p. 41 (Special Part),
[2] According to the Permanent Court of International Justice in the *Legal Status of Eastern Greenland Case* (Series A-B, (1933), p. 48) jurisdiction 'is one of the most obvious forms of the exercise of sovereign power'.
[3] *The Cristina*, [1938] A. C. 485, 496, 497.
[4] J. G. Starke, *An Introduction to International Law* (5th ed., 1963), p. 198.

preferential attachment to the territorial theory springs from the circumstance that in the territories under Anglo-American dominion sea frontiers predominate, and the free or unrestricted movement of individuals or of property to or from other countries did not in the past occur so readily or frequently as between States bounded for the most part by land frontiers. On the other hand, the European States take a much broader view of their jurisdiction precisely because the Continent is a network of land or river frontiers.

Such reasoning, however, is not convincing. It is open to much doubt whether European States take a broader view of the extent of their jurisdiction. Sovereignty is one of those facts of international life which are universal and the effects of which are identical and independent of facility of movement between States.

### III

Notwithstanding its somewhat elementary character, the territorial doctrine has not escaped criticism, to the evaluation of which it is now necessary to turn.

(1) The first attack was made in the name of private international law by two American scholars.

In an often cited article[1] Lorenzen rejected Story's maxims 'in so far as they suggest that the rules of the conflict of laws adopted by the English and American courts follow as a matter of logical and necessary deduction from the principle of the territoriality of laws'.[2] In support of this thesis Lorenzen gives numerous examples. Thus, he refers[3] to the rule that questions relating to land are subject to the *lex situs*. He says that the rule does not necessarily result from the exclusive jurisdiction of the State in which the land is situate, for many States recognize deeds relating to land as valid if they are executed according to the law of the place of execution rather than the *lex situs*. Or Lorenzen discusses the rule according to which chattels are subject to the *lex situs*, and points out that many questions relating to chattels are governed by the *lex domicilii*. He continues: 'To say that the law of the situs has "exclusive sovereignty and jurisdiction" with respect to chattels, is, therefore, only a vague and meaningless statement which does not express the existing law on the

[1] 33 (1924) *Yale L.J.*, 236, here quoted from *Selected Essays on the Conflict of Laws*, p. 1.
[2] p. 3.    [3] p. 3.

subject'.[1] He ends by speaking of 'the inadequacy of Story's maxims as a guide to the solution of the problems of the conflict of laws'.[2]

W. W. Cook[3] adopted a similar course, except that his arguments are primarily verbal and therefore even less attractive than Lorenzen's. Cook takes as an example the case of a resident of New York who owns land in California, which is taken from him by a Californian decree. Cook is concerned to show that the California decree, of course, affects and binds directly the California property and that notwithstanding the owner's residence in New York it 'binds' him. He says[4]:

it is impossible to create rights which 'affect' or 'bind' a 'thing' without at the same time also creating rights which 'affect' or 'bind' the person who has the rights relating to the thing. It follows that when this person is in one State and the 'thing' is in another, it is a logical impossibility to assign exclusive 'jurisdiction' over the person to one State and exclusive jurisdiction over the thing to the other.

Cook's conclusion is[5] that 'the postulates in question . . . contain inherently contradictory assertions, and so can never furnish a satisfactory basis for sound reasoning in the field of the conflict of laws'.

Private international lawyers[6] as well as those interested in semantics[7] will doubtless have much to say about the wholly unconvincing method of reasoning adopted by Lorenzen and Cook. The decisive answer to them, however, is that they have misunderstood Story who propounded, not rules of private international law, but much more fundamental, 'general

---

[1] p. 4.    [2] p. 8.
[3] *The Logical and Legal Bases of the Conflict of Laws*, 1942.
[4] pp. 59, 60.    [5] pp. 62, 63.
[6] See, generally, below p. 43. Since Story dealt with international jurisdiction, i.e. the right of regulation, he was, of course, not concerned with the specific application of the doctrine to the rules mentioned by Lorenzen. In any event, to take Lorenzen's first example, it would be open to the *lex situs* to provide that its own form must be employed, and if the *lex loci actus* is allowed to prevail this is the result of a decision taken by the *lex situs*. A similar comment applies to Lorenzen's second example.
[7] Cook's argument turns upon the meaning of the word 'bind'. In a sense the New York resident is 'bound' by the Californian decree. Yet it is equally clear that California cannot impose a personal duty upon and thus bind a New York resident: California would have no jurisdiction to require a New York resident to transfer to California all his lands, wherever they may be. This is what Story had in mind and expressed with such clarity that there is no room for misunderstanding.

maxims of international jurisprudence', of public international law and perhaps even of law as such. Although Story's maxims, if properly understood, do have a bearing upon private international law no less than on law in general, they express principles of public international law. As, probably on account of their lack of familiarity with this branch of the law, Lorenzen and Cook treated Story's maxims, not as what they were and were intended to be, but as a panacea for private international law only, the reader is relieved of any duty to embark upon further discussion.

(2) A wholly different departure from Huber–Storyan principles was initiated by the most authoritative exponent of public international law, i.e. the Permanent Court of International Justice or, perhaps, more accurately, by six of its twelve Judges in the *Case of the S.S. Lotus*.[1]

A French steamship, the *Lotus*, collided on the high seas with a Turkish collier. The latter sank and eight Turkish members of her crew lost their lives. When the *Lotus* reached Constantinople, one of her French officers was placed under arrest, prosecuted for manslaughter and eventually convicted in accordance with Turkish law which provided for the application of Turkish criminal law where a foreigner commits outside Turkey an offence against a Turkish subject. The question for the decision of the Court was whether Turkish law and procedure was in conformity with the rules of international jurisdiction. The Court decided in favour of Turkey, mainly on the ground that the French vessel's act could be said to have had its effect on the Turkish vessel and thus on what might be deemed to be Turkish territory and that, for this reason, the assumption and exercise of criminal jurisdiction was supported by traditional principles.[2] Even if the Court had not invoked the fiction relating to the locality of the crime, it would not by any means have been impossible to argue (though the majority of the Court refused to do so) that in the particular case of a criminal collision on the high seas the State to which the victim belongs was entitled to

---

[1] Series A, No. 10 (1927).
[2] See below p. 79. It should, however, be noted that the decision has, in effect, been overruled by certain treaties, in particular the Brussels Convention of 10 May 1952 (see Oppenheim, *International Law* (8th ed., by H. Lauterpacht, 1955), i.603) and the Convention on the High Seas of 29 April 1958, Art. 11 (Cmnd. 584).

assume criminal jurisdiction.[1] However this may be, as regards the general question of the territoriality of jurisdiction as a principle of international law, the importance of the decision lies in certain pronouncements of the Court which have suggested to some that no such principle exists and that a State's legislative jurisdiction is, under international law, free from any restrictions whatever. The majority of the Court said[2]:

> It does not, however, follow that international law prohibits a State from exercising jurisdiction in its own territory in respect of any case which relates to acts which have taken place abroad and in which it cannot rely on some permissive rule of international law. Such a view would only be tenable if international law contained a general prohibition to States to extend the application of their laws and the jurisdiction of their courts to persons, property and acts outside their territory and if, as an exception to this general prohibition, it allowed States to do so in certain specific cases. But this is certainly not the case under international law as it stands at present. Far from laying down a general prohibition to the effect that States may not extend the application of their laws and the jurisdiction of their courts to persons, property and acts outside their territory, it leaves them in this respect a wide measure of discretion which is only limited in certain cases by prohibitive rules; as regards other cases, every State remains free to adopt the principles which it regards as best and most suitable. This discretion left to States by international law explains the great variety of rules which they have been able to adopt without objections or complaints on the part of other States. . . . In these circumstances all that can be required of a State is that it should not overstep the limits which international law places upon its jurisdiction; within these limits its title to exercise jurisdiction rests in its sovereignty.

These sentences seem to propagate the idea of the delimitation of jurisdiction by the State itself rather than international law or, in the words of Sir Hersch Lauterpacht, they proclaim the principle of presumptive freedom of State action, and may, therefore, have to be read as countenancing a most unfortunate and retrograde theory. It can be confidently asserted that they have been condemned by the majority of the immense number of writers who have discussed them,[3] and today they probably

---

[1] It would not now be useful to develop the argument. It should, however, be noted that the question of the liability for damage resulting from a collision on the high seas is often held to be subject to the law more favourable to the victim.

[2] p. 19.

[3] For a particularly valuable analysis see Bourquin, 35 *Recueil* (1935 i) 5, 102–7, who states clearly that rules of jurisdiction 'dérivent de l'ordre juridique international'; Brierley, 58 *Recueil* (1936 iv), 145, 183; Rousseau, *Revue Générale*, 37 (1930), 420, 422 sqq.; Basdevant, 58 *Recueil* (1936 iv), 594; Fitzmaurice, 92

cannot claim to be good law. It is also true, as has often been pointed out, that they have only the status of an obiter dictum which should not 'mesmerize' even the most conservative adherent to the precept of *stare decisis*.[1] Again, the decision itself has, in effect, been overruled.[2] Moreover, the Court was concerned only with certain aspects of jurisdiction over crimes on the high seas and, notwithstanding the width of some of its opening remarks, there is no certainty that it was contemplating the doctrine of jurisdiction in general or any of its ramifications outside the field of criminal law. But even on the footing of the actual words used by the Court there is room for the suggestion that they are not as far-reaching as has sometimes been feared. The last of the sentences quoted above throws much light upon the preceding ones. The Court had stated that in determining the extent of its jurisdiction a State had 'a wide measure of discretion'. The Court ended by referring to 'the limits which international law places upon its jurisdiction' and which it 'should not overstep'. Perhaps it is the true explanation of the Court's statements that it intended, not to deny the existence of restraints upon a State's jurisdiction, but to reject the test of the strict territoriality of criminal jurisdiction which, according to the Court,[3] 'is not an absolute principle of international law', and to adopt a more flexible rule. Such an approach would considerably undermine the Huber–Storyan canons, but would not be inconsistent with the requirements of modern life.

## IV

It should, indeed, be obvious that the principle of territorial jurisdiction has to be reconsidered[4] for practical rather than

---

*Recueil* (1957 ii), 56 sqq. Cf. Lauterpacht, op. cit., p. 20 and pp. 359 sqq., and Waldock, 106 *Recueil* (1962 ii), 5, 165 sqq., who is perhaps less critical than most commentators.

[1] This point is well taken by Johnson, p. 34; see also Sir John Fischer Williams, *Chapters on Current International Law* (1929), p. 214, and Lauterpacht, op. cit., p. 361. This is of course reasoning peculiar to Anglo-American lawyers.

[2] Above, p. 25, n. 2.

[3] p. 20.

[4] Salmond, *Jurisprudence* (11th ed., 1957, by Glanville Williams), pp. 75 sqq. says that 'what is not so obvious is how law itself can be said to be territorial'. He continues by stating the territorial principle which he describes as 'only one possible answer'. One will agree with Salmond when he continues that 'it is an answer that can be stated only with great caution and with many qualifications'.

doctrinal reasons. What has to be assessed is the principle's ability to cope with borderline situations which its authors did not envisage and which have never been satisfactorily solved. It is at this point that, as the following few illustrations are designed to show, the principle fails to provide guidance.

(1) The complications of modern life are responsible for the steadily increasing reluctance to 'localize' facts, events or relationships. So long as it remains necessary to inquire whether certain facts have occurred within or outside the territory, one has to apply a somewhat mechanical test which is workable only by virtue of the view that in all but the simplest cases facts are deemed to have happened in more than one place. If A in Holland shoots at B in Belgium and if, as a result of the injury, B dies in France, the territorial test leads to the conclusion that the crime was committed in Holland, Belgium and, perhaps, France. This is a relatively simple set of circumstances. In many cases, however, it is very difficult to define the locality of an occurrence; much learning, acumen and even sophistry has been devoted to the problem in different connections. Yet a decision necessarily involving fine distinctions and based upon a review of steadily growing material is likely to rest on somewhat tenuous elements. Perhaps the most striking example is the well-known problem where a contract made by correspondence, teleprinter or telephone is concluded—a problem which, primarily for purposes of civil jurisdiction, is often of substantial importance. On the other hand, where, for instance, defamatory communications by wireless or television are concerned, where questions of passing-off or unfair competition arise in consequence of the distribution of advertising material in numerous forms and numerous countries, the territorial test is perhaps too readily satisfied and produces results which in a shrinking world may no longer be adequate. In short, a test developed in wholly different economic, social and technical conditions and at a time when corporations did not yet play a predominant role in international life is unlikely to satisfy a generation which is suspicious of rigidity and, indeed, of principles.[1]

(2) Even today it is impossible to quarrel with the proposition that the territorial sovereign controls aliens temporarily

---

[1] See Viscount Simonds in *Metliss* v. *National Bank of Greece*, [1958] A. C. 509, 524.

subject to his jurisdiction. Daily experience throughout the world provides much evidence in support of a firmly established and compelling principle. Nevertheless, it obviously requires some exceptions which the Huber–Storyan maxims fail to mention and the scope of which has received insufficient attention. Thus it would probably be universally admitted that if a State imposed a tax on the whole of the income of its aliens who are temporary visitors, who may be staying only for a few days to attend a meeting, or for a few weeks to spend a holiday, such legislation would constitute an excess of jurisdiction. Yet if the liability arises after a stay of six months (as, normally, it does in Germany)[1] no breach of international law can be suggested.[2] Even in the case of permanently resident aliens international law does not allow the territorial sovereign to make them subject to military service.[3] Presence within his territory does not give the sovereign such unqualified control over aliens as the test of territorial jurisdiction would indicate. Here, then, are further border-line situations which demand solution.

(3) The Huber–Storyan maxims would suggest that a State is always entitled to apply its legislative jurisdiction to its subjects resident abroad; though, of course, the local sovereign may, and usually does, restrict the methods of enforcing such legislation, this is frequently of little consequence, for in practice the mere existence of legislation necessitates obedience to it. In the course of the following discussion cases will have to be mentioned in which a State's policy of controlling its non-resident subjects has become subject to criticism; in certain contexts such a policy has even been stigmatized as an outgrowth of fascism.[4] Or suppose a Ruritanian corporation carries on a banking business not only in Ruritania itself, but also, through branches and wholly owned subsidiaries, in numerous other countries. Suppose further that Ruritania introduces legislation requiring all Ruritanian banks to disclose the names and assets of all their customers to the Ruritanian government. The Huber–Storyan approach would probably lend support to the legality of such a measure. Yet it cannot, or at least should not, be open to doubt that in so far as

---

[1] Section 14 of the Steueranpassungsgesetz (subject to exceptions obtainable in practice).

[2] See Oppenheim, p. 680, see below, p. 99.

[3] Oppenheim, pp. 290, 681; Dahm, p. 521.        [4] Below, p. 75.

branches and subsidiaries outside Ruritania are concerned the legislation will have to be ignored by them as lacking international validity. In this connection it is not without interest to notice the attitude of the Government of the Federal Republic of Germany. A statute of 1951 imposed the duty of exhibiting the federal flag upon shipowners of German nationality if they ordinarily reside within the Federal Republic. In the course of the *travaux préparatoires* the Government stated in terms that the last few words were necessary, because 'the federal law can impose duties only upon such Germans as are subject to the jurisdiction of the Federal Republic'.[1] Even if this may go far in the opposite direction there is clearly room for a reappraisal of traditional thought.

(4) The idea of the territoriality of legislation suggests that a State's legislation cannot be directed to the regulation of the conduct of foreigners in a foreign country.

There is, however, no doubt that if such conduct injures the legislating State itself or its nationals, the State may, in certain circumstances, impose criminal liability. The Turkish legislation which led to the *Case of the Lotus* presupposed that the offence was committed outside Turkey 'to the prejudice of Turkey or a Turkish subject'. This may have been unobjectionable in the case of a crime committed on the high seas, but it would be wholly unacceptable if an American who drives his motor-car in New York and knocks down a Turk would be subject to criminal prosecution in Turkey for an offence which, perhaps, exists only by Turkish law, if he were exposed to a penalty of which he had no inkling,[2] if the Turkish courts, perhaps, also assumed civil jurisdiction and applied Turkish law rather than the *lex loci delicti*. It is not surprising, therefore, that what has in criminal law been called the principle of passive personality, has, in the absence of severe qualifications, 'been more strongly contested than any other type of competence'.[3] Nor has it ever been suggested outside France, Holland, Luxembourg and Haiti[4] that international law would allow a State to vest in its courts civil jurisdiction over a non-resident foreigner

---

[1] 23 *Zeitschrift für ausländisches öffentliches Recht und Völkerrecht* (1963), 241.

[2] On these implications of the decision of the majority in *The Case of the Lotus* some members of the minority have commented. See also, for instance, Fischer Williams (above, p. 27, n. 1), pp. 218 sqq.

[3] *Harvard Research*, p. 579.     [4] See below, p. 67.

merely by reason of the fact that he has broken a contract made with a national.

The difficulties increase when jurisdiction is claimed in respect of the conduct abroad of foreigners towards foreigners. In international criminal law this is known as the principle of universality. Story does not seem to admit it at all. Yet in respect of piracy, counterfeiting of currency and other acts prohibited by the law of nations it prevails. Is it entitled to a wider range of application? Should it apply outside the sphere of criminal law? An American warehouseman negligently allows tobacco belonging to an American exporter to be destroyed by fire. Consequently the exporter cannot fulfil his contract with a British importer who suffers damage. Would international law permit Britain to assume civil jurisdiction in respect of an action by the British importer against the (absent) warehouseman?

## V

If the preceding remarks on the validity of the territorial doctrine of jurisdiction illustrate and establish its inadequacy, one would expect to meet with determined efforts at modernizing it. Only one such attempt, firmly based on the principle of territoriality itself, has been made. This is the Draft Restatement 1962 which has already been noticed more than once. Although it leaves much to be desired and is in many respects a poor successor to the outstanding contribution made in 1935 to the problem of criminal jurisdiction by the Harvard Research, it is unique and merits a short analysis.

The Draft Restatement recognizes four bases of jurisdiction, viz. territory, nationality, protection of certain state interests and protection of certain universal interests.[1]

The last two primarily, though not exclusively, contemplate criminal jurisdiction. It is more convenient, therefore, to deal with them under that specific heading.[2]

As regards nationality, the Draft Restatement proposes he abolition of the principle of passive personality[3]:

A state does not have jurisdiction to prescribe rules of law attaching legal consequences to conduct of an alien outside its territory merely on the ground that the conduct affects one of its nationals.

[1] Section 10.    [2] Below, p. 80.    [3] Section 30, subsection 2.

Within the realm of criminal jurisdiction the principle, we know, has been severely criticized.[1] Outside the field of criminal jurisdiction it has entirely failed to gain wide-spread application, still less general recognition.[2] Its formal disappearance[3] would make little practical difference. On the other hand, the Draft Restatement proposes to allow a State jurisdiction in regard 'to conduct of its nationals wherever the conduct occurs' (which is nothing new) and also 'relating to a thing, status or other interest of its nationals wherever the thing is located or the status or other interest is localized'.[4] This provision at first sight appears to be slightly obscure,[5] but it is probably no more than a possibly superfluous elaboration of the generally accepted rule just referred to that a national is subject in every respect to the jurisdiction of the State of which he is a citizen, though such jurisdiction cannot, of course, be enforced extraterritorially. It is, however, a grave problem whether national jurisdiction so stated does not go much too far,[6] and on this problem the Draft Restatement throws no new light.

Even more serious doubts surround the Draft Restatement's proposals as to the extent of jurisdiction based upon territory. In broad terms, the territorial test is so formulated as to distinguish clearly between conduct, thing, status or other interest[7] on the one hand and effect[8] on the other hand.

That a State has jurisdiction over conduct within its territory is plain.[9] It is equally clear that a State has jurisdiction over 'a thing located' in its territory. But where the Draft Restatement

---

[1] Above, p. 30, n. 2.    [2] See, however, above, pp. 30, 31.

[3] On the question whether the principle would, in fact, disappear, see below, pp. 78, 79.

[4] Section 30, subsection (1): 'A State has jurisdiction to prescribe rules of law (a) attaching legal consequences to conduct of its nationals wherever the conduct occurs or (b) relating to a thing, status or other interest of its nationals wherever the thing is located or the status or other interest is localized.'

[5] It is difficult to understand the difference between subsection (a) and (b). A State can control its non-resident nationals only insofar as their conduct is concerned. When subsection (b) refers to rules 'relating to a thing' and so forth, it only contemplates conduct, because the rule cannot directly affect a thing. Note also the peculiar contrast between 'located' and 'localized'.

[6] See above, p. 29.    [7] Section 17.    [8] Section 18.

[9] Section 17 makes it clear that it is irrelevant 'whether or not the significant effect, if any, of the conduct takes place within the territory'. This is the only place where reference is made to 'significant' effects. It is doubtful whether the quoted words are necessary and whether the word 'significant' means anything. Does the phrase intend to refer to one of the 'constituent effects'? See below, p. 34, n. 1.

puts 'a status or other interest localized in its territory' on the same level with conduct and with a thing, the difficulties begin. Thus one may ask: What is a status that is also an interest? What is an interest in this context? Where is a status localized? How is an interest localized? Do these words mean or achieve anything that would not be included in Story's simple reference to 'all property within its territory and all persons who are resident within it'? Unfortunately, the Comment throws no light on these questions, for it confines itself to giving an illustration which could not be more primitive: husband and wife are domiciled in B; the husband commits adultery; the wife petitions for divorce in B; the conclusion is that her 'status is subject to B's jurisdiction'. Is it conceivable that the contrary could be asserted?

Section 18 deals with jurisdiction in regard to effects within the territory and raises even more questions.[1] It contemplates conduct which occurs outside and 'causes an effect' inside the legislating State's territory.[2] In such a case the State where the effect occurs has jurisdiction if either of two entirely different conditions is fulfilled. Firstly, it has jurisdiction[3] if both the conduct and its effect[4] 'are generally recognized as constituent elements of a crime or tort under the laws of States that have reasonably developed legal systems'. Secondly, it has jurisdiction if[5]

the effect within the territory is substantial, occurs as a direct and foreseeable result of the conduct outside the territory, and the prescribing of a rule of law with a view to preventing or regulating such effect is not inconsistent with the principles of justice generally recognized by States that have reasonably developed legal systems.

The questions raised by these proposals are mainly concerned

[1] The predecessor of the section was subjected to searching and even today helpful criticism by Professor Jennings, 32 *Nordisk Tidsskrift for International Ret.* (1962) 209.

[2] The reference to causation which governs the whole of section 18 is perhaps a little unfortunate, particularly since subsection (b) (but not subsection (a)) contains a further reference to it when it speaks of effects occurring 'as a direct and foreseeable result of the conduct'. Is there in law any effect if it is not 'a direct and foreseeable result' of conduct? See, e.g., *The Wagon Mound*, [1961] A. C. 388.

[3] Probably general jurisdiction, not only in regard to crime or tort, although these are specifically mentioned in the text of subsection (a).

[4] Probably this refers to the particular effect which occurs within the territory, not to effects occurring elsewhere.

[5] Section 18, subsection (b).

with testing results achieved by them and with possible improvements and simplifications of phraseology. In substance the results are unlikely to differ from those produced by the traditional principle. It would appear, however, that certain of the worst features which in the past have been believed to be derivable from a loose interpretation of the word 'effect' are eliminated by the reference to generally recognized principles of justice. To base jurisdiction on nothing but 'attendant consequences or repercussions'[1] would become impossible. Yet the word 'effect' would not necessarily have to be confined, for instance, to facts which are 'constituent' elements of the offence. Accordingly, the Draft Restatement may constitute a reasonable compromise which in practice may not be unattractive. The general criticism which will probably be levelled against it is that it forces the rules of jurisdiction into a strait-jacket which will prove too tight. At the present stage of development and in the absence of that exhaustive and instructive documentation which made the Harvard Research so exemplary a piece of scholarship, a codification of those rules may be premature and unwise or, alternatively, should be attempted only if it is limited to broad and flexible statements. To put the point differently, even today the territorial principle in Story's simple, perhaps too simple, formulation may be preferable to a more elaborate and refined, but also more hazardous, version.

## VI

It is this very thought which leads to the question whether the time has not perhaps come for the international law of jurisdiction to liberate itself from the shackles of Huber–Storyan maxims rather than devote its energies to their modernization and improvement. It is, indeed, worthy of consideration whether there does not exist a different method of approach which may prove fruitful to international law and its progress.

(1) The problem, properly defined, involves the search for the State or States whose contact with the facts is such as to make the allocation of legislative competence just and reasonable.

---

[1] The avoidance of this practice was one of the principal demands made by Professor Jennings, op. cit., pp. 215, 218. He clearly pointed to the importance of attaching legal consequences to the 'constituent elements'.

It is, accordingly, not the character and scope inherent in national legislation or attributed to it by its authors, but it is the legally relevant contact between such legislation and the given set of international facts that decides upon the existence of jurisdiction.

The question thus formulated expects of the doctrine of jurisdiction a transformation not entirely dissimilar from that undergone in the course of the nineteenth century by the cognate doctrine of private international law. During the long period of the statutists this was derived from the grouping and the classification of statute law; were the statutes *personalia, realia* or *mixta*? The answer was found in their text, their content, their character. Gutzwiller has brilliantly described the idea and the technique[1]:

au lieu de prendre leur point de départ dans le rapport de droit en question; au lieu de déduire du pouvoir souverain constituant les lois les limites, pour chacune d'entre elles, de leur zone d'application; au lieu de prendre en considération avant tout la nature différente de droits subjectifs existants—ils envisagent les difficultés du conflit des lois sous un seul point de vue: pour eux tout le problème repose dans la règle de droit. C'est la loi par elle même, le résultat du processus législatif qu'il faut consulter. Sans avoir besoin de prescriptions spéciales réglant le conflit des lois, on les trouve contenues dans le texte des statuts; elles sont là, on n'aura qu'à les découvrir.

Although there were intermediate stages which for present purposes need not be explored, it was without any doubt only Savigny who revolutionized the subject by fastening, not upon the statute, but upon the legal relationship. In the words of Martin Wolff,[2]

he no longer asked, as the statute theoreticians ('the statutists') had done, what is the nature of this or that legal rule? Is it concerned with persons, things, or acts? Instead, he set out to classify the legal relationships, and it was his aim 'to ascertain for every legal relation that law to which, in its proper nature, it belongs or is subject', and thus to find out where a relationship has 'its seat', as he calls it.

Perhaps public international lawyers should now discard the question whether the nature of territorial jurisdiction allows certain facts to be made subject to a State's legislation. Rather should they ask whether the legally relevant facts are such that they '*belong*' to this or that jurisdiction.

---

[1] 29 *Recueil* (1929 iv), 312.    [2] p. 35.

As soon as attention is directed to the connection of facts with certain States, it becomes the foremost task, for purposes of international jurisdiction no less than for purposes of the choice of law in private international law, to identify the relevant points of contact, to localize the legal relationships. In pursuing this search private international lawyers employ as their tools various formulae such as 'the seat of a legal relationship', 'the nature of the thing', 'the centre of gravity', 'the most real (or closest) connection'. All of them have, in practice, the same meaning and effect.

Comparable phrases, similar tests and much useful material can be found in the field of constitutional law. Thus the necessity for drawing lines of demarcation has frequently arisen in British Inter-Imperial relations.[1] The Australian courts, have been confronted with the problem on numerous occasions.[2] But the most impressive and, at the same time, most confusing illustrations come from the vast number of cases decided in the United States of America, particularly by the Supreme Court, and bearing upon the right of the States to regulate matters connected with sister States of the Union. A foreign observer will hesitate long before he will venture to deduce a firm principle from the extremely varied and colourful picture produced by American discussions.[3] He cannot help gaining the impression that the decisive question is whether a State has a 'legitimate interest'

[1] See, generally, Salmond, *The Limitations of Colonial Legislative Power*, 33 *L.Q.R.* (1917), 117; H. A. Smith, *The Legislative Competence of the Dominions*, 43 *L.Q.R.* (1927), 380, and in particular O'Connell, *The Doctrine of Colonial Extraterritorial Legislative Incompetence*, 75 *L.Q.R.* (1959), 318.

[2] See, generally, W. A. Wynes, *Legislative, Judicial and Executive Powers in Australia* (3rd ed., 1962), pp. 86 sqq., and the cases there referred to. See also Cowen, 6 *Vanderbilt L.R.* (1953), 638.

[3] These are, of course, overshadowed by discussions and interpretations of the text of the Constitution itself, in particular the due process and the full faith and credit clauses. When the question is asked whether these clauses, for instance, *bind* a State to recognize the legislation of another State, a problem arises that hardly exists in public international law. From the point of view of the doctrine of international jurisdiction the material bearing upon this problem is confusing. In modern decisions or academic discussions that doctrine is hardly ever referred to. Thus Stumberg, *Principles of Conflict of Laws* (3rd ed, 1963), is not aware of it at all, although he has a whole chapter on legislative jurisdiction (pp. 51 sqq.) Apart from Rheinstein, 22 *University of Chicago L.R.* (1955), 755—an outstanding, though not always convincing contribution—the following writers should be consulted, though they are only of marginal interest to the international lawyer: Jackson, 45 *Col. L.R.* (1945), 1; Cheatham, 6 *Vanderbilt L.R.* (1953), 581; Weintraub, 44 *Iowa L.R.* (1958–9), 449.

in the subject-matter of its legislation and whether its significance is such as to 'outweigh' the interest of other States,[1] whether there are 'things done within the State of which the State could properly lay hold as the basis of the regulations'.[2] To put the point negatively, a careful perusal of American decisions indicates a tendency to abandon a purely territorial test and to substitute for it a flexible and largely discretionary notion based upon the degree of connection.[3]

(2) Since the doctrine of international jurisdiction is not at present concerned with exclusivity of jurisdiction, the legally relevant point of contact will have to be defined as indicating the State which has a close, rather than the closest, connection with the facts, a genuine link, a sufficiently strong interest.

Yet not every close contact will be legally acceptable. The question whether the contact is sufficiently close, though a question of degree, is answered, not by the idiosyncrasies or the discretion of States or judges, but by the objective standards of international law. All the circumstances will have to be taken into account, including, particularly, those to which the territorial doctrine attaches significance. These are in no sense to be discarded, but their presence is not invariably necessary or sufficient to support international jurisdiction. It must be possible to point to a reasonable relation, that is to say, to the absence of abuse of rights[4] or of arbitrariness. In the final analysis, however, the question will be whether international law, as embodied in the sources enumerated by Art. 38 of the Statute of the International Court of Justice, sanctions the exercise of jurisdiction, special regard being had to the practice of States and the general principles of law recognized by civilized nations. There will thus be definite barriers beyond which the exercise of jurisdiction is

---

[1] *Watson* v. *Employers Liability Assurance Co.*, 348 U. S. 66 (1954) at p. 73 per Black J.

[2] This is a phrase used by Brandeis J. in *Home Insurance Co.* v. *Dick*, 281 U. S. 397, n. 5 (1930). Among numerous other cases some of which will be referred to below, see *Alaska Packers Association* v. *Industrial Accident Commission*, 294 U. S. 532 (1935); *Pacific Employers Insurance Co.* v. *Industrial Accident Commission*, 306 U. S. 493 (1939).

[3] Cheatham, op. cit., p. 586, refers to 'substantial connection' as a prerequisite of legislative jurisdiction.

[4] The absence of 'reasonable relation to a legitimate end' still appears as the best definition of the abuse of rights. For references see 96 *Recueil* (1959 i), 92.

unlawful, there will be safeguards against any inclination to exaggerate flexibility.

The reference to the paramountcy of international law implies what one may call the requirement of non-interference in the affairs of foreign States.[1] More specifically, this important qualification renders unlawful such legislation as would have the effect of regulating the conduct of foreigners in foreign countries. It is not normally lawful for legislation to operate 'as applying to foreigners in respect of acts done by them outside the dominions of the sovereign power enacting. That is a rule based on international law, by which one sovereign power is bound to respect the subjects and the rights of all other sovereign powers outside its own territory.'[2] The difficulties in applying the principle of non-interference should not be underrated. The facts will not always be as clear as in a leading American case in which the Supreme Court refused to interpret an American statute in a sense likely 'to intervene between foreigners and their own law because of an act on a foreign ship not in our waters',[3] or as those put by Evatt J. in the High Court of Australia: could, say, New Zealand make punishable within its borders an assault committed upon French soil by a Frenchman upon a Frenchman? It could not, because the assault would 'bear no relation to New Zealand', because New Zealand would have to have 'some real concern or interest in the matter, thing or circumstances dealt with by the legislation'.[4] Conversely, could New Zealand threaten with punishment a foreigner who anywhere in the world assaults a citizen of New Zealand? Again, the answer should be in the negative, although the case is more doubtful.[5] In the last resort it is good faith and

---

[1] Rousseau, 37 *Rev. Gén.* (1930), 420, 444, speaks of 'le principe d'abstention'.

[2] *The Queen* v. *Jameson*, [1896] 2 Q.B. 425, 430 per Lord Russell of Killowen, adopted by the United States Supreme Court in *Lauritzen* v. *Larsen*, 345 U.S. 571 (1953) at p. 578.

[3] *Lauritzen* v. *Larsen* (preceding note) at p. 593. Of course, the question remains: when does legislation become intervention?

[4] *Trustees and Executors and Agency Co.* v. *Federal Commissioner of Taxation*, (1933) 49 C.L.R. 220, 235, 236. At p. 239 the learned judge added that 'the extent of extraterritorial jurisdiction permitted, or rather not forbidden, by international law cannot always be stated with precision. But, certainly, no State attempts to exercise a jurisdiction over matters, persons or things with which it has absolutely no concern.' Again, the question remains when a State has some sufficient concern.

[5] Rheinstein at p. 800 of the article quoted above, p. 36, n. 3, describes such a provision as an 'empty gesture' and as 'ineffective against one who neither comes

reasonableness in international relations that will be the rule of decision.

A further significant element in the process of assessing the closeness of connection will be supplied by what is a fact or an experience rather than a legal rule, namely the universality or mutuality of the character of jurisdiction.[1] Therefore, any contact believed to warrant application of a State's law to a foreign transaction will be an equally strong warrant for another State to apply its law to a transaction in the legislating State. International lawyers know that the remedy again lies in a policy of tolerance, reasonableness and good faith. As the Supreme Court of the United States has put it[2]:

in dealing with international commerce we cannot be unmindful of the necessity for mutual forbearance if retaliations are to be avoided; nor should we forget that any contact which we hold sufficient to warrant application of our law to a foreign transaction will logically be as strong a warrant for a foreign country to apply its law to an American transaction.

Or in the language of Mr. Justice Frankfurter,[3] 'the controlling considerations are the *interacting* interests of the United States and of foreign countries'.

(3) The conclusion, then, is that a State has (legislative) jurisdiction, if its contact with a given set of facts is so close, so substantial, so direct, so weighty, that legislation in respect of them is in harmony with international law and its various aspects (including the practice of States, the principles of non-interference and reciprocity and the demands of interdependence). A merely political, economic, commercial or social interest does not in itself constitute a sufficient connection. Whether another State has an equally close or a closer, or perhaps the closest, contact, is not necessarily an irrelevant question, but cannot be decisive where the probability of concurrent jurisdiction is conceded.

Such a suggestion is by no means out of step with some recent

---

into [New Zealand] nor owns any property there'. This is agreed. But if he comes into New Zealand could he be prosecuted? It is at this point that the foreigner's home State would be entitled to raise the problem of international jurisdiction. This is its 'element of contingency': see p. 8.

[1] Above, p. 10.

[2] *Lauritzen* v. *Larsen* (above, p. 38, n. 2) at p. 582.

[3] *Romero* v. *International Terminal Operating Co.*, 358 U. S. 354 (1959), 383, also 28 *International L.R.* 145 (italics supplied).

tendencies,[1] but special tribute should be paid to the valuable exposition by the late Professor Dahm[2] according to whom the extreme extension of domestic law

without regard to the foreign interests would involve the violations of the State's international duty to adopt in the international community an attitude consistent with the interests of the community. A State may subject foreign sets of facts to its jurisdiction and law only if their relationship with its own legal system is not too remote and the application of its domestic law to them does not lead to nonsensical or grossly unjust results. The subjection to domestic jurisdiction and the application of domestic law, therefore, presupposes a meaningful point of contact. Where it is wholly missing, the exercise of jurisdiction and the application of domestic law constitutes an excess, an abuse of State power, which could induce the foreign State to safeguard the interests of its nationals affected thereby.

The practical advantages of such a method of approach will have to be considered in relation to individual questions to which the following chapter will be devoted. But a few general points should be made in the present context.

On the one hand the mere fact that a person (including a corporation) is present within the territory of the legislating State does not necessarily make such person in all respects subject to the territorial sovereign's jurisdiction. What is required is a reasonably close contact between the person present within the territory and the subject matter of the legislation. An alien individual present within the territory for a day or so may be subject to duties of registration, but it does not by any means follow that he is also so closely connected with the territory as to render it lawful to subject him to taxation.

On the other hand the mere fact that a person not resident in the legislating State is its national does not necessarily make him subject to such State's jurisdiction in all respects. The rights and legitimate interests of the State of residence will have to be

---

[1] See, for instance, Jennings, *British Year Book of International Law*, 1957, 153. The same thought is frequently expressed in a negative form: no State has jurisdiction over facts which have no points of contact with it. See, in particular, Verdross, p. 221. Also, see the flexible approach which has characterized the practice of the International Court of Justice since its creation; *The Anglo-Norwegian Fisheries* case and *Nottebohm's* case are outstanding examples.

[2] ii.256, and 260. See also Wengler, *Völkerrecht* (1964), ii.937, who suggests that it is sufficient for the exercise of jurisdiction if those affected by the legislation participate in a manner corresponding to international usages in the facts localized within the territory.

considered. While a State is not debarred by any rule of international law from governing the conduct of its own citizens in foreign countries or upon the high seas, the rights of other nations or their nationals must not be infringed. Whether or no they are infringed can only be resolved 'by appraising the governmental interests of each jurisdiction and turning the scale of decision according to their weight'.[1]

It may be said that the test advocated in these pages would substitute vagueness for certainty. This would be formidable criticism if the principles of jurisdiction in fact were at present defined with certainty. But the simplicity of Huber–Storyan teachings is deceptive. The question, for instance, where a crime or tort is committed is subject to so much doubt that no certain answer can be suggested in any but the clearest cases; nor has the territorial test led to much certainty in the field of trade practices or taxation.

Finally, from the point of view of the progressive evolution of international law it would no doubt be desirable if the principle of exclusivity should come to be accepted for the purpose of jurisdiction, if, in other words, by common consent jurisdiction in respect of a given set of acts were exercised by one State only. Such a development cannot even begin while the doctrine of jurisdiction is embedded in the procrustean law of territoriality. It is, however, likely to be promoted by a doctrine which bases jurisdiction upon closeness of connection.

## 3. THE DOCTRINE OF LEGISLATIVE JURIS-DICTION (SPECIAL PART)

### INTRODUCTION

The suggestions made in the preceding part are of a very general character. They aim at no more than the definition of the basic point of contact which will confer jurisdiction upon a State. There remains the task of applying and adapting those suggestions to the principal specific topics which, in the past,

---

[1] This is another striking formulation of American origin: *Alaska Packers Association* v. *Industrial Accident Commission*, 294 U. S. 532 (1935) at p. 547 per Stone J. on behalf of the Court.

have given rise to the question whether in exercising legislative jurisdiction a State acted lawfully.

Seven such topics will be considered, although there are many more which this survey must ignore. Each of them would justify and, indeed, require a monograph. To write it would presuppose a comparative approach based on the most comprehensive research, for in each case the rules of municipal law would have to be ascertained and tested in the light of the international rule of jurisdiction. Each would involve the consideration of a vast amount of judicial and academic material which is unlikely ever to have been assembled completely. The following discussion can only attempt an outline, a broad picture, a statement of the guiding rules governing each subject. It will be based primarily, though not exclusively, on illustrations taken from English law.

It is sometimes said that the rules of jurisdiction which have been developed in several fields are 'established not by international law but by every country's own internal law by which they can be expanded or restrained in any way that may be deemed fit by the law-making agencies of the country in question',[1] and that, therefore, they should not be treated as part of the international order. Such a view overlooks that municipal law is one of the sources, or may at least be expressive of, international law; it also overlooks that what a State 'can' do it may not be able to do lawfully. The material of international origin which has a bearing upon the doctrine of jurisdiction is extremely meagre. The material of national origin is enormous. It follows that principles of international law will mainly have to be deduced from the latter category. It should be added that those who deny or doubt even the existence of rules of international jurisdiction cannot do better than to make themselves familiar with the selection from the available material, which follows. It supplies convincing proof of the fact that States have observed and adhered to limits of their legislative activity the details of which may not always have been clearly defined, but the substance of which is borne out by the reality of State practice. Professor Charles de Visscher has said[2] that 'la théorie qui ramène les droits étatiques à des compétences attribuées et repar-

---

[1] Rheinstein, 22 *University of Chicago L.R.* (1955), 775, 799.
[2] *Théories et Réalités en Droit International Public* (2nd ed., 1955), pp. 134, 135 (italics supplied).

ties par le droit international s'est trouvée trop en avance *sur les faits* et que la conception organiciste et hautement juridique dont elle procède n'est encore très largement qu'une vue de l'esprit'. It is satisfactory (and by no means the first time) that the realistic assessment of the sources of international law is the very weapon with which it will be possible to ward off 'realists' and their often unfortunate influence on law in general and international law in particular.

It might also be noted that the principles governing each of the seven topics are common to them all and that, therefore, there is no warrant for a method of presentation which treats the available material as pertaining to separate and distinct headings and thus precludes comprehensive investigation of the subject as a whole. Yet, in view of the lack of preparatory work on the doctrine of jurisdiction, it would seem to be preferable to adopt more traditional lines of inquiry and at the same time to invite the reader to follow his own process of blending: he will often find that material relating to one problem of jurisdiction has a bearing upon another.

## *Section 1*

### PRIVATE INTERNATIONAL LAW

### I

It is due to the close historical connection between the two subjects that private international law reflects the effects and requirements of the doctrine of legislative jurisdiction more faithfully than any other branch of the law. Private international law proves, in particular, the familiar reluctance to transgress those limits of jurisdiction which public international law recognizes, as well as the development from a strictly territorial to a more flexible doctrine of closeness of connection.

On the one hand, it is now accepted that the doctrine of jurisdiction does not by any means support the theory according to which a State is under a duty to enact 'one-sided'[1] or particular[2]

---

[1] Wolff, p. 96, uses this expression, which is probably not the happiest.

[2] This is the expression used by Morris, 'The Choice of Law Clause in Statutes', 62 *L.Q.R.* (1946), 170.

conflict rules. There have been writers[1] who have asserted the opposite: since all States enjoy an equal degree of sovereignty, each of them can only define the scope of its own legislation; without interfering with foreign sovereign rights it cannot lay down rules providing for the application of such foreign State's legislation; this could validly and effectively be done only by such foreign State itself. It is quite true that legislators have frequently preferred to enact 'one-sided' conflict rules. This is so not only in France and Germany, but also in England.[2] Indeed, the very familiar legislative technique of defining the international scope of a statute, of having 'spatially conditioned internal' rules[3] is nothing but the adoption of a 'one-sided' conflict rule: when the Copyright Act, 1956, provides that, primarily, it can be invoked only by persons of British nationality or domiciled or resident in the United Kingdom,[4] it supplies an example of a practice which most countries follow on frequent occasions, which is often convenient and certainly unobjectionable and which does not merit being described as 'a bastard hybrid',[5] or as 'parasitic legislative phenomena'.[6] However this may be, it is impossible to suggest that in adopting an 'all-sided' or general conflict rule the legislator would fail in his international duties. The conflict rule, whether particular

[1] Schnell, *Zeitschrift für internationales Privat- und Strafrecht* 5 (1895), 337, who had a few followers, particularly in Germany. It is said that the failure to enact, together with the German Civil Code, a detailed code of conflict rules as drafted by Gebhard, was due to some such reasoning as that propounded by Schnell: see Nussbaum, *Deutsches Internationales Privatrecht* (1932) 27, 28.

[2] Particularly significant examples are the rule that English divorce proceedings are invariably decided in accordance with English law, and the Adoption Act, 1958, which deals only with adoptions effected by an English Court, the jurisdiction being confined to cases in which the adopter is domiciled and both he and the infant are resident in England: section 1 (1) and (5). In such a case foreign law is probably immaterial: Cheshire, pp. 440, 441, with references. See also the Maintenance Agreements Acts, 1957, section 1 (3).

[3] This expression used by Nussbaum, *Principles of Private International Law* (1943), p. 71, is unfortunate, because it conceals the fact that a conflict rule is involved.

[4] Section 1 (5). The provisions of the Act are much more detailed and extend to many other categories of persons, but for present purposes precise reproduction is unnecessary.

[5] This is the characterization given by Dr. Morris (above, p. 42, n. 2), p. 172. Both Dr. Morris and Nussbaum are very critical of these 'particular' choice of law clauses, but their reasoning is unconvincing. It is impossible to see what harm is done by such clauses. See also De Nova, *Mélanges Jacques Maury* (Paris, 1960), p. 337. See, further, below, p. 58.

[6] Unger, 15 *Modern L.R.* (1952), 88, and 43 *Grot. Soc.* (1959), 96 sqq.

or general, is addressed solely to the courts of the legislator's own country. It tells them what they have to do, and does not prescribe what any organ of a foreign State should do in its own country. Nor would the existence of a set of 'one-sided' conflict rules be a meaningful measure, for the courts would not be slow to turn them into general rules. The argument is misconceived and today no more than a curiosity.

On the other hand, in laying down the conflict rules for application by their courts all countries have formulated them so as to follow the principle of 'non-interference'.[1] Private international law could have taken the view that it merely tells the judges of the forum what they should do in a given case and that, therefore, it does not have to have regard to the interests of any foreign country at all. No State has reasoned in this way. All States have introduced rules of private international law and, indeed, a strong body of opinion asserts that every country is under a duty to have rules of private international law, that it would be a breach of an international duty if the *lex fori* applied in all circumstances.[2] By allowing the foreign law to prevail the State refrains from any attempt to make foreign facts subject to its own regulations.

## II

In developing the substance of their choice-of-law rules the nations of the world have, on the whole, fully complied with the demands of the doctrine of jurisdiction.

The most significant fact is that all States apply to questions of status either the law of the person's nationality or the law of the person's domicile. No State simply submits such questions to its own law. No State is satisfied with the purely territorial test of presence or sojourn: questions of status are not submitted to the law of the country in which the person happens to be or has residence or has even habitual or ordinary residence.[3] The

---

[1] Above, pp. 40, 41.

[2] In this sense already in 1899 the unsurpassed observations made by Franz Kahn, *Abhandlungen zum Internationalem Privatrecht*, 1, 285 seq.; also Wolff, *Das Internationale Privatrecht Deutschlands* (3rd ed., 1954), p. 9; E. Kaufmann, *Recueil* 54 (1935 iv), 75; Dahm, p. 255, and others.

[3] The last-mentioned term has of late become very fashionable as a point of contact. If it is given the 'purely factual' meaning attributed to it by its advocates,

States select the connection which seems to them closest. In the British Commonwealth of Nations, it is true, the conception of domicile is in some respects so artificial and unrealistic as to make, in certain cases, the actual connection between a person and the country of his domicile somewhat tenuous.[1] Nevertheless, considered broadly, domicile, no less than nationality, is a conception founded upon a close factual connection with a given State, and, therefore, fully in harmony with the doctrine of jurisdiction.

Similar proof could be adduced in regard to most choice-of-law rules accepted by the principal legal systems. At the same time one could underline the development from a territorial approach to flexibility in the allocation of the right of regulation. Thus *locus regit actum*, originally an imperative rule derived from the territorial sovereignty over the transaction,[2] has in most countries become an optional rule in the sense that the form prescribed by the *lex causae* is equally available to the parties. Or until very recent times the validity of a contract was thought to be subject to the law of the place where the contract was made; the reason was that the local sovereign was thought to have control over the contract and its conclusion,[3] so that, as Story puts it,[4] the rule was 'founded, not merely in the convenience, but in the necessities of nations'. Today the proper law governs the whole of the contract.[5]

The problems, however, are not altogether solved. It is possible that a proper appreciation of the doctrine of international

---

it is subject to many and grave doubts: see Mann, *Juristenzeitung*, 1956, 466 (on whom see Nagel and Stoll, *Rabels Zeitschrift*, 1957, 187); 78 *L.Q.R.* (1962), 603 sqq.

[1] This is due to the interaction of the doctrine of domicile of origin, the doctrine of revival, the presumption operating in favour of an existing domicile and the effect of universality inherent in the rules of classification: an English Court always applies its own conception of domicile and it may happen therefore that a foreign national is domiciled in England merely because he has never aquired a domicile of choice and his father or grandfather had an English domicile of origin.

[2] Rabel, *Conflict of Laws*, ii.485 sqq., and numerous other textbooks.

[3] See, e.g., *P. and O. Steam Navigation Co.* v. *Shand*, 1(1865) 3 Moore P. C. C. (N.S.) 272, 290, per Turner L.J., or see Rabel, *Conflict of Laws*, ii.445.

[4] Section 242.

[5] The scission or 'morcellement' of the contract between conclusion and effect was maintained longest in Switzerland, but was abandoned in 1952 by the great decisions of the Federal Tribunal, *BGE* 77, ii.272; 78, ii.74; 79, ii.300. See, generally Batiffol, section 613, and in particular Vischer, *Internationales Vertragsrecht* (Basel, 1962) pp. 35–7.

jurisdiction will contribute to their solution. Three examples will perhaps indicate the type of re-assessment that is needed.

(1) It would seem to be a requirement of the doctrine of jurisdiction that the question of *liability for tort* should be subject to the law of the place where the tortious act is done. If this were not so a country could impose a liability which does not exist according to the *lex loci delicti*.[1] It would thus, in effect, prescribe what the defendant's conduct in the *locus delicti* should be. It is the law of the latter place 'to which the defendant owed obedience at the decisive moment, and it is by that law that his liability, if any, should be measured'.[2] In fact, the majority of States have adopted the principle that the *lex loci delicti* should govern. They have rejected Savigny's misconceived view, derived from pressing the analogy of criminal law too far, that the *lex fori* should apply. Nor have they shown any tendency, such as is all too noticeable in the field of criminal law,[3] of letting either the law of the victim's nationality[4] or of the wrongdoer's nationality[5] prevail, though exceptions in favour of the latter legal system[6] and in favour of the law of both parties' common nationality[7] are not unknown. But such exceptions are strictly limited in character and scope and do not affect the strength of the rule.

It is, however, the very existence of the rule which is doubtful in Britain, for there the law may be stated to be that the *lex fori*, i.e. English law, applies to all questions other than that of un-

---

[1] Or deny a liability which does so exist, though this would be a less serious case of 'interference'.

[2] Cheshire, p. 277.

[3] On this see below, pp. 75 sqq.

[4] This has nowhere been suggested, in regard to torts, but would be well in line with certain practices relating to criminal jurisdiction.

[5] This was suggested by Frankenstein, *Internationales Privatrecht* (1929), ii.362.

[6] See Art. 12 of the German Introductory Law according to which the claims made against a German national in respect of a tort committed by him abroad cannot exceed those which would arise under German law.

[7] As in Germany: see *BGHZ* 34, 222 (on which Beitzke, *Mélanges Jacques Maury* (Paris, 1960), p. 59), and *BGHZ* 35, 329; 40, 391, with further references. See, generally, Weiss, *Droit International Privé*, iv.416, among others. The view recently advocated in Britain that a foreign tort should be judged by the law of the country in which it has its 'social environment' (Dicey, p. 937, with reference to literature, particularly Morris, 64 *Harv. L.R.* (1950–1) 881) is, in its practical effects, unlikely to be different from the exception mentioned in the text. See now *Babcock* v. *Jackson*, 12 N. Y. 2d 473; 191 N. E. 2d 279 (1963) and the comments 63 *Col. L.R.*, (1963), 1219 sqq.

justifiability (*illicitiété, Rechtswidrigkeit*) which must exist also under the *lex loci delicti*.[1] This would seem to warrant the following result: Machado, a Brazilian resident in Brazil, libels in Brazil Fontes, another Brazilian resident in Brazil. The facts, therefore, were entirely Brazilian in character. By the law of Brazil the act is unjustifiable inasmuch as Machado was subject to criminal prosecution by the State, but under Brazilian law he was not under any civil liability towards Fontes at all. Yet the Court of Appeal held that the act was 'unjustifiable' in Brazil and that, therefore, Fontes could recover substantial damages from Machado in England.[2] This decision has, rightly, been described as 'regrettable' and as being 'at glaring variance with the rule of natural justice that the plaintiff should not reap an extra benefit by selecting a forum'.[3] The truth of the matter, it is submitted, is that the application of English law in the circumstances described was an excess of jurisdiction in the sense of international law.[4] For this reason, among others, the English rules on foreign torts are badly in need of re-examination.[5]

(2) If the English conflict rules relating to foreign torts pay too little respect to the doctrine of international jurisdiction, those on foreign immovables take an exaggerated view of the limitations imposed by that doctrine.

It has for long been a firmly established rule in Britain as well as elsewhere that the *lex situs* alone governs all questions concerning immovable property; the rule has been so inexorable

---

[1] This is the effect of the first rule formulated by Willes J. in *Phillips* v. *Eyre*, (1870) L. R. 6 Q. B. 1, 28, that 'the wrong must be of such a character that it would have been actionable if committed in England' and that 'the act must not have been justifiable by the law of the place where it was done'.

[2] [1897] 2 Q. B. 231; the facts are unfortunately insufficiently reported and it is, therefore, not certain whether they were absolutely identical with those stated in the text.

[3] Cheshire, p. 287, with references to literature.

[4] Could England have imposed criminal liability upon Machado? The answer is clearly in the negative: see below, p. 73. Why, then, should England have the right to impose liability for a tort?

[5] The root of the trouble lies in the exaggerated influence allowed to the *lex fori*. This is a *malaise* which pervades a large part of English private international law. It is believed, for instance, that the decision in *Kohnke* v. *Karger*, [1951] 2 K. B. 670, allowing the victim of a motor car accident in France damages far in excess of those awarded in France, would have given France just cause for complaint had the wrongdoer been French. The English practice as to the effect of statutes of limitation has similarly 'gone astray' (Cheshire, p. 685). The examples could be multiplied.

as to permit very few exceptions, the most important of them, relating to the forms of wills, having been introduced only by the Wills Act, 1963, with effect from 1 January 1964. The rule makes, of course, very good sense on grounds of expediency, particularly insofar as it applies to questions of entitlement, the type of rights capable of being enjoyed over immovables, the methods of alienation and transfer and other matters which, by their very nature, can effectively be regulated only by the *lex situs*. It is also inherent in the principle, and fully accepted on the Continent,[1] that, in general, only the courts of the situs have jurisdiction[2] to pass upon the rights to immovables.

In 1893, however, the House of Lords decided that the rule went so far as to preclude a court outside the situs from entertaining an action for damages for trespass, i.e. for interference with the possession and enjoyment of land.[3] This conclusion was, in part at least, based on the thought that[4]

in considering what jurisdiction our Courts possess, and have claimed to exercise in relation to matters arising out of the country, the principles which have found general acceptance amongst civilized nations as defining the limits of jurisdiction are of great weight.

Today, certainly, it is plain that there is no principle recognized by civilized nations, which forbids such personal actions for damages. It does not exist on the Continent[5] or in the United States of America.[6] Nor is it required by any rule of jurisdiction as developed by public international law, for even if in the course of an action for damages for trespass to land questions of title may incidentally have to be decided, this would not involve any attempt at regulating directly the title to foreign land.

(3) After criticism of the English private international law on the ground of the misapplication of the doctrine of international jurisdiction it is fitting, finally, to discuss a group of rules which clearly and commendably reflect that doctrine.

It is not now open to doubt that the title to property is

---

[1] Wolff, p. 92.

[2] Strictly speaking, the present discussion might have been in section 3, below, pp. 60 seq. But it seemed preferable to follow the traditional English view that the rule is substantive rather than procedural.

[3] *British South Africa Co.* v. *Companhia de Moçambique*, [1893] A. C. 602.

[4] p. 624 per Lord Herschell L.C.    [5] Wolff, p. 92.

[6] See the helpful note in 6 *Vanderbilt L.R.* (1953), 786; Ehrenzweig, *Conflict of Laws* (1962), p. 140.

governed by the *lex situs*. The idea of international jurisdiction
has played a large part in evolving the principle, though its
responsibility is neither exclusive nor decisive. Other considerations, such as the security of trade or expediency, were at work.[1]
But it is legitimate to suggest that these would not have carried
the day had they not produced results which were in harmony
with the requirements of public international law. The 'simple
rule' that generally property in England is subject to English
law and to none other,[2] explains, in particular, the confiscation
cases.[3] In connection with them the courts of many countries
have been strongly inclined to rely directly upon public international law in order to deny the extraterritorial effect of
confiscatory legislation.[4] It would, however have been sufficient
to invoke the *lex situs*, though this rule, in turn, is derived from
or at least influenced by public international law. To put it
differently, the epithet 'confiscatory' does not normally add
any legally significant element to the statement or application
of the rule.[5]

Among the problems which are still unsolved there is the
suggestion that a decree providing for the taking of property
if accompanied by the payment of compensation should have
extraterritorial effect.[6] But, as has been well said,[7] 'compulsory acquisition in return for compensation is still a manifesta-
tion of sovereignty', which no State may carry out so as to change
title to property in another State. If this were not so the decree
of a State would have greater legal effect in another State than
the dispatch of a battalion of soldiers. It is, therefore, not the
payment of compensation, but the character of the measure

---

[1] For a full and useful discussion see P. A. Lalive, *The Transfer of Chattels in the Conflict of Laws* (1955), pp. 103 sqq., particularly p. 107. For a convincing statement to the effect that in truth the maxim *mobilia sequuntur personam* always applied only to general assignments see *ibid.*, pp. 34 seq.

[2] *Bank voor Handel en Scheepvaart* v. *Slatford*, [1953] 1 Q.B. 248, at p. 260 per Devlin J. (as he then was).

[3] On the English confiscation cases see, for instance, Dicey, p. 665.

[4] This is particularly so in Germany: see, for instance, *BGHZ* 12, 79 or Wolff (Raiser), *Sachenrecht*, section 90, n. 6.

[5] This is the conclusion reached by Devlin J. in the case mentioned n. 2 above.

[6] This suggestion was first made by Wolff, section 501. It was taken up, in particular, by Seidl-Hohenveldern, *Internationales Konfiskations- und Enteignungs-recht* (1952), pp. 179 et sqq. But it was rejected not only by most writers, but also by the Swiss Federal Tribunal in *BGE* 82 i.196, also *Int. L.R.* (1956), 24.

[7] Dicey, *Conflict of Laws* (7th ed., 1958), p. 666.

that is decisive, for no State has jurisdiction so as to bind property outside its borders.

Or there is the question whether an exception should not perhaps be admitted insofar as the title to ships is concerned and whether, therefore, a State should be allowed the right to seize or requisition ships flying its flag even when they are in foreign waters. In regard to requisition at least Lord McNair advocates an affirmative answer, at any rate for the purpose of mere legislative jurisdiction.[1] This may be assumed to be an accurate statement, but it does not touch the crucial point which concerns the right to the actual taking of the ship. This can only be effected by the *lex situs*. Even if a ship were to be personified so as to be equiparated to a person having the nationality of the legislating State, it would be clear that the home State may impose, but cannot enforce, liability to military service.

Lastly, if the control of the *lex situs* is so obviously in conformity with the doctrine of international jurisdiction, it may be asked why it is that in matters of general assignment, such as succession on marriage, death, bankruptcy, or merger,[2] the personal law, whether it be the law of nationality or domicile, is allowed to prevail over the *lex situs*.[3] Does not the doctrine of jurisdiction require that even in the case of death, for instance, the *lex situs* should govern? It is remarkable that, except in regard to immovables, no such legal principle has made its appearance. The reason, it is suggested, is that from the point of view of international jurisdiction, general assignments are more closely connected with a person's status than with the situation of the person's property.

*Section 2*

STATUTORY INTERPRETATION

I

It is a matter of universal experience that in fact States do not ordinarily attempt to legislate in respect of matters outside their

---

[1] 31 *Grot. Soc.* (1946), pp. 30–46. Lord McNair expressly excepts enforcement in foreign waters and thus reduces the practical importance of the point to a minimum. See generally Dicey, p. 510.

[2] On this aspect see *Metliss* v. *National Bank of Greece*, [1958] A. C. 509.

[3] The distinction between general and particular assignments is clearly drawn by Devlin J. (above, p. 50, n. 2) at p. 257.

jurisdiction. As a rule they legislate solely for the purpose of regulating their own affairs, whether the statute be directed to their subjects or to facts and events occurring within their boundaries or to circumstances in which, for other reasons, they may fairly be said to have a legitimate concern. And no legislator, if asked whom or what he contemplates in enacting legislation, would assert his intention to reach beyond the confines of his lawful jurisdiction.[1] This is a point of some importance, for the legislator's intentions are everywhere the guide to the true construction of a statute and if they are limited in scope the statute will have to be given a meaning corresponding to such limitation. This aspect of statutory interpretation has received astonishingly little attention on the Continent where it is wholly exceptional for Professor Batiffol to refer to the 'principe élémentaire' according to which 'chaque État légifère sur les relations juridiques se déroulant sur son territoire, et l'ordre international sera satisfait en vertu de la maxime de bons sens "chacun chez soi"'.[2] But in England it is a well-founded and richly documented, though rebuttable, 'presumption that Parliament does not assert or assume jurisdiction which goes beyond the limits established by the common consent of nations'.[3] This is no more than the modern answer to the famous rhetorical question asked in 1808 by Lord Ellenborough[4] and (subject to adaptations) repeated by Lord Blackburn[5]: 'Can the island of Tobago pass a law to bind the rights of the whole

---

[1] See *Foley Bros.* v. *Filarda*, 336 U. S. 281 (1949), at p. 285 per Reed J. on behalf of the Court: 'Congress is primarily concerned with domestic conditions.'

[2] *Aspects Philosophiques du Droit International Privé* (1956), p. 260: see also Zitelmann, 'Geltungsbereich und Anwendungsbereich der Gesetze', *Festschrift für Bergbohm* (1919) 207, 227, and Riezler, *Internationales Zivilprozessrecht* (1949), p. 81. Nipperdey bei Enneccerus-Nipperdey, *Allgemeiner Teil* (14th ed. (1955), section 190, n. 3), refers to the fact that 'according to the principle of territoriality statutes and decrees can have effect only within the boundaries of their territorial sovereignty'. Henri Rolin, 77 *Recueil* (1950 ii), 307 seq., 370, must be quoted in full: 'L'Etat qui prétendrait légiférer, soit pour des territoires étrangers, soit pour des ressortissants de nationalité étrangère ne se trouvant pas fixés sur son territoire, commettrait une usurpation de compétence.'

[3] *Theophile* v. *The Solicitor-General*, [1950] A. C. 186, at p. 195 per Lord Porter, approving a statement now appearing in *Halsbury's Laws of England*, (3rd ed., 1961), p. 414. See the cases there quoted, in particular *Colquhoun* v. *Heddon*, (1890) 25 Q. B. 129, at pp. 134, 135 per Lord Esher.

[4] *Buchanan* v. *Rucker*, (1808) 9 East 192.

[5] *Schibsby* v. *Westenholz*, (1870) L. R. 6 Q.B. 155, p. 160.

world? Would the world submit to such an assumed jurisdiction?'

The necessity for reading legislation in the light of the limitations imposed by the doctrine of international jurisdiction has
been appreciated in the United States of America for an equally
long time. Already in 1818 Chief Justice Marshall emphasized
that general words in a statute 'must not only be limited to
cases within the jurisdiction of the State, but also to those
objects to which the legislature intended to apply them'.[1] This
rule, which merely illustrates the more basic principle that an
enactment 'ought never to be construed to violate the law of
nations if any other possible construction remains',[2] has since
been often reaffirmed[3] and is not open to doubt.

## II

What, then, are the limitations to which by the common consent of nations legislative jurisdiction is subject and which govern
the interpretation of statutes?

The typical problem arises where a statute uses such general
words as 'any person' or 'every' or 'whosoever' or 'any
property' and so forth. Is it intended to refer to all persons or to
all property in the world? If no, what is the qualification which
has to be read into phrases of such generality?

In the past the answer has almost invariably been formulated
in terms of the Huber–Storyan maxims. Speaking on behalf of
the Supreme Court Story himself said in 1824[4]:

And however general and comprehensive the phrases used in our municipal
laws may be, they must always be restricted in construction to places and
persons upon whom the legislature have authority and jurisdiction.

And in England as early as 1843 Lord Campbell gave expression
to them by stating negatively that 'the British Parliament
certainly has no general power to legislate for foreigners out
of the dominions and beyond the jurisdiction of the British
Crown'.[5] Since then they have been restated again and again,

---

[1] *United States* v. *Palmer*, 3 Wheat, 610, 631.

[2] *The Charming Betsy*, 2 Cranch 64, 118 (1804). The rule has frequently been
invoked; for some of the references see *Lauritzen* v. *Larsen*, 345 U. S. 571 (1953).

[3] *Lauritzen* v. *Larsen*, *ubi supra*, among numerous other cases.

[4] *The Apollon*, 9 Wheat, 362, 370.

[5] *Lopez* v. *Burslem* (1843) 4 Moo. P. C. 300, 305; similarly *The Amalia* (1863), 1
Moo. P. C. (N. S.), 471, 474 per Dr. Lushington.

both in the succinct form of a reference to 'the principle that, unless the contrary is made clear, an Act of Parliament is not intended to have extraterritorial effect',[1] and more elaborately[2]:

A State's authority, in the eyes of other States, and the courts that represent them is, speaking very generally, coincident with, and limited by, its power. It is territorial. It may legislate for, and give judgments affecting, things and persons within its territory. It has no authority to legislate for, or adjudicate upon, things or persons not within its territory.

A formula such as this remains, on the whole, acceptable today, but in accordance with earlier submissions should not be treated as an unalterable text. While it is appropriate in most cases, it is in others liable either to extend too far or to be too narrow. The overriding principle should be expressed in the more flexible terms which have been suggested.

For present purposes it must suffice to select, from the vast material,[3] three cases which vividly illustrate the Anglo-American approach to the problem.

*Buchanan* v. *Rucker*[4] arose from the legislation of the Island

---

[1] *Bank voor Handel en Scheepvaart* v. *Slatford*, [1953] 1 Q.B. 248, 258 per Devlin J. (as he then was).

[2] Dicey, *Conflict of Laws* (6th ed.), p. 13, approved by Atkinson J. in *Lorenzen* v. *Lydden & Co.*, [1942] 2 K.B. 202, at p. 205, and by Devlin J. (see preceding note) at p. 257. Notwithstanding such judicial approval Dicey's 7th edition seems to have omitted the sentence quoted in the text. Numerous judicial pronouncements to a similar effect are to be found in the cases mentioned in the following note.

[3] It is collected and discussed by Maxwell, *Interpretation of Statutes* (11th ed., 1962), 138 sqq.; Halsbury (Simonds), 36 *Laws of England* (3rd ed., 1961), p. 428, among others. The principal *English* cases are: *Jefferys* v. *Boosey* (1854) 4 H. L. L. R. 815, 926 per Lord Wensleydale; *Ex parte Blain* (1879) 12 Ch. D. 522, 526 per James L.J., p. 532 per Cotton L.J.; *R.* v. *Jameson*, [1896] 2 Q.B. 425, 430 per Lord Russell of Killowen; *Macleod* v. *Attorney-General for New South Wales*, [1891] A. C. 456; *Sirdar Gordyal Singh* v. *Rajah of Farikdote*, [1894] A.C. 670, 683 per Lord Selborne; *Cooke* v. *Vogeler*, [1901] A.C. 102; *Tomalin* v. *Pearson*, [1909] 2 K.B. 61, 64 per Lord Cozens-Hardy M.R. In the *United States of America* the development probably begins with *Rose* v. *Himely*, 4 Cranch, 241 (1808), at p. 297 per Chief Justice Marshall. The more important recent cases are *New York Central Railroad* v. *Chisholm*, 268 U. S. 29 (1925) according to which the Employers' Liability Act does not apply to an accident in Canada; *Blackmer* v. *United States*, 284 U. S. 421, 437 (1932); *Foley Bros.* v. *Filarda*, 336 U. S. 281, 285 (1949); *Lauritzen* v. *Larsen*, 345 U. S. 575, 577 (1953); *McCulloch* v. *Sociedad Nacional de Honduras*, 372 U. S. 10 (1963). See also *Vermilya-Brown Co.* v. *Connell*, 335 U. S. 377 (1948) relating to the application of the Fair Labour Act to Bermuda, where the majority of the Court used the very cautious formulation that Congress had 'power in *certain situations* to regulate the actions of our citizens outside the territorial jurisdiction of the United States' (p. 381, italics supplied).

[4] (1808) 9 East 192.

of Tobago according to which 'every defendant' who shall 'be absent from the island' and has failed to appoint an attorney, shall be deemed to be properly served with proceedings by 'the nailing up of a copy . . . at the entrance of the courthouse'. Lord Ellenborough was called upon to decide whether a judgment obtained in pursuance of service so effected against a defendant who had never been in Tobago was binding upon him. In refusing so to hold Lord Ellenborough based himself upon what he thought to be the true construction of the Tobago statute:

'By persons absent from the island must necessarily be understood persons who have been present and within the jurisdiction, so as to have been subject to the process of the Court; but it can never be applied to a person who for aught appears never was present within or subject to the jurisdiction.'

In a leading and most instructive American case[1] a Danish seaman, while temporarily in New York, signed ship's articles, written in Danish and governed by Danish law, with a view to serving on a ship of Danish flag and registry, and owned by a Danish citizen. Having been negligently injured aboard the ship while in Havana harbour, he claimed damages in the New York Courts under the Jones Act according to which 'any seaman who shall suffer personal injury in the course of his employment may . . . maintain an action for damages at law . . .'. In an opinion by Mr. Justice Jackson the Supreme Court of the United States proceeded to 'resolve conflicts between competing laws by ascertaining and valuing points of contact', such as the place of the wrongful act, the law of the flag, the allegiance or domicile of the injured, the allegiance of the defendant shipowner, the place of contract, the inaccessibility of the foreign forum, the *lex fori*. The Court did not decide what law was applicable to the claim vested in the plaintiff as a result of the accident. The Court was merely called upon to decide whether the Jones Act applied, and held that it did not apply, for it could 'find no justification for interpreting the Jones Act to intervene between foreigners and their own law because of acts on a foreign ship not in our waters'.[2]

---

[1] *Lauritzen* v. *Larsen*, 345 U. S. 571 (1953), followed and extended in *Romero* v. *International Terminal Operating Co.*, 358 U. S. 354 (1959), also Int. L.R. 28, 145.

[2] For an unconvincing attempt to distinguish this decision in a case in which the stock of the Honduran corporation owning the ship was owned by an American

Finally, there is another decision of the Supreme Court of the United States,[1] which is of quite unusual significance. The American National Labor Relations Act enables in entirely general terms the National Labor Relations Board to order an election of a trade union to represent the employees of a plant in negotiating collective agreements. The Board ordered an election to be held among the Honduran crew of a ship flying the Honduran flag and owned by a Honduran corporation; all members of the crew were resident in Honduras, had signed Honduran shipping articles and were members of a Honduran trade union. The United Fruit Company, a New Jersey corporation, owned all the shares of the Honduran corporation[2] and determined the voyages which for the most part were between Central and South American ports and those of the United States, as well as the vessels' ports of call, cargoes and sailings. In ordering the election the Board applied its own 'balancing of contacts theory'[3]: it held that the relative weight of the ship's foreign as compared with its American contacts was such as to produce 'substantial United States contacts, outweighing the numerous foreign contacts present'.[4] The Supreme Court disallowed the election. It asked itself 'whether the Act as written was intended to have any application to foreign registered vessels employing alien seamen'.[5] It found[6]

no basis for a construction which would exert United States jurisdiction over and apply its laws to the internal management and affairs of the vessels here flying the Honduran flag. . . .

In view of the generality of the statutory language it would not have been difficult to support the opposite conclusion. But since a question of international jurisdiction was involved the Supreme Court felt compelled to look for 'specific language',[7] and this was missing.

corporation, see *Zielenski* v. *Empress Hondurena*, 113 F. Supp. 93 (1953). See also *Bartholomeus* v. *Universe Tankship Inc.*, 263 F. 2d. 437 (1959), cert. den. 359 U. S. 1000 (1959), also Int. L.R. 28, 108.

[1] *McCulloch* v. *Sociedad Nacional de Marineros de Honduras*, 372 U. S. 10 (1963); see already *Benz* v. *Compania Naviera Hidalgo*, 353 U. S. 138 (1957), also Int. L. R. 1957, 167.

[2] Students of comparative law will note that in view of this fact the Court felt entitled to say that the United Fruit Company 'beneficially owns' the vessels. This would not be the English approach: *Bank voor Handel en Scheepvaart* v. *Slatford*, [1953] 1 Q. B. 248, 269 sqq.

[3] p. 19.     [4] p. 14.     [5] p. 19.     [6] p. 20.     [7] p. 19.

In ascertaining the scope of a statute Anglo-American courts have in the past often taken the position that international law permits a State to impose duties upon its non-resident citizens; no occasion has as yet arisen for investigating the question whether there are not exceptions to this rule. But English courts have also indicated that in questions of status and succession legislative jurisdiction will be held to extend to foreign citizens domiciled in the legislating State.[1] This would seem to be unobjectionable if the domicile is based upon actual residence. The English conception of domicile, however, is such as to make it possible for a person to have a domicile in a certain country with which he neither has nor has had any residential connection, but in which his ancestor has been resident. In such a case, it is submitted, a State is not entitled to legislate with effect upon the person in question. It has also been suggested that a State has legislative jurisdiction if a person in his life-time was domiciled in its territory.[2] This would seem to be wrong, because by giving up his domicile the person has, ex hypothesi, lost all legally material connection with the legislating State.[3]

## III

The rules of statutory interpretation which have just been discussed are, of course, rules of municipal law, but they are also a source, perhaps one of the main sources, of the principle of public international law that a State cannot legislate in respect of matters outside its jurisdiction. In other words the principles

---

[1] Lord Selborne in the case referred to above, p. 54, n. 3; *Pugh* v. *Pugh*, [1951] P. 482.

[2] See Lord Selborne's remarks (above, p. 59, n. 3). If after a person's death his status can retrospectively be changed by the law of the country where he was domiciled at some time during his life, this does not mean that while he is alive such country can change his status with effect in the country where he is domiciled at the date of the purported change.

[3] For this reason it would seem, for instance, that if the father had ceased to be domiciled in England before the Legitimacy Act, 1926, or the Legitimacy Act, 1959, came into force, the illegitimate child was not, as a matter of English law, legitimated, even if at the date of the marriage to the mother the father was domiciled in England and even if he is a citizen of the United Kingdom. In Australia and New Zealand the Courts so decided: see Dicey, p. 442, whose criticism is unjustified, because he disregards the material question whether the English Parliament can, and intends to, alter the father's status in these circumstances.

of public international law governing jurisdiction are both illustrated and proved by the municipal rules. Therein lies the
significance of the latter for present purposes.

These municipal rules of statutory interpretation, in effect,
constitute implied 'one-sided' or particular choice-of-law
rules.[1] As in the case of express rules of this type, difficult and
delicate problems are liable to arise when they come to be fitted
into a system of general choice-of-law rules.[2] In the present
context it is possible only to emphasize the following broad
distinction: for a court sitting in the legislating State it may
frequently be sufficient to ascertain, by interpretation, the scope
of a statute and to refrain from investigating the applicability
of any general rule of the conflict of laws.[3] But for a court sitting
in a third country the statute and its interpretation is a fit
subject for inquiry only after the law of the legislating State has
previously been found to be applicable. Thus suppose[4] that a

[1] See above, pp. 43, 44, and the literature there referred to.

[2] The problem will require much more attention than it has received in the past.
Most of the leading textbooks ignore it. One of the questions to be investigated is
whether there exists any difference between statute law and judge-made law.
Another is whether it is possible to distinguish various classes of cases. One class
would seem to include cases in which no choice-of-law problem arises at all, but
in which the plaintiff invokes a statutory right and the sole point for decision is
whether the statute applies to the facts of the case. This class comprises such cases
as *Tomalin* v. *Pearson*, [1909] 2 K. B. 61 in England and *McCulloch* v. *Sociedad
Nacional de Marineros de Honduras*, 372 U. S. 10 (1963) in the United States. The
extensive litigation relating to the Railway Labor Act provides other examples:
see, e.g., *Airline Stewards, etc.* v. *Northwest Airlines*, 267 F. 2d. 170, cert. den. 361
U. S. 901 (1959), also Int. L.R. 28, 115; *Airline Stewards etc.* v. *Trans World Airlines*
273 F. 2d 69 (1959) cert. den. 362 U. S. 988 (1960), also Int. L.R. 28, 125.

[3] But this method is not free from danger. See Mann. *The Variation of Trusts Act,
1958, and the Conflict of Laws*, 80 L.Q.R. (1964), 27. The Maltese Courts have
held that the rule of the law of Malta according to which a Roman Catholic
cannot marry otherwise than by canon law, applies to all Maltese wherever they
may be: see *Lepre* v. *Lepre* (1965) P. 52 and the earlier English decisions there
referred to. If the Maltese Courts had asked themselves whether a question
of capacity or of form was involved they would perhaps have avoided results
which outside Malta are unacceptable. In *Swift* v. *Attorney-General for Ireland*,
[1912] A. C. 276, it was rightly held that an Irish statute invalidating a marriage
between a Roman Catholic and a Protestant, if celebrated by a Roman Catholic
priest, related to form rather than capacity. On the other hand *Pugh* v. *Pugh*,
[1951] P. 482, relating to the Age of Marriage Act, 1929 ('a marriage between two
persons either of whom is under the age of sixteen shall be void') was decided on
the basis of statutory interpretation. The question whether the Act related to
capacity or to form was not put. Cf. the following note.

[4] The example is based on *Mount Albert Borough Council* v. *Australasian Temperance
and General Mutual Life Assurance Society*, [1938] A. C. 224. Another most instructive

creditor in Victoria lends money to a New Zealand debtor on the security of a mortgage on New Zealand land. The legislator in Victoria reduces the rate of interest payable in respect of 'any security for payment of money . . . over real or personal property'. If this provision is intended to reach a mortgage on New Zealand land, a judge in Victoria may have to apply it, although the mortgage may be subject to New Zealand law. But a New Zealand Judge will find it unnecessary and improper to consider the Victorian legislation if he has found the mortgage to be subject to New Zealand law. One will, therefore, always have to distinguish two different questions[1]: is the legal system of which the statute forms part applicable at all? If so, is the statute on its true construction intended to reach the matter in issue?

## IV

In pursuing that process of statutory interpretation which is frequently required to give effect to the demands of the doctrine of jurisdiction, no distinction arises between what is commonly described as public law on the one and private law on the other hand. Even if the contrast between the two branches of the law did not relate largely to procedure and, from a doctrinal point of view, were not wholly superficial, it would be impossible to assert that the scope of private law is necessarily wider than or different from that of public law, that legislative jurisdiction does not, and is not intended to, have the same extent in respect of both public and private law. When enacting a provision of a civil code for the limitation of the maximum rate of interest to 5%, the intention, the international right and the power of the

example is the decision of the German Supreme Court of 28 May 1936, below, p. 105. For an American case see *Foley Bros* v. *Filarda*, 336 U. S. 281 (1949) 119; An American building firm had made a contract under United States law in the United States with an American citizen, under which the firm was to do work in the Near East. He claimed that he had worked in excess of eight hours a day and that under the Eight Hours Law he was to be paid for such excess 'at not less than one and one-half times the basic rate of pay'. It was held as a matter of the interpretation of the Fair Labour Law that it was not intended to apply to work performed abroad. The question whether the Act did not perhaps apply merely by reason of the fact that the proper law of the contract was American was not even put. See the preceding note.

[1] See already Mann, *The Legal Aspect of Money* (2nd ed., 1953), p. 130, n. 2.

legislator in regard to the ambit of the statute (which is a private law statute) are in fact and in law the same as in the case in which he passes an emergency decree reducing the rate of interest to 5% (which, presumably, would be regarded as a public law decree). Accordingly, no rule of international jurisdiction requires or, indeed, permits any distinction in the scope of public and private law legislation.

It follows that international law lends no support to the dogma, so often asserted in France and Switzerland and, more recently, in Germany, that foreign public laws are to be disregarded because they 'sont strictement territoriales', are strictly territorial. If and insofar as it is intended to suggest that rights derived from foreign public laws cannot be enforced in the forum, that the forum will not allow a foreign sovereign State to exercise its prerogative rights, strong support can be found in the universal practice of civilized States. There is, however, no justification at all for the entirely different suggestion that outside the boundaries of the legislating State public law must be ignored in the sense that legal effects produced by it are to be treated as non-existent. It will appear later[1] that the opposite view has been taken by certain tribunals of high authority. In particular, the German Federal Supreme Court[2] derived far-reaching conclusions from the alleged fact that there was a 'fundamental distinction between the conflict of private laws and the conflict of public laws', that public law was dominated by a peculiar 'idea of territoriality' and that the forum could not give effect to or apply foreign public law. This is so unfortunate a development that it is necessary at once to expose it as legally unfounded.

## Section 3

### CIVIL JURISDICTION

### I

The jurisdiction of the courts in civil matters is an aspect of the activity of States, which is more effectively determined and

---

[1] Below, p. 125.

[2] 17 December 1959, *BGHZ* 31, 367, and (in French) *Rev. crit.* (1961), 313, with note by Mezger.

circumscribed by international rules of jurisdiction than many observers recognize or admit.[1] A judgment, viz. a command conveyed through the courts, is not essentially different from a command expressed by legislative or administrative action. It cannot claim international validity except if and in so far as it keeps within the limits which public international law imposes.

It will appear that in fact the municipal law of civil jurisdiction has everywhere taken notice of these limits and there exist but few cases in which doubts arise. Even on the Continent the actuality of the law does not support the type of academic statement which is exemplified by the assertion that the national rules of civil jurisdiction are determined by each State in its discretion,[2] that they depend 'à l'heure actuelle exclusivement de la législation nationale'.[3] This sounds uncompromising, but becomes less so when one reads later[4] that 'en principe les tribunaux d'un pays ne soient pas compétents pour connaître de contestations se référant à des faits étrangers ou à des personnes sans lien avec l'Etat qui les institue'; the difficulty, not discussed by the author, only lies in ascertaining the circumstances in which the necessary connection is missing. Or a German author admits that there are limits to civil jurisdiction and that in defining them the State 'should act so that, in Kantian language, the principle of its own regulation could serve as the principle of international legislation'.[5] There is still less justification for an American author to teach that a State may 'take hold of any judicial matter as the State sees fit'.[6] For in the British Commonwealth of Nations and the United States of America aware-

---

[1] Jessup, *Transnational Law* (1956), pp. 36–9, has rightly pointed out that international law books generally ignore civil jurisdiction. Professor Jennings, 'The Limits of State Jurisdiction', 32 *Nordisk Tidsskrift for International Ret.* (1962), 210, 211, suggests that public international law 'has little to say' on civil jurisdiction and that a principle qualifying it is 'otiose'. *Sed quaere.*

[2] Neuner, *Internationale Zuständigkeit* (1929), p. 13, with numerous references; Nussbaum, *Deutsches Internationales Privatrecht* (1932), p. 388; Gamillscheg, 'Zuständigkeit und Entscheidungsharmonie', *Berichte der Deutschen Gesellschaft für Völkerrecht*, Heft 3 (1959), 29, 32. Schnitzer, *Internationales Privatrecht* (4th ed., 1958), ii.797, believes that public international law includes no concrete rules for the demarcation of civil jurisdiction except the negative one: where there is 'no contact' with the forum, jurisdiction is missing. It remains to decide, however, in what circumstances there is no contact.

[3] Niboyet, *Traité de Droit International Privé Français*, (1949), vi.256.

[4] p. 270.     [5] Neuner, op. cit., p. 14.

[6] Nussbaum, *Principles of Private International Law* (New York, 1943), p. 192.

ness of the restrictions imposed by international law on civil jurisdiction has become very articulate indeed. There can be no doubt that once again the Huber–Storyan maxims dominate the scene.[1] Early tendencies[2] were epitomized by Mr. Justice Holmes with typical succinctness: 'The foundation of jurisdiction is physical power',[3] meaning sovereignty. Or as Chief Justice Warren remarked very recently,[4] all restrictions on the personal jurisdiction of courts 'are a consequence of territorial limitations on the power of the respective States'. In England Lord Russell of Killowen described civil jurisdiction as being 'based upon the principle of territorial dominion'.[5] and that jurisdiction should be exercised 'consistently with the general principles of international law which govern national jurisdictions',[6] is axiomatic. Yet it seems likely that in the modern world the territorial test fails to give complete satisfaction. Perhaps the exercise of a State's civil jurisdiction should presuppose no more than 'certain minimum contacts with it such that the maintenance of suit does not offend traditional notions of fair play and substantial justice'.[7] but at the present stage of development a suggestion on such lines could be put forward only with extreme diffidence and caution.

Civil jurisdiction, considered as an incident of the theory of international jurisdiction, cannot be adequately discussed except in conjunction with the problem of the recognition of foreign

[1] See Story, section 540.

[2] See *Pennoyer* v. *Neff*, 95 U. S. 714 (1878),—dicta only, for the case itself turned on a point of constitutional law.

[3] *McDonald* v. *Mabee*, 243 U. S. 90 (1917). Ehrenzweig's attack (pp. 77, 78) overlooks once again the implications of public international law. Against him Cheatham–Goodrich–Griswold–Reese, *Cases and Materials on Conflict of Laws* (4th ed., 1957), p. 95, n. 2.

[4] *Hanson* v. *Denckla*, 357 U. S. 235 (1958), another constitutional case.

[5] *Carrick* v. *Hancock* (1895) 12 T. L. R. 59; see also *John Russell & Co.* v. *Cayzer Irvine & Co.*, [1916[ 2 A. C. 298, 302, per Lord Haldane.

[6] *Tallack* v. *Tallack*, [1927] P. 211, 219, per Lord Merrivale.

[7] *International Shoe Co.* v. *State of Washington*, 326 U. S. 310, 316 (1945), per Chief Justice Stone. This was again a constitutional case. It is quoted here merely for the sake of the happy formulation referred to in the text. American literature on the Conflict of Laws makes abundant use of decisions which relate to the interpretation of the Due Process and the Full Faith and Credit clauses of the Constitution. Their relevance from an international point of view is open to much doubt. The recent Draft Uniform Interstate and International Procedure Act, published in *American Journal, of Comparative Law* 1962, 418, adopts a moderate attitude on questions of civil jurisdiction and related matters, but is dominated by considerations of constitutional rather than international law.

judgments, which, very largely, is identical with the problem of the jurisdiction of foreign courts. Both topics are, and should be recognized as, branches of the same tree. In order to be recognized by the forum, the foreign judgment must be pronounced by a court having jurisdiction in the international sense, viz. 'in such sense that in conformity with general jurisprudence and ordinary international law and usage the courts of other states will regard its judgments as binding'.[1] But this is precisely what is required of the rules of civil jurisdiction of the forum. It is in line with the interdependence of the two problems, it is, indeed, merely another description of the relationship between them that a principle of reciprocity is widely practised or at least favoured[2]: where the foreign court's judgment proceeds on a ground of jurisdiction known to the forum, it should be recognized by the latter, for it is impossible to suggest that the foreign country's rules do not merit recognition and are perhaps contrary to international law, when they correspond to the law of the forum. In other words, the limits of international jurisdiction should, broadly, be the same with respect to both aspects of civil jurisdiction.

## II

It would be tempting to consider all rules of civil jurisdiction with a view to ascertaining the extent to which they are consistent with rules of international jurisdiction. No divergence would probably come to light in so far as actions *in rem* are concerned. On the other hand problems of some gravity would have to be faced in connection with matters of status, particularly divorce. For present purposes it must suffice to draw attention to some specific types of proceedings *in personam*,[3] in which the effect of international jurisdiction on civil jurisdiction is subject to doubt.

[1] *Turnbull* v. *Walker*, 67 L.T.R. (1892), 767, per Wright J. On the connection between civil jurisdiction and the recognition of judgments see Nussbaum, 41 *Col. L.R.* (1941), 22.

[2] As to England, see Cheshire, pp. 651, 652, and Dicey, p. 1020. As to Germany, see section 328 of the Code of Civil Procedure. See also Gutteridge, Reciprocity in regard to Foreign Judgments, *British Year Book of International Law* (1932), 49.

[3] For a useful comparative survey (Switzerland, France, Germany) see De Vries and Lowenfeld, 44 *Iowa L.R.* (1959), 306, or Gutteridge, 44 *Recueil* (1933 ii), 118.

(1) In the case of actions *in personam* the defendant's territorial connection with the State of the forum provides the principal and almost universal basis of civil jurisdiction; such a point of contact is, of course, in complete harmony with the doctrine of international jurisdiction.

In most countries the territorial link is established by domicile or residence of the defendant, whether a natural or a legal person, within the State of the forum.[1] On the Continent this is usually the only method of justifying civil jurisdiction based on territorial connection, but in England and perhaps also in the United States of America it is a secondary ground.[2] It is 'presence' (or, in the case of corporations, the carrying on of business')[3] and service of proceedings within the State of the forum that is the primary and certainly a sufficient ground of civil jurisdiction.[4] As Martin Wolff has said,[5]

if an Irishman flying from Dublin to Amsterdam stops at Croydon for ten minutes he may there be served with a writ and English jurisdiction would thereby be established. . . . It makes no difference, finally, whether the facts of the case have any relation to England or not.

Such a result may be consistent with the territorial doctrine of jurisdiction, for this allows the sovereign to exercise jurisdiction over any person within his territory, merely by reason of such 'temporary allegiance'. Yet the English rule has frequently been criticized[6] and it is in fact arguable that it constitutes an excess of international jurisdiction: where there exists no sub-

---

[1] Express provisions to that effect can be found almost everywhere. For particularly detailed provisions see sections 12–22 of the German Code of Civil Procedure.

[2] For England see O. 11, r. 1 (c) of the Rules of Supreme Court. It should be carefully noted that in all cases covered by O. 11 it is a matter for the Court's discretion whether it will assume jurisdiction. The Court's discretion dominates the law of jurisdiction as a whole. Under O. 11, i.e., where the defendant is not served in England, the plaintiff is not entitled to, but it is for the Court, in its discretion, to grant or withhold leave. Where the defendant is present in England, the plaintiff is entitled to serve him, but in its discretion the Court may stay proceedings. See below, p. 65, n. 1.

[3] This test seems to be usual in the United States. For striking examples of American practice see *United States* v. *Scophony Corporation*, 333 U. S. 795 (1948) or *United States* v. *Watchmakers of Switzerland*, 133 F. Supp. 50 (1955). As to England see O. 9, r. 8, and Dicey, p. 178.

[4] As to England, see Cheshire, p. 107; Dicey, op. 176. As to the United States, see Ehrenzweig, p. 88, with references.

[5] p. 65.

[6] Cheshire, p. 108; M. Wolff, p. 65; Wortley, *Jus et Lex* (Festgabe für Max Gutzwiller, Basel, 1959), p. 351, seems to defend it.

stantial connection between England and the defendant, particularly where not even the cause of action has any connection with England, the requirements of an enlightened doctrine of international jurisdiction are unlikely to be met merely by service of the writ in England. It is a remarkable fact that, probably in deference to such misgivings, English courts have devised a remedy which is apt to remove all objectionable features from presence and service as a head of jurisdiction: where the plaintiff has taken advantage of the defendant's temporary presence in England in circumstances which would be productive of injustice, the court will order a stay of the proceedings.[1] In the crucial case, therefore, the old English rule is unlikely to be in conflict with the standards of modern public international law.

(2) In so far as civil jurisdiction is founded upon the subject-matter of the claim a sufficiently close connection with the State of the forum will readily be admitted where the claim arises from a tort committed within its territory[2] or from a contract made[3] or to be performed, but broken[4] within its territory, or from other circumstances which need not be set forth.[5] It should only be pointed out that there reappears in this connection the problem, so well known to other branches of the law of jurisdiction, whether the doing of an act in one, and the causing of consequences in another, State provides a basis of jurisdiction for both States or either of them.[6]

---

[1] See, e.g., *Re Norton's Settlement*, [1908] 1 Ch. 471. For a similar American rule, see Ehrenzweig, pp. 125, 126, and see, in particular, the important cases of *Latimer* v. *Industrias Matarazzo*, 175 F. 2d 184 (1949), cert. den. 338 U. S. 867 (1949), and 91 F. Supp. 469 (1950); *Burt* v. *Isthmus Development Co.* 218 F. 2d 353 (1955), cert. den. 349 U. S. 922 (1955).

[2] This again is a ground which is almost universally recognized: Germany, section 32 of the Code of Civil Procedure; section 244 of the Danish Code of Procedure; Art. 59 of the French Code of Civil Procedure, and so forth. In England O. 11, r. 1 (ee), applies; the jurisdiction is discretionary.

[3] The *forum contractus* is a discretionary ground in England (O. 11, r. 1 (e), (i) and (ii)), and exists elsewhere, particularly in certain American States. It is, however, relatively rare.

[4] In England O. 11, r. 1 (e) (iv)—a discretionary ground; in Germany section 29 of the Code of Civil Procedure. Similarly in numerous other countries.

[5] Such circumstances are the fact that the proceedings relate to property within the country, or submission, whether by prior agreement or appearance.

[6] See an illuminating article by Reese and Galson, 44 *Iowa L.R.* (1959) 249. See, in particular, pp. 261, 262 on the significance of consequences which are intended or could reasonably have been expected. The introduction of a subjective element should, if possible, be avoided.

In England, however, there exists one peculiar ground of civil jurisdiction which is of doubtful validity from the point of view of international jurisdiction. An English court may adjudicate merely by reason of the fact that the contract 'by its terms or by implication is to be governed by English law'.[1] This provision, as will readily be seen, is liable to lead to extraordinary results in cases in which there exists no other connection between the parties or the contract on the one and England on the other hand. Such an exercise of civil jurisdiction could not be justified by the territorial or, indeed, by any other test of international jurisdiction and, therefore, might well be held to be contrary to international law.

In practice no such danger exists, for in all these cases of the discretionary exercise of civil jurisdiction the English courts are very conscious of the fact that service of proceedings outside Britain is 'an exceptional measure', that 'the ordinary principles of international comity are invaded by permitting it' and that, accordingly, they 'should approach with circumspection any request for leave to serve a writ abroad'.[2] This rule places so heavy a burden on a plaintiff that his application will not succeed where he cannot prove a real and substantial connection with England.

(3) The French Courts always have jurisdiction over a defendant who is a French national: 'Un Français pourra être traduit devant un tribunal de France pour des obligations par lui contractées en pays étranger, même avec un étranger.'[3] A similar provision does not seem to exist elsewhere, but there is much to be said in favour of the not uncommon suggestion that the judgment of a foreign court is more likely to be accorded international recognition by the forum if the defendant is a national of the foreign State.[4]

Such consequences flow from the theory that a State has international jurisdiction over its citizens wherever they may be.

---

[1] O. 11, r. 1 (e) (iii)—a discretionary ground.

[2] These words occur in Lord Radcliffe's speech in *Vitkovice Horni* v. *Korner*, [1951] A. C. 869, 882, but similar statements have frequently been made. In practice the statement of the law made by Farwell L.J. in *The Hagen*, [1908] P. 189, 201, is particularly often relied upon.

[3] Art. 15 of the Code Civil.

[4] Cheshire, p. 652, with further references; Smith, 2 I.C.L.Q. (1953), 510, 529–31; Wortley (above, p. 64, n. 6), pp. 357–9. Cf. section 328 of the German Code of Civil Procedure.

They are, therefore, unobjectionable in law, particularly in view of the fact that a person can only in the most exceptional cases (if at all) claim the protection of public international law against his own country. This would seem to be so even where the defendant is a corporation.

In numerous cases, however, the French courts are given civil jurisdiction merely by reason of the fact that the plaintiff is a French subject, though the defendant is a non-resident foreigner. According to Art. 14 of the Code Civil 'l'étranger, même non résidant en France, pourra être cité devant les tribunaux français pour l'exécution des obligations par lui contractées en France avec un Français; il pourra être traduit devant les tribunaux de France pour les obligations par lui contractées en pays étranger envers les Français'. This is an almost unique provision[1] which has been much criticized[2] and can only be described as indefensible. In England a French judgment based upon it will be refused recognition.[3] In fact, it far exceeds the recognized limits of jurisdiction: it is impossible to think of a single argument in favour of the proposition that a State has jurisdiction over the whole world merely because it has entered into a contract with one of such State's nationals. It is not surprising that Niboyet could not justify Art. 14 otherwise than by describing it as a 'privilège politique'[4] and that Batiffol, ignoring the almost universal practice of other States, puts forward something akin to anticipatory retaliation: Art. 14 is necessary so long as the international order is not in a position to remedy 'défaillances éventuelles' of other jurisdictions.[5] It is a paradoxical aspect of this problem that in the field of civil jurisdiction Art. 14 is the counterpart of that theory of criminal jurisdiction which Turkish law has adopted, which France (unsuccessfully) attacked before the Permanent Court of International Justice in the *Case of the Lotus* and which almost all French jurists continue to condemn.[6] It is certain that a prin-

---

[1] See above, p. 29.

[2] See, in particular, the very illuminating article by Nadelmann, 'Jurisdictionally Improper Fora', in *Twentieth Century Comparative and Conflicts Law* (*Legal Essays in Honor of Vessel Yntema*), p.'321, with many references. Schnitzer (above, p. 61, n. 2), p. 810, speaks of the 'grave disturbance' caused by the French law.

[3] *Schibsby* v. *Westenholz*, (1870) L.R. 6 Q.B. 155.

[4] *Traité de Droit International Privé Français* (1949), vi.320.

[5] p. 757.     [6] See below, p. 79,

ciple of passive personality is even less maintainable in civil than in criminal jurisdiction.

(4) It has been said that Art. 14 of the Code Civil should be regarded as unobjectionable, because in practice, French plaintiffs do not bring actions in France against non-resident foreigners except in case the latter have property in France, so that Art. 14 is merely a substitute for another type of civil jurisdiction unknown to France, but known to other countries, viz. jurisdiction founded upon assets of the defendant within the forum. Such an argument lacks persuasiveness for many reasons.[1] It overlooks, in particular, that *forum patrimonii* jurisdiction exists, it seems, only in Germany, Austria, Japan, certain parts of Switzerland[2] and Denmark[3] and is itself not assured of recognition outside these countries. It will certainly not be recognized in Britain[4] or, perhaps, in other countries.[5] In principle it should probably be held that the existence within the forum of assets belonging to the defendant should be regarded as a sufficiently close link to justify the assumption of jurisdiction, but only to the extent of such assets. As the Supreme Court of the United States has said,[6]

Every State owes protection to its own citizens; and when non-residents deal with them, it is a legitimate and just exercise of authority to hold and appropriate any property owned by such non-residents to satisfy the claims of its citizens. It is in virtue of the State's jurisdiction over the property of the non-resident situated within its limits that its tribunals can inquire into that non-resident's obligations to its own citizens, and the inquiry can then be carried only to the extent necessary to control the disposition of the property.

In other words, civil jurisdiction based on the defendant's assets within the forum may claim international validity if, and only if, it is in its practical effect the same as the time-honoured *forum arresti* which, though it is said to have 'its origin in customary law developed and practised in the Mayor's Court of the

---

[1] See, generally, Nadelmann (above, p. 67, n. 2), p. 327.
[2] This is the list given by Nadelmann (above, p. 67, n. 2), p. 330.
[3] Allan Philip, *American-Danish Private International Law* (New York, 1957), p. 25.
[4] Dicey, p. 25; Cheshire, p. 650.
[5] This is suggested, but not proved, by Nadelmann, above, p. 67, n. 2. It would seem that the learned author has misunderstood the decision to be mentioned in the next note. It sanctioned the *forum patrimonii*, but it condemned the mode of service.
[6] *Pennoyer* v. *Neff*, 95 U. S. 714, 723 (1878).

City of London', [1] is not now known to English law, but exists in most other countries, including Scotland, South Africa and the American states. But the *forum arresti* jurisdiction is limited to the assets. From the point of view of the doctrine of international jurisdiction the objection to the *forum patrimonii* lies in the fact that assets of trifling value are said to justify civil jurisdiction in respect of claims of unlimited size.

## Section 4

### CRIMINAL JURISDICTION

### I

Civil jurisdiction is 'curial', that is to say, concerned with the question whether a State's rules for bringing a person before its *courts* conform to public international law. When one comes to criminal jurisdiction, a problem of a different nature falls to be considered: is the State of the forum, if it has 'curial' jurisdiction, entitled to make a person criminally *liable* for acts committed by him?

No such question can arise if the case involves no foreign element at all; if, in particular, all facts take place within the State of the forum: A, a Dutchman in Amsterdam, obtains by false pretences money from B, another Dutchman in Rotterdam. Only Holland is called upon to pronounce upon A's criminal liability. Only Dutch law applies. There is no room for any question of international jurisdiction.

It is inherent in what has just been said that another State such as France has no right to lay down rules which purport to deal with A's criminal liability. In the example given, France has no interest at all in A's criminal liability, and if she did purport to make him criminally liable this would be a clear case of the violation of the principle of non-interference and also an injustice in case A's act should have been lawful under the law of Holland: perhaps the pretence was only reckless and therefore not criminal under the law of Holland; it would be wrong if France, applying her own law, was allowed to hold it

[1] Nadelmann (above, p. 67, n. 2), p. 325.

criminal. This point of view which may safely be said to underlie all the opinions rendered in the *Case of the Lotus*[1] is of greater practical importance than may at first sight appear. It precludes France from arrogating to herself jurisdiction over A's Dutch activities if and when A enters French territory. It is, therefore, designed to promote security and certainty in international life, to prevent friction among nations. In fact, there is no authority which would support, and much authority which would condemn,[2] any such French legislation, and it is surely untenable to suggest, as a learned writer does more than once,[3] that 'the only, but decisive limitation which, in this respect, international law imposes on sovereign States is that, in the absence of permissive rules to the contrary, criminal jurisdiction must not actually be exercised outside the territory . . . of the State which claims such universal jurisdiction'.

It follows that in order to be entitled to assume legislative jurisdiction there must exist a close connection in an international sense between the person, fact or event and the State imposing criminal liability in regard to them. And the real problem of international law is to define the circumstances in which, according to the practice of States, the connection is sufficiently close. Most observers would probably still be inclined to answer in Huber–Storyan terms: a State may impose criminal liability if the act in question is committed within its territory or if the accused (or perhaps the victim) is its national. Yet while locality of the act or nationality are important points of contact, they are neither the only nor the invariably sufficient points of contact. It would go too far in the opposite direction if it were suggested that any connection with the legislating State should be sufficient. To see the limits of a State's criminal jurisdiction in the doctrine of the abuse of rights[4] comes nearer the truth, but is, perhaps, a less attractive formulation.

---

[1] P.C.I.J., Series A, No. 10 (1927).

[2] One can refer here to the whole of the literature dealing with the principle of non-interference (above, p. 38). See, further, Jennings, Extraterritorial Jurisdiction', and the United States Antitrust Laws, *B.Y.I.L.* (1957), 151.

[3] Schwarzenberger, *International Law* (3rd ed., 1957), i.254, and see p. 185; *Current Legal Problems* (1962), 248, 255.

[4] See, in particular, Bourquin, 16 *Recueil* (1927 i), 178 sqq., whose discussion remains very valuable; Dahm, i.260; Jennings, 'Extraterritorial Jurisdiction', p. 153. See also Sarkas, *The Proper Law of Crime in International Law*, 11 I.C.L.Q. (1962), 446.

## II

Thus it would seem to be clear that, to revert to the example given above, France is within her rights to impose criminal liability upon A if the letter containing the false pretences is sent by him from France to B in Rotterdam or, conversely, if A in Amsterdam sends the letter to B in Paris or if, as a result of false pretences communicated by A to B in Holland, money is obtained by A in France.[1]

To state the rule in general terms, one cannot do better than to repeat the time-honoured formula which is adopted by Art. 3 of the Draft Convention proposed by that excellent and unsurpassed undertaking, the Harvard Research in International Law[2]: A State has jurisdiction with respect to any crime committed in whole or in part within its territory. It is, of course, plain that within the limits so stated it is open to every State to define for itself the conditions under which it desires to impose criminal liability. Thus it has been held in England[3] that, if two persons agree to commit a criminal offence in and under the law of Germany, they cannot be convicted of conspiracy in England, even though the agreement was made there: no rule of international law required that result, and in many cases States punish for crimes initiated within their territory, but completed abroad.[4] Similarly, a State may treat as a crime an act which is completed within its territory, but commenced abroad.[5]

---

[1] This is certainly so if B hands the cash over in France. But would the result be the same if B hands to A in Holland a cheque drawn on a Paris bank? On a case of the type mentioned in the text see the Supreme Court of India in *Mobarik Ali Ahmed* v. *State of Bombay*, Int. L.R. (1957), 156.

[2] *Research in International Law* (1935), i.439 sqq. It is a great pity that this work has not been brought up to date and that, therefore, it cannot be taken for granted that the law is still as stated in 1935. We need much more work of the type and calibre of the *Harvard Research* which remains unique in character and quality. The Draft Restatement does not even attempt to be a comparable undertaking. On the problems discussed in the text see, in particular, sections 17, 18, and 19.

[3] *Board of Trade* v. *Owen*, [1957] A. C. 602.

[4] The *Harvard Research*, among others, calls this 'the subjective application of the territorial principle' (p. 484), a most unhappy phrase. On the principle see Jennings, 'Extraterritorial Jurisdiction', pp. 156 sqq.

[5] This is called the 'objective application' (see, e.g., *Harvard Research*, pp. 487 sqq),—an equally unhappy phrase. There exists an enormous amount of learning on this point. The rule stated in the text means that attempt or participation in any capacity is treated so that it may be punished wherever any part of the criminal

There exists, however, insufficient connection between the State and the allegedly criminal act or conduct, and jurisdiction in the international sense is, accordingly, lacking, if what occurs within the State is not an essential or constituent element of the crime.[1] As Art. 693 of the French Code de Procédure Pénale puts it,[2]

est reputée commise sur le territoire de la République toute infraction dont un acte caractérisant un des ses éléments constitutifs a été accompli en France.

Or as the German Supreme Court has consistently formulated the principle,[3] a crime is committed wherever 'irgend ein Teil des strafbaren Tatbestands verwirklicht worden ist, mag es sich um Ausführungshandlungen oder um *tatbestandsmässige Wirkungen* handeln'. It is necessary, therefore, in each case to analyse the factual requirements of the crime, as laid down in the rule, with a view to ascertaining whether at least one of them has occurred within the legislating State's territory.[4] Facts which do not constitute one of the requirements so defined are insufficient to justify the assumption of legislative jurisdic-

offence is committed either by the accused or his accomplices: *Harvard Research*, pp. 503 sqq.; Stimson, *Conflict of Criminal Laws* (1936), pp. 78 seq. As to Germany, in particular, see Schönke–Schröder, *Strafgesetzbuch* (11th ed., 1963), introduction to section 3, n. 5, with numerous references to decisions, particularly Supreme Court, 14 July 1936, JW 1936, 2655.

[1] This is a point which is frequently implied, but strongly and justifiably emphasized, for instance, by Jennings, 'Extraterritorial Jurisdiction', pp. 159, 160; 'Limits', p. 215; *Harvard Research*, pp. 494, 495; and especially the *Case of the Lotus* (above, p. 70, n. 1), p. 23: an offence is 'committed in the national territory if one of the constituent elements of the offence, and more especially its effects, have taken place there'. In the same sense Jescheck, *Internationales Recht und Diplomatie* (1956), 75, at p. 93. This is a brilliant and most persuasive contribution which, unfortunately, is not readily accessible, but which no student of the subject should overlook. For a good statement of English law see Halsbury (Simonds), x.318. This was accepted by the Supreme Court of India in *Mobarik Ali Ahmed* v. *State of Bombay*, Int. L.R. (1957), 156, 158.

[2] This Article gives statutory effect to previous judicial practice: see Bouzat–Pinatel, *Traité de Droit Pénal* (1963), ii.1300 seq., and, in particular, Cass. Crim. 29 July 1932, *Clunet* 1933, 636.

[3] See, for instance, Supreme Court, 2 March 1933, *RGStr* 67, 130, 138; 2 February 1940, *RGStr* 74, 56, and all textbooks.

[4] In private international law there frequently arises the cognate problem where a tort has been committed. In Anglo-American countries the law on this point is not yet settled: Dicey, p. 967; Ehrenzweig, pp. 545 sqq. On the Continent the solutions seem to be more in line with the practice in criminal cases: see, for instance, Batiffol, section 560; Swiss Federal Tribunal, *BGE* 76, ii.110 (1950), also *Jahrbuch für Schweizerisches Recht* (1952), 273, with note by Gutzwiller; for a recent comparative survey see Hillgenberg, *NJW* 1963, 2198.

tion, because in the eyes of the law they are, ex hypothesi, neutral and irrelevant, so that they cannot be regarded as a sufficiently close or, indeed, as any connection with the State. If A sends the letter containing the false pretences to B in Paris, but B has left for Rome and the letter is forwarded to him there, or if A writes the letter in France, but puts it in his pocket, returns to Holland and posts it there, no essential element of the crime of obtaining money by false pretences has taken place in France, although the letter has been on French territory. If a picture is stolen in Holland and the thief takes it to Germany and stores it there no element of the theft has occurred in Germany. Even if the thief destroys the picture in Germany, he cannot be prosecuted there for doing wilful damage to the property of another, because the destruction constitutes what in German criminal law is called a 'straflose Nachtat'.[1] If, while in Austria, the thief forms his intention to steal the picture in Holland, Austria would not have international jurisdiction to prosecute him for theft, because no constituent element of the crime took place in Austria. It may be that by Austrian law the thief is guilty of some other crime for which Austria is entitled to punish him. The point made here is that Austria is not entitled to punish him for the theft committed in Holland.

The requirement that what occurs within the State assuming criminal jurisdiction must involve an essential or constituent element of the crime should not, as Professor Jennings has so rightly insisted,[2] be obscured by the inexact use of the word 'effect'. The effect occurring within the country must be the fact which completes the offence; neither more nor less remote facts which could loosely be described as 'effects' are sufficient. What the law considers relevant is, as a rule, the necessary legal effect, not the ulterior effect economically or socially.[3] Words used, though not always the decisions reached, in certain

---

[1] See, e.g., Schönke–Schröder (above, p. 71, n. 5), Introduction before section, 73.

[2] 'Extraterritorial Jurisdiction', p. 159; 'Limits', p. 215. It is noteworthy that the new Convention on Offences Committed on Board Aircraft of 14 September 1963 allows a State to exercise jurisdiction over such offences if 'the offence has effect' on such State's territory: see Art. 4 (a) in *International Legal Materials*, (1963) ii.1042.

[3] Cf. *Commonwealth of Australia* v. *Bank of New South Wales*, [1950] A. C. 235, 307, per Lord Porter.

American cases[1] sometimes seem to be oblivious of this simple truth. They invariably invoke Mr. Justice Homes' statement in *Strassheim* v. *Daily*[2] which is *fons et origo* of this branch of American law, but properly analysed supports the view put forward here. While in Illinois Daily committed a fraud upon the State of Michigan, which took effect in Michigan in that the State made a payment there. Daily was held to have committed the offence in Michigan:

If a jury should believe that Daily did the acts that induced by fraud the payment by the State (of Michigan), the usage of the civilized world would warrant Michigan in punishing him, although he never set foot in the State until after the fraud was complete. Acts done outside a jurisdiction, but intended to produce and producing detrimental effects within it, justify a State in punishing the cause of the harm as if he had been present at the effect, if the State should succeed in getting him within its power.

Read in their context these words merely sanction, in a wholly traditional manner, the application of a well-established principle to the facts of a textbook-case.

The territorial principle of criminal jurisdiction, the main features of which have been described, is widely adhered to in the practice of States, particularly in Anglo-American countries, but it is by no means the only principle governing the exercise of a State's legislative jurisdiction in criminal matters. Nor is it a principle the observation of which is required by international law: 'The territoriality of criminal law ... is not an absolute principle of international law and by no means coincides with territorial sovereignty.'[3] There are other facts and rules which provide a State with sufficient contact with the crime and, consequently, with international jurisdiction. To treat them as exceptions to territoriality rather than as distinct aspects of a much wider principle is probably theoretically wrong, but does no harm. In truth, they are necessary as a matter of practical experience to take care of cases which

---

[1] See below, pp. 87, 88. Thus, to take an example from the law of libel, it is not a constituent element of the offence that the libelled person has knowledge of the libel, or suffers damage. Accordingly, the offence is not committed where such knowledge is acquired or damage is suffered. See German Supreme Court, 21 June 1943, *DR* 1943, 1101.

[2] 221 U. S. 281, 284, 285 (1911).

[3] *Case of the Lotus* (above, p. 70, n. 1), p. 20. It is possible that Professor Jennings would disagree; see, in particular, 'Limits', p. 214.

obviously engage a State's criminal jurisdiction, but which are not covered by the territorial principle; in fact, no legal system has found it possible to rely on the latter exclusively.[1]

## III

The most important of the alternative approaches to the problem of criminal jurisdiction is the principle of nationality.

(1) It cannot be doubted that international law does not preclude a State from imposing criminal liability upon its nationals in regard to crimes committed in foreign countries: if in the example given above A were a French subject, France would clearly be entitled to prosecute him. Nationality of the offender as a permissible general test of criminal jurisdiction is recognized not only by the territorial principle as understood by Huber and Story,[2] but also by the law of the United States of America,[3] France,[4] Germany[5] and many other countries[6]; this does not mean that, in fact, nationality is employed in these countries as a general test—in the United States, for instance, it has been adopted only seldom and only in specific cases. But on this footing, as will appear presently, exceptions to the principle of nationality become unavoidable. Hence, this system is not fundamentally different from the idea of strict territoriality which is taken as a starting point in Britain and a number of other countries, but which, in respect of a variety of crimes, has to be displaced by the test of nationality.[7] It is, of course, true that the principle of nationality lends itself to abuse and has been abused, in particular, by Italian fascism[8]

---

[1] Cf. Oppenheim, pp. 331, 332.     [2] Above, p. 20.

[3] *United States* v. *Bowman* 260 U. S. 94 (1922); *Blackmer* v. *United States* 284 U. S. 421 (1932); *Skioriotes* v. *Florida* 313 U. S. 669 (1941); *Steele* v. *Bulova Watch Co.*, 344 U. S. 280 (1952) and numerous other cases. See, generally, *Harvard Research*, p. 519.

[4] Art. 698 of the Code of Procédure Pénale.

[5] Section 3 of the Criminal Code.

[6] For the position in 1935 see *Harvard Research*, pp. 519 sqq. Art. 5 of its Draft Convention adopts the principle of nationality. See also Art. 4 (b) of the Convention on Offences on Board Aircraft, above, p. 73, n. 2, and the Report by Brierly and Charles de Visscher, *A.J.I.L.* (1926) (Special Supplement), pp. 252 sqq.

[7] The cases in which Britain asserts criminal jurisdiction over British subjects abroad are listed by Halsbury (Simonds), x.323, 324.

[8] See Drost, 43 *Zeitschrift für Internationales Recht* (1930–1), 111, at p. 137.

and German National-Socialism, so that it has become discredited. The Federal Republic of Germany has gone further: in the year 1940 Hitler substituted the test of nationality for that of territoriality[1] (both qualified by certain exceptions) and after the war the West German courts held these new rules to be reconcilable with the demands of the Constitution and the rule of law.[2] But the test of nationality remained subject to trenchant criticism,[3] and although at least one learned writer went too far, when he suggested that it was contrary to public international law,[4] the recent West German Draft of a new Criminal Code proposes its abolition and the return to a (qualified) principle of territoriality.[5]

The problem lies, not in the choice of a proper starting point, but in defining the limitations which, in the interest of a humane and progressive development and for the sake of a spirit of reasonableness and international neighbourliness, the nationality test must acknowledge. If Utopia were to enjoin all Utopians to drive on the left wherever they may be, a Utopian motorist driving in Holland would be breaking either Utopian or Dutch law. If Ruritania should prohibit all its nationals from doing business with certain countries and if such a discriminatory practice were a criminal offence in Holland, the Dutch branch of a Ruritanian corporation could not help committing an

---

[1] Sections 3–5 of the Criminal Code in the version of the decree of 6 May 1940. This was, of course, a measure of a highly political character.

[2] Federal Tribunal, 29 February 1952, *BGHStr* 2, 160; 12 July 1951, *NJW* 1951, 769. The development is fully discussed in all German books on criminal law.

[3] See, in particular, Jescheck's article, quoted above, p. 72, n. 1.

[4] Professor Hellmuth Mayer, *Juristenzeitung* 1952, 609. Jescheck (above, p. 72, n. 1), after having rejected (pp. 78, 80) the nationality principle 'as a piece of ideological strait-jacket which National-Socialism put over its nationals from the cradle to the grave', also expresses grave doubts about its legality under public international law (pp. 83, 84).

[5] Deutscher Bundestag, 3. Wahlperiode, Drucksache 2150: Draft Criminal Code, sections 3–6, and the Government's Statement of Reasons, pp. 99, 100, 103 sqq. See, in particular, p. 99: 'The disapproval of the nationality principle corresponds to the present trend of legal development. The historical instances which, for the purpose of the prosecution of and the punishment for offences, refer to the accused's nationality are today without validity. In the light of present relations between civilized nations the State's claim to subject nationals everywhere in the world to its own criminal law becomes questionable. A German national who resides abroad must be entitled to live according to the legal order of the country of residence. Most foreign laws, particularly in Western Europe and in Anglo-Saxon countries, accept this point of view.'

offence under either law. Accordingly, Oppenheim is fully justified in stating[1] that

> a State is prevented from requiring such acts from its citizens abroad as are forbidden to them by the Municipal Law of the land in which they reside, and from ordering them not to commit such acts as they are bound to commit according to the Municipal Law of the land in which they reside.

But a conflict is possible even if the law in both countries is the same: suppose a Utopian has committed an offence in Holland and is punished there for it. If Utopia could punish him again, it is not at all certain whether he could rely on the rule of *ne bis in idem*.[2] In these circumstances it is for the doctrine of international jurisdiction to avoid a clash between the territorial and the national rule. That doctrine can only suggest the test of closeness of connection. It demands, accordingly, a weighing up of elements connecting a set of circumstances with the local law and with the national law respectively. In a large number of cases the local law will have to be allowed to prevail, for every other solution would be destructive of justice and international intercourse.[3]

States which proclaim the test of nationality have given effect to such considerations, though not always so as to preclude an excess of jurisdiction. Thus, a French citizen can always be punished for a 'crime' committed abroad, but for a 'délit' only if it is punishable by the local law,[4] and in no case after final judgment has been pronounced in the foreign country.[5] A criminal act done by a German national outside Germany is at present not punishable in Germany 'if, in view of the peculiar factual conditions at the place of commission, the act, according to German legal conceptions, does not merit punishment'[6]; punishment already suffered abroad is treated as part of the

---

[1] p. 296.

[2] He could not do so in Germany (Bavarian Constitutional Court, *NJW* 1963, 1003), but he could do so in France (Art. 692 of the Code de Procédure Pénale) and probably in England (*R. v. Roche* (1775) 1 Leach 134, 135; *R. v. Aughet* (1918) 118 L. T. 658; Halsbury (Simonds), x.405).

[3] See Jennings, 'Extraterritorial Jurisdiction', p. 151. His statement that 'extraterritorial jurisdiction may not be exercised in such a way as to contradict the local law at the place where the alleged offence was committed' may be a little too rigid, but in principle deserves approval.

[4] Art. 689 of the Code de Procédure Pénale.

[5] Art. 692 of the Code de Procédure Pénale.

[6] Section 3 (2) of the Criminal Code.

punishment to be imposed in Germany.[1] These are methods of circumscribing the test of nationality which are not necessarily satisfactory and sufficient, and it may be more in harmony with the demands of a substantial connection if the test of nationality applies only to offences that are also punishable by the *lex loci delicti* or to enumerated offences of a certain degree.[2] It must, however, be admitted that it is difficult and perhaps impossible for restrictions upon the doctrine of international jurisdiction to operate at all in relation to the test of nationality, because international law cannot to any substantial extent limit the rights of a State over its own nationals.

(2) It is an entirely different question whether a State is entitled to exercise criminal jurisdiction over all persons who, according to its own law, committed a criminal act anywhere against one of its nationals. Does the nationality of the victim establish a sufficiently close connection? Although possibly far-reaching exceptions to the rule will have to be recognized,[3] by and large the answer can only be in the negative.[4] The paramount reason was forcefully stated by Sir John Fischer Williams[5]:

An American or a Japanese may be tried in Turkey without the observance of the forms of justice guaranteed to him by his own constitution for an act which perhaps in New York or Tokyo, the place where it was done, was no offence at all, but which violated a Turkish law of which he had never heard, framed under conditions wholly strange to him. He may be a national of a State which has abolished certain forms of punishment, e.g. the death penalty, or transportation overseas, and yet if he imprudently ventures into another State after committing in the territory of his home State an offence—or it may be even doing an act which the law of his home State does

---

[1] Section 7 of the Criminal Code.  [2] *Harvard Research*, pp. 523 sqq.

[3] These arise primarily from the principle of universality mentioned below. Whether there is any legitimate need for further exceptions is open to doubt. It is a matter of regret that the new German Draft Criminal Code (section 6) adopts section 4 (2), No. 2, of the present Criminal Code as altered in 1940, which had no precedent in the pre-Hitler era: German criminal law applies to acts done abroad against a German if the act is punishable by the *lex loci delicti* or the *locus delicti* is not subject to a State's criminal jurisdiction. The reasons given by the *Motives*, p. 106, are unconvincing.

[4] The vast majority of States probably agree. See the discussion by Jescheck (above, p. 72, n. 1), p. 92, who takes the view that the victim's nationality is a point of contact permitted by international law only if 'vital interests' of the victim are injured. Jescheck suggests that the principle of passive personality 'is contrary to a sound international order founded upon mutual confidence and the principle of division of labour, such as we must demand, create, and recognize'.

[5] *Chapters on Current International Law* (1929), p. 220.

not treat as criminal—he may be lawfully sent to the scaffold or into exile in a tropical climate.

Although in 1935 a number of countries seem to have followed the 'principle of passive personality',[1] the Harvard Research itself did not sanction it[2] and it should be treated as an excess of jurisdiction, though this would probably be impossible if the Convention on Offences Committed on Board Aircraft of 1963 should come into force, for it allows a State to exercise jurisdiction if the offence has been committed 'against a national or permanent resident of such State'.[3]

The reconcilability of that principle with the doctrine of jurisdiction could have been, but was not clarified by the Permanent Court of International Justice in the *Case of the Lotus*.[4] In this case, it will be remembered, the question was whether by international law Turkey was allowed to exercise criminal jurisdiction over the French captain of the *Lotus* which was responsible for the collision with the Turkish vessel. The Court found it unnecessary to pronounce upon the compatibility of the principle of passive personality adopted by Turkish criminal law with international law,[5] for it held that the Turkish prosecution could 'also be justified from the point of view of the so-called territorial principle', as the effects of the collision were produced on the Turkish vessel 'and consequently in a place assimilated to Turkish territory',[6] and that France had no exclusive jurisdiction over acts done on board a French ship on the high seas.[7] The latter reasoning was probably wrong[8] and is now obsolete.[9] The former is therefore without validity in its particular context, and in regard to the territorial principle as a whole merely reaffirms the well-known conditions of operation. In these circumstances it would seem tempting to conclude, as Lord Finlay said of the *Cutting* case,[10] that 'nothing was decided' in the *Lotus* case.[11]

[1] *Harvard Research*, p. 578.
[2] p. 579; the Draft Restatement, section 30 (2), also rejects it. Doubts about the alleged principle are expressed also by Germann, 69 *Schweizerische Zeitschrift für Strafrecht* (1954), 237, 249 sqq.
[3] Art. 4 (b), above, p. 73, n. 2.     [4] Series A, No. 10.     [5] pp. 22, 23.
[6] p. 23.     [7] pp. 24–7.
[8] It 'met with wide-spread criticism': Oppenheim, p. 334.
[9] See above, p. 25, n. 2.     [10] Series A, No. 10, p. 57.
[11] It remains remarkable that so progressive and outstanding a lawyer as Max Huber associated himself with the judgment of the majority.

## IV

Although the legislating State does not, in principle, have any rights of criminal jurisdiction in respect of acts done abroad by an alien, two exceptions had to be admitted and are now well established. Both of them stem from and illustrate the idea that in essence criminal jurisdiction is determined, not by such external, mechanical and inflexible tests as territoriality or nationality, but by the closeness of a State's connection with, or the intimacy and legitimacy of its interests in, the facts in issue. Both of those exceptions are among the strongest proofs of the inadequacy of the Huber–Storyan approach at the present time.

(1) Thus, no State can reasonably be expected to stand by in complete passivity while aliens abroad injure its own vital interests. Hence it is recognized that, according to the so-called protective principle, a State is entitled to punish aliens for offences of a certain character, though they were committed wholly outside its boundaries. The list of such offences includes attacks upon the security of the State,[1] perjury committed in proceedings pending in the State,[2] possibly disclosure of trade secrets owned by a domestic undertaking[3] and similar cases.[4] Although details vary and although British practice rejects the exception altogether,[5] it is clear that States must make a reasonable and just assessment of acts which so much affect their interests as to make it proper to impose punishment for them irrespective of the identity of place and person. It would be abusive if a State invoked the protective principle without due regard to the importance of the offence. In all cases, here as elsewhere, the standard is supplied solely by international law, i.e. by the general practice of civilized States.[6]

---

[1] France: Art. 694 of the Code de Procédure Pénale; Germany: section 4 (3), No. 2, of the Criminal Code. Art. 4 (b) of the Aircraft Convention, above, p. 73, n. 2.

[2] For instance, Germany: section 4 (3), No. 6, of the Criminal Code.

[3] From the point of view of international law this is a doubtful case mentioned in section 4 (3), No. 5, of the German Criminal Code.

[4] For a survey see *Harvard Research*, pp. 543 seq. The Draft Restatement, section 33, allows the protective principle to operate only where the conduct is generally recognized as a crime.

[5] Halsbury (Simonds), x.316, 317, 322.

[6] The necessity for an inquiry into the importance of the interests concerned is rightly stressed by Drost, 43 *Zeitschrift für Internationales Recht* (1930–1), pp. 136, 139 and Jescheck (above, p. 72, n. 1), p. 92.

This principle should be recognized as comprising those aspects of the principle of passive nationality which merit general acceptation: the nationality of the victim is a permissible point of contact for the purposes of criminal jurisdiction only where the offence itself is so seriously prejudicial to the State as to render it reasonable to impose punishment. It would be an excess of jurisdiction, if, for instance, every adverse speculation in bonds issued by the State or every prejudicial publication in the foreign press were said to affect its vital interests.[1]

(2) The second exception also arises from the character of certain offences. This may be such as to affect and, therefore, justify and perhaps even compel every member of the family of nations to punish the criminal over whom jurisdiction can in practice be exercised. These are crimes which are founded in international law, which the nations of the world have agreed, usually by treaty, to suppress and which are thus recognized not merely as acts commonly treated as criminal, but as dangerous to and, indeed, as attacks upon the *international* order. Traffic in women and children, trade in narcotics, falsification of currency, piracy and trade in indecent publications are crimes covered by such treaties, and therefore by the principle of universality.[2] By its very nature this principle can apply only in a limited number of cases, but the existence of a treaty is not a prerequisite of its application.[3] It is founded upon the accused's attack upon the international order as a whole.[4]

---

[1] These two examples of 'economic' and 'political defeatism' respectively were taken by Drost (see preceding note), p. 137, from the legislation of Fascist Italy. That the protective principle must be applied strictly and in a very limited number of cases is also emphasized by Germann, 69 *Schweizerische Zeitschrift für Strafrecht* (1954), 237, 246–8. It is possible that Fitzmaurice, 92 *Recueil* (1957 ii), 215 is too liberal in allowing a State to assume jurisdiction over acts committed 'against' it.

[2] For a list see *Harvard Research*, pp. 563 sqq. The *Harvard Research*, p. 561, and the Draft Restatement, section 33, treat counterfeiting of currency as covered by the protective principle. See Art. 4 (e) of the Aircraft Convention, above, p. 73, n. 2.

[3] Piracy is a familiar example of an 'international' crime not backed by treaty.

[4] It is, therefore, likely that Israel was entitled to exercise international jurisdiction in the *Case of Eichmann* which arose from a unique case of such an attack. See Judgment of the Supreme Court (published by the Ministry of Justice, Jerusalem, 1963) paragraph 12, pp. 35–46. On this judgment see Schwarzenberger, *Current Legal Problems* (1962) 248, 259; Green, 37 *Tulane L.R.* (1963), 641; *B.Y.I.L.* (1962), 457, and in particular Fawcett, ibid., p. 181, among others. But the *Harvard Research*, p. 573, and the Draft Restatement, sections 34–6, limit the prin-

## Section 5

### JURISDICTION OVER TRADE PRACTICES

## I

The State's international right to control restrictive practices gives rise to questions which are of so esoteric a character and have been so insufficiently clarified by judicial decisions that an introductory survey of the doctrine of legislative jurisdiction would perhaps do well to refrain from discussing it. On the other hand, this branch of the law throws vivid light on the interplay of several aspects of international jurisdiction. It may be instructive, therefore, to offer a few observations on the international implications of what in America is called antitrust legislation.

(1) The first comment arises from the necessity for distinguishing between such problems of international jurisdiction as relate to the local exercise of criminal[1] or administrative competence over the activities of non-resident aliens, and those which are created by the substantive regulation of restrictive practices adopted by non-residents. The former involve questions of wide impact and far transcend the narrow realm of the law of restrictive practices. Like many other American statutes the Clayton Act[2] provides for jurisdiction over a defendant 'who is found or transacts business' in the United States. Although it goes much too far to suggest that 'fairness is explicitly stated to be the nub of the issue of personal jurisdiction',[3] the practice of the American courts, particularly of lower courts, attributes extreme width to this phrase; the case in which the subsidiary is held to be no more than a branch of

ciple of universality so as to make it inapplicable in the circumstances of that case and of other cases in which it should be allowed to operate.

[1] In the international sense, of course. See Jennings, 'Extraterritorial Jurisdiction', p. 147.

[2] Section 12.

[3] This is said by Brewster, *Antitrust and American Business Abroad* (1958), p. 55, who, like many other American writers, makes the mistake of confusing two entirely different questions, i.e. whether according to the relevant substantive law a Court has local competence and whether that law conforms to the constitutional requirement of due process. *International Shoe Co.* v. *Washington*, 326 U. S. 310 (1945), related solely to the latter question.

the parent[1] will attract the special attention of any student who decides to inquire into such aspects of the doctrine of international jurisdiction as relate to the definition of residence, territorial subjection and so forth.

(2) A further complication illustrated by, though not peculiar to, the law of restrictive practices is that, having assumed competence in relation to a non-resident defendant, courts are liable to make orders which purport to enforce regulation of the defendant's conduct, not within the district of the court, but in foreign countries. This again, is a separate issue which concerns enforcement rather than legislative jurisdiction and to which it will be necessary to return.[2]

## II

(1) If traditional tests were applicable it would be open to a State to impose the duty of refraining from restrictive trade practices in foreign countries upon persons, whether natural or legal, who are its nationals: the United States could restrain its nationals operating a match factory in Ruritania from participating in the local match monopoly. The law of the United States does not so provide, for section 1 of the Sherman Act declares illegal 'every contract . . . in restraint of trade or commerce . . . with foreign nations', not in foreign nations. No country could so provide without contravening the paramount principle of international jurisdiction, i.e. the requirement of a close connection between the legislating State and the subject-matter of the legislation. A legitimate interest in the regulation of restrictive practices is not created merely by virtue of the participants' nationality. It cannot matter to a State whether one of its nationals is a party to a restrictive practice exclusively within the economy of another State, for a restrictive practice is not necessarily a heinous practice. If a State purported to regulate such activities of its nationals it would run the risk of exposing them to the dilemma of failing to give effect either to their permanent or their temporary allegiance. There would be the risk of a conflict with the local sovereign who would

---

[1] On these cases see Brewster, pp. 56–61. The principal cases are *United States* v. *Scophony*, 333 U. S. 795 (1948) and *United States* v. *Watchmakers of Switzerland*, 133 F. Supp. 40 (1955).

[2] Below, p. 132, and see p. 94, n. 1.

complain of interference with the local economy. It is not surprising that in fact no country has applied the test of nationality to the law of restrictive practices.[1]

(2) It is a much more difficult and elusive question whether the traditional test of the territoriality of jurisdiction is appropriate and sufficient for purposes of the law of restrictive trade practices. In most cases it may well be adequate. This applies, in particular, where the court is confronted with so special and unusual a situation as arose in the famous case of *American Banana Co.* v. *United Fruit Co.*,[2] which has perhaps been more frequently and more seriously misunderstood than most other decisions. This was a claim for triple damages brought under the Sherman Act and alleging a wrong done to and damage suffered by the plaintiff, a private person, in Costa Rica. In that country the Sherman Act did not apply, so that the plaintiff could not prove a tort in Costa Rica and was bound to fail. The decision has nothing to do with the case in which the United States, in the exercise of its sovereign power, proceeds in respect of a wrong alleged to have been done to it as a result of the infringement of its criminal legislation. The test of territoriality also covers those implications of the traditional doctrine which relate to participation in offences.[3] Thus, if one of the principals is subject to the State's jurisdiction, absent accessories or agents are similarly subject; if there exists jurisdiction over one of several conspirators, other conspirators may also be prosecuted. These rules explain such cases as *United States* v. *Holophane*,[4]

---

[1] This is different in the law of trade marks and unfair competition where the probity of citizens rather than economic policies of the State may be in issue: see above, p. 29. The decision in *Steele* v. *Bulova Watch Co.* 344 U. S. 280 (1956), also Int. L.R. (1956), 270, related to the Lanham Trade Marks Act and, notwithstanding certain dicta, is entirely consistent with the submissions in the text.

[2] 213 U. S. 347 (1909)—a famous judgment of the Court delivered by Mr. Justice Holmes. The explanation of the decision given in *United States* v. *Sisal Sales Corporation*, 274 U. S. 369 (1927), is wholly convincing. The *American Banana Co.* case would, so it may be confidently asserted, be decided in exactly the same way after more than fifty years.

[3] Above, p. 47, n. 7.

[4] 119 F. Supp. 114 (1935), affirmed by a memorandum of an equally divided Supreme Court at 352 U. S. 903 (1956), also Int. L.R. (1956), 130. For a forerunner in a different field see *Ford* v. *United States*, 273 U. S. 593 (1927). On proper analysis it appears that most international antitrust cases decided in the United States rest on the principle stated in the text. This applies, in particular, to *Timken Roller Bearing* v. *United States*, 341 U. S. 593 (1951), which is remarkable, not from the point of view of international law, but on account of the interpretation of the

where the court found an illegal agreement between an American, British and French corporation affecting world markets, including the American market. The decision in *United States* v. *Imperial Chemical Industries*[1] largely rests on a similar basis. Next, no difficulty will arise in those cases in which the activity complained of is carried out partly inside the legislating country, partly abroad. If, therefore, American companies combine in the United States to keep an American competitor out of Canadian markets, it is no defence under the Sherman Act that such part of the conspiracy as occurs in Canada is not unlawful there.[2] Finally, the traditional approach will likewise be sufficient in those cases in which all parties to a restrictive practice are, and act exclusively, outside the legislating State and leave its market completely unaffected: suppose a group of Dutch companies (some of which may be subsidiaries of an American parent) have factories in Holland and enter into a restrictive practice applicable only to the Dutch market. No case has decided that the United States could proceed against these companies in respect of a restraint which is wholly Dutch in character. When the Sherman Act forbids a 'restraint of trade .... with foreign countries', it contemplates, as should again be emphasized, the American trade *with* such countries; it excludes local trade *in* (or between) foreign countries. If any legislator should fail to exclude from his legislation restraints of trade of the latter type he would undoubtedly commit an international wrong.

There remains what may be described as the crucial case: suppose Dutch manufacturers enter in Holland into a minimum price agreement in respect of their products. The agreement is lawful under Dutch law. The products are sold by the Dutch manufacturers partly to consumers in Holland, the United

Sherman Act from which Frankfurter and Jackson JJ. dissented and of which the latter said (p. 608): 'this decision will restrain more trade than it will make free'.

[1] 100 F. Supp. 504 (1951).

[2] *Continental Ore Co.* v. *Union Carbide & Carbon Corporation*, 370 U. S. 777 (1962). The essence of this decision lies in the statement that the respondents 'are liable for actions which they themselves jointly took, as part of their unlawful conspiracy, to influence or direct the elimination of Continental (their American competitor), from the Canadian market' (p. 706). This would seem to be an obvious conclusion, and the similar case of *United States* v. *Learner Co.*, 215 F. Supp. 603 (1963) is equally plain.

States, and elsewhere, partly to Dutch distributors for resale. To a varying extent and in varying circumstances the Dutch restraint of trade affects the price level of competitive goods in the United States, among other nations. Is this an effect which, from the point of view of international law, entitles the United States to proceed against the Dutch manufacturers? To the implications of this type of situation[1] it is now necessary to turn.

## III

It is likely that traditional international law as expressed by the practice of nations does not permit an affirmative answer to the question just asked. In the example the contract is made in Holland. The essential element which brings about the consummation of the restraint occurs in Holland: it is the Dutch trade that is being restrained. Repercussions of that restraint will no doubt be felt, and are perhaps intended to be felt, in the United States and elsewhere. But such consequences are too remote, too indirect, too incidental to treat them as so essential a part of the contract in restraint that the latter can be said to have occurred outside Holland.[2]

It is, accordingly, plausible that, in order to extend the scope of a State's legislation, attempts have been made to find a substitute for the place of wrong as a test of jurisdiction in this field. Such attempts originate from developments in municipal law and may well serve as a means of ascertaining that close connection which the doctrine of international jurisdiction demands.

The discussion starts from and centres round the celebrated decision of the Court of Appeals for the Second Circuit (Learned Hand, Swan and Augustus N. Hand, Circuit Judges) in *United States* v. *Aluminum Company of America*.[3] A Swiss company known as Alliance had six shareholders who were corporations incorporated in France, Germany, Switzerland, Britain and Canada; the Canadian company known as 'Limited' was a co-defendant with Aluminum Company of America ('Alcoa').

---

[1] Which, as Van Hecke, 106 *Recueil* (1962 ii), 257, 290, says, 'n'a guère été éclairée jusqu'à présent'.
[2] See p. 94, n. 1, below.
[3] 148 F. 2d. 416 (1945).

By an agreement made in 1936[1] Alliance agreed with its six shareholders upon a quota for the production of aluminum. Each shareholder was to have a fixed free quota for every share it held, but as its production exceeded the sum of its quotas, it was to pay progressive royalties to Alliance which distributed them by way of dividends among its shareholders. Alcoa was in no way a party to the arrangements made by Alliance and did not join in any violation of the Sherman Act which these arrangements may have involved. Although the agreement 'was silent as to imports into the United States ... all the shareholders agreed that such imports should be included in the quotas'.[2] In an opinion delivered by Judge Learned Hand the Court held that, 'although the shareholders intended to restrict imports, it does not appear whether in fact they did so'. Hence the Court felt that prima facie the plaintiff Government failed. However, 'after the intent to affect imports was proved, the burden of proof shifted to' the defendants, and as they could not exonerate themselves, the plaintiff Government succeeded.[3] For present purposes the essential part of the decision lies in the proposition that the agreements 'were unlawful, though made abroad, if they were intended to affect imports and did affect them'. It rests on reasoning of great significance. Judge Learned Hand said, firstly, that there may be agreements which are not intended to, but do affect the American market. 'Congress certainly did not intend the Act to cover them'. *Mere effect upon the American market is, therefore, not suggested to be sufficient.* Secondly, the agreement may intend to affect American markets, but has 'no effect upon them'. The Court was prepared to assume, without deciding, that *mere intention to affect is equally insufficient.*

---

[1] The Court held that an earlier agreement of 1931 should be ignored 'since the shareholders almost at once agreed that the agreement of 1931 should not cover imports' (into the United States).

[2] It is perhaps not easy to follow this reference to the inclusion of imports. This was a cartel setting up quotas of production. How could such quotas 'include' imports? Presumably what is meant is that production required to satisfy American demand was included in the quota of *production* or, alternatively, was subject to royalty. It is also necessary to explain the Court's continuous reference to the 'restriction' of imports. No restriction in the strict sense occurred at all. Production for imports, if achieved outside the quota, was subject to a royalty. But this was doubtless a restraint of trade.

[3] This is not the place to discuss the shifting of the burden of proof. It may strike some observers as remarkable.

It is only where both conditions are satisfied that the Act applies.

The theory of the intended effect, approved by some,[1] criticized by most,[2] is responsible for, and at the same time generalized and refined by, the Draft Restatement.[3] This would require a 'substantial' effect occurring 'as a direct and foreseeable result of the conduct outside the territory', as well as consistency of the legisation 'with the principles of justice generally recognized by states that have a reasonably developed legal system'. On this basis the *Alcoa* would clearly involve an excess of jurisdiction. Another method of keeping that interpretation within acceptable bounds would be to require that, in the above example, the Dutch cartel should have 'executed the agreement within the United States to a significant degree' or 'extend its operation into the United States'.[4] This, again, would mean

---

[1] Mainly American writers. Outside the United States it is difficult to find support for the decision. The American attitude and perhaps even Judge Learned Hand's holding itself can be much more readily understood if it is remembered that the United States Constitution, Art. 1, paragraph 8, cl. 3, has the same language as section 2 of the Sherman Act in that it confers upon Congress the power to regulate commerce 'with foreign Nations, and among the several States'. This constitutional power is 'generally interpreted to extend to all commerce, even intrastate and entirely foreign commerce, which has a substantial effect on commerce between the states or between the United States and foreign': *Vanity Fair Mills* v. *Eaton Co. Ltd.*, 234 F. 2d 633 (Court of Appeals, 2nd Circuit, 1956) cert. den. 352 U. S. 871 (1956), also Int. L.R. (1956), 134, at p. 139, with many further references. Is it surprising that the rule of constitutional law was transplanted into international law? The constitutional rule about interstate commerce was, of course, of enormous significance in integrating the American nation into an economic unit. The integration of the world into a similar unit is a political matter which cannot be achieved (if it is to be achieved at all) except with the willing consent and co-operation of other nations.

[2] Haight, 63 *Yale L.J.* (1953), 639; Friedmann and Verloren van Themaat in Friedmann, *Anti-Trust Laws* (1956), 486 sqq.: see also Friedmann's wise warning (p. 556) that 'the United States cannot be content with sweeping and indiscriminate condemnations of any type of international arrangement that implies some restrictions of free competition'; Kahn–Freund, *American Bar Association Proceedings* (1957), p. 33; Jennings, 'Extraterritorial Jurisdiction', particularly p. 175; Seidl–Hohenveldern, *Aussenwirtschaftsdienst* (1960), 225; Verzijl, *Nederlands Tijdschrift voor Internationaal Recht* (1961), 30; Van Hecke, 106 *Recueil* (1962 ii) 257, 324, 325, and numerous other writers whom it is impossible to enumerate.

[3] Section 18. See above, p. 32.

[4] This interpretation is now favoured by Kronstein, *XXth Century Comparative and Conflicts Law* (Legal Essays in Honor of Hessel E. Yntema) (1961), pp. 432, 437, 438. This valuable essay seems to indicate a considerable qualification of the enthusiasm with which the author had previously welcomed the *Alcoa* doctrine; see, e.g., *Festschrift für Martin Wolff* (1952), pp. 225 sqq. It is possible, however, that

the reversal of the *Alcoa* ruling and a return to the test of the place of wrong, of the 'constituent element' or 'overt act'. On the other hand, a few of the legislative developments on the Continent tend in the opposite direction, probably because they were influenced by a misreading of the *Alcoa* case. Such comment, it is true, probably does not apply to the Austrian law of 1951 which, on the one hand, extends to foreign restraints of trade 'in so far as they are intended to be implemented in' Austria and, on the other hand, excludes from its scope cartels relating to foreign markets.[1] But it seems to apply to the Danish law of 1955 which apparently covers all such cartels as 'exert or may be able to exert an essential influence on price, production, distribution or transport conditions',[2] and, particularly, to the German law of 1957; this covers all restraints which 'have effect' within the Federal Republic, though they are not substantial and are put into operation abroad,[3] and does not seem to require any subjective element.[4]

In the light of these contradictory trends it is submitted that 'effect', whether intended or merely foreseeable or unexpected, does not constitute a sufficiently close connection with the importing country so as to permit the assumption of legislative

Professor Kronstein, like many others before him, continues to misinterpret the facts and findings of the *Alcoa* case (p. 436). Thus the Court did not hold 'that one of the purposes of the aluminum cartel was to restrict aluminum exports to the United States', nor is it fair to suggest that 'the facts of the *Alcoa* case indicate that substantial contacts with the American markets are a prerequisite of the application' of the Sherman Act. It is also necessary to take issue with the author's somewhat cryptic suggestion (pp. 437, 438) that 'international law does not define the jurisdictional limits which American antitrust authorities and courts (should?) have observed'. On a similar point made by Brewster, see above, p. 14.

[1] Art. 2. Probably the United Kingdom's Restrictive Trade Practices Act, 1956, should be mentioned here, for it applies only 'to any agreement between two or more persons carrying on business within the United Kingdom': section 6 (1). See, generally, Lever, 'The Extraterritorial Jurisdiction of the Restrictive Practices Court' in *Comparative Aspects of Antitrust Law* (1963), p. 117.

[2] Art. 2.

[3] Section 98 (2). On this section see the detailed and valuable discussion by I. E. Schwartz, *Deutsches Internationales Kartellrecht* (1962), reviewed by Mann, 126 *Zeitschrift für Handelsrecht* (1963), 165. See also Schlochauer, *Die Extraterritoriale Wirkung von Hoheitsakten* (1962).

[4] This is a remarkable and unexplained omission. The interpretation of the provision causes enormous difficulties. Kronstein (above, p. 88, n. 4), p. 442, seems to require that 'the foreign enterprise be active or effective within the Federal Republic'. No judicial decision has, it seems, thrown light on the point. For a comparative survey see Van Hecke, 106 *Recueil* (1962 ii), 257, 287, seq.

jurisdiction by the latter; from the point of view of public
international law the *Alcoa* decision cannot, therefore, be justified, and if the rules of statutory construction imposed by international law had been observed it is also unlikely to be supported
by a proper interpretation of the Sherman Act itself. The type of
'effect' which the *Alcoa* ruling has in mind has nothing in
common with the effect which, by virtue of established principles
of international jurisdiction, confers the right of regulation.[1]
The 'effect' within the meaning of the *Alcoa* ruling does not
amount to an essential or constituent part of the restraint of
trade, but is an indirect and remote repercussion of a restraint
carried out, completed and, in the legally relevant sense, exhausted in the foreign country. This is particularly clear where
the restraint is concerned with price maintenance, as it frequently will be. The price at which an exporter sells to the United
States may, it is true, be regulated by the latter's import restrictions or tariffs or subsidies, and these may make it even impossible
for the exporter to do business with the United States. But it is an
entirely different matter if the United States tells the foreign
exporter what prices he may or may not charge and how he has
to calculate them, and if the United States imposes liabilities
upon him in case he disregards its direction. To impose criminal
liability upon a foreign exporter for a price calculated or
charged in accordance with his own law constitutes an excess of
jurisdiction, because there is an altogether shadowy connection
between the United States and the criminality of the act.[2]
There is one piece of international practice which, perhaps,
lends a little support to the suggestion that the mere (intended)
'effect' of foreign restraints of trade does not confer legislative
jurisdiction over them. Almost all countries exempt from their
restrictive trade practices legislation all[3] or some[4] restraints

---

[1] See above, p. 72, where reference is made to Professor Jennings, 'Extraterritorial Jurisdiction'—a paper of particular value in the present context.

[2] Could it be suggested that if the United States introduces maximum or minimum prices a foreign exporter who offers goods for sale to the United States at
different prices has offended against American regulations? See on this very point
the German decision, above, p. 21, n. 7.

[3] For instance, Austria (above, p. 89); Germany (section 6); Netherlands
(section 4, subsection 1); Norway (section 5) Switzerland, Art. 5 (2) (d); United
Kingdom (section 8, subsection 8).

[4] In particular the American Webb–Pomerene Act of 1918.

relating to the export trade. Now, as has been well said,[1] 'what for one State is exports is imports for another'. If the 'effect' of restraints upon a market, rather than their operation in a market, were a permissible test of jurisdiction, then the immunity of export cartels would have to be lifted. The practice of nations cannot sanction the legality of export cartels, yet condemn their 'effects'. The importing State, therefore, is unlikely to enjoy international jurisdiction to legislate against the export cartels of another State.[2] Such a State has even less justification for assuming control over non-resident aliens merely because restraints of trade practised by them and touching their export trade have 'effects' upon the importing country.

Finally, the theory of the intended effect is incompatible with the mutuality which, as has been pointed out more than once, is so important an element in determining the extent of international jurisdiction. If State A were entitled to prescribe the terms on which the subjects of State B have to export their goods, State B would be entitled to prescribe the terms on which the subjects of State A have to import the same goods. The resulting confusion would be wholly opposed to the 'interacting interests' of the family of nations. The point has not as yet arisen in practice, because fortunately and very significantly the United States has so far been alone in arrogating to itself an international jurisdiction which the practice of States does not countenance.

The enormous and dangerous potentialities of the doctrine of the *Alcoa* case[3] were demonstrated by a United States District Court in a case against the Swiss watch industry and its organization.[4] The facts are too complicated to be set forth in the present context, but the Court held, in effect, that the arrangements made in Switzerland, with the assistance and approval of the Swiss Government, by Swiss manufacturers

---

[1] Schwartz, *Cartel and Monopoly in Modern Law* (Karlsruhe, 1961) ii.718.

[2] Whether this is subject to exceptions in cases, for instance, in which the cartel is actually operated and consummated within the importing State by the creation of a permanent sales organization or in some similar manner depends on the facts and is a question which cannot be pursued in the present context.

[3] *Ubi supra.* It is remarkable that in its judgment (for which see the following note) the court gave a long list of previous anti-trust cases, but very few of them, apart from the *Alcoa* case, would appear to have been in point.

[4] *United States* v. *The Watchmakers of Switzerland Information Centre* (1963) Trade Cases 77 414.

under the protection of Swiss law and regulating the manufacture and sale of Swiss-made watches, watch parts and watch-
making machinery were illegal under the Sherman Act, because
they were intended to, and did, 'affect' the United States.
Whatever the position may have been in regard to certain
American co-defendants, the judgment against the Swiss watch
industry[1] constitutes as clear an attempt to regulate the conduct
of Swiss defendants in Switzerland as has ever been made and,
therefore, an excess of international jurisdiction which, on
account of its manifold repercussions, is of unsurpassed gravity.
As the judgment finds,[2] the Swiss watch industry exports
approximately 95% of its production and the United States
is the largest single export market for Swiss watches. Hence the
District Court has in practice made the following decree[3]:
Unless the Swiss watch industry, 'one of the chief industries of
Switzerland',[4] conforms to the Sherman Act, officers and
representatives of the Swiss watch industry, when visiting the
United States, must expect to be taken into custody or fined[5]
and the industry's American property, in particular its patents,
will be liable to be taken over by the United States.[6] In the
absence of treaty provisions Switzerland has, it is true, no internationally recognized right to sell watches to the United States,
and if by import restrictions, subsidies or tariffs the United States
took steps to protect its domestic watch industry, Switzerland,
probably, could not complain. Again, if the United States del-
gates the exercise of such functions to its courts, this would
be unusual, but in law unobjectionable. But such considerations
would not be in point, for the object of the Sherman Act is not
to suppress, but to encourage competition—on its own terms.[7]

[1] In regard to many defendants it is not at all clear why and how they could be
said to be properly before the Court.

[2] Paragraph 64, p. 77 424.

[3] It is true that the terms of the order are so framed as to reserve to the defendants
certain liberties in Switzerland itself. But this does not by any means solve the
problem of jurisdiction. See further below, p. 134.

[4] Paragraph 72, p. 77 425.

[5] If not as principals, then at least as participants.

[6] This, it is presumed, would follow from the practice relating to contempt of
court, or from the law relating to the execution of judgments.

[7] One of the most remarkable legal aspects of the judgment is the suggestion
that 'if, of course, the defendant's activities had been required by Swiss law, this
court could indeed do nothing'. In other words, the court's powers derived from the
fact that 'the defendants' activities were not required by the laws of Switzerland',

There is, finally, no difference of principle between the case of the *Swiss Watch Industry* and the demand made in April 1964 by the United States Federal Maritime Commission that foreign shipowners who are members of a 'conference' and whose ships trade with the United States should terminate their 'dual rates' contracts with foreign shippers or in default pay a fine of $1000 a day. These contracts, it appears, allow a discount of 15% to such shippers as agree to use only conference ships, and influence the price of goods exported from the United States, because charges are considerably higher for American exports than for comparable items shipped from Europe.[1] In effect, therefore, the United States arrogates to itself the right to prescribe the rates charged, for instance, by English shipowners to their English customers for shipping goods from English ports to the United States. In substance it is not a new claim of the United States to be entitled to control the terms of transportation to or from United States ports. Already in the early part of the century the United States enacted legislation imposing upon shipping companies the duty to transport back to Europe free of charge such would-be immigrants as they had carried to the United States and as had been refused leave to land. This legislation which purported to regulate the terms of a contract of transportation was held by the United States Supreme Court to apply to a contract made at Bremen between a German shipping company and German passengers.[2] From the point of view of international law, however, there can be but little doubt that these American attempts to prescribe the terms of contracts made in foreign countries, between foreign parties constitute an excess of jurisdiction. The mere fact that such contracts involve transportation to and from the United States does not, in the eyes of international law, provide a sufficiently close nexus between the United States and the foreign activities of foreigners, for there does not seem to be any other State whose practice lends support to American tendencies in this field. These are unique in character and also inconsistent with the demands of

---

but merely permitted by them (pp. 77 456 f.). It is impossible to understand the basis of this distinction. If Swiss law was relevant at all, then, surely, all that matters is that by Swiss law the impugned arrangements were lawful. See below, p. 134, on the same point.

[1] *The Economist*, 4 April 1964, p. 39.

[2] *United States* v. *Norddeutscher Lloyd*, 223 U. S. 512 (1912).

commercial intercourse between nations, as would become apparent if any other nation pursued a similar policy of economic domination. It is significant that the United Kingdom felt compelled to confer power on the Government to prohibit compliance with foreign shipping measures, which 'constitute an infringement of the jurisdiction which, under international law, belongs to the United Kingdom'. [1, 2]

## Section 6

### FISCAL JURISDICTION

#### I

The international right to levy taxes (including estate duty) is today characterized by the existence of well over five hundred[3] Double Taxation Conventions. They follow a pattern which defines the limits of fiscal jurisdiction in a largely uniform manner and with the object of establishing exclusive rather than concurrent rights. It is this fact that gives rise to the question whether their terms have become so compelling as to have produced rules of customary international law. Is it possible to suggest, for instance, that royalties payable in respect of a patent are, for purposes of taxation, now beyond the reach of the State in which the patent is exploited? Or are capital gains made in a certain State by the residents of another State no longer within the fiscal jurisdiction of the former? Such questions do not seem to have as yet been answered or even investigated.

[1] Section 1 of the Shipping Contracts and Commercial Documents Act, 1964, on which see Mann, 13 *I.C.L.Q.* (1964), 1460. For a remarkable but unfortunate statement by the Attorney-General of England (Sir John Hobson, Q.C.) on the scope of international jurisdiction see 'Parliamentary Debates', *Hansard* (House of Commons), vol. 698, col. 1280.

[2] At this point some readers will perhaps expect a discussion of the extra-territorial effect of judgments and orders, particularly injunctions; of such decisions as *British Nylon Spinners* v. *Imperial Chemical Industries*; of discovery of documents, and so forth. Although the problem of presentation is difficult, it seemed preferable to treat all these questions below, pp. 127 sqq. They could not be discussed in the present context, because it would be quite wrong to give the impression that they are confined to trade practices.

[3] This is the figure mentioned for the end of 1960 by Bühler, 'Internationales Steuerrecht', in Strupp-Schlochauer, *Wörterbuch des Völkerrechts*, iii.377, 378. The Draft Double Taxation Convention prepared by the Fiscal Committee of the Organization for Economic Co-operation and Development (1963) is perhaps the most representative effort of establishing rules of international law in this field.

Hence, although the international law of fiscal jurisdiction enjoys the unique and outstanding distinction of being regulated by a network of treaties, it is open to doubt whether they are expressive of, or exceptions to, the rules of customary international law. They cannot, therefore, be taken as a conclusive guide, when such rules are to be ascertained.

The existence of any principles of customary international law limiting fiscal jurisdiction has, it is true, been denied altogether. Thus, a, French writer has said[1]: 'En vertu de leur souveraineté les Etats ont le droit de lever des impôts conformément aux principes qu'ils jugent équitables, opportuns et pratiques sans se préoccuper des mesures prises par leurs voisins.' Similar statements have been made by others.[2] Yet the truth is that from a relatively early day States have, on the whole, observed the implications of the familiar principle of territoriality. At the same time it is in the field of taxation that the necessity for a flexible approach was propounded with special emphasis. Already in 1892 a German economist, Georg von Schanz, developed the theory that the right of taxation depended on 'wirtschaftliche Zugehörigkeit', or 'economic allegiance'.[3] The idea of 'allégeance économique' was taken up and developed by Allix[4] who, however, limited its scope by attributing three elements to it, viz. domicile or residence, property, and economic activity within the taxing country. Although the terminology is not always the same, this principle is now widely accepted.[5] It is supported by similar and highly significant

---

[1] Oualid, 23 *Revue de Science et de Législation Financière* (1927), 5, here quoted from Isay (see following note) p. 121.

[2] For instance by Dorn, quoted by Ernst Isay, *Internationales Finanzrecht* (1934), p. 123; and see Isay, pp. 22, 23, where the view that international law imposes no limits on fiscal jurisdiction is described as prevalent. Isay himself rejects it (pp. 29–32), but his own views as expressed on pp. 36, 37, 50, are far from clear. Perhaps one should mention here Tillinghast in *Legal Problems in International Trade and Investment* (New York, 1962), p. 180, who thinks fit to speak of 'the bugaboo of jurisdiction' and says that 'a nation's assertion of legal jurisdiction is a policy decision like any other—a purely mortal development of how it is just or prudent to extend governmental power outside the territorial limits of the nation governed'. Cf. Brewster, above, p. 14.

[3] 9 *Finanzarchiv* (1892), 365, 368, 373.    [4] 61 *Recueil* (1937 iii), 545, 553 seq.

[5] Rodriguez Ramon, *Répertoire de Droit International* v.677; Seligman and others, quoted by Albrecht, The Taxation of Aliens under International Law, *B.Y.I.L.* (1952), 145, at p. 149, n. 1—a very valuable survey; 'Report on Double Taxation' submitted by the League of Nations Economic and Financial Committee (1923), here quoted from Bittker and Ebb, *Taxation of Foreign Income* (1960), pp. 5 sqq.

trends in the cognate field of constitutional law. Thus an Australian State which in relation to the Commonwealth of Australia is a subordinate legislature exceeds its fiscal jurisdiction if its tax legislation 'has no relevant territorial connection whatever with' the State, if there is no 'relevant nexus' between the taxed property and the State.[1] Or, as the Supreme Court of the United States has said,[2] 'visible territorial boundaries do not always establish the limits of a State's taxing power or jurisdiction', but due process (which, let it be repeated, does not essentially differ from such reasonableness as excludes arbitrariness or abuse of rights and is, therefore, demanded by international law) 'requires some definite link, some minimum connection between a State and the person, property or transaction it seeks to tax'.[3] It is submitted that such tests provide a useful guide to the analogous problem of international fiscal jurisdiction, for it is subordination that characterizes both the national legislature in relation to the international order and a state legislature in relation to the federation.[4]

## II

The traditional territorial test was expressed in America in 1870, when Mr. Justice Swayne on behalf of the Supreme Court said[5]:

If the legislature of a State should enact that the citizens or property of another State or country should be taxed in the same manner as the persons or property within its own limits or subject to its authority, or in any other manner whatsoever, such a law would be as much a nullity as if in conflict with the most explicit constitutional inhibition. Jurisdiction is as necessary to valid legislation as to valid judicial action.

And in 1889 in England Lord Herschell stated in strictly Huber–

---

[1] *Johnson* v. *Commissioner of Stamp Duties*, [1956] A. C. 331, at p. 350, where earlier Australian cases are referred to.

[2] *Miller Bros.* v. *Maryland*, 347 U. S. 340 (1954), at p. 342, per Jackson J. on behalf of the majority of the Court.

[3] Ibid., pp. 344, 345; for an application of the principle see *Scripto* v. *Carson*, 362 U. S. 207 (1960).

[4] For useful discussions of the problem of fiscal jurisdiction in international law see Hyde, i, section 205; Beale, i, pp. 1, 516–645, who only deals with cases arising under the American Constitution: Wurzel, 38 *Col. L.R.* (1938) 809; Λ brecht, above, p. 95, n. 5.

[5] *St. Louis* v. *The Ferry Co.*, 11 Wall. 423, 430.

Storyan terms[1] that British income tax legislation was to be so construed as to 'impose a territorial limit—either that from which the taxable income is derived must be situate in the United Kingdom or the person whose income is to be taxed must be resident there'.

(1) That the possession of property, if it has a not merely temporary character,[2] is a legitimate and, indeed, very usual source of taxation by the State of the *situs* cannot be open to doubt. 'The presence of property within a State's jurisdiction has always been regarded as a cogent reason for recognizing the right and power to tax that property.'[3] The reason frequently advanced is that property enjoys the protection of the State in which it is situate, and that taxation is the consideration for such protection,[4] but it is by no means certain whether such a far-fetched and specious argument carries the point further.

The State of the *situs* in which the income arises is entirely free to decide upon the type of tax it imposes. It may tax the local income of non-resident aliens.[5] The tax may be a property tax or estate duty, i.e. something in the nature of a capital levy.[6] No question of jurisdiction arises in this connection. It is, however, very necessary to distinguish clearly between the possession of property in a State as a source of income and, therefore, a

---

[1] *Colquhoun* v. *Brooks*, [1889] 14 A. C. 493, 504.

[2] On this requirement see Beale, pp. 547 sqq., who relies only upon constitutional cases which, though not directly in point, are of some interest.

[3] *Johnson* v. *Commissioner of Stamp Duties*, [1956] A. C. 331, at p. 352, per Lord Keith of Avonholme; similarly *Winans* v. *Attorney General*, [1910] A. C. 27, at p. 30, per Lord Loreburn L.C.; at p. 31, per Lord Atkinson; at p. 48, per Lord Shaw of Dunfermline. See also *Astor* v. *Perry*, [1935] A. C. 398, 406, per Lord Russell of Killowen; *Commissioners of Inland Revenue* v. *Kenmare*, [1958] A. C. 267, 282, per Lord Cohen; *London & South American Investment Trust Co.* v. *British Tobacco (Australia) Co.*, [1927] 1 Ch. 107, 118, per Tomlin J.

[4] All the Law Lords referred to in the preceding note; in the same sense *Whitney* v. *Inland Revenue Commissioners*, [1926] A. C. 37, per Lord Wrenbury, and also *Union Refrigeration Transit Co.* v. *Kentucky*, 199 U. S. 194 (1905), which contains a long and useful review of the principles relating to fiscal jurisdiction, though the decision itself gives rise to much doubt, and according to the U. S. Supreme Court itself cannot be applied in the international sphere: *Burnet* v. *Brooks*, 288 U. S. 378 (1933).

[5] From the point of view of constitutional law this was so decided in *De Ganay* v. *Lederer*, 250 U. S. 376 (1918); *Shaffer* v. *Carter*, 252 U. S. 37 (1920).

[6] That federal estate duty may be levied on the tangible and intangible property of a non-resident alien, which is situate in the United States would seem obvious, but was decided in *Burnet* v. *Brooks*, 288 U. S. 378 (1933) where Chief Justice Hughes delivered a very elaborate opinion.

permissible source of taxation, and the ultimate benefits to which that property and that income may give rise in another State and which, it is submitted, are not a legitimate object of taxation in the former State. The point is impressively illustrated by a decision of the Supreme Court of the United States in the cognate field of constitutional law.[1] A Connecticut insurance company carried on business in California. Other insurance companies which also carried on business in California entered into reinsurance contracts with the Connecticut company to indemnify them against losses incurred on policies which were written in California. Such reinsurance contracts were made, and the premiums payable in respect thereof were paid, in Connecticut. Was California entitled to tax these premiums and to enforce the tax against the Connecticut company's California branch? The Supreme Court answered in the negative. Mr. Justice Stone stated the principle[2]: 'the limits of the State's legislative jurisdiction to tax, prescribed by the Fourteenth Amendment, are to be ascertained by reference to the incidence of the tax upon its objects rather than the ultimate thrust of the economic benefits and burdens of transactions within the State'. Consequently, it is unreasonable to levy taxes merely 'because the corporation enjoys outside the State economic benefits from transactions within it'.[3]

(2) If and in so far as fiscal jurisdiction is based upon the residential nexus of the taxpayer with the taxing State, the right to tax extends to all the taxpayer's property wherever it may be situate[4] and all the income wherever it may arise and irrespec-

---

[1] *Connecticut General Life Insurance* v. *Johnson*, 303 U. S. 77 (1937).

[2] p. 80.

[3] p. 81. This is, of course, a point of general importance which should be borne in mind when anti-trust legislation is in issue.

[4] In Britain it seems to have been thought for many years that foreign immovables belonging to a deceased domiciled in Britain cannot or should not be subject to estate duty in Britain. No such rule of international law exists (see German Supreme Finance Court, *RFH* 27, 85, but see also Swiss practice referred to by Guggenheim i.333, n. 7) and the English rule was changed by section 28 of the Finance Act, 1962. As to the constitutional position in the United States, see Beale, section 118.D.2 with references. In the United States it is a rule of constitutional law that only the *lex situs* may tax *tangible* property *passing at death* and that the law of the owner's domicile has no such power: *Frick* v. *Pennsylvania*, 268 U. S. 473 (1925); *Treichler* v. *Wisconsin*, 338 U. S. 251, 256 (1949). This surprising rule certainly does not apply in international law.

tive of its receipt within the taxing State.[1] It is a matter for the State's discretion whether it makes domicile or residence the test,[2] but a person cannot be held to be resident if his presence is of a temporary or fleeting character. In Hyde's happy formulation,[3] the right to tax individuals (or, one may add, corporations) 'depends upon the intimacy and closeness of the relationship that has been established between itself and him'; this point, primarily developed in the field of taxation, is of wide and general importance to the international law of jurisdiction.[4] The doctrine of jurisdiction also throws light upon three particularly significant aspects of taxation, which arise in regard to so-called permanent establishments maintained by a resident taxpayer in foreign countries.

The law of many countries takes the view that in certain conditions foreign branches or subsidiary companies may, for tax purposes, be treated as part of the domestic enterprise.[5] The consequence is that the domestic enterprise becomes accountable for the foreign establishment's total profits as if they were its own and so that, for instance, accountability is not limited to dividends distributed by the foreign subsidiary. No problem of international jurisdiction occurs, because the domestic legislation is concerned solely with measuring the domestic taxpayer's tax liability. Thus if a Dutch company has a branch or a subsidiary in New York nothing precludes the Netherlands from treating the profits of the New York establishment as part of the Dutch parent's profits.

However, is the converse true? Suppose a Dutch company has a branch or a subsidiary in New York. Can New York treat the Dutch establishment's profits as part of the Dutch parent's profits, so that for instance, royalties or interest paid by the New York subsidiary to the Dutch parent are not deductible for tax

---

[1] In Britain certain types of income arising abroad are not subject to income tax unless and until remitted to and received in Britain. This is a matter of national policy, not of international law.

[2] On this question as well as on other points, such as the meaning of residence or the special problems of corporations or the *situs* of property, see in particular Albrecht (above, p. 95, n. 5), pp. 154 seq.

[3] i.665.

[4] See above, pp. 28, 29. And Henri Rolin, 77 *Recueil* (1950 ii), 307 sqq., 370, who, relying on Hyde, Guggenheim, and others, states that there is no international jurisdiction to tax 'des étrangers simplement de passage'.

[5] In such a case the foreign establishment is merely what in German tax law is

purposes? This is a problem of jurisdiction which, in a famous decision relating to the *Shell Group of Companies*, the German Supreme Finance Court answered in the affirmative.[1] The Double Taxation Conventions have usually answered it in the opposite sense,[2] and it is doubtful whether that German judicial practice, which, as a result of foreign representations, was rejected by the German tax authorities,[3] can today be regarded as consistent with international law.

There remains a third problem: if a Dutch company has an establishment in New York, would New York be entitled to tax the Dutch parent, not only in respect of the profits of the New York establishment, but also in respect of the profits made in the Netherlands and elsewhere outside the United States? In other words, does an enterprise, in respect of the totality of its profits, become subject to the fiscal jurisdiction of all countries in which it maintains a permanent establishment? The Double Taxation Conventions answer this question invariably in the negative by limiting fiscal jurisdiction to so much of the profits as is attributable to the permanent establishment.[4] This, it is submitted, is the only view consistent with a sensible doctrine of international jurisdiction, for, although through its permanent establishment an enterprise is to some limited extent and for some limited purposes subject to the law of the State in which the establishment is set up, the latter State does not thereby become so closely connected with the enterprise as a whole as to justify it in assuming jurisdiction over the foreign enterprise's conduct abroad. The Supreme Court of Pakistan, therefore, rightly held[5] that Pakistan could not tax an Indian company resident in India in respect of the Indian profits, for it is a

rule of international law that a legislature has authority . . . to tax foreigners only if they earn or receive income in the country for which that legislature has the authority to make laws.

called a 'Betriebsstätte', and if the foreign establishment is a subsidiary company it may be merely an 'Organgesellschaft': see sections 15, 16 of the Steueranpassungsgesetz.

[1] Reichssteuerblatt 1930, 148.
[2] Art. II (1) (e) of the Anglo–American and Art. II (1) (e) of the Anglo–German Convention, among others.
[3] See Friedrich, *Steuer und Wirtschaft* 1959, 17.
[4] See, for instance, Art. III of the Anglo–American or Art. III (1) of the Anglo–German Double Taxation Convention.
[5] *Imperial Tobacco Co. of India v. Commissioners of Income Tax*, 27 Int. L.R. (1958), 103.

## III

Among the numerous and largely unexplored problems of international fiscal jurisdiction there are four which the present survey should not ignore.

(1) Lord Herschell's statement referred to above[1] implies that nationality as such is not a legitimate test of fiscal jurisdiction. In fact, very few States have ever invoked it and already in 1923 scholars of great eminence stated[2]: 'In the modern age of the international migration of persons as well as of capital political allegiance no longer forms an adequate test of individual fiscal obligation. It is fast breaking down in practice, and it is clearly insufficient in theory.' The United States of America, however, continues to adhere to and even to extend the principle of nationality in taxation.[3] As between the national and his home country no problem of international jurisdiction can arise, but it is an open question whether the State of the national's residence is not itself in certain circumstances so injured as to entitle it to complain of the implications of taxation by virtue of nationality.

(2) There are, or at any rate there were, certain countries, the United States of America among them, which subject a non-resident alien to income tax in respect of dividends paid to him by a non-resident corporation of foreign nationality which derives some or most of its gross income from sources within the taxing State.[4,5] Is this a legitimate exercise of

---

[1] p. 96.

[2] Report of the League of Nations Committee (above, p. 96, n. 5), at p. 4. The authors of the Report were Professors Bruins, Einaudi, Seligman, and Sir Josiah Stamp. In 1889 von Bar, *Theorie und Praxis des Internationalen Privatrechts* (2nd ed.), thought (p. 319) that it was not contrary to public international law, but undesirable to extract tax from non-resident nationals. Von Bar is one of the few writers who discuss the international law of taxation (pp. 315 sqq.), and he does so with great insight. And see Isay (above, p. 95, n. 2) pp. 45, 46.

[3] See the recent legislation of the Kennedy Administration. That as a matter of constitutional law the United States has power to tax non-resident nationals was decided by *Cook* v. *Tait*, 265 U. S. 47 (1924).

[4] This, in substance, still seems to be the law in the United States: see section 861 (a) (2) (B) of the Internal Revenue Code. The constitutional validity of the statute was affirmed in *Lord Forres* v. *Commissioner of Internal Revenue*, 25 Board of Tax Appeals 154 (1932).

[5] In Australia, and it seems, in India similar legislation was or is in force. Its constitutional validity was upheld respectively in *Murray* v. *Federal Commissioners of Taxation*, 29 C.L.R. (1921) 134, and *Caltex (India) Ltd.* v. *Commissioners of Income Tax*,

fiscal jurisdiction? It is difficult to discover a sufficiently close or, indeed, any adequate connection between the taxing State and the dividends. It must be assumed that the foreign corporations' income derived from the taxing State has been taxed by it. The shareholder's dividends do not in any legally relevant sense arise in the taxing State. They are derived from the corporation, from the totality of its income out of which the dividends are declared. These arise exclusively in the country to which the corporation belongs. The country which only contributes to the fund from which they are paid, has, it is suggested, no jurisdiction to tax them.[1]

(3) Similarly, absence of a legally relevant nexus should lead to the condemnation of those statutes which impose a tax upon the non-resident purchaser of goods, who exports and sells them abroad at a profit. The legislation of India, for instance, requires the payment of income tax from an American manufacturer of carpets who buys wool in India, ships it to the United States, uses it there for the production of carpets and sells his products there, the tax being measured by such part of the ultimate profits as is reasonably attributable to the part of the operation carried on in India.[2] It may well be, as an Indian Court has held,[3] 'that the wise purchase of raw material must

---

54 *Bombay L.R.* (1951) 222, here quoted from Katz and Brewster, *International Transactions and Relations*, p. 239. For the reasons given in the text, as a matter of international law, such legislation cannot be justified. It is even more difficult to justify certain Indian legislation which imposes a tax upon persons resident outside India, not only in respect of their Indian income, but also in respect of their non-Indian income. Such legislation is referred to and upheld in *Wallace Brothers* v. *Commissioners of Income Tax* (1945) 7 F. C. R. 65 affirmed by the Privy Council (1948) 10 F. C. R. 1, here quoted from Katz and Brewster, op. cit., p. 226, where the contention that these provisions were extraterritorial in their operation and therefore beyond the powers of the Indian legislature was rejected. The reasoning is unconvincing. The profits arising outside India had no connection with India at all.

[1] It is the effect of section 17 of the German Income Tax Act that if a non-resident owns more than 25 per cent. of the capital of a German company and sells it to another non-resident, the excess of the sales price over the purchase price is subject to German income tax. The international validity of this provision is doubtful.

[2] Details of the legislation are set forth in *Webb Sons & Co.* v. *Commissioner of Income Tax*, 18 Income Tax Reports (1950), 33, here quoted from Katz and Brewster, *International Transactions and Relations* (1960), p. 719.

[3] ibid., at p. 721. The mere purchase of goods, without the interposition of a permanent establishment, cannot amount to the carrying on of a trade, and the reference to such cases as *Commissioners of Taxation* v. *Kirk*, [1900] A. C. 588 can only be due to a misunderstanding.

contribute to a considerable extent to the profits realized on the sale of manufactured products'. But many circumstances 'contribute' to profits without it being possible to describe them as a legally relevant source: thus the finance which the American manufacturer may have obtained in England contributes to the profits, yet it would be absurd to suggest that England should be entitled to levy a tax in respect of part of such profits. The truth is that in a loose sense profits arise from many 'sources', but the real and legally material source of the profits is the sale of the goods, and only the country in which such sales are made is so closely connected with the resulting profits as to be entitled to tax them. It is not surprising that Double Taxation Conventions almost invariably exclude the mere purchase of goods as a legitimate source of taxation.[1]

(4) Finally, to turn to the converse case, it is submitted that profits made from the mere sale of goods to a particular foreign country where no permanent establishment is maintained are not subject to the fiscal jurisdiction of that country. This would also seem to be borne out by the Double Taxation Conventions,[2] and it is not certain whether the contrary has ever been asserted or practised, but it is important to state that the sale of goods may lead to profits in many places, such as the place where the contracts are made or where the order is taken or where the trade is carried on and so forth. But it is not made in the country in which the goods are merely delivered, even if the buyer pays for them there. Again, such a nexus must be regarded as too insignificant to justify the imposition of a tax on profits of the seller.

## Section 7

### MONETARY JURISDICTION

There are few branches of the law where the doctrine of international jurisdiction has been invoked, or at least alluded to, with so much insistence and, on the whole, so little justification as in the case of monetary legislation. That monetary laws are

---

[1] Art. III (4) of the Anglo–American or Art. III (4) of the Anglo–German Convention.

[2] See the definitions of 'permanent establishment' in Art. II and III of the Anglo–American or of the Anglo–German Convention.

strictly territorial, that they have no extraterritorial effect—
these are catchwords which are wholly without foundation and
misleading, but which have often been proclaimed, particularly
in France, and by none with greater energy than by Arminjon
who made the fortunately unsuccessful attempt to have them
adopted by the *Institut de Droit International*.[1] In truth, of course,
no special problem of international jurisdiction usually arises in
relation to monetary legislation. Such features as are peculiar
to the law of money are readily explained and, indeed, covered
by the accepted principles governing the relationship between
the doctrine of international jurisdiction and private international law or statutory interpretation. Thus there is nothing
unfamiliar in the fact that, where a State changes, not the identity of its unit of account, but the substance or extent of
obligations (revalorization, devalorization), such legislation is
characterized by private international law as pertaining, not to
the *lex monetae*, but to the *lex causae*.[2] And if the legislation forms
part of the latter it may appear that certain of its provisions
cannot properly have, or be intended to have, effect in circumstances in which some definite connection between the legislating State and the transaction is lacking.

Although, then, these are in no sense remarkable phenomena,
it is a fact that, in particular for purposes of the abolition of gold
clauses and of exchange control, the doctrine of international
jurisdiction has figured prominently in certain decisions of
municipal tribunals. Hence it is probably helpful to an appreciation of that doctrine to review those two aspects of monetary
legislation.

I

When on 5 June 1933 the United States abrogated gold
clauses, the Joint Resolution of Congress did not indicate the
scope of its application except in so far as by its terms it was
limited to gold clauses attached to a promise to pay dollars. Did
it reach or intend to reach all dollar obligations, irrespective of

---

[1] 43 *Annuaire* (1950), ii.1. It is difficult to understand what Arminjon had in
mind, seeing that the explanations given by him two years later (Report of the
International Law Association's 45th Conference (Lucerne), pp. 250–2) make the
meaning and effect of his suggestions very doubtful.

[2] Mann, *The Legal Aspect of Money*, (2nd ed., 1953), pp. 237 seq., or, in German,
*Das Recht des Geldes* (1960), pp. 230 seq.

the proper law of the contract, the nationality and residence of creditor or debtor, and the place of payment? As a first step, so the judicial practice in all countries agreed,[1] the Joint Resolution could not be considered at all except in cases in which the contract was subject to the law of one of the American States, although an American court might, as a matter of public policy, require its application even if the proper law was not American,[2] and although a few non-American courts might, again as a matter of public policy, refuse to apply it in certain cases even if the proper law was American.[3] Yet even on the footing of American law being applicable, could or would the Congress of the United States legislate with reference to a case where, for instance, dollars were payable in Holland by one Dutchman to another Dutchman?[4]

A clear and convincing answer in the affirmative was given by the German Supreme Court.[5] Dollar bonds issued by a German debtor under New York law and providing for payment in New York were held by a German creditor. The Court of Appeal in Berlin[6] had taken the view that the Joint Resolution could operate only within the United States and, accordingly, could not reach a contract between a German creditor and a German debtor. This view of the limits of the legislative jurisdiction of the United States ('Grenzen der Gesetzgebungsgewalt') led the Court of Appeal to the conclusion that the Joint Resolution did not intend to apply in the circumstances of the case. The Supreme Court reversed:

It is impossible to see why, in the case of a contract submitted by the parties to its legislation or governed by the latter for other reasons of private international law, the United States, if it thinks it necessary for the purpose pursued by a general statute, should not be able to encroach upon the existence of an obligation, even where creditor and debtor are persons who are neither citizens nor residents of the United States and where payment is to be made outside its boundaries. It cannot be admitted that, where payments are to be made in its currency, the United States cannot in any cir-

[1] Mann, op. cit., p. 260, nn. 1 and 2.

[2] *Compañia de Inversiones* v. *Industrial Mortgage Bank of Finland*, (1935) 269 N. Y. 22, 198 N. E. 617; cert. den. 297 U. S. 705 (1936).

[3] Mann, op. cit., p. 268 (or German edition, pp. 259, 260).

[4] It is very remarkable that it was only in this type of situation that the Dutch Courts allowed public policy to reject the application of the Joint Resolution: see Mann, op. cit., p. 268, n. 2.

[5] 28 May 1936, *JW* 1936, 2058; Clunet 1936, 951.

[6] *IPRspr.* 1934, No. 92.

cumstances have any interest in including such payments in the measures taken by it; the object, declared in the Joint Resolution itself, of suppressing any attempt at forming a dual currency would justify, and would explain the intention to achieve, the extension of the statute to payments in foreign countries and between foreigners, provided they are made in dollar currency.[1]

It cannot, indeed, be suggested that a State does not have the right or power to enact legislation with a view to having it applied wherever and whenever, under the appropriate rules of the conflict of laws, its legal system prevails. Whether in a given case the State has the intention to exercise such right and power is another question to be answered as a matter of construction. In regard to the Joint Resolution it was never authoritatively decided whether it claimed application where payments were made outside the United States by and to foreigners.[2] Although the point is arguable, there does not seem to be any real ground upon which a restrictive interpretation could be based.

## II

Exchange control, by its very nature, is 'territorial', for its object is to preserve and protect the financial resources of the legislating State and, for this reason, to prevent their outflow as well as an increase of the foreign debt. The translation of this leading idea into legal terminology is not easy. Since most countries have, or have had, exchange control of a more or less comprehensive kind, a large part of the world has at various times been confronted with the problem. The solutions which were adopted by legislators display considerable variety.

One extreme is represented by an early German Exchange Control Decree made in 1917. It said nothing at all about its territorial scope. The Supreme Court did not resort to the principles governing criminal jurisdiction or the conflict of laws, but construed the decree by formulating a rule of some significance[3]:

[1] On the facts this reasoning is open to criticism, for under the bond payments had to be made in New York. In the German proceedings only a declaration was claimed.

[2] See, generally, Wahl, 52 *Zeitschrift für Internationales Recht* (1937–8), 277 seq.; Gutzwiller, *Der Geltungsbereich der Währungsvorschriften* (1940).

[3] 13 February 1922, *RGZ* 104, 50, 52; 16 January 1926, *IPRspr.* (1926), No. 12; 7 July 1926, ibid., No. 13; but see the decision referred to below, p. 108, n. 2.

According to general principles transactions which occur entirely abroad will not be touched by [the Decree]. It will always be a condition of its application that the transaction directly affects the German legal and economic system.

The Court thus affirmed the invalidity of a loan which had been granted in Switzerland under Swiss law to a German resident in Germany so as to burden the German economy with its repayment.

At the other extreme there is the English solution as embodied in the Exchange Control Act, 1947. It includes a somewhat elaborate scheme which, in respect of many transactions, rests on the broad distinction between acts done in the United Kingdom and acts done outside the United Kingdom. In the absence of permission, the former are not open to anyone, the latter are not allowed to be done by residents of the United Kingdom. Thus an American resident who is a temporary visitor in Britain cannot buy gold in Britain, while a British resident cannot buy gold either in Britain or elsewhere.[1]

The English legislation has, on the whole, worked well and succeeded in avoiding international incidents, because it has always been administered with exemplary reasonableness. Yet from a strictly legal point of view it is in many respects unsatisfactory, because it is liable to raise serious issues of international jurisdiction. Thus a person who is merely present in the United Kingdom—he may be a fleeting visitor—comes under the sway of some of the provisions of the Act, so that, for instance, he commits a criminal offence if he lends a sum of dollars to another visitor.[2] This, it is submitted, is a striking example of absence of substantial, real or, indeed, any connection between the legislating State and the 'offence', and constitutes an excess of international jurisdiction. In order to observe the requirements of such jurisdiction, exchange control regulations should apply only to residents or to property within the reach of the controlling State, but should not apply to transactions between non-residents.

This is well exemplified by a decision of the Supreme Court of Israel.[3] The English Defence (Finance) Regulations which

---

[1] Section 1.

[2] For other examples see Mann, op. cit., pp. 342 sqq. (or German edition, pp. 328 sqq.).

[3] *Amsterdam* v. *Minister of Finance*, Int. L.R. (1952), 229.

preceded the Act of 1947 were under the Mandate put into operation in Palestine and remained in force in Israel. Did they authorize orders requiring the transfer and surrender of securities which were actually held, and belonged to persons resident, outside Israel?[1] The Court decided in the negative. Its perhaps unnecessarily involved judgment invoked all the arguments supplied by the territorial rule of the Anglo-American system. But the result was hardly in doubt.

Lastly, it is submitted that it is not, as a rule, legitimate for a State to exercise exchange control in respect of persons who are its non-resident citizens. It is a matter of deep regret that, probably, the limits of international jurisdiction were disregarded and a serious breach of international law was committed by another provision of the Defence (Finance) Regulations as interpreted by the House of Lords in the memorable case of *Boissevain* v. *Weil*.[2] Reg. 2 provided that except with the permission of the Treasury 'no person other than an authorized dealer shall buy or borrow any foreign currency . . . from, or lend or sell any foreign currency . . . to any person'. According to section 3 of the Emergency Powers (Defence) Act, 1939, all Defence Regulations were to be so construed as to apply to all British subjects, unless a contrary intention appeared. A literal interpretation of these provisions meant that if a British subject resident during the war in Monaco borrowed a sum of French francs from a Dutch friend to save his son from a German concentration camp, the loan was, in English law, illegal and void and the Dutch lender could not obtain repayment in an English Court. Such a result will strike some as deplorable. It could and should have been avoided by the acceptance of an argument which Sir David Maxwell Fyfe, Q.C., later Viscount Kilmuir, L.C., seems to have presented to the House of Lords[3] and which would have put an 'intraterritorial construction'

---

[1] The Court also decided that if the owner resided in Israel the order was valid. This again was obvious. Apparently in a later case it was held that if the securities were in Israel, but belonged to foreign residents the orders were likewise invalid; *Rom* v. *Minister of Defence*, referred to in Int. L.R. (1952), 254 (note). This is very doubtful.

[2] [1950] A. C. 327. On this decision, see Mann, op. cit., p. 345, n. 3 (or German edition, p. 330, n. 54). A decision of the German Supreme Court of 21 June 1924, *JW* 1924, 1516, successfully avoided the result reached by the House of Lords in not entirely dissimilar circumstances, though the reasoning is far from convincing.

[3] p. 331.

upon the Regulation: it was not intended to and, therefore, did not apply where neither party was resident in Britain. Any other interpretation involved results of such absurdity that, in view of the criminal sanctions imposed by the Regulations, it cannot have been contemplated by the legislator. But if the Regulation had the meaning attributed to it by the House of Lords, then this would appear to be a case where nationality failed to establish a sufficiently close link with Britain. It is, in fact, a wholly inappropriate link for purposes of exchange control, for the State cannot have any reasonable interest in the borrowings of its non-resident subjects, unless the borrower should undertake to repay only out of funds which are within the control of his home State. The latter condition was no part of the contract in *Boissevain* v. *Weil*.[1] It is, therefore, unfortunately impossible to avoid the submission that the Defence (Finance) Regulations as interpreted by the House of Lords gave the Netherlands just cause of complaint against Britain.[2]

## CONCLUSION

Notwithstanding the length of the preceding survey, there remain many specific aspects of the doctrine of jurisdiction which it has not been possible to review, but which require further investigation. Among them there is the problem of the extraterritorial effect of bankruptcy[3] or the law of nationality which has often given rise to the question, for instance, whether and in what circumstances a State may impose its nationality upon non-residents.[4] Labour Law and the law of social

---

[1] It is important to appreciate that the plaintiff did not sue on the cheques drawn on an English bank, but claimed repayment of the loan.

[2] In fact nothing is known about any such complaint.

[3] For a recent survey see, in particular, Müller–Freienfels, 'Auslandskonkurs und Inlandsfolgen', in *Festschrift für Dölle* (*Vom Deutschen zum Europäischen Recht*) ii.359 (1963).

[4] Thus the Swiss Federal Tribunal and the German Supreme Court have held (wrongly) that Austria has the right and the power to reimpose Austrian nationality upon former Austrians who have become stateless and reside outside Austria: *BGE* 75 i.289, also Int. L.R. (1949), 184; German Supreme Court, 28 October 1959, *Rechtsprechung zum Wiedergutmachungsrecht* (1960), 37 with critical note by Mann, ibid. (1960) 182; German Supreme Court, 3 July 1963, ibid. (1963) p. 560, with critical note by Mann, ibid. (1964) 129. Cf. H. Lauterpacht, 'The Nationality of Denationalized Persons', in *The Jewish Yearbook of International Law* (1948), pp. 164, 171 seq. An even more famous problem is whether upon the

security,[1] certain aspects of air law and, of course general administrative law are other fields the international implications of which are influenced by the doctrine of jurisdiction.

Although, therefore, a final assessment of that doctrine, its nature and effect, is not at present possible, enough has been said to permit the conclusion that the general approach which has been suggested in Part 2 above, is borne out by the detailed investigation included in Part 3 above. A rigid territorial principle such as was favoured by Huber and Story is no longer practicable in the modern world. The flexible test of a close connection with the legislating State is likely to give more acceptable guidance. On the other hand, such a general formula, supported by the experience of municipal law and, in particular, of constitutional law, is at present probably the only one capable of embracing every sphere of a State's activity. In due course it may become possible to bring together various threads and to discover the idea unifying them; this, perhaps, can be done in regard to the meaning and relevance of 'effects'.[2] But such tasks exceed the scope of the present introductory study.


# 4. ENFORCEMENT JURISDICTION

## I

The problem of legislative jurisdiction, as will be obvious at the present stage of the inquiry, creates such difficulty, because

---

annexation of a State non-resident subjects of the annexed State acquire the nationality of the successor State: see, e.g., Mann, 5 *Modern L.R.* (1942), 218, with numerous references; Jellinek, *Der automatische Erwerb und Verlust der Staatsangehörigkeit durch völkerrechtliche Vorgänge* (1951); Paul Weis, *Nationality and Statelessness in International Law* (1956), pp. 140 sqq., and many others.

[1] The available material is too large to be set forth here. But there are two American cases the appreciation and assessment of which causes particular difficulty and which require special attention: *United States* v. *Norddeutscher Lloyd*, 223 U. S. 512 (1912): criminal liability in America for carriage from Bremen to New York made in Germany; *Sandberg* v. *McDonald*, 248 U. S. 185 (1918): advance wages paid under a foreign contract by a foreign ship to foreign seamen in a foreign port not unlawful under U. S. Seaman's Act. The former decision was probably unjustified, for the United States' connection with the contract of carriage was remote.

[2] See above, pp. 72, 88 sqq., 98, 107 and passim.

its fundamental aspects have to a large extent been left unexplored. Enforcement (or prerogative) jurisdiction is an even
more obscure topic. The books, it is true, frequently state the
platitude that, in the absence of consent, no State is allowed to
exercise jurisdiction within the territory of another State. Or in
the words of the majority of the Permanent Court of International Justice[1]:

the first and foremost restriction imposed by international law upon a State
is that—failing the existence of a permissive rule to the contrary—it may
not exercise its power in any form in the territory of another State. In this
sense jurisdiction is certainly territorial; it cannot be exercised by a State
outside its territory except by virtue of a permissive rule derived from international custom or from a convention.

It is perhaps remarkable that to the Draft Restatement this rule
is so plain that it does not even express it except by inference,
when section 20 suggests that a State 'has jurisdiction to enforce
within its territory rules of law that are validly prescribed by
it'. There is, however, nowhere to be found any comprehensive
explanation of what is meant by enforcement jurisdiction which
a State cannot exercise outside its territory.[2] Or, to put it differently, what is it that a State is or is not allowed to do in another
State in order to give effect to its legislation? Is it or is it not
open to a State to take any steps at all in a foreign State with a
view to securing obedience to its laws?

The issues raised by this question are by no means the same
as in the case of legislative jurisdiction. The latter is concerned
with the State's right to legislate within its own territory in
regard to matters which are of international impact in that they
may determine the conduct, the rights or the liabilities of persons abroad.[3] The problem of enforcement jurisdiction arises
when a State acts in foreign territory itself or at least takes
measures which, though initiated in its own territory, are

---

[1] *Case of the Lotus*, pp. 18, 19. For similar general statements about the local
sovereign's exclusive right to exercise acts of sovereignty see German Supreme
Court 26 June 1883, *RGStr* 8, 372, 375, 376; 28 February 1901, *RGStr* 34, 191. cf. 7
June 1921, *RGZ* 102, 251. In the same sense Swiss Federal Tribunal *BGE* 73, i.199
(revenue authorities), 73 iii.5 (1947) relating to execution.

[2] Sections 32 and 47 of the Draft Restatement, in particular, only deal with
enforcement on national vessels, etc., but omit any reference to the general
problems discussed in the present chapter.

[3] See above, pp. 7, 8.

directed towards consummation, and require compliance, in the foreign State. The assumption underlying this difference[1] is that a State may lack enforcement jurisdiction, although it has properly exercised its legislative jurisdiction. On the other hand, it is hardly possible for it to enjoy enforcement jurisdiction, when it is without legislative jurisdiction: if the assessment of a tax is not entitled to international validity there is no room for the question whether it can be recovered in a foreign country.

It is in line with the difference in the nature of the problems that entirely different legal principles govern legislative and enforcement jurisdiction respectively. A State which actually attempts to give effect to its legislation in the territory of another State comes into conflict with the latter's sovereignty. The problems of enforcement jurisdiction, therefore, fall to be considered exclusively from the point of view of the international rights of that State in which the enforcement takes place or is intended to take place. More particularly, they have to be considered from the standpoint of such State's territorial integrity: does the act which in fact occurs within its territory constitute, by international law, a violation of its own sovereign rights, so that it is illegal?

This, accordingly, is the sole test which governs enforcement jurisdiction in all its implications. Of these there seem to be mainly[2] five. Each of them will require separate investigation.

## II

The first case arises when a State exercises physical *force* in the territory of another State to assert its alleged rights: it sends its agents, for instance, to apprehend and remove fugitives from its justice or men liable to serve in its forces, and so forth. It is, of course, obvious that such exercise of force is illegal and no doctrine of jurisdiction is needed, or perhaps even pertinent, to

---

[1] It would have been desirable if section 7 of the Draft Restatement had made it clearer.

[2] The list is not intended to be exhaustive. Another case is, for instance, that of the Government in exile which, by consent, exercises its functions in the territory of another State: see the statement made by the Attorney-General in *Re Amand*, [1941] 2 K. B. 239. On the whole problem see the survey by Geck, *Hoheitsakte auf fremdem Staatsgebiet*, Strupp–Schlochauer, *Wörterbuch des Völkerrechts* i.795, with references.

establish so plain a violation of international law. The existence of a whole system of extradition treaties is conclusive evidence of the fact that customary international law condemns any unauthorized intrusion upon the elementary rights of other States. It is in the interest of the proper functioning of the international order to emphasize this without any ambiguity.

The principle is, indeed, so clear that no State has ever denied it.[1] Even Nazi Germany returned Mr. Jacob-Salomon who had been abducted from Switzerland.[2] That in the year 1963 France failed to return Colonel Argoud who was kidnapped in the Federal Republic of Germany is likely to be incapable of legal justification; there is, as has rightly been pointed out,[3] no warrant for the idea 'that international law need not be invoked if it would disturb a beautiful friendship between the two Governments involved'. Similarly, it is not open to doubt that Israel committed a breach of international law when its agents[4] abducted Eichmann from Argentina. Notwithstanding the diplomatic language employed by it, the Resolution of the Security Council of the United Nations passed on 23 June 1960[5] rightly condemned a regrettable act of illegality.[6] In circumstances which do not appear to have been made public, Argentina and Israel agreed on 3 August 1960 to treat the incident as

---

[1] See, generally, Oppenheim, p. 295, n. 1; Hyde, i, section 200; Dahm, p. 250; O'Higgins, 'Unlawful Seizure and Irregular Extradition', *B.Y.I.L.* (1960), 279; McNair, *International Law Opinions,* i. 69 sqq.

[2] For references see Oppenheim, op. cit.

[3] *The Times* (newspaper), 6 January 1964. The notes exchanged between France and the Federal Republic have so far apparently not been published. See on this and another case Clunet 1964, 187 sqq.; Kirchner, *NJW* 1964, 853.

[4] It seems to have been suggested that the persons who abducted Eichmann were 'volunteers' for whom Israel was not responsible: see Silving, *A.J.I.L.* 1961, 312. Even if as a matter of fact Eichmann's abduction should originally have been a private venture (which seems very doubtful) it became an act of the State of Israel when it was adopted and endorsed by Israel. The point would have been a good one if the abduction had been repudiated and Eichmann had been returned. See O'Higgins, op. cit., p. 296, and see the case of *Vincenti*: Hackworth, ii.320.

[5] The text is published by Silving (above, no. 4), p. 313.

[6] However revolting and unique Eichmann's crimes were and however desirable it was to bring him to justice, a deliberate breach of international law remains unpardonable. The view expressed in the text is developed by Schwarzenberger, *Current Legal Problems* (1962), 252, among others. The contrary view of Silving (above, n. 4), p. 338, that it could not be expected of Israel 'that she should abide by the law' is both untenable and disquieting. See also Green, 23 *Modern L.R.* (1960), 507, and in particular the excellent article by Fawcett, *B.Y.I.L.* 1962, 181.

'settled'. In its judgment in the *Eichmann* case, the Supreme Court of Israel inferred from this fact[1]

> that Argentina has condoned violation of her sovereignty and has waived her claims, including that for the return of the Appellant. Any violation of international law that may have been involved in this incident has thus been remedied.

But the correctness of this view is perhaps open to doubt. Would the compromise reached between Argentina and Israel have precluded the Federal Republic of Germany, if it had wished to do so, from taking up Eichmann's case and asserting the breach of international law?[2]

Forcible takings by or on behalf of one State in the territory of another State are no less illegal if they are directed against things rather than persons. Thus a State cannot compel entry into premises in a foreign country, nor can it take possession of a chattel such as a ship in the face of resistance by those in possession. The point is important, for instance, in the law of immunity: since an international wrong cannot give rise to an international right, a State should not be entitled to immunity in respect of property which it has obtained by the illegal exercise of force.[3]

## III

The *peaceable performance of acts of authority* by one State within the territory of another State should be considered in the light of the fact that throughout the world there exists an elaborate system of multilateral and bilateral treaties regulating the scope of the enforcing State's powers in foreign States. Consular Conventions, in particular, have been concluded between

---

[1] Judgment, paragraph 13, Int. L.R. 36, 5, at p. 26.

[2] It is, of course, an entirely different question whether a court sitting in the State which has wrongfully abducted the accused must or may decline jurisdiction. The majority of municipal courts seem to accept the old adage *male captus, bene detentus*: for references see Oppenheim, op. cit., and add, for instance, *United States* v. *Sobell*, 244 F. 2d 520 (1957), cert. den. 355 U. S. 873 (1957), also Int. L.R. 1957, 256. In the *Eichmann* case the Supreme Court of Israel also followed this rule: *Judgment*, loc. cit., paragraphs 40 sqq. This is a rule which perpetuates a dichotomy between international and municipal law and may at some time have to be reconsidered.

[3] The point was not decided in *The Cristina*, [1938] A. C. 485; see 2 *Modern L.R.* (1938–9), 57. The view expressed in the text is supported by the decision of the Court of first instance in *The Navemar*, 18 F. Supp. 153 (1937).

numerous countries. Although they display substantial variations, it would seem that the Vienna Convention on Consular
Relations which was signed on 24 April 1963[1] by only about
a dozen of the leading States of the world and is not yet in force
expresses fairly general State practice by including in the Consular office the function[2] of 'acting as notary and civil registrar
and in capacities of a similar kind' and of 'transmitting
judicial and extra-judicial documents or executing letters
rogatory or commissions to take evidence for the courts of the
sending State', in accordance with international agreements
and subject to the laws and regulations of the receiving State.
Even in the absence of express provisions of this type the mere
existence of a Consul in the receiving State may, by necessary
implication, invest him with the power to perform certain
official acts; as the Supreme Court of the United States has
suggested,[3]

while consular privileges in foreign countries are the appropriate subjects of
treaties it does not follow that every act of a consul, as, e.g., in communicating with citizens of his own country, must be predicated upon a specific
provision of a treaty. The intercourse of friendly nations, permitting travel
and residence of the citizens of each in the territory of the other, presupposes and facilitates such communications.

The widespread practice of regulating by treaty the performance
of official acts and of conferring the enforcing State's authority
upon consular officers in accordance with the terms of a treaty
makes it necessary to take a narrow view of the tasks which
customary international law allows the enforcing State and its
agents to perform in another State[4]—and it is customary

---

[1] Text in *A.J.I.L.* (1963), 995. On the function of Consuls generally see Zourek,
106 *Recueil* (1962 ii), 386 seq.

[2] Art. 5 (f) and (j).

[3] *Blackmer* v. *United States*, 284 U. S. 421, 439 (1932). On the other hand a
Consul cannot, for instance, perform a marriage ceremony in the United States:
*Miko Juny* v. *Rekusaburo Novaya*, 47 N. Y. Supp. 2d 48 (1946), also *Annual Digest*
(1946), No. 39.

[4] See Verdross, p. 267, who says generally that States are in principle under a
duty, 'in fremden Hoheitsräumen keinerlei Amtshandlungen ohne Genehmigung
des Territorialstaats vorzunehmen'. And see Dahm, p. 251, according to whom no
State has to put up with such activities of another State as involve the service of
documents, the making of investigations, the publication of official notices, the
execution of legal business of a non-contentious character, etc. About taking oaths
in foreign countries see section 6 of the (English) Commissioners for Oaths Act,
1889, as amended.

international law alone which the following observations are intended to clarify.

(1) Thus it would seem that no State has any right at all to employ its own officials or other agents to effect on its behalf *service of documents* in another State.

This conclusion is evidenced both by treaties and by State practice; nowhere is there any indication of a State being allowed to serve documents in another State except through its consular officers or through the instrumentalities of the receiving State itself. Among treaties pride of place must be given to the Hague Convention on the Law of Civil Procedure of 1954 to which a number of European States are parties and which re-enacts the Convention of 1905. The method normally envisaged by it is for the Consul of the forum State to request the competent authority of the receiving State to effect service.[1] A party may, however, apply direct to the competent authority in the receiving State or may serve through diplomatic or consular officers if either treaties so provide or the receiving State does not object; if the recipient is a citizen of the forum State and service is effected without the use of force by a diplomatic or consular officer an objection cannot be raised.[2] Any other method of service is impliedly excluded by the Convention. To take an example from municipal legislation, the notorious Art. 69, No. 10, of the French Code de Procédure Civile goes to the extreme of providing that a document intended for a person resident abroad is properly served when left with the local 'parquet'. By a 'faux-semblant, . . . une fiction' French law treats this as equivalent to service outside France, which, ex hypothesi, the French State would be unable to achieve.[3] According to the German Code of Civil Procedure[4] documents cannot be served outside Germany

---

[1] Art. 1.

[2] Art. 6. This is also American practice: Hackworth, ii.118, 119; Hyde, p. 644. Apparently out of twenty-three consular conventions made by the United States only those with the United Kingdom and Eire authorize American Consuls to serve documents: Jones, 62 *Yale L.J.* (1953), 519, 523, 536. Many bilateral Conventions follow the scheme of the Hague Convention: see, e.g. Arts. 2 and 5 of the Anglo-German Convention of 3 December 1928.

[3] On Art. 69 see, for instance, Rigaux, 'La Signification des Actes Judiciaires à l'étranger', *Rev. Crit.* 1963, 447, particularly pp. 467, 468, and the recent decision Cass. Civ. 23 February 1962, Clunet 1962, 986.

[4] Art. 199.

except in pursuance of a request addressed to the German Consul or to the competent authority of the foreign State.

Whether international law prohibits the service of documents by the despatch, through the post, of written communications from the territory of the forum State is open to doubt. In principle it would seem that this method of service should be treated as lawful, at any rate in those cases in which the document to be served contains merely a notification as opposed to a command[1] and does not include a threat of penalties in the event of non-compliance,[2] for in such cases the sovereignty of the receiving State can hardly be said to be impugned. On the other hand, the Hague Convention of 1954 allows service through the post only where treaties so provide or where the receiving State raises no objection.[3] The framers of the Convention seem to have thought, therefore, that by customary international law the receiving State may object; in fact it appears that Germany and Switzerland, for instance, do object.[4]

In the Anglo-American world documents may usually be served by any private person.[5] The admissibility of such service in a foreign country is likely to be subject to the same considerations as apply to service through the post.[6]

A special word, however, must be said about the subpoena of the Anglo-American system of law.[7] In England a subpoena cannot be issued at all if the addressee is resident outside the

---

[1] On the legality of serving a document containing a command see the following remarks about the subpoena. It is perhaps not without significance that, when leave has been obtained from an English court to serve outside the jurisdiction, the document actually to be served is a notice of a writ, for a writ contains a command to appear and this cannot properly be served abroad: see O. 11, r. 3, of the Rules of Supreme Court.

[2] This is emphasized by Riezler, *Internationales Zivilprozessrecht* (1949), pp. 683, 684, with references. The suggestion by Neumeyer, p. 496, that service abroad is illegal only if effected by registered, rather than ordinary, letter is untenable.

[3] Art. 6. In the same sense *Harvard Research* on 'Judicial Assistance' (supplement to *A.J.I.L.* (1939), pp. 64, 65, and Art. 6 of the Anglo-German Convention of 1928.

[4] Bülow, *Internationales Zivilprozessrecht*, p. 100a.

[5] From the point of view of Continental countries this is highly unusual and gives rise to much misunderstanding.

[6] In these cases it is not so much the method of service as the content of the document that causes difficulty.

[7] A subpoena contains the command of the sovereign to appear as a witness or to produce documents at a trial. The text does not deal with a subpoena served on a party to the suit.

United Kingdom[1]; an exception exists where a subpoena is served upon a British subject abroad to enforce a revenue claim.[2] A similar exception exists in the United States of America whenever the Attorney-General requires the attendance at a criminal trial of a person who is 'a citizen of the United States or domiciled therein'.[3] The constitutional validity of this provision was upheld by the Supreme Court in the much-discussed case of *Blackmer* v. *United States*,[4] where a United States citizen resident in France had been served with a subpoena by the American Consul in France.[5] Chief Justice Hughes, speaking on behalf of the Court, said[6]:

> The mere giving of such notice to the citizen in the foreign country of the requirement of his government that he shall return is in no sense an invasion of any right of the foreign government and the citizen has no standing to invoke any such supposed right.

No less an authority than Wigmore[7] has criticized this ruling on the ground that a subpoena cannot properly be described as a notice, but is a command which, in the absence of a treaty, cannot be served even upon a citizen resident abroad,

> for this would be an attempted exercise of State power within the territory o the foreign State—an intrusion impossible in legal theory and in international understanding.

This legal rule was, in fact, accepted by a recent decision of the Court of Appeals, Second Circuit.[8] In litigation between private parties a subpoena to produce documents situate in Canada was served upon the New York branches of Canadian banks which were only witnesses. It was held that the taking of evidence was possible only by letters rogatory or some similar

---

[1] Halsbury (-Simonds), *Laws of England* (3rd ed., 1956) xv.426. The same rule prevails in the United States: Wigmore, viii.92.

[2] See *Attorney General* v. *Prosser*, [1938] 2 K. B. 531. In this case the subpoena was served in France (p. 532).

[3] The extension of this provision to persons who are neither citizens of, nor resident in, the United States has rightly been criticized by Wigmore, below, n. 7.

[4] 284 U. S. 421 (1932).

[5] The method of service does not appear from the report, nor is it made clear whether the United States had any treaty rights in France.

[6] p. 439.

[7] 3rd ed. (1940), section 2195c (viii.92); see also Smit, 'International Aspects of Federal Civil Procedure', 61 *Col. L.R.* (1961), 1031, 1046.

[8] *Ings* v. *Ferguson*, 282 F.2d 149 (1960).

machinery and that the use of a subpoena was wrongful. As Judge Moore said[1]:

An elementary principle of jurisdiction is that the processes of the courts of any sovereign State cannot cross international boundary lines and be enforced in a foreign country. Thus service of the United States District Court subpoena by a United States Marshal upon a Montreal branch of a Canadian bank would not be enforceable.

If a subpoena cannot be served in Canada, service in New York for the purpose of securing obedience in Canada is likewise ineffective. Such reasoning should apply *a fortiori* to a case in which a prerogative claim is made: if the United States makes a tax claim against a taxpayer it cannot require the New York branch of a foreign bank to produce the foreign head office's documents. The result should be the same in the converse case in which the United States makes a tax claim against a taxpayer who is a non-resident alien and requires from the New York head office of an American bank the production of documents in the possession of its foreign branch. The Court of Appeals, Second Circuit, recently decided in the opposite sense and ordered a New York bank to produce the Panamanian branch's documents.[2] This unsatisfactory result is probably due to the failure to give sufficient effect to the independence of a branch.

(2) If, for the purpose of civil litigation pending in the forum State, it is necessary to *take evidence* in a foreign country, this cannot normally be done otherwise than with the assistance of the competent authorities of the foreign State. The assistance is granted either in pursuance of treaties such as the Hague Convention of 1954 or on the footing of municipal legislation such as the Foreign Tribunals Evidence Act, 1856, which is in force in the United Kingdom.[3] In France the right to judicial assistance has been recognized by the courts even in the absence of any

---

[1] p. 151.

[2] *First National City Bank of New York* v. *Internal Revenue*, 271 F. 2d. 616 (1959), cert. den. 361 U. S. 948 (1960), also Int. L.R. 28, 138. The only exception allowed is illegality under the *lex situs*. On this point see below, p. 134. See, generally, Roth, *New York Univ. L.R.* (1962), 295.

[3] A good survey is provided by Miller, *A.J.C.L.* (1960), 680, who rightly emphasizes that the United Kingdom has no objection to diplomatic or consular officers taking evidence from willing witnesses. For recent decisions on the interpretation of the Act see *Radio Corporation of America* v. *Rauland Corporation*, [1956] 1 Q. B. 618; *Penn-Texas Corporation* v. *Murat Anstalt*, [1964] 1 Q. B. 40; (No. 2), [1964] 2 All E. R. 594.

legislation, for 'en matière de besoins humains primordiaux l'humanité seule doit compter'.[1] Where, however, a witness is willing and the foreign State permits it, whether by treaty or otherwise, consular officers may take the evidence and administer oaths[2]; such a right may be limited to the evidence of nationals of the forum State or may be general. In no case, however, is the forum State entitled to send its officials or judges into foreign territory to take the evidence of witnesses even if they are willing[3]; in the absence of the consent of the State concerned the taking of such evidence by or on behalf of the forum State unquestionably constitutes an excess of international jurisdiction.

Nor is a State entitled to enforce the attendance of a foreign witness before its own tribunals by threatening him with penalties in case of non-compliance. There is, it is true, no objection to a State, by lawful means, inviting or perhaps requiring a foreign witness to appear for the purpose of giving evidence. But the foreign witness is under no duty to comply, and to impose penalties upon him and to enforce them either against his property or against him personally on the occasion of a future visit constitutes an excess of criminal jurisdiction and runs contrary to the practice of States in regard to the taking of evidence as it has developed over a long period of time.

(3) A further question is whether the officers of one State may exercise *notarial functions* in the territory of another State. The answer is in the negative, the exercise of such functions being a privilege of the local sovereign. The German Supreme Court in fact so decided.[4] And when Germany protested against the appointment of an American 'commissioner of deeds' in Germany, the United States of America did not persist in upholding it.[5] The rule is confirmed by the numerous consular

---

[1] Batiffol, section 732.    [2] Wigmore, viii.91 et sqq.; Batiffol, section 739.

[3] See Guggenheim, *Lehrbuch des Völkerrechts* (1951) i.332, n. 3, and Wigmore, viii.83: 'State A cannot send its officer into State B and there exercise power to compel witness W to answer.'

[4] 26 June 1883, *RGStr* 8, 372, 376, according to which it is 'a universally valid principle of the European public international law that no notary may act in foreign territory, no prosecution by courts or by the police may extend beyond the frontier, no official with public character may be appointed in foreign territory, without the placet or the exequatur of the foreign govenment'. See Dölle, *Rabels Z* (1962), 242.

[5] Hackworth ii.313, 314.

conventions which consider it necessary almost without exception to confer the right upon consular officers to authenticate documents, to receive and attest declarations and to legalize documents, when they are required by a national of the sending State outside the receiving State or by any person in the sending State.[1]

## IV

While it is thus clear that a State is without jurisdiction to perform official acts within the territory of another State, it is submitted that a State is also disentitled to carry out *investigations* in a foreign country, if it is their purpose to pursue and enforce its prerogative rights such as its criminal, administrative or fiscal jurisdiction.

It is necessary to stress this condition, for a State engaged in commercial activities, 'l'Etat Commerçant', is, of course, in no other position than any private person, and if it is involved in litigation about, say, a charterparty, it is free to make inquiries, take proofs from witnesses, consult experts or make other investigations in a foreign State. But the State acting as a sovereign, asserting its 'public' or prerogative rights or purporting to enforce its jurisdiction is intruding upon the corresponding rights of the State in the territory of which it acts, and cannot do so except with such State's consent.[2] This distinction will have to be emphasized more than once in the course of the following pages. It is a truly fundamental distinction, for without it the present international order could not function. It is based on the sovereignty of States, a concept necessitated by the absence of political and economic homogeneity in the world and guaranteeing the freedom of individual human beings living in them; to describe it as 'unfortunately still of unbelievable vigor'[3] is a singularly inept comment.[4]

[1] See, e.g., Art 17 (3) and (4) of the Consular Convention between the U.S.A. and Japan (published in *International Legal Materials* (1963) ii.748—perhaps the most recent and elaborate convention on the subject. The Vienna Draft Convention does not contain the qualifications stated in the text. Contrary to the view taken in the text Wengler, *Völkerrecht* (1964) ii.966 et seq., suggests that the rule embodied in consular conventions corresponds to customary law.

[2] This may, of course, be given generally by treaty or for a specific case.

[3] This phrase is used by Brewster, *Antitrust and American Business Abroad* (1958), p. 342, with reference to the enforcement of foreign penal and revenue laws. These, however, are merely one single aspect of the wider problem discussed in the text.

[4] For further discussion of the doctrine see below, p. 124.

In the absence of conventional arrangements such as those popularly known under the heading of 'Interpol'[1] a State cannot, therefore, send its police officers, even if they are in civilian clothes, into foreign States to investigate crimes or make inquiries affecting investigations in their own country.[2] Nor can it allow spies or informers to operate abroad.[3]

Similarly, the tax authorities of one State have no jurisdiction to send their officials to other States to look at books and records of taxpayers, to inspect properties for the purpose of valuation, to take statements from witnesses in the prosecution of tax litigation, and so forth. This, apparently, has not always been realized. In 1936 it was reported[4] that an agent of the American Internal Revenue Authorities 'who undertook to proceed to France to make an investigation was turned back at the port of entry by Governmental authority and refused admittance'. And three agents of the Dutch Ministry of Finance, who in 1949 in Lucerne took statements from a Dutch citizen in connection with tax claims are said to have been imprisoned by the Swiss authorities and to have been released only after the Netherlands had made appropriate amends.[5] (One cannot help adding that the American writer who reports this incident makes the disquieting comment: 'To an American observer the procedure [adopted by the Dutch] would appear routine').[6] What a State cannot lawfully do through its own officials it cannot achieve indirectly by employing a firm of lawyers, accountants or surveyors. Nor does it matter whether the taxpayer or witness consents to the investigation. The right to object, as well as the right to consent, belongs to the State concerned.[7] It is its jurisdiction within its own territory that is being infringed, not by the presence of certain individuals, whether they be officials or professional advisers of the enforcing State, but by the nature of their activity: they pursue the prerogative jurisdiction of the enforcing State in a territory to which it does not extend. These

---

[1] They do not seem to have been published.

[2] See the interesting German–Swiss incident described in Clunet (1913), 1430.

[3] See the illuminating French–Swiss incident reported in *Schweizerisches Jahrbuch für Internationales Recht* (1948), pp. 167, 168. Cf. Neumeyer, *Internationales Verwaltungrecht* (1910–36), iv.497.

[4] Angell, 36 *Col. L.R.* (1936), 908, 910.

[5] Jones, 62 *Yale L.J.* (1953), 519, 520.        [6] Jones, op. cit.

[7] It should be remembered that the consent of a willing witness is likewise insufficient to allow the enforcing State to take his evidence: see above, p. 119.

conclusions are supported by an important dictum of Germany's Supreme Tax Court[1]:

Without a treaty or without the foreign State's permission the officials of the German Tax Office may not *enter* the foreign territory. If, nevertheless, they do enter, they would commit, contrary to public international law, a violation of the territory of the foreign State.

Another type of investigation which a State is not allowed to carry out abroad arises in connection with exchange control. Nazi Germany, in particular, made it a practice to send official or professional representatives to England and other countries to check and supervise the assets of German nationals or residents which were subject to German exchange control, to inspect books and to interrogate the staff of German-controlled enterprises. In Switzerland such agents, when caught, were criminally prosecuted and convicted under a section of the Swiss Criminal Code,[2] but it is more important to stress that their activities engaged Germany's international responsibility on account of the excess of her enforcement jurisdiction.

For the reasons which have been explained it should, finally, not be open to doubt that investigations carried out in a foreign country in the interest of anti-trust legislation are, in the absence of consent by the State in question, not allowed to the enforcing State. Yet in this particular context the practice of the United States of America is stated to have developed in the opposite sense in that extensive investigations were carried out in foreign countries, nothing being known about any permission given by them.[3] Such investigations have been defended by some writers on the ground that they are made, not in pursuance of sovereign authority, but in reliance upon the willing co-operation of the persons to be investigated.[4] These American practices and the theories put forward in their support have rightly been described as 'astonishing'.[5] No State can exercise its jurisdiction in

---

[1] 27 September 1933, *Reichssteuerblatt* (1933), 1188, 1190 (italics supplied).

[2] *BGE* 65 i.39, also *A.D.* (1941–2), No. 2.

[3] Such incidents are mentioned by Schlochauer, *Die Extraterritoriale Wirkung von Hoheitsakten* (1962), p. 68, and Schwartz, *Cartel and Monopoly in Modern Law* (1961), ii.679, and *Deutsches Internationales Kartellrecht* (1962), p. 249.

[4] See the authors mentioned in the preceding note.

[5] Verzijl, *Nederlands Tijdschrift voor Internationaal Recht*, 8 (1961), 3, at p. 21. As to the views of the Swiss Government see *Schweizerisches Jahrbuch für Internationales Recht* (1957), 149.

the territory of another State except with the latter's consent
for which the consent of private persons is no substitute and
which, for reasons of constitutional law, in many countries cannot be readily given. And no form in which the investigating
process may be clothed can hide the fact that in substance it
constitutes a prerogative activity.

V

If, then, a State cannot exercise its jurisdiction outside its own
territory, whether by the use of force or by the peaceful performance of official acts or by mere investigation, the question
arises whether it can achieve its object by invoking the assistance
of the foreign State's courts. Is it open to a State to bring, in the
courts of another State, proceedings for the recovery of taxes?
Or for an injunction restraining the defendant from following
certain restrictive practices? Or for the surrender of foreign
exchange subject to the plaintiff State's control? Or for the
delivery up of documents? Or is it open to a State to vest in its
Custodian of Enemy Property a debt, a picture, a piece of
land or a ship belonging to an enemy, but situate in a foreign
country and then to start proceedings in such foreign country
to recover the property?

Merely to put these questions should be sufficient to make it
obvious that the answers can only be in the negative. The
reason is to be found in the broad principle of international law
according to which a State has no right to enforce in a foreign
court any claim which in substance involves the direct or
indirect enforcement of a prerogative right of the enforcing
State, or which is made by virtue of sovereign power.

The fundamental and far-reaching character of this rule was
developed and emphasized in 1955.[1] As a rule derived from
public international law and relating to the enforcement of
prerogative rights it has since met with a measure of approval.[2]
If it has not been generally accepted this is due to two main
causes. On the one hand, the rule is strictly limited to the
*enforcement* of prerogative rights; there is, in particular, no

---

[1] Below pp. 492 sqq. In German: 21 *Rabels* (1956), 1.
[2] Dicey, pp. 159 sqq.; Kegel, *Kurzlehrbuch des Internationalen Privatrechts* (2nd ed.,
1964), p. 389.

reason why it should be extended to the *application* of foreign public law, as public international law which is the source of the rule does not either justify or require such an extension.[1] On the other hand, the rule is by no means limited to what are frequently, but inaccurately, described as 'revenue or penal claims'.[2] Once the true basis of the rule precluding the extra-territorial enforcement of the latter claims is exposed the generality and usefulness of the rule is more likely to be appreciated.

However this may be, since 1955 the practice of the courts has produced new and striking illustrations of the principle and its scope. In the present context it is proposed to refer to four groups of cases from the United States, Scotland, Canada and the Netherlands.

Perhaps the most important case[3] is the decision of the Court of Appeals of New York in *Banco Do Brasil* v. *Israel Commodity Co.*[4] The plaintiff, 'an instrumentality of the Government of Brazil' and as such charged with the administration of Brazilian exchange control, brought an action in New York against a New York firm for damages for a tort allegedly committed in New York. The alleged conspiracy meant that, although Brazilian exporters received the amount of Brazilian cruzeiros to which they were entitled, the plaintiff did not receive such an amount

---

[1] The contrary is frequently asserted. The most unfortunate and at the same time the most outstanding example of the wider view is the decision of the German Supreme Court, 17 December 1959, *BGHZ* 31, 368, also in French *Rev. Crit.* (1961), 313, with note by Mezger; on the decision see Drobnig, *NJW* 1960, 1088, and Neumayer, 25 Rabels *Zeitschrift* (1960), 649, among others. In 1948, when both parties resided in Ruritania, X granted a loan to the defendant. At that time the law of Ruritania which governed the transaction provided that an assignment to persons resident outside Ruritania was not permitted by law. Nevertheless, X assigned the debt to the plaintiff who claimed payment from the defendant when, in 1957, he found him in the Federal Republic. The defendant relied on the law o Ruritania. The German Supreme Court regarded this as an attempt to enforce Ruritanian public law and rejected the defence. In truth, the defendant had invoked the rule of Ruritanian civil law that an assignment was excluded by statute (see section 399 of the German Civil Code) or that the prohibited transaction was void (see section 134 of the German Civil Code).

[2] The impression that the rule is so limited is given, e.g., by Cheshire, pp. 136 sqq., and many others.

[3] Another important decision of the United States Court of Appeals, Second Circuit, reaffirms the rule that foreign taxes cannot be recovered: *United States* v. *First National City Bank*, 321 F. 2d 14 (1963). See also *Rossano* v. *Manufacturers Insurance Co.*, [1963] 2 Q. B. 352, at pp. 376, 377.

[4] 12 N. Y. 2d 371, 190 N. E. 235 (1963) (a 4:3 decision), cert. den. 375 U. S. (1964).

of U.S. dollars as it would and should have received had its foreign exchange regulations been obeyed. After it had rejected a wholly untenable argument of the plaintiff founded upon Art. VIII (2) (b) of the Bretton Woods Agreement[1] the majority of the Court turned to the short and decisive point of the case, though its formulation was again unfortunate[2]:

Plaintiff is an instrumentality of the Government of Brazil and is seeking, by use of an action for conspiracy to defraud, to enforce what is clearly a revenue law . . . it is well established since the day of Lord Mansfield . . . that one State does not enforce the revenue laws of another.

To describe exchange control as a revenue law is, of course, a misnomer. But the meaning intended by the Court is clear and convincing: Brazil was attempting to enforce in New York a prerogative right, viz. its exchange control regulations, but had no international jurisdiction to do so.

The Scottish case was equally satisfactorily decided. The proceeds of sale of a French ship had been paid into court in Scotland. They were claimed partly by salvors for services rendered, partly by the French State in respect of contributions due from the owners of the ship as employers under State schemes for health insurance and family benefits. Lord Cameron held that these were 'nothing more nor less than taxes or at least charges or impositions of a like nature and that the sums so levied form part of the revenue of the State',[3] and were therefore not recoverable.

On the other hand, the almost incredible misunderstanding of the nature and function of a Custodian of Enemy Property[4] has unfortunately spread to Canada. The shares of a Dutch company were in 1957 vested in the State of the Netherlands on the ground that they belonged to German enemies. Thereupon the Dutch authorities appointed new managers of the company which owned all the shares of a Canadian subsidiary company. In proceedings instituted in Canada the substantial

---

[1] The Bretton Woods Agreement merely provides for the unenforceability of certain contracts. How this could possibly be said to create a liability for damages in tort or the extraterritorial enforceability of prerogative rights can only be described as mysterious.

[2] p. 377.

[3] *Metal Industries (Salvage) Ltd.* v. *St. Harle*, 1962 Scots Law Times Reports 114.

[4] On earlier instances in England see the paper reproduced below, p. 508.

question was whether the Dutch company, represented by its new Board, was entitled to its Canadian property. Apart from any question arising from special arrangements made by treaty, the answer can only be in the negative. McGruer C.J., however, before whom the real point was hardly argued,[1] allowed the Dutch company to recover.[2] Yet it is difficult to think of a clearer attempt to enforce a Dutch prerogative right in Canada. It constituted an infringement of Canadian sovereignty which Canadian courts were not entitled to countenance.

A much more doubtful case arose in Holland. In 1940 the German occupants of Belgium passed a decree providing for the payment of compensation to Belgians who during the first world war had supported Germany. A Belgian statute of 1944 revoked the German decree of 1940 and ordered the recipients to make restitution of the amounts paid to them. In a number of cases the Belgian Government started proceedings in the Dutch Courts to obtain repayment from Belgians resident in the Netherlands. All these actions succeeded,[3] although none seems to have reached the Supreme Court. It may be that in form the cause of action was based on the unjustified enrichment of the recipients, but in substance, it is submitted, the Belgian Government asserted sovereign rights. It attempted to enforce rights of government rather than property. In doing so it failed to have due regard to the sovereignty of the Netherlands.

## VI

(1) If, finally, a State cannot enforce its public law in a foreign country, whether by the use of force, by peaceably performing official acts, by mere investigation or by invoking the machinery of the foreign country's courts, there remains only one last possibility: is it open to a State to have resort to its own

---

[1] It would have been argued on appeal, but when this became apparent the case was settled.

[2] *Brown, Gow, Wilson* v. *Beleggings Societeit N.V.* (1961) Ontario Reports 815, discussed in 40 *Canadian Bar Review* (1962), 490, by Ziegler and Dunlop.

[3] Court of Appeal, The Hague, 2 August 1953, *N.J.* (1953), No. 589, also Int. L.R. (1953), 26; Court of Appeal, 's-Hertogenbosch, 29 June 1954, *N.J.* (1955), No. 24, 301, also Int. L.R. (1953), 28; Court of Appeal, The Hague, 3 November 1955, *N.J.* (1956), No. 1235, also Int. L.R. (1957), 38. For a New York case dealing with a cognate problem see *Land Nordrhein-Westfalen* v. *Rosenthal*, 232 N. Y. S. 2d 963 (1963); this also is a doubtful case.

legal system and, in particular, its own courts for the purpose of making the conduct of foreigners in foreign countries conform to its own commands? Or, to be more specific, can, for instance, a Dutch Court, in criminal proceedings against an American, order the forfeiture of the *instrumentum sceleris*, a car situated in New York? Or can the Dutch Court, in pursuance of Dutch legislation against restrictive practices, order General Motors in Detroit to grant a free licence of certain American and other patents so as to permit the import into the United States of Dutch products? Or, finally, to take an example from the law of exchange control: can a Dutch Court, in proceedings brought by the Dutch Government against the Chase Manhattan Bank as represented by its Amsterdam branch, order the bank to disclose all the accounts of Dutch nationals kept by it and its branches anywhere in the world? Could it do so if the defendant were a Dutch bank with branches overseas?

It would seem that the answers to the above questions must be in the negative. Any other result would be repugnant to one's commonsense and the dictates of justice, to that distribution of State jurisdiction and to that idea of international forbearance without which the present international order cannot continue. With one single exception the practice of all States seems to be in accord with this view. When that single State, viz. the United States of America, propounded the opposite philosophy, it was at once confronted with diplomatic protests. The decisions of its administrative agencies and its courts met with determined rejection by the legislatures and the courts of other States. Nor is it to be doubted that in the converse case the reaction of the American courts would have been similar.[1]

The strictly legal reasoning leading to this result rests on the submission that the judgment of a court or the order of an administrative agency no less than legislation in the narrow sense of the term[2] is internationally valid only within the limits of substantive jurisdiction. The mere fact that a State's judicial or administrative agencies are internationally entitled to subject a person to their personal or 'curial' jurisdiction, does not by any means permit them to regulate by their orders such person's conduct abroad. This they may do only if the State of the forum

---

[1] See below, p. 135, n. 2.
[2] For the definition of 'legislative jurisdiction' see above, p. 6.

also has substantive jurisdiction to regulate conduct in the manner defined in the order. In other words, for the purpose of justifying, even in the territory of the forum, the international validity of an order, not only its making, but also its content must be authorized by substantive rules of legislative jurisdiction. In those cases in which the enforcing State asserts a prerogative right and demands obedience to it abroad, an additional point of some significance is available. The enforcing State, as has been explained,[1] cannot achieve respect for its prerogative rights in foreign countries by proceedings taken there. It is precluded, *a fortiori*, from achieving its ends indirectly by having orders made in its own territory, which are to take effect abroad and thus attribute to themselves a power equal to that of an order which the foreign country could, but refuses to make. The crux of the matter lies in the fact that the enforcing State requires compliance with its sovereign commands in foreign countries where its writ does not run and where it cannot be made to run by clothing it in the form of judgments of courts, whether they be its own or those of the foreign country.

Where the enforcing State brings proceedings in its courts to assert prerogative rights against a person over whom it has personal jurisdiction, it might be suggested that no harm would be done if the order directed the defendant to do or not to do certain acts in foreign countries, for outside the country of the forum such an order would be *brutum fulmen* and would not be given effect.[2] Such an argument overlooks the fact that the defendant's assets in the State of the forum would be in jeopardy and that as a result of the disobedience to the order a number of individuals might risk their liberty on entering that State's territory.[3]

It would be equally wrong, on the other hand, to regard such judicial orders as something typical, as being in no way different

---

[1] Above, p. 124 et seq.

[2] In his most helpful article quoted above, p. 123, n. 5, Verzijl, after having posed the question discussed in the text (p. 12), lays grea stress on this argument. He believes that many cases mean no more than that the enforcing State is 'beating the air'. *Sed quaere.*

[3] Thus in *U.S.* v. *The Watchmakers of Switzerland Information Centre and Others* the final decree provides (paragraph iii) that it shall apply not only to any defendant, but also to 'its officers, directors, agents, servants, employees, subsidiaries, successors and assigns and to all other persons in active concert or participation with any defendant who shall have received actual notice of this final judgment'.

from orders traditionally made against a defendant over whom the court has personal jurisdiction, such as orders requiring the defendant to convey foreign land to the plaintiff[1] or to refrain from doing certain acts abroad.[2] In proceedings between private parties such orders are, of course, usual. But this does not by any means justify the conclusion that, by asserting its prerogative power within its own territory, a State is necessarily in a position to achieve its objects outside its territory just as if it was claiming merely the implementation of private rights. The two types of judgments are different in character,[3] as is shown by the fact that a prerogative right, even if embodied in a judgment, cannot be extraterritorially enforced, while a judgment enforcing a private right could: a Dutch judgment ordering B to convey New York land to A can no doubt be enforced in New York, while a judgment appropriating B's New York land to the State of the Netherlands could not. The same applies to other commands, such as injunctions,[4] even if they are obtained in proceedings said to be 'civil'. Their description is immaterial. The essential point is that in substance the State enforces its sovereign, governmental or public rights rather than rights of property.[5]

---

[1] Under the doctrine of *Penn* v. *Baltimore* (1750), 1 Ves. Sen. 44.

[2] As to England: *Ellerman Lines* v. *Read*, [1928] 2 K. B. 144. As to Germany: Supreme Court, 2 October 1956, *BGHZ* 22, 1, at p. 13.

[3] The distinction is overlooked, for instance, by Kronstein, in *XXth Century Comparative and Conflicts Law* (Legal Essays in Honor of Hessel E. Yntema) (1961), 432, at p. 438, who actually says that 'antitrust decrees . . . are patterned on the type of decree traditionally handed down by a court of equity' and who quotes *Penn* v. *Baltimore, ubi supra*, in support. In *U.S.* v. *Ross*, 302 F. 2d 831 (1962) the Court of Appeals, 2d Circ., confirmed the appointment of a receiver in respect of the property of the defendant, a non-resident U. S. citizen, to secure taxes alleged to be due from him. The Court said (p. 834): 'Personal jurisdiction gave the Court power to order to transfer property, whether that property was within or without the limits of the Court's territorial jurisdiction', and it relied on such cases as *Massie* v. *Watts*, 6 Cranch 148 (1810). All these cases were of the type of *Penn* v. *Baltimore, ubi supra*. None of them related to the enforcement of a prerogative right or supported the Court's ruling, though this was probably correct for entirely different reasons. On 'orders for foreign conduct' addressed to individuals at the instance of individuals see, generally, Nussbaum, *Principles of Private International Law* pp. 215, 216; Ehrenzweig, pp. 182 sqq.

[4] See, in particular, *Emperor of Austria* v. *Day* (1861) 3 De G. F. & J. 217, at p. 242, per Lord Campbell, and, generally, the paper reproduced below, p. 492, at pp. 34, 35.

[5] On the distinction which underlies the whole of the present section see the paper reproduced below, p. 492.

This, let it be repeated, it cannot do, because a State commits an excess of jurisdiction in so far as it requires performance of its prerogative rights by a foreigner in foreign countries. And in so far as the enforcing State requires compliance with its prerogative rights in its own territory it can do so only if and to such extent as it has substantive legislative jurisdiction. It cannot do so merely by reason of its personal (or 'curial') jurisdiction over the defendant.

(2) Even in the field of litigation between private persons it would be a mistake to believe that, once its competence is established, the court is necessarily free to proceed as its own law prescribes[1] and that the doctrine of legislative jurisdiction ceases to operate. An instance of its continuing operation is provided by the law relating to injunctions.[2] Where the plaintiff applies for an injunction against a non-resident defendant, two different questions may arise: Firstly, is the defendant properly before the court?[3] Secondly, if the answer is in the affirmative, is it proper for the court to grant an injunction restraining the defendant from doing some act abroad? The answer to the latter question is that according to English conceptions the defendant who is not a British subject[4] will not be restrained from doing in a foreign country what by the law of such country he is entitled to do, unless a sufficient 'connection with' England, is shown to exist. These pregnant words used by Lord Cranworth[5] mean that a foreigner[6] may pursue

---

[1] It has been said, it is true, that the moment a person is properly served with proceedings 'that person, so far as the jurisdiction of the court is concerned, is precisely in the same position as a person who is in this country': Re Liddell's Settlement Trusts, [1936] Ch. 365, 374, per Romer L.J. But although Megaw J. applied this dictum in Royal Exchange Assurance v. Compania Naviera Santi (The Tropaiofaros), [1962] 1 Lloyds L. R. 410, it is not easy to reconcile it with Re Vocalion (Foreign) Ltd., [1932] Ch. 196.

[2] For another example see the English doctrine of equitable jurisdiction in personam relating to foreign immovables. Cf. Cheshire, p. 623, who thinks it 'has been carried to an extent scarcely warranted by the principles of international law'.

[3] Where there is no other ground of jurisdiction, O. 11, r. 1 (f), gives an English court jurisdiction 'when any injunction is sought as to anything to be done within the jurisdiction'.

[4] For the case of a British subject see Ellerman Lines v. Read, [1928] 2 K. B. 144.

[5] Carron Iron Co. v. Maclaren (1855), 5 H. L. C. 439, 442. A similar tendency can clearly be discerned in Vanity Fair Mills v. Eaton, 234 F. 2d. 633, cert. den. 352 U. S. 871 (1956), also Int. L.R. (1956), 134; but see Steele v. Bulova Watch Co. 344, U. S. 280 (1956), also Int. L.R. (1956), 270.

[6] As to a British subject see Re Distin (1871) 24 L. T. 197; Dicey, pp. 692, 693.

abroad a claim against the foreign estate of an English bank-rupt[1] and if he subsequently comes to England he cannot be sued for the refundment of what he has recovered.[2] On the other hand, the court will in suitable cases restrain a party to English proceedings from bringing actions abroad,[3] or it will restrain a *resident* creditor from enforcing a claim against the foreign estate of a person who died domiciled in England and in respect of whose estate an administration action is pending in England.[4] And a sufficient connection with England has rightly been held to exist if a Greek resident in Greece pursues there proceedings against British subjects, which by Greek law he is entitled to take, but which are designed to reopen an earlier judgment given against him by an English Court.[5]

It is submitted that the principle upon which these English cases rest is sound and also highly significant from the point of view of the doctrine of international jurisdiction and that the cases which illustrate it are valuable examples of the test of closeness of connection and its advantages over the test of terri-toriality.

(3) The principles of international jurisdiction which have been stated came to the fore when, in a number of anti-trust cases against defendants who were non-resident aliens, the United States of America obtained from its courts orders which, in effect, required the defendants to make their conduct in their own countries conformable to United States anti-trust legislation.

Perhaps the most prominent of these cases is *U.S.* v. *Imperial Chemical Industries*[6] where the British defendant was ordered, inter alia, (i) to grant to any applicant against a reasonable royalty non-exclusive licences under certain British and other patents to import into Britain or any other country protected products manufactured in America and (ii) to refrain from disposing of its British and other patents except on terms preserv-ing the said rights to a compulsory licence. The judgment of

---

[1] *Re Chapman*, (1873) L. R. 15 Eq. 75. As to the position in case of the winding-up of a company, see the cases referred to by Dicey, p. 693, n. 24, and in particular *Re Vocalion (Foreign) Ltd.*, [1932] 2 Ch. 196.

[2] Cheshire, p. 528.     [3] Dicey, p. 1079.

[4] *Carron Iron Co.* v. *Maclaren*, (1855) 5 H. L. C. 439.

[5] *Royal Exchange Assurance* v. *Compania Naviera Santi (The Tropaiofaros)* [1962] 1 Lloyds L. R. 410.

[6] 105 F. Supp. 215 (1952).

Judge Ryan makes many points not all of which can be said to be of equal weight or persuasiveness, and it is, accordingly, very difficult to ascertain the ratio decidendi. But it does not seem far-fetched to suggest that it is to be found in the assertion that the court, 'acting on the basis of our jurisdiction *in personam*', may make whatever orders are necessary to suppress 'the effects of wrongful acts [I.C.I.] has committed within the United States affecting the foreign trade of the United States'. The court, it is true, hoped that it was 'not an intrusion on the authority of a foreign sovereign for this court to direct that steps be taken to remove the harmful effects on the trade of the United States', but within less than two weeks Upjohn J. and later the Court of Appeal restrained I.C.I. from complying with the American order.[1] The judgment of Lord Evershed M.R. again is perhaps not altogether free from precarious reasoning.[2] Yet it seems reasonably clear that the decision rests on the affirmative answer which, in effect, it gives to the 'somewhat serious question whether the order, in the form it takes, does not assert an extraterritorial jurisdiction which the courts of this country cannot recognize'.[3]

This, indeed, is the essence of the matter. The United States had obtained personal jurisdiction over the largest British industrial concern, because it had jurisdiction over what it treated as that concern's New York branch. It could, of course, enforce its laws against the branch in respect of the defendant's conduct in America. But to order the British defendant to implement American public laws outside America involved an excess of jurisdiction, because by their very nature those laws were incapable of extraterritorial enforcement.

However, the American practice has, in anti-trust cases, so far continued without change. In *U.S.* v. *General Electric*[4] the court made similar orders against the Dutch *N. V. Phillips* concern, though as a result of very strong diplomatic protests by the Netherlands the final decree lacked some of the extreme

---

[1] *British Nylon Spinners* v. *Imperial Chemical Industries*, [1953] Ch. 19. Kegel, *Internationales Privatrecht* (2nd ed., 1964) p. 416, suggests that the German courts should and would reach the same result.

[2] See, generally, a most useful note by Professor Kahn-Freund, 18 *M.L.R.* (1955), 65.

[3] p. 24.     [4] 115 F. Supp. 835 (1953).

features which the United States had originally demanded.[1] The most recent decree in the case of the *Swiss Watch Industry*[2] shows few such restraints: in includes many provisions which so plainly plant the anti-trust legislation of the United States into Swiss soil as to constitute a uniquely obvious excess of jurisdiction. It is not possible in the present context to analyse the long and complicated decision. It must suffice to refer, by way of example, to paragraph VII of the decree which orders Fédération Suisse des Associations de Fabricants d'Horlogerie and Ebauches S.A., a Swiss company, to amend the Collective Convention made in Switzerland in 1936 so as to provide that watch parts may be sold to any person in the United States without discrimination on the same terms as those on which such parts are sold to any person in Switzerland. The United States therefore purported to create for itself a national-treatment clause.

The only barrier which the United States at present recognizes is legislation in the foreign country which renders illegal what the American judgment commands the defendant to do. Such a 'savings clause' first appeared in *U.S.* v. *Imperial Chemical Industries*,[3] it has since been included in numerous consent decrees,[4] and in the case of the *Swiss Watch Industry*[5] the court restated the position as follows:

If, of course, the defendants' activities had been required by Swiss law, this court could indeed do nothing. An American court would have under such circumstances no right to condemn the governmental activity of another sovereign nation. In the present case, however, the defendants' activities were not required by the laws of Switzerland . . . Nonetheless, the fact that the Swiss Government may, as a practical matter, approve of the effects of this private activity cannot convert what is essentially a vulnerable private conspiracy into an unassailable system resulting from foreign governmental mandate.

The distinction drawn between acts required or prohibited, and acts tolerated, by the foreign law has no validity in international law. Nor does international law require a State to refrain from exercising its lawful jurisdiction merely because under the

---

[1] For details see Brewster, *Antitrust and American Business Abroad*, pp. 46, 47.
[2] The judgment is reported in *Trade Regulation Reporter*, 77, 414.
[3] 105 F. Supp. 215 (1952).
[4] See Note 63 *Col. L.R.* (1963–4), 1441, at pp. 1452, 1453.
[5] Above, n. 2.

municipal law of some other State a certain act is made illegal. The 'savings clause' of the American type indicates a limited awareness on the part of the court of its international responsibility and constitutes a half-hearted attempt to avoid some of the international wrong the court is committing, but in the crucial case it is without practical effect and, therefore, fails to solve the problem of international jurisdiction, which these decisions pose.

It must be added that, oddly enough, there is no evidence that in cases other than anti-trust cases American courts are equally ready to push aside the limits imposed by the rules of international jurisdiction. On the contrary, tax cases, in particular, show much respect for the requirements of international law. In a recent case of great significance the United States applied for an injunction restraining the defendant, First National City Bank, from disposing of any property, whether or not located within the United States, held by it or its branches for a Uruguayan corporation alleged to owe taxes to the plaintiff. The Court of Appeal, Second Circuit (Moore and Friendly, Circuit Judges, Hays, Circuit Judge, dissenting), held that the injunction could not be granted in regard to property held outside the United States.[1] Much of the Court's reasoning, it is true, rests on the unconvincing ground that it lacked personal jurisdiction over the Uruguayan taxpayer. Yet the Court clearly recognized the limitations imposed by the doctrine of international jurisdiction and concluded[2]:

In addition the rule suggested by the Government would have to work both ways ... However, it is inconceivable that the issuance of an injunction by a court of a foreign country against an American branch bank affecting the accounts or activities of the head office in the United States would be looked upon with favour. The untoward difficulties and potential conflict between the laws of different nations that such a doctrine would produce militate against giving it support here.

(4) In so far, finally, as the production of documents from a party to proceedings[3] is concerned, the practice of the United States has evolved the rule that, whenever personal jurisdiction over a party has been obtained, it becomes possible to order the

---

[1] *United States* v. *First National City Bank*, 321 F. 2d 14 (1963), re-argued *in banc* 325 F. 2d 1020 (1964).
[2] p. 24.
[3] As regards the right to obtain documents from third parties, see above, p. 117.

production of all documents in the possession of such party, wherever they may be situate, provided their production is not illegal by the law of their *situs*.[1]

The issue arose for the first time in 1952, when the United States commenced an investigation into alleged world-wide arrangements of the international oil industry, which were believed to involve a possible violation of the Sherman Act. As regards the Anglo-Iranian Oil Company the attempt made by the service of a subpoena to obtain a large quantity of documents situate in England failed, not on account of the diplomatic protest made by Britain, but on the truly 'astonishing ground'[2] that the Anglo-Iranian Oil Company was 'indistinguishable from the Government of Great Britain' and therefore entitled to sovereign immunity.[3] Strong diplomatic protests made at the same time by the Netherlands seem to have remained without effect.[4]

The next major attempt to obtain foreign documents occurred in 1960 when the Federal Maritime Commission requested some 180 foreign shipping companies to produce documents relating to foreign liner conferences. The request was made under section 21 of the United States Shipping Act, as amended, according to which the Commission may require 'any common carrier by water' to file, inter alia, 'any memorandum of any facts and transactions appertaining to the business of such

---

[1] Ontario made production of documents to a foreign government illegal: The Business Records Probation Act 1950. So did the Netherlands: Section 39 of the Economic Competition Act, 1956. The United Kingdom passed the Shipping Contracts and Commercial Documents Act, 1964, which enables a Minister to prohibit compliance with a foreign requirement to produce documents if it constitutes 'an infringement of the jurisdiction which, under international law, belongs to the United Kingdom'. On this Act see Mann, 13 *I.C.L.Q.* (1964), 1460.

[2] Jennings, 'Extraterritorial Jurisdiction', at p. 171.

[3] In *re Investigation of World Arrangements etc.*, 13 F. R. D. 280 (1952), also Int. L.R. (1952), 197. Both reports print the letters addressed to the Anglo-Iranian Oil Co. by Mr. Geoffrey Lloyd, the Minister of Fuel and Power, and by Sir Anthony Eden, the Foreign Secretary, ordering the company 'not to produce any documents which were not in the United States of America and which do not relate to business in the United States, without in either case the authority of Her Majesty's Government'. The constitutional basis of this order is mysterious. One would like to know what rule or provision of English law authorized the Government to make this order or preclude the company from disregarding it. It is remarkable that no such question was raised in the United States.

[4] Brewster, *Antitrust and American Business Abroad*, pp. 48, 49.

carrier'. In the words of Britain's Minister of Transport, the request thus raised 'the narrow issue of principle whether the United States can demand documents relating solely to transactions effected wholly within the United Kingdom and not within the substantive jurisdiction of the United States'.[1] Some ten countries made protests to the Department of State. These at first caused a District Court to reserve its opinion on the matter,[2] but a year later the Court of Appeals, District of Columbia Circuit, overruled all objections to the production of documents situate outside the United States.[3] No reason was given except that any limitation of the duty to produce would mean that 'the regulation of foreign flag carriers would be hampered to a substantial degree'.[4] At the end of 1963 a further conference of maritime nations took place in London and early in January 1964 eleven nations addressed protests to the United States. The Ministers responsible for shipping in the Governments of Belgium, Denmark, France, Germany, Greece, Italy and the Netherlands, Norway, Sweden and the United Kingdom (who were later joined by Japan) declared that[5]

they regard the Federal Maritime Commissioner's request to European shipowners to produce, under threat of penalties, documents and information outside the jurisdiction of the United States as an infringement of their countries' jurisdiction. They have urged their shipowners not to comply with such requests and to keep in close contact with their Governments.

In the field of taxation American Courts are likely to hold that in the course of making tax claims the United States may require the non-resident taxpayer to produce documents situate outside the United States.[6] The point has been expressly decided by the German Supreme Finance Court: A Swiss industrial undertaking has a branch in Germany which, in respect of its own profits, was liable to tax in Germany. The

---

[1] E. Lauterpacht, *The Contemporary Practice of the United Kingdom in the Field of International Law* (1962 i), 15–18, where the material is set forth in full.

[2] *Matter of Grand Jury Investigation of the Shipping Industry*, 186 F. Supp. 298 (1960).

[3] *Montship Lines* v. *Federal Maritime Board*, 295 F. 2d 147 (1961). Professor Verzijl (above, p. 123, n. 5) at pp. 22 sqq. rightly describes the American demands as contrary to international law.

[4] pp. 153, 154.  [5] *The Times* (newspaper), 14 December, 1963, p. 5.

[6] This is implied in *Application of Chase Manhattan Bank*, 297 F 2d. 611 (1962) and, in particular, in *United States* v. *Ross*, 302 F. 2d 831 (1962).

books relating to its affairs were kept in Switzerland. It was held that in so far as the books related to the branch's[1] affairs they had to be brought to and produced in Germany.[2]

Again, the only exception arises where the production of documents is prohibited and illegal according to the *lex situs* and a genuine attempt to obtain the permission of the local sovereign has been made, but has failed.[3] International law, as has been pointed out, [4] does not require any such exception, and it is noteworthy that Britain does not recognize it in cases in which a foreign claimant in prize is ordered by the Prize Court to make discovery, but under his own law is not allowed to disclose the documents.[5]

It is submitted that the American practice goes much too far and that the true legal position is as follows:

Firstly, where the enforcing State proceeds against the local branch with a view to the production of documents relating to the affairs of the branch itself, the demand cannot be resisted merely on the ground that the documents are abroad or belong to a non-resident alien. Thus, if the tax liability of the branch is in issue or if the branch is alleged to have embarked upon restrictive practices contrary to the local law discovery proceedings against the branch are lawful. The ultimate reason is that the State has proper legislative jurisdiction and asserts its enforcement jurisdiction only to the extent necessary to implement its legislative jurisdiction.

Secondly, if a non-resident alien appears as a claimant in the courts of the enforcing State, he must submit to the procedure of the courts to which he applies. An order for discovery which has properly been made and is not oppressive, cannot be resisted on the grounds of the documents being abroad.

Thirdly, in either of the above cases international law does not justify the refusal of discovery on the ground that according to the *lex situs* discovery is illegal.

Fourthly, if discovery has been properly ordered but is not

---

[1] This qualification is not expressly stated in the decision, but is implied in it and follows from the principles of general administrative law.

[2] 27 September 1933, *Reichssteuerblatt* 1933, 1188.

[3] *Société Internationale* v. *Rogers*, 357 U. S. 197 (1958); *United States* v. *Ross*, above, p. 137, n. 6; *Application of Chase Manhattan Bank*, ibid., and many other cases.

[4] Above, p. 134.

[5] *The Consul Corfitzon*, [1917] A. C. 550, 555, per Lord Parker of Waddington.

given by the non-resident alien, international law does not preclude the court from drawing appropriate inferences against him in accordance with the law of evidence or from making an order dismissing the claim or striking out the defence.

Fifthly, where the enforcing State proceeds against the local branch with a view to the production of documents situate abroad and relating to the affairs or activities abroad of the head office of the non-resident alien, the demand would be lawful only if the enforcing State had legislative jurisdiction to regulate and, therefore, to inquire into those affairs and activities. No such legislative jurisdiction is likely to exist. Without it the demand simply constitutes the illegal exercise of enforcement jurisdiction: a State cannot, by using the process of its own courts, so enforce its sovereign powers as to compel conduct abroad to conform to its commands. Thus, if a State were to impose a tax on a non-resident alien in respect of his foreign business it would act without legislative jurisdiction, and its attempt to enforce the tax against the local branch would be illegal. To the extent of such illegality the demand for discovery would be equally unlawful. Similarly, a restraint of trade practised and implemented abroad is beyond the legislative control of the State in which it may produce only 'effects',[1] and in the absence of such control the demand for documents relating to the restraint is not supported by international law.

Sixthly, it is a much more doubtful question what the law should be where the demand is made against the foreign branch of a citizen resident in the enforcing State. Probably the branch should be treated as sufficiently independent so as to make the principle stated in the preceding paragraph applicable.

[1] Above, p. 88.

# II

## REFLECTIONS ON A COMMERCIAL LAW OF NATIONS*

### I

IT is a well-known fact that in the course of the last few decades international law has become increasingly concerned with the far-reaching activities of States in the sphere of international economic relations.[1] The creation of numerous organizations and institutions, designed to establish co-operation in such matters as finance and banking, tariffs and taxation, the distribution of commodities or the exploitation of natural resources, has been one of the outstanding characteristics of the period. In the wake of these developments States have come to embark upon another, no less significant activity: they have gone into business and entered into contractual arrangements which in many respects do not fundamentally differ from what private traders have practised over the centuries.

It is perhaps too early to say that in consequence of such events a commercial law of nations has sprung into existence, for the available material is still scarce and restricted in scope. Yet it is permissible to suggest that the need for a commercial law of nations can no longer be denied. We are witnessing the growth of activities which occur in what to a considerable extent is a legal vacuum and for which the law remains to be found.

To evolve it or even to indicate its outlines is a task which at this stage would require research on so large a scale as to exceed the capacity of a single student. What can be attempted is no more than a modest introduction to and a preliminary study

---

* From *British Year Book of International Law* 1957, 20.

[1] Schwarzenberger, 'Standards of International Economic Law', 2 *I.C.L.Q.* (1948), p. 402; Alexandrowicz, *International Economic Organisations*; Scheuner, 'Die Völkerrechtlichen Grundlagen der Weltwirtschaft in der Gegenwart', *Verhandlungen des 40. Juristentags* (1953); Erler, *Grundprobleme des Internationalen Wirtschaftsrechts* (1956). These contributions are largely descriptive in character.

of some of the types of problems which arise and await solution.

It is for this very limited purpose that it will in the first place be necessary to gather some of the material, taken exclusively from British State practice and selected almost at random, and thus to draw attention to the nature of the legal inquiry to which the facts of international life give rise (Section II). Against the background of what is no more than a compilation it will be possible to draw some conclusions relevant to the general law of treaties (Section III) and thereafter to comment on the broad lines of approach which the commercial law of nations seems to demand (Section IV). This will lead to a discussion, by way of illustration only, of a modern case which will provide the opportunity of indicating methods for the application of theory to practice (Section V). Finally, the challenge which the commercial law of nations extends to lawyers will be re-stated in a few words of explanation (Section VI).

The commercial law of nations which this article has in view is understood as an ill-defined, though not a separate, branch of international law. To attempt to define its scope would be an unprofitable undertaking. In many continental legal systems, it is true, commercial law has a clear meaning: the commercial codes in force in France, Italy, or Germany define the particular persons or transactions to which they are intended to apply. In England, however,

the area which is covered by the term 'commercial law' is a matter of uncertainty. The use of the phrase 'commercial law' is, of course, purely conventional, and to speak of 'commercial law' as a separate branch of the common law is in any event unscientific. In our English legal system 'commercial law' is merely an extension of the general principles of the law of contract to special transactions of a mercantile character.[1]

Or, as another writer has put the point,[2] the selection of the portions to be included in commercial law

... is quite arbitrary. The law of England does not recognise any particular part of its system as being especially adapted to the requirements of persons engaged in commerce. Different writers upon the subject have accordingly differed in their views as to what part of the law ought properly to be included in a textbook on commercial law.

[1] Gutteridge, 51 *L.Q.R.* (1935), p. 91.
[2] Slater, *Mercantile Law* (13th ed., by Lord Chorley and O. C. Giles, 1956), p. xxxix.

In international law, as is to be expected, the position is almost identical with that prevailing in England. If a book on international commercial law came to be written it might well include the law relating to certain international organizations, just as English books on mercantile law deal with partnerships or companies. Again, it would be necessary to discuss not only customary rules of the commercial law of nations, such as minimum standards, but also the meaning and effect of conventional clauses, such as the most-favoured-nation clause or clauses guaranteeing national or equitable treatment, in the same way as an English book on mercantile law may analyse standard conditions in contracts. Furthermore, such a book would include a large part of the general law of treaties, just as some English authors on commercial law think that 'there is general agreement that the general principles of the law of contract . . . should be included in the subject',[1] though in the opinion of others only specific contracts, such as guarantees, bills of exchange, contracts of insurance and affreightment, should be covered by the subject.[2] In short, the commercial law of nations, like English commercial law, exists even in the absence of definition and comprises a variety of subjects which to some extent writers may determine according to their predisposition, on the selection of which opinions are likely to differ, by 'a predominant economic element',[3] by their similarity with what occurs in the sphere of private law.

Throughout the following discussion an assumption will be made which should be clearly understood. In an earlier article[4] it was suggested that, firstly, contracts made between States and private persons may be subject to public international law and, secondly, contracts between States in regard to matters of a non-political, commercial character may be governed by municipal law, the applicability of the one or the other legal system being determined by the intention of the parties. In the present article which is exclusively concerned with contracts between States or other international persons, the problem of the choice of law will not be further considered. It will be as-

---

[1] See preceding note.

[2] This is the course followed by Smith's *Mercantile Law* (13th ed., by Gutteridge, 1931).

[3] Schwarzenberger, op. cit., pp. 405, 406.

[4] Below, p. 179.

sumed that the contractual relationship between the States is governed by public international law. On this footing there arises the entirely distinct question of what are the substantive rules of public international law that are applicable to a commercial transaction between States. In an indirect way, however, a discussion of the commercial law of nations is likely to have the incidental effect of making a contribution to the problem of the choice of law considered thirteen years ago. The first limb of the rule then suggested, viz. the possibility of contracts between States and private persons being subject to public international law, met, it is true, with some approval[1] and found significant expression in an Award made by Lord Asquith of Bishopstone, when he said of a concession granted by a State to a private person that it was subject to 'principles rooted in the good sense and common practice of the generality of civilized nations—a sort of "modern law of nature"'.[2] But the rule has been criticized by others[3] on the ground that in fact public international law does not include a sufficiently developed body of law capable of governing the relationship between States and private persons. This criticism would lose much of its force if it should appear that such a body of law does exist and, indeed, must exist to regulate such commercial arrangements between States as are subject to public international law. The commercial law of nations which, in the appropriate cases, governs the relationship between States and which, admittedly, is *in statu nascendi*, also applies to the relationship between States and private persons.

## II

There exist grounds for the suspicion that the archives of the British Government contain the texts of many treaties which would be of great value for the present discussion, but which have never been published.[4] Charterparties made during the

---

[1] Jessup, *A Modern Law of Nations*, p. 139.

[2] 'In the Matter of an Arbitration between Petroleum Development (Trucial Coast) Ltd. and the Sheikh of Abu Dhabi', 1 *I.C.L.Q.* (1952), p. 247, at p. 251.

[3] Martin Wolff, *Private International Law* (2nd ed., 1950), p. 417, and 35 *Grot. Soc.* (1950), pp. 143, 150–2; Fawcett, *B.Y.I.L.* (1948), 44, n. 3; Friedmann, *A.J.I.L.* (1956), pp. 483, 484.

[4] See, e.g., the extracts from the Anglo-Greek Shipping Agreement of 20 May 1941 reported in *Royal Hellenic Government* v. *Vergottis* 78 (1945), Ll. L. R. 292.

war under Lend-Lease, bulk-purchasing contracts entered into by the Ministry of Food, agency agreements whereby the Custodian of Enemy Property collected monies on behalf of foreign governments, are probably so buried. Although it is to be hoped that these and similar documents will soon see the light of day, it may properly be claimed that the published material is amply sufficient to justify and permit preliminary classification:

*Sale.* On 4 March 1948 the Government of the United Kingdom and the Royal Danish Government entered into an Agreement to make further provision for the supply of certain aircraft and equipment to Denmark.[1] The two governments agreed as follows:

### Article 1

1. Subject to the provisions of paragraphs 2 and 3 of this Article, the Government of the United Kingdom agree to sell, and the Royal Danish Government agree to purchase, the aircraft and equipment specified in the Appendix to this Agreement.

2. The aircraft and equipment specified in the Appendix shall be delivered as soon as possible, and the Government of the United Kingdom will endeavour to complete deliveries within six months from the date of signature of this Agreement, or the date of return by the representatives of the Royal Danish Government of approved schedules referred to at Note 2 of Appendix hereto, whichever is the later. In the event of unforeseen shortages arising every effort will be made by the Government of the United Kingdom to find acceptable substitutes.

3. The aircraft and equipment specified in the Appendix and any substitutes therefor which may be supplied in accordance with paragraph 2 of this Article shall be in accordance with Royal Air Force standards of serviceability; nevertheless the Royal Danish Government shall be entitled to appoint a receiving commission in the United Kingdom to whom the United Kingdom Government shall, on request, afford reasonable opportunity to inspect any aircraft, mechanical transport vehicle, or other major item of equipment, prior to delivery. The quantities of items of equipment to be supplied shall be calculated from Royal Air Force consumption data and based on Royal Air Force rates of effort.

4. If the Royal Danish Government desire any aircraft or equipment specified in the Appendix to be delivered by air, such delivery shall be at the

---

[1] Cmd. 7660. This is the latest version of an agreement of sale. For earlier versions see Agreement between the United Kingdom and Denmark for the Supply of Aircraft, 16 August 1946, Cmd. 7141, and Agreement between the United Kingdom and the Netherlands, concerning the Supply of Aircraft and Equipment, 4 December 1946, Cmd. 7011.

expense and risk of the Royal Danish Government whether or not the aircraft are flown by pilots of the Royal Air Force.

5. In so far as the aircraft and equipment specified in the Appendix of the Agreement includes items of equipment which have been obtained by the Government of the United Kingdom from the Government of the United States of America on Lend-Lease terms, the delivery and price of such items will be subject to the completion by the Government of the United Kingdom of appropriate arrangements with the Government of the United States. If any such items are not available from existing United Kingdom stocks and no acceptable substitutes can be found, the Government of the United Kingdom will refund to the Royal Danish Government a sum equivalent to the value of such items as included in the Agreement.

6. Subject to paragraph 4 above, the aircraft and equipment to be supplied shall, if coming from the United Kingdom or from a source outside Europe, be delivered by the Government of the United Kingdom free alongside ship at the port of embarkation; or if coming from the United Kingdom will be delivered to a station or depot in the United Kingdom if so required by the Royal Danish Government. The cost of all shipment, including any handling or dock charges and the risks of transport from the point of delivery to Denmark, shall fall upon the Royal Danish Government. Aircraft and equipment to be supplied and coming from Royal Air Force Depots or Units in Europe or to be delivered to a station or depot in the United Kingdom shall be deemed delivered by the Government of the United Kingdom at those depots or units and the Royal Danish Government shall assume the cost and all risks of transport to Denmark; such conditions apply equally in those instances where sea transportation is arranged by the Government of the United Kingdom.

7. It is the intention of the two Governments that all aircraft shall be delivered by air from the United Kingdom, and that as far as possible all the equipment should be supplied from sources in the United Kingdom or in Europe and should be delivered to ports of embarkation to be agreed upon between the Government of the United Kingdom and the receiving commission referred to in paragraph 3 above.

## Article 2

1. The Royal Danish Government will pay for the aircraft and equipment specified in the Appendix the sum of £225,000 to the Government of the United Kingdom.

2. The above-mentioned sum of £225,000 is payable in sterling in two instalments as follows: (a) £168,750, (b) £56,250. Payment of the sum of £168,750 as an advance was effected on 31 December 1947; and payment of the balance of £56,250 shall be made not later than 31 October 1948.

## Article 3

The present Agreement shall come into force as from this day's date.
In witness whereof the undersigned, duly authorized by their respective

Governments, have signed the present Agreement and affixed thereto their Seals.

Done in London in triplicate this fourth day of March 1948.

Agreements for sale are also sometimes included in treaties which primarily cover other transactions. Thus in a treaty between the United Kingdom and Portugal the latter agreed 'to sell to the Rhodesia Railways the section of the line between Umtali and the frontier of Mozambique on conditions to be agreed between the two Governments'.[1] The Agreement between the United Kingdom and the Republic of Iceland concerning the transfer of Reykjavik Airfield to the Icelandic Government[2] provides that, on the one hand, the Reykjavik airfield, runways and all immovable installations constructed thereon and owned by the United Kingdom shall 'revert to and become the property of the Republic of Iceland without any payment' and, on the other hand, all movable installations and equipment and a direction finding station shall be made available to Iceland 'at a price to be agreed upon separately'.

*Barter.* The most conspicuous instance of an agreement for the barter of goods is contained in the Agreement which the Government of the United Kingdom and the Government of the United States of America concluded on 23 June 1939 to provide for the exchange of cotton against rubber.[3] The United States Government undertook to supply to the Government of the United Kingdom 600,000 bales of raw cotton, the price to be fixed on the basis of the average market price for spot delivery at New Orleans. The Government of the United Kingdom undertook to supply to the Government of the United States rubber in bales 'to a value equivalent to that of the total value of the cotton'. The Agreement contains detailed provisions on the calculation of prices, the quality of the goods, inspection and acceptance, settlement of disputes about quality 'in accordance with the normal custom of the trade', disposal of stocks and other matters.

An Agreement of a similar nature was made between the United Kingdom and the United States of America on 5 June

[1] Article IX of the Agreement of 17 June 1950, Cmd. 7983, referred to below, p. 150, n. 6.

[2] Agreement of 4 July 1946, Cmd. 6994, which was substituted for an earlier Agreement of 12 October 1944, Cmd. 6993.

[3] (23 June 1939), Cmd. 6048.

1956 for the sale by the latter of $12 million worth of tobacco.[1] The sterling equivalent of the dollar cost, calculated 'at the buying rate for telegraphic transfers on New York in the London market at the close of business on the dates of such dollar disbursements', was to be deposited to the account of the United States Government. It was to be made available to the United Kingdom 'for the procurement of military facilities for the common defence' and for this purpose to be used for the construction of 'military dependents' housing and/or community facilities' of the United States Air Force stationed in the United Kingdom 'at the nominal rent of £1 per unit per annum for as long as and to the extent that they may be required in connection with the presence in the United Kingdom of units of the United States military forces'. The two Governments agreed, *inter alia*, to 'take reasonable precautions to ensure that no sales of tobacco within the terms of this Memorandum will unduly disrupt world prices of tobacco, displace usual tobacco marketings of the United States or other friendly countries or materially impair trade relations among the countries of the free world'.

*Loans.* Loan agreements are among the oldest commercial agreements made between States and British practice supplies numerous examples; the existence of the European Payments Union has recently led to a series of such agreements.[2] Usually they provide for the granting of a loan, whether by the advance of specific sums or by allowing the borrower State to draw upon a credit opened in its favour.[3] Other agreements are more

---

[1] (5 June 1956), Cmd. 9793.

[2] Agreements between the United Kingdom and the Netherlands (9 July 1954) Cmd. 9266; Belgium (9 July 1954), Cmd. 9279; Germany (10 July 1954), Cmd. 9267; Switzerland (16 July 1954), Cmd. 9254.

[3] For recent instances see Loan Agreement between the United Kingdom and Spain, 18 March 1940, Cmd. 6230; Agreement between the United Kingdom, France, and Poland for a Loan to Poland, 7 September 1939, Cmd. 6110; Agreement between the United Kingdom and Turkey regarding an Armaments Credit for Turkey, 27 May 1938, Cmd. 6119; Agreement between France, the United Kingdom, and Turkey, 19 October 1939, Cmd. 6165; Financial Agreement between the Governments of the United States and the United Kingdom, 6 December 1945, Cmd. 6708; Loan Agreements between the United Kingdom and the Export–Import Bank of Washington, 26 October 1948; 16 February 1949; 26 January 1950; 20 September 1950, Cmd. 8126; 25 February 1957, Cmnd. 104; Exchange of Letters between the United Kingdom and the United States of America on the subject of a loan for the development of certain port facilities in Kenya and

elaborate and envisage the issue of promissory notes by the debtor government.[1] Sometimes the economic effect of a loan is achieved by a transaction of a different legal character, viz. the purchase by the lender State of promissory notes issued by the borrower State.[2] Ancillary clauses relate to interest and its calculation,[3] the assignability of promissory notes,[4] the purposes for which the loan is to be used,[5] exemption from taxation or transfer restrictions and similar privileges.[6]

In this connection it is necessary to mention agreements made after the date of the loan and regulating the method of discharge. A particularly elaborate type is an Agreement with Belgium which imposes a duty upon the United Kingdom to repay a loan of 1,250 million Belgian francs by causing British manufacturers to deliver to the Belgian Government certain defence equipment and by settling their invoices, but so that the United Kingdom 'assumes responsibility for the execution of the orders'.[7] In one case a novation agreement was made whereby the borrower undertook to pay the equivalent of the loan in local currency and to make it available for the purchase of local goods.[8] In another case the repayment of the loan was deferred by the issue of new promissory notes.[9]

---

Tanganyika, 26 June 1953, Cmd. 8965; Agreement between the United Kingdom, Australia, India, Pakistan, Ceylon, and Burma regarding a Loan to Burma, 28 June 1950, Cmd. 8007.

[1] See the Agreements included in Cmd. 8126 and referred to in the preceding note or Loan Agreement between the United Kingdom and Belgium, 7 September 1949, Cmd. 8365.

[2] Exchange of Notes between the United Kingdom and Yugoslavia for the granting of credits to Yugoslavia: 26 December 1949, Cmd. 7880; 28 December 1950, Cmd. 8149; 11 January 1951, Cmd. 8172; 10 May 1951, Cmd. 8313.

[3] See, for example, Article 2 of the Agreement with Turkey, Cmd. 6119; Article 3 of the Agreement with Spain, Cmd. 6230; Article 5 of the Agreement with Burma, Cmd. 8007.

[4] See, for example, Article 6 of the Agreement with Belgium, Cmd. 8365.

[5] See, for example, Clause 5 of the Agreement with the United States of America, Cmd. 8965.

[6] See, for example, Article IV of the Agreement with Belgium, Cmd. 9258.

[7] Agreement between the United Kingdom and Belgium, 30 June 1952, Cmd. 9258.

[8] Exchange of Notes between the United Kingdom and Turkey constituting an Agreement regarding the repayment of certain credits granted to Turkey relating to armaments, 11 February 1954, Cmd. 9120.

[9] Exchange of Notes between the United Kingdom and Turkey regarding certain financial obligations of the Yugoslav Government, 22 December 1954, Cmd. 9382.

*Lease.* Leases have also long been known to international practice.[1] Yet it seems appropriate to draw attention to some modern examples. Among them pride of place belongs to the remarkable arrangements which the United Kingdom and the United States of America made on 27 March 1941 relating to the bases leased to the United States in the West Indies and Newfoundland. The transaction was preceded by an Exchange of Notes of 2 September 1940[2] which provided for the transfer of fifty United States destroyers to the United Kingdom. The Agreement relating to the bases leased to the United States is a document of considerable length.[3] By Article I it confers upon the United States

all the rights, power, and authority within the Leased Areas which are necessary for the establishment, use, operation, and defence thereof, or appropriate for their control, and all the rights, power, and authority within the limits of territorial waters and air spaces adjacent to, or in the vicinity of, the Leased Areas, which are necessary to provide access to and defence of the Leased Areas or appropriate for control thereof.

There follow provisions about non-user, jurisdiction, security legislation, arrest, service of process, shipping and aviation, immigration, customs and other duties, abandonment, removal of improvements, assignment and underletting, and numerous other matters. The Annex to this Agreement contains the forms of leases which were executed. The operative words of the lease relating to Newfoundland, for instance, are:

witnesseth that in consideration of the premises the Newfoundland Government hath demised and leased and by these presents does demise and lease unto the United States of America all those six several pieces or parcels of land (hereinafter referred to as the Leased Areas) described in the Schedule to these presents and delineated on the plans hereto annexed: TO HAVE and TO HOLD the same for the full end and term of ninety-nine years to begin and to be computed from the date of these presents free from the payment of all rent and charges other than compensation as aforesaid AND the United States of America agrees that it will not during the term hereby granted use the Leased Areas nor permit the use thereof except for the purposes specified and on the terms and conditions contained in the aforesaid Notes and

[1] See Lauterpacht, *Private Law Sources and Analogies of International Law*, pp. 181 et seq. A lease is also included in the Anglo-Belgian treaty referred to below, p. 150, n. 4. It amends a similar Agreement of 15 March 1921 (Treaty Series, No. 11 (1921), Cmd. 1327) and provides that a site in the port of Dar-es-Salaam 'shall be leased in perpetuity to the Belgian Government at a rent of one franc per annum'. The Agreement includes an interesting interpretative Note on the assignability of the Belgian rights under the treaty of 1921.
[2] Cmd. 6224.     [3] Cmd. 6259 as amended by Cmd. 7000 and Cmd. 8076.

Agreement, which are incorporated in and form part of these presents except such parts thereof as refer specifically to territory other than Newfoundland.

Since then the United Kingdom has entered into treaties in the nature of tenancy agreements for the establishment of long-range proving grounds for guided missiles with the United States of America relating to the Bahama Islands[1] and with the Dominican Republic.[2]

*Work and Labour.* Among treaties similar to contracts for work and labour[3] the most interesting is perhaps the Agreement between the United Kingdom and Belgium relative to the construction of a deep-water quay at the Port of Dar-es-Salaam for the use of the Belgian Government.[4] The Government of the United Kingdom undertook to cause to be built for the use of the Belgian Government a deep-water quay on a site leased to the latter.[5] The British Government was to negotiate and conclude the necessary contracts 'in such terms as it shall consider most appropriate', but only after consulting the Belgian Government, and further was to ensure that the quay 'shall be of design and capacity similar to the two quays at present under construction and shall be equipped in substantially the same manner'. The Belgian Government accepted sole responsibility for the cost of the construction and equipment and agreed to reimburse the British Government. The quay will, however, 'be operated and maintained by or on behalf of and at the cost of the Belgian Government'.

A more complicated Agreement was made between the United Kingdom and Portugal relative to the Port of Beira and Connected Railways.[6] By Article III the Portuguese Government undertook

to maintain the Port of Beira and the Beira Railway in a state of efficiency adequate to the requirements of the traffic proceeding to or from Southern Rhodesia, Northern Rhodesia, and Nyasaland, to which end they will promote the execution of the works and the acquisition of the equipment necessary for the technical and economic development of the Port of Beira

---

[1] Cmd. 8109 and Cmd. 9810 where certain other agreements are referred to.
[2] Cmd. 8546.
[3] See also the Agreement between the United Kingdom and Egypt regarding the construction of the Owen Falls Dam in Uganda, Cmd. 9132.
[4] (6 April 1951), Cmd. 8240.
[5] In exchange for the site referred to in the 1921 treaty: above, p. 149, note 1.
[6] Cmd. 7983.

and the Beira Railway and in order to expedite the handling of cargoes and clearance of ships and railway traffic.

On the other hand, among the duties assumed by the British Government there is, in particular, an obligation to avoid discrimination 'against traffic for which the Port of Beira, on account of its proximity to sources of consumption or origin, is the natural inlet or outlet'. The Agreement provides for the establishment of a free zone, for the appointment of an Advisory Board and other incidental matters.

*Exchange of Information.* In industrial life it has become a matter of frequent occurrence that undertakings interested in a particular field of research and technical development enter into agreements for the exchange and joint exploitation of knowledge; by the nature of things such agreements are usually of considerable complexity. The examples which are met in the sphere of public international law are of no different character.

In August 1942 the United States of America and the United Kingdom signed an Agreement for the Interchange of Patent Rights and Information,[1] which was reformulated by a further Agreement made in March 1946.[2] Its overriding term was that 'each Government, in so far as it may lawfully do so, will procure and make available to the other Government, for use in war production, patent rights, information, inventions, designs or processes requested by the other Government'. Each Government was to bear the cost of the procurement of such rights from its own nationals. There followed detailed provisions about the manner in which the rights were to be exploited, the terms on which the rights were to be acquired, the indemnities to be provided by the respective Governments and similar matters.

After the war the same Governments entered into an Agreement on the Principles applying to the Exchange of Information relating to the synthesis of Penicillin.[3] 'All information pertaining to the purification, structure and synthesis of penicillin and/or a therapeutic equivalent' was to be exchanged during the period from 1 December 1943 to 31 October 1945.[4] Neither Government was to permit the transmission of information to persons who had not concluded a standard form of

---

[1] Cmd. 6392.    [2] Cmd. 6795.    [3] Cmd. 6757.
[4] It appears, therefore, that by the time the treaty was made the period of exchange had already expired.

agreement with either of the two Governments. The Agreement also provided for the disposition of patent rights and the grant of licences.

Another Agreement made in January 1953 between the United States of America and the United Kingdom relates to the facilitation of the interchange of patents and technical information for defence purposes.[1] Finally, there comes a whole series of Agreements for Co-operation in the peaceful uses of Atomic Energy. The United States of America, which by July 1955 had entered into twenty-six agreements of this kind,[2] made its agreement with the United Kingdom on 15 June 1955[3] and, subsequently, the United Kingdom concluded similar agreements with a number of countries, e.g. with Belgium.[4]

## III

The first question to which the preceding survey of some commercial treaties (a term not intended to be synonymous with treaties of commerce) gives rise is whether and to what extent they throw light on international law in general, namely, on those problems which are common to all treaties of whatever description.

For this purpose it would not be fruitful to devote attention to the effects of such matters as formation, mistake, fraud or duress, discharge, waiver, estoppel, damages, limitation of claims, and so forth—matters which the practice and literature of international law have for long had occasion to consider. They arise independently of the character and terms of a particular treaty. The commercial law of nations cannot probably make any particular contribution to their treatment by public international law as a whole. Nevertheless, there are certain other rules of customary international law the establishment and clarity of which has much to gain from the commercial law of nations.

(1) In the first place it appears that the doctrine of consideration finds no room in international law.[5] It is true that, at any

---

[1] Cmd. 8757.

[2] See Wit, 'Some International Aspects of Atomic Power Development', in *Law and Contemporary Problems* (1955), xxi.148, 175 et seq.

[3] Cmd. 9560 as amended by Cmd. 9677 and 9789. See also Cmnd. 20.

[4] Cmd. 9632 as amended by Cmd. 9794.

[5] Lauterpacht, *Private Law Sources and Analogies of International Law* (1927), pp. 177, 178.

rate in Anglo-American practice, lip-service is sometimes paid to that doctrine. Thus the Note[1] with which the United States of America accepted the British proposal for the leasing of bases and facilities in the Western Hemisphere states that 'in consideration of the declarations quoted above the Government of the United States will immediately transfer to His Majesty's Government Fifty United States Navy Destroyers generally referred to as the twelve-hundred tons type'. And the Lease,[2] or rather the 'Indenture of Lease', as it was called in this single case, which in pursuance of the same arrangements Newfoundland executed in favour of the United States of America, 'witnesseth that in consideration of the premises the Newfoundland Government hath demised and leased and by these presents does demise and lease unto the United States of America' the Leased Areas. But these are exceptional cases which do not in any way indicate that consideration was treated as a customary rule of law. Had it been so regarded it would surely have found its way into the Loan Agreements which do not record a loan, but the promise to make a loan.[3] In none of these Agreements, not even in those made between Great Britain and the United States of America, is consideration mentioned.

(2) On the other hand, one of the essential requirements of a treaty, as of a contract in private law, is an intention to create legal relations. Whether or no such intention exists is a matter of construction. In private law the existence of that intention is presumed. It is believed that a similar presumption prevails in public international law.

Sir Hersch Lauterpacht has suggested[4] that such a presumption arises only if a treaty is registered with the United Nations in accordance with Article 102 of the Charter. It would seem to be more likely, however, that the registration of a treaty does not add to, and that failure to register does not detract from, the contractual character of a treaty. The function of registration is merely to achieve publicity, to preclude or minimize secret

---

[1] Above, p. 149, n. 2.     [2] Above, p. 149.

[3] Under English law such a promise would not be enforced by an order for specific performance. It is believed that no such rule prevails in public international law.

[4] *Second Report on the Law of Treaties*, U.N. Doc. A/CN/4/87, pp. 4 et seq.

arrangements. Consequently registration has no bearing upon the legal character of the document: a mere statement of policy should not be presumed to have contractual character if it is registered and the legal effect of a contractual obligation *stricto sensu* should not be presumed to be diminished if the treaty remained unregistered. Hence it must be doubted, with respect, whether the presence or absence of registration permits or negatives a presumption on the point under discussion.

Moreover, it may be difficult to accede to the suggestion,[1] made apparently *de lege ferenda*, that international agreements are presumed not to create legal relations and that this presumption can be rebutted only if the agreement is governed by public international law, the general principles of law or a specific system of municipal law, or if the parties have provided for the compulsory judicial settlement of disputes. The former of these conditions does not seem to do more than to state the obvious: all international agreements must be governed by some system of law; an agreement governed by no system of law is unthinkable. The presumption would, therefore, always and automatically be rebutted. The latter condition is derived from the mechanical application to international disputes of experience gained in private law. It involves, in effect, the adoption of the view that there can be no law where there is no possibility of compulsory enforcement. It thus attaches too much significance to the question of jurisdiction. The binding character of customary international law 'does not depend upon the existence of a compulsory machinery'[2] for its enforcement. And if States set up a judicial or arbitral tribunal to decide an actual dispute arising from a treaty they recognize rather than create the legal character of the treaty. In other words, the submission of an existing dispute to judicial or arbitral jurisdiction cannot convert a non-contractual arrangement into a contract. Jurisdiction in international law is a distinct issue, a matter of procedure rather than a matter of substantive law. Even an arrangement between two States who have accepted the Optional Clause without qualification would not have contractual character if on its true construction it appeared

---

[1] Fawcett, 'The Legal Character of International Agreements', in *B.Y.I.L.* (1953), xxx.381.

[2] Lauterpacht in *Second Report* (quoted above, p. 153, n. 4), at p. 10.

to be a mere statement of policy. Similarly, a tribunal would not necessarily be precluded from treating an arrangement as non-contractual, although it includes an express submission to compulsory jurisdiction.

(3) Another essential requirement of a treaty, as of a contract in private law, is a sufficient degree of certainty: its terms must be ascertained or capable of being ascertained.

The fact that obligations imposed by a treaty are 'indefinite and elastic' or 'can be fulfilled by a somewhat nominal act of the parties'[1] does not, as Sir Hersch Lauterpacht has pointed out, render a treaty so uncertain as to lead to unenforceability. Whether a State has discharged its duty to co-operate 'to the fullest degree'[2] can be ascertained by a tribunal. Similarly, by a Treaty of 31 March 1936 the United Kingdom sold to Iraq the railway system of Iraq for a sum of £400,000, one of the terms being that certain posts were for twenty years to be filled by British subjects 'on equitable conditions'.[3] This phrase supplies an objective standard, so that the terms, though *prima facie* uncertain, could, if necessary, be rendered certain by a decision of a tribunal. A treaty which creates nothing but mutual duties to consult or to negotiate about certain matters or in certain contingencies would give rise to contractual obligations. They would not be far-reaching, but they are capable of being defined and they must be discharged in good faith. They are light, but not uncertain in character. This applies even more strongly where, as frequently happens in the case of commercial treaties,[4] the arrangements between the parties include clauses providing for consultation or further negotiations. Such clauses do not in any way detract from the binding and enforceable character of the instruments in question.

Much more difficult problems arise where *prima facie* the subject-matter of the obligation is undefined. There are instances of treaties whereby governments have agreed to make available

---

[1] Lauterpacht, *Second Report on the Law of Treaties*, U.N. Doc. A/CN/4/87, p. 5, and *First Report on the Law of Treaties*, U.N. Doc. A/CN/4/63, p. 25.

[2] For an example of such a duty see Lauterpacht, *First Report* (referred to in the preceding note), p. 5.

[3] Cmd. 5282: *League of Nations Treaty Series*, 172, 175. The provision referred to in the text is in Article 4. The treaty was later terminated: *United Nations Treaty Series*, pp. 149, 221.

[4] Most of the treaties mentioned in Section II, above, include such clauses.

to each other 'such equipment, materials, services or other military assistance as the contracting Government furnishing such assistance may authorize in accordance with detailed arrangements from time to time to be made between them'.[1] It would seem very likely that these words introduce so strong an element of uncertainty that they are incapable of objective definition and the agreement is unenforceable. It does not help to describe such clauses as being in the nature of a *pactum de contrahendo*, for even such a *pactum* has no legal effect unless it incorporates all the essential terms of the final contract. The Agreement between the United Kingdom and Iceland relating to Reykjavik Airfield[2] confers upon Iceland the right to purchase certain installations 'at a price to be agreed separately'. Or by Article IX of the Convention between the United Kingdom and Portugal relative to the Port of Beira,[3] Portugal, as has been pointed out above, agreed to sell a certain section of a railway line 'on conditions to be agreed between the two Governments'. It may be a possible conclusion that, in the absence of agreement between the parties, the express terms are so indeterminate as to render the clause ineffective and unenforceable; in that event the further question arises whether the treaty as a whole is ineffective or whether the clause in question is capable of being severed. Another solution may be that, failing agreement, reasonable terms or prices apply and may be judicially fixed. Again it may be possible to hold that the selling State has the overriding right to determine the conditions of the sale.[4] The usual methods of interpretation may lead to the implication of a term into the treaty. Where, as will frequently happen, they do not help, the question remains: how will a solution be found?

---

[1] Mutual Defence Assistance Agreement between the United Kingdom and the United States of America of 27 January 1950, Cmd. 7894.

[2] Above, p. 146, n. 2.

[3] Above, p. 150, n. 6.

[4] The first of the solutions referred to in the text seems to prevail in France: Planiol–Ripert, *Traité de droit civil français* (2nd ed., 1956), x, No. 36. It may also apply in England, though there seems to be a tendency to favour the second solution: *Foley* v. *Classique Coaches Ltd.*, [1934] 2 K. B. 1, distinguishing *May & Butcher* v. *R.*, (1929) ibid., p. 17. As to American law see Williston, *On Contracts*, section 41. The second solution in effect also prevails in Germany by virtue of section 316 of the Civil Code, though the determination is primarily the privilege of the creditor who, however, must act reasonably.

## IV

It is this question, then, which indicates the fundamental problem of the commercial law of nations. While the commercial law of nations is known to exist, its content is unknown. Where and how is it to be discovered?

It is, of course, plain that the treaty itself constitutes the primary source of the law applicable to it; the whole of the subsequent discussion is subject to this overriding proviso. The municipal lawyer is wont to ask whether the text of a contract displaces the rule of law with which he is familiar. The international lawyer frequently, and in connection with commercial treaties almost invariably, proceeds from the opposite standpoint. He must first exhaust every possibility of deducing the result intended by the parties from the minute scrutiny of the provisions of the treaty which is itself a source of law. In very many cases such interpretation of the treaty will render it superfluous to search for the rule of common law which in international commercial law is often merely a secondary force. In contradistinction to the contract under private law the primary source of law applicable to a commercial treaty is to a large extent the treaty itself.

Yet, notwithstanding this extensive qualification, that vast *terra incognita*, the commercial law of nations, must be discovered—not for the sake of mere speculation, but on account of the undeniable necessity for resorting to and applying it where the treaty gives no or insufficient guidance or where legal rules other than those connected with a treaty are in issue. If, to repeat the example just referred to, the parties have stipulated for 'a price to be agreed separately', is the treaty, or the particular clause included in it, invalid or, alternatively, what price is payable in default of agreement? If part of the equipment sold by the United Kingdom to Denmark under the treaty of 4 March 1948[1] is defective, can Denmark, claim rescission or damages or delivery of equipment of the agreed quality? If a State fails to implement its promise to make a loan, can the borrowing State claim specific performance or damages only?[2] If between the date of the treaty which imposes the duty to make a loan and the agreed date of implementation the

---

[1] Above, p. 144.   [2] Above, p. 153, n. 3.

circumstances of either party materially change, is the lending State entitled to repudiate the treaty? What are the lessor State's rights in regard to dilapidations? What are the lessor State's rights in the event of the demised premises being destroyed by fire? Does the commercial law of nations recognize agency of necessity or a claim for unjustified enrichment and, if so, what are its limits? Does the commercial law of nations recognize the existence of equitable rights or the grantor's obligation not to derogate from his grant? These are only some very few examples of questions to which the treaties themselves usually give no answer and which are typical of, though perhaps not necessarily peculiar to, the general commercial law of nations.

In one sense it is not difficult to find this law. It is included in those general principles recognized by civilized nations to which Article 38 of the Statute of the International Court refers. It cannot have any other source.

One thus turns to the practice and doctrine relating to the general principles of law recognized by civilized nations in order to see whether they give guidance to the commercial law of nations. It is perhaps not surprising that the available decisions of international tribunals have so far contributed very little to the development of the commercial law of nations: it is a body of law which is in its infancy and which as yet has hardly come up for consideration by an international tribunal. Those decisions which have a bearing on the commercial law of nations, as opposed to international law in general, and which are discussed in the third part of Sir Hersch Lauterpacht's book on *Private Law Sources and Analogies of International Law* conclusively prove the controlling force of the principles of private law. But none of these cases of which, in the present context, the *Russian Indemnity* case is of particular interest, throws much light on the methodological problem of how the law is to be found. On many occasions the existence of a general principle relating to the assessment of damages, waiver, *force majeure* and other matters has been asserted by international tribunals. In many instances it would not be difficult to show that the principle so asserted is perhaps not quite as general and unequivocal in private law as the tribunal seemed to think. The remarkable fact remains that international tribunals have on many occasions failed to elucidate the route which led them to their assertions. They have thus not only made it difficult to check the correctness of the results, but may also have deprived their decisions of much of the value which attaches to a precedent that is based on exhaustive documentation and a detailed explanation of the process of reasoning. Any tendency to state general principles in general terms should, therefore, be avoided. While it is sufficient to teach us where we are to dig to find the source, it does not tell us which tools we should use and how we are to handle them.

That, on this problem of method, the vast literature on the general principles within the meaning of Article 38 proves to be largely unhelpful is a matter for real disappointment. This literature in the first place has seen its task in the enumeration of the general principles which in the past have been accepted or alluded to by international tribunals.[1] Such catalogues tell us that *restitutio in integrum*, estoppel, waiver, the prohibition of an abuse of rights, *res judicata* and many similar institutions or conceptions of private law have been recognized as general principles of law. There are, secondly, writers[2] who attempt to extract from available decisions broad maxims which are said to be general principles, but which constitute merely a reformulated catalogue. Thus reference is made to the principle of responsibility, of self-preservation, of good faith. Thirdly, doctrinal discussion seems to be interested in a somewhat speculative and frequently verbal analysis of Article 38. One reads about the nature of the general principles and their connection with natural law,[3] about general principles as a source of international law and about the question whether they are an independent source.[4] It is not intended to deny the usefulness of these contributions. But it is intended to submit that many of the earlier discussions[5] have failed to pay sufficient

---

[1] See, for example, Rousseau, *Principes généraux du droit international public* (Paris, 1944), i.901 et seq.

[2] See Bin Cheng, *General Principles of Law as applied by International Courts and Tribunals* (London, 1953).

[3] Rousseau, op. cit., p. 892, with further references.

[4] Rousseau, op. cit., p. 894, with further references.

[5] The greater part of the vast literature has been consulted, but only a small part of it is being referred to in these notes. For the reasons which have been given in the text many earlier contributions do not throw light on the present problems, so that the selection of characteristic views is likely to suffice. Tribute

attention to the overriding problem of ascertaining how general principles are to be discovered. This is a purely practical problem of *method*. Its solution provides an answer to the question how the commercial law of nations can be found.

It is believed that some slight progress can be made if the following submissions are accepted:

(1) The general principles as a whole and the commercial law of nations in particular are determined and defined by comparative law, i.e. by the process of comparing municipal systems of law. Although publicists rarely refer in terms to comparative law as a 'source'[1] of international law, the great majority is likely to agree. This is so for the obvious reason that since the elimination of the direct influence of Roman law there does not exist any system or branch of law, other than comparative law, which could develop general principles.[2] Moreover, the positivist will derive support for the conclusion from a remark made by Lord Phillimore in the course of the deliberations of the Committee of Jurists of 1920. He explained[3] that the general principles were those principles which applied in *foro domestico*. He thus referred expressly to comparative law as their source. So did, for instance, Ripert[4] when he reached the conclusion 'que c'est dans les législations positives qu'il faut chercher les principes généraux du droit'.

(2) The fact that a rule is of a technical character does not mean that it does not, or cannot, constitute a general principle. To put the same point differently, it is the generality of the application of the rule, not the generality of the legal idea underlying it, that determines whether or not it is a general principle. Very little, if anything, is therefore to be gained by drawing a distinction between principles and rules, a distinc-

---

must, however, be paid to Sir Hersch Lauterpacht's important and, indeed, fundamental works on the subject, without which this article could not have been written: *Private Law Sources and Analogies of International Law* (1927), and *The Function of Law in the International Community* (1933).

[1] Although comparative law is, of course, only a method of study, it does not seem to be unjustifiable to describe some of the results achieved by the comparative method as a source of law.

[2] It should be obvious that natural law in the traditional sense cannot help. The 'modern law of nature' referred to by Lord Asquith (above, p. 143, n. 2) is, of course, something different.

[3] *Procès-Verbaux of the Proceedings of the Committee* (1920), p. 335.

[4] 44 *Recueil des Cours* (1933), pp. 569 et seq., at p. 579.

tion which is largely verbal, which has never been satisfactorily defined and should be discarded. This view is opposed to the prevailing trend of opinion. Thus Ripert,[1] whose outstanding contribution should be acknowledged, starts from the premiss that 'les principes du droit sont les règles essentielles sur lesquelles sont greffées des règles secondaires d'application et de technique'. He elaborates it in words which merit quotation in full[2]:

Pour définir les principes généraux du droit interne des nations civilisées, il n'est pas nécessaire d'envisager toutes les règles positives adoptées par ces nations. Le principe commande les règles; ou peut changer une règle sans renverser un principe, mais si on change un principe il faut modifier une série de règles. Les règles sont établies sur des considérations d'ordre pratique et d'après une certaine technique. Elles ont presque toujours un caractère national, parce que les besoins ne sont pas partout identiquement les mêmes et que la technique dépend, jusqu'à un certain point, de l'esprit national. Les principes, au contraire, se retrouvent semblables dans les principales législations. Il y a accord sur les principes, bien que diversité dans les règles. Les nations civilisées ont, à l'heure actuelle, un droit qui est établi sur des principes communs, bien que leur droit codifié ait un caractère technique particulier.

To mention another writer of authority with a different background, Verdross[3] propounds a similar theory:

On doit ainsi distinguer nettement la technique du droit interne et les principes généraux qui se trouvent à sa base. Il ne suffit donc point de rechercher les règles formulées par la science du droit comparé pour les appliquer aux relations internationales, il est nécessaire de pénétrer jusqu'aux principes généraux supposés par le droit positif.

There are many reasons which enjoin the rejection of these suggestions. Firstly, the wording of Article 38 does not by any means necessitate their adoption. A generally accepted rule may well be described as a general principle. A denial of this proposition would demand so narrow and verbal an interpretation as to make the argument an inadmissible play with words. Secondly, such international practice as is material to the point does not support the suggested distinction. Thus in the Award which the Senate of the City of Hamburg made in 1861 in an arbitration between Great Britain and Portugal[4] the amount of interest to which the claimant Government was entitled was

---

[1] Ibid., p. 575.    [2] Ibid., p. 582.
[3] 52 *Recueil des Cours* (1935), pp. 195 et seq., at p. 205.
[4] Lapradelle–Politis, *Recueil des arbitrages internationaux*, ii.72 et seq., at p. 108. For criticism see ibid., p. 108.

held to be limited to the amount of the capital. This decision was based on the rule of *alterum tantum* developed by Roman law. The rule which has not at any time formed part of the common law and has not found its way into the modern codifications of continental countries is of a technical character. It does not appear to be derived from any basic principle of law. Yet it was applied in 1861 and, if it still existed, could be applied today.[1] Thirdly, it must be doubted whether it is always possible to find a 'principle' which underlies each technical rule. Fourthly, it is probably wrong to think that principles 'se retrouvent semblables dans les principales législations' and that, therefore, the problem is solved in practice if one penetrates to the principles as opposed to the rules. Fifthly, however, the distinction between principles and rules ignores the requirements and perhaps even the existence of the commercial law of nations. It is of the very essence of commercial law that it is frequently concerned with technicalities of the law. The commercial law of nations would be poorly served and could, indeed, not be developed at all if it could not be built upon generally recognized rules of a technical character, but had to rely on 'principles' or maxims which are necessarily vague, colourless, and ambiguous. In particular, the principle of good faith which unquestionably pervades public international law should not be regarded as a sufficient substitute for a more detailed commercial law of nations. The opposite view would, it is believed, be mistaken because it ignores the teachings of private law. In a sense it is quite true that all law and all legal systems incorporate and are based upon some such maxims as find expression in the maxims of English equity, in Article 1134 of the French or in section 242 of the German Civil Code or in similar provisions of codified law. Many, if not most, of the specific rules and provisions accepted in the systems of municipal law can be said to be manifestations or applications of such maxims. Yet 'general clauses', as they have been called, have been proved to be an unsatisfactory guide and dangerous to legal development. While no legal system has found it possible to do without them none has found it possible to work with them alone. They leave much room for a subjective approach by the

---

[1] The Award should not, on this point, be treated as a precedent, because the alleged principle does not now exist.

court. They leave the result unpredictable. They lack that minimum degree of precision without which every legal decision would be wholly uncertain. They may, on occasions, be useful to fill a gap but in essence they are too elementary, too obvious and even too platitudinous to permit detached evaluation of conflicting interests, the specifically legal appreciation of the implications of a given situation. In short they are frequently apt to let discretion prevail over justice. For these reasons they cannot be the sole source of a sound and workable commercial law of nations.

It is, of course, not intended to suggest that rules should invariably be preferred to 'principles' or that 'principles' should be ignored. The argument is directed against overrating the legal strength of principles and against the exclusion of technical rules from the ambit of Article 38—a provision which, if it is to fulfil its purpose, requires the most elastic and liberal interpretation and application.

(3) A principle of law is a general one if it is being applied by the most representative systems of municipal law.

That universality of application is not a prerequisite of a general principle of law is emphasized by almost all authors.[1] It should be equally clear that a single system of municipal law cannot provide a general principle within the meaning of Article 38. What is usually required is that the principle pervades the municipal law of nations in general.[2] It is believed, however, that a more specific formula ought to be found.

Where a rule of customary international law or a treaty between States having heterogeneous legal systems is in issue a wide field of application is normally both necessary and sufficient to establish a general principle. The numerical aspect is likely to be of little consequence. Rather it is the weight, the quality, status, prestige of the principle or rule that matters. Regard should be had to those imponderables which are enshrined in the reference to the representative character of a municipal system of law. A long line of decisions, possibly rendered by the highest tribunals over a long period, may carry greater authority than a longer line of statutes or decrees. His-

---

[1] Ripert, op. cit., p. 579; Verdross, op. cit., p. 205, and many other writers.
[2] Article 38 speaks of principles recognized 'by civilized nations', not 'by the civilized nations'.

torical developments will frequently provide guidance.

The process of comparison should be different where the issue arises from a treaty between States having related legal systems. In this case a principle common to the law of the countries in question may be treated as a general one and may even prevail over a different principle accepted by all or most other countries of the world.[1] Let it be supposed that a treaty provides for the sale of equipment by one State to another 'at a price to be agreed separately' and that according to the municipal law of both parties in default of agreement the seller determines the price. Let it be supposed, further, that in such circumstances most systems of municipal law provide for the payment of a reasonable price. Would it not be more satisfactory and in closer harmony with the intention of the parties to let the law of the parties prevail over what in another case may have to be treated as a general principle of law? A common denominator may and sometimes should outweigh an alien, albeit general denominator. It indicates, in the given conditions, the more representative legal systems.

(4) A principle of law is a general one even though the constituent rules of the representative systems of law are similar rather than identical.

Comparative lawyers will regard it as almost platitudinous that complete identity, extending to all the details of a legal rule, hardly ever exists between the legal systems of two or more countries; even if the wording of a statutory provision is the same, its judicial interpretation may differ from country to country. On the other hand comparative lawyers will not hesitate to testify to the existence of a surprising degree of similarity of rules or at least results, arrived at frequently by differing means, processes of reasoning or classification. It is this similarity which permits the deduction of general principles. Perhaps it will be thought that the facts do not warrant so optimistic and even sweeping an assessment of the help which comparative law can render. By the very nature of things only impressions or beliefs can be formed. No doubt they will not be shared by all, but they are likely to be supported by most of those who have the benefit of practical experience.

---

[1] A similar view has been expressed by a comparative lawyer, René David, in his *Traité élémentaire de droit civil comparé* (Paris, 1950), p. 101.

It is, of course, likely that even the most comprehensive investigation does not always produce an unequivocal solution in that, for instance, several groups of legal systems may emerge which differ in respect of the rule in question from each other and each of which may claim to have representative character. In such a case the international judge, unless he feels compelled to reach the desperate and wholly unsatisfactory verdict of *non liquet*, will have to make a choice in the spirit of the legislator. By his decision he will create a general principle and thus exercise a function which in all countries of the world a judge, though he purports to apply the law, in fact frequently performs.[1] No text confers such power upon an international judge who is not expressly authorized to decide *ex aequo et bono*. Yet that power is inherent in the judicial process in general and should be affirmed, because without it neither international law as a whole nor international commercial law could live and develop.

In short, the commercial law of nations should be approached in a manner corresponding to the attitude which, before the nineteenth century, English jurists adopted towards the law merchant. Sir John Davies in 1656[2] and many later writers, including Malynes, Molloy, and Blackstone, envisaged the law merchant as 'a branch of the law of nations'[3] and judges described it as 'jus gentium',[4] as 'a system of equity, founded on the rules of equity and governed in all its parts by plain justice and good faith'.[5] This meant no more than that the law merchant 'was free from certain technical rules of the common law'.[6] The terminology should not be misunderstood: the earlier English jurists did not intend to attribute to the law merchant the quality of public international law in the modern sense. Rather were they thinking of a universal law, of usages which, notwithstanding local variations, were common to the

---

[1] This is clearly seen by Lauterpacht, *The Function of Law in the International Community*, pp. 60 et seq.

[2] *Concerning Impositions*, p. 17 [quoted from Sir John Macdonell in Smith, *Mercantile Law* (13th ed., 1931, by Gutteridge), Introduction, p. ccviii].

[3] Smith, op. cit.

[4] *Mogadara* v. *Holt* (1691), 1 Shower 318.

[5] *Master* v. *Miller* (1791), 4 T. R. 340, per Buller J.

[6] Smith, op. cit.

Western world.[1] Today so cosmopolitan an outlook has disappeared in municipal law. It should be revived for the purpose of moulding the commercial law of nations. International lawyers will succeed in discharging their task if they follow the example of their forebears who discovered and developed the law merchant.


V


It was originally intended at this point to discuss a hypothetical case founded upon one of the treaties referred to in section II and affording a suitable illustration of the method of approach which is suggested by the preceding observations. It is, however, possible now to adopt the more satisfactory course of taking an actual case as an example and submitting its methodological basis and reasoning to scrutiny. This is the case of the *Diverted Cargoes*, which led to an arbitration between Greece and the United Kingdom and to an Award made in 1955 by the sole Arbitrator, Monsieur René Cassin, Vice-President of the Conseil d'État in Paris.[2]

The facts may in a considerably simplified form be summarized as follows. In April 1941 ships bound for Greece were diverted by British forces to territories outside Greece, where their cargoes, the property of the Greek consignees, were discharged and taken over by the British authorities for use in the war against the common enemy. In February 1942 the Governments of Greece and the United Kingdom entered into a treaty[3] the short effect of which, in so far as it is relevant for present purposes, was that the Greek Government undertook to prevent the owners of the cargoes from making any claim against the British Government, and the latter Government undertook to

---

[1] See Sir Frederick Pollock's valuable Introduction to the 'Commercial Law of Great Britain and Ireland', being vol. i of the *Commercial Laws of the World* (ed. by Bowstead), p. 11.

[2] The Award, written in the French language, is published in *Revue critique de droit international privé* (1956), p. 278, with a Note by Batiffol. The quotations in the text are taken from an English translation published Int. L.R. 1955, 820. A valuable Note on the case by Mr. J. L. Simpson appeared in 5 *I.C.L.Q.* (1956), p. 427. For a critical but very helpful comment upon some of the questions of monetary law arising from the Award see Dach, 5 *A.J.C.L.* (1956), p. 512.

[3] It is printed in Cmd. 9754.

credit the Greek Government with 'the f.o.b. cost of such cargoes'. Some of them had been bought in the United States of
America against dollars. Before September 1949, when sterling
was devalued, the two Governments had agreed that in repect of
goods bought against sterling the Greek Government was entitled to a credit of £1,438,600 and that the f.o.b. value of goods
bought against dollars was $4,051,401, which, on the basis of
'une conversion comptable', was agreed to be equal to
£1,012,850. Furthermore, in August 1949 the Greek Government agreed to credit the British Government with a sum of
£1,666,700[1] and in March 1950 agreed to discontinue a claim
to a sum of $3,999,235.48. On the other hand, in August 1951
the British Government admitted the f.o.b. value of cetain
goods bought in the United States at $2,057,698.94. The issue
before the Arbitrator was whether the f.o.b. cost of goods purchased in the United States was to be converted into sterling
at the post-devaluation rate of $2.80 to the pound (as the Greek
Government contended) or at the pre-devaluation rate of
$4.03 to the pound (as the British Government contended). It
is to be noted that the parties had expressly agreed by their
Terms of Reference[2] that actual payment was to be made in
sterling and that, accordingly, sterling was the money of payment.

In order to decide that issue the Arbitrator asked himself
three questions.

The first was: What was the currency—dollar or sterling—
which the parties chose in 1942 as the *monnaie de contrat* for the
effective settlement of the claim? The Arbitrator had no difficulty in concluding that the Agreement created a single account
in a single currency, viz. sterling. Hence the dollar was not

---

[1] It thus appears that, had an account been taken in August 1949, the Greek
Government was entitled to £1,438,600 plus £1,012,850 less £1,666,700, i.e.
£784,150 only. Or to put the point in a different way, in August 1949 more than
the sterling equivalent of $4,051,401 was wiped out by the amount of £1,666,700
due from Greece, and even if the latter sum was credited against the sum of
£1,438,600 about £228,700 was available to reduce at that time the dollar amount
by almost $1,000,000. Yet the Award ordering payment at the rate of $2.80 to the
£ seems to apply to the whole of the sum of $4,051,401, and this is in the face of the
fact that according to the Arbitrator conversion had to be effected 'on the day on
which the credit due to the Hellenic State is given' ('au jour où aura lieu l'inscrip-
tion du crédit dû à l'État hellénique'). See below, p. 168, n. 3.

[2] Cmd. 9754, Terms of Reference, clause 5 (A): 'the Royal Hellenic Government
accepts that the credit to be given even for the aforesaid cargoes will be in sterling'.

adopted as the 'monnaie de contrat, c'est-à-dire de paiement effectif'.[1]

The second question was whether the sterling credit thus to be given was to be calculated by reference to the dollar regarded as the unit of value and as the money of account ('comme étalon de valeur et comme monnaie de compte'). It is difficult to understand how this question could ever arise or how, as the Arbitrator records, the British Government could ever contend for a negative answer. If the f.o.b. value of goods bought in the United States against dollars is to be ascertained, one necessarily starts from the dollar as the money of account. The obligation of the British Government can only have been for '$x$ dollars payable in sterling' or for 'such sum of sterling as corresponds to $x$ dollars'. In either case the result was probably the same,[2] but having rejected the former alternative by his answer to the first question, the Arbitrator was bound to answer the second by holding that the dollar was the money of account.

He thus reached his third and last question which, it is believed, was the only one of substance that arose in the case: Which rate of exchange—the rate on the day on which the debt arose or the rate of the day of payment or settlement—should be used to calculate the sterling amount to be credited to Greece? The Arbitrator held that the rate of exchange of the date of settlement[3] had to be applied. After some introductory remarks the Arbitrator stated:

> The international practice in legislation, agreements and cases as well as the practice of the great majority of nations recognizes that the rate of conversion from the money of account into the money of payment is that prevailing at the date on which the debt is settled.

---

[1] It is submitted with respect that the Arbitrator's terminology is confusing. He seems to draw a distinction between *monnaie de contrat* and *monnaie de compte*. No such distinction exists. Moreover, the phrase referred to in the text and numerous similar phrases which occur in the Award make it clear that to the Arbitrator's mind *monnaie de contrat* and *monnaie de paiement effectif* are interchangeable conceptions. In truth the dollar may be the *monnaie de contrat* or the *monnaie de compte*, yet sterling may be and, as a result of the Terms of Reference, clearly was the *monnaie de paiement effectif*. On the distinction see Mann, *The Legal Aspect of Money* (2nd ed., 1953), p. 158.

[2] In both cases the same problem of construction would arise.

[3] This expression, used in the English translation, means the date of payment. It is, however, noteworthy that in the fifth paragraph of his concluding summary the Arbitrator equiparates the date of payment to the 'day on which the credit due to the Hellenic State is given' (see above, p. 167, n. 1). These two dates do not necessarily coincide and did not coincide in the present case.

He then referred to Article 41 (in fact he wrote '49')[1] of the Geneva Uniform Law in Bills of Exchange which, he said, provided 'one of the most striking instances of the great importance attached to the rate of conversion at the date of the payment of the debt'. He proceeded to discuss at some length the decisions of the Permanent Court of International Justice in the cases of the *Serbian* and the *Brazilian Loans*[2] and concluded his investigation of the law by stating:

> After reference to so decisive a monument of international case law it is unnecessary to add either the long list of decisions of courts of many countries in support of the principle of conversion on the day of actual payment (see for example the reasons given in support of this thesis by Nussbaum, op. cit., p. 361) nor an analysis of the cases of the common law countries which, starting from a different conception, that of conversion on the day of the breach of the contract, frequently arrive in practice at conclusions very similar to those of other systems of law (see criticism by Nussbaum, op. cit., p. 370).

Finally, the Arbitrator turned to the Agreement before him and set forth the specific reasons 'which combine to require the application to the present dispute of the principle of conversion on the day of actual payment'.[3]

The preceding summary is, it is hoped, sufficient to lay the foundation for a discussion of the three general questions to which the Award gives rise within the context of this article: What was the source of law to which the Arbitrator resorted? How did he proceed to ascertain the law? Does the law which he thus purported to apply in fact have the effect assumed by him?

(1) As to the source of the law applicable by him the Arbi-

---

[1] This error is not without interest. It also occurs in Nussbaum, *Money in the Law, National and International Law* (2nd ed., 1950), p. 361, one of the few books referred to by M. Cassin (see below, p. 171, n. 1), although Nussbaum prints the full text in n. 5.

[2] *Collection of Judgments* (1928–30), Series A, Nos. 14, 15.

[3] These reasons are unconvincing. The first was that by virtue of the undertaking to credit Greece 'with the f.o.b. cost of the cargoes' the British Government's obligation 'must necessarily be ascertained by a conversion on the very day on which the credit is actually given'. This statement merely begs the question. The second reason rests on the 'non-profit making and strictly compensatory character' of the treaty. It involves not only a *non sequitur*, but is also, at least in part, derived from the unfounded belief that Greece was entitled to a credit only 'on condition that the Royal Hellenic Government themselves repaid the owners of the cargoes requisitioned'. The treaty contains no such express or implied condition.

trator made only two pronouncements. On the one hand he thought that his decision had to rest 'upon the basis of respect for law' in accordance with Article 37 of the first Hague Convention of 1907. On the other hand, he started from the undeniable premiss that the Agreement of 1942 was 'unquestionably governed by international law'. Yet it is clear that he found the law applicable to the case before him, in so far as it was not merely the construction of the treaty that was in issue, in the municipal practice of the family of nations, however 'technical' in character it may have been. It is true that the Arbitrator did not in every respect accept the controlling character of the analogy of the institutions or rules of municipal law; thus he did not think it right to have recourse 'to the alleged existence of a huge current account between the two Governments which is a conception of municipal law'. Nevertheless, taken as a whole, the Award rests on reasoning which is exclusively derived from municipal law and which, indeed, could not possibly be derived from any other source. The broad distinction, fundamental to the Award, between the money of account and the money of payment has hitherto been unknown to public international law *stricto sensu*. The rule that conversion is to be effected according to the rate of the date of payment, almost in terms proclaimed by the Arbitrator as a generally accepted principle of law and thus given the status of a rule of international law, is derived from no source other than municipal law. This method of approach may have been self-evident, simply because nowhere else could guidance possibly be found. But it merits express and unqualified welcome and approval, particularly in view of the fact that the issue related, not to one of those broad and, perhaps, primitive general principles which underlie municipal law, but to 'lawyers' law', to very specific aspects of a specific branch of municipal law.

(2) The Arbitrator's method of deriving general principles of law from municipal law is perhaps less exemplary and should not without hesitation be accepted as a precedent.

In the first place it is remarkable that in connection with a point of law arising between Greece and the United Kingdom no reference was made by the Arbitrator to Greek or to English law. No Greek or English statutory provision, decision, or academic authority on private law is mentioned in the Award.

Nor were American sources consulted, though references to American writers occur.[1] On the other hand, in a case which had nothing to do with France reliance was to a considerable extent placed upon French law. A thesis submitted to the University of Paris[2] or a Note on certain French decisions published in a French legal periodical are put on the same level as leading French textbooks[3] and both sources are preferred to French decisions which are ignored altogether, though by no means all of them give unqualified support to the statements made by the writers consulted by the Arbitrator. Moreover, no comparative material available in other countries was resorted to. Even the full significance of the Geneva Convention on Bills of Exchange was not emphasized: no mention is made of the fact that it applies in seventeen countries.

It is submitted that such treatment of comparative law as a source of international law is insufficient to establish the existence of principles of general application and to secure the necessary respect and authority for international decisions which are based on municipal law. Where a bilateral treaty is involved the law of the contracting States should not be ignored. The law of a third State, not concerned with the treaty, can only serve as an example, not as the sole source of international law. Intensive research and, in particular, close investigation of judicial practice is required if comparative law is to serve as a satisfactory yardstick to international law. In the discharge of this task the parties and their representatives will have to take a considerable share. In fairness to Monsieur Cassin it must be added that the pleadings in the present case have not been published and that it is, therefore, impossible to say to what extent he received all the assistance which he could expect.

(3) Although the broad results reached by the Arbitrator

---

[1] They were Nussbaum, op. cit., and Domke, 'International Loans and the Conflict of Laws', *Grot. Soc.* (1937), (which really deals with the gold clause).

[2] Penciulesco, *La Monnaie de paiement dans les contrats internationaux* (Thèse, Paris, 1937).

[3] The Note (which is by no means the most illuminating contribution to monetary law which the French legal world has produced) is by Loussouarn, *Revue critique du droit international privé* (1953), p. 389. The textbooks are Planiol–Ripert, *Traité pratique de droit civil*; Ripert–Boulanger, *Manuel de droit civil*; and Batiffol, *Traité élémentaire de droit international privé*. The last-mentioned work (2nd ed., 1955), pp. 675 et seq., does not deal with the particular problems which confronted the Arbitrator.

may have been correct, the statements made by him on the effects of municipal law are open to criticism. In view of the methods employed for the purpose of finding the municipal law this is perhaps not surprising. Five points require consideration.

The conflict between conversion at the rate of exchange prevailing at the date of maturity (maturity-date rule) and conversion at the rate of exchange prevailing at the date of payment (payment-date rule) has developed over the centuries in connection with a specific situation: in the words of the Geneva Convention on Bills of Exchange[1] it arises when an obligation 'is expressed to be payable in any currency other than that of the place of payment'. Thus, if dollars are payable in London, it is probably both the law of England and a general principle of law that the debtor has the option of paying in sterling.[2] Where such occasion for conversion occurs, it becomes necessary to choose between the maturity-date rule and the payment-date rule. In the case of the *Diverted Cargoes* this particular occasion for conversion did not arise, for by his answer to his first question the Arbitrator held that the United Kingdom had not undertaken to pay dollars, but had undertaken to pay such sum of sterling as corresponded to a certain sum of dollars. Even on this footing, of course, it became necessary to choose the date determining the rate of exchange. But the question was one of construction and the vast body of law developed in regard to the case in which a sum of money is payable in a currency different from that of the place of payment could, at the most, be material by way of analogy. The point is by no means of merely formal significance, for in answering his third question, the essential question in the case, the Arbitrator was so clearly influenced by what he regarded as the governing general principle of law that it is impossible to say what his conclusions would have been if he had realized that that principle was not directly applicable.

Even assuming, however, that the body of law to which the Arbitrator referred was, directly or indirectly, applicable, it is by no means certain that the payment-date rule can be said

---

[1] Similar words occur in the Geneva Convention on Cheques.

[2] See Mann, op. cit., pp. 272–85. See also the survey by Dach, 'Conversion of Foreign Money', *A.J.C.L.* (1954), p. 155.

to be supported by 'so decisive a monument of international case law'. As will be shown below, the Geneva Convention on Bills of Exchange confirms it only to a limited extent. The decisions of the Permanent Court of International Justice in the cases of the *Serbian Loans* and the *Brazilian Loans*[1] relate to the gold clause and are not germane to the issue.[2] The payment-date rule seems to exist only in Greece, Austria, Germany, and South Africa.[3] There are many countries in which, at any rate outside the law of bills of exchange, the maturity-date rule prevails[4]—in Italy this rule was reaffirmed as recently as 1942 when the new Civil Code was introduced. There are also countries which regard the problem as one of construction. This solution which, it is believed, demanded application in the present case for more than one reason, has possibly been adopted in England,[5] and is very likely to prevail in France where, consequently, the practice of the courts does not by any means establish the uniform control of the payment-date rule.[6] It must suffice to refer to one decision of the Cour de Cassation[7] where it is said

qu'il est de principe, en effet, que tout paiement fait en France, quelle qu'en soit la cause, doit être effectué en monnaie française et *que le solde d'un marché fixé en dollars doit être évalué selon le cours du dollar au jour où le débiteur devait payer.*

and to quote from the relevant section, ignored by the Arbitrator, of Planiol–Ripert's authoritative work[8] where French practice is summarized: 'La Cour de Cassation estimait que la date dépend encore de la volonté implicite des parties.' The niceties of French law on the point cannot and need not be pursued here: all that matters for present purposes is to note 'les contradictions apparentes'[9] of French practice.

[1] Above, p. 169, n. 2.

[2] The reference to the decisions mentioned in the text indicates an almost incomprehensible *lapsus* on the part of the arbitrator. There is, however, a widespread tendency in French literature to rely on them in suppport of propositions with which they are not concerned: see, for example, Batiffol, op. cit.

[3] Mann, op. cit., p. 278, n. 1.

[4] Mann, op. cit., p. 278, n. 2, where, however, the reference to Italy is wrong.

[5] Mann, op. cit., p. 285.       [6] Mann, op. cit., pp. 278–80.

[7] Req. 17 February 1937, Clunet (1937), p. 766.

[8] *Traité de droit civil français* (2nd ed., 1954), vol. vii, No. 1161. The sentence quoted in the text is followed by the remark that ordinarily resort is had to the rate prevailing on the day of maturity.

[9] Mater, *La Monnaie* (1925), p. 270.

Next, in support of the general character of the payment-date rule the Arbitrator relied on the Geneva Convention on Bills of Exchange which, he thought, provided 'one of the most striking instances'. In truth, that Convention provides that 'the sum due may be paid in the currency of the country at the rate of exchange on the day of maturity', but 'if the debtor is in default', the creditor may require payment at the rate on the day of payment. However, the Award does not hold that there was any default on the part of the British Government.[1] The Geneva Convention, therefore, did not assist the Arbitrator.

Again, as has been shown, the payment-date rule has been developed in contradistinction to the maturity-date rule. But on the facts of the case of the *Diverted Cargoes* it is not even clear, and the Arbitrator did not decide, when the United Kingdom's debt fell due. This again shows that the body of municipal law on which the Arbitrator relied was not relevant. Moreover, the British Government, as the Award records, had argued in favour of the rate of the day on which the debt arose. This probably meant 1941 or 1942. The true issue raised by the British Government was, it seems, that the Treaty of 1942 by implication included a provision to the effect that conversion was to take place on the basis of the rate of exchange of 1942, or a clause such as '$4.03 = £1'.[2] If this is right, the issue, treated as one of construction, is hardly reflected in the Award.

Finally, it is necessary to mention a point which may have influenced the Arbitrator, to which he merely alludes, but

---

[1] On the other hand the Arbitrator held expressly that there was no evidence of the delay in the negotiations being due to the fault of the creditor.

[2] The British Government's case was, therefore, the same as that of the defendant in whose favour the Cour de Paris rendered the decision of 22 December 1951, *Revue critique de droit international privé* (1953), p. 379; it is one of the decisions commented upon by Loussouarn (above, p. 171, n. 3) upon whom the learned Arbitrator relied. The defendant, acting for a party of travellers, had hired from the plaintiffs, a Swedish company, through their Paris agency, a coach for travelling from Stockholm to Paris. The agreed price was expressed in Swedish currency. But the defendant submitted that in the circumstances the equivalent in French francs, calculated at the rate prevailing at the date of the contract, was the real *monnaie de contrat*, the money of account. This submission was upheld. In the case before Monsieur Cassin the dollar amount was, of course, at the date of the contract unknown. It may well be that if in accordance with the teachings of comparative law he had attached weight to the decision of the Cour de Paris rather than Loussouarn's comment on it he would have found it easier to appreciate the real nature of the British case.

which, notwithstanding its immense significance, he does not develop. It is expressed in one sentence:

'The creditor is entitled to reject, in so far as it would affect the substance of his claim, the effect of any action taken by the debtor State itself to devalue its currency.

If this sentence is intended to lay down the theory that in inter-State relations the debtor State cannot rely on the effects of nominalism flowing from its own monetary legislation, then great regret would have to be expressed at the appearance of a fundamental rule which, for reasons developed elsewhere,[1] cannot be accepted as sound, and at the absence of any reasoning designed to support it.

There thus exists considerable doubt whether the learned Arbitrator applied municipal law correctly. Private law, while it must be the principal source of the commercial law of nations, cannot be a safe source except by the employment of the utmost care and precision. It would be unfortunate if the commercial law of nations came to be built upon a foundation of false analogies of private law.

## VI

The commercial law of nations thus constitutes a challenge to the international and the comparative lawyer alike. It is only by their co-operation that it can be developed into a workable system of law.

The international lawyer must become familiar with the functions and methods of a branch of the law of which, usually, he has little experience. He is bound to run considerable risks if he should believe that the art of comparing can be practised without training and education. This applies not only to the international judge, but also to the advocate appearing before an international tribunal and, in particular, to the draftsman of international documents.

The task of supplying the material with which large parts of the commercial law of nations will be built is primarily, however, imposed upon the comparative lawyer. For him the commercial law of nations opens a field which has hardly been ex-

---

[1] Mann, op. cit., pp. 451, 452.

plored, but has, perhaps, the strongest claim to his attention. Very few comparative lawyers have shown themselves aware of the nature and extent of the contribution which they are called upon to make.[1] There is room for the impression that even the late Professor Gutteridge who devoted a remarkable essay[2] to the relationship between comparative law and the law of nations did not fully appreciate the specific requirements of the commercial law of nations. He felt that general principles of private law which are recognized by civilized nations 'must be rare, partly because there is little or no scope for the employment of any save the main principles of law for this purpose, and partly because such exploration of the field as has been attempted appears to indicate that there are few principles of this description'.[3] This conclusion was due to the fact that the learned author was thinking mainly of international law in general rather than its several branches and did not contemplate the particular branch with which this article is concerned. This is made clear by his discussion of the principle of impossibility of performance. He felt[4] 'grave doubt' whether it was possible to discover in the English doctrine of frustration, in the French theory of imprévision, and in the German principle of good faith 'some underlying principle which is common to all these attempts to solve the problem, and whether such principle, if it exists, could be adapted to the settlement of international disputes'. He continued, significantly, as follows[4]:

> It is, of course, obvious that the environment in which such a principle would be required to function is not the same in the international as in the private sphere. This is so ... because the problem as it arises in private law has an economic background which is very different from the political considerations which surround it in international law.

It is possible that this view is too narrow. It cannot be shared by anyone who realizes the 'economic background' on which the commercial law of nations rests. Professor Gutteridge continued to express the opinion that in any event there was not 'much hope of the discovery of a principle [relating to impossibility of performance] which is recognized by all systems or even by a

---

[1] This also applies to Rabel, 'Rechtsvergleichung und internationale Rechtsprechung', 1 *Rabels Zeitschrift* (1927), pp. 5, 17–19, but does not apply to David referred to above, p. 164, n. 1.

[2] *Comparative Law* (2nd ed., 1949), pp. 60–71.

[3] Ibid., pp. 65, 66.        [4] Ibid., p. 67.

majority of them'.[1] Here again a broader approach would seem to be desirable. In the first place, as has been indicated above, international law does not confine the usefulness of municipal law to the case in which comparative lawyers can prove the existence of a rule in identical form in all or most systems: existence of the rule in the most representative systems is sufficient to render municipal law a source of international law. Secondly, however, it is at the present stage of the development not really a question of formulating a common 'principle'. It is tempting to suggest that the search for the formulation of a 'principle' is both confusing and irrelevant. Rather is it necessary to consider the particular point or problem or issue and to ascertain how this point, this problem, this issue is in fact solved by the law of the most representative countries. It must be stressed again that a detailed investigation of practice and doctrine is likely often to disclose a widespread identity or, at least, similarity of result in a given case, though the starting point, that is to say, the legal rule or 'principle' may vary considerably in formulation as well as in character. What the commercial law of nations is concerned with is the result rather than its origin or derivation. In a given case the first system may work with the conception of the implication of terms, the second may have an express statutory provision, the third may rely on the requirements of good faith, the fourth may refer to judicial discretion—these are merely relatively unimportant questions of method. What matters is whether they lead to the same or to similar results.

From this point of view, then, the most effective assistance which the comparative lawyer can render in the development of the commercial law of nations can be defined with a fair degree of precision. It is true that, as Professor Gutteridge concluded,[2] comparative law furnishes the international lawyer 'with an objective by which he can measure the justice of a principle' and also with 'a corrective to any tendency ... to employ concepts or rules which either belong exclusively to a single system or are only to be found in a few of such systems'. Yet comparative law has also a much more important, a much more direct function: it provides, or at least it ought to provide, the international lawyer with a pattern which will guide him

<hr />

[1] Ibid., p. 67.    [2] Ibid., p. 71.

to the solution of his practical problems and which will protect him against the many dangers and pitfalls involved in any process of comparison. It is, of course, impossible to compile a treatise or digest which would describe in a comparative fashion everything that could conceivably be of interest to the commercial law of nations. But it is feasible and, indeed, imperative to select isolated subjects and to show how far they have received solutions which may be described as common to the representative systems of law and, therefore, as expressive of a general principle. International law supplies an abundance of typical questions which lend themselves to comparative research on these lines. It may well be that the international lawyer will never be confronted with an actual case upon which such specific studies would have a bearing. But if he is conversant with them, then he will have a better idea of how he should proceed when he is faced with a problem requiring a similar type of investigation. It is for comparative law to evolve the methods of research and to define the standards of identity, affinity or similarity which are adapted to the peculiar requirements of the commercial law of nations and will in the future mould it into a coherent branch of the law. International law is designed to have the benefit of this work, but ought not to be called upon to do it. In many respects the commercial law of nations, therefore, may have to be developed primarily by the comparative lawyer who is aware of its existence and needs and who, since the days of Saleilles and Lambert[1] has become familiar with the task of ascertaining 'the principles which are common to all civilized systems of law', rather than by the international lawyer whose equipment may not always be commensurate to the task.

[1] See Gutteridge, op. cit., p. 5, with further references.

# III

# THE LAW GOVERNING STATE CONTRACTS*

## I

THE growing assumption by the State of commercial and industrial activities, both in the domestic and the international field, is a phenomenon which in many respects requires a revision of traditional legal thought.

The necessity for a new approach is particularly evident in connection with the classification of State contracts from the point of view of international law. At present this legal analysis is overshadowed by the widely accepted dogma, not necessarily confined to those subscribing to the dualistic view of international law nor altogether opposed by the monistic doctrine, that there exists a clear-cut dichotomy of international public and private law in the following directions:

First, the relationship between States or other international persons is subject to public international law, while the relations between private persons or between a private person and a foreign State is governed by some municipal system of law (which is determined by the rules of conflict of laws), except in so far as universally recognized principles of customary international law have been incorporated into such municipal rules so as to become an ingredient thereof.[1]

---

* From *British Year Book of International Law* 1944, 11.

[1] The statement in the text is supported by numerous authors. The following remark of Sir John Fischer Williams is typical (*Chapters on Current International Law and the League of Nations*, 1929, at p. 259): 'When the debt is from State to State, we have at once a relationship within the sphere of international law . . .; where the contract from which the debt arises is between a State and a foreign individual, the matter becomes one of international law in the strict sense only if and when the State of the individual makes his cause its own and addresses itself diplomatically to the contracting State.' Or see the Arbitral Tribunal France–Chile, Award of 5 July 1901, in Descamps–Renault, *Recueil* (1901), 370: 'Les rapports entre l'Etat emprunteur et les particuliers preneurs de l'emprunt . . . relèvent exclusivement du droit privé et ne peuvent en aucun cas tomber sous l'empire des règles du droit de gens qui régissent les rapports juridiques des Etats entre eux . . . et non pas les rapports contractuels formés entre un Etat et un particulier.'

Second, municipal tribunals are bound to apply municipal law, whether domestic or foreign; they have no authority to enforce an international right or duty, since the underlying transaction is needs 'governed by other laws than those which municipal courts administer'.[1] On the other hand, it is open to international tribunals to have resort to such legal conceptions of private law as express general principles.[2]

Whatever the theoretical or jurisprudential justification of these distinctions may be, modern economic and social developments have resulted in blurring them to an appreciable extent and in blending the two branches of law. These tendencies have produced the effect, among others,[3] that, on the one hand, there are what *prima facie* appear to be transactions under municipal law which are based upon and determined by inter-state arrangements and that, on the other hand, there are inter-state arrangements, *prima facie* governed by public international law, which are 'commercialized', i.e. to use for the moment a neutral description, brought under the influence of some municipal system of law. This tendency is shown nowhere more clearly than by a variety of international financial transactions, chiefly of the inter-war period.

It is one of the objects of the following observations to submit that, taking cognizance of these developments, both municipal and international tribunals should, in certain cases, be guided by considerations which may tentatively be formulated as follows:

It is not impossible that transactions between national persons are, at least partially, governed by those supra-national principles of law which are the tools of public international law, and that transactions between international persons are governed by a national system of law. A problem of the choice of law is involved; it is the intention of the parties that determines the 'proper law' of the contract in the sense of the branch of law applicable to it.

If it were the only purpose of this paper to make these sug-

---

[1] *Secretary of State* v. *Kamachee Boye Sahaba* (1859), 13 Moo. P. C. C. 22, 75, per Lord Kingsdown; Lord Halsbury L. C. in *Cook* v. *Sprigg*, [1899] A. C. 572, 578.

[2] See Art. 38 of the Statute of the Permanent Court of International Justice; Lauterpacht, *Private Law Sources and Analogies of International Law* (1927); and the literature collected in Oppenheim (–Lauterpacht) (5th ed.) i.22.

[3] See Friedmann, *B.Y.I.L.* (1938), p. 118.

gestions of a somewhat academic character, they would perhaps not at present merit publication, having regard to the further refinements and subtleties with which they would seem to overburden a topic already bristling with difficulties. Their justification lies in the hope that they may contribute not only to the elucidation of the particular field of the law of international finance which, but for some studies of great value,[1] has received only scant attention from international lawyers[2] and to which the present writer hopes to revert in a more comprehensive manner at a later date, but also to the development of that general body of international law of the future which will have to 'embrace economic and social as well as political matters'.[3] Writing on 'International Law and International Financial Obligations arising from Contract', Sir John Fischer Williams remarked twenty years ago[4]: "The task of the international lawyer in this field is not so much to build up a law of contract ... as a law of international execution and bankruptcy.' Today this view would appear to be too narrow. At a time when suggestions for the international organization of currency, banking, food, aviation, and so forth are being authoritatively discussed, the realization of such plans clearly requires, *inter alia*,[5] an international law of contract. But if a review of some aspects of the present position would do no more than to bring home prevalent shortcomings and to indicate the directions in which reform is necessary, its wider purpose would be achieved.

One of these directions should perhaps be mentioned at once. None of the problems touched upon in the following remarks would arise if draftsmen availed themselves of the remedy which is at their disposal, viz. to make express provision for the law applicable to the transactions which they are called upon

---

[1] Particularly the various lectures by Sir John Fischer Williams collected in *Chapters*, pp. 257–419; also Hague Academy, 34 *Recueil des Cours* (1930), p. 81; Borchard, *Proc. American Soc. Int. Law* (1932), p. 134.

[2] The available literature is largely of a descriptive character and concentrates on what is called state bankruptcy and execution.

[3] Report on the 'Future of International Law', 27 *Grot. Soc.* (1942), p. 291.

[4] *Chapters*, p. 262.

[5] See Jenks, 'Some Legal Aspects of the Financing of International Institutions', 28 *Grot. Soc.* (1943), p. 87; Friedmann, 'International Public Corporations', *Modern Law Review* vi (1943), 185.

to bring into legal shape. But it is only in exceptional cases that such provision has been made. Since one must exclude as an explanation the draftsmen's desire to keep their fellow lawyers busy, this phenomenon remains mystifying. The present writer would have no regrets if he contributed to its burial.

## II

The legal character of debts of States to foreign individuals has of late become fairly clear inasmuch as all attempts[1] to regard them otherwise than as contractual obligations in the sense of private law have failed. It is no longer possible to say that the obligation of the debtor State is binding not in law, but in honour only[2]; that it is a 'public' debt, not only in the sense of a State's internal financial administration or constitutional law, but also in the sense of a debt subject to mere administrative discretion[3]; that its recognition or non-recognition no less than its creation is an act of unfettered sovereignty.[4] These views were derived partly from a confusion of the constitutional power or authority of making contracts and the duty of fulfilling them, when validly made,[5] partly from a misunderstanding of the true nature and significance of sovereignty, and partly from an exaggeration of the impact of the fact that, unless they waive their rights, States are immune from the jurisdiction of courts other than their own and that some[6] States are not even subject to the jurisdiction of their own courts. In a memorable

---

[1] The most important among them is connected with the name of Dr. Luis Drago, then Foreign Minister of the Argentine Republic, and the doctrine which he propounded in his Note of 29 December 1902 to the United States of America and, subsequently, in several articles. See the literature collected in Oppenheim (–Lauterpacht), i.253, n. 3, and the criticism by Fischer Williams, *Chapters*, pp. 272 sqq.

[2] This view, which was already rejected by Grotius, Book II, ch. 14, s. vi, was expressed *obiter* by Sir G. Jessel M.R. in *Twycross* v. *Dreyfus*, (1877) 5 Ch. D. 605, 616, and by many writers, particularly v. Bar, *Private International Law* (trans. Gillespie) (1892), p. 112; Politis, *Les Emprunts d'état en droit international* (1894). And see the writers quoted by Borchard, op. cit., p. 144, n. 20.

[3] See Borchard, op. cit., also Jèze, Hague Academy, 7 *Recueil des Cours* (1925), 174.

[4] This was the essence of Drago's doctrine.

[5] This point is rightly stressed by Strupp, 'L'Intervention en matière financière', Hague Academy, 8 *Recueil des Cours* (1925), 1, at p. 64.

[6] But by no means all of them. In pre-Nazi Germany, e.g., the contracts of the Government were 'civil disputes' in respect of which the courts had unrestricted jurisdiction.

decision which is both influenced[1] by and highly important for public international law, the Supreme Court of the United States of America said[2]: 'But the right to make binding obligations is a competence attaching to sovereignty.[3] ... The fact that the United States may not be sued without its consent is a matter of procedure which does not affect the legal and binding character of its contracts.' There are in fact many recent decisions in which the highest courts of various countries have recognized the binding quality of the State's debt to foreign creditors[4]; and it is on this basis that public international law will have to put a State's foreign indebtedness when it comes to deal with such matters as are its primary concern, viz. State responsibility, intervention, execution, financial control.[5]

Nor is it helpful to distinguish between State debts in general and bonds of public debt in particular[6] or to say the latter

---

[1] The sentence quoted in the text is supported by a reference to Oppenheim (4th ed.) i, sections 493, 494. The Court points out that international engagements are not without legal force even though there may be no judicial procedure by which they could be enforced.

[2] *Perry* v. *United States*, 294 U. S. 330, 353, 354 (1934), per Chief Justice Hughes.

[3] It is remarkable how similar the language of the Permanent Court of International Justice was in *The S.S. Wimbledon* (Series A, No. 1, at p. 25); 'But the right of entering into international engagements is an attribute of State Sovereignty.'

[4] *England: International Trustee for the Protection of Bondholders A.G.* v. *The King*, [1937] A. C. 500; *France:* Cass. Civ., 31 May 1932, *Rev. Crit.* (1934), 909 (Etat Français *c.* Carathéodory); *Sweden:* Supreme Court, 30 January 1937, *B.Y.I.L.* (1937), 215, and 36 *Bulletin de l'Institut Juridique* (1937), *Norway:* 8 December 1937, 38 *Bulletin de l'Institut Juridique* (1939), 71; *Austria:* 26 November 1935, 9 *Zeitschrift für ausländisches und internationales Privatrecht* (1935), 891; 10 July 1936, ibidem 11 (1937), 269; *Switzerland:* Court of Appeal at Bâle, 29 November 1935, 34 *Bulletin de l'Institut Juridique International* (1936), 322 (*obiter*); *Morocco:* Trib. Mixte at Tangier, 18 May 1935, *Rev. Crit.* (1936), 131. As to *Germany* see Supreme Court, 14 April 1932, *RGZ* 137, 1 (not an international case). Strupp, Hague Academy, 8 *Recueil des Cours* (1925), 1, 61 sqq., recognizes the contractually binding character of the State debt, but concedes to the State 'le pouvoir de modifier ce contrat par la voie législative' (p. 65), provided that the modification is not arbitrary—an untenable suggestion. The private-law character is also accepted by Sack, *Les Effets des Transformations des Etats sur leurs Dettes Publiques* (1922), pp. 30–6, and by a growing number of modern authors: see Borchard, *Proc. American Soc. Int. Law* (1932), 145, n. 21. It is noteworthy that the contracts of the Soviet Trade Delegations were everywhere subject to the local law: see, e.g. German-Soviet Treaty, 10 October 1925, (*RGBl.* (1926 ii) 14), Art. 3; Franco-Soviet Treaty, 11 January 1934 (*Rev. Crit.* (1934), 521), Art. 6.

[5] See the literature referred to by Oppenheim (–Lauterpacht), i.278, n. 1 (on Responsibility); p. 255, n. 3 (on Intervention and Control); and Strupp, Hague Academy, 8 *Recueil des cours* (1925), 1.

[6] This distinction, originally suggested by Drago, is strongly emphasized by

type of transaction that it is of 'a mixed private and public nature', 'that it is not purely an international contract, for this could be concluded only by States and not by a State and the subjects of another State', but that it is 'by its nature under the protection of international law and is what Bluntschli called a quasi-international contract'.[1] Such descriptions in reality explain, not the legal character of a State contract, but diplomatic practice relating to its international protection which, it would appear, is very largely discretionary and hardly lends itself to the rigour of legal principles.

If, then, a State debt to foreigners is a contract within the accepted meaning of municipal law, the question arises of determining its 'proper law'. It is generally recognized that, although a State debt is in the usual case 'charged on and issued out of'[2] the State's public funds, it may be subject to a law other than that of the debtor State[3]; the only controversy is to what extent the personality of the debtor raises a presumption in favour of its own legal system.[4] The law governing a State debt as well as that governing any other debt is the law of a specific country which is determined by the express or implied intentions of the parties.[5]

---

Borchard, *The Diplomatic Protection of Citizens Abroad* (1928), pp. 284 sqq., but is rejected by Hall, *International Law*, p. 334; Hyde, *International Law*, i.560; Eagleton, *The Responsibility of States* (1928), pp. 176 sqq.

[1] Borchard, op. cit., pp. 302 sqq., 304, 305. It has not been possible to identify Borchard's reference to Bluntschli, *Das Moderne Völkerrecht der Civilisierten Staaten*, (3rd ed, 1878), sections 433 (b), 442. The French editions of 1870 and 1895 under the title *Le Droit International Codifié* do not appear to contain a statement supporting Borchard's statement. Schmitthoff, 'The International Government Loan', 20 *Journal of Comparative Legislation* (3rd Series, 1937), 179, asserts that the international government loan is a contract of a peculiar character which cannot be classified under any existing category. This is of little positive value.

[2] This is the phrase usually employed in British legislation authorizing the issue of bonds or guarantees; see, e.g. Austrian Loan Guarantee Act, 1933, section 1, and many similar statutes.

[3] See the decisions mentioned above, p. 183, n. 4.

[4] The existence of the presumption is asserted by the Permanent Court of International Justice in the *Case of Serbian and Brazilian Loans* (Series A, Nos. 14 and 15), at pp. 42, 121, and German Supreme Court, 14 November 1929, *RGZ* 126, 196.

[5] That the proper law of a contract is determined by the parties is an indisputable doctrine which is firmly established in this country (see, e.g. *International Trustee for the Protection of Bondholders A.G.* v. *The King*, [1937] A. C. 500, 529, per Lord Atkin) as well as abroad (see Haudek, *Die Bedeutung des Parteiwillens im Internationalen Privatrecht* (1931), or Mann, *B.Y.I.L.* (1937), 97, and the cases and litera-

It was the traditional method of localizing a transaction which lawyers employed when they came to deal with certain State contracts which, owing to their origin, character, and object, presented new and somewhat revolutionary aspects. If the British Government's issue of $5\frac{1}{2}$ per cent Gold Dollar Bonds of 1917 which had to be considered by the House of Lords in *The King* v. *International Trustee for the Protection of Bondholders A.G.*,[1] is being compared with such transactions as a number of loans issued under the auspices of the League of Nations,[2] the German External Loan 1924 (Dawes Loan)[3] or the German Government International $5\frac{1}{2}$ per cent Loan 1930 (Young Loan), it becomes evident that the latter type of transaction involves features making it clearly distinguishable from the well-known and orthodox structure on which the British issue of 1917 was built. In fact these circumstances are such as to justify the question whether they necessitate something other than the traditional approach and its concomitant attempt of determining a territorial 'seat' or, in other words, of localization. The import of this question is impressively shown by the Young Loan which may conveniently be selected for more detailed discussion.

ture there mentioned). It is, however, to some extent doubtful whether the parties' freedom of choice is subject to any restrictions; see below, p. 190, n. 2. All the formulations of the doctrine express the necessity for submitting the contract to the law of a particular country.

  [1] [1937] A. C. 500.
  [2] Particulars of the bonds issued by Austria, Hungary, Greece, Danzig, Bulgaria, and Esthonia are published in the Annual Reports of the League Loans Committee (London) and of the Council of Foreign Bondholders. The Austrian Government Guaranteed Loan, 1923–43, made in pursuance of the Agreement of 4 October 1922 (Cmd. 1765), and authorized by section 2 of the Trade Facilities and Loans Guarantee Act, 1923, and the Austrian Government Guaranteed Conversion Loan, 1934–59, made for the conversion of the old issue in pursuance of the Protocol of 15 July 1932, and authorized by the Austrian Loan Guarantee Act of 1933, section 1, are particularly interesting from a legal point of view. They involve both the appointment of Trustees and State Guarantees and seem to have influenced in many respects the International Convention on Financial Assistance signed at Geneva on 2 October 1930 (Cmd. 3906, and Hudson, *International Legislation*, v, No. 270). The original loan led to an opinion by the Austrian Supreme Court (26 November 1935, 9 *Zeitschrift für ausländisches und internationales Privatrecht* (1935), 891), which is discussed by Plesch and Domke, *Die Oesterreichische Völkerbundsanleihe* (1936); Pirotte, 34 *Bulletin de l'Institut Juridique International* (1936), 7. The Austrian International Federal Loan of 1930 led to a decision of the Austrian Supreme Court of 10 July 1936, mentioned at p. 183, n. 4.
  [3] Issued in accordance with the 'Reports of the Expert Commmittees appointed by the Reparation Commission' (1924), Cmd. 2105.

The German Government International 5½ per cent Loan
1930 originated in the following circumstances: In its report
published in June 1929[1] the Young Committee recommended
that Germany be permitted to discharge its reparation debt
by certain annuities which were to be partly unconditional
and non-postponable, and partly postponable, and of which
the former were later fixed at RM 612,000,000.[2] It was one of
the essential features of the plan that it provided 'for the conversion of the reparation debt from a political to a commercial
obligation'[3] and aimed at assimilating that debt 'as closely as
possible to an ordinary commercial obligation("commercialization")'[4] so as to remove it 'from the sphere of inter-Governmental relations'.[5] This object was to be achieved by the
formation of the Bank for International Settlements. The Hague
Conference accepted these recommendations.[6] The decision to
form the Bank was carried into effect by an agreement with
Switzerland[7] to which the Constituent Charter was annexed and
in pursuance of which the Bank was incorporated in Switzerland; it is therefore fairly evident that the Bank cannot be regarded as an international person, but is a Swiss Corporation.[8]
Under a Trust Agreement (Contrat de Mandat, Treuhand-
vertrag) settled at The Hague[9] the Bank was appointed the
Creditor Governments' 'joint and sole trustee to receive,
manage and distribute the annuities' which were to be 'employed and distributed' as laid down in the Agreement 'on the
understanding that the obligations of the Trustee in regard to
the said sums shall be only those normally incumbent upon a
banker for the execution of a trust agreement'.[10] Consequently,

---

[1] Cmd. 3343.

[2] Art. VII of Annex I to the Hague Protocol of 31 August 1929. The text of the
Hague Agreements is published in Cmd. 3764 and in Hudson, *International Legislation*, v.

[3] Ibid., p. 5.     [4] Ibid., p. 28.     [5] Ibid., p. 7.

[6] Clause 2 of the Hague Protocol of 31 August 1929; Agreement of 20 January
1930.

[7] Convention respecting the Bank for International Settlements of 20 January
1930.

[8] Gutzwiller, *Mitteilungen der Deutschen Gesellschaft für Völkerrecht* (1933), 116;
Martin Wolff, *Internationales Privatrecht* (1933), p. 73, n. 27; Hudson, *A.J.I.L.* (1930),
561; Schwarzenberger, *Die Internationalen Banken* (1932), 51 sqq.; *contra* Schlüter,
*Die Bank für Internationalen Zahlungsausgleich* (1932), 380 sqq., 400.

[9] Annex VIII to the Agreement of 20 January 1930.

[10] Preamble and Art. IV of the Trust Agreement.

the German Government handed to the Bank a Debt Certificate containing 'a solemn engagement' to pay the annuities to the Bank.[1]

The Young Committee, however, in this respect following the example of the Dawes Committee of 1924,[2] also envisaged the 'mobilization' of portions of the unconditional annuities,[3] i.e. the device 'of raising money by the issue to the public of Bonds representing the Capitalization' of those portions. Accordingly the Hague Agreement included a Mobilization Agreement[4] promising Germany facilities for the issue on the international markets of reparation bonds of a total amount of 300 million dollars and providing for such operations to be 'carried out through the Bank for International Settlements'. This agreement was amplified by a further Agreement signed in Paris on 10 June 1930[5] in which the terms of the General Bond submitted by the Bank for International Settlements were approved by the Creditor Governments; this bond which was attached to the Paris Agreement became part, and was printed on the back of, the Definitive Bonds issued later in nine European countries on the basis of a prospectus advertised on 12 June 1930.[6] It contained the German Government's acknowledgment that it was indebted to the Bank in the total amount of the loan (Art. VII), and its undertaking to pay the service moneys 'in accordance with the provisions of the Hague Agreements' to the Bank (Art. IX) and also a covenant to pay principal and interest to the Bondholders (Art. VII). The Bond included a well-defined gold-clause,[7] but while, in the event of a divergence, the English text was made to prevail (Art. III), there was no clause dealing with the law applicable to the Bond or the question of jurisdiction.[8]

[1] Annex III to the Agreement of 20 January 1930.

[2] Cmd. 2105.    [3] Cmd. 3343, p. 28.

[4] Arrangement as to the mobilization of the German annuities.

[5] Hudson, *International Legislation*, v, No. 261.

[6] The prospectus advertised in *The Times* and other national newspapers of 12 June 1930, is very instructive. It stated that the issue was made with the approval of H.M. Government under the Hague Agreements of 20 January 1930.

[7] Art. VI, sub-clause (f) gives the Bank for International Settlements wide powers of interpretation. The full text of the General Bond, which is a document of fascinating interest, is published in Hudson, *International Legislation*, v, pp. 575 sqq.

[8] When in 1932 the Powers met at Lausanne 'with the firm intention of helping to create a new order', they put a complete end to German Reparations: Agree-

Of the numerous interesting and important legal (as well as political and financial) problems to which this Bond gives rise, a few had to be decided by the Swiss courts.[1] Notwithstanding the fact that in September 1931 Sweden went off the Gold Standard, the Reich continued until the end of 1932 to pay interest on the Swedish tranche of the loan at the gold rate. In May 1933, however, i.e. after Hitler's accession to power, the Reich notified the Bank that in future it would pay interest on the English, American, and Swedish branches of the loan at the nominal value,[2] and it adhered to this attitude in spite of the Bank's protest.[3] When the service moneys were received by the

---

ment of 9 July 1932, Cmd. 4126; Hudson, *International Legislation*, vi, No. 311. In the absence of ratification this Agreement never came into force. According to Art. VII is was without prejudice to the rights of the bondholders of the Young Loan, but it also provided that any necessary adaptation of the machinery relating to the Reich's obligations in respect of the Young Loan was a matter for mutual agreement between the Reich and the Bank for International Settlements. It is very difficult to see how the Bank could have entered into such arrangements so as to bind the bondholders.

[1] Civil Court at Bâle, 20 April 1935, 33 *Bulletin de l'Institut Juridique International* (1935), 148; Court of Appeal at Bâle, 29 November 1935, 34 ibidem (1936), 322; Federal Tribunal, 26 May 1936, 62 *BGE* (1936), ii.140; *Rev. Crit.* (1937), 138.

[2] On 8 May 1933, the Reich's Minister of Finance wrote to the Bank referring to English judgments which, notwithstanding the presence of a gold clause, permitted payment at the nominal value. These probably were the decisions of Farwell J and of the Court of Appeal in *Feist* v. *Société Intercommunale Belge d'Electricité*, [1933] Ch. 684, rendered on 27 October 1932 and 17 March 1933, respectively. They were reversed on 15 December 1933 by the House of Lords: [1934] A. C. 161. When the court of first instance at Bâle pronounced judgment the Reich's argument had therefore collapsed. In so far as can be seen from the Reich's letters published in the Swiss reports, they do not contain any hint of the reprisal theory mentioned in the Federal Tribunal's judgment and indicated below.

[3] It would be very interesting to know why the Bank felt entitled to refrain from further action of the kind indicated in the text below. The Reich defaulted in respect of the payments due both under the General Bond and under the Hague Agreements (which served as security under Art. IX of the Bond). The Bank's reply to the Reich of 18 May 1933 gives the impression that it intended to claim against the Reich only 'in the event of bondholders claiming damages from the Trustee on account of alleged breaches of its duties resulting from the General Bond'. The attitude subsequently adopted by the Bank appears from its Annual Reports. As from 1 July 1934 the Reich failed to make any payments to the Bank at all, but it made certain special arrangements with various Governments which, according to its 8th Annual Report (pp. 109, 110) the Bank 'considered as incompatible with the General Bond and the international agreements relating thereto'. The special arrangements with this country are contained in the Anglo-German Transfer Agreement, 1934 (Cmd. 4640), Art. 2, the Anglo-German Payments Agreement, 1935 (Cmd. 4963), Art. 7, and the Anglo-German Transfer Agreement, 1938 (Cmd. 5788), Art. 2. It was expressly provided that, without prejudice to the rights of holders, coupons would be purchased on the basis of the nominal value and not on a gold basis.

Bank, it allocated them to the seven tranches according to the nominal value, so that the holders of bonds denominated in currencies which had depreciated received less in terms of gold than those holders whose bonds were denominated in such currencies as at the time were still on a gold basis. The plaintiffs, holders of bonds of the Swedish tranche, brought an action for damages against the Bank, alleging that the payments received by the Bank ought to have been distributed equally among all the holders. There was little substance in this claim and the dismissal of the action would appear to have been inevitable.[1] The really interesting point lies in the line of reasoning adopted by the courts. They were faced with the problem of defining the duties of a 'trustee' of a most special character. In the traditional manner they set out to discover the law governing the Bank's obligations. They held that, since there was no express stipulation in the bond and since both the place of performance and the Bank's domicile were in Switzerland, Swiss law applied, and the Court of Appeal at Bâle added that according to Swiss rules of classification even the German Government's obligations were subject to Swiss law. According to Swiss law, which does not include a law of trusts and trustees, the Bank's duties arose under a contract which the Federal Tribunal described as a tripartite agreement *sui generis* and the effect of which was to be exclusively determined by the terms of the bond. The Federal Tribunal continued that the bondholders had direct rights of action against the Reich and that the Bank was not 'sole debtor',[2] but mere intermediary between the bondholders as creditors and the Reich as debtor and, at the same time, representative of the bondholders. On this basis it

---

[1] If the Bank had acted in the manner contended for by the plaintiffs it would have violated the principle of equality and exposed itself to a claim by the holders of bonds denominated in currencies still on a gold standard. The Bank's defence made this point, but also made others which make astonishing reading. It said that by protesting it had done the 'only proper and possible' thing. *Sed quaere.* It also said that Art. VI (f) gave it an 'absolute discretion' and that 'without considerable limitation of its responsibility . . . it would, in view of the obscure legal situation, not have accepted the office of trustee'—an office, let it be remembered, for which the Bank was formed.

[2] This passage suggests that the Courts had great difficulty in appreciating the conception of a trust. There is a clear confusion between the debt of the Reich towards both the bondholders and the Bank under the General Bond and the debt of the Bank towards the bondholders in respect of the amount paid by the Reich and available for distribution.

was concluded that the Bank could disregard the Reich's instructions only if 'they constituted an absolutely unjustifiable violation of the contract'. While the Tribunal regarded the Reich's attitude as irreconcilable with the terms of the bond, it inferred from the Reich's arguments that

from the point of view of public international law a reprisal against those States was involved, which, having abandoned the gold standard, have injured the interests of German subjects by their failure to fulfil obligations subject to a gold clause. The defendant was not called upon to decide whether the Reich had such right of reprisal or whether the non-observation of the terms of the contract was justifiable from the point of view of public international law. . . . It sufficed for the defendant that the Reich's point of view was not manifestly untenable. . . . Since it expressly reserved the rights of the bondholders against the Reich, it is impossible to say that it has broken the duties imposed upon it by the contract of loan towards the bondholders.

This decision, which certainly cannot be counted among the outstanding achievements of that august Court, proves the hopelessness of the attempt to press a highly unusual transaction into forms not made to fit it. It would have been equally inappropriate in conformity with the defendants' argument to apply 'Anglo-Saxon' law.[1] No careful reader of the General Bond will find it difficult to think of rules of English law which it would be unreasonable to apply to this instrument.

In these circumstances it is suggested that the formula according to which a contract is to be localized in a particular country is too narrow. It is the *legal system* to which a contract is subject. This legal system may be chosen by the parties. It is disputed to what extent the parties' freedom of choice is restricted. But whether it is *mala fides*, unreasonableness or lack of actual connection that invalidates their decision,[2] if one

---

[1] The Courts pointed out that no such law existed.

[2] According to the Privy Council in *Vita Food Products Inc.* v. *Unus Shipping Co. Ltd.*, [1939] A. C. 277, 290, the parties may select any legal system, provided the selection is made bona fide. The opinion, delivered by Lord Wright, has been attacked by Cheshire and Morris, 56 *L.Q.R.* (1940), 320, and discussed by Gutteridge, 55 *L.Q.R.* (1939), 323; Falconbridge, 18 *Canadian Bar Review* (1940), 77; Kahn-Freund, 3 *Mod. L.R.* (1939), 61, and others. On the various tests which have been suggested, see Martin Wolff, *Juridical Review* (1937), 110; Mann, *B.Y.I.L.* (1937), 98, 99. To a large extent the prevailing conflict of opinions lacks reality. No case has become known in which the parties' selection was held to be *mala fide*, unreasonable or arbitrary. For the purposes of the argument in the text the question need not be discussed at length.

party to a contract is an international person, particularly a State, there exists *ipso facto* a sufficient connection with supranational rules of law which, on any view of the proper law theory, may enable and justify the parties to de-localize their contract and to submit it to what may be called public international law, i.e. to internationalize it. They may do this in order to make applicable the provisions of a treaty giving rise to their transaction or those general principles of law recognized by civilized nations with which publicists are conversant and which, though by no means fixed or easy to ascertain, are yet not so vague as to render a submission to them void for uncertainty. Such general principles as are referred to in Art. 38 of the Statute of the Permanent Court of International Justice will largely be private law to be ascertained on a broad comparative basis or to be deduced from the law of the particular group of countries with which the transaction is predominantly connected (Common Law, Latin Codifications, etc.) or even from the legal system of a particular country; but the law so found will have to be interpreted with such liberality and freedom as is allowed to an international court which is not compelled to 'apply' foreign law in the strict sense and is, therefore, not bound by strict rules of construction, precedents, or similar peculiarities. If the conception of a trust or trustee is to be analysed it would thus be possible to have resort to 'Anglo-Saxon' principles (as opposed to technicalities), although neither English nor American law would 'apply' to the clauses in question or would even have to be considered in other respects.

But the parties to a State contract may also refer to rules of strict public international law. Thus it is a principle of public international law that no State can rely on its own legislation to limit the scope of its international obligations.[1] A State contract which, according to the intention of the parties, is internationalized, may include a contractual adoption of that principle. It would be *nihil ad rem* to argue that its invocation is open only to persons who are subjects of international law; for that principle of public international law would apply, not *ex lege*, but *ex contractu*. In State bonds it has become usual to

---

[1] See, e.g. P.C.I.J., *Case concerning the Free Zones of Upper Savoy and the District of Gex (Series A)*, No. 24, p. 12.

provide that payments shall be made without deduction for taxes imposed by the debtor State and that payments shall be made in time of war as well as of peace and no matter whether the bondholders are subjects of a State friendly or hostile to the debtor State.[1] The difficulties to which such provisions obviously give rise if the bond is subjected to the law of a particular country or even to the law of the debtor State, are overcome by the internationalization of the contract. Such a view would ensure, generally, that municipal legislation, for instance, the abrogation of gold clauses or similar enactments, could not interfere with the terms of a contract which has international character; for a municipal court there would be only one restriction, viz. the public order of the forum. It would thus be possible to restrict the effect of that 'absurdity' which, in an all too little known decision, the Supreme Court of the United States exposed; it held that, in view of Art. I, section 10 of the Constitution preventing a State from 'impairing the obligation of contract', a city could not so use its taxing power as to deduct taxes from the interest payable on its bonds:

The truth is, States and cities, when they borrow money and contract to repay it with interest, are not acting as sovereignties. They come down to the level of ordinary individuals. . . . Hence, instead of there being in the undertaking of a State or city to pay, a reservation of a sovereign right to withhold payment, the contract should be regarded as an assurance that such a right will not be exercised. A promise to pay, with a reserved right to deny or change the effect of the promise, is an absurdity.[2]

---

[1] These clauses are to be found in many State bonds issued in recent years: Young Loan (General Bond, Art. XVI); Austrian Government Guaranteed Conversion Loan, 1934–59, particularly Art. XX of the General Bond; Agreement between Roumania and J. Henry Schröder & Co. Ltd. of 4 July 1928, 2 *Zeitschrift für ausländisches öffentliches Recht und Völkerrecht* (1931 ii), p. 322; French Loan mentioned below, p. 193, n. 2; and others. Such provisions raise many difficult problems of law which have not yet been investigated. Could the British Government which has guaranteed payments to enemy holders of the Austrian Loan, rely on the Trading with the Enemy Act? It is submitted that the answer should be in the negative, for this among other reasons that the British guarantee is subject to public international law. Even if this is not accepted, the clause derives its validity from section 1 of the Austrian Loan Guarantee Act, 1933, which authorized the Treasury to guarantee 'in such manner as they think fit', and is not superseded by the Trading with the Enemy Act, 1939.

[2] *Murray* v. *Charleston*, 96 U. S. 432, 445, (1877), per Mr. Justice Strong, Miller and Hunt JJ. dissenting on the ground that the contract was made subject to the power of taxation. Vattel, *The Law of Nations*, Book II, sections 214, 216, seems to equiparate State contracts with treaties made between sovereigns, and says the rights of the creditors of a State are 'indefeasible'.

There exist a few instances of State contracts which, though *prima facie* subject to municipal law, have been submitted by the parties to international law rather than to the law of a particular country. The 5 per cent 1932 and 1937 Bonds of the Czecho-slovak Republic guaranteed by the French Government and concluded with French bankers contain the following clause[1]:

Any disputes which may arise as to the interpretation or execution of the present provisions shall be subject to the jurisdiction of the Permanent Court of International Justice at The Hague acting in execution of Art. 14 of the Covenant of the League of Nations. The Czecho-Slovak State undertakes to lay such disputes before the Permanent Court of International Justice whose jurisdiction it accepts.

The contract of loan entered into between Dutch bankers and the French Government in 1934 provides[2]:

L'Etat Français accepte de soumettre tous différends auxquels le présent Bon de Trésor donnerait lieu à la juridiction de la Cour Permanente de Justice Internationale de la Haye.

According to generally recognized principles[3] the submission to the jurisdiction of a specific court implies the submission to the law of such court. The above clauses, therefore, would appear to contain an almost express reference to the law which Art. 38 of its statute enjoins the Permanent Court to apply.[4]

It is this law which, it is suggested with diffidence, a municipal court should and can apply when dealing with an internationalized contract of a State.

In the absence of an express reference a State contract should be regarded as internationalized, if it is so rooted in international

---

[1] *Report of the Committee for the Study of International Loan Contracts*, League of Nations Publications (Economic and Financial, 1939, II, A 10), p. 39.

[2] 30 *Bulletin de l'Institut Juridique International* (1934), 279. The Bon du Trésor provides for payment 'nonobstant toute disposition législative ou réglementaire éventuelle'.

[3] See, e.g., Dicey (–Keith), *Conflict of Laws* (5th ed.), pp. 667 sqq., or Batiffol, *Les Conflits de lois en matière de contrats* (Paris, 1938), sections 149 sqq. See recently Lord Wright in *Vita Food Products Inc.* v. *Unus Shipping Co. Ltd.*, [1939] A. C. 277, 280.

[4] The Trust Agreement between the Creditor Governments and the Bank for International Settlements (p. 186, n. 10), the interpretation and application of which was subject to the jurisdiction of the special Tribunal provided for in the Hague Agreement of January 1930, would also have to be regarded as an international contract, although the bank is a Swiss corporation. It would be impossible to find a localized system of law to which it could be subject. In the result, Schlüter, *Die Bank für Internationalen Zahlungsausgleich* (1932), p. 400, is of the same opinion.

law as to render it impossible to assume that the parties intended to be governed by a national system of law.[1] The Young Loan is a prominent example of such implied internationalization. It contains no reference to the law governing it—an omission which in a document of this type is hardly accidental. It resulted from the Hague agreements between the Creditor Governments and Germany to which the General Bond makes frequent reference. Its legal shape was determined or at least approved by the Powers. It has, as a superficial perusal of the bond discloses, no special connection with any of the nine countries participating in the issue.[2] Its lay-out is supranational rather than municipal. This becomes particularly clear, if regard is had to the fact (entirely disregarded by the Swiss Federal Tribunal) that the service moneys which the Reich acknowledged to owe both to the bondholders and the Bank for International Settlements are 'secured' by the Reich's undertaking (Art. IX) to pay them in equal monthly instalments to the Bank 'in accordance with the provisions of the Hague Agreement', two-thirds of such payments operating to discharge not only the debt under the bond, but also the unconditional annuities payable in substitution for the former reparations. Suppose the bondholders brought an action for damages against the Bank on the ground that it had failed to enforce the gold clause or any other of the Reich's liabilities. They would have to prove the Bank's duty to proceed, the remedies which would have been open to the Bank, and their success. They could allege not only the possibility of suing the Reich in its own courts or in the courts of any country where, under Art. 281 of the Treaty of Versailles, Germany has waived her immunity, but also, under Art. IX of the bond, the possibility of invoking the special Arbitral Tribunal set up under the Hague Agreements.[3] In such an action a Swiss Court would have to decide what result that Arbitral Tribunal would probably have reached. For this purpose public international law would undoubtedly have to be considered. There is no reason why a municipal court which may thus consider inter-

---

[1] At present these cases are, of course, exceptional. It is by no means intended to lay down any hard-and-fast rule or anything in the nature of a presumption.

[2] That the English text prevails (Art. III of the General Bond) is, of course, in no way decisive, though not irrelevant.

[3] Agreement of 20 January 1930, Art. 15 and Annex XII.

national law incidentally, should not also apply it directly so as to secure the submission of a single and indivisible instrument under a single legal system.

These suggestions[1] are made in full knowledge both of their tentative nature and of the necessity for further investigation and elaboration.[2] They are made with an equally clear realization of the fact that the developments which have been alluded to and which may come to be regarded as the kernel of much wider schemes of the future, involve a new departure requiring new methods. The intention of the parties, though often overworked, has long been known as one of the vehicles that connect old and new ideas. Although in the end it will lose its force and attraction as a doctrinal explanation, it has often proved to be, and may again become, a useful stepping stone at the beginning.

## III

The conception of inter-State transactions primarily calls to mind those legal relations between States which, as Professor Lauterpacht[3] has put it, have 'their roots in the ordinary and public functions of the State's imperium' and, accordingly, create 'rights and duties of States as political entities endowed with attributes of government' so that they represent, 'not a case of

---

[1] It may be of interest to remind the reader that, in a special and limited sense, a doctrine of a 'contrat international' emerged in France. According to J. Donnedieu de Vabres, *L'Evolution de la Jurisprudence Française en Matière de Conflit des Lois* (1938), pp. 553 sqq., 561, these tendencies prove 'qu'il y a une activité économique internationale échappant à la souveraineté des législateurs particuliers et revêtue d'un statut juridique propre, irréductible au simple concours des lois internes en conflit'.

[2] Four main points will have to be distinguished: (1) Can contracts be internationalized in the sense discussed in the text? (2) What type of contract may be so internationalized? The text only deals with State contracts. It is very doubtful whether and to what extent contracts between two private persons could be internationalized. (3) What are the consequences of partial or total internationalization, particularly in connection with the principle of State sovereignty? (4) What are the circumstances in which internationalization may be implied? In order to avoid misunderstanding it should also be made clear that we are not concerned with mere 'incorporation' in the sense mentioned by Lord Wright in *Vita Food Products Inc.* v. *Unus Shipping Co. Ltd.*, [1939] A. C. 277, 291, 399, or by Dicey (–Keith), *Conflict of Laws*, (5th ed.), p. 45, n. r, or by Mann, *B.Y.I.L.* (1937), 101. The 'incorporation' of public international law into a private law contract would, of course, be possible, but its effects would be very different from those discussed in the text.

[3] *Private Law Sources and Analogies of International Law* (1927), p. 4.

*meum* and *tuum* in the judicial but in the political sense'.[1] Such relations spring from treaties (in the narrow and, perhaps, popular sense of the word) made between States as sovereignties in respect of matters about which no person other than a sovereign State can contract. These transactions are clearly subject to public international law. They are not amenable to municipal jurisdiction on the principle that 'wherever sovereign nations have contracted upon sovereign matters, the effect is a species of obligation *ex quo non oritur actio*'.[2] They are of no interest to the following discussion except in so far as it is necessary to emphasize the two points of contact which they may have with private law. Conceptions or rules of private law may serve as a source, or analogy, of public international law applicable to the interpretation of the treaty.[3] Moreover, such treaties may refer to municipal law by that process which is known as incorporation,[4] reception,[5] or *renvoi*.[6] Nationality, taxation, currency, and many similar matters belong to municipal law and are, therefore, broadly speaking, subject to independent and unfettered regulation by a State. If and in so far as a treaty of the type in question refers to such aspects of a municipal system of law, there is, again broadly speaking, no longer room for the application of that fundamental principle of public international law according to which a State cannot, by the exercise of its legislative power, modify its international engagements.[7] Consequently, to paraphrase a dictum of Mr. Justice Cardozo,[8] such treaties, when dealing with a subject-matter which lies within the control of municipal law, have a 'congenital infirmity'. Thus, if a treaty makes provision for the nationals of a country, that country's law determines the per-

---

[1] *Cherokee Nation* v. *Georgia*, (1831) 5 Peters 1, 28, 29, per Mr. Justice Johnson.

[2] *Nabob of the Carnatic* v. *East India Co.* (1791), 1 Ves. Jr. 370, at pp. 389, 390, per Lord Thurlow; similarly same case, (1793), 2 Ves. Jr. 56, at p. 59, per Chief Baron Eyre. These decisions were referred to with approval in the American case quoted in n. 1, above.

[3] This is the theme of Lauterpacht's book mentioned above, p. 195, n. 3.

[4] Dicey (–Keith), *Conflict of Laws* (5th ed.), p. 45, n. r; see above, p. 195, n. 2.

[5] This is the expression used by Triepel, 'Völkerrecht und Landesrecht' (1899), and 'Les Rapports entre le Droit Interne et le Droit International', Hague Academy, 1 *Recueil des cours* (1923), 77 sqq.

[6] This expression is used but criticized by Kaufmann, Hague Academy, 54 *Recueil des cours* (1935), 447.

[7] See above, p. 191, n. 1.

[8] *Holyoke Water Power Co.* v. *American Writing Co.*, 300 U. S. 324 (1936).

sons who are or are not nationals. Or if a treaty provides for the payment of a certain sum of money expressed in the currency of a particular country, it is the national law of that country that fixes the value of the currency; this means that the principle of nominalism[1] controls in the sphere of public international law no less than in private law. But if a gold clause is added, this probably does not involve the incorporation of municipal law,[2] so that municipal legislation cannot affect it.[3] Difficult problems of classification and construction arise in connection with delimiting the extent of the incorporation of municipal law into treaties, but they are of a somewhat exceptional character and do not impair the general rule that treaties in the narrow sense of the word are exclusively subject to public international law.

With the political treaty, 'actus ... regis qua regis ad (quem) civiles leges non pertinent', already Grotius[4] contrasted another type of inter-State transactions: 'quod si tales sint actus qui a rege sed ut a quovis alio fiant, etiam civiles leges in eo valebunt'. It is indeed widely admitted[5] (though often ig-

---

[1] See generally, Mann, *The Legal Aspect of Money* (1938), pp. 59 sqq. The existence of the nominalistic principle in public international law requires further investigation which must have regard to the legal nature and effect of incorporation and to such decisions as *Murray* v. *Charleston*, 96 U. S. 432 (1877), above, p. 192, n. .2

[2] Serious questions of the type indicated in the following sentence are involved. The problem arose in acute form in connection with the Panama Canal Treaty between the United States of America and Panama of 18 November 1903 (Martens, *Nouveau Recueil Général* (Série 2), (1904 xxxi), 599), which provided for the payment to Panama of an annuity of $250,000 in gold coin of the United States. Relying on the Joint Resolution the United States at first refused to pay in gold, but subsequently abandoned this point of view by the Convention of 2 March 1936 (*A.J.I.L.* (Supplement) (1940), 139). See Wolsey, *A.J.I.L.* (1937), 300.

[3] In recent years a practice has arisen according to which treaties do not only contain a gold clause, but refer to and define an imaginary unit of currency: see, e.g., Art. 29 of the Universal Postal Convention of 20 March 1934 (Hudson, *International Legislation*, vi, No. 367) and many other treaties defining the franc as 'the gold franc of 100 centimes of a weight of 10/31 of a gramme and of a fineness of ·900'.

[4] *De Jure Belli ac Pacis* (1625), Book II, ch. 14, section vi.

[5] See the authorities mentioned below, p. 204, n. 1, and, in addition, Hold–Ferneck, *Lehrbuch des Völkerrechts* (1930) i.16; ii.8, 157; Feilchenfeld, *Public Debts and State Succession* (1931), p. 650. Some writers, however, maintain that all agreements between States are governed by public international law: Von Bar, *Private International Law* (trans. Gillespie, 1892), pp. 1122, 1123; De Louter, *Droit International Public* (1920), i.468; Hatschek, *An Outline of International Law* (trans. Manning, 1930), p. 164; Jèze, Hague Academy, 53 *Recueil des cours* (1935), 381, 383; Sir John Fischer Williams, *Chapters*, p. 259.

nored) that there are contracts made between States which may be and, perhaps, often are subject to private law determined by the ordinary rules of private international law[1] and which are, accordingly, amenable to the jurisdiction of municipal courts. The growth of State activities in the commercial and industrial field makes it a matter of daily occurrence that States and their administrative departments contract with each other in a manner which in no way differs from that prevailing between private persons or government-controlled companies. As a Swiss author has said,[2] from the legal point of view it is essentially immaterial whether Switzerland (where railways are state-owned) sells locomotives to a French railway company or to Germany (where railways are also state-owned). This group of inter-State contracts comprises such transactions as the sale of goods, the sale or leasing of land, loans, chartering a ship, issuing a bill of lading, and so forth. No case, however, seems to have come before the courts which involved litigation between modern sovereign States, and it is even difficult to find texts of inter-State agreements which are clearly subject to private law.[3] Perhaps the most significant instance is furnished by the Agreement of 9 August 1919, by which Great Britain made a loan of £2,000,000 to Persia.[4]

In these circumstances the problem arises of defining the legal nature of such inter-State transactions as cannot readily be classified either as political treaties or as commercial contracts, or, in other words, of delimiting the boundaries between both categories. The intermediary class which necessitates serious consideration of this problem is very large and includes, in particular, agreements for the sale of war supplies, the

---

[1] Lauterpacht, *Private Law Sources and Analogies*, p. 5, while admitting that there may be inter-State transactions subject to private law, doubts whether the law to be applied is the municipal law of a particular country or 'a universal private law, a kind of modern *jus gentium* based on comparative jurisprudence'.

[2] Ruck, *Staatliches und Überstaatliches Handelsrecht, Festgabe für Carl Wieland* (Bâle, 1934), 320, 329.

[3] Lauterpacht, op. cit. and p. 184, mentions the treaty between Columbia and Venezuela of 20 July 1925, League of Nations Treaty Series, xxxix.15, and the Treaty between Italy and Czechoslovakia, ibidem, xxxii.251.

[4] State Papers, 112, 761; see also the agreement between Netherlands and Germany of 11 May 1920, State Papers 113, 1060, whereby Holland extended a credit of Fls. 200,000,000 to Germany, and Germany undertook to deliver coal, '*force majeure* always excepted'.

acquisition of sites for battle monuments, the settlement of war debts, the division of booty, the joint construction of a tunnel or railway, and similar transactions originating from activities *regis qua regis*.

To a large extent the tests which have been suggested in the past coincide with those applied in certain continental countries for the purpose of qualifying the principle of State immunity in foreign courts.[1] Where the personal status of the defendant is held to be insufficient to secure immunity, the form of the transaction or its nature or the capacity in which the defendant State acted has been relied upon to decide whether the business was done *jure imperii* so as to guarantee immunity. All these tests, singly and in combination, recur in connection with the question under discussion. Decisive weight is being attached to the form of the transaction—was it concluded as a treaty or as a contract?[2]; to its nature—was it done *in commercio*[3] or in the exercise of and with reference to sovereign rights?[4]; to the functions assumed by the contracting States—did they act as sovereigns or as *fisci*?[5] A peculiar, but unfortunate, distinction was sug-

---

[1] For references, see Oppenheim (–Lauterpacht), i.222, n. 4; Van Praag, *Revue de Droit International et de Législation Comparée* (1934), 652; (1935), 100; Stoupnitzky, ibidem (1936), 801; Niboyet, 43 *Revue Générale de Droit International Public* (1936), 525; Brookfield, *Journal of Comparative Legislation* (3rd series) (1938 xx), 1; Fox, *A.J.I.L.* (1941), 632.

[2] Chailley, *Traités Internationaux*, *Répertoire du Droit International* (Supplément, 1934), No. 10.

[3] See the very interesting remarks of Lord Shaw of Dunfermline in *Food Controller v. Cork*, [1923] A. C. 647, 667, 668 (although they do not relate to inter-State contracts).

[4] This seems to be the view of Heilborn, *Handbuch des Völkerrechts* (1912), i.14. Although the important decision of the French Cour de Cassation of 31 May 1932 in Etat Français *c.* Carathéodory (*Rev. Crit.* (1934), 909, with note by Niboyet) relates to a contract between a State and a foreign private person, it should be mentioned here, since it submits to private law contracts which 'tant par leur nature que par la forme en laquelle ils ont été passés rentrent dans la catégorie des conventions de droit privé', and since it qualifies a transaction as a private law lease if 'ce bail n'a procédé en rien d'un acte d'autorité de l'Etat Français, assimilable à la réquisition au séquestre ou à toute autre mesure consécutive à l'état de guerre; qu'il ne relève pas que le bail ait contenu aucune stipulation dérogatoire au droit commun et de nature à lui imprimer un autre caractère que celui d'un véritable contrat civil'.

[5] This seems to be the predominant view. See e.g., Bluntschli, *Le Droit International Codifié* (Paris, 1895), section 442 (note); Triepel, Hague Academy, 1

gested by the *Harvard Research on the Law of Treaties*[1] which defines a treaty within the meaning of the Draft Convention as a 'formal instrument of agreement by which two or more States establish or seek to establish a relation *under international law* between themselves'; the italicized words which are meant to exclude State contracts governed by municipal law contain no more than a begging of the question, and the *Comment*'s conclusion does not make the matter clearer; it requires of a treaty that the 'obligation assumed is one between States, the engagement is recorded in a formal instrument and is governed by the rules of international rather than those of the municipal law of any party'.[2]

The available literature, however, seems to have overlooked some judicial pronouncements which, in so far as the law of this country is concerned, have in a large measure disposed of the matter without undue emphasis upon fine distinctions of formulation rather than substance. All the cases arose out of Indian events, the earlier ones resulting from the double character of the East India Company as a British corporation and a sovereign State. They proceeded on the basis of the familiar principle that a treaty between sovereigns 'is not a subject of private, municipal jurisdiction'[3] or, to put it in a less procedural way, that 'the transactions of independent States between each other are governed by other laws than those which municipal courts administer; such courts have neither the means of deciding what is right nor the power of enforcing any decision which they may make'.[4] In order to justify the jurisdiction of the courts and the application of municipal law, therefore, the plaintiffs alleged that the transaction did not fall within the principle, since it involved not a treaty or an act of State, but a commercial contract. In *Nabob of the Carnatic* v.

---

Recueil des cours (1923), 101; Liszt (–Fleischmann), *Völkerrecht*, (12th ed., 1925), p. 238, with further references and interesting material; Anzilotti, *Cours de Droit International* (1929), pp. 53 sqq., 341 sqq.; Lauterpacht, *Private Law Sources and Analogies*, p. 4; Ruck (above, p. 198, n. 2), p. 329; see also the P.C.I.J. in the *Case Concerning the Serbian and Brazilian Loans* (Series A), Nos. 14 and 15, p. 41: 'Any contract which is not a contract between States in their capacity as subjects of international law is based on the municipal law of some country.'

[1] Supplement to the *A.J.I.L.* (1935), Part III, Draft Convention, Art. 1.
[2] Ibidem, pp. 693 sqq., 695.
[3] *Nabob of the Carnatic* v. *East India Company* (1793), 2 Ves. Jr. 56, 59.
[4] *Secretary of State* v. *Kamachee Boye Sahaba* (1859), 13 Moo. P. C. C. 22, 75.

*East India Co.* the facts were as follows: the plantiff, being indebted to the defendants, assigned to them by way of security certain districts of the Carnatic the revenues of which they were to receive and account for. By a later agreement the plantiff was restored to his territories and the receipt of the revenues. By his bill the plaintiff alleged that the defendants had received moneys in excess of their debt, and claimed an account. While the first decision, rendered by Lord Thurlow on demurrer, turned mainly on questions of pleading,[1] at the trial Chief Baron Eyre said[2] (though he was not called upon to give a full judgment) that the transaction arose out of a treaty entered into with the defendants 'not as subjects, but as a treaty between two sovereigns' and that therefore the dismissal of the action would have been inevitable.

The next case is *The Ex-Rajah of Coorg* v. *The East India Co.*[3] The Ex-Rajah had advanced money to the defendants and held their promissory notes for an aggregate amount of 857,840 rupees and interest. In 1834 the defendants declared war against the Rajah and seized his property except the notes which, being in the possession of his agents, could not be seized, but subsequently came into the defendants' possession. The Ex-Rajah claimed payment of the amount of the notes. The problem before the Court was so concisely stated by Sir John Romilly that the material part of his judgment should be set out in full[4]:

The principal difficulty that I have felt in this case has arisen from the double character filled by the defendants, the East India Company. They were both a company of merchants trading to the East Indies, and a sovereign power, and so far as the Rajah of Coorg was concerned, a sovereign State wholly independent and at war with him. From hence it follows that the acts done by the defendants are frequently of an ambiguous character and that it becomes extremely difficult to ascertain whether any particular act is to be attributed to the exercise of the political power of a sovereign State, or to the functions of a company of merchants trading to the East Indies. If this case can be fairly represented to be an instance of a foreign power taking prisoner a private individual who is an enemy, and while so holding him, obtaining possession of documents which established his right to recover a debt due to him in his private capacity, then I am clear

---

[1] *Nabob of the Carnatic* v. *East India Co.* (1791), 1 Ves. Jr. 370.

[2] See above, p. 200, note 3. See also *Moodolay* v. *Morton and East India Co.* (1785), 1 B. C. C. 468, which, though the plaintiffs were not sovereigns, is of some interest.

[3] (1860), 29 Beav. 300.          [4] pp. 308, 309.

that the plaintiff is entitled to relief, and that the circumstance that the defendants constitute both the conquering power and the debtor, does not in any respect vary the position. But if the notes were the property of the plaintiff in his character of Rajah of Coorg and if they were taken possession of by the defendants in the exercise of their sovereign and political power, then I am equally clear that this Court cannot interfere.

The learned Master of the Rolls was satisfied that the notes belonged to the plaintiff 'in his character of Rajah of Coorg and not in any private character apart from such office', that they were 'part of the jura regalia', and that they were taken possession of by an act which had 'no mercantile character', but which was done in the exercise of the defendants' sovereign and political power.

The last and most significant case on the question is the decision of the Privy Council in *Secretary of State* v. *Sardar Rustam Khan*.[1] In 1903 an agreement was made between the Khan of Kalat and an agent to the Governor-General in Baluchistan, which was confirmed by the Viceroy and Governor-General in Council and provided that in consideration of certain rents the Khan of Kalat 'makes over and cedes in perpetuity to the British Government the entire management of the Nasirabad Niabat absolutely and with all the rights and privileges, State or personal, as well as full and exclusive revenue, civil and criminal jurisdiction, and all other powers of administration, including all rights to levy dues and tolls'. In 1906 the Government of India decided that there should be a settlement of the territory. For this purpose the lands were divided into three classes, one of which 'was to be entered as government unoccupied lands'. The plaintiffs claimed certain of these lands on the ground that they were comprised in their grants from the Khan of Kalat and that, therefore, the Government had no title to them. The Government's defence was that the treaty of 1903 gave them full sovereign rights over the territory, and that their acts done under the treaty were acts of State for which they could not be impleaded. Lord Atkin, who delivered the opinion of the Board, agreed that it was necessary to define the juristic effect of the treaty[2]:

According to the plaintiffs, it was merely what their counsel styled a 'commercial contract' intended only to effect a more convenient method of

_____

[1] [1941] A. C. 356.    [2] At p. 368.

collecting revenue and granting powers only for that object. Their Lordships cannot take this view. It is opposed to the plain wording of the
document and to the obvious construction when the treaty is regarded as a
whole.

It is not necessary to review in detail Lord Atkin's reasoning
or to refer at length to a considerable number[1] of other Indian
decisions the essence of which is similar, though they did not
arise out of contractual relations between two sovereigns, but
involved the allegation that the plaintiff sovereign's property
held by the defendants had been taken by them under colour
of legal title in trust for the plaintiff rather than by way of seizure, i.e. an act of State. Enough has been said to show, firstly,
that the courts have admitted the possibility of an inter-State
transaction being a commercial contract subject to municipal
law and amenable to municipal jurisdiction, and, secondly,
that no single test has been evolved to distinguish the two
categories. The nature of the transaction, the capacity in which
the parties acted, the wording and contents of the agreement
have been relied upon to determine its character.

It is thus perhaps permissible to suggest that, provided acts
are in question which have clearly no 'political' aspect or, to use
the words of Grotius, which 'a rege sed ut a quovis alio fiant',
it is in reality the intention of the parties that determines the
application of private law or of public international law. In the
absence of express stipulation that intention is to be deduced
by methods similar to those employed by the private international lawyer who ascertains the 'proper law' of a contract:
it depends on all the material circumstances of the case. Very
clear evidence will have to be required before it can be assumed that sovereign States have contracted on the basis of
private law,[2] particularly if it is remembered that by forming
companies and doing their business through them States can

---

[1] *Secretary of State* v. *Kamachee Boye Sahaba* (1859), 13 Moo., P. C. C. 22; *Salaman* v.
*Secretary of State*, [1906] 1 K. B. 613; *Secretary of State* v. *Bai Rajbai* (1915) L. R.
42, Indian Appeals 229; *Vajesingji Joravarsingji* v. *Secretary of State* (1924) L. R. 51,
Indian Appeals 357.

[2] It should not be objected that the idea of sovereignty will usually prevent
States from contracting on the basis of private law. States are known to submit
readily to a legal system other than their own when contracting with private
persons (above, p. 183, n. 4); there is no reason why greater doctrinairism should
be imputed to them when they contract with their equals about commercial
matters.

so easily clarify their intention of securing the control of private law. On the other hand, it would probably not be justified to speak of a presumption that public international law applies.[1]

It is against this theoretical background that the grave legal problems should be viewed which are involved in certain aspects of the settlement of the war debts incurred between 1914 and 1918; they merit closer attention than they have so far received or can be given within the ambit of this paper.

By the British-American Agreement of 18 and 19 June 1923 which had been negotiated by Mr. Baldwin and is often referred to as the Baldwin Settlement,[2] Great Britain's indebtedness, agreed at $4,600,000,000, was to be funded into bonds. It was intended to issue to the United States, 1,000 bonds of $4,600,000 each, which, at the request of the United States, were to be exchanged for marketable obligations. The form of bond exhibited to the Agreement is, as Sir John Fischer Williams has remarked,[3] 'in the style commonly adopted in lawyers' offices in London and New York for private "business" arrangements':

GOVERNMENT OF THE UNITED KINGDOM 62 YEAR 3–3½ PER CENT GOLD BOND.

The Government of the United Kingdom, hereinafter called Great Britain, for value received, promises to pay to the United States of America, hereinafter called the United States, or order, on . . . the sum of $4,600,000. . . . All payments on account of principal and/or interest shall be made at the Treasury of the United States in Washington or, at the option of the Secretary of the Treasury of the United States, at the Federal Reserve Bank of New York. This bond is payable as to both principal and interest in gold coin of the United States of America of the present standard of weight and fineness or . . .

The principal and interest of this bond shall be exempt from all British taxation, present or future, so long as it is in the beneficial ownership of the

---

[1] Cf. Triepel, Hague Academy, 1 *Recueil des cours* (1923), 77, 102, 103: 'les normes d'un droit privé interne déterminé sont applicable à des traités internationaux au cas seulement où les Etats ont indiqué ce droit par un accord spécial, soit en y renvoyant expressément, soit en faisant connaître, par des actes concluants, que ceci ou cela devra être apprécié d'après les règles d'un droit civil déterminé'. The suggestion made in the text is supported by H. Kraus, Hague Academy, *Recueil des cours*, 50 (1934 iv), 327.

[2] Cmd. 1912; State Papers 126 (1927 i), 307. The full text of the agreement is reproduced by Sir John Fischer Williams, *Chapters*, pp. 361 sqq.

[3] op. cit., p. 348.

United States or of a person, firm, association or corporation neither resident
nor ordinarily resident in the United Kingdom.

. . .

This bond is issued by Great Britain pursuant to the Proposal, dated the
18th day of June, 1923, and to the Acceptance of Proposal, dated the 19th
day of June, 1923.

In Witness Whereof etc.

The same form of Agreement was adopted by the United States
for the earlier settlement with Finland and the thirteen further
settlements made over a period of three years.[1] In a standardized
manner they set out the terms as to principal, interest, method
of payment, marketing, notices, and so forth, and exhibited the
form of bonds issued by the debtor State to the United States.
These bonds, however, which are of predominant interest for
present purposes, disclose a number of variations. Some of them
are of minor importance,[2] but the significance of one of them
may be considerable. The last clause of the Finnish bond reads:

This bond is issued under an Agreement dated May 1, 1923, between
Finland and the United States to which this bond is subject and to which
reference is made for a further statement of its terms and conditions.

Substantially the same wording is to be found in the thirteen
later bonds.

[1] *Finland:* 1 May 1923; *Hungary:* 25 April 1924; *Lithuania:* 22 September 1924;
*Poland:* 14 November 1924; *Belgium:* 18 August 1925; *Latvia:* 24 September 1925;
*Czechoslovakia:* 13 October 1925; *Estonia:* 28 October 1925; *Italy:* 14 November
1925; *Roumania:* 4 December 1925; *France:* 29 April 1926; *Yugoslavia:* 3 May 1926;
*Germany:* concluded in pursuance of the Hague Conferences, 1929 and 1930, see
the German publication, *Entwürfe zu den Gesetzen über die Haager Konferenz*, Part IV.
All the above agreements, with the exception of the German agreement, are
published by H. G. Moulton and L. Pasvolski, *World War Debt Settlements* (New
York, 1926), pp. 241–374. The French settlement is also reproduced in State
Papers 127 (1927 ii), 511, and Lucien Petit, *Le Règlement des Dettes Inter-Alliées*
(1919–22) (Paris, 1932), p. 671. For the Italian and Lithuanian settlements see
also Martens, *Nouveau Recueil Général* (3e Série) (1932 xxv), 30 and (1934 xxix),
658, respectively. For the Polish settlement see also Lucien Petit, op. cit., p. 561,
who on p. 539 reproduces a 'certificat de dette' as issued by France to the United
States during the war. Already that certificate contained an undertaking to pay
'aux Etats-Unis d'Amérique ou à leurs ayants droit'.

[2] Exemption from taxation was extended to such beneficial owners of the bond
as were corporations not organized under the laws of the debtor State. The words
'for a further statement of its terms and conditions' in the clause of the Finnish
bond mentioned in the text were omitted from the Belgian and all following bonds.
The Roumanian, Italian, French, and Yugoslavian bonds read 'to which Agreement' instead of merely 'to which' in the last clause mentioned in the text. There
are other variations of the clause dealing with payment which need not be indicated in detail.

The Agreements which Great Britain concluded with eleven debtor States[1] closely followed the American pattern, although as to four of them this statement is only in the nature of a guess, since their text does not seem to have been published. Moreover, all the Agreements, except that with France, contain forms of a bond. The bond given by Estonia is as follows:

> The Government of the Republic of Estonia, for value received, promises to pay to the Government of Great Britain or order on the . . . the sum of . . . pounds sterling.
>
> This bond is payable in pounds sterling at the Bank of England in London.
>
> This bond will be paid without deduction for and will be exempt from any and all tax and/or charge, present and future, imposed by authority of the Government of Estonia or its possessions or by any political or taxing authority within the Republic of Estonia.

In the case of Roumania the wording of the bond was different:

> The Government of the Kingdom of Roumania, for value received, promises to pay to the Government of His Britannic Majesty or order on the . . . the sum of . . . pounds sterling at the Bank of England in London.
>
> The payment due under this bond shall be exempt from all Roumanian taxation, present or future, so long as it is in the beneficial ownership of His Britannic Majesty's Government or of a person, firm, association, or corporation neither domiciled nor ordinarily resident in Roumania.
>
> This bond is issued by the Government of the Kingdom of Roumania pursuant to the agreement of the 19th October, 1925, for the funding of the Roumanian war debt to Great Britain.

The bonds issued by Italy, Portugal, Greece, and Yugoslavia were *mutatis mutandis* in identical terms except that the second paragraph was worded more shortly:

> . . .
> The payment due under this bond shall be exempt from all Italian taxation, present or future.
> . . .

---

[1] *Poland:* 2 December 1924 (not published, but mentioned *Survey of International Affairs*, 1925 (Supplement), p. 155); *Estonia:* 24 July 1925 (Martens, *Nouveau Recueil Général* (3e Série) (1928 xviii), 169); *Latvia:* 13 August 1925 (not published, but mentioned *Survey*, ibidem); *Roumania:* 19 October 1925 (Cmd. 2990, State Papers 123 (1926 i), 562); *Czechoslovakia:* 3 November 1925 (not published, but mentioned *Survey*, ibidem); *Belgium:* 31 December 1925 (not published, but mentioned *Survey*, ibidem); *Italy:* 27 January 1926 (Cmd. 2580, State Papers 123 (1926 i), 526); *France:* 12 July 1926 (Cmd. 2692); *Portugal:* 31 December 1926 (Cmd. 2791, State Papers 123 (1926 i), 559); *Greece:* 9 April 1927 (Cmd. 2848, State Papers 126 (1927 i), 262; *Yugoslavia:* 9 August 1927 (Cmd. 2973, State Papers 126 (1927 i), 294).

It is submitted that the differences between the various types of bond which have been pointed out have a bearing upon the problem of determining the legal system to which these bonds are subject.

The bond of the American standard type, such as the Finnish bond, is probably subject to public international law. This is the legal system governing the Agreement between creditor and debtor State. The bond is expressly made subject to the terms and conditions of the principal Agreement. In case of the German bond, in particular, there is no indication in the text that any person other than the United States was contemplated to become a creditor. The consequence is that if such bonds are assigned or (where they contain an order clause) indorsed in favour of a third party and if the successor in title is a private person,[1] public international law will have to be applied not only as between the holder and the debtor State, but also as between the holder and an indorser: if the United States indorses a British bond to the Guaranty Trust Company of New York, who indorses it in favour of the Royal Bank of Canada, the latter's rights against the former are not affected by British, American, or Canadian legislation, except in so far as the public policy of the forum has to be considered; since both under the Joint Resolution of Congress of 5 June 1933, and under the Canadian Gold Clauses Act, 1937, a gold-clause obligation is declared to be contrary to public policy, neither an American nor a Canadian Court will enforce such an obligation, but an English Court could and would have to do so. The traditional view would probably lead to the conclusion that, so long as the bonds are owned by the creditor State, they are subject to public international law and that upon transfer to a private person they become subject to private law.[2] It is not a very attractive proposition to attribute such chameleon-like character to one and the same instrument. A deviation from traditional teaching is inevitable. Notwithstanding the

---

[1] This was quite clearly contemplated, as appears from the clause granting exemption from taxation.

[2] Jèze, 'Les Défaillances d'Etat', Hague Academy, 53 *Recueil des cours* (1935), 381, 383, in fact says that if a state issues bonds *and* they reach the public, they become a commercial debt subject to private law, but if the second condition is missing, they remain political debts (whatever their origin or nature) subject to public international law.

order clause and the clause dealing with taxation a uniform submission under private law seems to be excluded by the incorporation of the principal agreement. On the other hand, a uniform submission under public international law will not terrify those who believe in the possibility of 'internationalizing' a contract to which a State is a party. They will not even be deterred by the necessity for developing an international law of negotiable instruments to deal with problems to which the order clause of the bonds may give rise. They will assume this task rather than engage in the hair-splitting distinctions inevitably involved in any other method of approach.

The form of bond issued by Great Britain to the United States and signed by the majority of Great Britain's debtors, e.g. Roumania perhaps is of a different character. These bonds are not expressed to be subject to the agreements from which they result. They refer to the funding agreements in pursuance of which they are issued. This, it may be argued, is not a contractual clause, but merely a statement made *informationis causa*, viz. for the purpose of indicating the debtor government's authority for the issue. This difference between what one may call the British and the American standard type of bond presumably was intentional. The parties apparently intended to sever all connection between the instrument and its political origin. Owing to their form and phraseology, to the order clause and the tax-exemption clause which so clearly envisages a transfer to private persons, all these bonds, of whatever type, have a commercial character. Unless the funding agreements were mentioned, all the bonds might be said to be subject to municipal law and, more particularly, to the law of the creditor State.[1] This conclusion may in fact be drawn where the bonds omit to incorporate the terms and conditions of the funding agreements.

These views, put forward with much doubt and hesitation, may perhaps be more confidently expressed in regard to the Estonian bond. This makes no mention at all of the funding agreement under which it is issued. It seems to be a purely commercial document governed by English law.[2]

---

[1] The connection with the creditor country's law is established by the fact that the bonds are payable in, and are expressed in the currency of, that country.

[2] The bond probably is a promissory note the 'interpretation' of which would be

## IV

The interrelation of international and private law shown by the preceding discussion and the necessity for a revision of many an inveterate dogma are impressively demonstrated by the law of State guarantees. Within the framework of this paper no attempt can be made to treat it adequately.[1] But it entails in a singular fashion a combination of some of the features which have been alluded to above, and it is therefore fitting to devote to it a few words by way of postscript.

In its simple form a guarantee creates a tripartite relationship between creditor and debtor, creditor and guarantor, and guarantor and debtor. If both debtor and guarantor are States and if the creditor–debtor and creditor–guarantor relationship is subject to private law while the guarantor–debtor relationship is subject to public international law, there arises a curious situation in the event of the guarantor State being called upon to implement its guarantee: By way of subrogation (*cessio legis*) it acquires the creditor's claim against the debtor State. Since this claim is subject to private law and municipal courts have jurisdiction over it, the guarantor State would appear to have two entirely different rights against the debtor State, the one under private law, the other under the convention between the States, i.e. *prima facie* under public international law.

'Ceci donne à réfléchir,' said Sir John Fischer Williams of this situation, and he continued[2]:

Il paraît un peu anormal lorsqu'il s'agit d'une garantie que les droits des créanciers—des individus porteurs—soient considérés comme dépendant d'un droit (et d'un tribunal) autre que celui qui régit (ou est compétent pour juger) les rapports du gouvernement garant avec le gouvernement débiteur. Et cette anomalie s'accentue quand on se rend compte qu'au

---

subject to the law of the place where the contract is made: section 72 (2) Bills of Exchange Act, 1882. This is the place of the first delivery: sections 84, 21, 2, ibidem.

[1] See, in particular, Jèze, 'La Garantie des Emprunts Publics d'Etat', Hague Academy, 7 *Recueil des cours* (1925), 155, and the literature there referred to. For guarantees in which Great Britain participated see, e.g., the Egyptian Guarantee (Convention of 18 March 1885, State Papers 76, 348), the Greek Guarantee (Convention of March 1898 in Schedule to Greek Loan Act, 1898), the Austrian Guarantee referred to above, p. 185, n. 2.

[2] 'La Convention pour l'Assistance Financière aux Etats victimes d'aggression', Hague Academy, 34 *Recueil des cours* (1930), 81, at pp. 137, 138.

cas où le garant paie il a le droit de se faire subroger dans le droit du créancier vis-à-vis du débiteur. Ces droits, par le fait même de ce transfert, cesseraient-ils appartenir au régime national pour s'élever au domaine international?

The implications of these questions have not always been fully realized by the draftsmen of international government loans.[1] The authors of the International Convention on Financial Assistance signed at Geneva in 1930[2] seem to have thought that the elimination of a direct claim by bondholders against guarantor States, the interposition of trustees and the control of the trustees by public international law,[3] would dispose of the difficulties.[4] Sir John Fischer Williams hoped that these problems would find a practical solution, and sought a somewhat academic refuge in the monistic character of law, 'au moins pour les questions financières'.[5] Neither method is quite satisfactory. So long as a comprehensive and radical reform of this field of law remains a hope for the future, there is no alternative but to approach the problems by a realistic manipulation of available tools. It is in this spirit that an attempt has here been made to furnish an initial contribution to a practical, though by no means easy, or ideal, solution.

[1] The Austrian loan, e.g., would appear to give rise to grave problems.

[2] Cmd. 3906; Hudson, *International Legislation*, v, No. 270. The Convention has never entered into force, but is interesting as a precedent for legal machinery.

[3] The guarantor States have to pay to the trustees (Art. 18). The amounts paid by the guarantor States constitute a debt due from the borrowing government to the trustees (Art. 17 (1) (c), 20 (1)). The liabilities between governments are to be settled through the intermediary of the trustees (Art. 17 (1) (d)) who have the right to settle all questions subject to appeal by any government to the Council of the League of Nations (Art. 22 and see Art. 27) which would no doubt have the right to obtain the opinion of the Permanent Court.

[4] The Convention pays little attention to the rights of the bondholders.

[5] loc. cit., pp. 138, 139.

# IV

# THE PROPER LAW OF CONTRACTS CONCLUDED BY INTERNATIONAL PERSONS*

SOME fifteen years ago it was submitted[1] that there are, on the one hand, contracts between international persons, which are subject to a national law, and, on the other hand, contracts between international and private persons, which are subject to public international law, and that in both cases the governing legal system is determined by the express or implied intention of the parties.

The developments, both factual and legal, which have taken place since then and which have a bearing upon that thesis have been substantial. This is due mainly to the large number of international persons other than States, which have come into existence since 1944 and which enter into contracts of varying types. There have also appeared some doctrinal contributions which, whether they were critical or approving in character, have thrown fresh light upon certain aspects of that thesis, its justification, correctness and effect. Hence, although legal writers should normally consider themselves subject to the rule *ne bis in idem* and nothing is intended to derogate from its strictness, weighty extenuating circumstances may be pleaded if it is now proposed once more to review a problem of growing practical importance. The purpose will be, not to repeat, but to reconsider in the light of experience what was said earlier on contracts between international persons (below, Section I) and between international and private persons (below, Section II) and, finally, to define the problems in the light of some broader aspects of legal development (below, Section III).

---

* From *British Year Book of International Law* 1959, 34.

[1] 'The Law Governing State Contracts', above, p. 179. The present article is supplementary to the earlier one. It is a development of a recent paper by the present writer in *Jus et Lex, Festschrift für Max Gutzwiller* (Basel, 1959), p. 465, which appeared in German under the title 'Die Verträge der Völkerrechtssubjekte und die Parteiautonomie'.

# I

(1) Contracts between international persons, particularly States, are, in general, subject to public international law.

This principle which is not open to doubt implies, of course, the existence of a body of public international law capable of being applied to contractual arrangements between international persons. No international lawyer will experience any difficulty on this score. While he is conscious of the rudimentary character of international law in many respects, he will fill gaps by invoking the general principles of law recognized by civilized nations, as directed by Article 38 of the Statute of the International Court of Justice. In order to find these principles he will resort to private law on a comparative basis. It is at this point that the methodological problem raises its head: how is the process of comparison to be operated so as to lead to the ascertainment of general principles?

This question arises with particular urgency in connection with those treaties which come under the heading of the commercial law of nations and, accordingly, display the greatest degree of similarity with contracts subject to private law or concluded by private persons.[1] For international persons have everywhere gone into business. They have, on the footing of both public international and municipal law, formed corporate bodies in order to engage in banking,[2] render rivers navigable[3] or finance the supply of railway material.[4] Furthermore, on the footing of public international law, they enter into transactions

---

[1] See, generally, 'Reflections on a Commercial Law of Nations', above, p. 140.

[2] e.g., the Bank for International Settlements, a legal person created by Swiss law, and the International Bank for Reconstruction and Development, a legal person created by public international law.

[3] For a recent example see the treaty between France, the Federal Republic of Germany and Luxembourg relating to navigation on the Moselle of 27 October 1956 (BGBl (1956 ii), 1838), which provides for the formation of the Internationale Mosel-Gesellschaft m.b.H., a limited company created under German law.

[4] See the treaty between Yugoslavia and Albania of 28 November 1946 relating to the formation of an Albanian company intended to build and operate railways, United Nations Treaty Series, cxi.127. (For other treaties between these two States see ibid., pp. 95 and 115.) And see the treaty of 20 October 1955 (BGBl (1956 ii), 907), which was concluded between thirteen European States and provides for the formation of Eurofima, a limited company created under Swiss law for financing the purchase of railway equipment.

of a commercial character. A complete investigation of international practice is not yet available. A survey of British practice[1] has produced significant examples of contracts for the sale or exchange of goods, contracts for work and labour, leases, loans, and contracts for the exchange of patents and technical information. Fresh examples continue to come to light. Thus a recent treaty between the United Kingdom and Turkey[2] concerns the purchase of certain ships of the British Reserve Fleet by the Turkish Government. The treaty is said to be 'constituting an agreement between the two Governments in this matter', yet it also records the fact that 'agreement was reached in principle' only. A treaty between the United Kingdom and the Republic of the Lebanon[3] sets forth the terms on which a free loan of arms, ammunition, and equipment was made in November 1956 to the latter State, and again exemplifies the numerous legal problems which are likely to arise. What is the scope of the obligation of the borrower State to make good the cost of repairing damage to equipment 'except for fair wear and tear'? What is the precise extent of the borrower State's obligation to *replace* equipment which has been lost, seeing that the treaty provides for the setting up of an Anglo-Lebanese Commission to study the question of *compensation* for such losses? Treaties of a commercial character are, however, by no means a peculiarity of British State practice. The volumes of the *United Nations Treaty Series*, of which about three hundred have so far appeared, as well as the new series of the *United States Treaties and Other International Agreements*, contain numerous examples of such treaties to which Great Britain was not a party and which require compilation and scholarly analysis.[4]

---

[1] In addition to the treaties discussed on pp. 143 et seq. above, see treaty of 27 November 1875 relating to the purchase of shares in Suez Canal Company, printed by Hurewitz, *Diplomacy in the Near and Middle East* (1956), i.179; Loan Agreement between Great Britain and Persia of 6 August 1919, Cmd. 300 or Hurewitz, op. cit., ii.64; Agreement of 18 July 1951 between the United Kingdom and the United States of America relative to the development of the Rhodesia Railways, *United Nations Treaty Series*, cxvii.49; Agreement of 28 November 1951 between New Zealand and the United Kingdom concerning sugar supplies, ibid., cxxvii.263.

[2] Cmnd. 260.          [3] Cmnd. 518.

[4] See, for example, Convention of 2 March 1936 between the United States of America and Panama relating to the construction of the Trans-Isthmian Highway, *League of Nations Treaty Series*, c.205 with Supplemental Agreement of 31 August and 6 September 1940, *United Nations Treaty Series*, cxxiv.210; Agreement between

That there are and, indeed must be legal rules applicable to commercial treaties of this type will be obvious and is, in fact, proved by daily experience, though the number of cases capable of serving as precedents is as yet small and the number of unsolved problems of both substance and method is large. One of the few modern decisions, the significant, though in many respects highly unsatisfactory case of the *Diverted Cargoes*[1] was, within a short time, followed by another case relating to the international law of money, viz. *Switzerland* v. *Federal Republic of Germany* decided by the Arbitral Tribunal for the Agreement on German External Debts.[2] In respect of certain debts contracted by German debtors the Agreement on German External Debts signed in London on 27 February 1953[3] provides[4] that such debts 'expressed in Gold Marks or in Reichsmarks with a gold clause as have a specific foreign character shall be converted into Deutsche Mark at the rate of 1 Goldmark, or 1 Reichsmark with a gold clause = 1 Deutsche Mark'. Debts have a 'specific foreign character' if[5] it was 'expressly agreed under the original written debt arrangements that the place of payment ... is situated abroad'. A contract made in 1931 between a Swiss vendor and a German purchaser provided that payment of

the United States of America and Panama of 23 March 1940 relating to the construction of a highway between Chorrera and Rio Hato, ibid., p. 196; Agreement of 17 May, 1946 between the United States of America and Portugal relating to the supplying of Portuguese colonial sisal, ibid., cxxvi.3; Agreement of 2 July 1947 between New Zealand and France regarding the granting of credits for the purpose of financing purchases of wool and other produce of New Zealand, ibid., xvi.219; Agreement of 11 September 1946 between the United States of America and the Philippines for the sale of certain surplus war property, ibid., xliii.231; Convention of 23 December 1946 between Yugoslavia and Roumania concerning the loan of grain, ibid., cxvi.33; Loan Convention between Belgium and Netherlands of 7 September 1949 between Belgium and the Netherlands (with form of promissory note), ibid., cxvii.3; Loan Agreement of 7 September 1949 between Belgium and France (with form of promissory note), ibid., cxxiii.13; Loan Agreement of 23 March 1948 between United Nations and the United States of America, ibid., xix.43.

[1] *Revue Critique de Droit International Privé* (1956), p. 278; Int. L.R. (1955), p. 820, discussed by Simpson, 5 *I.C.L.Q.* (1956), p. 427; Simpson and Fox, *International Arbitrations* (1959), p. 135; Dach, 5 *A.J.C.L.* (1956), p. 512; Mann, above, pp. 166 et seq.; 96 *Recueil des cours* (1959 i), 101 et seq.

[2] Reports No. 1 and (in a German extract) 19 *Zeitschrift für ausländisches öffentliches Recht und Völkerrecht* (1958), p. 761, discussed by Johnson, in *B.Y.I.L.* (1958), xxxiv.363 and W. Lewald, *Neue Juristische Wochenschrift* (1959), 1017.

[3] Cmd. 8781.

[4] Annex II, Article V (3).

[5] Annex VII, section I, paragraph 2 (a).

the purchase price was to be made 'free of charge to the vendor'. The question, accordingly, arose whether these words constituted an express agreement that the place of payment was in Switzerland. The Arbitral Tribunal held by a majority (Messrs. Daehli, Michelson, Richard, Phenix, and Hinderling, Messrs. Barandon, Wolff, von Caemmerer, and Makarov dissenting) that the words 'place of payment' had their natural as opposed to their technical meaning, and signified the place where the creditor is entitled actually to receive payment, not the place at which the money is to be dispatched to the creditor or any other step preparatory to actual payment is to be taken. Although the result, derived from a comparative approach, may be said to be based on a construction of the London Agreement, it would seem to be permissible to deduce from the decision the rule that in public international law the place of payment is the place where payment is actually to be made to the creditor. For the majority assigned to the expression an independent meaning, a meaning determined by public international law. The minority took the view that the concept had to be taken from the contractual relationship between the parties, in the present case from German law according to which the place of payment was in Germany. It is not necessary for present purposes to take a position on these or other controversial aspects of the decision,[1] for it is sufficient to note the emergence of a satisfactory and acceptable rule of the commercial law of nations, according to which in public international law the place of payment is prima facie in the creditor State.[2] Nor does the pursuance of such questions fall within the scope of the argument which it is intended to submit. This merely requires proof of the existence of a branch of public international law which deals with and is capable of regulating treaties of an economic character. That that branch is in an early stage of development must be regarded as a challenge to scholars rather than a negation of its existence.

[1] The decision of the majority is open to criticism on the ground, among others, that probably there was no *express* agreement in regard to the place of payment and that, consequently, the discussion of the meaning of that term was otiose.

[2] It should be made clear that the decision is not conclusive on this point. In the first place, as mentioned above, it may be said to rest on construction of the treaty. Secondly, the treaty does not embody a commercial transaction between international persons, but has a law-making character. Yet it supports the rule mentioned in the text.

(2) Although international persons usually contract on the footing of public international law, there does not exist any legal rule which precludes them from submitting their transactions to a system of municipal law selected by them.

Until recently it was not easy to indicate treaties of an economic character by the terms of which the parties have in fact provided for the application of a system of municipal law. There is now available, however, the example provided by a number of loan agreements which the International Bank for Reconstruction and Development, an international person, in the early years of its existence concluded with several States and which invariably contained the clause[1]

The provisions of this Agreement and of the Bonds shall be interpreted in accordance with the law of the State of New York, United States, as at the time in effect.[2]

This is an express choice-of-law clause which makes the whole of the law of New York applicable to the Agreement. A different view has been suggested by three authors who belong to the Legal Department of the Bank.[3] Their observations, although not entirely clear, are apparently intended to mean that the clause contemplates merely the incorporation of New York rules of interpretation, but does not exclude the application of public international law to which reference is allegedly made by another clause reading as follows[4]:

---

[1] For examples see Article IX (2) of the Agreement of 18 August 1949 and 18 April 1950 (Loan Number 17 In and 23 In) with India, or Article IX (2) of the Loan Agreement of 6 January 1949 between the Bank and Nacional Financiera S.A., a Mexican Company, and Article VI (2) of the Agreement of Guarantee of the same date with the United States of Mexico both published in the *United Nations Treaty Series*, cliv.4, 18. The precise date when the use of the clause was discontinued is not known, but it is no longer included in the Agreement of 18 December 1952 between the Bank and the India Iron & Steel Co. Ltd. as borrower and India as guarantor (Loan Number 71 In).

[2] It is believed that the last-mentioned words are intended to refer to the time when the interpretation takes place. If they should be intended to refer to the time when the contract is made, they would, indeed, involve a case of mere incorporation, not a choice of New York law.

[3] Sommers, Broches, and Delaume, 'Conflict Avoidance in International Loans and Monetary Agreements', *Law and Contemporary Problems* (1956), pp. 463 et seq., 479. Similarly Adam, *Revue Générale de Droit International Public* (1951), pp. 41, 55, and see Broches and Boskey, *Nederlands Tijdschrift voor International Recht* (1957), pp. 159, 169. The view taken here is supported by Sereni, 96 *Recueil des cours* (1959 i), 206.

[4] This clause occurs in all agreements made by the Bank.

The rights and obligations of the Bank and the Borrower under the Loan Agreement and the Bonds shall be valid and enforceable in accordance with their terms notwithstanding the law of any State or political subdivision thereof to the contrary.

The distinction between incorporation and choice of law is, of course, a well-known and real one,[1] though to draw it accurately is frequently not an easy task. Even Scrutton L.J. thought[2] that the clause in a contract 'to be construed in accordance with English law' required only the application of English rules of construction to a contract which in all other respects was subject to the law of Palestine. But the Judicial Committee of the Privy Council consisting of Lords Atkin, Russell of Killowen, Macmillan, Wright, and Porter rejected that suggestion.[3] It described the distinction between the formula 'to be construed in accordance with English law' and the clause 'shall be governed by English law' as 'merely verbal'. Both clauses involve a choice of law, because[4]

The construction of a contract by English law involves the application to its terms of the relevant English statutes, whatever they may be, and the rules and implications of the English common law for its construction, including the rules of conflict of laws. In this sense the construing of the contract has the effect that the contract is to be governed by English law.

This reasoning, it is believed, is unanswerable and leads to the conclusion that where the contracts between the International Bank for Reconstruction and Development and a borrowing State refer to interpretation according to the law of New York they are subject to the law of New York. It follows, moreover, that the attempt to attribute overriding force to the tenor of the document by the clause 'notwithstanding the law of any State or political subdivision thereof to the contrary' was futile and ineffective. Similar attempts have often been made and always failed, because it is for the legal system chosen by the parties rather than the parties themselves to determine whether and to what

---

[1] See, for example, Dicey, *Conflicts of Laws* (7th ed., 1958), pp. 728, 729 and the English authorities there collected. For Germany see, in particular, Haudek, *Die Bedeutung des Parteiwillens im internationalen Privatrecht* (1931), pp. 37 et seq.

[2] *The Torni*, [1932] P. 78, at p. 84. In other instances the somewhat unfortunate influence of Scrutton L.J. upon public and private international law in England was not so soon rectified by a superior tribunal.

[3] *Vita Food Products* v. *Unus Shipping Co. Ltd.*, [1939] A. C. 277.

[4] At p. 298, per Lord Wright.

extent the terms of the contract are superseded by changes in the law.[1] Nor can that clause be treated as a reference to public international law, for in the face of a reference to New York law the intention to remain unaffected by any State law cannot be equiparated to the intention to submit a contract to a specific legal system such as public international law. In other words, a clause which is not a choice-of-law clause but merely expresses a negative intention cannot displace a clause which affirmatively refers to and adopts a specific system of municipal law. Nor is there, finally, any advantage to be derived from the suggestion made by a Belgian author[2] that the clause purporting to confer exclusive effect upon the terms of the contract was 'capitale', 'exclut toute application du droit interne d'un Etat quelconque ... et fait du contrat lui-même la seule loi des parties'. This is, of course, not possible, for a contract which is not subject to a specific legal system, whether it be a municipal law or international law, is inconceivable.

If, as is undeniable, international persons are at liberty to, and in fact do, submit their treaties to a system of municipal law by virtue of an express clause, such a choice of law may occur also impliedly, and it thus becomes a matter of the parties' intention whether public international law or a system of municipal law is the proper law applicable to the contract.[3]

---

[1] The problem has frequently arisen in connection with gold clauses and has invariably been dealt with in the sense put forward in the text: for references see Mann, *The Legal Aspect of Money* (2nd ed., 1953), p. 266. The point is really an obvious one and it is difficult to understand why draftsmen of important international documents continue to insist upon the insertion of clauses which cannot be effective.

[2] Jean Salmon, *Le Rôle des Organisations Internationales en matière de Prêts et d'Emprunts* (1958), p. 228. Of the clause referring to the law of New York Salmon says that it 'ne droit tromper personne. Interpréter à la lumiere d'un droit, ce n'est pas appliquer un droit.' This is one of the many observations which show that the learned author has failed to appreciate the manifold problems of public and private international law to which he alludes. See also below, p. 231.

[3] This is now accepted by Jessup, *A Modern Law of Nations* (1948), pp. 139 et seq.; Martin Wolff, *Deutsches Internationales Privatrecht* (3rd ed., 1955), p. 144, and Van Hecke, *Problèmes Juridiques des Emprunts Internationaux* (1955), pp. 29 et seq.; Sereni, 96 *Recueil des cours* (1959), ch. ii, s. 3, who, however, overrates the significance of registration. Perhaps it may be mentioned here that the question whether a document is a 'treaty' or an 'international agreement' within the meaning of Article 102 of the Charter of the United Nations and therefore requires registration has nothing to do with the problem discussed in the text. An agreement may be caught by Article 102, although it is subject to a system of municipal law. Conversely, an agreement may be subject to public international law, though it does not come

This intention is to be ascertained in the same way as private international lawyers employ, when they have to ascertain the proper law of the contract. The submission of a treaty to a municipal system of law is, however, so unusual a step that it ought not be inferred from other than the most compelling evidence.

No such evidence exists in the case of the Loan Agreement made on 23 April 1954 between the United States of America and the European Community for Coal and Steel,[1] or the supplementary Pledge Agreement made between the European Community for Coal and Steel as borrower and the Bank for International Settlements.[2] It has been said[3] that both are subject to 'droit américain'. This conclusion is being based on the fact that the Loan Agreement was concluded in the United States, that the money was raised and is to be repaid there, that dollars constitute the money of account, that the Agreement is made in the English language and that the terminology 's'en refère au droit anglo-saxon'. It is, however, obviously impossible to speak of an American or an Anglo-Saxon law of contract, neither of which exists. The place of the contract as well as the place of performance are inconclusive factors when international persons contract among themselves. Since the family of nations has no currency system of its own, no inferences can be drawn from the use of a certain national currency. For similar reasons no weight should be attached to the use of a particular language, least of all the English language. In all the circumstances it is clearly preferable to submit the Loan Agreement to public international law,[4] and the same solution

---

within the ambit of Article 102. On Article 102 see Broches and Boskey (above, p. 216, n. 3) and Lauterpacht, *Report* and *Second Report on the Law of Treaties* ( U.N. Doc. A/CN.4/63 p. 27 and A/CN.4/87, p. 10).

[1] *United States Treaties and Other International Agreements* (1954 v), Part 1, p. 525 (TIAS 2945), and Part 3, p. 2647 (TIAS 3126).

[2] ibid., Part 3, p. 2655. For further discussion of this Agreement see below, p. 235.

[3] Blondeel and Vander Eycke, *Revue de la Banque* (1955), pp. 249, 274, whose arguments recall the unfortunate decision of the Swiss Federal Tribunal referred to below, p. 234, n. 3.

[4] In the same sense Sommers, Broches, and Delaume (above, p. 216, n. 3) at p. 478; Salmon (above, p. 218, n. 2), p. 292. The latter author reaches the correct result, because for him 'l'application d'une loi locale est écartée par le fait que les deux contractants réels sont des sujets de la communauté internationale'. His reasoning thus rests on the obsolete theory that international persons cannot

should apply to the Pledge Agreement, though the latter suggestion raises different problems to the consideration of which it is now necessary to turn.

## II

(1) Contracts between an international person, on the one hand, and a natural person or a legal person created under a domestic legal system, on the other hand, are, as a rule, governed by the system of municipal law chosen by the parties.

Here again the starting-point is free from doubt. The familiar problem of the conflict of laws as to how, in the absence of an express reference, the proper law is to be found need not, for present purposes, be pursued with particularity. It is only necessary to warn against the inclination to overrate the significance of the problem whether there exists a presumption in favour of the law of the contracting international person, i.e. the State.[1] Those who, like the Permanent Court of International Justice[2] or the German Supreme Court,[3] contended in favour of such a presumption did not contemplate more than a readily rebuttable presumption. On the other hand, those who reject the presumption do not doubt that in searching for the proper law 'great weight'[4] or 'considerable weight'[5] or 'great, if not decisive, weight'[6] is to be attached to the fact that one of the contracting parties is a State. The practical difference between both methods of approach is, accordingly, likely to be small, yet the existence of a presumption must be denied, for it could be of no use in those numerous cases in which the contract is made

---

contract between themselves otherwise than on the footing of public international law. He has unfortunately failed to provide any argument in support of that theory. But see Sereni, 96 *Recueil des cours* (1959 i) 163.

[1] In the case of an international subject other than a State the presumption cannot, of course, operate.

[2] In the case of the *Serbian and Brazilian Loans* (Series A), Nos. 20/21, 42, 121, 122.

[3] 14 November 1929, *RGZ* 126, 196, at p. 206.

[4] *International Trustee for the Protection of Bondholders A.G.* v. *The King*, [1937] A. C. 500, 531 per Lord Atkin; for other decisions belonging to this group see Van Hecke, *Problèmes Juridiques des Emprunts Internationaux*, p. 71.

[5] ibid., p. 567, per Lord Maugham.

[6] *Bonython* v. *Commonwealth of Australia*, [1951] A. C. 201, at p. 221, per Lord Simonds.

with international persons who are not States and who, therefore, do not possess their own legal system.

It is perhaps more important to state that the application of
the principle has not always been satisfactory, and, although the
point may not be wholly germane to the main argument developed in these pages, its elaboration within the context of an
article on the contracts of international persons is likely to be
permissible. No criticism, it is true, can be levelled against the
line taken by Lord Simonds delivering the opinion of the Privy
Council in *Bonython* v. *Commonwealth of Australia*.[1] In that case
bonds issued by the Governor-in-Council by the authority of
the Parliament of Queensland under the Act 58 Victoria No.
32 were held to be subject to the law of Queensland. Lord
Simonds said[2]:

> As has been pointed out, the debentures were issued on the authority of a
> Queensland Act which empowered the Governor-in-Council to raise by
> way of loan not more than £2,000,000 for the public service of the Colony.
> By the same Act the loan was secured on the public revenues of the Colony,
> and was made repayable on January 1, 1946. These circumstances cannot
> but be of great, if not decisive, weight in determining what is the proper
> law of the contract.

It is, however, not easy to reconcile this decision with the view
adopted by the House of Lords in *International Trustee for the
Protection of Bondholders A. G.* v. *The King*[3]—a case which provokes
criticism also on another point. It will be remembered that it
concerned bearer bonds issued by Great Britain in New York in
1917. The issue was made in pursuance of the War Loan Act,
1916, which authorized the Treasury to contract a loan of
$250,000,000 and to repay it out of public funds. Relying on this
provision Sir William Jowitt argued[4] that it was inconceivable
that a foreign legislator such as the United States of America
could increase or, by abrogating the gold clause, reduce the
liability of the Crown. Yet it was held by the House of Lords
that the War Loan Act, 1916, was 'a domestic matter which
only concerns the authority to pay'[5] and carried no weight in
determining the proper law. The House of Lords preferred the
view that the bonds were subject to the law of New York.
It may well be that this solution could be readily defended by

---

[1] [1951] A.C. 201.       [2] p. 221.       [3] [1937] A. C. 500.
[4] p. 527.                [5] p. 532 per Lord Atkin.

the wording and form of the bonds. But the House of Lords supported it primarily by the American character of certain antecedent transactions which were not reflected in the bond. Such reasoning, it is believed, ran counter to the legal nature of a bearer bond which is a negotiable instrument, to the whole tradition of the law merchant and to the practical requirements and the experience of a sound bond market. As Nussbaum has said,[1] the law of negotiable instruments does not permit 'an interpretation vitally affecting the rights of the bondholders to be based on circumstances entirely outside the bond'. The House of Lords does not seem to have given consideration to a point which, it is submitted, carries great force and ought to have made the evidence of the earlier documents inadmissible.

(2) It is possible, however, for contracts between parties only one of whom is an international person to be subject to public international law.[2]

A reconsideration of this submission demands an inquiry into (a) its scope and effect, (b) its legal justification, (c) its illustration by an express or implied choice of law, and (d) its status in the light of the practice developed in the course of certain arbitrations.

(a) According to the theory referred to, a contract could be 'internationalized' in the sense that it would be subject to public international law *stricto sensu*; that, therefore, its existence and fate would be immune from any encroachment by a

---

[1] *Money in the Law, National and International* (1950), pp. 424–6.

[2] In the same sense Jessup, *A Modern Law of Nations* (1948), pp. 139 et seq., but especially Lord Asquith of Bishopstone as Sole Arbitrator in the matter of an arbitration between *Petroleum Development (Trucial Coast) Ltd. and the Sheikh of Abu Dhabi;* 1 *I.C.L.Q.* (1952), p. 247, at p. 251; Int. L.R. (1951), p. 144. The following observations do not in any way contemplate that doctrine which is unique to France, which is unacceptable as a principle of law and unattractive *de lege ferenda* and according to which in the event of a *paiement international* the parties are at liberty 'de convenir, même contrairement aux règles impératives de la loi interne appelée à régir leur convention, une clause valeur-or'; Cass. Civ. 21 June 1950, Clunet (1950), 1196; 24 January 1956, Clunet (1956), 1012; Trib. Com. Seine, 11 March 1957, Clunet (1958), 994 (*Messageries Maritimes*). For the time being this practice relates only to gold clauses and Goldman (Clunet (1958), 1000) goes, therefore, too far when he speaks of 'l'édifice de l'immunité financière internationale'. If that practice were extended, it would lead to the submission to public international law of contracts between private persons. Contrary to the suggestion in the text it would apply to contracts to which no State is a party; this would be an unacceptable solution. The theoretical basis too, would be entirely different from that developed here.

system of municipal law in exactly the same manner as in the case of a treaty between two international persons; but that, on the other hand, it would be caught by such rules of *jus cogens* as are embodied in public international law.

The public international law which would prevail and which the domestic judge or arbitrator having jurisdiction over the contract would apply in all matters governed by the proper law of the contract, would largely be derived from those principles of law accepted *semper ubique et ab omnibus*, which govern the treaties, particularly the 'commercial treaties', between international persons and which were shortly referred to above. This means that there is little force in the objection made by Martin Wolff[1] and others,[2] according to which the 'internationalization' of a contract could in practice not be carried out, because public international law has allegedly not yet succeeded in developing, or sufficiently developing, the necessary legal rules. Such an argument overlooks the fact that in regard to treaties between international persons, the nature and subject-matter of which frequently are not substantially different from contracts between international and private persons, those legal rules have been, or are capable of being, and, in any event, must be developed. The law which is available for application to the one type of contractual arrangement, can, without difficulty, be applied to the other group of contracts. And the material as well as the method of judicial reasoning with which an international tribunal may and, indeed, must equip itself may likewise lead the experienced judge or arbitrator of a domestic tribunal to a decision: it would be both wrong and disrespectful to suggest that the judge of a domestic tribunal has necessarily less ability in ascertaining the relevant rules of international law than the international judge. This is a conclusion which will be disapproved only by those who are not fully alive to public international law and its factual background or are inclined to underestimate its vitality and its potentiality.

Furthermore, what is being contemplated is a reference to

---

[1] *Private International Law* (2nd ed., 1950), p. 417, and 35 *Grot. Soc.* (1950), pp. 143, 150–2.

[2] Fawcett, *B.Y.I.L.* (1948), xxv.44, n. 3; Friedmann, *A.J.I.L.* (1956), pp. 483, 484, also in *Law in a Changing Society* (1959), p. 472.

public international law in the sense of a real choice of law, a reference such as, in regard to type, quality and effect, is familiar to the conflict of laws and opposed to mere incorporation (*materiellrechtliche Verweisung*).[1] Hence it is impossible, or would at any rate be inexact, to speak of the application of the general principles of law recognized by civilized nations. The general principles are not a law or a legal system that can be applied or referred to. If it was only the application of those principles that was being envisaged, then the internationalization of a contract would not be different in character from a contract which the parties have submitted, say, to Roman law or into which they have embodied the Sale of Goods Act, 1893: the parties would have done no more than to provide for the incorporation of certain rules of public international law, however far-reaching or extensive they may be, and the contract as such would remain subject to the legal system applicable to it, so that, to mention only one of many consequences, changes introduced in that legal system would affect it. One of the main purposes of a true 'internationalization' of a contract would fail in that the contract would be subject to rather than exempt from interference by its proper law. (It is, of course, necessary to guard against mere terminological sophistry. The reference to the general principles will not usually be mere incorporation, but will be tantamount to a reference to or a choice of public international law as the governing law.[2] This, however, is not necessarily so.) The fundamental distinction which it has been attempted to draw is liable to be overlooked. Lord McNair,[3] who has recently given attention to the problem of internationalization, somewhat surprisingly considers the general principles as affording, in certain cases, 'the choice of a legal system', and, indeed, describes them as a 'system of law'.[4] Yet it is hardly open to doubt that, unless they are equiparated to public international law, the general

---

[1] On these terms see above, p. 217, n. 1.

[2] See below, p. 232. It is likely that the editors of Dicey, *Conflict of Laws* (7th ed., 1958), p. 736, merely commit a terminological *lapsus* and contemplate the application of public international law, when they mention the application of the general principles of law.

[3] *B.Y.I.L.* (1957), xxxiii.1, particularly at pp. 6, 10, 19. Similarly already Fawcett, (1953), xxx.399, and Sereni, 96 *Recueil des cours* (1959), ch. iv, ss. 4 and 5.

[4] pp. 1, 19.

principles are not a legal system at all, and Lord McNair clearly refuses so to equiparate them. For he submits that the contracts he has in mind are not 'governed by public international law *stricto sensu*', but 'should be governed by the general principles of law recognized by civilized nations'. The contrast so created is one, not of terminology, but of substance, since Lord McNair explains that in his view public international law cannot apply, because 'this system is an inter-State system —*jus inter gentes*', and the contracts under discussion 'are not inter-State contracts and do not deal with inter-State relations'.[1] This argument does not, it is respectfully submitted, do justice to the nature of a genuine choice of law, a reference to a legal system. Moreover, if a choice of public international law is possible at all[2] it cannot miscarry merely by virtue of the fact that normally[3] public international law regulates relations between international persons. Swiss law is an 'inter-Swiss system' and envisages legal relations between Swiss citizens, 'inter-Swiss relations'. Yet no student of the conflict of laws would challenge the view that, if an Englishman and an Italian submit their contract to Swiss law, this legal system applies also to the contractual relations between the Englishman and the Italian by virtue of the choice of law, by virtue of the reference permitted by private international law and notwithstanding the inter-Swiss character of Swiss law. Nor is it doubtful that, for the same reason, the *jus cogens* included in either English or Italian law does not affect a contract governed by Swiss law, but that Swiss *jus cogens*, whether it is anterior or subsequent to the contract, does touch it. It follows that Lord McNair must allow the *jus cogens* of the proper law to override the general principles which are merely incorporated into it. It is thus not unlikely that his interpretation of the 'internationalization' of contracts defeats one of the very objects which that doctrine is intended to achieve, and which, it is believed, he desires to accomplish.

(*b*) The question whether and under what circumstances it is

---

[1] pp. 10, 19.      [2] On this point see section (*b*) below.

[3] This qualification would in any event be required, for the statement that public international law is only an inter-State system of law is no longer accurate.

open to an international person[1] and a private person to submit their contract to public international law relates to the
doctrine of the proper law in private international law rather
than to public international law.

According to most legal systems the principle is firmly established: it is left to the parties to choose the proper law. Whether
their choice is subject to any restrictions is being much discussed by legal writers, but none of the numerous formulae
which are designed to limit the parties' freedom of choice would
preclude the choice of public international law where a contract with an international person is in question and where,
therefore, by the nature of things a close connection with public
international law exists from the outset. The fear lest the ad-
mission of a reference to public international law might involve
political or social dangers would be justified if and only if its
unrestricted recognition, particularly as between private persons, were being advocated.

It is, moreover, true that the conflict of laws has in mind the
localization of legal relationships and that, therefore, the conflict rule normally refers to a locally defined legal system. But
this is no more than a form of words from which no dogma
should be derived. When Savigny uses the well-known metaphor
of the 'seat of a legal relation', he certainly contemplates
territorially defined systems of law. But an all too literal interpretation would not be in harmony with his genius. Von Bar's
phrase of the 'nature of the thing', Gierke's formula of the
centre of gravity, and especially Westlake's figure of the law
with which a contract has the most real connection no longer
maintain the idea of localization[2] and prove that the reference
to a legal system which is not territorially defined is fully reconcilable with the traditional doctrine of the conflict of laws.
In any event, it must be emphasized, considerations of a conceptualist character cannot be decisive. The real justification of
the possibility of 'internationalization' is provided by the requirements of international intercourse. There are cases in

---

[1] It seems likely that 'internationalization' should also be permitted where the
contract is concluded, not by the international person itself, but by one of its instrumentalities, including a State corporation.

[2] See the helpful remarks made by Martin Wolff, *Private International Law* (2nd
ed., 1950), p. 37, n. 2, p. 425, n. 1.

which no solution other than the choice of public international law is practicable. In particular, States are frequently not prepared to submit to foreign law, while private persons either refuse to submit to the law of the contracting State or would be willing to do so, but are confronted with the absence of any such law; the latter difficulty arises, for instance, in connection with certain undeveloped States of the Middle East and Africa. In such circumstances the reference to public international law is often the expedient which satisfies the factual conditions, the interests of the parties and the demands of a progressive economic policy.

Nor is the theory of the possible 'internationalization' of contracts defeated by the exception to the control of the proper law which was propounded by Dicey and according to which a contract is, in general, invalid in so far as its performance is unlawful by the law of the country where the contract is to be performed.[1] This exception might be said to be relevant in circumstances which are exemplified by the following set of facts: By a contract governed by public international law an English firm has undertaken towards the Government of Utopia to build a railway in Utopia at a price of £100 a foot. While operations are proceeding Utopia enacts legislation prohibiting the building of railways at a price exceeding £50 a foot. If Dicey's exception was good law, the contract would be discharged as a result of the supervening Utopian legislation and the contractors would be left without a cause of action, notwithstanding the submission of the contract to public international law. In other words, in many crucial cases the 'internationalization' of a contract would not afford protection against encroachments by the contracting State. In truth, however, this danger does not exist. In the first place, the exception does not seem to have support anywhere outside England and, perhaps, the Commonwealth. Secondly, however, in spite of the judicial approval frequently and emphatically, though invariably obiter, given to the exception[2] it may be confidently asserted that it does not form part of the conflict of laws at all, but is a rule of the English law of contracts, an aspect of the English doctrine

---

[1] *Conflict of Laws* (7th ed., 1958), p. 788.
[2] They are collected by Dicey, op. cit., p. 788, n. 6.

of frustration.[1] If this is correct, then the consequences of any legislation by the State in which performance takes place are to be judged exclusively by the proper law, i.e. public international law, not by that State's law, the *lex loci solutionis*. The question what effect public international law attributes to the *lex loci solutionis* lies outside the scope of this article, but admits of a short and unequivocal answer: no State can avoid its international obligations by invoking its own or, indeed, any municipal law.[2]

Finally, the 'internationalization' of contracts is by no means precluded by the dictum of the Permanent Court of International Justice,[3] according to which

any contract which is not a contract between States in their capacity as subjects of international law is based on the municipal law of some country.

The pedant may argue that the 'internationalization' of a contract is reconcilable with this dictum, because an internationalized contract is in fact based on the municipal law, viz. on the private international law of some country, and is referred by that law to public international law. A more convincing argument is to the effect that in 1929 the Permanent Court of International Justice cannot have intended, by a dictum unsupported by reasons, to negative a progressive development of the law by a doctrine of internationalization. Nor did that Court have the power of doing so. It is true that a different but all too literal effect was attributed to the Permanent Court's dictum by the Arbitrators in the dispute between *Saudi Arabia and The Arabian American Oil Company (Aramco)*, Professor Sauser-Hall, Mr. Mahmoud Hassan and Sir Aba Habarchy,[4] who stated that[5]

as the Agreement of 1933 has not been concluded between two States, but between a State and a private American corporation, it is not governed by public international law.

---

[1] This submission was first made in *B.Y.I.L.* (1937), xviii.97, 103 et seq., and has since been adopted by a number of legal writers, particularly by Cheshire, *Private International Law* (5th ed., 1957), pp. 236 et seq., and others referred to by Dicey, op. cit., p. 790, n. 11, where it is also made fairly clear that if they did not feel bound to pay lip-service to Dicey's exception his editors would delete it from a work devoted to the conflict of laws.

[2] See, for instance, *Treatment of Polish Nationals in Danzig* (1932) (Series A/B), No. 44, p. 24; *Free Zones of Upper Savoy and the District of Gex* (1932) (Series A/B), No. 46, p. 167.     [3] *Serbian Loans* (1929) (Series A), Nos. 20/21, p. 41.

[4] Int. L.R. 27, 117.     [5] p. 165.

It is, however, doubtful, how much weight can be attached to the Arbitrators' decision which is perhaps not characterized by an outstanding degree of precision or conciseness[1] and which, moreover, does seem to permit a measure of internationalization, as appears from the following sentence[2]:

> The Tribunal holds that public international law should be applied to the effects of the Concession, when objective reasons lead it to conclude that certain matters cannot be governed by any rule of the municipal law of any State, as is the case in all matters relating to transport by sea, to the sovereignty of the State on its territorial waters and to the responsibility of States for the violation of its international obligations.

Although this remark is far from clear, it may not be entirely consistent with the earlier dictum which may thus suffer a further loss of authority.

While the foregoing reasons tend to support or, at any rate, not to disprove the theory of an internationalization of contracts, they render it impossible, on the other hand, to subscribe to certain suggestions which, without consideration of the whole of the available material or of the teachings of private international lawyers, Professor Verdross recently put forward.[3] He speaks of the 'quasi-public-international contract'[4]

---

[1] When the reader has reached p. 172 and perhaps only p. 202, the real nature of the issue and its remarkable simplicity become apparent. The question was whether a Concession Agreement of 1933 conferred upon Aramco the exclusive right to transport across terrestrial and maritime frontiers of Saudi Arabia. The Arbitrators held that the answer was in the affirmative. Since they also held that ratification of Agreements by Royal Decree did not affect their 'purely contractual nature' (p. 204), it was obvious that the rights granted by the Agreement of 1933 could not be prejudiced by a later inconsistent Agreement made between Saudi Arabia and Mr. Onassis. The Award is not an international decision at all, but belongs to the group of cases referred to below, pp. 236 et seq.

[2] p. 172. The sentence states that at any rate in respect of certain matters a contract may be internationalized. But the examples given are not matters which come within the province of the proper law chosen by the parties and to 'be applied to the effects of the Concession'; on the contrary, at least two out of the three examples are matters which are of necessity subject to public international law, irrespective of it being or not being 'applied to the effects of the Concession'.

[3] 18 *Zeitschrift für ausländisches öffentliches Recht und Völkerrecht* (1958), p. 635.

[4] This expression is said to have been used by Schwarzenberger, *Internationa Law* (3rd ed., 1957), i.578. However, discussing the place of unjustified enrichment in public international law and the Award in the case of *Lena Goldfields Ltd.* (below, p. 238), Dr. Schwarzenberger says merely that the latter 'belongs in the sphere of quasi-international law'. This phrase is different from, and certainly less objectionable than, Verdross' term mentioned in the text. It may be added that, adopting accepted terminology, Dr. Schwarzenberger (pp. 146 et seq.) speaks of public contracts which, if concluded between an international person and

between a State and an alien corporation, whereby 'a specific concession granted to such a corporation is submitted to the *lex contractus* of this contract'.[1] Such contracts are said to be governed neither by the municipal law of a State nor by public international law, 'as they are not concluded between international persons'.[1] Accordingly, they constitute 'a third group of contracts, which is characterized by the fact that it subjects such private rights as the contract establishes to a new legal system created by the agreement of the parties, that is to say, to the *lex contractus* agreed by them'.[1] Such *lex contractus* 'created by a quasi-public-international contract is an independent legal system which exhaustively regulates the relations between the parties. Naturally, for the purpose of construing its provisions and of filling possible gaps the *lex contractus* may refer to the legal system of the contracting State or to the legal system of the other party *or to public international law*, but all these legal systems are applicable only in so far as they are substituted by the *lex contractus*, as this defines the parties' mutual rights and duties in a sovereign manner.'[2]

The idea that contracting parties are at liberty not only to choose the legal system applicable to their contract, but also to create their own legal system which is independent, exhaustive and sovereign and to which municipal systems of law and public international law are inferior—that idea is doctrinally so unattractive, so impracticable, so subversive of public international law, so dangerous from the point of view of legal policy and so unnecessary that its novelty will not cause surprise. It hardly requires emphasis that every legal relationship in general and every contract in particular must of necessity be governed by a system of law and is otherwise unthinkable.[3] Of course, in the words of the Code Civil,[4] 'les conventions légalement formées tiennent lieu de loi à ceux qui les ont faites';

---

foreign nationals, 'are not necessarily excluded from international law' (p. 146). Though this formulation is perhaps capable of clarification, the learned author later (pp. 147, 149) states that a public contract, while normally governed by municipal law, may be subject to international law. This is not very different from the submission repeated in the present article.

[1] p. 638.
[2] p. 641 (italics supplied).
[3] See already above, p. 218.
[4] Article 1134.

but freedom of contract does not exist independently of the legal system which grants it or confer any measure of sovereignty upon the contracting parties. Nor can contracts either in law or in fact regulate the parties' relationship exhaustively. Contracts are written against the background of a system of law, its *jus cogens*, its rules of construction and so forth. Recognizing this Professor Verdross proposes to reverse the usual order and to allow such a system of law to operate only if and in so far as the parties refer to it. In many cases, perhaps, this view will lead, in a circuitous way, to results which are identical with those reached by familiar doctrine. It remains, however, remarkable that Professor Verdross who first proclaims the dogma that contracts 'not concluded between international persons' cannot be subject to public international law considers it possible for parties to refer to public international law as a subsidiary source of law. An international lawyer, in particular, cannot give approval to a theory according to which there is any *lex* higher than, or uncontrolled by, public international law. Can the *lex contractus* created by the parties validate a contract which is not only contrary to elementary demands of a domestic *ordre public*, but also violates fundamental human rights? If Nazi Germany had granted to a Ruritanian corporation the contractual right to carry on commercially some of her opprobrious activities, would that contract really have been sovereign and could no legal system have condemned it? And why, so one asks in conclusion, should a doctrine such as that propounded by Professor Verdross be necessary? Its object can be directly and in a less radical manner achieved by the internationalization of contracts, which Professor Verdross admits only indirectly, i.e. where the *lex contractus* refers to public international law. If there is any force in the unsubstantiated dogma according to which international law cannot apply except as between international persons and which Professor Verdross seems to put forward as the only objection to internationalization as suggested here, then one would expect the indirect no less than the direct reference to public international law to be rejected.

(c) If it is open to contracting parties, one of whom is an international person, to choose public international law as the proper law of their contract, the exercise of their choice becomes a matter of their intention, whether it be express or implied.[1]

No contract could be found, which the parties in terms submitted to public international law as such (as opposed to the general principles of law). But it would seem to be legitimate to treat a clause which provides for the jurisdiction of the International Court of Justice as equivalent to such a submission. A recent example of this type of clause is, it appears, contained in the Loan Agreement which the Belgian Régie des Télégraphes et Téléphones as borrower and the Belgian State as guarantor contracted in the year 1947 with a group of Swiss bankers and which provides that all disputes 'shall be decided exclusively by the International Court of Justice in The Hague, or in default thereof by the Swiss Federal Tribunal at Lausanne'.[2] It is clear that this clause is primarily intended to deal with jurisdiction and it is in that very connection that it may lead to considerable difficulties.[3] But irrespective of the problem of jurisdiction and whichever tribunal ultimately assumes jurisdiction, the old rule *qui elegit judicem elegit jus* must be given effect, at any rate where the circumstances are so peculiar.[4]

Similarly, an express reference to public international law will usually be embodied in a clause providing for the application of the general principles of law.[5] What may be the first of such

---

[1] Rabel, *Conflict of Laws* (1950), iii.14, 15 described it as 'confusing' to believe that a contract was internationalized, delocalized, or deprived of its national character merely because one party to it was a State. No such suggestion has ever been made by anyone; it has certainly not been made by the present writer.

[2] The text does not seem to have been published. The above remarks are based on the information given by Delaume, 6 *A.J.C.L.* (1957), pp. 189, 206, who, however, hardly does justice to the clause. The Federal Tribunal has jurisdiction only, when the International Court of Justice has ceased to exist. So long as it does exist, it has sole jurisdiction. For this reason and in view of the fact that the clause determines the proper law it cannot be described as a 'sham provision'. See also the following note.

[3] As Delaume (above) rightly points out, the International Court of Justice has jurisdiction only in respect of disputes between States. A clause such as that mentioned in the text or on p. 20 of the article referred to above, p. 211, n. 1 will, therefore, have to be construed as meaning that the contracting State submits to the jurisdiction of The Hague Court and recognizes the right of the State to which the contracting private persons belong to invoke the jurisdiction of The Hague Court for the benefit or in the interest of such persons.

[4] On the other hand, the fact that the decision of disputes by a municipal tribunal must have been within the contemplation of the parties does not by any means exclude their intention to submit the contest to public international law. Only the express choice of a court usually implies the choice of the law of such court.

[5] See already above, p. 224.

clauses is to be found in the concession which Persia granted in 1933 to the Anglo-Persian Oil Co. Ltd. and which directed arbitrators to base their award 'on the juridical principles contained in Article 38 of the Statutes of the Permanent Court of International Justice'.[1] The more elaborate Article 46 included in the so-called Consortium Agreement which after the termination of the concession of 1933 was concluded with a group of international oil companies is to the same effect[2]:

> In view of the diverse nationalities of the parties to this Agreement it shall be governed by and interpreted and applied in accordance with the principles of law common to Iran and the several nations in which the other parties to this Agreement are incorporated, and in the absence of such common principles then by and in accordance with principles of law recognized by civilized nations in general, including such of those principles as may have been applied by international tribunals.

In a much-discussed concession made in 1939 the parties declared 'that they base their work in this Agreement on goodwill and sincerity of belief and on the interpretation of this Agreement in a fashion consistent with reason'. Of this clause Lord Asquith of Bishopstone as Sole Arbitrator declared[3] that it was inconsistent with the idea

> that the municipal law of any country, as such, could be appropriate. The terms of that clause invite, indeed prescribe, the application of principles

---

[1] See Article 22 (F), also Article 21 of the Concession which is printed in Cmd. 8425, p. 17 and by Hurewitz, op. cit., ii.188. It was held in the *Anglo-Iranian Oil* case, I.C.J. Reports (1952), pp. 111, 112, that the Concession was not a treaty or convention within the meaning of the declaration whereby Persia accepted the jurisdiction of the International Court of Justice. This was no doubt correct, but has nothing to do with the question discussed in the text. The Concession of 1933 led to one of the gravest injustices which the history of international law records: for reasons and in circumstances which are discussed by Johnson, in *B.Y.I.L.* (1953), xxx.152 and which can only be deplored, the arbitration clause became abortive, and in Italy and Japan the Courts failed to give redress against an obvious international tort: Court of Venice, 11 March 1953, *Foro Italiano* (1953), i.719 or Int. L.R. (1955), p. 19; Civil Court of Rome, 13 September 1954, *Foro Italiano* (1955), ii.256 or *Revue Critique* (1958), p. 519, with note by De Nova or Int. L.R. (1955), p. 23; Court of Appeal Tokyo, Int. L.R. (1953), p. 305. The reasoning of these decisions to the effect that the Persian legislation afforded adequate compensation is wholly unconvincing.

[2] The text is published by Hurewitz, op. cit., ii.346. Similarly Article 40 of the Agreement made in September 1957 between an Italian Oil Company and the National Oil Company of Iran: Wall, 7 *I.C.L.Q.* (1958), pp. 736, 739. The last-mentioned company is not an international person, but an instrumentality of the Persian State, and this is likely to be sufficient to permit internationalization: see above, p. 226, n. 1.

[3] For references see above, p. 222, n. 2.

rooted in the good sense and common practice of the generality of civilized nations—a sort of 'modern law of nations'.

This statement, which provides the most authoritative support for the doctrine of the 'internationalization' of contracts, rightly regards words of a very general character as a sufficiently clear reference to public international law.

The most frequent case of an implied reference is that of the contract of employment made by every member of the international civil service. These contracts which raise numerous problems and the detailed consideration of which would far exceed the scope of the present observations[1] are, of course, primarily subject to the staff codes or staff regulations which so many international organizations have put into force. But these codes or regulations themselves are governed, and gaps are filled, by public international law. Nothing else is or can be intended by the statement, often encountered in legal literature, but meaningless unless understood in the sense suggested here, that such employment contracts are governed by the internal law of the organization, 'le droit interne de l'organisation'.[2]

There remain numerous agreements of a financial character, the construction of which leads to the inference that they are governed by public international law.[3] Among them pride of place is due to the loan agreements made in recent years by the International Bank for Reconstruction and Development with private borrowers and guaranteed by the State to which the borrowers belong.[4] The terms of these agreements are silent about the proper law. The jurisdiction of municipal courts is

---

[1] For numerous cases on the rights and liabilities of international officials see the recent volumes of Int. L.R.

[2] This is the phrase used, for instance, by Bastid, 'Les Tribunaux Administratifs Internationaux et leur Jurisprudence', 92 *Recueil des cours* (1957), pp. 347, 471 et seq. Similarly Sereni, 96 *Recueil des cours* (1959), 143.

[3] Some of the earlier ones are referred to in the paper reprinted above, p. 179. Even today the Young-Loan (published by Hudson, *International Legislation*, v.575) is likely to be most interesting. Its interpretation by the Swiss Federal Tribunal in the decision *BGE* 62, ii.140 remains highly unsatisfactory.

[4] The view that these agreements are subject to public international law is shared by Adam (above, p. 216, n. 3), pp. 55 et seq., and Sommers, Broches, and Delaume (above, p. 216, n. 3), p. 477, though without detailed discussion. The clause set forth above, p. 216, n. 4 is of some significance in the present connection, for, although it does not contain a choice of law or a reference to public international law, in cases in which there is no such choice or reference it is one of the elements leading to the ascertainment of the parties' intention.

excluded by an arbitration clause. It cannot reasonably be held that the Bank intended to be subject to the law of the borrower's nationality or residence. It is equally unlikely that the parties intended to apply the law of the District of Columbia, as opposed to the law of New York, Canadian or English law, merely because the Bank's seat is in Washington D.C. The very fact that the proper law is not defined, that arbitration is provided for and that every loan to a private borrower is supplemented by a State guarantee is a compelling reason for applying a legal system which permits and assures the control of the general principles of law. And though it is possible for the principal debt and the guarantee to be subject to different legal systems, it is, in the absence of express regulation, legitimate to impute to the parties the intention to submit two closely connected transactions to a single legal system. It would certainly be a less attractive solution if the contract between the Bank and the borrower were held to be governed by some undefined system of municipal law and the contract between the Bank and the State guarantor were subject to public international law.

Similar arguments justify the conclusion that the 'Act of Pledge' made on 28 November 1954 by the High Authority of the European Coal and Steel Community[1] is subject to public international law.[2] This document was executed for the purpose of securing the notes which the High Authority might issue to lenders, 'by pledge of the obligations which the High Authority shall receive from the enterprises to which it relends the borrowed funds'. The Act of Pledge, it is true, was declared before a Notary in Luxembourg and constitutes a contract with the Bank for International Settlements, a Swiss company. Yet is has no substantial connection with the law of either Luxembourg or Switzerland, the only systems of municipal law which could possibly have been intended by the parties.[3]

---

[1] See above, p. 219, n. 2.

[2] Against this view, in particular, Blondeel and Vander Eycke, above, p. 219, n. 3, and Sereni, above, p. 216, n. 3.

[3] Although the document is expressed in the English language, it can hardly be suggested that it is subject to the law of any country in which the English language is used: nothing in the Agreement points to the law of the District of Columbia, New York, or any other of the States of the Union, of Canada, England, Australia, and so forth. 'Anglo-Saxon law' does not, of course, exist. Sereni, op. cit., suggests that Swiss law should apply.

As in the case of the Young Loan, no solution other than the application of public international law would appear to be reasonable and practicable.

(*d*) On the other hand, it must be emphasized that there is no room for the doctrine of the possible 'internationalization' of contracts except in cases in which the parties, judge, or arbitrator consciously and specifically refer to or apply public international law as such. No such conscious or specific reference or application is indicated by the mere fact that the judge or arbitrator fails to state the law he is applying or purports to apply the law of more than one country or substitutes broad statements, diffuse reasoning, or generalities for judicial terseness and precision.

From this point of view it is necessary to express grave doubt about the significance and value of a number of awards which may be thought, but probably ought not, to be relevant to the present discussion. On many occasions arbitrators who were called upon to decide disputes arising from contracts between States and private persons have proceeded in a manner which may give rise to the impression that they applied public international law or at any rate the general principles of law which form part of it. Close analysis, however, proves that, except in the case of one not altogether satisfactory award, such an impression would be wrong; that in most cases the arbitrators applied a specific municipal law, but supported their conclusions by a process of comparison with other legal systems familiar to them, just as a municipal judge in England might test his views by referring to, say, Roman or New York law; that even where arbitrators did not in terms base their award on a certain system of municipal law they were not conscious of applying public international law or, indeed, any specific legal system at all; that, accordingly, their awards, while sometimes useful as studies in comparative law and, accordingly, indicative of the methods leading to the ascertainment of general principles, ought not to be treated or reported as if they were authorities on international law. International law would fall into disrepute and suffer great harm if every award on a dispute between a State and an alien came to be regarded as an example of 'internationalization' or as representative of the substance of public international law.

Thus no relevance, for present purposes, is to be attached to the *Alsing* case[1] which arose from contracts made in 1926 between the Greek Government and the Swedish Match Company or its associates and which in 1954 led to an award by M. Louis Python, then President of the Swiss Federal Tribunal. The contracts were held to be governed by Greek law.[2] When, in the course of his reasoning, the Arbitrator referred to Swiss, French, or German law, he did so merely in order to fill gaps in Greek law or to test or illustrate his results by a process of comparison.[3,4]

A different tendency of arbitrators is exemplified by a case involving the Radio Corporation of America and China.[5] The Award does not purport to apply any specific legal system at all. Whatever authoritative value it may have in other respects,[6] it cannot be invoked as an example of 'internationalization' or as a contribution to the substance of public international law which the arbitrators did not profess to have had in mind and which is unlikely to have been applicable.[7]

[1] Schwebel, 'The Alsing Case', 8 *I.C.L.Q.* (1959), p. 320; Int. L.R. 1956, 633.

[2] pp. 326, 327. It is important to note that the Arbitrator recorded the parties' agreement (p. 327) that 'given the interdependence and the common source of the systems of law in force in Continental Europe, the question of the law to be applied is rather a question of principle without much practical significance'.

[3] It is difficult to see the significance of the case for any branch of the law except, possibly, comparative law. If it became a practice to afford space to the numerous awards made in private arbitrations and employing the comparative method, the existing facilities for publication would be wholly insufficient.

[4] The Award made in the arbitration between *Saudi Arabia and The Arabian American Oil Company* (above, p. 228, n. 4) could be mentioned here, but since it was not published in 1959, a discussion would at that time have been of little advantage to the reader. The case was not one relating to international law at all. References in the Award to the law in some European countries were clearly by way of illustration.

[5] *Radio Corporation of America v. The National Government of the Republic of China; Reports of International Arbitral Awards* (1935), iii.1623.

[6] It is difficult to understand why it was thought helpful to report this case. It is even more difficult to understand why the report found its way into publications which are concerned with public international law.

[7] In the writings of international lawyers one sometimes finds a reference to the Award made in the case of *The Administration of Posts and Telegraphs of the Republic of Czechoslovakia v. Radio Corporation of America; A.J.I.L.* (1936), p. 523. The Agreement out of which this arbitration arose provided in Article 11 as follows: 'This Agreement, as to the obligations and responsibilities hereunder of the Corporation and the Administration respectively, shall be construed, interpreted and enforced according to the laws of the State of New York, U.S.A., and of the Republic of Czechoslovakia respectively.' The comment made in the preceding note applies with special force.

A special case is the Award in the arbitration between *Lena Goldfields Ltd. and the Soviet Government.*[1] Article 89 of the Concession granted by the Soviet Union to the Claimants provided[2]

The parties base their relations with regard to this Agreement on the principle of goodwill and good faith as well as on reasonable interpretation and the terms of the Agreement.

It has been shown that Lord Asquith of Bishopstone regarded an astonishingly similar clause as importing a choice of public international law as the proper law of the contract,[3] and the same result could possibly have been reached in *Lena Goldfields* case. It could also have been held that the Concession was subject to Soviet law, and that the words quoted above expressed no more than a pious hope; this is in fact the view of Professor Nussbaum.[4] The Arbitrators, however, decided, in accordance with the applicants' submission, that Soviet law applied as to performance in the Soviet Union, but that in other respects the general principles of law prevailed.[5] It is doubtful whether any such scission which is justifiably criticized by Nussbaum was possible in law. It is still more doubtful whether in the circumstances of the case there was any warrant for it. However, if and in so far as reference was made to general principles, the award does throw some light upon certain aspects of public international law and indicates what internationalization of a contract can accomplish.[6]

# III

The commercialization of treaties as well as the internationalization of contracts are different aspects of the same funda-

---

[1] Nussbaum, 'The Arbitration between the Lena Goldfields Ltd. and the Soviet Government', 36 *Cornell Law Quarterly* (1950–1), p. 31 where the Award is printed in full. The extract in *Annual Digest* (1929–30), Cases No. 1 and No. 258, is unfortunately insufficient.

[2] p. 50.     [3] Above, p. 223.     [4] p. 36.     [5] pp. 50, 51.

[6] Except in so far as the case is an example of internationalization and of the application of general principles, it is not an international case. See Lauterpacht, *Annual Digest* (1929–30), p. 428. It is perhaps appropriate to refer here to the lectures which Professor Jessup published in 1956 under the title of *Transnational Law*. The term is not unattractive, but it must be doubted whether there is any advantage in advocating transnational law, unless the scope of its application and the method of ascertaining it are explained with precision. Only when this is done will it be possible to say whether and to what extent the idea of a 'transnational law' is in any way different from and superior to traditional legal conceptions.

mental idea. It is no longer attractive to suggest that public international law and private law respectively have fields of application, which are clearly and perhaps even inflexibly defined and which are determined by *a priori* or conceptualist reasoning, such as the formula that public international law is applicable only as between international persons or that relationships between international persons are necessarily subject to public international law. Both branches of the law are branches of the same tree. They apply in conformity with the demands of reasonable justice and practical convenience. They overlap and pervade each other. Both are called upon to contribute to the progressive evolution of the law. From this point of view the two doctrines advocated in this article (and any attack upon them) must in the last resort rest on arguments which are broad rather than narrow and which stem from substantive rather than formal grounds.

In adopting practical usefulness as one of the operative tests due regard should be had to the problem of the assignment of treaty rights[1] and of contractual rights. The assignment of such rights may occur *ex lege*, as in the case of the subrogation of a guarantor to the rights of the creditor whom he has paid, or it may be voluntary, as in the case of a contractual assignment of a debt or the endorsement of negotiable instruments. If treaty rights which are governed by public international law can be, and are, assigned to a private person, will they cease to be subject to public international law and become subject to some (undefined) system of municipal law? If the rights of a private person, which arise from a contract with a State and are governed by a municipal system of law are assigned to a State, do they become subject to public international law? Perhaps it will not be seriously challenged that the answer to both questions should be in the negative. It may be that the traditional view would lead to the opposite results. If so, their appropriateness may have to be reviewed in the light of modern practices and requirements. On the other hand, it would go too far to submit, as Professor Sereni[2] does, that 'national law also applies to a situation, transaction and relationship if it is contemplated that the rights and duties arising thereunder may be transferred

---

[1] Below, p. 360.  [2] 96 *Recueil des cours* (1959), p. 163.

to entities which only have the status of subjects within national systems of law'. This view is intended to lead to the conclusion that the numerous bonds which international persons have issued to other international persons 'or order' are automatically subject to some municipal system of law (which Sereni does not define), merely because title may become vested in private persons. Such a solution would frequently be quite contrary to the parties' intention and hardly invites approval.

The critical reader should not, in conclusion, overlook the fact that the question whether public international or municipal law may, and is intended to, apply to a contractual arrangement has a counterpart in the sphere of domestic law, which in some respects may serve as an illuminating analogy. In many countries[1] there exists the necessity for distinguishing the governmental from the proprietary contract,[2] the *contrat administratif* from the *contrat commercial*,[3] the *öffentlichrechtliche Vertrag* from the *privatrechtliche Vertrag*,[4] Both types of contract may be subject to different rules. They may serve the same purposes and it may be open to the parties to make a choice. To the extent to which there exists interchangeability of legal rules in the municipal sphere, a corresponding conclusion put forward with a view to the international sphere would lose much of its novelty. The inquiry into the existence, validity, and effect of the analogy will require a separate study.

----

[1] See in general, Mitchell, *The Contracts of Public Authorities* (London, 1954), containing a survey of English, American, and French law; Langrod, 'Administrative Contracts', 4 *A.J.C.L.* (1955), 325. The problem of the administrative contract was discussed in the arbitration cases mentioned on pp. 228, 237, above.

[2] Williston, *On Contracts*, ix, s. 195.     [3] Mitchell, op. cit., pp. 164 et seq.

[4] Forsthoff, *Lehrbuch des Verwaltungsrechts* (7th ed., 1958), pp. 250 et seq.; as to Switzerland, see Imboden, *Der verwaltungsrechtliche Vertrag* (Basel, 1958).

# V

## ABOUT THE PROPER LAW OF CONTRACTS BETWEEN STATES*

SINCE the problem of the proper law of State contracts was first discussed in the pages of the *British Year Book of International Law*[1] a great development has taken place in so far as concerns contracts between States (or international organizations) and alien private persons, whether physical or legal. Much material has been collected and an immense literature has illumined it.[2] It has become, it is now possible to suggest, the prevailing view that a contract between a State and a foreigner may be subject to 'internationalization'[3] in the sense that, if the parties so intend, it is governed by public international law, or, as some prefer to put it, by the general principles of law recognized by civilized nations (though these are, not a legal system, but merely one of the sources of a legal system, namely public international law). No doubt there remain numerous detailed points of law and formulation to be clarified. Much additional experience will have to be gained in drawing acceptable lines of demarcation. Such difficulties do not jeopardize the growing evolution of a useful guide to decision.

On the other hand, what was described as the 'commercialization of treaties',[4] namely the submission of treaties between States[5] (or other international subjects) to municipal law, has

---

* Not previously published.
[1] Above pp. 179, 211.
[2] It must suffice at present to mention the latest contributions in the French and German language respectively: Prosper Weil, 128 *Recueil des cours* (1969 iii), p. 95; Böckstiegel, *Der Staat als Vertragspartner ausländischer Privatunternehmen* (1971).
[3] Above, pp. 191 to 195; 222 sqq.     [4] Above, p. 238 and passim.
[5] The expression is intended to include agencies of the State such as Ministries or Government Departments or other instrumentalities acting on behalf and for the account of the State. The question whether it is the State itself that is acting will frequently give rise to difficulty, particularly where the instrumentality is in law a separate corporation. See, for instance, *Baccus S. R. L.* v. *Servicio Nacional*, [1957] 1 Q. B. 438. One of the most doubtful cases is that of the Export–Import Bank of the United States in Washington. At least two Agreements providing for a Line of

been less fully documented and, consequently, has received little academic attention. None of the early examples[1] of such a practice can be said to be conclusive. The clause which in the early years of its existence the International Bank for Reconstruction and Development inserted into its loan agreements with borrowing States and which seemed to make the agreements and bonds subject to the law of New York has for many years fallen into disuse.[2] Its character about which scholars have failed to agree was never judicially considered. There has been no other unambiguous evidence of international persons having expressly or by clear implication contracted on the footing of a municipal system of law.

Such evidence can now be adduced. It has come to light as a result of work done by members of the seminar on International Commercial Law which for more than ten summer terms the writer has conducted at the University of Bonn.

Between 1966 and 1968 Denmark entered into five Loan Agreements with Jordan,[3] Brazil,[4] Malawi,[5] Iran[6] and

Credit and made between the United Kingdom and the Bank on 25 February 1957 and 11 February 1965 (Cmnd. 104 and 2610) contained the following clause: 'All questions with respect to the execution or interpretation of this Agreement and the notes or with respect to performance or non-performance hereunder or thereunder shall be interpreted according to New York law' (Article XVI and/or Article X). The Attorney-General of the United States, it is true, has stated in an opinion dated 30 September 1966 'that Eximbank's contractual liabilities constitute general obligations of the United States backed by its full faith and credit and that persons in whose favour it has incurred contractual liabilities in accordance with law have acquired valid general obligations of the United States and are therefore in a position to reach beyond Eximbank and its assets to the United States for a source of payment if necessary' (see *The Economist*, 29 January 1972, p. 93). Yet section 2 of Public Law 341 of 31 July 1945 which defines the Bank's status and organization describes the Bank as 'a banking corporation organized under the laws of the District of Columbia as an agency of the United States'. It is far from certain whether the Bank may be treated as an emanation of the United States. If the answer were in the negative then its Agreements with the United Kingdom or other States, which render the law of New York applicable, would be different in character from those to be discussed in the text. The nature of the Export–Import Bank's Agreement is rendered even more obscure on account of the fact that the latest Agreement with the United Kingdom (3 November 1969, Cmnd. 4226) fails to deal with the applicable law.

[1] Above, pp. 208, 209, 216 sqq.

[2] Delaume, *Legal Aspects of International Lending and Economic Development Financing* (1967), p. 85.

[3] 28 June 1966, U.N.T.S., vol. 574, p. 3.

[4] 8 July 1966, ibid., vol. 581, p. 95.

[5] 1 August 1966, ibid., vol. 586, p. 3.

[6] 2 November 1967, ibid., vol. 638, p. 217.

Malaysia.[1] The agreement with Malawi, signed by the Danish Minister for Foreign Affairs and the Minister for Finance of Malawi, reads as follows:

The Government of Denmark and the Government of Malawi desiring to strengthen the traditional co-operation and cordial relations between their countries, have agreed that, as a contribution to Malawi's Development Plans, a Danish Government Loan will be extended to Malawi in accordance with the following provisions:

### Article I

#### THE LOAN

The Government of Denmark (hereinafter called the Lender) agrees to make available to the Government of Malawi (hereinafter called the Borrower) a development Loan in an amount of 15 (fifteen) million Danish Kroner for the realization of the purposes described in Article VI of this Agreement.

### Article II

#### LOAN ACCOUNT

Section 1. An account designated 'Government of Malawi Loan Account' (hereinafter called 'Loan Account') will be opened with Danmarks Nationalbank (acting as agent for the Lender) in favour of the Reserve Bank of Malawi (acting as agent for the Borrower). The Lender will ensure that sufficient funds are always available in the Loan Account to enable the Borrower to effect punctual payment for goods and services procured under this Loan, provided that the amounts successively made available to the Borrower shall not, in the aggregate, exceed the Loan amount specified in Article I.

Section 2. The Borrower (or the Reserve Bank of Malawi acting as agent for the Borrower) shall be entitled, subject to the provisions of this Agreement, to withdraw from the Loan Account amounts needed for payment of equipment or services procured under the Loan.

### Article III

#### RATE OF INTEREST

The Loan will be free of interest.

### Article IV

#### REPAYMENT

Section 1. The Borrower will repay to the Lender the principal of the loan withdrawn from the Loan Account in 30 (thirty) semi-annual instalments of 500,000 (five hundred thousand) Danish Kroner each, commencing on October 1, 1971 and ending on April 1, 1986.

[1] 29 February 1968, ibid., vol. 640, p. 30.

Section 2. The Borrower has the right to repay in advance of maturity all or any part of the principal amount of one or more maturities of the Loan specified by the Borrower with such variations in the amount of instalments as may thereby be rendered necessary.

## Article V

### PLACE OF PAYMENT

The principal of the Loan will be repaid by the Borrower in convertible Danish Kroner to Danmarks Nationalbank to the credit of the current account of the Ministry of Finance with Danmarks Nationalbank.

## Article VI

### USE OF THE LOAN BY THE GOVERNMENT OF MALAWI

Section 1. The Borrower will use the proceeds of the Loan to finance imports (including transport charges from Denmark to Malawi) of such Danish capital equipment as will be agreed upon between the Lender and the Borrower.

Section 2. The proceeds of the Loan may also be used to pay for Danish services required for the implementation of Malawi's Development Plans, including, in particular, pre-investment studies, preparation of projects and the provision of consultants during the implementation of the projects, or during the assembly or construction of plant or buildings, and technical and administrative assistance during the initial period of the undertakings established by means of the Loan.

Section 3. A proportion of the Loan not exceeding 25 per cent may be drawn for the purpose of financing non-Danish capital investment costs related to the projects for which Danish capital equipment is procured under this Agreement, provided that (a) contracts for supplies of the Danish capital equipment have been approved by the Lender, and (b) the amount thus utilized does not exceed $33\frac{1}{3}$ per cent of the value of the Danish capital equipment procured for all projects.

Section 4. The Borrower will cause the proceeds of the Loan to be applied exclusively to the provision of goods and services needed to implement contracts approved by both Parties. The particulars of the methods and procedures for the payment of such goods and services, beyond those already set forth in Article II, shall be determined by agreement between Borrower and Lender.

Section 5. The concurrence of the Lender as to the eligibility of a contract under the Loan shall not be interpreted in such a manner as to imply that the Lender takes upon him any responsibility for the proper implementation or subsequent operation of such contracts.

Section 6. The terms of payment stipulated in contracts or documentation to the effect that an order has been placed with a Danish exporter or contractor for supplies or services of the nature described above shall be considered as normal and proper whenever such contracts contain no clauses involving special credit facilities from Danish exporters or contractors.

Section 7. The proceeds of the Loan may be used only for payment of supplies and services contracted for after the entry into force of the Agreement.

Section 8. The Borrower may draw on the account with Danmarks National bank referred to in Article II for up to three years after the entry into force of the Agreement or such other date as shall be agreed by the Lender and the Borrower.

Section 9. If the proceeds of the Loan have not been fully utilized within the time limit stipulated in Section 8 above, the semi-annual repayments shall be reduced by a proportion equal to the ratio between the unutilized amount of the Loan and the principal of the Loan.

## Article VII

### NON-DISCRIMINATION

Section 1. In regard to the repayment of the Loan, the Borrower undertakes to give the Lender no less favourable treatment than that accorded to other foreign creditors.

Section 2. All shipments of equipment covered by this Agreement shall be in keeping with the principle of free circulation of ships in international trade in free and fair competition.

## Article VIII

### MISCELLANEOUS PROVISIONS

Section 1. Prior to the first drawing against the Account referred to in Article II the Borrower will satisfy the Lender that all constitutional requirements and other requirements laid down by statute in the Borrower's home country have been met so that this Loan Agreement will constitute a valid obligation binding on the Borrower in the terms of the Loan Agreement.

Section 2. The Borrower will furnish to the Lender evidence of the authority of the person or persons who will, on behalf of the Borrower, take any action or execute any documents under this Agreement, and authenticated specimen signatures of all such persons.

Section 3. Any notice or request under this Agreement and any agreement between the parties contemplated by this Agreement shall be in writing. Such notice or request shall be deemed to have been duly given or made when it has been delivered by hand or by mail, telegram, cable or radiogram to the party at such party's address specified in Article XV, or at such address as such party shall have indicated by notice to the party giving such notice or making such request.

## Article IX

### PARTICULAR COVENANTS

The principal of the Loan shall be repaid without deduction for, and free from, any taxes and charges, and free from all restrictions imposed under the laws of the Borrower. This Agreement shall be free from any present and future taxes imposed under the laws of the Borrower, or laws in effect in its territories or in connection with the execution, issue, delivery or registration thereof.

## Article X

### CANCELLATION AND SUSPENSION

Section 1. The Borrower may, by notice to the Lender, cancel any amount of the Loan which the Borrower shall not have withdrawn.

If any of the following events shall have happened and be continuing, the Lender may, by notice to the Borrower, suspend in whole or in part the right of the Borrower to make withdrawals from the Loan Account:

(a) a default shall have occurred in the payment of principal under the Agreement or under any other financial commitment entered into by the Borrower in relation to the Lender; or

(b) a default shall have occurred in the performance of any other covenant or agreement on the part of the Borrower under the Agreement.

Section 2. The right of the Borrower to make withdrawals from the Loan Account shall continue to be suspended in whole or in part, as the case may be, until the event or events which gave rise to such suspension shall have notified the Borrower that the right to make withdrawals has been restored, whichever is earlier, provided however, that in the case of any such notice of restoration the right to make withdrawals shall be restored only to the extent and subject to the conditions specified in such notice, and no such notice shall effect or impair any right, power or remedy of the Lender in respect of any other or subsequent event described in this Article.

If the right of the Borrower to make withdrawals from the Loan Account shall have been suspended with respect to any amount of the balance of the Loan or any part thereof for a continuous period of sixty days, the Lender may, by notice to the Borrower, terminate the right of the Borrower to make withdrawals with respect to such amount. Upon the giving of such notice such amount of the Loan shall be cancelled.

Section 3. Notwithstanding any cancellation or suspension all the provisions of the Agreement shall continue in full force and effect except as is specifically provided in this Article.

## Article XI

### REMEDIES OF THE LENDER

If any event specified in subparagraphs (a) and (b) of Section 1 of Article X shall occur and shall continue for a period of sixty days after notice thereof has been given by the Lender to the Borrower, then at any subsequent time the Lender, at his option, may declare the principal of the Loan then outstanding to be due and payable immediately, and upon any such declaration such principal shall become due and payable immediately, anything in the Agreement to the contrary notwithstanding.

## *Article XII*

### APPLICABLE LAW

Unless otherwise provided for in the Agreement, the Agreement and all the rights and obligations deriving from it shall be governed by Danish law.

## *Article XIII*

### SETTLEMENT OF DISPUTES

Section 1. Any dispute between the Contracting Parties arising out of the interpretation or administration of the present Agreement, which has not been settled within six months through diplomatic channels, shall, at the request of either Party be submitted to a tribunal of arbitration, consisting of three members. The chairman of the tribunal shall be a citizen of a third country and shall be appointed by common consent of the Contracting Parties. Should the Parties fail to agree on the appointment of the chairman of the tribunal, either Party may request the President of the International Court of Justice to make the appointment. Each Party appoints its own arbitrator; if a Party abstains from appointing an abitrator, the latter may be appointed by the chairman of the tribunal.

Section 2. Each Contracting Party will observe and carry out awards given by the tribunal.

## *Article XIV*

### DURATION OF THE AGREEMENT

Section 1. This Agreement shall come into force on the date of signature.

Section 2. When the entire principal amount of the Loan has been repaid, the Agreement shall terminate forthwith.

## *Article XV*

### SPECIFICATION OF ADDRESSES

The following addresses are specified for the purposes of this Agreement:
For the Borrower:

> Secretary to the Treasury
> Ministry of Finance
> P.O. Box 53
> Zomba

Alternative address for cablegrams and radiograms:

> Finsec
> Zomba Malawi

For the Lender with respect to disbursements:

> Ministry of Foreign Affairs
> Secretariat for Technical
>   Co-operation with Developing Countries
> Copenhagen

Alternative address for cablegrams and radiograms:

> Dacomta
> Copenhagen

For the Lender with respect to servicing of the Loan:

> Ministry of Finance
> Copenhagen

Alternative address for cablegrams and radiograms:

> Finans
> Copenhagen

IN WITNESS WHEREOF, the Parties hereto acting through their representatives duly authorized for this purpose, have caused this Agreement to be signed in two copies in the English language in Copenhagen this first day of August, 1966.

> For the Government of Denmark:
> Per HAEKKERUP
> For the Government of Malawi:
> J. Z. U. TEJBO

In each case the Agreements are supplemented by an Exchange of Letters. The Agreement with Malawi includes a Letter in the following terms:

> Copenhagen, August 1st, 1966

EXCELLENCY,

I have the honour to refer to the Development Loan Agreement of today's date between the Government of Denmark and the Government of Malawi and have the honour to propose that the following provisions should govern private Danish investments in Malawi guaranteed by the Danish Government in projects financed under the Loan:

(1) The Government of Denmark shall consult the Government of Malawi regarding private Danish investments, properties, rights or other pecuniary interests (hereinafter called investments), which the Government of Denmark would be prepared to guarantee.

(2) The Government of Denmark shall not guarantee such investments unless the Government of Malawi approves the activity to which the investment relates and recognizes that the Government of Denmark may guarantee such investments.

(3) Such investments belonging to Danish Nationals, Companies or other

Danish Investors (hereinafter called Danish Investors) shall be subject to just and equitable treatment.

(4) Such investments of Danish Investors in Malawi shall not be accorded a treatment less favourable than the Government of Malawi accords to any other similar investments in its territory belonging to its own Nationals or Companies or to Nationals or Companies of third countries.

(5) The Government of Malawi shall not subject the activities of Danish Investors in connection with their investments guaranteed by the Danish Government to conditions less favourable than it imposes on activities in connection with any other similar investments in its territory.

(6) Such investments by Danish Investors should be accorded no less degree of protection than the Government of Malawi accords to any other similar investments in its territory belonging to its own Nationals or Companies or to Nationals or Companies of third countries.

(7) The Government of Malawi shall take no measures of expropriation nationalization or any other dispossession either direct or indirect against such investments in the territory of Malawi and belonging to Danish Investors except for public benefit and against compensation.

(8) If the Government of Malawi expropriates or nationalizes such investments of Danish Investors or if it takes any other measures with a view to direct or indirect dispossession of Danish Investors, it shall provide for the payment of effective and adequate compensation.

(9) Such compensation shall represent the equivalent of such investments effected at the time of expropriation, nationalization or any other form of dispossession, it shall be realisable and freely transferable and shall be made without delay. Provision shall be made in an appropriate manner at or prior to the time of dispossession for the determination and payment of such compensation.

(10) Danish Investors whose investments may suffer losses in the territory of Malawi owing to war or other armed conflict, revolution, a state of national emergency, or revolt, shall be accorded treatment not less favourable than the Government of Malawi accords to its own Nationals and Companies or to Nationals and Companies of third countries as regards restitution, indemnification, compensation or other similar valuable consideration. Such payments shall be freely transferable.

(11) If the Government of Denmark makes payment to any Danish Investor under a guarantee it has assumed in respect of an investment in Malawi, the Government of Malawi shall recognize

(a) the assignment, whether under Danish law or pursuant to a legal transaction in Denmark of any right or claim from such Investor to the Government of Denmark, as well as
(b) the subrogation of the Government of Denmark to any such right or claim which the Government of Denmark shall be entitled to assert to the same extent as its predecessor in title.

Payments to be made by virtue of such assignment or subrogation shall be freely transferable.

(12) In conformity with provisions of present legislation, legal and

administrative practice or of any future more favourable legislation, legal and administrative practice the Government of Malawi shall authorize the transfer of

(a) the net return yielded by an investment guaranteed by the Danish Government such as interest, dividends, royalties, payments for licences and other claims of Danish Nationals or companies, formed or registered in the territory of Malawi,

(b) amortization, or the proceeds of the total or partial liquidation of guaranteed Danish investments in Malawi,

(c) an adequate portion of the wages, salaries and other remuneration of Danish Nationals authorised to exercise activities in Malawi.

(13) Any dispute between the Government of Denmark and the Government of Malawi arising out of the interpretation or administration of the present exchange of letters should be settled in accordance with the provisions of Article XIII of the Loan Agreement of today's date between the Government of Denmark and the Government of Malawi.

If the foregoing provisions are acceptable to the Government of Malawi I have the honour to suggest that this letter and Your Excellency's reply to that effect should constitute an Agreement between our two Governments on this matter.

Please accept, Excellency, the assurance of my highest consideration.

For the Government of Denmark:

Per HAEKKERUP

The Loan Agreement, on account of its Article XII, is a document of unusual interest and calls for certain comments.

(1) The nature, effect and extent of the reference to Danish law depends on the conflict rules of the legal system to be observed by the tribunal of arbitration that, under Article XIII, will have to decide disputes. It is by no means certain whether the tribunal envisaged by Article XIII is one functioning under public international law or under national law and whether, in the latter case, the conflict rules of the country of the tribunal's seat or Denmark apply.[1] Since the conflict rules

---

[1] These questions are not directly germane to the principal point discussed in the text. See, generally, below, pp. 256 et seq. It would seem very likely that the arbitration provided for by Article XIII would proceed under public international law, for there is nothing to suggest that the High Contracting Parties intended municipal law to apply even outside the field defined by Article XII. Perhaps it is permitted in this context to mention that in 1967 it was stated (at pp. 13, 14) that the procedure under the Convention on the Settlement of Investment Disputes between States of 1965 was 'the only one that renders a procedure under public international law available to a private person for the enforcement of a State contract'. This is incorrect. There is at least one other case of an arbitration procedure which was set up by treaty, to which a State and a private person may

accepted by public international law are ill developed, since the seat of the tribunal is not fixed and since the conflict rules are by no means uniform in all countries, it is impossible to suggest solutions which are likely to be in harmony with the conflict of laws of the legal system eventually found to be primarily applicable. It is, therefore, not intended to do more than to indicate some problems and their solutions which are believed to be common to many countries of the Western world. But all suggestions here made with considerable diffidence will have to be carefully tested and reconsidered in the light of the conflict rules which the tribunal will have to follow and which alone have the power of determining the scope of the reference to Danish law.

(2) Where the terms are so general as to submit to Danish law 'the Agreement and all the rights and obligations deriving from it' it is clear that the reference comprises all questions relating to the contract that may arise and, includes, in particular, the conclusion, validity, interpretation, discharge, and breach of the Agreement.

This means, on the one hand, that the law of Malawi has no role to play. It is the proper law of the contract that governs, not the debtor's law. If, for instance, Malawi were to introduce a moratorium, such legislation would have to be disregarded.[1] It follows that Article IX of the Loan Agreement is otiose.

On the other hand, the public international law, whether customary or conventional law, is, in so far as it relates to questions of contract, equally irrelevant. The rule that in relation to other States no State is entitled to rely upon its own legislation in order to justify its failure to observe international law is inapplicable. Similarly it is Danish law that decides upon such matters as *jus cogens* or the operation of the *clausula rebus sic stantibus* or what public international law would consider as abuse of rights.

To avoid misunderstanding it should be repeated that

be parties and which is subject to public international law: see Articles 46, 157–78 of the Petroleum Convention between France and Algeria of 29 July 1965. *International Legal Materials*, (1965), iv.809 et seq. There are probably other arbitration tribunals of a similar type.

[1] In England, at any rate, it is now clearly established that the effect of a moratorium depends on the proper law of the contract: *National Bank of Greece* v. *Metliss*, [1958] A. C. 509.

Danish law governs only questions of a contractual character. Their definition is a matter of classification. And, according to widely accepted practice, classification is determined by the arbitrators' *lex fori*, the *lex arbitri*, rather than the proper law of the contract. Thus it depends on the *lex arbitri* whether questions of prescription or limitation of actions are to be treated as forming part of the law of procedure or the law of contract. Similarly the *lex arbitri* determines whether the borrower has, in the event of the Lender's breach, the remedy of specific performance or can only claim damages.

(3) It is implied in what has just been submitted that any illegality, whether initial or subsequent, will have to be judged exclusively by Danish law. But a peculiar point arises in regard to exchange control regulations. According to Article VIII (2) (b) of the Bretton Woods Agreement exchange contracts which involve the currency of any member and are contrary to the exchange control regulations of that member maintained consistently with the Agreement are unenforceable. Does this provision apply to the Loan Agreement? It forms part of a treaty to which both Denmark and Malawi are Parties and which no doubt has been incorporated into the municipal law of both States. Private parties could not assert the irrelevance of an infringement of Malawi exchange control regulations on the ground that Danish law applies. Are Denmark and Malawi similarly entitled to invoke Article VIII (2) (b)? Could Denmark, to take an extreme case, refuse performance on the ground that the Loan Agreement is contrary to Danish exchange control regulations? It is believed that neither State can rely upon the Bretton Woods Agreement. It is not easy to formulate a compelling reason for this conclusion. Probably the best argument is that by entering into an Agreement such as the Loan Agreement both States must be taken to have waived any such defence as Bretton Woods would supply.

(4) Perhaps the most interesting question is whether Article XII extends to the interpretation and performance of the terms laid down by the Letter which has been set forth. It is submitted that the answer should be in the negative. In the first place it is noteworthy that the Parties thought it necessary to state expressly in paragraph (13) that Article XIII of the Loan Agreement should apply to any dispute arising from the

Exchange of Letters, but refrained from rendering Article XII applicable. If the application of Article XIII to the Letter was not considered obvious, then it can hardly be maintained that Article XII necessarily governs the terms of the Letter. Secondly, the subject-matter and character of the Letter is such as to render its submission to a municipal system of law peculiarly inappropriate. The Letter which, by its terms, has hardly any connection with Denmark but is primarily to be performed in and by Malawi, is almost in the nature of a Treaty of Friendship and Commerce. It includes clauses, such as paragraph (3) imposing the duty of just and equitable treatment or paragraphs (4), (5) and (6) guaranteeing most-favoured-nation and national treatment or detailed provisions guaranteeing the property of Danish investors or their rights to transfer moneys, which one does not normally find in, and cannot very well construe with reference to, a system of municipal law. In short, the Letter deals with legal aspects which are distinct from the Loan Agreement as such and are more readily appreciated from the point of view of public international law.

(5) Another question of difficulty arises from the fact that Article VI of the Loan Agreement and the first of the Letters attached to it, but not reproduced above, clearly envisages the conclusion of a series of further and distinct agreements between Danish concerns and the Government of Malawi or, perhaps, Malawian firms. Is Article XII to be so construed as to apply also to those secondary agreements? The wording ('rights and obligations deriving from' the Loan Agreement) is possibly wide enough to comprise such agreements. It may well be that, where in connection with one or the other of such agreements the proper law has to be ascertained, Article XII is one of many circumstances which may be taken into account. But it could hardly be considered conclusive and, generally, it would not seem that Article XII necessarily governs secondary agreements or is even material to the determination of their proper law. A distinction will have to be drawn between agreements to which the Government of Malawi is or is not a Party. In the former event Article XII is a weighty element in the process of construction that has to be gone through where no express choice of law has occurred. On the other hand, where

the parties are both private who, perhaps, do not even know of the Loan Agreement, it may in law be inadmissible to draw an inference from an Agreement made *inter alios*. Even in the absence of any such legal impediment only very little weight can in such circumstances be attached to Article XII. In the more usual case of the Loan Agreement being governed by public international law it could hardly be argued that all agreements made by private parties in consequence of it should or could be subject to the same legal system.

(6) To a lawyer's mind the existence of an express clause subjecting the Loan Agreement to Danish law compellingly supports the earlier suggestion that it is open to States impliedly to agree upon the application of a municipal system of law to their contracts, though the implication must be clear and necessary to override the presumption according to which, normally, States contract under public international law. The Agreements under discussion do teach, however, that it would be wrong in the course of the process of construction to attach much significance to the form of the document. Denmark's Agreements are in a form which could equally be employed for treaties in the strict sense of the term.

A process of reasoning which would certainly not be permissible would be to the effect that similar Loan Agreements made by other States, or, indeed, by Denmark herself should be treated as governed by the lender State's law. The United Kingdom, for instance, has entered into a large number of Loan Agreements; perhaps it will suffice to mention recent ones with Peru,[1] Indonesia,[2] Jordan,[3] Afghanistan,[4] Ecuador,[5] and Turkey.[6] There is nothing in these Agreements to support the view that they are subject to English law, though certain arrangements made in pursuance of them, such as bank accounts opened by the borrowing States with London banks, are almost certainly governed by English law.

(7) The question whether Denmark's Loan Agreements are, or may be described as, treaties is merely a terminological one and without interest or substance. That the Secretariat of the United Nations Organization has considered them to be treaties

[1] Cmnd. 3379.    [2] Cmnd. 3770, 3771, 3980, 4535.    [3] Cmnd. 4252.
[4] Cmnd. 4597.    [5] Cmnd. 4344.
[6] Cmnd. 3374, 3876, 4231, 3472, 4586, 4602.

or international agreements within the meaning of Article 102 of the Charter is neither surprising nor illuminating. The legal character of a document is not determined by the Secretariat's refusal of, or acceptance for, registration.[1] But if in some context the point is of importance it is suggested that submission to a municipal system of law does disqualify a document from coming within the definition of a treaty, though it is an international Agreement. Article 2 of the Vienna Convention[2] on Treaties excludes from the definition of a 'treaty' such international agreements as are not governed by international law. It is by no means unlikely that this exclusion is in conformity with the prevailing understanding.

(8) There is, however, one provision which may require some decision on the legal character of the Agreement. Article VIII imposes the duty upon Malawi to satisfy Denmark 'that all constitutional requirements' in the Borrower's home country have been met. It is possible that under the law of Malawi the Agreement is a 'treaty' and, for this reason, is not, in the municipal law of Malawi, binding upon Malawi unless and until certain constitutional requirements have been observed. It might be said that the control of Danish law made it unnecessary, except for questions relating to capacity or authority, to have regard to the law of Malawi at all. But for Parties contracting on the footing of municipal law it was a useful precaution to ensure the enforceability of the Loan Agreement according to the municipal law of Malawi.

It is a little more difficult to appreciate the reasons for Article IX. A provision of Malawian law which, for instance, requires the deduction of tax is, outside Malawi, unlikely to be material in the context of a Loan Agreement subject to Danish law. On the other hand, if enforcement in Malawi should become necessary such a provision would probably have the effect of overriding Article XII on the ground of *ordre public*. Hence Article IX may well be otiose, although similar provisions are frequently included in private loan documents which in the case of the Danish–Malawian Agreement may have served as a precedent.

[1] Above, p. 218 n. 3.    [2] 63 *A.J.I.L.* (1969), p. 875.

# VI

## STATE CONTRACTS AND
## INTERNATIONAL ARBITRATION*

THERE are three types of international arbitration arising from contractual obligations,[1] namely arbitration between States (or other international persons); arbitration 'between parties subject respectively to the jurisdiction of different contracting States'[2]; and arbitrations between States and private persons of foreign nationality or residence.

The purpose of the present contribution is to investigate the peculiarities of the last-mentioned type of arbitration. However, in order to define and to comment upon these peculiarities, it is necessary to view them against the background of the other two types of arbitration; hence, by way of introduction, these will be shortly discussed.

### I

Arbitration between States under treaties concluded by them is almost invariably regulated by the *compromis*. Even where there exists an earlier treaty providing for the submission of future disputes to arbitration, it cannot usually be given

---

* From *British Year Book of International Law* 1967, 1.

[1] There is a fourth type, namely arbitration set up by a treaty between States, to which private parties are or may be parties and which is intended to settle private disputes of all kinds and by no means arising from contract only. The most prominent examples are the Mixed Arbitral Tribunals created by the treaties of peace after the First World War. A more recent example is the Arbitral Commission on Property Rights or Interests in Germany set up under the Convention on the Settlement of Matters Arising out of the War and the Occupation (Cmd. 9368, p. 104), which by Art. 8 is expressly instructed to 'apply the general principles of international law and of justice and equity'. These arbitrations, on which see Hallier, *Völkerrechtliche Schiedsinstanzen für Einzelpersonen und ihr Verhältnis zur innerstaatlichen Gerichtsbarkeit* (1964), are arbitrations under public international law. They are disregarded in the present context. While they are founded on treaties, they do not arise from treaties or contracts between States made for the purpose of settling their own disputes, as opposed to those of their nationals.

[2] See the definition in paragraph 1 of the Geneva Protocol of 1923.

effect without a further special agreement or *compromis* 'to define the question to be referred to arbitration and the method by which the tribunal is to be constituted',[1] as well as any other point of practice that may have to be settled. Thus the *compromis* frequently deals with the procedure to be followed, the law to be applied and the publication of the award to be rendered by the arbitrators. The details included in the *compromis* vary considerably, but the broad terms are now fairly well established.[2] The Hague Convention of 1907 establishing the Permanent Court of Arbitration[3] and the Model Rules on Arbitral Procedure adopted in 1958 by the International Law Commission[4] in many respects point the way.

Though there is no compelling reason of principle or logic why in a given case States should not decide upon arbitration under the law of a particular State, it has so far been the uniform practice to divorce arbitration between States entirely from any system of municipal law, and to submit it to public international law. This seems to be generally accepted or assumed, but is hardly ever stated in express terms. The tribunal cannot help of course, having its seat and its hearings in national territory, and this probably presupposes the consent of such territory's sovereign.[5] But his law does not reach the arbitration between States. Thus the arbitration will follow its own procedural rules, whether they are laid down in the *compromis* or derived from a multilateral Convention such as the Hague Convention of 1907 or from general international law. It follows that the arbitrators may be at liberty to hear witnesses on oath even where the *lex loci* precludes arbitrators from administering oaths.[6] Or, to take another example, the award is not subject to the requirement, known to many systems of municipal law, according to which it must be deposited with the local court.[7] Or if an arbitration under international law takes place in England the Arbitration Act 1950 does not apply to it, so that, for instance, the High

---

[1] Simpson and Fox, *International Arbitration* (1959), pp. 44–5.

[2] For a model draft see Carlston, 47 *A.J.I.L.* (1953), pp. 203 et seq.

[3] See Oppenheim, *International Law* (7th ed., by Lauterpacht, 1952), ii.36 et seq.

[4] *Yearbook of the International Law Commission* (1958 ii), p. 81.

[5] The point is not covered by authority, but would seem to follow from general principles.

[6] As it does, for instance, in Germany: section 1035 of the *Code of Civil Procedure*.

[7] Where one party requests it, this is the position, for instance, in Zurich: section 368 of the *Rules of Civil Procedure*.

Court of Justice cannot exercise the supervisory powers normally vested in it. The exemption cannot be deduced from the terms of the Act. It rests on the broad ground that arbitrations between States are outside the jurisdiction of the territorial sovereign. Those who prefer a narrower and more technical ground will invoke the well-established, though ill-documented, rule according to which arbitrators appointed under a *compromis* are immune from judicial process in the country in which they exercise their official functions.[1]

Similarly, the law applicable in arbitrations between States is almost always, though perhaps not necessarily,[2] international law. It has been held[3] and suggested[4] that international law applies even in the absence of a clause to such effect in the *compromis*. The fact that a rule of the local law has the character of *ordre public* is, accordingly, without relevance.

Next, there is the question whether the award rendered by international arbitrators in pursuance of the *compromis* is enforceable,[5] not only by such methods as public international law permits, but also in the manner of a municipal award. Suppose a treaty provides for the sale by the United Kingdom of aircraft to Denmark[6] and arbitrators have awarded to Denmark a large sum of money as damages for the defective quality of the engines. Suppose, further, that the United Kingdom fails to pay. Could Denmark bring an action in the English Courts founded upon the award? Could the successful, State obtain in the courts of third countries, such as Belgium, the *exequatur* to the award? The question has not arisen in

---

[1] See Art. 46 of the Hague Convention of 1907 and Simpson and Fox, op. cit. (above, p. 257, n. 1), at p. 102.

[2] There may be exceptional cases in which contracts between States are governed by a municipal system of law and have thus been 'commercialized': see above, p. 238 with further references.

[3] In the case of the *Diverted Cargoes* between the United Kingdom and Greece, Int. L.R. (1955), p. 820, the sole Arbitrator, Monsieur Cassin, held that in the absence of any express provision he had to decide 'on the basis of respect for law' as required by Art. 37 of the Hague Convention of 1907 and that this meant international law. See the much more explicit Arts. X and XI of the Model Rules on Arbitral Procedure referred to above, p. 257, n. 4.

[4] Carlston, *The Process of International Arbitration* (1946), p. 140; Simpson and Fox, op. cit. (above, p. 257, n. 1), at pp. 128–30.

[5] A very similar question relates to the setting aside, the annulment or revision of award.

[6] Cf. Cmd. 7660.

practice.[1] It would seem, in general, to demand an answer in the negative,[2] for the awards which the rule of municipal law envisages are, it is submitted, normally awards made in, or under the sovereignty of, foreign States. As a matter of construction, awards made under international law by virtue of a *compromis* between States will only rarely be within the contemplation of municipal provisions relating to the enforcement of (domestic or foreign) awards.[3]

Finally, there is clear and convincing authority for the proposition that arbitration proceedings between States cannot attract the international responsibility of the State in the territory of which they take place.[4] Just as the Netherlands cannot be held responsible for the activities of the International Court of Justice, so it has no responsibility for the Permanent Court of Arbitration when it decides disputes between States. This is another consequence of the fact that, although the local

---

[1] It did not arise in the case of *Société Commerciale de Belgique* v. *Greece, Revue critique de droit international privé* (1952), p. 111, also Int. L.R. (1951), p. 3, for in that case the application to the Belgian Court was made by virtue of an award obtained by the applicant, a private person, in arbitration proceedings against Greece. The fact that, in proceedings between Belgium and Greece, the Permanent Court of International Justice had held that award to be binding (Ser. A/B, No. 78) was of little legal relevance. The Permanent Court's judgment is one of the most confusing and confused decisions rendered by it: see Verzijl, *The Jurisprudence of the World Court* (1965), i.584. On the Belgian decision see Rosenne, *The International Court of Justice* (1957), pp. 85–9, whose criticism appears unjustified, and Schachter, 54 *A.J.I.L.* (1960), pp. 12–14.

[2] C. Wilfred Jenks, *The Prospect of International Adjudication* (1964) devotes chapter 12 to 'Methods of Securing Compliance with International Decisions and Awards' (p. 663). He seems to envisage decisions rendered in proceedings between States (or other international persons). It would seem from pp. 706 et seq. that the learned author differs from the view expressed in the text, and would, accordingly, consider it possible to enforce a truly international award in a municipal court. He says of the Belgian case referred to in the preceding note that it 'represents a constructive approach' (p. 706). Since the case has no bearing upon the type of award under discussion in the text, it is possible that Dr. Jenks gives to the term 'International Decisions and Awards' a wider meaning so as to include the problems discussed in Section III, below.

[3] See below, pp. 353–4.

[4] See the decision in *Salem's* case *Annual Digest* (1931–2), Case No. 98 and the decision of the European Commission for Human Rights at Strasbourg (*Yearbook of the European Convention on Human Rights*, ii.256, also Int. L.R. 25 (1958), p. 190) where the Supreme Restitution Court at Nürnberg was held not to be subject to German jurisdiction. Neither of these cases arose from an arbitration between States, but the principles laid down in them have general validity, though their application to the facts of the latter case give rise to doubt. See, e.g., Vasak, *La Convention européenne des Droits de l'Homme* (Paris, 1964), pp. 100–3.

sovereign's consent to the setting up of the tribunal in his territory is necessary he has no control over its activities; the purely negative control which he could exercise by revoking his consent is insufficient to support the affirmative conclusion that he has control and therefore incurs responsibility.

## II

Arbitration under a contract between two private persons resident in different States is in every respect the very antithesis of the arbitration between States which was surveyed in the preceding section. In particular, such arbitration is altogether subject to a municipal system of law, namely the legal system of the country in which the tribunal has its seat. This *lex arbitri*, this *loi de l'arbitrage* determines all questions of procedure as well as of private international law. Although many laws allow much freedom of choice to the parties or the arbitrators, it is always the *lex arbitri* in the above sense that decides whether and to what extent such freedom exists.[1] In order to illustrate these principles it may be helpful, by way of example, to refer again to the question of arbitrators taking the evidence of witnesses on oath. It would be quite wrong to make a general statement such as this: arbitrators are entitled to regulate procedure and therefore they decide whether witnesses can be heard on oath. The law differs from country to country. Hence no general statement is possible. The first task is to find the *lex arbitri*. This is the law of the tribunal's seat. The *lex arbitri* so identified provides the solution: perhaps it says that arbitrators cannot administer oaths at all; perhaps it allows the parties to regulate the procedure, and includes the question of sworn evidence among the matters subject to the parties' decision; perhaps it gives these powers to the arbitrators. It is always the *lex arbitri* which, primarily, regulates procedure.

These views which may claim to be supported, in substance, by traditional thought as well as by reasons of principle and sound legal policy, have in recent years been challenged by several scholars who aim at the 'internationalization' of inter-

---

[1] These views are more fully developed by Mann, 'Lex Facit Arbitrum', in *International Arbitration, Liber Amicorum for Martin Domke* (1967), p. 157.

national commercial arbitrations.[1] Perhaps this method of approach is most concisely represented by Professor Fragistas.[2] According to him, it is open to the parties to an international arbitration by their contract to detach the arbitration from every municipal system of law so as to render it 'supranational' and to submit it to public international law.

L'arbitrage supranational doit donc être un arbitrage international, c'est-à-dire un arbitrage qui échappe à l'emprise de tout droit national pour être soumis directement au droit international.

There are, so the learned author recognizes, difficulties in application, but they will be overcome by reference to the general principles of law which govern all questions of procedure, private international and substantive law. The difficulties have to be overcome, for 'l'arbitrage privé supranational est un fait social, une réalité que l'on ne peut pas méconnaître'. The parties' wish to 's'élever au dessus de tout ordre étatique' is particularly pronounced in the case of arbitrations subject to the rules of the International Chamber of Commerce. Where these rules apply, 'les parties ont l'impression de soumettre leur litige à un arbitrage qui se trouve au dessus de tout ordre étatique'. An author who seems to have been the first to suggest that certain contracts to which a private person is a party may be 'internationalized'[3] has the particularly clear duty to state unequivocally that a theory such as that propagated by Professor Fragistas is unacceptable, undesirable and legally unjustifiable.

First, the parties' wishes and impressions are irrelevant and should be left out of account. Nor can it be admittted that there is any cogent evidence of 'arbitrage supranational' being a social fact. It is true that certain awards, made under the auspices of the International Chamber of Commerce, have been referred to as evidence of a tendency to detach arbitrations from municipal legal systems.[4] But the authors of these

---

[1] See, in particular, Goldman, 'Les Conflits de lois dans l'arbitrage international de droit privé', 109 *Recueil des cours* (1963 ii), p. 351; Fouchard, *L'Arbitrage commercial international* (1965).

[2] *Revue critique de droit international privé* (1960), p. 1, at pp. 14–17.

[3] Above, p. 191. It was made clear that the extension of that doctrine to contracts between private persons was not contemplated and could not be defended: see, e.g., above, p. 226.

[4] They are discussed by Fouchard, op. cit., above, n. 1.

awards are unknown. There is room for the impression that such awards may involve a violation rather than a progressive application of the law. Finally, it is a matter of speculation whether in given cases the 'supranational award' has satisfied or disappointed the parties.

Secondly, there is in law no basis whatever for the application of public international law, of general principles of law or of some odd systems of discretion, frequently honoured by the name of 'equity', except upon the basis of a municipal system of law which permits the control of such rules in all or some respects. No municipal system of law is known that includes a permissive rule to that effect, where the arbitration arises between two private persons.

Thirdly, the proposed 'internationalization' of arbitrations between private persons would be liable to become the source of grave political and social dangers and must, for this reason alone, be firmly rejected. The supranational arbitration which Professor Fragistas advocates for use between private persons would not in any way differ from the arbitration between States, which the *compromis* usually submits to public international law. Private persons, however, cannot and should not enjoy the privileges open to, or be exposed to the risks accepted by, States.

## III

International arbitrations[1] arising from a contract between a State and an alien do not, by definition, come within either of the categories discussed in the preceding sections. Should they be equiparated to arbitrations between States, which are subject to public international law? Or should they be put on the same level as arbitrations between two private persons, which are subject to the *lex arbitri*, i.e. the municipal law prevailing at the tribunal's seat?

(1) It is submitted that, in principle, it is the latter question

---

[1] Two points should be made clear. First, there are arbitrations between a State and an alien which take place within the territory of the State concerned. These are not international arbitrations within such meaning as is usual or is employed here. Secondly, arbitration is not the same thing or is not always subject to the same law as the contract from which it arises. This study is concerned with arbitration only.

that requires an affirmative answer. This, as has been pointed out, does not mean that it is impossible for the *lex arbitri*, to the extent and for the purposes determined by it alone, to allow the application of rules created by the parties themselves or of another legal system, including possibly public international law, to which they may refer. Accordingly, the problem of international arbitration cannot be discussed except against the background of a given *lex arbitri;* the legal systems of the world differ so considerably that no general rule can, or is intended to, be put forward. It follows that, in principle and always subject to such freedom of choice as it may allow, the *lex arbitri* governs the validity and effect of the submission; the constitution of the tribunal; the procedure; the law applicable by the arbitrators; the making, publication, interpretation, annulment and revision of the award; and, where this arises for purposes of enforcement, the nationality of the award, for this has necessarily a national character and does not constitute an instrument created by public international law. It may well be that in many State contracts 'there is evidence of the intention that arbitration is to be "international", in the sense that it is not to be conducted under the laws of any of the States directly related to the transaction'.[1] But this intention does not in any way deprive the arbitration of its municipal character. Nor is that intention expressed merely by provisions relating to the appointment of the arbitrators or the umpire.[2] It can be carried into effect only by express or implied provisions sanctioned by the law of the tribunal's seat. Finally, the country of the arbitration tribunal's seat supplies the *lex arbitri* even in those cases in which the agreement is made between an international organization and a private person and stipulates for the arbitration to take place in the premises of the international organization. Such premises are not 'extraterritorial'[3] and the Headquarters Agreements which usually cover them do not, for the purposes material to the present discussion, confer 'extraterritoriality' upon them. Thus the Agreement of 21 November 1947 between the United States of America and the United Nations Organization expressly provides that in general 'the federal, state, and local law of the United States shall apply

---

[1] Spofford, 113 *Recueil des cours* (1964 iii), p. 182.    [2] Spofford, ibid.
[3] See, in particular, Brandon, *B.Y.I.L.* (1951), xxviii.96.

within the headquarters district'.[1] Accordingly, an arbitration between the United Nations Organization and a New York building contractor will be a New York arbitration even if, pursuant to the agreement, it takes place in the United Nations building.

The fundamental approach which is thus suggested and the detailed implications of which will have to be considered is exemplified by numerous cases of arbitrations between States and private persons occurring in almost daily practice. Yet it has not always been followed, although it is possible that deviations from it have occasionally sprung from inexact terminology or have for other reasons been unguarded rather than deliberate. There is, for instance, a series of awards[2] which, in disputes between a State and a private person, were made under a municipal system of law, but as they are reported in publications normally devoted to public international law and as they are frequently referred to in the context of the peaceful settlement of disputes with States, they have been misunderstood and treated as if they were awards made under public international law. One of the earliest and clearest examples is the award made in London in the case of *Lena Goldfields Ltd.* v. *Soviet Government*.[3] With some hesitation the late Sir Hersch Lauterpacht published it in the *Annual Digest of Public International Law Cases*.[4] The arbitration arose from a Concession Agreement made between the Soviet Government and Lena Goldfields Ltd. Its terms have never been published in full. The *lex arbitri*, it is submitted, was clearly English, so that the English Arbitration Act, English procedure, and English private international law applied, and the arbitration was not

---

[1] Section 7.

[2] Nussbaum, 'The Arbitration between the Lena Goldfields Ltd. and the Soviet Government', 36 *Cornell L.Q.* (1950 i), p. 31, where the Award is printed in full; *Radio Corporation of America* v. *The National Government of the Republic of China*, *Reports of International Arbitral Awards*, iii.1623; *The Administration of Posts and Telegraphs of the Republic of Czechoslovakia* v. *Radio Corporation of America*, A.J.I.L. (1936) p. 523; *Petroleum Developments (Trucial Coast) Ltd.* v. *The Ruler of Abu Dhabi*, I.C.L.Q. (1952) p. 247. On these and the other cases to be mentioned in the text see above, pp. 236–8.

[3] See the preceding note; it is difficult to understand how Friedmann, *The Changing Structure of International Law* (1964), p. 146, comes to suggest that the case is derived 'from the Mixed Claims Commissions constituted after the first world war'.

[4] 1929–30, p. 428.

subject to public international law. It may well be that the law which the arbitrators were instructed, or decided, to apply was, at any rate, public international law.[1] But this is the effect of the English conflict of laws which applied on account of the *lex arbitri* being English. It does not mean that the arbitration arose under or was subject to public international law: the fact that an English judge or arbitrator has to apply Italian law leaves him in all other respects subject to English law.

A more recent example which is sometimes put forward as an international case[2] but which should never have been published, is the case of *Alsing Trading Co.* v. *Greece.*[3] It arose from a concession made under Greek law.[4] Arbitration was held in Lausanne.[5] No question of public international law arose or should be read into the award. It was an arbitration on the footing of municipal law between a State and a private person, such as merits no comment. It should, perhaps, be added that contracts made between a private person and a corporation wholly owned by a foreign State[6] are even less problematical.

The preceding submissions do not require any qualification where the contract is a concession. It has sometimes been argued that a concession is a contract under public or administrative law and cannot therefore be put on a par with an ordinary commercial contract. Whether this is a valid and material distinction depends on the proper law applicable in a given case. Even if a concession is a *contrat administratif* it is still a contract under municipal law. Neither it nor any arbitration flowing from it belongs to the realm of public international law. It is, therefore, difficult to understand the precise point which Professor Friedmann has in mind, when, introducing a lengthy discussion of the nature of international concession agreements, he refers to the 'often bitter debate' on the

---

[1] See the article printed above, p. 211, and Lord McNair, *B.Y.I.L.* (1954), xxxi.10.

[2] It is, however, quite clear that the umpire made no such mistake. In particular, he held that the award was subject to the law of the Canton of Vaud. The contract was subject to Greek law with ample references to comparative material.

[3] Int. L.R. (1956), p. 633.    [4] Ibid., p. 637.    [5] Ibid., pp. 638–9.

[6] This was the position in the case of *Sapphire International Petroleum Ltd.* v. *National Iranian Oil*, 35 Int. L.R., p. 136, on which see J. F. Lalive, *Annuaire suisse de droit international* (1962), p. 273; and Suratgar, 3 *Columbia J.I.L.* (1965), p. 152. The arbitrator correctly treated the arbitration as being subject to Swiss law, this being the *lex arbitri*.

question 'whether concession agreements made between the government controlling the resources to be exploited by the concession and the foreign party should be treated as genuine civil contracts or whether, on the other hand, the right to terminate such agreement at any time should be regarded as a non-negotiable aspect of the power and duty of governments to serve the social and economic welfare of their peoples by the exercise of their sovereign legislative and administrative powers'.[1] This is not a matter on which international law has any contribution to make; nor is it a question which can possibly be put in general terms, without reference to a specific system of municipal law. The classification, and the consequences flowing from it, are determined by the proper law of the contract. Here as elsewhere propositions of great width are unlikely to be helpful. Nor is any legally relevant point made by the suggestion that a particular contract or concession has the character of an 'economic development agreement'.[2] This is not a conception which, for present purposes, the law recognizes or finds useful. Even if it were accepted as a descriptive term, it would have no effect upon the control of municipal law, though, let it be repeated, the conflict rules of the *lex arbitri* may permit or require the application of public international law as the law chosen by the parties for their contract, however this may be described.

If one leaves aside doctrinal misunderstandings there is room for the impression that there exists only one award which explicitly adopts the opposite view and does so on grounds that must be described as wholly unconvincing but which, happily, are entirely *obiter*. The award was made by the late Professor Sauser-Hall as umpire and by M. Hassan and M. Saba Habachi as arbitrators in the case of *Saudi Arabia* v. *Arabian American Oil Co.*[3] The dispute arose from a concession which, apparently, did not define the legal system controlling it, but by the submission the arbitrators were instructed to decide the dispute in accordance with Saudi Arabian law, in so far as matters

---

[1] *The Changing Structure of International Law* (1964), pp. 200 et seq.

[2] This is a description to which Suratgar unjustifiably attached importance; see above, p. 265, n. 6.

[3] 27 Int. L.R. (1963), p. 117. For a summary of the decision (without apparent disapproval of its character or reasoning) see Mme Bastid, *Annuaire français de droit international* (1961), p. 300.

within the jurisdiction of Saudi Arabia were concerned, and, in regard to other matters, in accordance with the law deemed by the arbitrators to be applicable. The concession provided for arbitration at the Hague, but later the parties agreed that the seat of the tribunal should be at Geneva. In the course of a discussion of 'the law to be applied', but without explaining the relevance of its observations[1] the tribunal made the following statement:

Although the present arbitration was instituted, not between States, but between a State and a private American corporation, the Arbitration Tribunal is not of the opinion that the law of the country of its seat should be applied to the arbitration. The jurisdictional immunity of States (the principle *par in parem non habet jurisdictionem*) excludes the possibility, for the judicial authorities of the country of the seat, of exercising their right of supervision and interference in the arbitral proceedings which they have in certain cases. . . . The Courts of Geneva have applied the law of Geneva to arbitrations between foreign corporations which, in the *compromis*, had established the seat of their arbitration tribunal in Geneva. . . . The question of the applicability of Swiss law to an arbitration in Switzerland to which a foreign State is a party does not appear to have ever been decided by the Courts of Geneva or by Swiss Courts. Considering the jurisdictional immunity of foreign States, recognized by international law in a spirit of respect for the essential dignity of sovereign power, the Tribunal is unable to hold that arbitral proceedings to which a sovereign State is a party could be subject to the law of another State. Any interference by the latter State would constitute an infringement of the prerogatives of the State which is a party to the arbitration. This would render illusory the award given in such circumstances. For these reasons the Tribunal finds that the law of Geneva cannot be applied to the present arbitration. It follows that the arbitration, as such, can only be governed by international law.

In the first place, it is obvious that the arbitrators could not, and probably did not intend, to decide finally the question whether and to what extent Swiss law applied to the arbitration. In case of need, this was a question for decision by the Swiss courts. Their jurisdiction could not be taken away or limited by the arbitrators. Secondly, the tribunal could not help being subject to the sovereignty, i.e. to the law, of the

---

[1] 27 Int. L.R. (1963), p. 155. What difference would it have made if the tribunal had held that the arbitration was subject to the law of Geneva? In other words, why was it necessary to make the observations which in part are referred to in the text? This is only one of the many points which establish that the award is a diffuse and poorly reasoned contribution of very little value. See above, p. 229.

country where it was sitting. The arbitrators thought it right to suggest that any interference by Switzerland 'would constitute an infringement of the prerogatives of the State which is a party to the arbitration'. And what about 'an infringement of the prerogatives of the State' in which the arbitration, exempt from its jurisdiction, takes place? Had Switzerland given its consent to an arbitration proceeding in its territory which was subject to international law and which, therefore, Swiss law could not reach? Thirdly, the arbitrators assumed without discussion that the principle of immunity applied to a contract and an arbitration of the type they were concerned with. In truth, it is almost certain that in Switzerland the principle does not comprise acts done *jure gestionis*. Fourthly, it is necessary to draw attention to the inadmissible consequences of the arbitrators' ruling. Perhaps reference may once again be made to the question of administering oaths to witnesses appearing before the arbitrators. Should Professor Sauser-Hall, M. Hassan and M. Saba Habachi be able to administer oaths in the face of an express prohibition by the law of Switzerland or Geneva? Moreover, would it really be in the interest of the parties if the award made by these arbitrators were an international award which, in all probability, could not be enforced in a municipal court?[1] Fifthly, and most significantly, it is submitted that the tribunal completely misunderstood the nature and effect of immunity. Let it be assumed that there may be circumstances in which in arbitration proceedings immunity may have a role to play.[2] Nevertheless, it is certain that, once a State has submitted to the jurisdiction of a judicial or arbitral tribunal, it has lost all its privileges; it is exposed to certain counter-claims, it has to provide security for costs, it has to pay costs when unsuccessful, it may become a respondent in an appeal, and so forth.[3] It is, therefore, plainly wrong to suggest that after submission to arbitration a State remains, within the framework of the same arbitration, entitled to any jurisdictional immunity. Hence, it is not surprising that the views expressed by the arbitrators in the present case are unique.[4] They are, not

---

[1] See above, pp. 258–9.    [2] See below, p. 274.

[3] For these elementary propositions see, for instance, Oppenheim, *International Law*, (8th ed., 1955, by Lauterpacht), i.266 and *Guaranty Trust Co.* v. *United States*, 304 U. S. 126 (1938). Or Dahm, *Völkerrecht*, i.246.

[4] The only author who holds that the local law, i.e. the *lex arbitri*, is inapplicable

reflected in any other case. They are in particular, contrary to the arbitral practice in England,[1] where, as is well known, the doctrine of sovereign immunity has generally been allowed greater scope than in any other country.

If, in accordance with the preceding suggestions, an arbitration between a State and a private person, arising under a State contract, is subject to municipal law, then the award resulting from such arbitration has the 'nationality' of the country under whose law it is rendered, and can be enforced as such. In particular, it comes within the terms of any Convention which may apply to the international enforcement of such country's awards. The Geneva Protocol of 1923 extends to arbitration clauses agreed between 'parties, subject respectively to the jurisdiction of different contracting States'. Dr. Jenks has suggested[2] that in view of these terms the Protocol can 'have no direct application to an arbitration clause, one of the parties to which is an international body corporate which by definition is not subject to the jurisdiction of a contracting State'. A State which enters into an arbitration clause with a private person and becomes subject to arbitration under a municipal system of law may be said to have itself assumed the character of a private person and, therefore, to be under its own jurisdiction for the purpose of the Protocol of 1923. The broad policy pursued by the latter is such that there is no intrinsic reason why arbitration to which a State is a party should be excluded from its scope.

(2) If an arbitration between a State and a private person is, irrespective of the nature of the contract, invariably and necessarily subject to the *lex arbitri*, i.e. a municipal system of law (though this may refer to or allow reference to some other law), there remains the question whether this principle also applies in the case of arbitration proceedings under the auspices of certain institutions.

No exception is possible where the parties avail themselves

---

in the case of an arbitration between a State and a private person, seems to be Bourquin in 15 *Business Lawyer* (1960), 860, at pp. 870–1. But although he relies on the jurisdictional immunity of States as his argument, he does not develop the point, or define the law which is applicable in substitution for the local law, or consider waiver.

[1] Above, p. 268, n. 3.
[2] *The Proper Law of International Organizations* (1962), p. 246.

of the facilities offered by the International Chamber of Commerce.[1]

A problem of greater difficulty arises in the case of the Rules of Arbitration and Conciliation for Settlement of International Disputes between two parties of which only one is a State, elaborated in 1962 by the Permanent Court of Arbitration.[2] This organization was originally created for the pacific settlement of disputes between States. The Convention of 1907 provides[3] that 'the Bureau is authorized to place its office and staff at the disposal of the *Contracting Powers* for the use of any special Board of Arbitration'. This provision, one would have thought, contemplates disputes between 'contracting powers' only, but, as appears from Article 1 of the Rules of 1962, the Bureau considered that 'in case of arbitration in an international dispute between two parties of which only one is a State, the International Bureau of the Permanent Court of Arbitration ... is authorized to place its premises and organization at the disposal of the parties'.[4] This is a highly doubtful interpretation of Article 47, but up to a point it is an innocuous one, for nothing precludes a State and a private person from agreeing upon any set of rules of arbitration that appeals to them. The only question is whether by invoking the prima facie inapplicable Article 47 of the Convention of 1907 the Bureau intends to impress the international character, which would clearly attach to proceedings between contracting powers, upon proceedings between a State and a private person. If this is the intention, it has not succeeded, for Article 47 certainly does not confer so far-reaching an authority. Arbitration proceedings under the Rules of 1962 would seem to be subject to Dutch law except that this may provide for another law to prevail. An award rendered as a result of such proceedings is a Dutch award and as such enforceable outside Holland.

The legal position is different in the case of the Convention on the Settlement of Investment Disputes between States and

---

[1] See on such cases Böckstiegel, 59 *A.J.I.L.* (1965), p. 579.

[2] For the text see 57 ibid. (1963), p. 500. On the new Rules and their background see Schlochauer, 12 *Archiv des Völkerrechts* (1964–5), p. 173, who at p. 187 prints the French text.

[3] Art. 47.

[4] See François, *Annuaire suisse de droit international* (1959), xvi.285, 289.

nationals of other States which, under the auspices of the International Bank for Reconstruction and Development, was signed in March 1965, and has been ratified by numerous countries. This provides for the creation of the International Centre for Settlement of Investment Disputes between contracting States and nationals of other contracting States,[1] the High Contracting Parties having recognized, by virtue of the third recital, the benefits of 'international methods of settlement' in the case of such disputes. The Centre which lays down its own rules of procedure,[2] has 'full international legal personality' and enjoys the usual immunities.[3] So do the arbitrators and other persons engaged in the proceedings.[4] The award is not 'subject to any appeal or any other remedy except those provided for' in the Convention,[5] and is recognized and enforceable in each contracting State.[6] This, therefore, is a truly international tribunal which the contracting States have created for themselves and their nationals, which rests on a treaty and is 'self-contained', i.e. independent of any municipal law except in so far as concerns enforcement. Accordingly, in the United Kingdom the Arbitration (International Investment Disputes) Act 1966, made special provision for the registration of Convention Awards,[7] but in addition it anticipated that an arbitration tribunal set up under the Convention might function in England. Therefore, it not only recognizes the immunities and privileges granted by the Convention,[8] but also declares that, subject to two exceptions, the Arbitration Act, 1950, 'shall not apply to proceedings pursuant to the Convention'.[9] The elimination of the English Courts' supervisory powers over arbitration proceedings in England confirms the international character of arbitration under the Convention. This is even more clearly emphasized by the terms of the statute with which the United States of America ratified the Convention. It provides[10] that an award made by the Centre's arbitration tribunal 'shall create a right arising under a treaty of the United States'. It continues that 'the pecuniary obligations imposed by such an award shall be enforced and shall be given

---

[1] Arts. 1 and 2. The text of the Convention is printed as a Schedule to the Arbitration (International Investment Disputes) Act, 1966.
[2] Art. 6.  [3] Arts. 18–20, 23, 24,.  [4] Art. 21.  [5] Art. 53.
[6] Art. 54.  [7] Sections 1 and 2.  [8] Section 4.
[9] Section 3 (2).  [10] *International Legal Materials* (1966), v.820.

the same full faith and credit as if the award were a final judgment of a court of general jurisdiction in one of the several States' and that the Federal Arbitration Act shall not apply. An arbitration under the Convention is, therefore, the only one that renders a procedure under public international law available to a private person for the enforcement of a State contract, although, as a rule, this remains subject to a municipal system of law.[1]

At the same time, an award made in pursuance of the Convention is the only award made under public international law that is enforceable through the medium of municipal procedure. In addition, if it is made against a contracting State and remains unsatisfied, the State of which the successful party is a national is entitled to espouse its national's claim; this certainly applies to the claim arising under the municipal judgment into which the award has been converted and also applies to the award itself, for the provisions of Article 53 according to which an award is not subject 'to any appeal or any other remedy' cannot be read as excluding the possibility of diplomatic protection. The fact that this remains available does not necessitate the conclusion that the proceedings leading up to the award are not international in character.

(3) At this point is becomes possible to end the discussion of the general principles governing international arbitration under State contracts and to turn to the peculiarities and to some of the specific problems to which such arbitration is likely to give rise.

(a) *The validity of the submission.* There are certain countries which render it unlawful for the State and its organs to submit to arbitration. This is so in France where articles 83 and 1009 of the Code of Civil Procedure provide that 'on ne peut compromettre . . . sur aucune des contestations' which concerns the State. It was until recently difficult in France to assess the significance of this prohibition in the realm of international

---

[1] Art. 42. The Tribunal will decide 'in accordance with such rules of law as may be agreed between the parties'. In the absence of such agreement the law of the contracting State party to the dispute, including its conflict rules, shall apply together with 'such rules of international law as may be applicable'. The great significance of this provision cannot be discussed in the context of the present article. See, however, Delaume in *Clunet* 1966, pp. 20–3, or (in English) 1 *The International Lawyer* (1966), pp. 77–9.

arbitration. Is it without effect on the ground that it relates only to proceedings in France? Does it apply only where French law governs the contract? Or, on the contrary, is it perhaps a principle of *ordre public*? Or does it create an incapacity even on the part of the French State to submit to arbitration? It was only in 1966 that the Cour de Cassation finally answered these questions by its decision in the case of *Galakis*. In 1940 the French Admiralty chartered a Greek ship under a charter-party which provided for arbitration in London. This took place in 1953, when Galakis obtained an award against the French State. In 1954 it was declared enforceable in France and this decision was affirmed in 1966 on the ground that the prohibition 'ne soulève pas une question de capacité', that the rule was 'édictée pour les contrats internes' and that it was inapplicable to 'un contrat international passé pour les besoins et dans les conditions conformes aux usages du commerce maritime'.[1]

It is to be hoped that this liberal decision will be followed wherever fetters similar to those prevailing in France are imposed upon the State's ability to submit to arbitration. But whether or not this is so depends primarily on the *lex arbitri*. If the arbitration takes place, for instance, in England and if already in the course of the arbitration, i.e. before the award, the respondent State invokes provisions such as those of the French Code of Civil Procedure, they afford a defence only if they invalidate the submission or impose an incapacity and if in either case the law of the respondent State governs. In deciding the question of the governing law and the classification, the arbitrators will follow the conflict rules of the *lex arbitri* or of the legal system to which the *lex arbitri* refers.

Normally, one would expect the arbitrators to pass upon any such problem in the course of the arbitration, though their decision cannot foreclose the right of review vested in the court of a country in which the award is enforced. The trouble which arose in the case of *Losinger & Cie* and which led to a dispute between Switzerland and Yugoslavia[2] was caused by the arbitrator's refusal to pronounce upon the effect of a Yugoslavian

---

[1] Cass. Civ., 2 May 1966, *Clunet* 1966, p. 648, with note by P. Level; see also Cass. Civ., 14 April 1964, *Clunet* 1965, p. 645, with note by Goldman.

[2] P.C.I.J. (1938), (Series C), No. 78.

law according to which 'les procès contre l'État ne peuvent être intentés que devant les tribunaux réguliers de l'État'.[1] Instead, the arbitrator, M. Henri Thélin, suspended the arbitration and left to the parties 'le soin de soumettre cette question à l'autorité compétente'.[2] The precedent will not, it is hoped, be followed. It was the source of the trouble which eventually brought Switzerland and Yugoslavia before the Permanent Court of International Justice.

(*b*) *Immunity.* It has already been pointed out that once a State has submitted to arbitration it is, in regard to the conduct of the proceedings, in no different position from any other litigant. The problem of immunity arises only when it comes to enforcing (i) the submission agreement or (ii) the award against a recalcitrant State in a court of law outside the contracting State.

(i) It is usually assumed that in both respects the answer is supplied by the general law relating to immunity rather than any specific rules relating to international arbitration. As regards the enforcement of the submission in particular, in almost all countries except Britain and the Communist world this depends on whether the contract under which it arises constitutes a private or commercial activity *jure gestionis* or a political or public act *jure imperii*. The latter is, the former is not, entitled to immunity. Accordingly, an arbitration arising from a charter-party between a private shipowner and a government for the transport of wheat is a commercial act, with the result that the courts of the *lex arbitri* are entitled to lend their assistance in procuring the constitution of the arbitration tribunal.[3] On this footing it only remains to define the State contracts which can be classified as commercial. According to the prevailing American practice[4] not only legislative, administrative, and diplomatic acts, but also 'public loans' would be treated as public. Loans taken up and bonds issued by a State are, however, by their nature not different from those to which

---

[1] For the text of the law see ibid., p. 118.

[2] See the award ibid., p. 116. The contract as a whole was subject to Yugoslavian law (p. 133). The arbitration was held in Switzerland, though in accordance with the arbitration clause the award was rendered in Yugoslavia (pp. 7–8).

[3] *Victory Transport Inc.* v. *Comisaria General*, 336 F. 2d 354 (1964), also 35 Int. L.R., p. 110, a decision of the United States Court of Appeals, 2nd Circuit.

[4] See the dicta in the case mentioned in the preceding note.

a private corporation is a party. Nor is their purpose necessarily different. Their form and legal structure are usually identical in both cases. Arbitration clauses may occur in both. It would be a great disservice to international investment if the lender of money to a State were told that in law he is participating in a transaction *jure imperii*.[1] It is quite true that according to the Supreme Court of the United States[2] Treasury Notes issued by the Republic of China were 'Sovereign obligations, *jure imperii* in form, of the highest public character'. But even if this was so in the case of Chinese Treasury Notes, it would be wrong to propound a principle of general application.

The problem is more doubtful in the case of concession agreements. These normally involve a grant made by the State in the exercise of its sovereign powers. Such an origin strongly points to the public character of concession agreements. Yet it will not always be decisive, for the agreement as a whole may disclose an intention to separate its content and operation from its origin, i.e. from the granting State's public law.

It is, however, submitted that within the context of the present discussion the character of the agreement as a commercial or public act is irrelevant and that, whether the agreement arises *jure imperii* or *jure gestionis*, the mere presence of an arbitration clause should be treated as an implied waiver of the plea of immunity.

In England, it is true, such a proposition is at present contrary to the law as laid down by the Court of Appeal in the unfortunate and unjust decision of *Kahan* v. *Federation of Pakistan*,[3] where the express submission in a contract to the jurisdiction of the English Courts was denied effect on the ground that a waiver of immunity was invalid except if made *in facie curiae*. This doctrine, which no doubt extends to arbitration clauses, has no basis in international law, as appears from the Optional Clause embodied in the Statute of the International Court of Justice[4]; when States 'declare that they recognize as compulsory, *ipso facto* and without special agreement, in relation to any other State accepting the same obligation, the jurisdiction

---

[1] Cf. Delaume, 6 *A.J.I.L.* (1957), p. 189; 3 *Columbia Journal of Transnational Law* (1964), p. 3.
[2] *National City Bank of New York* v. *Republic of China*, 348 U. S. 356 (1955).
[3] [1951] 2 K. B. 1003.      [4] Art. 36 (2).

of the Court in all legal disputes', they enter only into an 'obligation', yet it has never been doubted that the declaration operates as a submission or as the actual waiver of the right to allege lack of jurisdiction. The law (not only the English system of equity) regards that as done which is agreed to be done. Thus, private persons who agree upon the exclusive jurisdiction of a particular court, waive the jurisdiction of any other tribunal and cannot escape by alleging the promissory character of their respective undertakings. Nor is there any other argument of logic, common sense, or justice that supports the English practice.[1] It is open to the House of Lords to reject it, for even if, contrary to its plain meaning and effect,[2] *Duff Development Co.* v. *Kelantan*[3] had to be treated as an actual decision on the waiver implied in an arbitration clause, it would now be open to the House 'to depart from a previous decision when it appears right to do so'. It is possible, therefore, that even in Britain a better view may come to prevail.

But outside Britain there is no reason at all why a State should not be held to its contractual undertaking and why an arbitration clause should not be considered as an implied waiver of the plea of immunity. It is difficult to conceive circumstances which more clearly point to a waiver of immunity than an arbitration clause. It implies exclusivity of the tribunal contemplated by it. One cannot give business efficacy to such a clause if one assumes it to have the effect of allowing one party unilaterally to repudiate it. And if the officious bystander had asked the parties or any reasonable man whether such repudiation was intended to be permitted a very clear answer in the negative would have been forthcoming.[4] In 1932 the

---

[1] For criticism see, in particular, Cohn, *B.Y.I.L.* (1958), xxxiv.260. He is the only writer who has put forward an explanation of the curious doctrine that submission to jurisdiction is ineffective except if declared *in facie curiae*. It is a purely English doctrine which is based on unacceptably narrow and dogmatic reasoning.

[2] The decision quite clearly relates exclusively to the enforceability of an award by judicial proceedings. This is an entirely different question from that discussed in the text.

[3] [1924] A. C. 797.

[4] This is a wholly traditional method of approaching the question of waiver and very much less extreme than what has from time to time been done in this field. See, on the one hand, the decision of the Appellate Division of the Supreme Court of New York in *Hannes* v. *Kingdom of Roumania Monopolies Institute*, 20 N. Y. S. 2d 850 (1940), where it was considered possible that the usual provisions in a statute creating a corporation according to which it may sue and be sued constituted a

*Harvard Research* suggested that a State should not be entitled to immunity if it has previously consented to the institution of proceedings by a contract upon which the proceedings are based. Its authors described this result as 'so obviously equitable that its general acceptability may be assumed'.[1] Their view was in fact supported by decisions of the Supreme Courts of Germany and of Greece.[2] Since then, the American Law Institute's *Foreign Relations Law* seems to have adopted the same rule.[3] It is, indeed, a rule that is both legally sound and intrinsically meritorious.

Nevertheless, it will always be prudent for parties to avoid all doubt by framing the arbitration clause so as to ensure its efficacy without resort to any tribunal. Thus, the clause should provide machinery for the appointment of an arbitrator or umpire if the State fails to co-operate, whatever the reason may be.[4] It should provide, moreover, for the right of the arbitrator to pronounce upon the validity and effect of the arbitration clause as well as upon his own jurisdiction. And, finally, it should make it clear that the arbitration is to be held outside the territory of the contracting State.

(ii) Enforcement of the award by execution against the State is, in the absence of consent, impossible even in most of those States which do not extend the doctrine of sovereign immunity to acts done *jure gestionis*.[5] Enforcement of the award,

---

waiver of the plea of immunity. And see, on the other hand, the decision of the English Court of Appeal in *Baccus S.L.R.* v. *Servicio Nacional*, [1957] 1 Q.B. 438, where a similar provision was, rightly, considered immaterial to the problem of waiver (see at p. 472, per Parker L.J.), but where an appearance entered and maintained for eighteen months was held not to constitute waiver in the absence of knowledge of the legal position on the part of, and authority given by, the sovereign; Singleton L.J.'s dissenting judgment is wholly convincing. It is not certain that the argument addressed to the Court on behalf of the unsuccessful plaintiffs was as broadly based as would have been desirable.

[1] *A.J.I.L.* (1932) (Supplement) 453, 548. For the text of Art. 8 and comment see p. 548.

[2] *Juristische Wochenschrift* 1926, p. 804, and *Annual Digest* (1927–8), Case No. 109, respectively.

[3] The text of section 70 is perhaps not entirely clear, but the illustration on p. 219 leaves no doubt about the author's intention.

[4] In doing so, the pitfalls should be avoided which came to light in the *Anglo-Iranian Oil Company* case and which are discussed below, p. 280.

[5] The problem of enforcement seems to have been involved in *N.V. Cabolent* v. *N.I.O.C.*, *International Legal Materials* (1966), v.477, the Dutch sequel of the *Sapphire International* case mentioned above, p. 265, n. 6, and below, p. 284, n. 2.

however, comprises not only execution in the accepted sense of the term, but also turning the award into a judgment or a title equivalent to a judgment by providing it with an *exequatur* or some similar judicial certificate. Is the latter type of enforcement sanctioned by the waiver of immunity included in the arbitration clause and the submission to arbitration proceedings? Or has it to be considered from the point of view of execution? In other words, does the judgment constitute the final point of the arbitration or the beginning of, or at least a preliminary to, execution?

This was, it is submitted, the real problem with which the House of Lords was confronted in *Duff Development Co.* v. *Government of Kelantan.*[1] An award against Kelantan had been made by arbitrators. The application to the Court by the successful contractors was for an order that the award be made a judgment of the Court. The House rejected the application. The reason given by Viscount Cave[2] with whom, in effect, Lord Sumner[3] and Lord Dunedin[4] agreed, was that such an order could only be made if the Government had actually submitted to the jurisdiction of the Court and that mere agreement to submit was insufficient. This reason is, as has been pointed out[5] unconvincing and, indeed, inadequate today. It is also lacking in precision, for the existence of an agreement to submit to the jurisdiction of the Court was assumed without discussion. Lord Finlay[6] approached the heart of the matter much more closely when he asked whether the Government had 'waived objection to execution upon their property in this country'. The answer was bound to be in the negative. Neither the arbitration clause nor the submission to arbitration implies submission to the Court. An application for enforcement serves no useful purpose except as a first step towards execution. This being precluded by the doctrine of immunity and no express or implied consent to the jurisdiction of the courts for purposes of execution having been given, the defence of immunity was rightly allowed to prevail.

---

The decision can perhaps be justified on the ground that the plaintiffs attempted to execute the award.

[1] [1924] A. C. 797.    [2] Ibid., 809, 810.    [3] Ibid., 819.
[4] Ibid., 821.    [5] Above, p. 276.
[6] *Duff Development Co.* v. *Government of Kelantan*, [1924] A. C. 797, at 820.

(c) *A third person's failure to appoint an arbitrator.* If a third person[1] such as the President of a court, bank, chamber of commerce or some similar body, or the secretary of a trade association is, according to the terms of an arbitration clause, intended to appoint an arbitrator or umpire but fails to do so, a well-drawn arbitration clause or, alternatively, the *lex arbitri* may provide machinery for filling the gap. Where, however, a remedy is not available or where, in the absence of such appointment, the *lex arbitri* cannot even be determined, the arbitration clause becomes frustrated.[2]

An arbitration clause which confers a power of appointment upon a third person, does not and, indeed, cannot impose an enforceable legal duty upon a person not a party to the contract. Compliance with such an invitation is rarely more than a *nobile officium.* Failure to give effect to the invitation may, in view of the danger of frustrating the arbitration clause, involve great injustice and financial damage and thus attracts heavy, albeit moral, responsibility.

In view of the very numerous contracts[3] which, without creating a legal duty, authorize a third party to make appointments, it is necessary to make it clear that such a person or body does not in any circumstances perform any judicial function in exercising the power. By making the appointment it renders no decision in the dispute between the parties, expresses no opinion on a procedural aspect or on the merits of the case nor precludes the arbitrators (or any competent court) from reviewing the validity and effects of the appointment that is made. The third party acts in a purely ministerial capacity and without prejudice to the decision of the competent tribunal. Thus, the fact that one

---

[1] It is necessary to make it very clear that this section deals with the refusal of the appointor to make an appointment. Where the respondent refuses to make an appointment entirely different problems arise which will be referred to below, p. 285.

[2] That this is the consequence in law is clearly established by judicial practice in Germany (see Court of Appeal, Karlsruhe, *Neue Juristische Wochenschrift* 1958, p. 1148), but must be so in all countries in which the law makes no provision for a substitute appointor.

[3] A list of the treaties which provide for appointments to be made by the President of the International Court is to be found in the Court's *Yearbook* (1963–4), pp. 255 et seq. A list of contracts including such clauses is not known. But the *Yearbook* for 1964–5 states (p. 36) that 'such requests are generally acceded to' and that 'the usual practice is to consult the President in advance and to submit the draft contract to him'.

party to the dispute alleges the invalidity of the contract or of the arbitration clause may lead to an issue to be decided by the arbitrator or by a court. But it should have no influence on the mere administrative act which the appointing body performs. This is so even in case the third person is a judge. The identity of the appointor is in law a fortuitous fact and the judicial appointor cannot have any different or larger rights, duties, or functions of inquiry or decision than a chamber of commerce or any other non-judicial body. Nor does the judge act under the supervision or as a representative of his court. He acts in his private capacity. His appointment stems from a clause which, if fully spelt out, would define him, for instance, as 'the gentleman who at the relevant time will occupy the office of President of the Swiss Federal Tribunal'.

It is possible that if these considerations had been borne in mind an incident would have been avoided which is subject to serious criticism and which it is difficult to describe with academic detachment. The concession granted by Iran to the Anglo-Iranian Oil Company provided that, in the event of one party's refusal to appoint an arbitrator, the President of the Permanent Court of International Justice should be asked to appoint the sole arbitrator who would have the power, *inter alia*, to determine the place of the arbitration. Iran having failed to make an appointment, the company, on 25 May 1951, applied to the President of the International Court of Justice for the appointment of the sole arbitrator.[1] On 28 May 1951 M. Basdevant replied.[2] He referred to the proceedings which the United Kingdom had instituted against Iran in the International Court of Justice and stated that these proceedings and the Company's request had 'certain points in common and that, consequently, I am unable to deal at present with that which you have submitted to me'. It is impossible to understand the reason for this inability. It may, however, be assumed that the common points were those which M. Guerrero was to indicate more than a year later. For after the Court had rejected the United Kingdom's application on the ground that the concession was not 'a treaty or convention' within the meaning of Iran's submission to the jurisdiction of the Court, M.

---

[1] C.I.F. Pleadings (1952), in the *Anglo-Iranian Oil* case, p. 387.
[2] Ibid., p. 391.

Guerrero wrote to the Anglo-Iranian Oil Company on 11 October 1952 in terms which do not seem to have been published in full, but included the point that[1]:

> He did not consider himself entitled to proceed to the appointment of an arbitrator. . . . He pointed out that that Agreement had conferred power to appoint upon the President or Vice-President of the Permanent Court of International Justice; no request had been addressed to the International Court of Justice by the parties to the contract to undertake functions similar to those entrusted to the President or Vice-President of the Permanent Court. Moreover, Article 37 of the Statute could not be applied since that provision related only to the settlement of cases of jurisdiction provided for in a treaty or convention between States.

It is possible that this reasoning was wrong. A question of construction was involved. The question was whether the concession had to be so construed as to refer to the President of that Court which was then known as the Permanent Court or to its successor. Article 37 of the Statute could have no bearing upon this question. It deals with cases in which 'a treaty or convention in force provides for reference of a matter to a tribunal . . . or to the Permanent Court of International Justice'. It does not affect the power of appointing an arbitrator conferred upon M. Basdevant, the President for the time being of the (International) Court, rather than upon the Court itself. It follows that M. Guerrero rendered a decision or expressed a view upon a point which was entirely outside his jurisdiction. The summary of his letters is published in the *Yearbook* of the International Court as an example of the 'extra-judicial functions' which 'the Court, or its President, are sometimes requested to perform'.[2] This is a correct characterization, and if M. Guerrero had adhered to it he would simply have refused to act[3] or would have made the appointment without prejudice to the decision which those called upon to perform judicial functions would render on the validity of his ruling and on the underlying question of construction. By failing to act extra-judicially M. Guerrero assumed the responsibility of depriving Anglo-Iranian Oil Company of its remedy. The Vice-President's conduct is

---

[1] *Yearbook of the I.C.J.* (1952–3), p. 45.    [2] Ibid., p. 44.

[3] This would have been possible, but difficult, seeing that on 21 October 1933 the Court had stated that 'it sees no obstacle to the acceptance by its President and Vice-President of the functions conferred upon him by Art. 22 of the said Agreement'. I.C.J. Pleadings (1952), p. 272.

aggravated by reason of the fact that, if and in so far as he had the right and intention to act judicially, he had the clear duty to hear the applicant before causing it irreparable damage.

Notwithstanding its almost tragic character, M. Guerrero's refusal does not seem to have led to much scholarly discussion. Professor Johnson's contribution[1] is an exception. His reasoning, which gives the impression of an attempted vindication, cannot be accepted. He says that 'the President remains a judge, and the senior judge of the Court, and a situation may easily arise in which the effect of an appointment of an arbitrator by the President may be to prejudge some issue which either is, or may come, before the Court'.[2] He therefore attributes to M. Basdevant 'the very proper fear' that 'a decision either to grant or to reject the Company's request for the appointment of an arbitrator would have prejudged a principal issue in the case between the two Governments'.[3] It can only be repeated that there was no 'decision' nor any possibility 'to prejudge some issue'. Professor Johnson also poses, but does not answer, the question 'whether, in appointing arbitrators, the President acts in a purely personal capacity or ultimately under the control of the Court'.[4] With the greatest respect for the eminent office which the President holds, it is suggested that, when he appoints an arbitrator, he acts in no other capacity than the Secretary of the National Association of Fishmongers who is called upon to perform the same task: he acts as a fair-minded person who may be expected to be a man of the world and to find the right man for the job about the legal existence, the nature and the extent of which others will have to reach a decision.

At this point it becomes possible and necessary to review comprehensively that part of the *Anglo-Iranian Oil Company* case in the International Court of Justice, which related to the enforcement of the arbitration clause in the Concession Agreement of 1933. It was the United Kingdom's original claim (on which, of course, no decision was pronounced) that the Court should[5]

... declare that the Imperial Government of Iran are under a duty to submit the dispute between themselves and the Anglo-Iranian Oil Com-

---

[1] *B.Y.I.L.* (1953), xxx.153 et seq.    [2] Ibid., p. 155.    [3] Ibid., p. 156.
[4] Ibid., pp. 157–8.    [5] I.C.J. Pleadings, (1952), p. 18.

pany Ltd. to arbitration . . . and to accept and carry out any award issued
as a result of such arbitration.

The Memorial resumed the same thought, though in different
words and with an eye to *restitutio in integrum*. The United
Kingdom asked for a declaration that Iran

. . . is bound, within a period fixed by the Court, to restore the Anglo-
Iranian Oil Company Limited to the position as it existed prior to the said
Oil Nationalization Act and to abide by the provisions of the aforesaid
Convention, including the obligations of Article 22 thereof, providing for the
arbitration of any differences of any nature whatever between the Imperial
Government of Iran and the Anglo-Iranian Oil Company Limited . . .

On 26 May 1951, when this application was submitted, or on
the date of the Memorial—10 October 1951—it was not known
that the President (or the Vice-President) of the Court would
frustrate the arbitration by his refusal to make the appointment. The substantial point at that time was that Iran alleged
the ineffectiveness of the arbitration clause on the ground that,
as a result of its nationalizing legislation, the concession agreement in general and the arbitration clause in particular had
been abrogated or invalidated. However, the decision on this
point was, as the United Kingdom itself seemed to recognize in
its pleadings, vested in the arbitration tribunal. Had there been
such a tribunal in existence, the International Court of Justice
would not even have been entitled to pronounce the declaration for which the United Kingdom asked. It would have been
for the arbitrators to proceed with the reference, even in the
absence of Iran, and reach a decision on the issues. On this
footing, therefore, the United Kingdom asked the International Court of Justice to do something that was contrary to
the judicial function.[1] But the arbitration tribunal was, in fact,
not constituted. Had the International Court had jurisdiction,
it should, therefore, have told the United Kingdom that its
national, the Anglo-Iranian Oil Company, should proceed with
the arbitration. Again, there was no room for the declaration
for which the United Kingdom asked. Finally, let it be assumed
that the Vice-President had already communicated that refusal
to make the required appointment, which he was to express a

[1] Within the meaning of the decision in the *Northern Cameroons* case, I.C.J.
Reports (1963), p. 15.

year later. In that event the arbitration would have been frustrated and the claim to a declaration made in the proceedings in the International Court would have been unjustified. Iran may well have been under a duty to appoint an arbitrator and the United Kingdom may well have been entitled to *restitutio in integrum*; but if, as a result of the Vice-President's attitude, the contemplated machinery for filling the gap broke down, this did not supply the United Kingdom with a cause of action with a view to compelling Iran to make an appointment.[1] It follows that the United Kingdom's claim to a declaration was unfounded. Whether there was an arbitration tribunal in existence or not, the International Court could not intervene, because in either case intervention was pointless. What the United Kingdom should have done was to await the outcome of the application for the appointment of the arbitrator, which had been addressed to the President. If the appointment had been made, the arbitration ought to have been proceeded with. In the absence of an appointment by the President, the arbitration was frustrated by him and there was no basis for alleging any duty on the part of Iran to make an appointment itself, or for any damage caused by Iran's refusal to arbitrate. The damage arising from the frustration of the arbitration clause was caused by the Vice-President. In so far as the United Kingdom's claim was directed towards observance of the arbitration by Iran it was mistaken.

It only remains to be added by way of postscript that, for the reasons which have been outlined, it is not possible to recommend the Swiss practice relating to the status of the appointor. Thus, in the case of *Sapphire International* v. *National Iranian Oil Company*,[2] the arbitration clause provided that in the event of

---

[1] See in a different, though cognate, field the case of *Interpretation of Peace Treaties with Bulgaria, Hungary and Roumania*, I.C.J. Reports (1950), pp. 65, 211, which concerned a treaty. The Court held that reference to a Commission at the request of one State imposed the duty upon the other party 'to co-operate in constituting the Commission, in particular by appointing its representative. Otherwise the method of Settlement by Commissions provided for in the treaties would completely fail in its purpose' (p. 77). At the same time, however, the refusal to make the appointment, though involving a breach of treaty, 'cannot alter the conditions contemplated in the treaties for the exercise by the Secretary-General of his power of appointment' (p. 228).

[2] 35 Int. L.R., p. 136, at p. 167. On this see, in particular, J. F. Lalive, *Annuaire suisse de droit International* (1962), p. 273, and *I.C.L.Q.* (1964), p. 987.

one party's failure to appoint its arbitrator the President of the Swiss Federal Tribunal should appoint the single arbitrator. The President made the appointment, but its validity was disputed by the respondent. On this point the arbitrator held that the arbitration clause had entrusted the appointment *à une autorité judiciaire* whose decision had *force de chose jugée*.[1] In another case between two private parties[2] the President of the Swiss Federal Tribunal refused to make the appointment on the ground that the validity of the arbitration was in issue and that, therefore, the arbitrators had to decide about it, while he was precluded from doing so. Why in either of these cases the President was called upon or had the power to make a judicial decision has remained unexplained[3] and appears to be contrary to principle and good sense.

(*d*) *Progress of the arbitration in the event of the State's absence or a party's failure to appoint its arbitrator.* In the event of a party to the State contract and, in particular, the State refusing to participate in the arbitration the remedy available to the claimant is, in principle, not open to doubt: the arbitration can proceed unilaterally in such manner as the arbitration clause or, alternatively, the *lex arbitri* may permit with a view to setting the arbitration in motion.

In practice, numerous and serious difficulties are liable to occur, particularly in case the arbitration clause fails to lay down the machinery for creating the tribunal without both parties' co-operation. Thus, the *lex arbitri* may be uncertain, because the seat of the tribunal is not determined in the arbitration clause, but is a matter for decision by the arbitrator or umpire. Or the *lex arbitri* may not provide a remedy against a party refusing to appoint its arbitrator. In such circumstances arbitration is effectively stultified.[4] In the result, the claimant party may be compelled to consider whether it should pursue any remedy open to it in the ordinary courts, including the

---

[1] See Lalive, op. cit., in the preceding note, at p. 283. Against this part of the decision Suratgar, 3 *Columbia Journal of Transnational Law* (1965), pp. 152, 176 et seq. whose reasoning is somewhat diffuse, but in essence convincing.

[2] *BGE* 88 i.100 (7 July 1962).

[3] The decision is particularly unsatisfactory in that no arbitration tribunal could ever decide upon the validity of the arbitration clause, unless it had previously been appointed. Yet the President made the appointment impossible.

[4] For a very clear example, see the cases between France and Lebanon referred to below, p. 288, n. 3.

courts of the defaulting State. If, on the other hand, notwithstanding the absence of the State, the arbitration can proceed in accordance with the *lex arbitri*, the tribunal will hear the case and eventually render an award which is binding upon the defaulting State and entitled to international recognition.[1]

Where the State's failure to co-operate stems from the purported abrogation of the arbitration clause[2] or of the contract as a whole, the legal position is, in principle, the same, but requires some additional explanations.

(i) Any such abrogation cannot possibly be material except in the event of the law of the abrogating State being applicable. If, according to the conflict rules of the *lex arbitri*, the contract or the arbitration clause is subject to a legal system other than that of the abrogating State, consideration of the latter's legislation is in any case precluded.

(ii) Even if, *prima facie*, the law of the abrogating State is applicable, this does not necessarily impede the progress of the arbitration, for the arbitrators may well reach the conclusion that for reasons of *ordre public* or on some similar grounds, they cannot give effect to the abrogating legislation.

(iii) It is, accordingly, not open to a court or other body to refuse, for instance, to appoint an arbitrator on the ground that there may be doubt about the continued validity of the arbitration clause or of the clause conferring powers of appointment upon the court or other body or of the agreement as a whole. For the reasons already outlined, the effects of total or partial invalidity is a question to be decided by the arbitrators when constituted.[3] Similarly, it would be wrong to argue that in the absence of a valid arbitration clause no tribunal can have jurisdiction. It is for the arbitrators to decide upon their jurisdiction and, for this purpose, to pronounce upon the continued validity of the arbitration clause.[4]

No discussion of these matters has taken place in England

---

[1] This happened, for instance, in the *Lena Goldfields* case, above, p. 264, n. 2, and in the case of *Sapphire International,* above, p. 284, n. 2.

[2] Jimenez de Aréchaga, *Mélanges Gidel* (1961), p. 375, seems to take the view that it is never open to a Government to abrogate the arbitration clause in a contract to which it is a party.

[3] See above, pp. 279–80.

[4] In the case of *Losinger & Cie,* P.C.I.J. (1938) (Series C), No. 78, the arbitrator wrongly failed to do this; see below, pp. 290–91.

where section 10 of the Arbitration Act, 1950, confers power
upon the High Court or a judge thereof to make appointments
in a number of circumstances, e.g. where 'an arbitration agreement' provides for a reference to a single arbitrator and the
parties are unable to select him. It should be sufficient that
there appears to be 'a written agreement to submit present or
future differences to arbitration'.[1] It is not the function of the
court, when making the appointment, to investigate the
validity of the agreement, for if it were to hold the agreement
invalid, it would render arbitration impossible and thus prevent
a decision by the appropriate body on the very question at
issue. Similarly, if the court were to treat the agreement as
valid, there would be the great danger that the arbitrators would
consider themselves bound, whether in law or in fact, to accept
and follow the court's ruling, and thus once again to forgo their
own right and duty of decision. The court merely makes the
appointment. Its decision on this point is binding and renders
the arbitrator's position invulnerable, even if the arbitration
agreement should be invalid. While the court necessarily acts
judicially, it does not, in such cases, perform the judicial functions of deciding an issue.[2] It must, however, be added that a
different view seems to prevail in Germany where section 1029
of the Code of Civil Procedure in certain events allows the
court to make appointments.[3] The point, however, has not
been discussed in depth. It should certainly not be decided by
asserting the judicial function which the court normally performs (this is undeniable) and which is (wrongly) said to presuppose the right to inquire into the existence of a valid arbitration agreement.

(e) *Refusal of arbitration as a denial of justice.* It follows from
the preceding observations that there are many circumstances
in which the attitude of one party to an arbitration clause and,
in particular, of the contracting State results in the impossibility of setting up or operating the arbitration tribunal.
Usually this is the direct responsibility of the State; as, for instance, when the State fails, and no other person or body is

---

[1] Section 32 of the Arbitration Act, 1950.
[2] On the characteristics of the judicial power and function see *United Engineering
Workers' Union* v. *Devanayagam*, [1968] A. C. 356.
[3] See Baumbach–Schwab, *Schiedsgerichtsbarkeit*, pp. 109–10.

authorized, to appoint an arbitrator. Or the responsibility is indirect as, for instance, when an arbitrator withdraws from the proceedings, perhaps even at the request of the State, and there is no machinery for appointing a substitute. Can such or similar lack of co-operation on the part of the respondent State, which frustrates arbitration, be considered as a denial of justice so as to permit the State entitled to protect the interests of the contracting alien to invoke the rules of international responsibility? An affirmative answer has been given by Switzerland,[1] the United Kingdom,[2] and France,[3] though, not unnaturally, the opposite view has been taken by their opponents, namely Yugoslavia, Iran, and Lebanon respectively. Thus, the United Kingdom formulated its submissions as follows[4]:

(d) In rejecting arbitration, the means provided by Article 22 of the Convention for settling 'tous différends de nature quelconque entre les parties'. . . the Imperial Government of Iran have denied, or are attempting to deny, to the Company the exclusive legal remedy expressly provided for in the Convention.

(e) In purporting unilaterally to annul or alter the terms of the Convention with the Company, and in denying, or attempting to deny, to the Company the exclusive legal remedy expressly provided for in the Convention, the Imperial Government of Iran have been or will, if they persist in the denial of this remedy, be responsible for a denial of justice against a British national.

The point has, however, never been decided. Nor has it been fully argued. It is necessary, therefore, to consider the three different cases which are liable to arise.

(i) Does the mere refusal or failure to arbitrate in accordance with an arbitration clause amount to a denial of justice?

It would be wrong to fasten upon the fact that mere non-performance or breach of a contract made between a State and an alien does not necessarily constitute a tort within the meaning of the rules of State responsibility,[5] and to conclude that the repudiation of an arbitration clause cannot, as such, be treated

---

[1] Case of *Losinger & Cie, S.A.* (*Switzerland* v. *Yugoslavia*), P.C.I.J. (1938) (Series C), No. 78.

[2] *Anglo-Iranian Oil Company* case (*United Kingdom* v. *Iran*), I. C. J. Pleadings (1952), p. 120.

[3] *Electricité de Beyrouth Company* case (*France* v. *Lebanon*), ibid. (1954), pp. 14, 56; case concerning the *Compagnie du Port, des Quais et des Entrepôts de Beyrouth and The Société Radio-Orient*, ibid. (1960), p. 39.

[4] Above, n. 2, at p. 12.  [5] See below, p. 292, n. 5.

as a denial of justice. Whatever the position may be in regard to contractual obligations in general, the repudiation of an arbitration clause has a distinct and special character in that it involves the denial of access to the only tribunal which has jurisdiction and upon which the parties have agreed. The failure to afford access to tribunals has traditionally been treated as a peculiar and particularly grave instance of State responsibility. It is submitted, therefore, that it would be in line with the accepted tendency of international law, sound doctrine and the demands of justice to hold that a State which repudiates an arbitration clause denies justice.[1] In the past, it is true, denial of justice in the strict and narrow sense of the term implied the failure to afford access to the tribunals of the respondent State itself. But there is no reason of logic or justice why the doctrine of denial of justice should not be so interpreted as to comprise the relatively modern case of the repudiation of an arbitration clause. The respondent State which, wilfully and as a result of its own initiative, has failed to implement an arbitration clause, can hardly allege that it has afforded justice in general or the agreed justice in particular, or complain that it is aggrieved by being held responsible for its own deliberate acts. Nor should it be argued that denial of justice presupposes the failure of the State as sovereign to provide proper access to its tribunals, while the State which simply disregards an arbitration clause acts, not as a sovereign, but in the same manner as any private person could do. This would be a somewhat conceptualist reasoning. In its practical effect the failure of a contracting State to implement an arbitration clause is tantamount to barring access to the tribunal which could, should, and is agreed to, be available. Obstruction by a State has a different quality from obstruction by a private person.

(ii) There are occasions when the failure to implement an arbitration clause results from specific legislation directed against the contracting alien. This is really an *a fortiori* case. It occurred in its most classic form when the property of the Anglo-Iranian Oil Company was taken by Iran in 1951. This

---

[1] In the same sense O'Connell, *International Law*, ii.1071–2. Cf. Hyde, *International Law* (2nd ed., 1945), ii.879, according to whom a State is under a duty to afford access to a tribunal and Eagleton, *Responsibility of States in International Law* (1928), pp. 167–8, who says that a State commits an international wrong if it 'does not permit judicial action against itself'.

entailed the purported annulment of the concession (falsely called 'Convention') granted to the Company in 1933 and the repudiation of the arbitration clause included in it. To treat such incidental effects of a far-reaching scheme of spoliation as a denial of justice may be a little artificial and disproportionate, and it is by no means obvious why in the *Anglo-Iranian Oil Company* case[1] the United Kingdom decided to put so much emphasis on the Company's right to arbitration. This right is, in such circumstances, overshadowed by the rights flowing from violations of the most elementary rules of public international law. One expects such violations to provide the primary cause of action. Arbitration about them is not in private life a familiar experience.

(iii) Much more difficult questions arise where the State's failure to arbitrate results from general and in every respect unobjectionable legislation which it enacts. This is, for present purposes, assumed to have occurred in the case of *Losinger & Cie*, which led to proceedings between Switzerland and Yugoslavia before the Permanent Court of International Justice.[2] A contract governed by Yugoslavian law was made in 1929 between a Swiss firm and the Yugoslavian Government. In August 1934 it was repudiated by the Yugoslavian Government. The Swiss firm commenced arbitration proceedings. Before the Swiss umpire whose award, according to the express terms of the contract, had to be rendered in Yugoslavia,[3] the respondent Government relied on a Yugoslavian law of July 1934 which provided[4]: 'Les procès contre l'État ne peuvent être intentés que devant les tribunaux réguliers de l'État.' The umpire committed an obvious error in that he failed to pronounce upon the Yugoslavian defence and held (wrongly) that he was without jurisdiction to do so. Accordingly, he suspended the arbitration proceedings and decided to 'laisser au Parties le soin de soumettre cette question a l'autorité compétente'.[5] The Swiss firm, however, did not apply to the Yugoslavian (or Swiss) Courts. Switzerland took up its national's case and started proceedings in the Permanent Court of International Justice, alleging a breach of the principles *pacta sunt servanda* and *abus de droit*, though not relying expressly and formally on

---

[1] Above, p. 208, n. 2.   [2] P.C.I.J. (1938) (Series C), No. 78.
[3] See Art. XVI, ibid., p. 7.   [4] Ibid., p. 118.   [5] Ibid., p. 117.

denial of justice. It is possible that the Swiss case failed to show any cause of action; in particular, no denial of justice had taken place, for the (wrong) decision of the arbitrator bound the parties and compelled the Swiss firm to apply to the courts for a ruling. If one disregards this aspect of the matter, the question remains whether the Yugoslavian statute of July 1934 involved a denial of justice.

If, as appears likely, the *lex arbitri* was Yugoslavian and if, accordingly, Yugoslavian law was material at all, the statute could not be ignored. Its construction and effect may, it is true, have been the same as that of the cognate provision of French law.[1] But if it invalidated the submission, then, on the basis of the umpire's decision, there was no warrant for treating it as a denial of justice. It was, so it is assumed, a general, non-discriminatory law enacted by the *lex arbitri* and held by the umpire to have a decisive effect upon the arbitration. A government which acts in accordance with such a law cannot be said to frustrate an arbitration clause and thus to commit a denial of justice. Even if the umpire had not rendered a decision, but the Yugoslavian Government had kept aloof from the arbitration in reliance on the law of 1934, a denial of justice would not have occurred, for the failure to participate would have been sanctioned by a general law enacted by the *lex arbitri*.

It only remains to add that if, on the other hand, the *lex arbitri* had not been Yugoslavian, the statute of July 1934 could not possibly be material. The umpire should have proceeded with the arbitration and no occasion for considering a denial of justice would have arisen.

(*f*) *Failure to comply with award as an international wrong.* Is the State's international responsibility engaged by reason of its failure to satisfy an award (or, indeed, a judgment) rendered against it?

There has been singularly little discussion of this question, but in 1939 Belgium submitted, and Greece did not deny, that the answer should be in the affirmative. This occurred in the *Société Commerciale de Belgique* case which came before the Permanent Court of International Justice.[2] The decision itself[3] is of very limited effect in that it merely established the binding

---

[1] Above, pp. 272-3.          [2] P.C.I.J. (1939) (Series A/B), No. 78, p. 21.
[3] For references see above, p. 259, n. 1.

character of the award rendered in an arbitration between Société Commerciale de Belgique and Greece—a result that could hardly be open to doubt. But before the picture became obscured by several changes of position in the parties' pleadings, Belgium put forward the thesis that 'le refus de l'éxécution' of the award was an international wrong on the ground that it signified 'une méconnaissance de droits acquis par une société étrangère et constitue une violation des principes de droit international'.[1] Greece did not by any means dissent from this proposition, but alleged that it was impossibility, not refusal of performance, that was in issue.[2] The point does not seem, however, to have been developed at length. Nor is it carried much further by Hyde's assertion[3] that the refusal 'to heed the adverse decision of a democratic court' involves a denial of justice.

Such a view is certainly attractive and merits support, but in the present state of the law it is not easy to discover its legal foundation. The idea that a State may be sued at all is of comparatively recent origin and, perhaps, not yet generally followed. According to the law of many countries execution cannot be levied in respect of a judgment rendered against the State; this is so, for instance, in English law,[4] and applies even where the State has agreed to submit and has submitted to the jurisdiction of the tribunal. Such a rule has the effect that the obligations of the State, whether contractual or not, suffer from a congenital infirmity of which alien contractors must be aware and which makes it difficult to speak of a generally recognized legal duty to satisfy a judgment or award. Moreover, it is likely that the mere non-performance of a State's contractual obligations does not constitute an international wrong.[5] Although an award (or judgment) may be described as a specially solemn obligation or, in the terminology of the common law, as a 'contract of record', this, therefore, does not carry the argu-

---

[1] p. 23. No international tort is indicated by this phrase. For a different view, apparently, see Jiménez de Aréchaga. *Mélanges Gidel* (1961), pp. 380–1.

[2] P.C.I.J. (1939) (Series A/B), No. 78, p. 100.

[3] *International Law* (2nd ed., 1945), ii.990.

[4] Section 25 (4) of the Crown Proceedings Act, 1947.

[5] On this problem see below, p. 302; Amerasinghe, 58 *A.J.I.L.* (1964), p. 881; Schwebel, *Proc. American Soc. Int. Law* (1959); Jennings, *B.Y.I.L.* (1961), xxxvii.156; and many others.

ment much further. It is certainly true that, as the Permanent
Court of International Justice held,[1] 'en signant le compromis
le Gouvernement Héllénique s'était engagé de manière irrévo-
cable à respecter et à éxécuter la sentence qui interviendrait',
but this applies to all arbitrations and, indeed, all agreements
and does not, by itself, permit the treatment of non-performance
as an international tort.

Yet it is suggested that the rule is defendable on the ground
of its inherent justice. What is decisive is the attitude in fact
adopted by States towards judicial decisions adverse to them
and rendered by a tribunal of competent jurisdiction. Whatever the strict legal position may be and whatever excuses a
State may in law be able to put forward, in fact such decisions
are, it is believed, almost invariably obeyed by all those nations
which, by their devotion to the judicial process and its dignity,
determine the minimum standard. If this were not so, grave
injustice would arise, for after years of litigation and after
much expenditure the alien would be deprived of the fruits of
his efforts. In the broad sense of international law a State
would be guilty of an *abus de droit* if it claimed the right thus to
lead the alien contractor by the nose.

In this connection it is necessary to draw attention to Article
27 of the Investment Disputes Convention, according to which
'no Contracting State shall give diplomatic protection or bring
an international claim, in respect of a dispute which one
of its nationals and another Contracting State shall have consented to submit or shall have submitted to arbitration under
this Convention, unless such other Contracting State shall have
failed to abide by and comply with the award rendered in such
dispute'. This provision clearly assumes that non-compliance
by a State with an award might lead to an international claim.
In this limited sense it lends support to the submission made
above.

(*g*) *The exhaustion of local remedies.* Until recently the relevance
of this problem of international arbitration had been discussed only in a haphazard fashion, but attention has now been
drawn to it in a fairly comprehensive, though not altogether

---

[1] *Société Commerciale de Belgique* case (*Belgium* v. *Greece*), P.C.I.J. (1939) (Series
A/B), No. 78, p. 2.

happy, article by Schwebel and Wetter.[1] The principal criticism arises from their omission to distinguish between the three different questions that may occur. First, is the arbitration itself dependent upon the prior exhaustion of local remedies? Secondly, can the State's failure to co-operate in the constitution of the tribunal or the conduct of its proceedings be made the subject-matter of an international claim before the exhaustion of local remedies designed to compel the State to participate in the arbitration? Thirdly, can the failure by the State to implement an award rendered against it give rise to an international claim in the absence of prior exhaustion of local remedies?

(i) In the first of these cases there is, or should be, no room at all for the operation of the rule. This has to be considered where a State espouses the interests of one of its nationals against another State; it makes good sense that the respondent State should not be exposed to an international claim, unless the claimant State's national has first established that redress cannot be obtained from the respondent State's municipal tribunals, namely the normal forum for the prosecution of claims in municipal law. Where, on the other hand, a State submits its dispute with a private person to the jurisdiction of a particular tribunal outside its own territory, whether it be a court or an arbitrator, it submits, as has been shown, to a municipal system of law, the *lex fori* or the *lex arbitri*, as the case may be. It is accordingly, neither confronted by a State nor exposed to an international claim. Rather it faces a private person on the footing of municipal law. Accordingly, the whole idea that the rule of exhaustion could be germane to the normal conduct of international arbitration is misconceived. If, in disregard of an arbitration clause accepted by it, a State were to refuse arbitration on the ground of non-exhaustion of local remedies, this would simply be a fallacious point which could not be allowed to hold up the arbitration.[2]

Probably, therefore, in the present context the point would

---

[1] 60 *A.J.I.L.* (1966), p. 484.

[2] *Foreign Relations Law of the United States* (1965), section 209, Comment (*a*); Spofford, 113 *Recueil des cours*, (1964 iii), p. 168. Schwebel and Wetter, op. cit., in the preceding note, at pp. 485–7, seem to have doubts, but they are without justification.

not have come to the fore had not Article 26 of the Convention on the Settlement of Investment Disputes between States and Nationals of other States been framed in the following terms:

> Consent of the parties to arbitration under this Convention shall, unless otherwise stated, be deemed consent to such arbitration to the exclusion of any other remedy. A contracting State may require the exhaustion of local administrative or judicial remedies as a condition of its consent to arbitration under this Convention.

This provision may be said to be superfluous in that it merely expresses the obvious, yet its first sentence has the advantage of eliminating a doubt which could have arisen. It must be regarded as an established principle that the conclusion of an arbitration agreement between two States does not involve the abandonment of the claim to exhaust all local remedies in cases in which one of the contracting States espouses the claim of its national.[1] The Convention is a treaty between States, although arbitrations taking place in pursuance of it will be between a State and the national of another State. In these circumstances the rule referred to might have been said to be applicable. The second sentence of Article 26 preserves the parties' right[2] to incorporate special provisions into their contract. And such special provisions may well make good sense. Suppose that an 'economic development agreement' which includes an arbitration clause confers freedom from local taxation upon the investor, and suppose a dispute arises as to whether a certain charge is a tax. In the absence of special provisions such a dispute would have to be decided by the arbitrators, but it could be well understood if the parties allowed the arbitrators to decide only after the locally competent courts or authorities had established the legal character of the charge. Article 26 preserves, but does not create, the right so to agree.

[1] The strongest case is probably the *Interhande* case, I.C.J. Reports (1959), p. 6, but see also *Salem* case (*Egypt* v. *United States*), *Reports of International Arbitral Awards*, ii.1189, with many references. The contrary view taken by the *Foreign Relations Law of the United States* (1965), section 209, Comment (*b*), is inconsistent with prevailing practice.

[2] It is not without interest to remember that the consent to which Art. 26 refers is that mentioned in Art. 25. This deals with a dispute 'which the parties to the dispute consent in writing to submit to the Centre'. It is a contractual consent. It is quite different, for instance, from the optional clause conferring jurisdiction upon the International Court of Justice.

But in the absence of such agreement or outside the scope of the Convention on International Investment Disputes a State that has submitted or agrees to submit to arbitration with an alien cannot resist arbitration on the ground that local remedies should first be exhausted to ascertain, for instance, the character of a charge in the nature of a tax. As a rule consent to arbitration excludes all other remedies. To put it differently, the right and duty of arbitrators to decide disputes covered by the submission is absolute and comprehensive.

(ii) If the contracting State fails to participate in the arbitration and if the arbitration clause or the *lex arbitri* does not provide machinery enabling the arbitration to proceed even in the absence of the State's co-operation, the State to which the contractor belongs may, as a matter of international protection, in circumstances that have been outlined,[1] claim relief for denial of justice. Is it in such a case open to the respondent State to plead that, notwithstanding the arbitration clause, the international claim cannot be pursued before the alien has exhausted the remedies available to him in the ordinary courts of the contracting State itself?

In its purest form the problem arose in the two cases of the *Beyrouth Companies*.[2] The *lex arbitri* in respect of an arbitration between the French companies and the Lebanon was undoubtedly French. In the face of the Lebanon's refusal to participate in the constitution of the arbitration tribunal the arbitration, it would appear, could not proceed under French law. Hence arbitration as contemplated by the contract was stultified. Could the French Republic's right to protect its nationals be resisted on the ground that these nationals should first have proceeded in the Lebanon in accordance with remedies available there? While in one of the two cases Lebanon did not file a pleading, in the other case it confined itself to asserting an affirmative answer to this question.[3] The case of *Losinger & Cie, S.A.* is hardly more illuminating, for, although the defence was clearly raised by Yugoslavia, the case was not really an international one (as the *lex arbitri* was Yugoslavian) and, moreover, was bedevilled, as has been shown,[4] by the umpire's

---

[1] Above, p. 287.     [2] Above, p. 288, n. 3.
[3] Case concerning the *Compagnie du Port, des Quais et des Entrepôts de Beyrouth . . .*, I.C.J. Pleadings (1960), pp. 67–70.     [4] Above, pp. 273, 290.

decision which was binding upon the parties and therefore minimized the effect of the rule of customary international law. The case of the *Anglo-Iranian Oil Company*, it must be repeated,[1] is not a typical case illustrating the frustration of an arbitration clause; but it involved an international tort of such gravity and intensity as to overshadow the incidental repudiation of the arbitration clause and to render Iran's policy of frustrating it a minor step in a vast scheme of spoliation. Yet it was in this case that one finds a statement, though no reasoned development, of the argument in support of the view that, where the law of the respondent State does not provide the *lex arbitri*, such State's international responsibility for the repudiation of the arbitration clause does not presuppose the exhaustion of remedies available under its law. Iran took the point that 'l'accusation de déni de justice ne pourrait donc intervenir conformément au droit international général qu'après épuisement préalable des instances internes'.[2] The United Kingdom's reply was to the effect that the concession of 1933 'provided for arbitration and that, on any view, therefore, the company was not obliged or even permitted to have recourse to the Iranian municipal courts'.[3]

It is necessary to leave aside the much wider issues raised by a claim for illegal confiscation, and to confine the discussion to the narrow point of a denial of justice inherent in the failure to implement an arbitration clause. The local remedy which bears upon the latter point is, not a remedy to test the legality of the confiscation or to recover compensation, but solely a remedy to procure the constitution or the operation of the arbitration tribunal. Where a local remedy of this type is available, it will probably have to be exhausted. The only reason for suggesting that a principle of general application should be disregarded could be a waiver by the respondent State. Such a waiver would have to be communicated to the claimant State; it cannot be derived from any contractual arrangement made with the contracting alien. In particular, the arbitration clause as such does not imply it, nor can it be inferred from the fact that, *ex hypothesi*, the *lex arbitri* is, and is agreed to be, different from the law of the respondent State. International law includes no rule which defines the local remedies that must be exhausted

---

[1] Above, pp. 289, 290.    [2] I.C.J. Pleadings (1952), p. 291.    [3] Ibid., p. 365.

as those only which are provided by the forum chosen by the contract between the respondent State and the alien. There is a strong argument to the contrary, namely that the rule contemplates the local remedies provided by the respondent State itself. The rationale of the rule points in the same direction; if an application to the ordinary courts of the respondent State can undo the wrong suffered by the alien, it is in the interests of the peaceful settlement of disputes between States to have this done before international litigation is started.[1]

It is likely that Schwebel and Wetter take a different view[2]:

> Conversely, where the arbitral process is not governed by the municipal law of the contracting State, then no municipal remedies of the contracting State need be exhausted; arbitration within the four corners of the agreement to arbitrate is the sole remedy which the alien must exhaust.

It is, however, doubtful whether the learned authors' minds were directed to the same point as that which is now under discussion, i.e. the case in which arbitration cannot proceed under the *lex arbitri* which differs from the law of the contracting State and, therefore, does not effectively provide the sole remedy. But if they do contemplate this case, their answer, which is not supported by reasoning, cannot be accepted.

If the result appears unsatisfactory this is inherent in the rule of local remedies. Its operation can be avoided only if, and in so far as, the absence of a 'genuine link' with the contracting State may serve as an exception. Suppose that under an English contract and for a sum payable in sterling in England a shipyard in England builds a merchant ship for a foreign State and undertakes to make delivery in England, and suppose that the arbitration in England which the contract contemplates cannot take place on account of the foreign State's obstruction. There is much to be said for the view[3] that the link with the foreign

---

[1] In the same sense Professors Sohn and Baxter, quoted by Schwebel and Wetter, op. cit., (above, p. 294, n. 1), at p. 499, n. 67.

[2] Ibid., p. 499; cf. Hyde, 105 *Recueil des cours* (1962 i), p. 352. See also Olmstead, 49 *California L.R.* (1961), p. 504, at pp. 510–11, according to whom 'the inclusion of an arbitration clause in a foreign investment agreement may indicate a waiver of the local remedies rule, but the question ultimately depends upon the intention of the parties'. This is open to much doubt. Would even an express waiver in a contract under municipal law have effect and validity so as to permit an international claim?

[3] Meron, *B.Y.I.L.* (1959), xxxv.83, at pp. 94 et seq.

State, its territory, its tribunals, its law is so tenuous as to render the exhaustion of local remedies inappropriate and unjust.

(iii) There remains the question whether the State against which an award has been rendered, which fails to comply with it and which, therefore, in principle, attracts international responsibility, may require remedies available against it in its own municipal courts to be exhausted. Suppose an arbitration between a British corporation and Utopia has taken place in Geneva and resulted in an award under which Utopia has to pay a large sum of money. Utopia does not pay. The United Kingdom takes up its national's claim and is met by the answer that the British corporation should and could have applied to the Utopian courts with a view to enforcing the award.

In principle such a defence is well founded. If there is a remedy under Utopian law it must be exhausted. There is no argument in favour of a different result. In particular, there is no waiver that could possibly extend to the enforcement of the award. Nor is there any reason of legal policy or justice which could be said to relieve the claimant of the duty to exhaust local remedies. Nor has the existence of any such exemption ever been asserted.

## IV

It seems convenient to conclude by summarizing the principal results which, it is submitted, the preceding discussion is likely to establish.

(1) While arbitration between States is governed by public international law, arbitration between a State and an alien is, like arbitration between private persons generally, governed by a municipal system of law, namely the law of the country where the arbitration tribunal has its seat (*lex arbitri*).

(2) Such arbitrations between States and aliens are neither subject to nor illustrations or sources of public international law to any, or any greater, extent than decisions of municipal tribunals which may in certain circumstances contribute to the development of general principles of law recognized by civilized nations.

(3) The only type of contractual arbitration between a State

and an alien that, exceptionally, is subject to public international law is an arbitration under the Convention on the Settlement of Investment Disputes.

(4) Where, under its own law, a State is precluded from submitting to arbitration, the *lex arbitri* will pronounce upon the scope and effect of such disability; but the recent French practice refusing to treat it as a case of incapacity and rendering it inapplicable to international contracts should be welcomed as exemplary.

(5) The enforcement of an arbitration agreement against the contracting State is not precluded by the latter's immunity, for the arbitration clause implies the waiver of immunity.

(6) The doctrine of immunity precludes the enforcement of the award by execution as well as by a (preliminary) order for an *exequatur* of the award. This is different only in countries which permit execution of judgments or awards rendered in respect of commercial matters.

(7) If the arbitration agreement provides for a third person to appoint an arbitrator or umpire, such third person does not act judicially and therefore is neither entitled nor bound to enter upon any discussion relating to the validity, construction or effect of the contract or the arbitration agreement. He should make the appointment and leave it to the arbitrators to decide all questions of substance. If he refuses to make the appointment and thus frustrates arbitration, his moral responsibility is heavy.

(8) In the event of the contracting State refusing to participate in the arbitration, the arbitration agreement or the *lex arbitri* may provide machinery for permitting the arbitration to proceed, but if a court is called upon to intervene it should do so without deciding any question of substance such as the validity of the arbitration agreement. In such cases the court does not perform a judicial function.

(9) Where a State refuses to proceed to arbitration as contemplated by the arbitration agreement it is guilty of a denial of justice. This does not apply, however, where such refusal stems from general legislation which is not discriminatory or confiscatory or otherwise inconsistent with the minimum standard and which, according to the *lex arbitri*, invalidates the arbitration agreement.

(10) A State which fails to implement an award rendered against it is guilty of an international tort.

(11) In the cases contemplated by the two preceding paragraphs the rule requiring the exhaustion of local remedies applies and, if disregarded, provides a defence.[1]

---

[1] Nothing has been said in this article about the substantive law which may govern contracts between States and aliens and which the arbitrators may have to apply. This is an entirely distinct problem of some importance, which is dealt with in two earlier contributions above, pp. 179, 211. It may in due course be necessary to revert to it at some length in order to consider the rapidly growing literature on the subject, and also a significant observation by Megaw J. in *Orion Cia. Española de Seguros* v. *Belfort Maats.* (1962), 2 Ll. L.R. 257, at 264, and by Judge Cavin in *Sapphire International* v. *National Iranian Oil Co.* (1963), 35 Int. L.R., pp. 136, 172–5.

# VII

## STATE CONTRACTS AND
## STATE RESPONSIBILITY*

In an age in which trading activities of the State are increasing everywhere, in which the economic progress of underdeveloped countries has become the object of international and national concern, but in which, on the other hand, the rights and legitimate expectations of alien investors have in many countries suffered more frivolous and alarming setbacks than at any other time—in such an age the problem of the State's international responsibility for losses arising out of contractual relations between States (or other international persons) and aliens is clearly of great actuality. Yet, among the many uncertainties, ambiguities, and doubts still surrounding the law of international torts, it is subject to a particularly remarkable degree of confusion. This was pointed out by Dunn[1] more than twenty-five years ago and continues to be the position today. The following observations are intended to resume the discussion and, for this purpose, in the first place to define the circumstances in which there may be room for the question whether a State's failure to discharge its contractual obligations towards an alien may constitute a distinct and independent international tort (below, Section I); thereafter to review the authorities on the subject so defined (below, Section II); and, finally, to consider whether and to what extent proper legal analysis permits (below, Section III) and the progressive development of public international law requires (below, Section IV) the recognition of 'breach of contract' as a separate head of international responsibility.

## I

The typical factual background is as follows: A State has entered into a contract with a private person, the national of

---

* From *A.J.I.L.* (1960), p. 572.
[1] *The Protection of Nationals* (Baltimore, 1932), p. 163.

another State. Under the contract the alien may undertake, for instance, to build a railway or to supply goods or make a loan, whether on the security of bonds or otherwise, or may be granted a concession. After the conclusion of the contract the alien alleges that the contracting State has failed to perform its obligations under the contract. The contracting State invokes its own legislative or executive act to justify non-performance. The State to which the alien belongs espouses his claim before an international tribunal. Hence the claimant State will have to allege and prove a cause of action under international law, it usually[1] being insufficient to allege a breach of duty arising under municipal law only.

One is thus confronted with the duality of the contracting State's capacities (and its firm appreciation is likely to assist in exposing the heart of the problem). The contracting State, as a fisc, is under contractual duties towards the alien to whom it is bound on the footing of private law; yet, in addition to or in place of that liability in private law, the contracting State, as a sovereign, may be under a delictual liability in international law towards the claimant State. The tort, if any, is of a very specific character: Is it unlawful for a State to invoke its own legislative or executive measures, taken by it as a sovereign, to justify what *prima facie* constitutes a breach of its own contract made by it as a fisc? This definition of the problem implies two important points of delimitation.

In the first place the peculiar problem demanding a solution cannot arise unless the contract in issue, either as a whole or in part, is governed by the law of the State whose responsibility is invoked, for, according to established principles of private international law, it is only in such event that the contracting State's act can possibly be relevant at all. If the contract is subject to the law of a country other than that of the contracting State, a defence derived from the proper law cannot be tortious (and a defence derived from the law of the defendant State must needs be immaterial). Thus the United Kingdom may have issued bonds in the United States of America which are governed by the law of New York. The bonds include a gold

---

[1] The rule does not apply where the dispute is submitted to an international tribunal by way of *compromis*. See the *Serbian and Brazilian Loan Cases*, P.C.I.J. (Series A), Nos. 14, 15.

clause, but by the law of the United States gold clauses are abrogated and for this reason the United Kingdom refuses to implement the gold clause or to pay more than the nominal amount due in accordance with the proper law of the contract.[1] It has not been, and cannot be, suggested that in such circumstances the debtor State commits an international wrong if it relies on the proper law. It does not even break the contract, for it performs its obligations in conformity with the law which governs them and which is not its own.[2]

Secondly, no relevance attaches, for present purposes, to those acts and events which, by reason of their objectionable nature, attract the State's international responsibility, irrespective of whether or not the State is a contracting party. These are acts and events which are not specifically related to State contracts only. That they affect State contracts, among other contracts, is fortuitous. Such cases are governed by the general principles applicable to the State's tortious liability: if the State is delictually responsible at all, its responsibility arises from the nature of the act or event and extends to all contracts without regard to the identity of the contracting party. The specific type of State responsibility which falls for investigation in the present context is founded, not upon the character, quality or content of the act, but exclusively upon the fact of its having been done by the State with whose contractual duties it is apparently incompatible. The act itself is unobjectionable, but it is criticized, because it encroaches upon a contract to which its author, the State, is a party. This, then, is the peculiar problem of State responsibility in relation to State contracts: Is an act of sovereignty, which in regard to all other contracts is innocent, capable of attracting the inter-

---

[1] These were the facts in the case of *International Trustee for the Protection of Bondholders* v. *The King*, [1937] A. C. 50; having found that the bonds issued by the British Government were governed by the law of New York, the House of Lords had no hesitation in giving effect to the Joint Resolution of Congress abrogating the gold clause.

[2] To be sure the defendant state may be guilty of an international tort in that it may fail to provide adequate judicial remedies and thus commit a denial of justice, or its rules of private international law may not conform to the minimum standard which public international law prescribes. In these and similar circumstances, however, the international tort, if any, does not lie in conduct peculiarly relating to State contracts. The problem of liability is a general one and, for the reasons given in the following paragraph of the text, irrelevant in the present context.

national liability of the State in so far as it affects contracts made by the State? Or, in other words, as a matter of the international law of torts, is the State's responsibility in respect of its own contracts higher than or different from its responsibility in respect of contracts to which it is not a party? This means that a number of cases which have arisen or are liable to arise in practice are outside the scope of a discussion devoted, not to the law of State responsibility in general, but to the peculiar problem of State responsibility for State contracts.

(1) Non-performance by the defendant State may occur without colour of legal right. Without invoking any legal rule or contractual clause as justification for its attitude the State expressly or impliedly repudiates its liability. It may fail to pay or refuse to allow the alien to carry out the work or revoke the concession. Such conduct (displayed, for instance, by Russia after 1918 in respect of pre-revolutionary obligations) is likely to amount to a breach under the municipal law applicable to the contract, but, irrespective of whether or not this is so, clearly involves an international tort of the traditional type: such headings as the minimum standard, the principle of non-discrimination, the protection of alien property, the denial of justice, the abuse of rights, will provide the claimant State with an effective remedy.[1] In this situation it is the arbitrary exercise of sovereign power, coupled with the disregard of the alien's legitimate interests, that constitutes internationally unlawful conduct. There exists, of course, a breach of contract, but the lawlessness which, *ex hypothesi*, the defendant State exhibits and professes is such as to render it unnecessary to treat that breach as a separate international tort.

(2) There is the case in which the debtor State puts forward an interpretation of its legal duties (whether they be governed by its own or any other legal system), which is controverted by its creditors and the State protecting them. There thus exists a dispute which, so it is assumed, is a genuine one and arises from the law as existing at the date of the contract. If the debtor State's interpretation of the legal position is mistaken, a 'breach of contract' may have occurred, yet the case is unlikely to give rise to a claim for 'breach of contract' in international law.

---

[1] We are, of course, not concerned here with questions of jurisdiction or with any such defence as the lack of exhaustion of local remedies.

In practice the point in issue will be decided judicially, either in the ordinary courts of the debtor State or by arbitration, and it is normally only in the event of a denial of justice that an international case will become possible and necessary. It will then be founded upon that denial of justice rather than breach of contract.

(3) The breach of contract is alleged to result from the fact that the defendant State whose law governs the contract has, in the exercise of its legislative or executive powers, taken measures specifically designed to terminate or interfere with the particular contract in issue. Here the international tort consists in the confiscatory, discriminatory, or arbitrary character of the exercise of the defendant State's sovereignty or, in short, in the *abus de droit* of which it is guilty and which is sufficient to attract its liability.

A good example of this type of case is provided by the arbitration between the United States of America and Guatemala in the matter of *Shufeldt's Claim*.[1] A contract between Shufeldt, a citizen of the United States, and Guatemala, held to have been validly concluded, was brought to an end by a special decree cancelling it. The two States submitted the dispute to Sir Herbert Sisnett as Sole Arbitrator to decide whether Shufeldt had a 'right' to indemnification. The Arbitrator asked himself whether there had been an 'injustice to an alien subject, in which case the Government ought to make compensation for the injury inflicted'.[2] It is true that the Arbitrator avoided the real problem of international law, when he said:

> What does the word 'right' in this question mean? It can only mean an equitable right of which international law takes cognizance. It cannot mean a legal right enforceable only in keeping with Guatemalan law, for if that was so this case would never have been referred to an international tribunal which does not administer municipal law.[3]

But if the Arbitrator had embarked upon an evaluation of the decree he would undoubtedly have reached the conclusion that the Government of Guatemala was guilty of internationally unlawful conduct when it issued a decree directed against Shufeldt alone. The law itself which the Government enacted and then invoked constituted an international tort.

---

[1] 2 Int. Arb. Awards 1081 et seq.    [2] Ibid., 1095.    [3] Ibid., 1098.

A similar situation arose in the recent case of the *Anglo-Iranian Oil Company*. By a Concession of 29 April 1933[1] Persia granted to the Anglo-Iranian Oil Company 'the exclusive right, within the territory of the Concession, to search for and extract petroleum as well as to refine or treat in any other manner and render suitable for commerce the petroleum obtained by it' (Article 1). The Concession was granted for a period ending 31 December 1993 (Article 26). It could not be withdrawn or annulled by Persia nor could its terms be altered (Article 21). Although it did not constitute a treaty,[2] it was a contract governed by public international law.[3] In 1951 Persia nationalized the oil industry, dispossessed the Anglo-Iranian Oil Company and annulled the Concession.[4] It was not open to doubt that these measures were directed against that company only.[5] They unquestionably involved a breach of contract which was subject to arbitration in accordance with the Concession (Article 23).[6] But from the point of view of the United Kingdom which, espousing the cause of the company, invoked the law of international responsibility, Persia's conduct was tortious because it involved the taking alien property without compensation,[7] or discrimination against the company,[8] or an abuse of rights.[9] To treat the mere breach of contract as an

---

[1] Cmd. 8425, p. 9, or *Anglo-Iranian Oil Co. Case*, Pleadings, p. 72.

[2] This was the conclusion rightly reached in the *Anglo-Iranian Oil Co. Case*, [1952] I. C. J. Rep. 93; digested in 46 A. J. I. L. 737 (1952).

[3] This followed from Art. 22 (F) of the Concession, according to which any award was to be based 'on the juridical principles contained in Article 38 of the Statutes of the Permanent Court of International Justice.' On the possibility and effect of a submission to public international law, see above, pp. 179, 211, and the literature there referred to.

[4] The Persian legislation is printed in Cmd. 8425, p. 29, and *Anglo-Iranian Oil Co. Case*, Pleadings 36. It is of a very rudimentary character.

[5] In *Anglo-Iranian Oil Co.* v. *Jaffrate (The Rose Mary)*, [1953] 1 W. L. R. 246, at 251, 252, this was admitted.

[6] On the deplorable fate of the arbitration proceedings, see Johnson, *B.Y.I.L.* (1953), xxx.153.

[7] This was the view taken by Campbell J. in the case referred to above, n. 5.

[8] This was the view taken by Upjohn J. in *Re Helbert Wagg & Co. Ltd.*, [1956] Ch. 323, at 346.

[9] It is a matter of regret that in Italy and Japan the courts failed to give redress against an obvious international tort: Court of Venice, 11 March, 1953, 78 *Foro Italiano* (1953), i.719; Int. L.R. (1955), 19; Civil Court of Rome, 13 September 1954, *Foro Italiano* (1955), i.256; *Rev. Crit. de Droit Int. Privé* (1958), 519, with note by De Nova, Int. L.R. (1955), 23; Court of Appeal, Tokyo, Int. L.R. (1953),

international wrong would have been both confusing and unnecessary. If the Concession had been granted by a municipal authority or a private owner rather than the Iranian State, its cancellation and the dispossession of the company would have been no less tortious conduct by the Persian State, not only on account of the character of the legislation enacted by it, but also because, as will appear from Section III (3) below, that legislation involved the clearest possible case of a taking of property.

(4) This leaves the last type of alleged breach: the defendant State's refusal to perform the contract according to its tenor is said to be justified by legislative or executive measures of general impact taken since the conclusion of the contract by the defendant State whose law governs the contract, and which, as such, are not open to attack: A State has undertaken to pay interest at the rate of 8 per cent to its creditors. By a general law of that State the rate of interest in respect of all contracts is reduced by 2 per cent. Or a State has agreed to buy a large quantity of wheat. All import licences are revoked and importation of any kind and by anybody becomes impossible. Or a State has granted to an alien the sole right to produce and sell beer. After the alien has built a brewery and sold its output for a number of years the State introduces prohibition.

This is the crucial case. There is, so one assumes, no ground for an allegation of discrimination, *abus de droit*, denial of justice, or any other international tort of the traditional type. Is the defendant State's responsibility engaged solely by reason of the fact that it is unwilling to perform its obligations otherwise than in accordance with its own general law, this being the law governing the contract?

## II

(1) An emphatic answer in the affirmative was suggested by Switzerland and France, when they were claimants, while, not

---

305. The reasoning of these decisions to the effect that the Persian legislation afforded adequate compensation is wholly unconvincing. The failure to give redress against acts of remarkable lawlessness must forever be a source of disappointment for international lawyers.

unnaturally, the opposite was contended for by Yugoslavia and Norway, respectively, as defendants.

In the *Losinger & Co.* case[1] a Swiss firm had in the year 1929 entered into a contract with Yugoslavia for the building of a railway. The contract, which was admittedly governed by the law of Yugoslavia,[2] contained an arbitration clause. While the arbitration proceedings were pending, legislation was enacted in Yugoslavia, whereby the procedure in the case of claims against the Yugoslav State was regulated, and arbitration clauses to which the Yugoslav State was a party were declared null and void.[3] Relying on this statute the Yugoslav State refused to participate any longer in the arbitration proceedings.[4] Switzerland took up the cause of its national and asked the Permanent Court of International Justice to declare the Yugoslav attitude unlawful. In support of her case Switzerland invoked the principle of *pacta aunt servanda* and attributed the following meaning to it:

L'État ne peut se libérer d'obligations contractuelles valables ni par son droit privé interne, ni par ses dispositions légales de droit public. La thèse contraire équivaudrait à rendre aléatoire tous les contrats conclus par les étrangers avec un État, puisque celui-ci aurait toujours la faculté d'anéantir ses engagements en promulguant des lois spéciales, comme il l'a fait en l'espèce. La validité d'une obligation assumée par un État doit évidemment s'apprécier d'après la législation en vigueur au moment où l'obligation est née. Cette règle de simple bon sens ne souffre aucune discussion.[5]

Professor Sauser-Hall, the author of this formulation, adhered to and developed it with force in the course of the oral argument which he submitted to the Court on behalf of Switzerland.[6]

Independently of this precedent France took a similar line

---

[1] P.C.I.J. (Series C), No. 78. It did not become necessary for the Court to render a decision.

[2] Ibid., 32, 238.        [3] The statute is printed ibid., p. 118.

[4] In view of such refusal the Arbitrator stayed the proceedings: see pp. 113 et seq. This decision which caused the trouble was probably mistaken. It was for the Arbitrator to decide upon his own jurisdiction, even in a case in which it was alleged that a submission, valid at the time of the contract, became invalid as a result of later legislation.

[5] Ibid., 32.

[6] Ibid., 295. For the Yugoslav argument presented by M. Stoykovitch, see pp. 242, 254 et seq., 333, 334.

in the case of *Certain Norwegian Loans.*[1] In the early part of the twentieth century Norway had issued several series of bonds, a large part of which were held by French nationals. Later Norway passed legislation abrogating the gold clause. The bondholders, whose case was espoused by France, alleged that their bonds contained a gold clause and that the Norwegian legislation abrogating it involved a breach of international law. The French case was originally put as follows:

> Une loi intérieure ne peut modifier la substance des contrats internationaux consentis par un État; admettre le contraire serait sortir du droit pour entrer dans la voie de l'arbitraire. Le Gouvernement de l'État emprunteur ne peut se trouver dégagé à l'égard de l'étranger par sa propre législation; s'il suffisait de promulguer une loi pour être libéré de son obligation internationale, il n'existerait plus entre le prêteur et l'emprunteur de rapport contractuel, mais seulement un rapport de sujet à souverain mettant le premier à la merci du second.[2]

At a later stage France submitted that a State was internationally responsible

> chaque fois qu'il y a rupture arbitraire d'un contrat, atteinte essentielle à l'équilibre des relations contractuelles ou encore, pour reprendre la terminologie anglo-saxonne, 'breach of contract'.[3]

Finally, in the course of his oral argument Professor André Gros submitted that

> lorsqu'un État a conclu avec un particulier étranger un contrat quelconque, il ne peut l'en dépouiller, directement ou indirectement, sans engager sa responsabilité à l'égard de l'État protecteur de cet étranger.[4]

No other State seems to have adopted the Swiss-French doctrine. The practice of the United States of America has, for more than a century and a half, been clearly opposed to it. Since 1803 it has not been usual for the United States to assist its citizens in the prosecution of claims founded on contracts with foreign governments except by rendering 'its good offices'[5] and except in cases in which there is 'an arbitrary wrong', lack of good faith or abuse,[6] or in which, in short, the

---

[1] [1957] I. C. J. Rep. 9, digested in 51 *A.J.I.L.* (1957), 777. The Court was not called upon to render a decision on the merits.

[2] 1 Pleadings 34.    [3] ibid., 404.

[4] 2 Pleadings 61. And see pp. 63, 181, 182. For the Norwegian answer see 1 Pleadings 485 et seq.; 2 ibid., 134 et seq.

[5] Moore, 4 *Digest*, 705; Hackworth, 5 *Digest*, 611.

[6] Moore, op. cit., 289, 723 et seq.; Hackworth, op. cit., 611 et seq.

foreign government is guilty of a tort as opposed to a breach of contract, this being the distinction expressly and formally adopted by the President and entire Cabinet in 1847.[1] Little is known about British practice, but it has recently come to light[2] that in 1858 and 1859 the British Government was advised by Harding, Q.C., that it should not afford protection to a British subject who had entered into a contract with a foreign government, 'unless and until they have suffered a denial or flagrant perversion of justice or some gross wrong'.

(2) As regards academic opinion, Professor Bourquin was fully justified in stating that

la question de la responsabilité internationale des États pour manquement à des obligations contractuelles a retenu souvent l'attention des juristes. Il faut reconnaître, cependant, qu'elle a été rarement étudiée d'une manière approfondie. La plupart des auteurs qui s'en sont occupés se contentent d'émettre à ce sujet des idées sommaires et quelquefois assez vagues.[3]

Some authors shortly express views which, in effect, conform to United States practice and involve the rejection of 'breach of contract' as a head of international responsibility. Thus Lapradelle and Politis explain that liability depends on abuse and similar circumstances:

dans ces hypothèses et autres semblables, à la responsabilité contractuelle, interne, se substitue la responsabilité délictuelle qui est internationale; le débiteur est recherché, non pour l'inexécution du contrat, mais pour la mauvaise foi, l'iniquité notoire ou l'injustice flagrante dont il s'est rendu coupable.[4]

Neither this view nor the opposite theory is supported by analysis or reasoning. Thus Hyde, after correctly explaining the American practice,[5] expresses doubt[6] 'whether the mere breach of a promise by a contracting State with respect to an alien is generally looked upon as amounting to internationally illegal conduct', and requires a denial of justice as a condition

---

[1] Moore, op. cit., 708; Eagleton, *The Responsibility of States* (1928), 161.
[2] 2 McNair, *International Law Opinions*, pp. 202–4.
[3] Case of *Certain Norwegian Loans*, 2 Pleadings 134.
[4] 2 *Recueil des Arbitrages Internationaux*, 548 (Note Doctrinale). See also, e.g., Van Hecke, *Problèmes Juridiques des Emprunts Internationaux* (1955), pp. 279, 280; Eagleton, *The Responsibility of States* (1928), pp. 165, 166; Lipstein, *B.Y.I.L.* (1945), xxii.134, 135, 142.
[5] *International Law*, p. 988.    [6] ibid., pp. 989, 990.

of international responsibility. He then continues, however, as follows:

Again, a State may, in the exercise of its power as a sovereign, alter or destroy its contractual obligations and so pursue a course in relation to its undertaking that is not only harmful to the alien party thereto, but also at variance with the theory on which the arrangement was concluded and with what that party had reason to anticipate. Such action, manifestly in one sense a breach of the agreement and effected by it (*sic*), constitutes also tortious conduct that possesses an internationally illegal quality.[1]

This is no more than a singularly bare and unconvincing assertion.[2]

(3) When one comes to judicial practice, it would appear that no international tribunal has ever expressed approval of the Swiss-French doctrine; indeed, it seems that no international tribunal was at any time confronted with the issue. Several decisions have been invoked as favouring the one or the other theory, but on analysis are not in point. This applies, in particular, to certain decisions of the United States–Mexican General Claims Commission. In the case of the *North American Dredging Company of Texas*[3] the question arose whether the Calvo clause deprived the Commission of jurisdiction: it was held that this was not so in those cases in which 'a claim is based on an alleged violation of any rule or principle of international law'.[4] It is against the background of this decision that the case of *International Fisheries Co.*[5] will have to be approached. Again the question was whether the Calvo clause precluded the investigation of a claim arising from the cancellation of a contract. The majority of the Commission (Nielsen dissenting) answered in the affirmative, the reason being that the cancellation in question 'was not an arbitrary act, a violation of a duty abhorrent to the contract and which in itself might be considered as a violation of some rule or principle of international law'.[6] The case of *Illinois Central Railroad Company*[7] was again concerned

---

[1] ibid., p. 991.

[2] For a similar assertion, see Borchard, *State Insolvency and Foreign Bondholders* (1951), i.137, whose observations cannot readily be followed. They are limited to the cases of currency devaluation and the abrogation of the gold clause. Against this view, see Sir John Fischer Williams, *Chapters on Current International Law* (1929), pp. 257 et seq., 291.

[3] 4 Int. Arb. Awards 26.     [4] ibid., p. 33.     [5] ibid., p. 691.

[6] ibid., p. 699; see also p. 700.     [7] ibid., p. 21.

with jurisdiction only. The claim was founded upon the alleged non-performance of a contract. Mexico denied that 'contract claims' came within the terms of the convention which authorized the Commission to pass upon 'all claims . . . for losses and damages'. The objection was overruled. These decisions have no bearing upon the point now under discussion,[1] because none of them touches upon the question whether a State commits a tort if, in defence to a claim made against it under a contract which is subject to its law, it relies on a general change in that law.

## III

(1) It is submitted that the Swiss-French doctrine, as formulated by its authors, stems from a fundamental error which would not have arisen if public international lawyers had had due regard to the character and teachings of private international law: in the type of case where there is room for the problem at all under customary public international law, no breach of contract in fact occurs and, consequently, the principle of *pacta sunt servanda* is not infringed.

Contracts are governed by the law determined by the private international law of the forum. That law 'not merely sustains but, because it sustains, may also modify or dissolve the contractual bond'.[2] These words of Lord Radcliffe express a principle of universal application. It is nowhere doubted, and has frequently been affirmed by the highest tribunals,[3]

---

[1] It is difficult to understand how the last-mentioned case came to be relied upon by France in the case of *Certain Norwegian Loans*, 1 Pleadings 404. From time to time learned writers have referred to such decisions as *The Administration of Posts and Telegraphs of the Republic of Czechoslovakia* v. *Radio Corporation of America*, 30 A.J.I.L. (1936), 523, or *Radio Corporation of America* v. *The National Government of the Republic of China*, 3 Int. Arb. Awards (1623), but a perusal of these cases makes it obvious that they are immaterial to the point under discussion; these were private law arbitrations in the course of which no point of public international law arose. Nor is any help to be derived from the award made by the Permanent Court of Arbitration in the case of *French Claims Against Peru*, 16 A.J.I.L. (1922), 480: the claim of Dreyfus Bros. against Peru was admitted by the Peruvian President in 1880. A Peruvian law of 1886 declared all the internal acts performed by the President null and void. It was held that 'this law cannot be applied to foreigners who treated in good faith'. The case depended on the effects of recognition and on the fact that the acknowledgment of 1880 was not an internal act.

[2] *Kahler* v. *Midland Bank*, [1950] A. C. 24, at 56.

[3] England: *Re Chesterman's Trusts*, [1923] 2 Ch. 466, 478; Belgium: Cass., 24

that a contract is subject to its proper law as it exists from time to time. If, therefore, the debtor relies on changes in the proper law, he does what he is entitled to do and cannot be charged with a breach of contract, his undertaking being limited to perform in accordance with the terms of the contract as sanctioned by the provisions of the proper law. This would be so even if the parties had expressly agreed upon the application of the proper law as existing at the time when the contract was made, and had thus excluded the application of subsequent changes, unforeseen and unforeseeable by the parties. The validity and effect of such a clause is doubtful in many respects.[1] It is clear, however, that it is the proper law of the contract that decides the question whether the change in the law overrides the clause. If the governing law is the law of the country which has enacted the change the clause will usually be abortive. Thus, if a contract containing a gold clause is subject to American law, the Joint Resolution will have the effect of abrogating the gold clause, notwithstanding the parties' attempt to render changes in the law inapplicable; if the contract is subject to a legal system other than that of the United States, the Joint Resolution necessarily is without effect and again the clause is abortive.

These rules of private international law demand the rejection of any idea of 'breach' of contract also in the case in which the State enacting the new law of general impact is itself a party to the contract.

(2) An argument in support of the Swiss-French doctrine might be derived from the well-known principle that as a matter of public international law no State can rely on its own legislation to limit the scope of its international obligations.[2]

February 1938, 39 *Bulletin de l'Institut Juridique International* (1938), 105; Germany: Supreme Court, 28 May 1936, *JW* 1936, p. 2058; Sweden: Supreme Court, 30 January 1937, 36 *Bulletin de l'Institut Juridique International* (1937), pp. 334; see, generally, Rabel, *Conflict of Laws* ii.564 et seq.; Van Hecke, *Problèmes Juridiques des Emprunts Internationaux* (1955), 195, 196, and numerous other writers on the conflict of laws.

[1] For a fundamental discussion see Rabel, 10 *Rabels Zeitschrift* (1936), pp. 492, 508 et seq. One of the principal questions is whether such a clause does not involve only the incorporation of a foreign law, i.e. a case of *materiellrechtliche Verweisung*. Probably the answer should be in the affirmative.

[2] P.C.I.J., Case concerning the *Free Zones of Upper Savoy and the District of Gex*, (Series A), No. 24, p. 12, and many other decisions rendered by that tribunal.

But this rule contemplates obligations governed by public international law and has no bearing upon the scope of obligations which are subject to a system of municipal law, such as the law of the debtor State. If under the latter system of law no breach of contract occurs, it is not open to public international law to assert the contrary. Where the debtor State does wrong to its alien creditor, public international law may impose a delictual liability. The existence of a tort towards the creditor's State is independent of any question of breach of contract.

A somewhat strongly worded Report of the Committee on the Nationalization of Property recently set up by the American Branch of the International Law Association has described the view here advanced as 'formalistic':

No government would suggest that it has a legal right to breach a loan agreement it concludes with the International Bank for Reconstruction and Development. Can it seriously be contended that a government has the legal 'right' to breach a loan agreement with the Chase Manhattan Bank? Acceptance of the argument that the former contract is intergovernmental, and consequently governed by international law, while the latter has but one government as a party, and consequently is governed by municipal law, even if formalistically satisfying—as it is not—adds nothing to the rule of international law. It may detract from the flow of international investment. The unsoundness of treating the legal rights arising from contracts between States and aliens as being of a lower order than those arising from agreements between governments or their agencies merits further illustration. Afghanistan recently granted the Soviet Techno Export Organization rights to explore for oil in Afghanistan. A breach by Afghanistan of the pertinent agreement would be a breach of international law. But a contract with a privately owned oil company, for the same object, of the same substance, upon the same terms, breached in the same way, by the same State, would not be a breach of international law in the eyes of some formalists. In fact, some would go so far as to say that if the contract were governed by Afghanistan law and that law were altered to authorize the contract's breach, no law, international, municipal, or other, would be violated by breach.[1]

This argument, it is believed, breaks down for reasons of justice and substance rather than form. To hold the parties to their own choice of a legal system as the proper law of their contract and to judge the existence or non-existence of a 'breach' by the law so chosen is imperatively demanded by any legal order which cherishes certainty, equitable treatment, and

[1] *Proceedings* (1957–8) and Committee Reports of the American Branch, 70, 71.

sound results.[1] It is not a question of certain contracts being 'of a lower order' than others. The point is that certain contracts belong to *different* orders from others. The 'order' is determined by the parties themselves and cannot be changed merely because the expectation of one of them is disappointed.

(3) It is a more serious question whether general legislation which the contracting State enacts and which interferes with such State's contracts in a manner prejudicial to the alien is to be treated as expropriation, so that in the absence of reasonable compensation it would be illegal in international law. It would be merely a different formulation of the same question if, in accordance with some well-known American decisions,[2] it were asked whether a State must be treated as having impliedly waived rather than reserved its power to change its law to the detriment of the alien with whom it contracts.

No State can be fixed with responsibility for expropriation unless the act complained of can fairly be said to involve the taking of property within the meaning attributed to that conception by the general principles of law recognized by civilized nations. These principles cannot be ascertained otherwise than by comparative law.[3] While contracts are undoubtedly property

---

[1] Perhaps it should be emphasized at this point once again that cases of discrimination, denial of justice, abuse, and so forth, are not within the contemplation of this article.

[2] See, in particular, *Murray* v. *Charleston*, 96 U. S. 432, 445 (1877), and other cases, all of which relate to contracts made by American States or municipalities granting exemption from taxation. Since *Piqua Branch of the State Bank of Ohio* v. *Knoop*, 16 How. 369 (1853), such contracts are valid. These cases rest on very special reasoning which does not lend itself to generalization. They can possibly be supported on the ground that they envisage only partial exemption from taxation, are predicated upon consideration and establish a rule which, as the example of charities shows, does not endanger essential governmental activities. See, generally, J. D. B. Mitchell, *The Contracts of Public Authorities* (1954).

[3] This point requires emphasis. It is unfortunate that no international lawyer discussing expropriation, confiscation or nationalization has as yet to any appreciable extent investigated the municipal law on such fundamental matters as the conception of property, the conception of taking, the ambit of the duty to compensate and so forth. This is the principal reason why most studies of the international law relating to the taking of property are so unsatisfactory. They rest on insecure and insufficient foundations, with the result that on a number of crucial points they have only positivistic assertions to offer. As indicated, 75 *Law Q.R.* (1959), p. 219, n. 43, the writer hopes soon to resume his studies of the municipal law of expropriation as an essential preliminary to the study of the international law of expropriation. The doubts about this programme expressed by Drucker, 228 *The Law Times* (1959), p. 86, only serve to emphasize the urgency of the task.

creating vested rights,[1] legislative interference with their terms does not necessarily constitute the taking, but may amount to mere regulation, of property.[2] More particularly, those measures which matter in the present context, namely, general legislation or executive provisions put into force for the benefit of the community at large, do not involve the taking of property even if they affect the rights of the owner or the value of his property.

This proposition derives its strongest support from the unsurpassed wealth of material supplied by the judicial practice of the United States of America, as well as from decisions rendered in Germany and, to some extent, in the United Kingdom and France.[3] General legislation passed for the protection of public health, public safety or general welfare, i.e., for purposes falling within the 'police power' as known to American Constitutional law, cannot ever involve the taking of property, because 'no person has a vested right in any general rule of law or policy of legislation entitling him to insist that it shall remain unchanged for his benefit'.[4] Thus where a State introduces prohibition, the owner of a brewery is without remedy, although he loses his business and the value of his factory premises is greatly reduced[5]; similarly, a creditor who suffers loss as a result of the depreciation of currency or the abrogation of gold

---

[1] *Lynch* v. *U.S.*, 292 U. S. 571 (1933), at pp. 576, 577, 579, per Mr. Justice Brandeis. Similarly *Brooks-Scanlon Corporation* v. *U.S.*, 265 U. S. 106 (1923), which has its international counterpart in the case of *Norwegian Claims*, Scott, Hague Court Reports, p. 38, and should be contrasted with *Omnia Commercial Co.* v. *U.S.*, 261 U. S. 502 (1923).

[2] The distinction between regulation and taking is both fundamental and universal. It is sanctioned by so many American and German decisions that they cannot even be listed. It was recently recognized in an impressive manner by the House of Lords in England: *Belfast Corporation* v. *O.D. Cars Ltd.*, [1960] A. C. 490.

[3] Much useful material on the law of England, the United States, and France has been collected by Professor Mitchell (above, p. 316, n. 2). It will, of course, be appreciated that most of the cases used, in particular the American cases, are grounded in express Constitutional provisions, such as the due process clause and the prohibition of State impairment of the obligations of contract. But these provisions, in turn, rest on fundamental ideas of universal validity.

[4] *Chicago and Alton Railroad Co.* v. *Tranbarger*, 238 U. S. 67 (1915), at p. 76, per Mr. Justice Pitney on behalf of the Court. See also *New Orleans Gas Light Co.* v. *Louisiana Light and Heat Producing and Manufacturing Co.*, 115 U. S. 650, 672 (1885); *Pennsylvania Railroad Co.* v. *Miller*, 132 U. S. 75, 83 (1889); *Pennsylvania Coal Co.* v. *Mahon*, 260 U. S. 393 (1922).

[5] *Mugler* v. *Kansas*, 123 U. S. 623 (1887).

clauses cannot allege the invalidity of the legislation on the ground that it interferes with his contractual rights and, therefore, takes his property without compensation.[1] The extent of the 'police power' has never been defined,[2] but it is clearly established that the financial enrichment of the public purse is not a legitimate purpose covered by it.[3]

Where the State itself is a party to the contract, the same principles apply. Thus, where the United States has sold silk for delivery on a certain date, but fails to deliver it on account of a general embargo placed by its Railway Administration on the shipment of silk by freight, it cannot be held liable for damages, for it is settled law 'that the United States when sued as a contractor cannot be held liable for an obstruction to the performance of the particular contract resulting from its public and general acts as a sovereign'.[4] Or where a State in 1867 granted to a corporation the monopoly of carrying on a lottery, but in 1869 made all lotteries illegal, no complaint can be made, for

the legislature cannot bargain away the police power of a State. Irrevocable grants of property and franchises may be made if they do not impair the supreme authority to make laws for the right government of the State, but no legislature can curtail the power of its successors to make such laws as they deem proper in matters of police.[5]

Again, if the monopoly rights of a railway company, granted in 1870, are infringed by a statute of 1907 which imposes the duty

---

[1] *Knox* v. *Lee,* and *Parker* v. *Davies,* 12 Wall. 457, 551 (1870), per Mr. Justice Strong; *Norman* v. *Baltimore and Ohio Railroad Co.,* 294 U. S. 240, 306 (1935), per Chief Justice Hughes; German Supreme Court, 1 March 1924, *RGZ* 107, 370; 4 November 1925, *RGZ* 111, 320; 20 May 1926, *RGZ* 114, 27.

[2] What *prima facie* is 'regulation' may become a 'taking'. The question is one of degree: *Pennsylvania Coal Co.* v. *Mahon,* 260 U. S. 393 (1922); *New Orleans Public Service* v. *City of New Orleans,* 281 U. S. 682, 687 (1929); *Belfast Corporation* v. *O.D. Cars Ltd.,* [1960] A. C. 490, at p. 519, per Lord Simonds.

[3] *Lynch* v. *U.S.,* 292 U. S. 571, 580 (1933), where Mr. Justice Brandeis said that 'to abrogate contracts in the attempt to lessen government expenditure would not be the practice of economy, but an act of repudiation'. Cf. *Von Hoffmann* v. *City of Quincy,* 4 Wall. 535 (1866). In the same sense German Supreme Court, 10 February 1932, *RGZ* 136, 113, 123.

[4] *Horowitz* v. *U.S.,* 267 U. S. 458 (1925), at p. 460, per Mr. Justice Sanford on behalf of the Court. In the same sense the Court of Appeal in England: *William Cory and Son Ltd.* v. *City of London,* [1951] 2 K. B. 476.

[5] *Stone* v. *Mississippi,* 101 U. S. 814, 817, 818 (1879), per Chief Justice Waite. See also, e.g., *New Orleans Public Service Co.* v. *City of New Orleans,* 281 U. S. 682 (1929).

to construct an opening through a railway embankment to prevent land from being flooded, this is not the taking of property, but the legitimate exercise of governmental powers for the benefit of the community at large.[1] There are numerous similar cases in some of which the guiding principle is stated as follows:

> But into all contracts, whether made between States and individuals or between individuals only, there enter conditions which arise not out of the literal terms of the contract itself; they are superinduced by the pre-existing and higher authority of the laws of nature, of nations or of the community to which the parties belong; they are always presumed, and must be presumed, to be known and recognized by all, are binding upon all and need never, therefore, be carried into express stipulation, for this could add nothing to their force. Every contract is made in subordination to them and must yield to their control, as conditions inherent and paramount, wherever a necessity for their execution shall occur.[2]

Yet where a legislative measure cannot fairly be described as being adopted for the benefit of the general public or, in other words, by way of regulation, the interference with contractual rights constitutes a taking. Thus, where a corporation is granted the exclusive right to produce and distribute gas in the City of New Orleans, a subsequent statute of Louisiana purporting to abolish 'the monopoly features in the charter of any corporation' other than a railway company is invalid: it would be open to the State to modify the charter upon payment of just compensation under the power of eminent domain, but the police power cannot be invoked, because a contract contemplating the distribution of gas is for the general benefit and 'is not, in any legal sense, to the prejudice of the public health or the pubic safety',[3] it being clear that nothing can 'restrict the power of the State to protect the public health, the public morals or the public safety, as the one or the other may be involved *in the execution of such contracts*'.[4] To take a more

---

[1] *Chicago and Alton Railroad Co.* v. *Tranbarger*, 238 U. S. 67 (1914).

[2] *The West River Bridge Co.* v. *Dix*, 6 How. 507, 532 (1848), per Mr. Justice Daniel on behalf of the Court; *Home Building and Loan Association* v. *Blaisdell*, 290 U. S. 398, 435 (1933); *East New York Savings Bank* v. *Hahn*, 326 U. S. 230 (1945).

[3] *New Orleans Gas Light Co.* v. *Louisiana Light and Heat Producing and Manufacturing Co.*, 115 U. S. 650, 671, 673 (1885).

[4] ibid., at p. 672. For a similar application of the principle see *Manigault* v. *Springs*, 199 U. S. 473, 480, 481 (1905). The leading case is *Charles River Bridge* v. *Warren Bridge*, 11 Pet. 420 (1837).

recent case, in which the opinion of the Court was delivered by Mr. Justice Brandeis: by virtue of the War Risk Insurance Act passed during the First World War the United States issued policies for the benefit of the dependants of serving soldiers. In 1933 a new statute repealed 'all laws granting or pertaining to' such insurance and thus rendered enforcement of payments due under the policies impossible. Contracts being property, their annulment without compensation constitutes a taking, 'unless, indeed, the action falls within the federal police or some other paramount power',[1] and this, clearly, cannot be asserted.[2]

There is only one type of contract which, if concluded by the United States, constitutes a distinct category and in connection with which regulation becomes taking, viz., the contract whereby the United States borrows money. The United States cannot by legislative measures annul or modify the obligations it has undertaken towards its lenders. Accordingly, if the United States abrogates the gold clause, this cannot affect bonds issued by the United States.[3] There would seem to be no justification for founding upon this exception a general principle of law applicable to State loans.

It is certainly difficult and perhaps impossible to devise a verbal formula capable of explaining the line of demarcation between regulation and taking, between measures designed to define the content and scope of substantial rights in general and measures of expropriation. Nor is it easy to find the phrase which exposes the distinction, for instance, between the prohibition of lotteries, a regulating measure, and the invalida-

---

[1] *Lynch* v. *U.S.* (above, p. 318, n. 3), at p. 579.

[2] Because the Act of 1933 was enacted to economize, and this is insufficient justification for regulation: above, p. 318, n. 3. Moreover, it was directed against a specified and limited group of persons and therefore lacked generality.

[3] *Perry* v. *U.S.*, 294 U. S. 330 (1935). Although a distinguished writer (Professor H. M. Hart, 'The Gold Clause in United States Bonds,' 48 *Harvard L.R.* (1935), 1057) has suggested that 'few more baffling pronouncements . . . have ever issued from the United States Supreme Court', the reason is both clear and at the same time a very special one. It is derived solely from two provisions of the American Constitution, according to which Congress is authorized 'to borrow money on the credit of the United States' (Art. I, section 8), and the 'validity of the public debt of the United States, authorized by law . . . shall not be questioned' (14th Amendment, section 4). The analysis by Mitchell, op. cit., pp. 148 et seq., is unsatisfactory, because he overlooks these essential points.

tion of monopolies (including lotteries, but excluding railway companies), a case of taking. The attempt to draw that elusive line must be left for a later occasion, though this obvious point may perhaps be made: if a State prohibits lotteries in general so as to prevent its citizens from gambling, this, it is true, invalidates lottery monopolies granted by it, but does not amount to a taking, because neither the State itself nor any other person within its boundaries will carry on the business of a lottery.[1] For present purposes it must suffice to conclude that there is no evidence in support of the proposition that, as a matter of general principle and, consequently, of international law, State contracts enjoy a greater degree of protection against regulation (as opposed to expropriation) than other contracts.

(4) This leaves the last question whether a State commits an international wrong at any rate in the case in which, by a general law, it modifies its own contractual obligations in disregard of an express prior undertaking not to do so or to exempt them from any such change. Such a clause, as has been shown,[2] was included in the concession granted by Persia to the Anglo-Iranian Oil Company. Since that concession was governed by public international law, it could not be reached by Persian measures, and the express exemption clause was otiose. If the concession had been governed by Persian law, its repudiation was presumably valid from the point of view of the proper law and there is, therefore, little difference between the case of an express exemption clause and the factual situation discussed in the preceding Section 3. Such a difference seems to have been asserted by the United Kingdom in the course of its submission in the *Anglo-Iranian Oil Co. Case*, but these were unfortunately not characterized by close and convincing reasoning. After starting with a far too general proposition,[3] the United Kingdom submitted the much more specific thesis that the termination of a concession was unlawful if the grantor State 'has

---

[1] In other words, if the State itself carries on the lottery, the case would clearly be one of taking.

[2] Above, p. 307.

[3] Pleadings 78; it was to the effect that there was '*always* prima facie an *international* obligation upon a State to observe the terms of a concession granted to a foreigner . . . the *international* responsibility of the grantor State is engaged if there is a breach of this obligation and if municipal remedies have been exhausted without success' (italics supplied).

expressly undertaken ... not to terminate it unilaterally'.[1]

No evidence in support of this proposition was adduced nor can it be found anywhere. In particular, it cannot be found in the law of the United States, where it is firmly established that the power to regulate for the general benefit is paramount[2] and 'inalienable even by express grants'.[3] The truth is that even in international law the express exemption from the effects of future legislation is redundant. Such exemption cannot and ought not to preclude the genuine exercise of the State's police power. On the other hand, where, in substance, the State takes property without compensation, its international liability is engaged even in the absence of the clause.

# IV

If the preceding submissions, based on the present state of customary international law are correct, the question arises whether, *de lege ferenda*, a different rule should be recommended. It is by no means certain that the answer should necessarily be in the affirmative.

The idea that contracts must in all circumstances be performed according to their tenor, that in regard to interference by a competent legislator they are sacrosanct, that they are entitled to an almost unique status of immunity—that idea, so it may be argued, is opposed to the daily and universal experience of mankind and to the requirements of good sense and justice. If an alien who contracts with a foreign State desires to be protected against legislative encroachments by that State upon his contractual rights, he must insist upon the submission of the contract to a legal system other than that of the contracting foreign State. If the alien fails to do so, he is

---

[1] Pleadings 81. The argument was developed at pp. 87 et seq. At its conclusion the thesis was submitted (p. 92) that 'a State can validly bind itself by treaty *or by contract* with a foreign national not to interfere with concessionary rights' (italics supplied). A similar argument is put forward by Friedmann, *Law in a Changing Society* (1959), pp. 455, 456.

[2] Above, p. 319, n. 4; and see *Home Building and Loan Association* v. *Blaisdell*, 290 U. S. 398 (1933).

[3] *Chicago and Alton Railroad Co.* v. *Transbarger*, 238 U. S. 67 (1914), at p. 76, per Mr. Justice Pitney on behalf of the Court. See Mitchell, op. cit., pp. 90 et seq., for a large number of other cases on the same point. It is, however, difficult to agree with the analysis suggested by the learned author.

disentitled to complain about the consequences flowing from the application of the foreign State's law to a contract voluntarily concluded and submitted to that law which, *ex hypothesi*, is unobjectionable in content and, in particular, does not involve the taking of property. In other words, if, by implication a contract concedes to the State the power of interference and if the exercise of such power is not subject to criticism, international law ought not to impose responsibility for what is not tortious.

Against this it may be urged that in practice private persons frequently have no option but to agree to the application of the legal system of the State with which they contract; that the alien should not be left unprotected against the effects of legislation enacted by the contracting State itself; that any willingness to allow *prima facie* validity to such legislation would give rise to an invidious discussion of such objectionable features as can be discovered in it; that, therefore, in the interest of justice in a broad sense, it is preferable to deny altogether international validity to any such legislation, in so far as State contracts are concerned; that, moreover, the flow of international investments and the economic progress of many countries demand the possibility of giving an absolute and indefeasible assurance against interference by the State which is the recipient of benefits under a contract governed by its own law.

It is difficult to choose between these two views. The former, probably, is sound in law and attractive to the lawyer, but the latter seems to be regarded as conforming more closely to practical needs, for it appears that for thirty years or so reformers and codifiers have attempted to find a formula to express it. Their motive for so doing has frequently been lacking in clarity and persuasiveness. Yet they must have been inspired by the conviction that their endeavours were supported and, indeed, demanded by reasons of substance. It would, therefore, be retrograde and unhelpful to condemn those efforts as unnecessary or misplaced and to refrain from a contribution to a legal development which so many regard as desirable. What, then, should be the definition of the international tort which it is intended to create?

The Bases of Discussion drawn up by the Preparatory Committee of the Hague Conference of 1930[1] distinguished between contracts in general and debts. As regards the former the Committee suggested the affirmation of responsibility for such legislation as 'directly infringes' contractual rights, but where general legislation is incompatible only with the operation or performance of a contract, responsibility 'depends on the circumstances'. It must be doubtful whether a solution on such lines would add anything to the existing law, particularly if it is remembered that the direct infringement of contractual rights is likely almost invariably to involve the taking of property. As regards debts, the cancellation or repudiation was intended to involve absolute liability, but in the case of the suspension or modification of the service or in the case of a failure to pay, liability should exist only in the absence of 'financial necessity'. The distinction cannot easily be drawn or justified. Moreover, it is contrary to legal principle and practical requirements that in the case of monetary obligations the debtor should be allowed to invoke financial difficulties as an excuse for non-performance. It is not surprising that the Third Committee of the Hague Conference of 1930[2] in effect abandoned these suggestions and submitted a draft of extreme conservatism: The Committee proposed to limit the State's responsibility for legislation to the case in which this is incompatible with the State's 'international obligations', i.e., obligations resulting from treaty, custom or the general principles of law (as opposed to obligations resulting from municipal law). Such a provision would, of course, merely express what is obvious and elementary.

The Draft Convention which the Harvard Research prepared in 1929[3] intends to be more progressive, but is also more obscure: International responsibility is said to flow from the 'non-performance' of a contractual obligation owed by the State to an alien who has exhausted local remedies. The Comment does not by any means make the matter clearer by stating that the proposed provision implied 'of course an unlawful or wrongful non-performance'. But can there be 'non-

---

[1] Nos. 3, 4, 8, and 9, conveniently printed in *I.L.C. Yearbook* (1956), ii.223; see also 24 *A.J.I.L.* (Supplement) (1930), 48 et seq.

[2] Art. 6, *I.L.C. Yearbook* (1956), ii.225.

[3] Art. 8, 23 *A.J.I.L.* (Special Supplement) (1929), 167 et seq.; *I.L.C. Yearbook* (1956), ii.229.

performance' and, still less, unlawful or wrongful non-perform-ance if the contract is subject to the law of the debtor State and this provides justification for the failure to perform? It seems likely that in the crucial case the Draft Convention would be ineffective.

The latest attempt at codification comes from Professor F. V. García Amador, the International Law Commission's Special *Rapporteur*. In his Second Report on State Responsibility[1] he distinguishes between contractual obligations in general and public debts. Apart from the obvious and quite distinct cases of discrimination, denial of justice and expropriation, the 'non-performance' of State contracts involves an international tort, if it 'is not justified on grounds of public interest or of the economic necessity of the State'. Similarly, in the case of the State's public debts[2] international responsibility is attached to the acts of repudiation and cancellation (not, apparently, modification and suspension) except where 'the measure in question is justified on grounds of public interest' (not eco-nomic necessity).

In the first place it must be objected that there is no good reason for any distinction between contractual obligations and public debts. Both types of obligation should be on the same level,[3] because, notwithstanding the peculiar policy embodied in the American Constitution,[4] there is no room in the modern world for the proposed differentiation: whether the State is liable for money lent or for the price of goods sold and delivered or whether it has to deliver goods which it has sold, but for which it has refused to grant an export licence—in these and many similar cases identical solutions are required of inter-national law.

Secondly, the Report does not define the terms non-per-formance, repudiation and cancellation. It is necessary to explain the distinction between three different conceptions.

---

[1] *I.L.C. Yearbook* (1957), ii.104, 116.

[2] This term, unfortunately, is not defined.

[3] Some of the material on this point is collected above, pp. 182 sqq. It is not really open to doubt that the distinction between contracts and public debts (if it ever existed), is obsolete and unjustified. In the same sense Eagleton, *The Responsibility of States* (1928), pp. 176 et seq., and Van Hecke, *Problèmes Juridiques des Emprunts Internationaux* (1955), pp. 17 et seq.

[4] Above, p. 320, n. 3.

It is even more important to state the legal system which determines whether any such breach as is contemplated by the Report has occurred.

Thirdly, it is difficult to give approval to the disappointing suggestion that any failure to perform contractual obligations or public debts, which, *ex hypothesi*, must be unjustifiable under the proper law of the contract, is, in international law, capable of being justified on grounds of public interest. This must be the public interest of the State whose responsibility is in issue. No elaboration is required to bring home the point that acceptance of any such exception would in practice exclude the possibility of establishing the contracting State's responsibility.[1]

It may be that a workable solution of the problem can be found only by generalizing an established principle of international law and at the same time taking a leaf out of the American Constitution and out of the books of authority to which it has given life: without prejudice to its liability for any other tort (such as denial of justice, discrimination, expropriation), the State shall be responsible for the injuries caused to an alien by the non-performance of its obligations stipulated in a contract with that alien if and in so far as such non-performance results from the application of the State's law enacted after the date of the contract; this shall not apply where the law so enacted is required for the protection of public safety, health, morality, or welfare in general.

---

[1] In the case of contractual obligations, economic necessity is suggested as an additional justification. 'Public interest' is so wide a term that it is likely to comprise economic necessity.

# VIII

# THE ENFORCEMENT OF TREATIES BY ENGLISH COURTS*

THE student who embarks upon a re-examination and an analysis of the decisions of English Courts (other than Prize Courts[1]) relating to treaties is bound to notice much uncertainty and vagueness. This is due, mainly, to two circumstances. In the first place it appears that there has frequently been a failure, on the part of pleaders and Counsel, to distinguish clearly between the different purposes for which a treaty may be invoked in a given case. It will be necessary, therefore, to attempt by the following observations a restatement and a re-classification of well-known material. Secondly, there exists sometimes, on the part of the Judiciary, a pronounced tendency to fight shy of an investigation into the meaning and effect of a treaty. Yet it is a fact of outstanding importance, which will have to be kept in mind throughout the following discussion, that English law knows no such rule as that which has been developed by the French Courts and according to which the interpretation of treaties involving political questions is withdrawn from the jurisdiction of the courts and the interpretation of treaties involving private law is primarily, though not exclusively, a matter for the Governments concerned.[2] On the contrary there is a long line of English cases in which the courts were called upon and felt both bound and entitled to consider and execute the terms of a treaty where they become relevant as an incidental point in the course of the judicial process.[3]

---

* From 44 *Transactions of the Grotius Society* (1958–9), 29.
[1] It would only be confusing to refer to the practice of Prize Courts, as this is not necessarily identical with or even indicative of that of English municipal courts.
[2] For references see Batiffol, *Traité Elémentaire de Droit International Privé* (2nd ed., 1955), p. 39.
[3] *Imperial Japanese Government* v. *P. and O. Steam Navigation Co.*, [1895] A. C. 644, particularly at p. 657; *Philippson* v. *Imperial Airways Ltd.*, [1939] A. C. 332; *Parke Davies and Co.* v. *Comptroller-General*, [1954] A. C. 321 and many other cases; see also *Re Ning Yi-Ching*, 56 (1939–40) T. L. R. 3, at p. 6, and *Adeyinka Oyekan* v. *Musendiku Adele*, [1957] 1 W. L. R. 876, where Lord Denning, delivering the opinion of the

The manner in which, in such circumstances, English Courts have approached a treaty, does not seem to, and indeed cannot, be determined by any specific principles of law and, therefore, does not require or lend itself to discussion. Nor is it necessary to inquire again into the question whether and to what extent treaties may constitute a guide to the interpretation of English statutory law.[1] Rather is it intended to review those cases in which a treaty may be relied upon in the course of municipal litigation as a source of rights and duties, viz. as a source of English law (below Section I) or as a source of international law or public policy (Section II) or as a cause of action for the benefit of a contracting State (Section III) or as a cause of action for the benefit of or against third parties (Section IV). Finally it will be asked whether any significance attaches to describing a treaty as an act of State (Section V).

# I

It is a commonplace that a treaty as such cannot be a source of English law or, in other words, impose duties or confer rights on anyone except the Crown in its international relations.[2] Were this not so the Crown would have the power of legislation. Consequently, in order to become binding upon subjects a treaty must be incorporated into the law of England by parliamentary legislation. What is sometimes loosely referred to as 'ratification' will not be sufficient.[3] Parliament may approve the conclusion

---

Privy Council, said: 'Their Lordships desire to point out that the treaty of cession was an Act of State. . . . In these circumstances the Courts of Law will not take it upon themselves to construe the treaty.' *Sed quaere.*

[1] See 'The Interpretation of Uniform Statutes', below, p. 614.

[2] Internationally a treaty to which the Crown is a party binds the Crown even if there has been no ratification of any kind. This is elementary and probably not denied, though sometimes concealed by loose formulations. Thus, when it is said of a treaty to which the United Kingdom is a party that in order to be binding it requires legislation, what is referred to is only the binding character of the treaty in municipal law.

[3] In the United Kingdom ratification in the strict sense of the term is the act of the Crown upon the advice of the appropriate Minister: McNair, *Law of Treaties*, p. 87. Such ratification does not normally occur without the approval of Parliament to be inferred from the fact that before ratification the treaty has been lying on the Table of both Houses of Parliament for 21 days: McNair, op. cit., pp. 32, 33; Oppenheim (–Lauterpacht) (8th ed. 1955), p. 905, n. 6. The ratification so given is insufficient to make the treaty part of the law of the country.

of a treaty and it may even pass legislation connected with a treaty, but a treaty cannot become part of English law otherwise than by the strictly legislative process Thus the various treaties which are known as 'Documents relating to the Termination of the Occupation Regime in the Federal Republic of Germany'[1] were ratified and approved by Parliament after they were signed at Bonn in May 1952 and Paris in October 1954, yet they do not form part of English law except in so far as the German Conventions Act, 1955, adopts certain of their provisions. The legal position is summarized by a dictum of Lord Atkin which must today be regarded as *locus classicus*[2]:

> Within the British Empire there is a well-established rule that the making of a treaty is an executive act, while the performance of its obligations, *if they entail alteration of the existing domestic law*, requires legislative action.

This comprehensive principle does not gain in clarity or ambit if it is supplemented by what, in effect, are mere sub-rules or illustrations. Thus it has been suggested that parliamentary sanction in the form of a statute is necessary not only for treaties requiring for their execution a change in the law, but also for treaties the execution of which presupposes the grant to the Crown of some new powers not already possessed by it or which create a direct or contingent financial liability upon Great Britain.[3] The measures contemplated by the three last-mentioned cases involve a change in the law and, therefore, merely illustrate the application of the principle.

The rule as formulated by Lord Atkin is of so fundamental a character in the British constitutional system that it is not, as has sometimes been suggested,[4] and, indeed, cannot be subject

---

[1] Cmd. 8571.

[2] *Attorney-General for Canada* v. *Attorney General for Ontario*, [1937] A. C. 326, 347. There are, of course, numerous other cases in which the existence of the principle is expressed or assumed. It may suffice to mention *Walker* v. *Baird*, [1892] A. C. 491 or *Hoani Te Heuheu Tukino* v. *Aote District Maori Land Board*, [1941] A. C. 308 where Lord Simon said (at p. 324): 'It is well settled that any rights purporting to be conferred by such a treaty of cession cannot be enforced in the Courts, except in so far as they have been incorporated in the municipal law.'

[3] Such a list of sub-rules which are merely illustrations of the principal rule is frequently presented by learned writers; see e.g., McNair, op. cit., p. 22.

[4] For instance by McNair, op. cit., pp. 18 sqq. The distorted proposition to be found in so prominent a work as Halsbury (–Simonds), *Laws of England* (3rd ed.), vii.287, is more dangerous and wholly inaccurate: 'treaties concluded by the Crown are in general binding upon the subject without express parliamentary sanction; but the previous consent of, or subsequent ratification by, the legislature is legally necessary to their validity in certain cases.'

to any exceptions. Rather is it necessary to solve the problem of the scope of the rule. The words 'if they entail alteration of the existing domestic law' as used in the context of Lord Atkin's dictum have no technical meaning; they are of wide, but uncertain impact. Hence there arises the frequently difficult task, not of finding exceptions to a rigid rule, but of defining the circumstances in which a treaty does or does not alter the law or, to put the same point differently, in which a treaty impinges upon the supremacy of parliamentary control of the law or falls solely within the purview of the Crown's prerogative in foreign affairs.

A treaty does not alter the law and, therefore, does not require legislation if it keeps wholly and exclusively within the limits of the Royal Prerogative or, in other words, if it constitutes such exercise of the Prerogative as is consistent with the existing law. In this case the treaty is binding upon the subject, because, it is the law itself that confers upon the Crown the power to make it so. That the Crown acts by treaty rather than, e.g., by Proclamation is merely fortuitous.

On the other hand legislation is required if the provisions of the treaty expressly contemplate or their performance necessarily presupposes a change of the law and, under the existing law, the Crown cannot make the change by the exercise of its Prerogative. This is the most comprehensive class and there is room for the impression that it is being given a very generous ambit, although there are cases in which, ignoring the limitations upon its constitutional powers, the Crown has effectively deprived British subjects of their property without legislative authority. This occurred as a result of the established rule of international law according to which a State is competent, on behalf of its nationals, to effect a transfer of their rights of property, 'as if the cessions had been made personally by the owner concerned'.[1] The United Kingdom has exercised this power on numerous occasions. Thus by treaties made after the Second World War with Yugoslavia, Czechoslovakia, Poland, Bulgaria, and Hungary, the British Government accepted certain sums as compensation for the expropriation of British property in these countries. In each of the treaties[2] the British

---

The Blonde, [1922] 1 A. C. 313, at p. 335, per Lord Sumner.
[2] Art. 2 of the Agreement with Yugoslavia of 23 December 1948, Cmd. 7600 or

Government declared 'on their own behalf and on behalf of British nationals that the conclusion of the present Agreement and compliance by the [Czechoslovak] Government with its terms shall be accepted in full satisfaction and final discharge of all liability to British nationals, owners whether legal or beneficial, of the claims' to all British property, rights, and interests affected by Czechoslovakian measures. In the unlikely event of the point having to be tested judicially and English law being applicable,[1] the British owner or creditor could not be held to have lost his right to his property or debt under the treaty,[2] unless, of course, he has accepted his share of the compensation distributed under the Foreign Compensation Act, 1950.[3] In most cases, however, the treaty has effectively deprived him of his property.[4] Hence the Crown ought to have obtained parliamentary authority.

There remains the case of a treaty which, on its face, does not fulfil the conditions just stated, but seems to fall within the limits of the prerogative, yet has the merely incidental effect of bringing about a change in the legal position or status of all or some members of the nation. This, it is submitted, is not a treaty involving an alteration of 'the existing domestic law'. The law remains unaltered, but as a result of the international facts created by the Crown the law of England calls for the application of a particular set of its existing rules. In consequence of

State Papers cli.198; Art. III of the Agreement with Czechoslovakia of 28 September 1949, Cmd. 7797 or State Papers cliv.74; Art. 5 of the Agreement with Bulgaria of 22 September 1955, Cmd. 9625; Art. 5 of the Agreement with Hungary of 27 June 1956, Cmd. 9820; Art. 5 of the Agreement with Poland of 11 November 1954, Cmd. 9343.

[1] The treaties only apply to property situate in the expropriating country and title would, therefore, be lost by virtue of the *lex situs*, though this may, of course, change. Moreover, if foreign law applies it will probably be found that the treaty has become part of it.

[2] He may have lost it under the local law. See the preceding note.

[3] The Orders which have been made under it and which regulate the assessment of compensation make it clear that no claimant can receive compensation except upon surrender of all rights to his property and all documents of title and upon renunciation of his debt; Foreign Compensation (Czechoslovakia) Order, 1950, S.I. 1950, No. 1191, clause 21; Foreign Compensation (Yugoslavia) Order, 1950, S.I. 1950, No. 1192, clause 22; Foreign Compensation (Poland) Order, S.I. 1956, No. 618, clause 21. Owners who claim under the Act, therefore, lose their property as a result of an assignment against some compensation.

[4] A recent case in which a treaty, not being incorporated into English law, has failed to have this effect and in which its conclusion has left private rights undisturbed, is the London Debt Settlement of German Pre-War debts (Cmd. 8781).

the Crown's declaration of war, for example, the common law rules about trading with the enemy come into operation or ships are liable to be requisitioned.[1] This follows from, and, therefore, does not constitute an alteration of, the existing law, though individual rights and duties are necessarily affected. Or English law includes a set of rules applicable to unrecognized governments and another set applicable to recognized governments; if the Crown grants recognition to a government the law provides for the application of the one in substitution for the other set of rules. In a similar manner a treaty may have legal effects on the footing of the existing law: the treaty may change, not the domestic law itself, but its operation.

It is, accordingly, not possible to support the delimitation which was suggested by Sir William Holdsworth and which, as will be observed, is open to the further criticism that it introduces a vague element of intention and would possibly permit such alteration of the law by the Crown as is merely incidental in character. Sir William said[2]:

What, then, is the test to be applied to ascertain whether an alteration of rights of the subject is an alteration which the Crown cannot effect by treaty because it amounts to an alteration of the law, or whether an alteration of the rights of the subject is merely the incidental effect of a treaty, so that the Crown is able to make the treaty? The test is, I think, this: If the object of the treaty is the doing of an act which the Crown has power to do, e.g. the recognition of the status of a foreign sovereign or a public ship or a cession of territory, the fact that it will have the effect of altering the rights of the subject will not preclude the Crown from making it. But if ... its object is to alter the rights of the subject, it cannot take effect without the consent of Parliament, because in this case it amounts to an alteration in the law.

The problem which has been discussed is liable to arise in many connections, but has in the past come up for consideration mainly in four cases.

(1) It has been suggested that it is not only a convention, but a legal rule of the constitution that the cession of British territory must be authorized by legislation, the reason being that the

---

[1] Halsbury (–Simonds), op. cit., p. 292.

[2] 58 L.Q.R. (1942), 175 sqq., 183. This article contains much useful material of a historical character. The suggestion made below, p. 394, that the necessity for legislation depends on whether on its face the treaty purports to alter the law or is only concerned with the conduct of foreign affairs is too narrow.

inhabitants of the ceded territory lose British nationality.[1] The controversy was perhaps always a little sterile, since for very many years no cession has occurred that was not authorized by Parliament. It must now be regarded as obsolete, for by virtue of the British Nationality Act, 1948, no subject of the United Kingdom and the Colonies loses his nationality as the result of the cession of territory.[2] The strict legal rule, if it has not fallen into desuetude, would therefore be that the Crown can cede territory without the consent of Parliament.[3]

(2) The question whether from the point of view of constitutional law the Crown has power to impose upon its subjects a Treaty of Peace so as to make it binding upon them is equally academic, seeing that in recent history Parliament has invariably legislated to give effect to the treaty. As a matter of strict law it would appear that the powers of the Crown depend on the terms of the treaty. If it provides merely for the conclusion of peace and for terms of a purely international character (such as the return of prisoners of war or of booty) the Crown's powers are unfettered, but legislation is necessary if and in so far as the law is intended to be altered by the imposition of financial charges or by altering the title to property and so forth.[4]

A contrary view, it is true, was expressed in Canada by no less an authority that Duff J. (as he then was) who, speaking of the Treaty of Versailles, said that, being a treaty of peace, it 'had the effect of law quite independently of legislation'.[5] But although the dictum was adopted by another Canadian judge,[6] a third Canadian judge[7] voiced dissent and laid down what, it is believed, is the better doctrine:

[1] The problem is discussed at length and with many further references by McNair, op. cit., pp. 24 sqq.; Holdsworth, op. cit., and in all textbooks on constitutional law.

[2] Clive Parry, *British Nationality* (1951), p. 163, but see J. Mervyn Jones, *B.Y.I.L.* (1948), 158, at p. 175.

[3] This, as appears from the quotation in the text, was already in 1942 the view of Sir William Holdsworth, though, of course, he relied on different reasons.

[4] The point has received very little attention in England. Halsbury (–Simonds), op. cit., p. 288, seems to assume that the Crown's power to make and implement treaties of peace is in law unfettered.

[5] *Secretary of State for Canada* v. *Alien Property Custodian for United States*, (1931) 1 D. L. R. 890, 902.

[6] Angers J. in *Ritcher* v. *The King*, (1943) 3 D. L. R. 540.

[7] Thirson, J. in *Bitter* v. *Secretary of State for Canada*, (1945) 3 D. L. R. 272 or A. D. 1943–5, No. 86. It will be appreciated that the prerogative to wage war ends

While a Treaty of Peace can be made only by the Crown, it still remains an act of the Crown. While it is binding upon the subjects of the Crown in the sense that it terminates the state of war, it has never, so far as I have been able to ascertain, been decided or admitted that the Crown could by its own act in agreeing to the terms of a treaty alter the law of the land or affect the private rights of individuals.

(3) A much more serious question arises in regard to treaties affecting belligerent rights.

The present extent of the Prerogative in war-time is a matter of some doubt.[1] Perhaps it continues to be almost unlimited except in so far as Parliament has either restricted it in terms or conferred upon the Crown statutory powers to do what formerly could be done by virtue of the Prerogative, in which event the Crown cannot now act otherwise than subject to the conditions of the statute.[2] It would seem to follow that, if and in so far as the prerogative rights of the Crown in war-time prevail, the Crown can, by treaty no less than by proclamation, alter the common law, for to that extent it is in pursuance of the existing domestic law that the Crown alters it.[3]

A doctrine such as this may well underline the decision of the full Court of Appeal (Lord Reading L.C.J., Lord Cozens-Hardy M.R., Buckley, Kennedy, Swinfen Eady, Phillimore, and Pickford, L.JJ.) in *Porter* v. *Freudenberg*,[4]—a case which, it cannot be denied, must cause 'some heart-searching',[5] but has met with singularly little analysis. The broad problem before the Court, it will be remembered, was the status of persons resident in enemy territory for the purpose of legal proceedings in England. 'Having stated the common law of England in regard to the question of an alien enemy's right to sue in our Courts of Law', the Court proceeded 'to consider whether the Hague Convention of 1907 upon the Laws and Customs of War on Land, Article 23 (h) of Chapter 1 of section 2 of the Annex entitled "Regulations respecting the Laws and Customs of War on Land" has any bearing upon the question we have to

---

at the moment when peace is made and cannot, therefore, justify any alteration of the law contemplated by the treaty of peace.

[1] See, generally, Halsbury (–Simonds), op. cit., p. 292.

[2] *Attorney-General* v. *De Keyser's Hotel*, [1920] A. C. 508.

[3] Statute law and common law in their relationship with the prerogative are therefore not necessarily on the same level.

[4] [1915] 1 K. B. 857.  [5] McNair, *B.Y.I.L.* (1928) 65.

determine'.[1] That Article makes it illegal 'to declare abolished, suspended or inadmissible the right of the subjects of the hostile party to institute legal proceedings'. The conclusion which the Court reached and which is based on the construction of the Article is couched in the following language[2]:

Suffice it to say that the substantial question being whether the operation of this paragraph is or is not to abrogate the old rule ... that an alien enemy's rights of action are suspended during war, jurists of eminence have expressed widely divergent views upon the point, and this Court has given to those views its very careful consideration. We are all clearly of the opinion that the paragraph in question cannot be treated as effecting any such abrogation.

It is obvious, therefore, that the Court of Appeal thought it possible that Article 23 (h) of the Hague Regulations, though not incorporated into English law by any statute, could 'abrogate' a rule of the common law. The Court's pronouncement might conceivably be decribed as an obiter dictum, for the actual decision is to the effect that on their true construction the Regulations limited the rights of 'the military commander of a belligerent force in the occupation of the enemy's territory'[3] and did not apply to proceedings in Great Britain. However, it would not be consonant with the weight to which this judgment is entitled to discard any part of its reasoning on technical grounds. It must, on the contrary, be accepted that not only the Court, but also the Attorney-General, Sir John Simon, attributed to the Hague Regulations the power to supersede the common law. The explanation can only be found in the view that, in the absence of any relevant restriction by Parliament of the Crown's prerogative in war-time, the Crown could by treaty alter the common law.[4]

---

[1] pp. 874, 875.       [2] p. 877.       [3] p. 878.

[4] Lord McNair, *B.Y.I.L.* (1928), pp. 63 sqq. and *Law of Treaties*, p. 337, seems to think that the Hague regulations constitute a treaty affecting belligerent rights and therefore bind the subject. Similarly, Wade and Phillips, *Constitutional Law* (4th ed. 1950), assert the binding character of treaties affecting belligerent rights, because waging war comes under the prerogative. There is probably not much difference between these formulations and the statement of the rule suggested in the text. However, the conception of belligerent rights originates from public international law and is not germane to English constitutional law. The latter regards treaties as binding only if and in so far as the prerogative of the Crown prevails. If it does not prevail even treaties affecting belligerent rights cannot bind the subject.

The uncertainties surrounding the extent of the Crown's prerogative are liable to create many doubts whenever the doctrine sanctioned by the Court of Appeal is relied upon; by way of example reference may be made to Article 93 of the Geneva Convention relative to the Treatment of Prisoners of War of 1949, according to which offences committed by prisoners of war with the sole intention of facilitating their escape and which do not entail any violence against life or limb shall occasion disciplinary punishment only.[1] The Geneva Conventions Act, 1957, did not incorporate Article 93 into the law of this country, yet it may be that Article 93 would effectively encroach upon the ordinary jurisdiction of the Courts.

(4) The question whether, in the absence of legislation, a treaty conferring immunity has municipal effect is, perhaps, the most difficult and, in practice, the most important one. It is submitted that, notwithstanding its prerogative in the conduct of foreign affairs, the Crown has no power to grant immunities, by treaty or otherwise, to any class of persons, which under the established law is not entitled thereto, though the Crown has the sole right of determining the members of the class on which the law confers immunity. On the other hand, the Crown has power to enter into a treaty restricting or reducing the immunities to which a foreign State or its representatives would normally be entitled.

The former part of the suggested principle rests on the fact that the creation of a new category of immunities involves a change of the law. This can be demonstrated by the extreme case in which the treaty assures the nationals of a foreign State who visit this country for business purposes, of immunity from legal proceedings. However, the result must be the same in cases which are less remote. Thus, if under English law foreign government officials or state-owned corporations are not entitled to immunity,[2] then a treaty cannot confer it upon them in a municipally binding manner. Were this not so there would have been no legal necessity for the passing of such statutes as

[1] Cmd. 8033, at p. 71.

[2] As to government officials see Oppenheim (–Lauterpacht) (8th ed., 1955), pp. 256 and 861, and as to State-owned corporations see ibidem, p. 265, with many references to which should be added *Miller* v. *Ferrocarril Del. Pacificio de Nicaragua*, 137 Maine 251; 18 A. (2d.) 688 or A. D. (1941–2), No. 51, and German Supreme Court, 7 June 1955, NJW 1955, 1435.

the International Organizations (Immunities and Privileges) Act, 1950, or the Diplomatic Immunities (Commonwealth Countries and Republic of Ireland) Act, 1952, but the Crown, in the exercise of its prerogative, could have achieved the objects pursued by these Acts. These statutes may, therefore, be invoked in support of the principle which has been suggested and which, of course, does not encroach upon the Crown's prerogative in two directions clearly covered by it: If there is no doubt as to the title to immunity of the class under consideration, it falls upon the Crown to determine the members of the class and such determination is for judicial purposes conclusive.[1] It is conceivable that the Crown will agree to treat a particular person as a member of a class to which he does not belong, and will thus clothe with immunity a person not entitled to it.[2] However, in these matters of state (the prerogative over which can always be restricted by Parliament) an argument founded upon the possibility of an abuse of power or of a factual determination made otherwise than *uberrimae fidei* cannot be carried too far.

The authorities which have considered that point are few and conflicting. It was Sir Robert Phillimore who first gave judicial expression to the doctrine which the present observations attempt to elaborate.[3] He had found that 'neither upon principle, precedent nor analogy of general international law' the *Parlement Belge* belonged 'to that category of public vessels which are exempt from process of law and all private claims'.[4] On the footing of this premise he had to investigate whether immunity, ordinarily non-existing, was conferred by the terms of the Anglo-Belgian Convention of 1876 whereby vessels such as the *Parlement Belge* were, in effect, equiparated to ships of

---

[1] *Engelke* v. *Musman*, [1928] A. C. 433. The distinction between the determination of the class (which is a question of law) and the determination of its members (which is a question of fact) underlies Lord Warrington's statement in that case at p. 457: 'It must be borne in mind that all that is directly in issue is the fact of the appellant's status. Whether, that fact being established, a defendant is entitled to the immunity he claims is a further question, which might have to be determined by the Court.' See also the Attorney-General's argument at pp. 436, 437.

[2] Since *Engelke* v. *Musman*, *ubi supra*, even in such circumstances recognition by the Crown would normally be conclusive (see, in particular, Lord Buckmaster, at p. 446). However, that case may not preclude the Court from denying effect to the recognition by the Crown if this is obviously inconsistent with the law.

[3] *The Parlement Belge* (1878–9), 4 P. D. 129.     [4] p. 149.

war, while in a British port. The learned judge had no difficulty in holding that this was a use of the treaty-making power
of the Crown which was 'without precedent and in principle
contrary to the laws of the Constitution'.[1] The decision on the
first point, as is well known, was reversed by the Court of
Appeal,[2] but the decision on the second point remains an
authority. Its force is in no way diminished by an obiter dictum
which fell from Atkin L.J. (as he then was) and will presently
be referred to in full.[3] It regards it as possible in law that sovereign States agree upon the enlargement of their envoys'
immunities. No argument has been advanced in support of a
view which implies a substantial and undesirable extension of
the Crown's prerogative.

Conversely, it is justifiable on grounds of principle and
precedent to suggest that even in the absence of legislation
Courts must give effect to such curtailments of the immunities
existing under the general law as are agreed upon by treaty (as
opposed to the unilateral act of the Crown). Such a treaty would
not involve a change of the law which the Crown is unable to
carry out. Rather would it amount to a waiver of the foreign
State's rights, which the law permits and which it is open to the
Crown to accept. The English Courts have, it is true, developed
the questionable doctrine that waiver of a foreign State's rights
can occur only as the result of steps taken in the course of proceedings.[4] But this doctrine has never been, and ought not to
be, pushed so far as to render nugatory the terms of a treaty
made between sovereign States. It is for these reasons that the
decision of the Court of Appeal in *Fenton Textile Association Ltd.*
v. *Krassin*[5] merits respectful approval. At a time when the
Government of Soviet Russia was recognized de facto only a
Trade Agreement was concluded between the United Kingdom
and Soviet Russia, which provided, inter alia, that official
agents sent by Soviet Russia to this country were exempt from
taxation, arrest and search. The defendant claimed that the
Agreement also involved immunity from civil jurisdiction.
The Court, and in particular Scrutton L.J., was inclined to

---

[1] p. 154.    [2] (1880) 5 P. D. 197.    [3] Below, p. 339.
[4] See, in particular, *Duff Development Co.* v. *Kelantan Government*, [1924] A. C. 797.
[5] (1922) 38 L. T. R. 259.

think (wrongly, it is believed)[1] that, had there been no treaty,
the defendant would have been entitled to full immunity.
Yet it rejected the claim to immunity, because, in the words of
Scrutton L.J.,[2] it found the position governed, not 'by any
general law of nations or common law, but by the special
agreement between the two countries', which did not mention
immunity from legal proceedings and, therefore was construed
according to the maxim *expressio unius est exclusio alterius*. Or,
as Atkin L.J. said by way of an obiter dictum[3]

> I see no reason why Sovereign States should not come to an agreement
> as to the rights and duties of their respective envoys, ordinary or extra-
> ordinary, or why such agreements should not enlarge or restrict the immuni-
> ties which would otherwise be due under the well established usage of na-
> tions.

That similar principles apply to the immunity of property,
such as ships, should not be open to doubt and is, in fact, inherent in the decision of Sir Robert Phillimore[4] to which, for
the sake of convenience, reference has been made above in another connection and which, strictly, relates only to the status of
property. It is, however, remarkable that the Crown has apparently never claimed the right to determine or agree upon
the categories of foreign property entitled to immunity or,
indeed, the question whether a particular piece of property
falls within the category or not.[5] On the analogy of the position
in regard to foreign envoys it would not have been surprising
if the Crown decided upon the status, e.g., of a particular ship
as a public vessel. This restraint, however, is well justified.
While the status of a person accredited to the Crown may be
supposed to be 'necessarily within the cognizance of the
Crown',[6] the same cannot be said of the status of property
claimed by a foreign State.

---

[1] See Oppenheim (–Lauterpacht) (8th ed. 1955), pp. 137, 789, 861, and Lauterpacht, *Recognition in International Law* (1947), p. 344. In *Engelke* v. *Musman, ubi
supra*, Lord Phillimore speaks of the 'special envoy' who is entitled to diplomatic
immunity. It is, however, obvious that he uses the expression in the sense of Envoy
Extraordinary in which this term has been used since the Vienna Congress: see
Oppenheim (–Lauterpacht), p. 776.

[2] p. 260.        [3] At p. 262.        [4] Above, p. 338.

[5] Lyons, *B.Y.I.L.* (1946), p. 259 seems to claim the latter right for the benefit of
the Crown. The authorities other than *The Parlement Belge* do not support this
suggestion.

[6] *Engelke* v. *Musman, ubi supra*, at p. 443, per Lord Buckmaster.

## II

Although a treaty which has not been incorporated into English law in general lacks the force of law in England, an English judge may yet have to regard it as a legally relevant rule of decision. This may be so either because the treaty is expressive of a rule of customary international law or because it constitutes a head of public policy, it being frequently difficult in theory and immaterial in practice to draw a clear line of distinction between the two conceptions.

In appropriate cases an English judge will give effect to a rule of customary international law. It may, therefore, be incumbent upon him to ascertain that rule. For this purpose he may and, indeed, must consider a treaty as a source or as evidence of customary international law, even though the Crown may not be a party to it.[1] However, for a number of reasons the practical significance of this proposition is but slight. In the first place the range of questions which an English Court will hold to be governed by international law *per se* is relatively restricted. Secondly, customary international law cannot in any event displace an existing rule of English law, whether it be derived from legislation or precedent. Thirdly, where a rule of customary international law is not clearly established, an English Court will be inclined to deduce it only from such treaties as indicate a uniform and comprehensive practice; treaties of isolated occurrence or limited scope will be resorted to rather for the purpose of supporting an *argumentum e contrario*. This attitude may not always be in harmony with the weight which international lawyers may be prepared to attach to a treaty, but it follows so clearly from the case of *The Franconia*[2] that it must be taken as a firm guide, however precarious the authority of the actual decision in that case may now be.

On the other hand, it cannot be gainsaid that public international law stands a greater chance of prevailing in an English Court if it provides a specific head of public policy, for it is of the essence of public policy that in a particular connection it is

---

[1] This follows clearly from *Regina* v. *Keyn* (1876), 2 Ex. Div. 63, 202 per Cockburn C.J.

[2] *Regina* v. *Keyn, ubi supra.*

capable of overriding an established rule of English law such as freedom of contract. In this sense, therefore, public policy may be stronger than a rule of customary international law. Thus in 1824 Best C.J.[1] said with reference to a contract made in England that

> it was contrary to the law of nations (which in all cases of international law is adopted into the municipal code of every civilized country) for persons in England to enter into engagements to raise money to support the subjects of a government, in amity with our own, in hostilities against their government.

A similar idea underlies the rule laid down in 1929 according to which it 'would be contrary to our obligations of international comity as now understood', i.e. to international law, to enforce an English contract 'if the real object and intention of the parties necessitates them joining in an endeavour to perform in a foreign and friendly country some act which is illegal by the law of such country'.[2] This rule was recently applied and much extended by the House of Lords in a case in which Lord Simonds put it on the ground that public policy demanded 'deference to international comity'.[3] It must be doubted whether as a matter of public international law any of these pronouncements were accurate at the time when they were made or are accurate today.[4] Yet they have established unquestionable rules of English public policy and also render evident the rationale: it is the inconsistency with the law of nations that creates the illegality. As the breach of a treaty to which the United Kingdom is a party is contrary to the law of nations, it might be suggested that public policy precludes any decision which involves the approbation of such a breach. Hence, to a considerable extent, treaties internationally binding upon the Crown, but not incorporated into English law, would become indirectly enforceable in England.

Such a proposition demands the utmost caution. In view of the authorities it is perhaps not a cogent reason for hesitation that, in general, the circumstances in which public policy can

---

[1] *De Wütz* v. *Hendricks* (1824), 2 Bing 314, 315.

[2] *Foster* v. *Driscoll*, [1929] 1 K. B. 470, 521, per Sankey L.J. (as he then was).

[3] *Regazzoni* v. *K. C. Sethia* (1944) *Ltd.*, [1958] A. C. 301, 757.

[4] See Oppenheim (–Lauterpacht) (8th ed., 1955), i, section 127a, with further references. From this point of view the above three decisions throw a remarkable light on the attitude of English judges towards public international law.

assert itself, are rare. But there is the more specific and more powerful reason that it would be wrong to do indirectly, viz. through the conception of public policy, what cannot be done directly through the application of the law: a treaty to which the legislature has failed to attribute the force of law cannot be given that very same force by the judiciary. This point is so fundamental that it necessarily imposes severe limitations upon the ambit within which treaty obligations may constitute a head of public policy. The mere fact that a particular decision would be inconsistent with the terms of a treaty concluded by the Crown and, therefore, would involve a breach of this country's treaty obligations cannot lead to a decision in the opposite sense. This conclusion is in line with the fact that the Executive cannot, under the English system of Government, exercise any control over the public policy as applied by the courts.[1] Nor is there anything startling or incongruous in the consequence that in English law treaties enjoy a considerably lesser degree of efficacy than the rules of customary international law. It is no more than an aspect of the established differentiation between customary international law and treaties[2] that English public policy will not normally permit a breach of the former, while it will be indifferent to a breach of the latter.

Considerations such as these should guide the approach to the problem what effect, if any, an English Court can give to those provisions of the Charter of the United Nations which enjoin the protection of human rights, in particular to Article 55 (c) which imposes upon the United Kingdom the duty to co-operate with the United Nations to promote 'universal respect for, and observance of, human rights and fundamental freedoms for all without distinction as to race, language, or religion'. For the purpose of this discussion it must be assumed not only that the relevant provisions of the Charter constitute legal obligations of the members of the United Nations and of the Organization as a whole,[3] but also that they are 'self-executing'[4] in the sense that had the Charter been

---

[1] *Bank voor Handel en Scheepvaart* v. *Slatford*, [1953] 1 Q.B. 248, 266, per Devlin J. See below, p. 418.

[2] See Lauterpacht, Transactions of the 25 *Grot. Soc.* (1939), 73 sqq.

[3] Oppenheim (–Lauterpacht) (8th ed., 1955), pp. 738 sqq.

[4] In American practice a treaty is described as self-executing if it 'prescribes by its own terms a rule for the Executive or for the Courts of . . . creates obligations

incorporated into the law of England they would, even in the absence of further legislation, effectively confer rights and impose duties upon individuals. Yet there is no room for the suggestion that the very general terms of the Charter afford evidence of any rule of customary public international law designed to protect human rights and fundamental freedoms. If any such rule exists independently of the Charter,[1] it is limited to a few cases which are unlikely to come before an English Court. Thus it will not be extravagant to suggest, for instance, that the right to life and the corresponding duty not to murder is so recognized. Yet it is difficult to see how this somewhat platitudinous statement could assist an English Court in any given case. On the other hand, when one comes to consider the marginal cases in which the existence of a human right may in practice become a matter of substantial significance, such as the right to the sanctity of the home or the right to a nationality, one finds that customary international law has failed to develop any accepted principle, so that, even if the Charter, in this respect, contained any definite legal rule, a decision would not be facilitated by having resort to it. As has been observed above, while the Charter could corroborate the existence of a rule of customary international law to which English public policy might give effect, the Charter cannot by itself achieve the creation of a rule of English public policy.

For these reasons the solution which the problem has found in Canada merits approval. In *Re Drummond Wren*,[2] it is true, Mackay J. sitting in the High Court of Ontario held that in view of the provisions of the Charter a restrictive covenant precluding the sale of land to Jews was void as being offensive to the public policy of Canada. However, in the later case of *Re*

---

for individuals enforceable without legislative implementation': see Evans, *B.Y.I.L.* (1953), p. 185. The term is not usual in this country, but aptly expresses a situation which may arise everywhere. It indicates a differentiation which is recognized, for instance in Germany: see *BGHZ* 17, 309; 18, 26 with reference to earlier cases.

[1] Although in his various contributions, particularly in *International Law and Human Rights* (1950), Sir Hersch Lauterpacht discusses very fully what may be described as the moral and philosophical background of the problem of human rights, he does not assert that *customary* international *law* has developed any specific rules on the subject. See, in particular, op. cit., p. 407. In Oppenheim (8th ed., 1955), p. 1,641, it is said to be 'generally recognized' that customary international law does not acknowledge the existence of the 'rights of mankind', though they have frequently been asserted by learned writers.

[2] (1945) Ontario Reports 778 or A. D. (1943–5), No. 178.

*Noble and Wolf* another judge of the High Court of Ontario[1] as well as the Court of Appeal[2] of Ontario refused to follow Mackay J.'s judgment. The broad ratio decidendi was that freedom of contract, itself a principle of public policy, could not, upon the issue then before the Court, be restricted by a treaty such as the Charter which had not been made part of the law of the land.

The preceding conclusions, should not, however, be carried to the length of suggesting that the provisions of a treaty as such are necessarily and wholly immaterial to the question of public policy. There are perhaps two cases in which a connection between this question and treaties is apparent and becomes a fit subject for further enquiry.

(1) A special question arises where an action is brought against the Crown itself, where the plaintiff relies on the provisions of a treaty made by his own sovereign with the Crown and where the Crown puts forward the defence that the treaty has not been incorporated into English law. Unless the Crown can show that the treaty was submitted to Parliament for the purpose of giving it effect in England, but that Parliament refused to do so, such a defence ought to fail. This follows from the principle of public policy according to which no man will be allowed to invoke and take advantage of his own wrong.[3] For it would be a breach of international law if a treaty which is internationally binding is not made effective in municipal law, and that breach will be within the cognizance of every Court which does not adhere to an unjustifiably extreme dualist doctrine about the relationship between international and municipal law.

If *Republic of Italy* v. *Hambros Bank*[4] was a case in which a treaty fell to be considered as a source of law rather than a

---

[1] (1948) Ontario Reports 579 or (1948) 4 D. L. R. 123 or A. D. (1948), 302.
[2] (1949) Ontario Reports 504 or (1949) 4 D. L. R. 374 or A. D. (1948), 308. The decision was reversed on other grounds: (1951) 1 D. L. R. 321. These cases are discussed by Lloyd, *Current Legal Problems* (1955). The American decisions on the point which are collected by Oppenheim (8th ed., 1955) (by Lauterpacht), p. 1,740, n. 4 are not relevant for present purposes, because the constitutional law of the United States on the position of treaties is wholly different from English law. It should perhaps be added in the present connection that the solution of the problems discussed in this article is hardly assisted by foreign material.
[3] Broom, *Legal Maxims* (10th ed., 1939), pp. 191 sqq.
[4] [1950] Ch. 314, discussed 14 Mod. L.R. (1951), 64.

cause of action, then it requires discussion in the present context. By treaty[1] with the plaintiff Republic the Government of the United Kingdom agreed to 'transfer to the Italian Government all the liquid assets now held as Italian property' by the Custodian of Enemy Property. Contrary to the terms of the treaty the Custodian of Enemy Property, at the direction of the Board of Trade, transferred certain liquid assets held by him as Italian property to Hambros Bank as the attorney-administrators of the English estate of the original Italian owner. The Republic of Italy claimed a declaration and other relief, not only against Hambros Bank but also against the Custodian of Enemy Property. The plaintiffs argued that the treaty had become part of the law of this country. The argument failed and, accordingly, Vaisey J. dismissed the action. The question whether it was open to the Custodian of Enemy Property to rely on the absence of statutory recognition of the treaty was not raised. Since the Custodian is the servant or agent of the Crown,[2] he could not be in a better position than his master or principal, i.e. the Crown who, it is submitted, was precluded by public policy from setting up a defence derived from its own wrong. On behalf of the Custodian it was said that he understood the plaintiffs' grievance perfectly well,[3] and the learned Judge himself repeatedly confessed[4] that he was disturbed and bewildered by what had occurred and resulted in the Republic of Italy being deprived of its treaty rights. In so far as the Custodian was concerned it would have been both possible and necessary to translate these feelings into legal effect by holding him to the terms of the treaty.

An argument on these lines was probably in the mind of the claimants in the case of *Bataafsche Petroleum* v. *War Damage Commission*[5] which came before a special Appeal Board in Singapore and the facts of which can, for present purposes, be summarized as follows. Property of the claimants was confiscated by the Japanese authorities during the occupation of the Netherlands East Indies, but was later found in Singapore and seized there by the Crown from whom the claimants demanded

---

[1] Cmd. 7118.
[2] *Bank voor Handel en Scheepvaart* v. *Slatford*, [1954] A. C. 584.
[3] p. 323.        [4] pp. 324, 329.
[5] Int. L.R. 1956, 810.

compensation. If the Japanese had acquired a title valid by the law of the Netherlands East Indies at the time of the confiscation, the Crown's title was *prima facie* unassailable. This is so even if it is assumed, further, that by the law of the Netherlands East Indies the title of the Japanese was subsequently invalidated with retrospective effect.[1] However, if the Crown had, by treaty undertaken not to recognize the title acquired by the Japanese authorities, but to give effect to the subsequent invalidation by the Dutch, the principle suggested above would have assisted the claimants, it being immaterial that no legislation had been enacted to implement the treaty. It was held that there was no treaty requiring, or capable of, implementation and, moreover, that in the absence of legislation no regard could be had to the terms of the treaty if any. It is the latter part of this reasoning that may be open to challenge. It was, however, intended to reject the claimants' argument that the alleged treaty involved a mitigation or waiver of the Crown's belligerent rights and therefore did not require legislation.[2] It is believed that an argument so formulated was rightly held to be unacceptable.

(2) Where a rule of the conflict of laws requires an English judge to apply the provisions of a foreign legal system, it is, or ought to be, much more readily open to him to reject them by virtue of English notions of public policy or of a rule of public international law.[3] Consequently, there ought to be no doubt that an English judge will not give effect to the implications of the law of a foreign country in so far as they are opposed to the treaty obligations of that country, particular if the United Kingdom is also a party to the treaty. This is a point of considerable practical significance. It has never been decided in England whether English law will recognize disabilities created by religious belief, race or caste, though it is the almost unanimous opinion of textbook-writers that such disabilities will not be recognized.[4] Within the framework of the European Convention for the Protection of Human Rights and Fundamental Free-

---

[1] On the significance of this point see *B.Y.I.L.* (1954), p. 245.

[2] On this point see above, p. 334.

[3] The situation envisaged in the text does not really raise a question of public policy: see below, p. 376.

[4] Cheshire, *Private International Law* (4th ed.), pp. 146 sqq; Martin Wolff, *Private International Law* (2nd ed., 1950), p. 173, Dicey, *Conflict of Laws* (6th ed., 1949), pp. 465 sqq.

doms it is clear law that 'men and women of marriageable age have the right to marry and to found a family, according to the national laws governing the exercise of this right'[1] and that the enjoyment of this right 'shall be secured without discrimination on any ground such as sex, race, colour, language, religion, political or other opinion, national or social origin, association with a national minority, property, birth, or other status'.[2] It is submitted that an English Court could not now reach a decision similar to that rendered by the German Supreme Court[3] some twenty-five years ago and according to which a foreign law prohibiting a marriage between a Christian and a Non-Christian did not offend against German public policy.

Some support for this suggestion may be found in the decision of Atkinson J. in *Royal Hellenic Government* v. *Vergottis*.[4] The facts are too complicated to be summarized here. It must suffice to say that the case arose out of the—unpublished— Anglo-Greek Shipping Agreement of 20 May 1941[5] which provided for the chartering to the British Government of Greek ships requisitioned by the Greek Government. The latter claimed from the defendant certain moneys held by him and derived its alleged rights, *inter alia*, from certain Greek legislation which, in the view of the learned judge, was inconsistent with the Agreement of 1941. It was on this ground that the Court refused to apply the Greek legislation in question[6]:

No English Court can be asked to give effect to a legislative act of a foreign Government which is in the very teeth of the Agreement which that Government has made with the British Government.

It is difficult to ascertain from the report whether the Agreement of 1941 was a treaty. If it was an agreement made on the footing of municipal law, the learned judge's dictum would, it is submitted, apply *a fortiori* in the case of a treaty.

---

[1] Cmd. 8969, Art. 12 and Art. 14.

[2] It is submitted that the words 'according to the national laws governing the exercise of this right' in Art. 12 are limited by, but do not control Art. 14.

[3] 16 May 1931, *RGZ* 132, 416. It is unlikely that the decision would be followed in Germany today.

[4] 78 Ll. L.R. (1945), 292.

[5] It is partly reproduced at pp. 313, 314.

[6] At p. 328.

# III

The question whether a treaty can afford a cause of action in an English Court in the sense that proceedings can be founded upon it and be the means of its enforcement as a contract has received curiously little attention from scholars. It may well be that many, if not most, of them would agree with Westlake[1] who, fifty years ago, observed that it was 'beyond controversy' that treaties could not be the subject of private municipal litigation:

To deny it would involve the consequence that if a treaty of peace stipulated the payment of a sum of money by one sovereign to another, the latter might sue the former for the amount in a court of justice,—quod est absurdum.

There is, indeed something absurd in the idea of proceedings by a foreign State against the Crown, whereby, under the provisions of Order 14 of the Rules of Supreme Court, a sum of possibly hundreds of millions of pounds due for reparations is sought to be recovered before a Master of the Queen's Bench Division. The reason for that impression lies primarily in the fact that it is impossible to imagine that the Crown, having made default in the discharge of its obligations, would satisfy a judgment so recovered against it without obtaining parliamentary assistance designed to nullify the proceedings in the courts. Yet it is not certain whether the problem raised by Westlake's hypothetical case is capable of being disposed of by description rather than discussion.

When one turns to judicial authorities it is necessary to beware of that long line of cases[2] which have established the broad rule first formulated by Lord Kingsdown[3]:

The transactions of independent States between each other are governed by other laws than those which municipal Courts administer; such Courts have neither the means of deciding what is right, nor the power of enforcing any decision which they may make.

This statement, it is true, refers to 'transactions of independent

[1] 22 *L.Q.R.* (1906), 14, 21.

[2] *Cook* v. *Sprigg*, [1899] A. C. 572, 578, per Lord Halsbury: *Secretary of State for India* v. *Bai Rajbai*, (1915) 42 Ind. App. 229; *Vajesingji Joravarsingji* v. *Secretary of State for India*, (1924) 51 Ind. App. 357.

[3] *Secretary of State in Council of India* v. *Kamachee Boye Sahaba* (1859), 13 Moo. P.C.C. 22.

States between each other' and is, therefore, wide enough to comprise treaties and thus to withdraw them from cognizance by English Courts. But so far-reaching an interpretation of the dictum is hardly tenable. It is, in the first place, not open to doubt that on many occasions courts are called upon to, and in fact do, consider such transactions between sovereign States as are treaties. There exists, as has been pointed out,[1] a long line of English authorities which show that courts have not found it improper or difficult to give effect to rights and duties flowing from treaties. Secondly, the dictum is, on analysis, not intended to deal with treaties as a cause of action: it relates to seizures effected by the Crown as an act of state, whether in pursuance or in defiance of a treaty, but it does not, in its context, relate to the enforceability of a treaty in municipal courts as a cause of action rather than a source of law.

This problem seems to have come before the courts on three and possibly four occasions. The leading case is still *Nabob of the Carnatic* v. *East India Company*.[2] The plaintiff, an Indian Prince, was indebted to the defendants who, in the context, had the status of sovereigns. He assigned to them by way of security certain districts of the Carnatic the revenues of which they were to apply to the reduction of the debt. By a later agreement the plaintiff was restored to his territories and the receipt of the revenues. In the proceedings the plaintiff claimed an account of the revenues received by the defendants and payment of such sums as exceeded the amount of the indebtedness. The first decision rendered by Lord Thurlow turned almost exclusively on points of pleading and it is not easy to ascertain to what extent the Court expressed its own views on the substantive questions involved in the case; in particular, the oft-quoted statement that 'wherever sovereign nations have contracted upon sovereign matters the effect is a species of obligations *ex quo non oritur actio*'[3] is more likely a summary of the argument than an expression of the Court's considered opinion. When the case came before the Court again,[4] judgment had to be given in circumstances of some haste; accordingly it was very short and rendered *ex tempore*. The claim was dismissed:

---

[1] Above, p. 327, n. 3.    [2] (1793) 2 Ves. Jr. 56.
[3] (1791) 1 Ves. Jr. 371, 390.    [4] (1793) 2 Ves. Jr. 56, 60.

It is a case of mutual treaty between person acting in that instance as States independent of each other. . . . That treaty . . . is the same as if it was a treaty between two sovereigns, and consequently is not a subject of private municipal jurisdiction.

The next, and no doubt, the most important case was *Salaman* v. *Secretary of State for India*[1] the relevant facts of which were as follows. By the terms of Lahore made in 1849 between an Indian Prince, the Maharajah Duleep Singh, and the defendant's predecessor in title, the East India Company, the latter promised to pay to the Prince a certain pension for the support of himself, his relatives, and the servants of the State. The Maharajah died in 1893 and his estate passed to Prince Victor of whose property the plaintiff was in 1902 appointed trustee in bankruptcy. One of the claims made by him was that the defendant was a trustee of the annual sums allegedly due to the Maharajah and the Prince which had not been paid. The action was summarily dismissed as frivolous and vexatious. Vaughan Williams L.J. said[2]:

There does not appear to me the very slightest ground upon the face of this document for treating it as a contract of any kind. It is to my mind, perfectly plain that the granting of these terms . . . was an act of State over which a municipal court has no jurisdiction whatsoever.

Stirling L.J. expressed himself in similar vein.[3] Fletcher Moulton L.J.[4] started 'from the premiss that the claims are not necessarily beyond the cognizance of municipal courts merely because their origin is connected more or less directly with an act of State'. The learned Lord Justice proceeded to say[5] that the treaty indicated 'no intention on the part of the Government to pay to the Maharajah Duleep Singh any allowance of such a character as to be capable of determination by a court of law', but that even if this were not so the plaintiff could allege what[6] 'would at most be only a breach of contract on the part of the Government'. This short summary will, it is hoped, be sufficient to show that the majority of the Court of Appeal based its decision on the absence of jurisdiction, while Fletcher Moulton L.J. was prepared to hold the Terms of Lahore justiciable, but found their provisions so indeterminate as to be incapable of supporting a claim for breach of trust as opposed to a breach of contract.

[1] [1906] 1 K. B. 613.  [2] At p. 628.  [3] p. 635.
[4] p. 641.  [5] Ibidem.  [6] Ibidem.

The third case which may be, but is not necessarily relevant is *Republic of Italy* v. *Hambros Bank*.[1] The facts which have already been summarized seem to raise the issue whether the plaintiff Republic could, and did in fact intend to, rely on its treaty with the Crown to enforce contractual rights. It is not certain whether the treaty was pleaded as an agreement, as a cause of action; probably it was not, since, as the learned judge pointed out, the Crown was not a party to the proceedings, and, moreover, the argument, in so far as it is reported, seems to have been directed to the wholly distinct point whether the treaty had become incorporated into English law and thus been made a source of law. However this may be, the action was dismissed on the ground that the treaty was 'not cognizable or justiciable in this Court'.[2] This probably meant that the treaty was disregarded, because it was not 'forming part of our municipal or domestic law'.[3] If this interpretation is correct, the *Republic of Italy's* case is not, but could and ought to have been material to the point now under discussion, for that the treaty with Italy was not incorporated into English law was hardly open to doubt.

The last case is Devlin J.'s decision in *Bank voor Handel en Scheepvaart* v. *Slatford*,[4] in which the plaintiffs sued as assignees of a foreign sovereign to enforce, inter alia, the so called Property Agreement made in 1944 between the Government of the United Kingdom and the Government of the Netherlands. It provided for the release to the Netherlands of certain property held in this country. The plaintiffs pleaded the treaty as an agreement and claimed, in effect, its specific performance. The learned judge found it unnecessary to deal at length with the enforceability of the treaty, but he made the following significant observation[5]:

> The Solicitor-General is, I think, right in saying that the agreement is not justiciable, and that neither its language nor that of its accompanying letters is suited to legal interpretation.

It thus appears that the courts' refusal to allow the enforcement of a treaty as an agreement has in the past been supported by several different reasons. In order to examine their strength an elaborate and far-reaching inquiry into their foun-

---

[1] [1950] Ch. 314.    [2] p. 329.    [3] p. 325.
[4] [1953] 1 Q.B. 248.    [5] p. 254.

dation (such as Sir Hersch Lauterpacht has undertaken in regard to the justiciability of international disputes)[1] may well be necessary, for this may be one of those cases in which the recorded judicial pronouncement conceals the undisclosed reluctance to enter unfamiliar and possibly embarassing ground —a reluctance the explanation of which in terms of history, jurisprudence and psychology would far exceed the scope of this article. Yet their review in a somewhat cursory manner will, it is hoped, be sufficient to support the submission that they do not carry conviction.

The first reason would seem to be that treaties cannot be justiciable, i.e. subject to municipal jurisdiction. It is, indeed, undeniable that in public international law no less than in private law there are certain disputes which are not justiciable: they may shortly be described as disputes of a political character. Such disputes are usually or at least frequently withdrawn from the jurisdiction of international tribunals.[2] In municipal law, too, it is clear, for instance, that a court 'would not grant an injunction against the French Republic marching an army across the Rhine or the Alps'[3]: equally, no court would or could grant such an injunction against the British Crown. But disputes of a strictly legal character are pre-eminently within the cognizance of an international tribunal, although it is a very large question how they are to be distinguished from political issues. It is not by any means clear why legal issues arising from a treaty should necessarily be incapable of being decided by a municipal court if they arise in an action for the enforcement of a treaty. There is no rule of positive law or logic or legal policy which would demand such a result, seeing in particular that treaties are clearly justiciable where their construction is incidental to the decision upon disputes arising from private law.

That, secondly, treaties are usually governed by public international law does not disqualify a municipal court from pronouncing upon legal issues involved in them. Municipal courts are frequently called upon to administer justice by applying a legal system other than English law, and, more

---

[1] *The Function of Law in the International Community* (1933).

[2] See Oppenheim (–Lauterpacht) (7th ed., 1952), ii.30.

[3] *Duke of Brunswick* v. *King of Hanover* (1848), 2 H. L. C. 1, at p. 27, per Lord Campbell. This is so, of course, even independently of the principle of immunity.

specifically, to apply public international law. There is no warrant for the suggestion that municipal judges do not have the means for deciding what is right by the rules of public international law.

Thirdly, it is unjustifiable to refuse municipal enforcement to a treaty on the ground that it is allegedly couched in the language of diplomacy rather than law and therefore incapable of 'legal' interpretation. This is a point which at the present stage of the development of public international law cannot be maintained. It involves a denial of the legal character of public international law—a denial that strikes at the root of our civilization. It may be, of course, that a certain document is merely a Declaration of a Protocol or some other type of programmatic statement without binding force. Assuming, however, that a treaty in the established sense of the term has been concluded its legal character and, consequently, the applicability of rules of legal interpretation is unquestionable.

If it is said, fourthly, that a municipal court which would attempt to enforce a treaty would be without the power of enforcing its judgment, this is an argument which has for long, but unsuccessfully been used to throw doubt upon the efficacy of international litigation and which is not more convincing when used in connection with municipal litigation. In none of the cases which came before English Courts in the past and which have been summarized above would it have been impossible for the court to enforce its judgment; nowadays section 25 of the Crown Proceedings Act, 1947, makes an argument based on the alleged unenforceability of a judgment largely untenable. That argument would in any event be of no avail where the court is asked to make a declaration.

The conclusion so far reached is that if a treaty is relied upon as a cause of action and the issue is of a legal character an English Court is not under an inherent disability to render judgment.

The real obstacle, it is believed, arises, not from municipal law, but from public international law, from the treaty itself. It arises from the fact that the pacific settlement of legal disputes has for over a century and a half been conceived as a matter for international tribunals to whose jurisdiction States are not subject in the absence of express submission; that the enforcement of treaty rights by municipal tribunals has only infrequently been attempted and never succeeded; and that, therefore, a treaty may well have to be so construed as to contain an implied term excluding the jurisdiction of municipal tribunals in cases in which the treaty is relied upon as a cause of action. This view is likely to impose itself most forcefully and almost inevitably where, for instance, by their acceptance of the Optional Clause States have agreed upon an international forum competent to decide their disputes or where they have designed other machinery for the enforcement of treaty rights. But even where this condition is not fulfilled the result will, in general, be the same. At the present stage of development and experience it would probably be rash to state the point more categorically: a problem of construction is involved. There may be treaties, admittedly exceptional in number and character, the terms of which do not exclude the jurisdiction of municipal courts. The court will and ought to be slow in so interpreting a treaty as to permit its municipal enforcement as an agreement. Thus a clear finding to the effect that the issue is of a legal rather than a political nature will not often be possible. Moreover, the process of construction will have to be influenced by the idea of reciprocity: if the plaintiff State could not in its own courts be sued by the Crown on the treaty in issue an English Court should almost invariably find it impossible to allow that plaintiff State to enforce the treaty by action here.

If, in the light of these considerations, the four cases referred to above are again examined, it will appear that in *Bank voor Handel en Scheepvaart* v. *Slatford*[1] the jurisdiction of municipal courts is likely to have been excluded, because by Article 16 of the treaty it was provided that 'a Committee shall be established to execute this Agreement'. In *Republic of Italy* v. *Hambros Bank*[2] the position was more doubtful. There was apparently in April 1947 no machinery in force for the settlement of disputes between Italy and the United Kingdom. The dispute was clearly of a legal character. And, above all, it was one so intimately connected with matters of municipal law that the submission of a dispute to a municipal court cannot *a priori* be said to have been outside the contemplation of the parties. The other cases were of inter-imperial origin. There was and is

---

[1] [1953] 1 Q.B. 248.      [2] [1950] Ch. 314.

no machinery in existence for the decision of legal disputes between members of the British Commonwealth of Nations. It is likely that the judicial practice inaugurated by the *Nabob of the Carnatic's* case[1] has given rise to the intention to exclude the jurisdiction of municipal courts. As a matter of principle, however, the inclination of Fletcher-Moulton L.J. (as he then was) to treat the failure to pay a pension due under a treaty as a breach of contract cognizable by and enforceable in English Courts may have to be preferred to the view expressed by the majority of the Court of Appeal.

# IV

That a treaty which is not a source of English or international law or of public policy but is invoked as an agreement cannot be enforced by anyone except a party to it is an elementary consequence of its contractual character. It is quite true that within narrow limits treaty rights may be capable of an assignment[2] and that, where this is permitted, a third party may be able to set it up to the same extent as its assignor. But this is a possibility which keeps strictly within the framework of the normal contractual relationship.

It is a wholly distinct question whether third parties who are not assignees may derive benefits from or be bound by the terms of a treaty for the purpose of proceedings in an English Court in which the treaty is relied upon as an agreement. It is a question which can arise only if, in accordance with the tentative suggestions made in the preceding section, it is assumed that in some special cases it is in fact possible to enforce a treaty by action in an English Court.[3]

---

[1] (1793) 2 Ves. Jr. 56.

[2] Below, p. 360.

[3] Many of the problems discussed in the following paragraphs are exemplified by the Agreement regarding the Repayment of certain Credits made between the United Kingdom and Turkey on 11 February 1954, Cmd. 9120. By this treaty the United Kingdom agreed to give full discharge to Turkey 'of all their obligations to Vickers-Armstrongs Ltd.', while Turkey undertook to pay to Vickers-Armstrong Ltd. the equivalent of the sterling amount due to them in Turkey in Turkish liras and to 'abandon to the Company the materials in the possession of the Company in the United Kingdom'. It is not difficult to visualize circumstances in which both Turkey and Vickers-Armstrong Ltd. might desire or be compelled to invoke this treaty in proceedings in an English Court.

(1) In international law it may be regarded as settled that third parties (including individuals) may acquire rights under a treaty made between sovereign States.[1] If, therefore, an English Court can enforce a treaty at all, it can do so for the benefit of a third party, subject to two qualifications.

The Crown's intention to create treaty rights in favour of its subjects or some of them must be expressly declared. It is a clearly established rule of English constitutional law that, in general, the Crown does not act as agent or trustee for its subjects.[2] But Lord Atkin has added the significant proviso that it is open to the Crown 'expressly to declare that it is acting as agent'.[3] It should, however, not be assumed that the constitutional law of other countries is necessarily the same. Yet such generalization occurs in the judgment of Maugham J. (as he then was) in *Administrator of German Property* v. *Knoop*.[4] In this case the defendant, a German subject, relying upon a treaty made between the United Kingdom and Germany, claimed the release of certain property held by the plaintiff. It was argued on his behalf that the treaty was entered into by the German Government on behalf of German nationals in the sense that the German Government was either a trustee or an agent for German nationals who were intended to have benefits under the treaty. This argument, it is submitted, could not be rebutted by considerations founded upon English decisions, but depended on German law about which, however, nothing seems to have been proved except the probably irrelevant fact that the treaty had become part of German law.[5] On the other hand, it is plain that a heavy burden rests upon a litigant who sets out to prove rights vested in him personally under the treaty. But this is an obvious caveat which affects the practical import of the principle rather than the extent of the exception now under discussion.

The second qualification likewise arises from a rule of English constitutional law; if by a treaty of cession the Crown assumes obligations towards the inhabitants of the territory ceded to the Crown, 'the right to enforce remains with the high

---

[1] Permanent Court of International Justice in the *Case of the Danzig Railway Officials* (1928) (Series B), No. 15.
[2] *Civilian War Claimants Association* v. *The King*, [1932] A. C. 14.
[3] At p. 26.    [4] [1933] Ch. 439.    [5] p. 455.

contracting parties' and cannot be asserted by any of the inhabitants.[1] This doctrine, it is true, may be said to rest on
obiter dicta, for it does not seem to have been laid down in any
case in which the treaty was relied upon as an agreement and
that treaty included a term conferring benefits upon the plaintiff. But the principle has been stated in at least three decisions
of the Privy Council and must, therefore, be accepted as part of
the law of England.

(2) In international law it is also a settled rule that a
sovereign State is competent to make a cession of rights by
treaty 'which would bind its nationals and effect a transfer of
their rights and property as if the cession had been made personally of their rights of property'.[2]

If, therefore, by treaty with the Crown, a foreign State
assigns certain of its subjects' rights to the Crown, the question
arises whether the Crown can assert the rights so acquired
against a foreign national in the English Courts. Thus, to take an
imaginary case, a foreign State may agree to transfer to the
Crown the British patents which its nationals may have obtained in a certain field of invention. Can the Crown claim a
transfer of such patents from a foreign patentee resident in
England? It would be *nihil ad rem* to point out that the Crown
could not by treaty in a municipally binding manner dispose
of its own subjects' property: the case depends on the international competence of a foreign State. Nor would it be relevant to argue that the treaty in question does not form part of
English municipal law: the Crown relies on the treaty as an
agreement rather than generally binding law. If the hypothesis
on which the present discussion rests is correct, then the
Crown's claim should succeed in the same way as the individual
plaintiff should succeed in the converse case in which he sues
the Crown in reliance upon the provision in a treaty made for
his benefit.

If, on the other hand, it is the Crown which, by treaty,
disposes of the property of its subjects in favour of a foreign
State, the result is necessarily different. The foreign State is

---

[1] *Vajesingji Joravarsingji* v. *Secretary of State for India* (1924) Ind. App. 357, at
p. 360, per Lord Dunedin; *Secretary of State* v. *Sardar Rustam Khan*, [1941] A. C.
356, *Hoani Te Heuheu Tukino* v. *Aotea District Maori Land Board*, [1941] A. C. 308.
[2] *The Blonde*, [1922] I A. C. 313, 335, per Lord Sumner.

unable to claim under the treaty against a British subject. The treaty is, *ex hypothesi*, not incorporated into English municipal law. Under English constitutional law, as opposed to international law, the Crown cannot, in the absence of legislation, so act on behalf of its subjects as to affect their legal rights.[1]

## V

The conclusions reached by the preceding observations, which, it is hoped, speak for themselves and need not be summarized, should be amplified in one respect. No reference has been made to a treaty as an act of State, though treaties have frequently been so described. The reason is that probably no advantage is to be derived from any such description.

Treaties may be acts of State in the sense that they belong to that group of international occurrences about which, for certain purposes, the courts obtain information from the Executive. How far this practice extends in the case of treaties is obscure. Thus it may be for the courts to decide for themselves, without reference to the Executive, whether a treaty has come into existence, for instance, if a high contracting party has merely signed but not ratified it.[2] It is probably also a judicial question to be decided by the courts whether a treaty has come to an end.[3] That it is both the right and the duty of the courts to undertake the interpretation of a treaty further curtails the significance of a treaty being an act of State.

Act of State denotes a defence. It is open to the Executive or its agents, when a non-resident alien purports to found a claim upon an act of the Executive done as a matter of policy in the course of its relations with another State.[4] In one case the defence can be relied upon even if the claim is made by a British subject or resident aliens: this happens where the act complained of was done in the exercise of prerogative powers in the annexation of foreign territory.[5] In both cases the existence

[1] See above, p. 331.

[2] See *Philippson* v. *Imperial Airways*, [1939] A. C. 332.

[3] See the decision of the District Court for the Southern District of California in *Artukovic* v. *Boyle* 107 (1952) Fed. Supp. 11, at p. 24.

[4] This definition was first put forward by Professor Wade, *B.Y.I.L.* (1934), 98, at p. 103, and is now generally accepted.

[5] See the cases mentioned, p. 357, n. 1.

or non-existence of a treaty is irrelevant. It is the act that matters. It cannot be rendered lawful by a treaty[1] nor does the mere absence of a treaty render it actionable. It follows that the conception of a treaty as an act of State is confusing and otiose and ought to be discarded.

[1] *Walker* v. *Baird*, [1892] A. C. 491.

# THE ASSIGNABILITY OF TREATY RIGHTS*

IT is, of course, clear that there are many treaties in connection with which it would be unthinkable to treat rights arising from them as assignable. Rights to political or armed support, rights to the extradition of criminals, rights to the recognition or enforcement of judgments—these are a few examples of cases in which obviously there cannot be any question of an assignment. Yet it is to be noted that contracting States have on occasions thought it necessary to make express provision about assignments. By the Agreement made on 27 March 1941 between the United Kingdom and the United States of America and relating to the Leased Areas in Newfoundland and the West Indies, the United States of America was given comprehensive rights of user and jurisdiction in the Leased Areas.[1] Article XXIII of the Agreement provides that 'the United States will not assign or underlet or part with the possession of the whole or any part of any Leased Area or of any right, power or authority granted by the Leases or this Agreement'. An Agreement made between the same two States on 21 July 1950[2] confers upon the United States similar rights in the Bahamas Islands for the purpose of establishing and maintaining a long-range proving ground for guided missiles. According to Article XX 'the Government of the United States of America shall not assign or part with any of the rights granted by this Agreement'. On 26 November 1951 the Governments of the United States of America and the United Kingdom entered into a similar Agreement with the Dominican Republic[3]; this, however, does not contain a covenant against assignments. In a different field the picture to be derived from the practice of States is equally varied. Treaties of a financial character have long been known to include frequently clauses permitting the assignment

---

* From *British Year Book of International Law* (1953), p. 475.
[1] Cmd. 6529.    [2] Cmd. 8109.
[3] Cmd. 8546.

of the debt. Thus, when the inter-allied debts came to be settled after the First World War, the bonds issued by their debtor states to the United States of America and the United Kingdom respectively embodied the promise to pay certain sums to the creditor State 'or order'.[1] By virtue of the policy of economic co-operation the Government of the United States of America caused several lines of credit to be established in favour of the United Kingdom. Thus the Loan Agreements which the United Kingdom concluded with the Export–Import Bank of Washington provided for the execution by the borrower of promissory notes containing the promise to pay 'to Export–Import Bank of Washington, an Agency of the United States of America, its successors or assigns'.[2] By an Agreement of 7 September 1949 Belgium opened in favour of the United Kingdom a credit in Belgian francs equivalent to $28 million for the purpose of financing the deficit of the sterling area with the Belgian monetary area.[3] The promissory note executed by the United Kingdom provides for repayment to the Belgian Government, but by Article 6 of the Agreement the latter 'undertakes not to · assign, pledge or mortgage any promissory note given by the Government of the United Kingdom ... except in favour of one or more Belgian Government Agencies or Institutions. In the event of such assignment, pledge or mortgage the Belgian Government shall notify the Government of the United Kingdom within thirty days'. However, no corresponding term is included in the Agreement of 30 June 1952 between the United Kingdom and Belgium whereby the former acknowledged to be indebted to the latter in the sum of 1,250 million Belgian francs and undertook to discharge the debt by the supply of defence equipment or, in certain events, by payment. Nor is anything said about assignment in the Agreements covering the loans made by the United Kingdom and France to Poland on 7 September 1939,[4] by the United Kingdom to Turkey on 27

---

[1] For references see above pp. 204, sqq.

[2] The Agreements are conveniently collected in Cmd. 8126 which, in effect, supersedes Cmdd. 7550, 7636, and 8053. It is, of course, arguable that these Agreement and promissory notes are not subject to public international law at all. But this problem (on which see the paper referred to in the preceding footnote) is outside the scope of the present observations.

[3] Cmd. 8365, which supersedes Cmd. 7811.

[4] Cmd. 6110.

May 1938,[1] or to Spain on 18 March 1940,[2] or by the United Kingdom and other members of the Commonwealth to Burma on 28 June 1950.[3, 4]

In these circumstances it is apparent that assignments are sometimes expressly permitted, sometimes expressly precluded. Neither of these courses adopted by contracting Governments is of assistance in dealing with treaties which are silent on the question of assignability. According to established principles the existence of particular stipulations in a treaty, e.g. for or against assignments, does not mean that in general, that is, in the absence of such stipulations, the reverse would be true.[5] Nevertheless, the differences in State practice do show, first, that a problem exists which draftsmen have solved sometimes in the one, sometimes in the other sense; secondly, that the assignability of treaty rights is by no means a conception which would be necessarily and *a priori* alien to and inconsistent with international law; and thirdly, that a rule of customary international law must be found so that it may apply where draftsmen fail to make specific provision.

The problem is *primae impressionis*, and its solution would not be facilitated if reference were made to the much-discussed fate of treaties in case of State succession—a question to which Dr. Jenks has recently made a weighty contribution.[6] The succession to treaties, i.e. to contractual arrangements involving both rights and duties, is as different from the assignability of treaty rights as is in private law the succession to contracts from the assignability of debts or choses in action.

The fundamental argument which is likely to be levelled against the assignability of treaty rights is derived from the fact that every treaty is founded upon a background of relationships between the contracting States which is of a political and, consequently, of a personal character, and that, therefore, in the absence of express provisions, the promisor State cannot be expected to allow an assignee, whether it be a State or a

---

[1] Cmd. 6119.      [2] Cmd. 6230.      [3] Cmd. 8007.

[4] The credits granted by the United Kingdom to Yugoslavia in pursuance of the Agreements of 28 December 1950 and 11 January 1951 (Cmd. 8149 and Cmd. 8172) are secured by promissory notes issued by Yugoslavia and made payable to bearer.

[5] See McNair, *The Law of Treaties* (1938), p. 255.

[6] See *B.Y.I.L.* (1952), xxix.105–44.

private person, to intrude upon an obligation which is indicative of peculiar and delicate ties. This line of reasoning, it is true, is so obvious and so forceful that it requires neither illustration nor amplification. Yet it proves too much. Indeed, it is of a rigidity which is typical for a legal system that still finds itself in an early and primitive stage of development. For centuries the same reasoning used to hold the private law of all nations in thrall. Thus, before Justinian, Roman law did not permit the assignment of debts,[1] and the common law was no less slow in developing the assignability of choses in action.[2] Both legal systems were unable to overcome the conceptualist difficulty of the *vinculum juris*, of the strictly personal nature of the obligation which, so it was thought, precluded a change in the identity of the creditor. It was only in modern times that it became possible to devise a flexible solution, based on the interests of the three persons concerned rather than on a preconceived dogma. In broad terms it may be stated that the assignment of debts and other choses in action is nowadays permitted everywhere save, in the words of the Swiss Civil Code,[3] if and in so far as the agreement or the specific character of the obligation demands otherwise. This is a rule which, by and large, is probably common to all modern systems of private law and which may be regarded as a general principle of law.

It is submitted that the formula should yield satisfactory results in public international law, though non-assignability which in private law is the exception will in fact be the rule in public international law. It will in each case be necessary to weigh the circumstances prevailing at the time of the conclusion of the treaty, the interests of both parties, the terms of the treaty itself, the significance of the identity of the assignee, and the effect of an assignment upon the *debitor cessus*—the paramount rule being that his position is not to be prejudiced as a result of the assignment. Since the matter depends, therefore, on factual rather than legal considerations it is not easy to give examples of cases in which the assignment of a treaty right

---

[1] See Buckland, *Roman Law* (2nd ed., 1950), p. 407; Kunkel, *Römisches Privatrecht* (1949), p. 205.

[2] See, for example, Pollock, *Principles of Contract* (13th ed. by Winfield, 1950), p. 570; Holdsworth in 33 *Harvard L.R.* (1919–20), pp. 1018 ff.; S. J. Bailey in 47 *L.Q.R.* (1931), 516, and ibid, 48 (1932), 248, 547.

[3] Article 183.

is clearly permissible. It cannot even be asserted that purely financial claims (such as claims to the repayment of loans) are necessarily assignable or are assignable to anyone. In view of the modern mechanics of international trade and finance and, in particular, the implications of exchange control, it may be, for instance, that the assignment of such a claim to another Government is excluded, but its assignment to a national of the assignor State is unobjectionable. But these are details. They do not affect the principle that rights arising from treaties are capable of being assigned.

Such an assignment occurred, and was not challenged, in the case of *Bank voor Handel en Scheepvaart* v. *Slatford*[1]—a decision which in more than one respect contains some important observations on the effect of treaties in English law, though they are not made readily apparent by the very concise judgment delivered by Devlin J. The plaintiffs, a Dutch Bank, were the owners of gold bars and certain bank balances in England. As a result of a vesting order made by the Board of Trade in July 1940 the gold bars were sold by the Custodian of Enemy Property who, in May 1950, transferred the proceeds to the second defendant, the Administrator of Hungarian Property, on the ground that all the shares in the plaintiff Company were owned by a Hungarian national and that, therefore, the plaintiff Company's own assets were subject to the charge which the Treaty of Peace with Hungary imposed upon the property of Hungarian nationals. The plaintiffs' objection to this transfer rested on two propositions. They said that at the material time, i.e. in September 1947, the proceeds of sale were payable to the State of the Netherlands which in 1950 had assigned them to the plaintiffs, and thus did not constitute Hungarian property. They also said that the assets of a Dutch limited company were not the property of its shareholders. The plaintiffs succeeded on the latter ground, and it was for this reason that the learned Judge did not feel called upon to say much about the former. For the academic lawyer, however, it does remain of some interest.

The plantiffs' argument was derived from the Anglo-Dutch Property Agreement of 2 October 1944, which has never been published but is very similar to the Anglo-Belgian Property

---

[1] [1953] 1 Q.B. 248.

Agreement of 6 October 1944.[1] The Agreement, in short, provided for the release to the Dutch Government of property situate in the United Kingdom which fell within the definition of enemy property in the Trading with the Enemy Act, 1939, but belonged to Dutch nationals. By a document in writing of which notice was given to the Board of Trade the Dutch Government assigned to the plaintiffs its right to the payment of the proceeds of sale, which arose under the Treaty of October 1944. This, it is submitted, was a legitimate assignment and, as mentioned above, its legality was not challenged by the Solicitor-General. It is, of course, another matter that the learned Judge refused to allow the plaintiffs to recover by virtue of the Treaty on the ground that this was held to be not 'justiciable' and incapable of 'legal interpretation'.[2]

It would be contrary to the main submission made in this Note if an attempt were made to classify the types of treaties in which an assignment of rights may or may not be possible. The only test of a general character which may perhaps be suggested and which in some cases may assist in solving the problem of construction and may have been applicable to the case decided by Devlin J. is the following: where a provision in a treaty appears to be made for the benefit of third persons,[3] an assignment of treaty rights to such third persons may be more readily sanctioned than an assignment in cases in which the contracting States do not contemplate a third party as a beneficiary.

[1] Cmd. 6665.      [2] At p. 254.
[3] See Oppenheim, *International Law* (7th ed., by Lauterpacht, 1948), i.829 ff.

# X

## INTERNATIONAL DELINQUENCIES BEFORE MUNICIPAL COURTS*

### I

THE attitude which municipal courts should adopt towards public international law has been considered from two points of view.

Public international lawyers have to determine whether and to what extent municipal law has so accepted the rules of public international law as to make them applicable by municipal courts. This is a matter which does not permit uniform treatment, because largely, if not exclusively, it depends on the constitutional law of each State. It certainly does not fall solely within the purview of public international law. Where public international lawyers have referred to the conflict of laws, they have usually done so merely for the purpose of explaining that this is a branch of municipal law which is distinct from and independent of the law of nations.[1]

Private international lawyers, on the other hand, have discussed the problem whether and to what extent the conflict rules of a particular country are derived from public international law. In fact, for well over a hundred years private international lawyers have been divided into 'nationalists' and 'internationalists'.[2] The former take the view that the conflict rules of each country form part of the national system of law and that each State is free from restrictions in the formulation of those rules; this is a wholly pragmatic approach which is widely followed in practice and to which Lord Parker gave

---

* From 70 *L.Q.R.* (1954), 181.

[1] Although the Permanent Court of International Justice has accepted the principle that conflict rules 'form part of municipal law', it has emphasized that this is not so where conflict rules have been established by international conventions *or customs* and where, therefore, conflict rules 'possess the character of true international law governing the relations between States': *Case of Serbian Loans* (Series A), Nos. 20 and 21, p. 41.

[2] See, e.g., Beale, *Conflict of Laws* (1935) iii.1942 et seq.; Starke, 52 *L.Q.R.* (1936), 395; or Lipstein, 27 *Grot. Soc.* (1942), 142, with numerous references.

classical expression when he said[1]: 'private international law is really a branch of municipal law'. The latter start from Savigny's idea of an 'international common law of nations having intercourse with one another',[2] and use and develop it for the purpose of explaining and postulating the existence of certain aspects of the conflict of laws. The dispute would seem to relate primarily to two problems: First, why is it that we apply foreign law? Is there any duty imposed by public international law to allow a certain set of circumstances to be governed by foreign law rather than the *lex fori*? Secondly, what foreign law ought we to apply where the judge is given liberty in the choice of law? Are such universally applied principles as the control of the *lex loci actus* over matters of form or of the *lex situs* over immovables founded upon public international law?

So formulated, these questions may justly be described as sterile and speculative, and there is force in the statement that their solution cannot be 'scientifically founded upon the reasoning of jurists, but is beaten out on the anvil of experience'.[3] Yet it would be surprising if the endeavours of so many scholars who for years have expended a vast amount of learning upon this doctrinal controversy did not originate from the knowledge, or at least the suspicion, of the existence of an actual and solid connection between the two branches of the law. In fact the discussion acquires a substantial measure of reality if language is employed which is familiar to the public international lawyer, but of which far too many private international lawyers are unaware. Thus, firstly, the internationalists may claim that they were the first to perceive what is now known as the monistic view of the relation between international and municipal law. This, in itself, is a valuable contribution on account of the strong ethical appeal to legal conscience made by a philosophy which asserts the absolute and homogeneous character of right and wrong and which denies and combats the principle that what public international law condemns is yet right in municipal law and that what the municipal laws of the world provide for is yet irrelevant for the purposes of public international law.

---

[1] *Dynamit A. G.* v. *Rio Tinto*, [1918] A. C. 292, 302.

[2] *A Treatise on the Conflict of Laws* (transl. by Guthrie, 1849), p. 70.

[3] Cheshire, *Conflict of Laws* (4th ed., 1952), p. 44; and see the discussion at pp. 35 et seq.

Secondly, it is by no means without interest or significance to ask whether the municipal rules of the conflict of laws are subject to any minimum standards. This is a question which many private international lawyers answer in the affirmative, though they differ on its practical implications in general and on the definition of the individual standards prescribed by public international law.[1] Thus, in France Bartin[2] whose work will not be denied representative and authoritative character speaks of the fact that each State

se considère comme tenu en principe, sous ce point de vue, de certaines obligations internationales: il reconnaît, en principe, que son autonomie, son indépendance, sa maîtrise chez soi, ne vont pas, ne peuvent pas aller jusqu'à la totale et absolue méconnaissance, par ses juridictions, de l'effet des lois étrangères ou de la compétence des juridictions étrangères, bref, jusqu'à la territorialité absolue.

So moderate and cautious a scholar as Martin Wolff has emphasized the guiding rule, based upon the idea of the community of nations, according to which it is incumbent upon each State to make its private international law conform to the 'communal spirit'. He regards grave infractions of that rule as tantamount to the breach of an international duty. He mentions by way of example that no State may prescribe the exclusive application of the *lex fori* or arbitrarily prohibit the application of the law of a foreign country that is *prima facie* applicable or may introduce rules which are inconsistent with such respect for the rights of aliens as international law requires.[3] The list of authors who have made similar suggestions could be continued for long. Enough has been said, it is hoped, to indicate the very practical points involved in what is frequently regarded as mere doctrinal discussion.

However, even within this ambit of research the role of public international law in the sphere of the conflict of laws is usually

---

[1] For a survey see Makarov, *Völkerrecht und Internationales Privatrecht, Mélanges Streit* (1939), p. 535, or Gutzwiller, *Internationalprivatrecht*, pp. 1553 et seq. On the Continent it is today almost generally accepted that the strictly nationalist view of private international law is unfounded. It is believed that the practice of the English Courts in developing rules of the conflict of laws is in fact much influenced by public international law: see below, p. 370, n. 3.

[2] *Principes de Droit International Privé* (1930), i.113.

[3] *Das internationale Privatrecht Deutschlands* (3rd ed., 1954), pp. 7 et seq. This is a most valuable contribution which, unfortunately, is very much shortened in *Private International Law* (2nd ed., 1950), pp. 12 et seq.

confined to determining the character and content of the *lex fori*, i.e., the principles which should or must guide the legislator or judge in developing his own conflict rules. There remains, therefore, the task of defining the attitude which a municipal judge should adopt towards public international law when he applies the foreign law to which he is referred by his own conflict rule. It is at this point that a third aspect of the relationship between public and private international law makes its appearance—a relationship which is neither as remote nor as theoretical as some earlier research, much influenced by the dualistic approach, would suggest. The question is what decision a judge should arrive at when he finds that the foreign law which he is called upon to apply involves an international delinquency[1] bearing upon the issue of the case.[2]

The present article is devoted to the elucidation of this problem which is, or in many connections is liable to become, of considerable practical importance. The inquiry will be concerned, not with the existence or formulation of rules of international law, but with the method of giving effect to rules of international law assumed to be in force when applying foreign law.

## II

While it is easy to think of imaginary cases[3] in which the problem indicated in the preceding section may arise, it is difficult to trace those cases in which courts were actually confronted with it. Many statements which can be found in the books and at first sight seem relevant are so inseverable from their peculiar context as to have no bearing upon the precise

[1] This term is intended to indicate any breach of customary or conventional international law.

[2] The question is put by Miss Morgenstern, 4 *Int. L.Q.* (1951), 326. The author reviews the traditional means whereby municipal courts may exclude foreign law as being contrary to public international law.

[3] Cf. Mann, *The Legal Aspect of Money* (2nd ed., 1953), p. 232, n. 1: 'Does the principle of nominalism as explained in the text apply if, for example, a State depreciates its currency in breach of its obligations under the Articles of Agreement of the International Monetary Fund? It is believed that such a breach should be refused recognition and treated as ineffective.' The problem would also arise if public international law came to recognize such human rights as the right to marry without discrimination on any ground of race, colour, religion and so forth. (See Art. 14 of the European Convention for the Protection of Human Rights and Fundamental Freedoms of 4 November 1950, Cmd. 8969, to which the United Kingdom is a party.)

point under discussion. This arises only if the municipal law of the forum has not developed or accepted for itself an overriding rule of international law, if it provides for the application of foreign law and if the latter involves an international delinquency.

Thus where courts have discarded foreign law because they have acted upon a rule of public international law accepted by and therefore necessarily binding upon them, their conclusions are not directly relevant for present purposes. This situation arises, for instance, whenever the foreign law does not keep within the acknowledged limits of territorial or personal jurisdiction: if, to take an example which has been put,[1] a State were to impose its nationality upon all persons residing outside its territory, but within a distance of 500 miles from its frontiers, no State would recognize such legislation, simply because by international law the foreign State would lack the jurisdiction necessary to the validity of its law. Moreover, no help can be derived from cases which throw light only on the municipal law of the forum itself, and, in particular, upon its reconcilability with international standards of conduct. It is for this reason that, e.g., the question of a municipal court's jurisdiction over seizures effected by its own State in violation of international law (a question to the elucidation of which Miss Morgenstern has recently made a helpful contribution[2]) is not in point.[3] Further,

---

[1] Harvard Law School's *Draft Convention on Nationality* (Special Supplement), *A.J.I.L.* (1929), 26. It will appear later that the conception of international jurisdiction is of considerable value in the present connection.

[2] *B.Y.I.L.* (1952), p. 265. After discussing arrests effected in violation of international law, seizure of vessels in territorial waters and seizures on the high seas in circumstances not authorized by international law, Miss Morgenstern submits 'that municipal courts should decline to exercise jurisdiction over persons or property which have been seized in violation of international law'. This suggestion would be material to the present inquiry if it dealt with the question how an English Court should exercise its jurisdiction over persons or property seized *by a foreign State* in violation of international law. Miss Morgenstern's suggestion cannot provide an *a fortiori* argument, since she does not sufficiently distinguish between cases in which the court is bound by its municipal law (as it was, e.g., in *Molvan* v. *Att.-Gen. for Palestine*, [1948] A. C. 531) and cases in which it is free to apply customary or conventional international law.

[3] It should be remembered, however, that, when they develop their conflict rules, English judges frequently adhere to what they describe as the comity of nations, i.e., public international law: see, e.g., the cases relating to foreign judgments or to jurisdiction of the courts (as to the latter aspect *British South Africa Co.* v. *Companhia de Moçambique*, [1893] A. C. 602, at p. 624, per Lord Herschell; *Tallack* v. *Tallack*, [1927] P. 211 and others).

it would be unprofitable to analyse cases in which the foreign law might have been said to violate rules of public international law, but in which those rules were not even invoked before the court (or were of doubtful authority) and in which, therefore, the decision was founded upon wholly different considerations. Finally, nothing is to be gained from decisions of international tribunals. That in the discharge of their duties they apply international law is elementary, but also immaterial to what municipal courts do or may do.

There are at least four types of cases which illustrate the manner in which municipal courts treat international delinquencies committed by the foreign country the law of which is applicable (*lex causae*). They will be discussed, not with a view to elaborating the solution or to providing a full documentation of each type of case, but merely as examples of the subject of inquiry in general.

(1) The law of nationality includes particularly significant material. It is obvious that the question whether a person possesses the nationality of a certain State can only be answered by the law of that State. Does it follow, then, that that answer will inevitably and universally be accepted? As a matter of international law Article 1 of the Hague Convention on the Conflict of Nationality Laws of 1930[1] imposes a duty of recognition only in so far as the law 'is consistent with international conventions, international custom and the principles of law generally recognized with regard to nationality,'[2] and, consequently, acknowledges the existence of rules of international law which have a restrictive effect upon the content of municipal legislation. Will the English Courts reject foreign legislation on nationality when it infringes those rules?

It may be expected that the answer will be in the affirmative. Where a State imposes its nationality upon persons resident within and therefore subject to its territorial jurisdiction, and dispenses with the necessity for a voluntary application for naturalization, it probably commits an international delin-

---

[1] Hudson, *International Legislation*, v.359.

[2] On these see, among others, Makarov, *Allegemeine Lehren des Staatsangehörigkeitsrechts* (1947), pp. 68 et seq.; Verdross, *Völkerrecht* (1950), pp. 209 et seq.; Briggs, *Law of Nations* (2nd ed.), pp. 209 et seq. with much further material.

quency.[1] Municipal courts ought to treat such naturalization as null and void. For many years the law of Mexico provided that foreigners who owned real property in Mexico or who had children of Mexican nationality, automatically became Mexican nationals, unless they expressed a contrary intention. Diplomatic practice[2] as well as the practice of numerous international tribunals[3] condemned that law as unwarranted by the law of nations. Although municipal courts do not seem to have been called upon to pronounce upon the validity of the Mexican law, they would in all probability reach the same result, notwithstanding the principle of the conflict laws from which they would start. In fact, this occurred in France in connection with a Brazilian law which imposed Brazilian nationality upon all foreigners who were resident in Brazil on 15 November 1889, but failed within six months to notify the authorities of the retention of their national status. The Tribunal de la Seine held[4] that, although it was for Brazilian law to determine who were Brazilian nationals, the law for 1889 contained 'dispositions exorbitantes du droit international' and had to be disregarded.[5]

(2) It is a rule of the law of money that the *lex monetae* determines the rate at which, in the event of a currency alteration, sums expressed in the former currency are converted into the terms of the succeeding currency.[6] On the other hand, international law recognizes the State's monetary sovereignty, but

---

[1] See, e.g., Makarov, op cit., pp. 76, 100. German Federal Tribunal, 29- Dec. 1953, *NJW* (1954), 510, 512. The text does not refer to compulsory naturalization as a result of cession.

[2] Moore, *International Arbitrations*, iii.2468 et seq.

[3] Feller, *Mexican Claims Commissions* (1935), pp. 98, 100.

[4] 13 July 1915, *Revue de Droit International Privé* (1915–16), p. 67. Cf. the decision of the Brussels Court of First Instance, 31 January 1948, A.D. (1948), No. 66.

[5] Another example taken from the law of nationality is provided by legislation by which States have discriminatorily expatriated certain groups of their nationals. It must today be regarded as an open question whether such legislation involves an international wrong to which recognition should be refused. The only judicial decision dealing with the point would seem to be that of the Swiss Federal Tribunal, *BGE* 60, 67; *Annual Digest* (1933–4), Case No 115. For literature see Oppenheim (–Lauterpacht) (7th ed., 1948), 598; Makarov, *Festschrift für Raape* (1948), pp. 258, 259; Lauterpacht, *Jewish Y.B.I.L.* (1949), p. 180; Verdross, op. cit.; Martin Wolff, *Private International Law* (2nd ed., 1950), pp. 129, 130, who speaks of a violation of international law leading to non-recognition.

[6] Mann, *The Legal Aspect of Money* (2nd ed., 1953), p. 230.

limits it by the prohibition of any abuse of right.[1] When Poland introduced the zloty currency in the territories ceded to her by Germany under the Treaty of Versailles, the rate of conversion of mark debts imposed by Poland was universally binding. That rate was 1 zloty = 1 mark and therefore, so it was thought in Germany, took no account of the fact that the zloty currency had seriously depreciated in terms of marks, so that mark creditors suffered heavy prejudice. It became necessary for German courts to decide whether they should give effect to the rate enacted by Poland. In numerous decisions the Berlin Court of Appeal, apparently with the approval of the German Supreme Court,[2] decided that the Polish rate was inconsistent with German public policy on the ground that it was an arbitrary and discriminatory measure. It might have been said (if the facts warranted it, a matter which is not to be investigated here) that the Polish rate was due to an abuse of monetary sovereignty and therefore constituted a legally ineffective international delinquency.

(3) It is a widely accepted rule of the conflict of laws that the title to property is subject to the *lex situs*. It may happen that the *lex situs* is inconsistent with public international law. Will a municipal judge follow and apply the *lex situs* to which he is referred or the law of nations?

The problem has arisen where the transfer of movables results from the illegal requisitioning of private property by a belligerent occupant.[3] Suppose that during the last war the German authorities requisitioned in Holland the picture of a private individual in a manner unauthorized by the Hague Regulations, sold it to a dealer in France and the latter resold it to a Swiss buyer. Suppose, further, that an English Court has to decide whether and on what conditions the Swiss buyer acquired title to the picture. There is strong authority for suggesting that the English Court should disregard any special legislation introduced in Holland or France, treat the picture as stolen and hold title to have passed only to such extent as under the general law

---

[1] ibid., pp. 419 et seq.

[2] ibid., pp. 231, n. 1, 424; see German Supreme Court, 7 December 1921, *RGZ* 103, 259, 262; 5 December 1922, *JW* (1924), 1357 *in fine*.

[3] See, generally, Oppenheim (–Lauterpacht) (7th ed., 1952), ii.410, n. 1; McNair, *Legal Effects of War* (3rd ed.), pp. 336, 337; Morgenstern *B.Y.I.L.* (1951), pp. 305, 316, 317.

of the *lex situs* title to stolen property may be acquired. In this sense the Supreme Courts of Poland[1] and Hungary[2] seem to have proceeded after the First World War, and after the Second World War the Federal Tribunal of Switzerland and a United States District Court have followed suit. The former stated that 'an object seized from its owner in a manner contrary to international law has, without doubt, the character of stolen or lost property within the meaning of Article 934 (1) of the Swiss Civil Code.'[3] In the latter court Goddard J. even stated, albeit *obiter*, that if in the circumstances described above a Dutch, French, or Swiss court would recognize valid title in the Dutch transferee, 'such recognition would not be in accord with the public policy of New York State and the United States, and could hardly be acceptable to this court. Plainly, under the rules governing land warfare of the Hague Convention the confiscation of private property by a belligerent is expressly prohibited.'[4,5] If this represented a correct statement, it would be in line with the rule prevailing in a different, though cognate, branch of the law: *pirata non mutat dominium.*[6]

(4) The same rule of the conflict of laws is the starting point when one comes to consider the effect of a foreign State's confiscatory legislation upon property situate in that State. In principle there cannot today be any doubt that if by virtue of the legislation of the *lex situs* title to local property is transferred such transfer will be recognized everywhere. Will a municipal court sitting in another country afford similar recognition if the legislation is confiscatory and involves a violation of those rules of international law by which the property of aliens is protected?

Notwithstanding the vast amount of decisions and literature dealing with the effects of confiscatory legislation, the specific problem has not attracted the attention of many scholars[7] and

---

[1] 15 June 1921, *Annual Digest* (1919–22), Case No. 342.

[2] ibid., p. 482.

[3] ibid. (1948), Case No. 150.

[4] *State of the Netherlands* v. *Federal Reserve Bank*, 99 F.Supp. 655 (1951); on appeal the question was left open: 201 F. 2d 455 (1953).

[5] The decisions referred to in the text are supported by Seidl-Hohenveldern, *Internationales Konfiskations- und Enteignungsrecht* (1952), pp. 31–33.

[6] Wortley, *B.Y.I.L.* (1947), p. 258, particularly at pp. 267–271.

[7] The controversy relates to the question whether confiscation in violation of international law merely attracts the liability of the confiscating State to pay

has only rarely been considered judicially. It does not, of course, arise in such countries as France where, in the absence of 'une juste et préalable indemnité,' a confiscatory transfer of property is in any event contrary to public policy.[1] Nor are American decisions, in so far as they are directed to the point, of any real value, since to a very large extent, as will be shown below,[2] they rest on the implications of the constitutional organization peculiar to the United States. The problem in its acute form seems to have come up for judicial consideration on two occasions.[3] In 1942 a Dutch creditor of a nationalized Latvian corporation invited the Court of Appeal at Amsterdam to deny effect to the nationalization on the ground that the Latvian Soviet Republic had failed to take over the liabilities of the corporation or to indemnify the owners. Although it is very doubtful whether an international delinquency had occurred at all, the court declined to assume jurisdiction 'even if the measures under consideration should have been taken contrary to Latvian law and to the general principles of international

---

damages or involves the invalidity of the confiscation. In the latter sense Wortley, 33 *Grot. Soc.* (1948), 30; Raape, *Internationales Privatrecht* (3rd ed., 1950), p. 429, in regard to movables only; Niederer, *Der völkerrechtliche Schutz des Privateigentums* in *Festschrift für Hans Lewald* (Basle, 1953), p. 547: Although according to the author it is a principle of public international law that an illegal confiscation only attracts the liability of the confiscating State to pay damages (p. 552), a municipal court may have to treat such confiscation as contrary to *ordre public* and, therefore, as null and void (p. 554). In the former sense Seidl-Hohenveldern, op. cit., p. 36, although this view cannot easily be reconciled with the passage referred to above, p. 374, n. 5; Beitzke, *Festschrift für Raape* (1948), pp. 96, 97; Lewald, *Beiträge zum Deutschen Recht* (1950), p. 418.

[1] Cass. Req., 5 March 1928, Clunet (1928), 674; Cass. Civ., 14 March 1939, Clunet (1939), 615; *Annual Digest* (1938-40), Case No. 54. Italian Law, if one can take it from the decision of the Court of Venice in ' *The Miriella*', *I.C.L.Q.* (1953), 628, would appear to be different. Dealing with the Anglo-Iranian Oil Company's claim to oil which had been confiscated in Persia, sold in Persia to the defendants and carried by them to Italy, the Court primarily relied on the fact that Italian public policy was not violated by the mere 'acceptance of effects' accomplished in Persia; on this point see below, Section III (1). In the alternative the Court held that the Persian law did 'not rule out compensation' and that 'any question relating to the amount of compensation and the time of its payment remains outside the ambit of public policy' (p. 631). In Italy, apparently, compensation need not be 'juste et préalable.'

[2] p. 384

[3] No German decision entitled to anything in the nature of persuasive authority seems to have considered the point. Decisions rendered by German county courts should be ignored.

law.'[1] The opposite result was reached by a British court when the Anglo-Iranian Oil Company claimed title to oil which after nationalization the defendants had purchased in Persia from the Persian Government. The plaintiffs contended that the Persian Government's title to the oil should not be recognized, because, first, its acquisition was contrary to public policy, and because, secondly, it was contrary to international law. Campbell J. of the Supreme Court of Aden found[2] that there existed a clear rule of international law which made the Persian confiscation illegal. He did not state whether he accepted the first or the second or both of the plaintiffs' contentions to take account of that illegality, but concluded simply 'that, following international law as incorporated in the domestic law of Aden, this court must refuse validity to the Persian Oil Nationalization law in so far as it relates to nationalized property of the plaintiff which may come within its jurisdiction. I find the oil in dispute to be still the property of the plaintiffs.'[3]

The catalogue of illustrations could probably be considerably extended.[4] However, what has been said is, it is hoped, sufficient to define the problem, to emphasize the generality of its character, to indicate its treatment in judicial practice and to depict the background against which its solution must be attempted.

## III

The preceding survey shows that, although municipal courts usually seem to have succeeded in denying legal effect to international delinquencies committed by a foreign country, they have not yet evolved a consistent and comprehensive principle guiding them to their decisions. Is there any such principle?

(1) Public policy (*ordre public international*) has frequently been resorted to, but is not a wholly satisfactory rule of decision.

The definitions of public policy which are current in England are, it is true, by no means inapt to comprise the case of international delinquencies committed abroad. Thus, an English

---

[1] 3 December 1942, *Annual Digest* (1919–42), Case No. 75. The observation quoted in the text was only an *obiter dictum*, as the decision rested on the point mentioned below, p. 385, n. 1 where other Dutch decisions are referred to.

[2] *The Rose Mary*, [1953] 1 W. L. R. 246.    [3] p. 259.

[4] The law relating to the recognition of foreign judgments may be mentioned as a further case in point. It was considered on previous occasions, particularly by Miss Morgenstern, above, p. 369, n. 2.

court must disregard the sale of a British ship effected abroad under a foreign judgment *in rem* which ignores the rights of English mortgagees and, therefore, is 'contrary to law and to what is required by the comity of nations.'[1] Consequently, it is by no means revolutionary to expect that an English judge, called upon to pronounce upon international delinquencies *stricto sensu*, would have no difficulty in overcoming his well-known reluctance to invoke public policy or in discarding the wide and for international purposes inappropriate statement which, in the atmosphere of the year 1902, Lord Halsbury felt entitled to make and according to which no court 'can invent a new head of public policy.'[2] Nor should it strain ingenuity to reduce to its true proportions the 'obvious exaggeration'[3] contained in Scrutton L.J.'s dictum[4] that it would be 'a serious breach of international comity' and possibly a *casus belli* if foreign legislation were held to be contrary to essential principles of justice and morality. In France, too, it has been suggested by so judicious an author as Lerebours-Pigeonnière[5] that

l'exception d'ordre public réagit contre l'application de lois étrangères qui méconnaîtraient les principes de droit public ou privé commun aux nations civilisées, expression de la morale et de la justice objective (d'autres diront qu'elles sont une necessité de l'ordre civilisé) que certains auteurs qualifient de principes internationaux. En bref nous visons les lois étrangères contraires à la morale et au droit naturel.

Nevertheless, public policy is an inadequate guide on account of the relativity of the conception. It is relative from the point of view of both space and time, so that French scholars have rightly spoken of the *mobilité et actualité de l'ordre public*.[6]

Thus what is against public policy in one country is not necessarily against public policy in another. No court, when it has to apply the law of a foreign country, gives effect to that country's public policy. In other words, public policy only comes into play if the vital interests of the State of the forum are concerned.

[1] *Simpson* v. *Fogo* (1863), 1 H. & M. 195, 248, per Sir W. Page Wood (as he then was).

[2] *Janson* v. *Driefontein Consolidated Mines*, [1902] A. C. 484, 491.

[3] Martin Wolff, *Private International Law* (2nd ed., 1950), p. 177, n. 1.

[4] *Luther* v. *Sagor & Co.*, [1921] 3 K. B. 532, 558, 559.

[5] *Précis de Droit International Privé* (1948), p. 344. The learned author was a member of the Cour de Cassation.

[6] ibid., p. 345; Niboyet, *Traité de Droit International Privé* (1944), iii.534, and others.

It follows that English Courts would not be assisted by the conception of public policy if they had to pronounce upon the effects of an international delinquency committed by Ruritania against Utopia. Moreover, public policy depends upon the interests and requirements of the State of the forum as they exist from time to time. Thus it was possible for Dicey to suggest in 1922 that the status of adoption, being unknown to English law, would not be recognized here, but since the Adoption of Children Act, 1926, such a view is untenable.[1] As the French Cour de Cassation has put it in terms which, though they strike an English lawyer as exaggerated, emphasize the point very clearly, public policy depends 'dans une large mesure de l'opinion qui prévaut à chaque moment en France.'[2]

It can be concluded, therefore, that public policy, while it is a sufficient weapon in many cases, lacks such comprehensiveness and precision as is required in the present context, for not every international delinquency involves a violation of public policy (nor, of course, does every violation of public policy involve an international delinquency).

(2) In these circumstances it is submitted that the true principle of decision is public international law itself: when dealing with international delinquencies committed by a foreign State a municipal court ought to be bound by international law in the sense that this overrides the foreign law which, though applicable to a given set of facts, is objectionable. In other words, foreign law, *prima facie* applicable to a case, should be refused effect by a municipal court if and to such extent as public international law so requires. Or, if an international tribunal would apply 'the essential principle contained in the actual notion of an illegal act—a principle which seems to be established by international practice and in particular by the decisions of arbitral tribunals—that reparation must, as far as possible, wipe out all the consequences of the illegal act and re-establish the situation which would, in all probability, have existed if that act had not been committed',[3] then a municipal tribunal should similarly 'wipe out' the international delinquency by disregarding it.

---

[1] Dicey, *Conflict of Laws* (6th ed., 1949), p. 512.

[2] Cass. Civ., 22 March 1944, S. (1945), 1.77 with report by Lerebours-Pigeonnière and note by Niboyet.

[3] Permanent Court of International Justice in *Case of Chorzow Factory* (Series A), No. 17, p. 47.

A view similar to, though not quite identical with these submissions was expressed as early as 1897 by Zitelmann, who probably was the first to see the problem and whose observations merit extensive quotation[1]:

> Finally, there exists, I believe, a third point which, exceptionally, *justifies* the refusal to apply foreign law that is prima facie applicable: it is that the foreign law does not conform to the requirements of public international law. The principal instance would arise where the foreign law prejudices aliens, in relation to citizens, in a manner inconsistent with the requirements of public international law; and a similar case would arise if, in relation to those adhering to a different faith, Christians should be discriminated against, assuming this is possible at all in a State subscribing to the rule of law. Such foreign provisions must be inapplicable, not because they are immoral (whether or no the application of the foreign law leads to a result which in our eyes is immoral is immaterial), nor because they are unjust, although discrimination always involves injustice, but exclusively because that injustice is tantamount to an international delinquency. And in this case the non-application must go much farther than in cases of immorality; the correct formulation would be: we treat the provision of the foreign law as altogether non-existent or treat it as so amended that aliens and citizens, Christians *inter se* as well as in relation to non-Christians enjoy the same rights. How far aliens in relation to citizens or Christians in relation to the adherents of another religion must be discriminated against to create a breach of international duties is not to be investigated here; the conclusion, however, that we *need* not apply the foreign law as soon as we recognize the existence of such a breach, is likely to be justified by itself. . . . In other directions the foreign law may be inconsistent with the requirements of international law. In particular it is conceivable that it has failed to make its municipal law conform to what it ought to be under the terms of a treaty. . . . In such a case one cannot expect the other High Contracting Party to apply the foreign law as it is: it should be entitled to treat the rule required by international law as part of the foreign legal system, although this is not so in fact, and to apply it therefore as foreign law in the place of the existing.

A principle on these lines has much to commend it. In the first place it is consonant with the dignity, moral force and inherent vitality of public international law to enforce it as such, by means of direct application rather than in an oblique fashion by using public policy as a back door. If 'we admit unreservedly

---

[1] *Internationales Privatrecht* (1897), i.378–80 (italics supplied). Zitelmann's view has generally been rejected in Germany, not on account of its unsoundness but because it was considered unnecessary in view of the wide scope of public policy in Germany (Art. 30 of the Introductory Law to the Civil Code). Against Zitelmann's thesis also recently Vallindas, *Zeitschrift für ausländisches und internationales Privatrecht* (1953), pp. 1 et seq., at p. 7.

the supremacy of international law', [1] it would not be fitting if it had to be harnessed to the unruly horse of public policy. Secondly, the relative objectivity and uniformity of its standards, as compared with the varying notions of public policy, makes public international law a more attractive guide to judicial decision. To invoke public policy means a condemnation on grounds which are liable to create the impression of special pleading and which thus conceal, behind the interests involved in the case, the peculiarly legal quality of the issue. Thirdly, the judicial application of international law is, and ought to be, a matter of duty, not, as Zitelmann suggested, of mere right. In other words the requirements of public international law are absolute and leave no room for the relativity of public policy. Foreign measures which do not affect the forum are not contrary to its public policy. Yet a judge who, in a case involving an international delinquency committed by State A against State B, applies the law of the former, may assist in the consummation of that delinquency and thus engage his own Sovereign's international responsibility. The often expressed apprehension [2] that a judicial decision might produce that consequence is most effectively allayed by scrupulous compliance with the requirements of international law. The opposite view according to which a municipal court may have to sanction what international law condemns can hardly be said to be attractive. [3]

If, then, the rejection of foreign law involving an international delinquency may be regarded as producing a satisfactory result, it remains to show that it rests on a legally sound foundation. The dogmatic justification lies in the fact that in so far as a State violates international law it lacks jurisdiction in the international sense and, consequently, acts *ultra vires*. We know that inter-

---

[1] Sir Arnold McNair, 30 *Grot. Soc.* (1945) 12.

[2] It underlies Scrutton L.J.'s dictum referred to above, p. 377, n. 4, and the alleged maxim that in international relations a Sovereign cannot speak with two voices (*Taylor* v. *Barclay*, 2 Sim. 213, 221, per Shadwell J.; *The Arantzazu Mendi*, [1939] A. C. 256, 264, per Lord Atkin; Sir Arnold McNair, *B.Y.I.L.* (1921–2), p. 65 and others).

[3] See now Halsbury (Simonds), *Laws of England* (3rd ed., 1954), vii.8, 9, where the distinguished author states that English law will withhold recognition or enforcement of foreign law when it is 'not conformable to the usage of nations'.

nationally the jurisdiction of a State is limited in a territorial as well as a personal sense: a State cannot, e.g., legislate in regard to property outside its boundaries or in regard to non-resident aliens. Similarly, its international jurisdiction is subject to substantive or intrinsic limits. In the words of the Permanent Court of International Justice, a State cannot rely on its own legislation 'with a view to evading obligations incumbent upon it under international law or treaties in force'[1] or 'to limit the scope of [its] international obligations'.[2] These limitations are cognizable by municipal courts not less than limitations of territorial or personal jurisdiction. Once one sees the problem under discussion as one of international jurisdiction, the key to its dénouement is available. That it is one of international juris-diction must to some extent be a submission or an *ipse dixit*[3] incapable of conclusive proof, though the history of legal thought,[4] jurisprudential teachings on the relationship between the right and the power to do an act and analogies from private law may not be without value. That international law in general, that its very existence as a system of law implies restric-tions of a State's jurisdiction (or sovereignty) can no longer be open to controversy.

## IV

It remains to deal with the criticism which may be levelled against the suggestions made in the preceding section.

No objection can be based upon what is no more than an obsolete theory of international law, viz., on the doctrine that international law is binding and operative only between States or, being a separate system of law, has no direct effect in munici-pal law.[5] The realities of legal development, too manifold and

---

[1] Permanent Court of International Justice, *Case of Polish Nationals in Danzig*, (Series A/B), No. 44, p. 24.

[2] Permanent Court of International Justice, *Case of Free Zones of Upper Savoy*, (Series A/B), No. 46, p. 167.

[3] It is not intended to suggest that others have not already expressed similar views.

[4] cf. the history of the principle 'lex est supra principem' which at least since Bracton's time has taken the place of the Hellenistic and post-classical principle 'princeps legibus solutus est'; see Schulz, 60 *English Historical Review* (1945), 136.

[5] The doctrine referred to in the text is responsible for the view that discriminatory expatriation of nationals does not justify non-recognition (see above, p. 372, n. 5) or that confiscation in violation of international law only justifies a claim for dam-ages (above, p. 374, n. 7). See the Court of Appeal at Kiel 26 March 1947,

too impressive to require restatement at the present time, make such a doctrine untenable. It cannot in any event find room in such countries as Germany,[1] Japan,[2] or Italy[3] where the supremacy of international law is embedded in the Constitution.

Nor can any counter-argument be derived from the fact that by the constitutional law of the majority of countries international law has no such direct effect as is suggested here. The constitutional law of the forum is not in issue: even if the State of the forum does not allow its courts to apply international law in derogation of existing municipal law, this does not imply the necessity for an analogous approach to the law of a foreign country. As regards the constitutional law of the latter, it would be a *petitio principii* if weight were attached to its refusal to allow international law to prevail: the question whether such refusal can be recognized is not answered by pointing to the existence of the refusal. To put the same point differently, the true construction of the conflict rule by which the judge is referred to the foreign law is that it prescribes the application of such foreign law as is internationally lawful.

Nor can it be said that the forum ought not to apply another standard to foreign law than it maintains in its own affairs. It may well be that, to a greater or lesser extent, the State of the forum does not give effect to public international law in the absence of express municipal legislation. In some respects this is unfortunately so in England where it was said, for instance, that, although 'according to the well-understood rules of international law a change of sovereignty by cession ought not to affect private property, . . . no municipal tribunal has authority to enforce such an obligation'.[4] However, nothing would permit or compel a judge to emphasize what in itself may be an international delinquency by extending it to a sphere to which it is not meant to apply, viz., the realm of foreign law. The fact that judges have found themselves in the unenviable position in which they had to apply their municipal law knowing it to be

---

*Süddeutsche Juristenzeitung* (1947), 323; *Annual Digest* (1948), Case No. 125, at p. 420 'According to international law international delinquencies give rise only to a duty on the part of States to pay compensation.'

[1] Art. 25 of the Constitution of 1949.
[2] Art. 98 of the Constitution of 1946.
[3] Art. 10 of the Constitution of 1947.
[4] *Cook* v. *Sprigg*, [1899] A. C. 572, 578.

contrary to international law[1] is a matter of regret, not a source of authority for similar indifference to the requirements of international law, when the constitutional law of the forum does not operate as a shackle.

Nor can reliance be properly placed on the fact that in many directions international law continues to be in a state of development and, accordingly, has failed to establish definite rules of law. This is an objection which is made, not against the suggested principle, but against the scope of its application. It is answered, therefore, when it is emphasized that a judge will not attribute the character of an international delinquency to a foreign law unless there has been a clear breach of a clear international duty, whether it may arise from customary or from conventional international law. But where this is the case, the judge, it is submitted, is equally clearly bound not to perpetuate that delinquency, but to 'wipe out' its consequences.

Finally, a municipal court's power of denying effect to a foreign country's breach of international duties is not impaired by the fact that an international delinquency cannot occur except as the result of an act of State, whether it be committed by the foreign State itself or whether it be authorized by it so as to attract its vicarious responsibility. A foreign act of State has been said to be protected by a measure of sacrosanctity in the sense that 'the courts of one country will not sit in judgment on the acts of the Government of another done within its territory'[2] and that any remedy must be asserted through local courts or through diplomatic channels.[3] If this principle exists and applies to the problem under discussion, then the submission made in this paper would be untenable and a municipal court could not even treat a foreign act of State as contrary to public policy.

It has been suggested[4] that the maxim of the sacrosanctity of the foreign act of State is far too widely formulated and that its true ambit is as follows: provided that according to the conflict

---

[1] See, e.g., *Administrator of German Property* v. *Knoop*, [1933] Ch. 439 or *Republic of Italy* v. *Hambros Bank*, [1950] Ch. 314, discussed 14 Mod. L.R. (1951), 64. In these cases the courts had to apply English municipal law, although it was inconsistent with the United Kingdom's treaty obligations.

[2] *Underhill* v. *Hernandez* 168 U. S. 250, (1897) the *fons et origo* of the maxim. The words 'within its territory' are responsible for the fact that the maxim has never been applied to confiscation of property outside the confiscating State or in such cases as *Central Air Transport Corporation* v. *Civil Air Transport Inc.*, [1953] A. C. 70.

[3] Below, p. 387, n. 2.     [4] Below, p. 420.

rule of the forum the foreign act of State is recognizable or relevant at all, its validity may be inquired into to the extent defined by the law of the country from which it emanates or, as Niboyet has explained,[1] according to the rule *auctor regit actum*, and in so far as public policy requires it may even be disregarded. Since then nothing has occurred that would necessitate a revision of this thesis. On the one hand it may now be claimed that there exists powerful support for the view that an English Court is not as a matter of principle precluded from investigating the constitutional validity of foreign legislation, for the Court of Appeal held in terms that it could treat a foreign statute as unconstitutional and void[2]—a conclusion which is supported by a growing number of writers.[3] On the other hand American Courts have persisted in applying, or at least referring with approval to, the maxim. But even if it had the full effect which its formulation implies[4] it could not be brought to bear upon an international delinquency. This could be done only if either the maxim were

---

[1] *Traité de Droit International Privé Français* (1949) vi.1 et seq.

[2] *A/S Tallina Laevauhisus* v. *Tallina Shipping Co.*, [1947] 80 Ll. Rep. 99, at p. 114, per Tucker L.J. (as he then was) with whom Scott L.J. expressly agreed. The observations of Rowlatt J. in *King of the Hellenes* v. *Brostram*, [1923] 16 Ll. Rep. 190 cannot be regarded as a considered statement of the law. The text is, of course, concerned only with the court's powers of investigation. That an English court will, and ought to be, reluctant to exercise it and will not readily be prepared to hold foreign legislation unconstitutional are other matters which may safely be left to judicial discretion.

[3] Martin Wolff, *Private International Law* (2nd ed., 1950), pp. 174, 214. Lipstein, 35 *Grot. Soc.* (1950), 178–80, and Niboyet's views are now set forth in *Traité de Droit International Privé Français* (1944), iii.404 et seq. A different view is taken by Dr. Morris, 68 *L.Q.R.* (1952), 127. Cf. *Seidl-Hohenveldern*, op. cit., p. 44.

[4] It is very difficult to obtain a clear picture of American practice in all its aspects. It may be that the courts of New York differ in some respects from the practice of the Federal Courts. Thus it was held in *Vladikavkazsky Ry.* v. *New York Trust Co.*, 263 N. Y. 369 (1934); *Annual Digest* (1933–4), Case No. 27, after the recognition of Soviet Russia, that the arbitrary dissolution of corporations and the confiscation of their assets was 'contrary to our public policy and shocking to our sense of justice and equity'. In the recent case of *Sulyok* v. *Penzintezeti Kozpont Budapest*, 279 App. Div. 528 (1952), affirmed without opinion 304 N. Y. 704 (1952) the plaintiff claimed in New York payment of a pension which was payable in Hungary under a Hungarian contract, but which was extinguished by a Hungarian decree of 1948 depriving an employee of his pension rights if he left Hungary and remained abroad for more than three months. The Court held that the decree was 'invalid and ineffective as contrary to our public policy' and relied on *Plesch* v. *Banque Nationale de la République d'Haïti*, 273 App. Div. 224 (1948), affirmed 298 N. Y. 573 (1948); *Annual Digest* (1948), Case No. 7. On identical facts the Court of Appeal at Zurich reached the same result: *Schweizerische Juristenzeitung* (1953), 281. On these cases see Sommerich, *A.J.C.L.* 1954, 87.

itself a rule of international rather than municipal law or if, being a rule of municipal law, it would at least serve rather than pervert the true purpose of international law. Neither condition exists.

The alleged sacrosanctity of the foreign act of State finds no support in the judicial practice of any country outside the Anglo-American sphere of legal influence and Holland.[1] No international tribunal has ever adopted it. There is no evidence of any diplomatic protest against a judicial decision which has failed to adhere to it. Textbooks of acknowledged authority have not given greater support to it than can be inferred from a reference to the practice of Anglo-American and Dutch Courts and in England a note of serious doubt was sounded by Professor Lauterpacht.[2] It is, indeed, unlikely that international law should demand or at least sanction that practice, for it is difficult to see what internationally recognized right would be infringed by a court inquiring into the validity of a foreign act of State.[3]

If, then, the sacrosanctity of the foreign act of State is treated as a rule of the municipal law of the United States, Britain, and Holland, it cannot be so extended as to lead to the legalization of an international wrong. Such a consequence would be opposed to the very 'comity of nations' which was invoked to

---

[1] See District Court of Middelburg, 2 August 1938, *Annual Digest* (1919-42), Case No. 7; Court of Appeal of The Hague, 4 December 1939, ibid., p. 18; District Court of Rotterdam, 31 July 1939, ibid., p. 19, all dealing with the confiscation of Mexican oil; Court of Appeal of Amsterdam, above, p. 376, n. 1, dealing with the nationalization of a Latvian corporation. In the last-mentioned decision it is described as a principle of international law that 'the courts of a sovereign State have no jurisdiction to enter into an examination of the legality of governmental acts of measures taken by another State jure imperii'.

[2] Oppenheim (7th ed.) i.242.

[3] Sometimes reference has been made to the independence or the dignity of a foreign State which, in the absence of the maxim, would allegedly be threatened. On this reasoning see, in a different context, Lauterpacht, *B.Y.I.L.* (1951), 229-31. Even if one does not agree with the learned author's views on the question of immunity, he is, particularly in the present context, entitled to full support when he rejects 'these strained emanations of the notion of dignity . . . as a rational basis' for legal principles and submits that 'a State does not derogate from the dignity of another State by subjecting it to the normal operation of the law under proper municipal and international safeguards', and that 'the time has probably come for abandoning what is now no more than an incantation alien to the conception of the rule of law, national and international, and to the true position of the State in modern society'. It is to be hoped that these words will contribute to the removal of much false sentiment that continues to take the place of clear legal reasoning.

justify the maxim. On the contrary, as has already been suggested, if a State commits an international wrong and the court of another State, the forum, refuses recognition to that wrong, the latter does what international law expects it to do and what it must do in order not to become an accessory to the delinquency.

Accordingly, it is not surprising to find that, whatever the true ambit of the dogma may be and howsoever it has been formulated, it has not even in the United States been consciously employed for the purpose of granting immunity to an international delinquency committed by a foreign State. Three American cases seem to be relevant in this connection.[1] However, on analysis they appear to be distinguishable, for they did not relate to an international delinquency at all or they rested on the peculiar conception of the relationship between Judiciary and Executive which characterizes American practice in these matters and which the foreign observer finds so difficult to appreciate, unless and until he recalls the constitutional background typical to the United States.

In *Oetjen* v. *Central Leather Co.*[2] the Supreme Court was concerned with title to a quantity of hides which had belonged to a Mexican subject and had been seized and sold in Mexico by Mexican insurgent forces which subsequently became the recognized Government of Mexico. In *Ricaud* v. *American Metal Co.*[3] the facts were almost the same except that the goods seized in Mexico had at all times belonged to United States nationals. In the former case two references to international law were made. The plaintiff had apparently invoked the Hague Regulations, but they were held to be immaterial because they did not apply to civil war, because the rule that private property could not be confiscated did not, in the view of the Court, 'have the scope claimed for it' and because according to the Convention itself cases not provided for in the Regulations were governed by the principles of the law of nations which, obviously, the Court did not find to be affected. In a later passage the Court refused to consider 'the validity of the levy of the contribution made by the Mexican commanding

---

[1] No English case accepting the principle of the sancrosanctity of the foreign act of State (such as *Luther* v. *Sagor*, [1921] 3 K. B. 532) can be said to have involved anything in the nature of an international delinquency.

[2] 246 U. S. 297 (1917).     [3] 246 U. S. 304 (1917).

general, under [unspecified] rules of international law applicable to the situation, since the subject is not open to re-examination by this or any other American Court'.[1] The meaning of this observation is made clearer by the only sentence in *Ricaud's* case in which the Court rejected the relevance of the plaintiff's American nationality: 'Whatever rights such an American citizen may have, can be asserted only through the courts of Mexico or through the political departments of our Government.'[2] It will be seen, therefore, that no international delinquency had occurred in either of these cases,[3] that in *Oetjen's* case the Court expressly so held and that in both cases any violation of international law was treated as what American lawyers call a 'political question', i.e., one falling within the exclusive jurisdiction of the executive branch of the Government.[4]

The impact of the last-mentioned aspect upon the problem is most impressively shown by a third case, the remarkable decision of the United States Court of Appeals, Second Circuit, in *Bernstein* v. *Van Heyghen*[5] (Learned Hand and Swan JJ., Clark J. dissenting), by which a statement of claim alleging substantially the following facts was struck out as failing to disclose a cause of action: in the early part of 1938 a German Jew, while in the custody of Nazi officials acting on behalf of the German Government and while under the threat of indefinite imprisonment, bodily harm, and even death, executed documents transferring title to one of his ships to a nominee of the Nazi Government. The transaction was invalid under German

---

[1] ibid., p. 304.    [2] ibid., p. 310

[3] The reasons are given by Oppenheim (7th ed. by Lauterpacht, 1948), i.332.

[4] An English Court will not decline the application of legal principles in deference to the attitude of the Executive: *Bank voor Handel en Scheepvaart* v. *Slatford*, [1953] 1 Q.B. 248, at p. 266, per Devlin J. The 'political question' as understood in the United States urgently requires re-examination by an American lawyer. A foreign observer cannot help feeling that judicial control is continuously being reduced to an extent which must cause anxiety. Outside the United States the problem seems to have been largely ignored. See, however, Mann, below, p. 391; *Süddeutsche Juristenzeitung* (1950), 545; François Payot, *Les instructions du Gouvernement lors de l'interprétation judiciare du droit international* (Lausanne, 1950), and on the specific aspect of certification, Lyons, *B.Y.I.L.* (1946), p. 240 (United Kingdom); ibid. (1947), p. 116 (United States of America); ibid. (1948), p. 180 (Continent and Latin-America).

[5] 163 F. 2d 246 (1947), cert. den. 332 U.S. 772; also in *Annual Digest* (1947), Case No. 5. For critical comment see 27 *Col. L.R.* (1947), 1061; 57 *Yale L.J.* (1947-8), 1008; 60 *Harv. L.R.* (1947), 1351; House, 37 *Cal. L.R.* (1949), 38.

law then in force and odious to the standards of justice accepted by the civilized world. In 1939[1] the defendants, in full knowledge of these facts, purchased the ship from the Nazi Government's nominee. The ship having become a total loss in 1942, the plaintiff claimed payment of the insurance money. The Court started from the rule that it could not sit in judgment on the acts of the government of another State done within its territory. Thus the alleged invalidity under German law became immaterial. The Court then proceeded to ask itself whether the Government of the United States had already so acted as to relieve its courts of the restraint upon the exercise of their jurisdiction which was imposed upon them under the Constitution in general and under the particular rule that the courts 'should not so act as to embarrass the executive arm in its conduct of foreign affairs'.[2] That question was answered in the negative.[3] Consequently the action failed. The *ratio decidendi* was that the Court assumed (wrongly, as it turned out)[4] that the Government had not lifted its ban on the exercise of the Court's jurisdiction. The implications of the international delinquency

[1] It may be that to some extent the Court was influenced by the thought that it had to decide the case as if it were sitting in 1939. However, the language of the court is such as to make this explanation far-fetched.

[2] For other instances of this rule see *United States* v. *Pink*, 315 U. S. 202, 232 (1942) (recognition); *Republic of Mexico* v. *Hoffmann*, 324 U. S. 30, 35 (1945) (immunity).

[3] The result is open to grave doubts. First, the Court applied the maxim (derived from the respect for the independence of foreign sovereign States) to the acts of a State which at the time of the decision had unquestionably ceased to be a sovereign one, which had no foreign relations of its own, the leaders of which had been executed for crimes against humanity (including the type of crime in issue) and international law and which was occupied and administered by the Allies, including the United States. Consequently a review of the acts of its (former) officials could not possibly, in the words of *Oetjen's* case (at p. 304), 'imperil the amicable relations between Governments and vex the peace of nations.' Secondly, notwithstanding the judgment of the International Military Tribunal at Nuremberg, the pronouncements of the United States Government on the Nazi régime in general and the restitution of the property of dispossessed Jews in particular, the court took it upon itself to ascertain whether there was 'positive evidence' of a policy *permitting* the exercise of jurisdiction. It held that the absence of such evidence was tantamount to a restraint on jurisdiction. One would have expected that the opposite was true and the absence of evidence restraining the exercise of jurisdiction implied liberty to assume it.

[4] Letter from the Department of State in *Bulletin of the Department of State* (1949), 592: 'This Government has consistently opposed the forcible acts of dispossession of a discriminatory and confiscatory nature practised by the Germans on the countries or peoples subject to their controls. . . . The policy of the Executive, with respect to claims asserted in the United States for the restitution of identifiable property (or

which, it may be suggested, was at the root of the case and which the Court was prepared to 'accept arguendo' did not fall to be considered. It may be expected that if the Court had felt able to give a different answer to the 'political question' the allegation that rights cannot be founded upon an international wrong would not have been held demurrable.

It follows that there does not seem to be any decision even in the United States which allows the alleged rule of the sacrosanctity of the foreign act of State to override an international delinquency and which would be opposed to the submissions made in this article.

## V

They lead to conclusions which cover a narrow field and may appear to be disproportionate to the somewhat elaborate discussion on which they rest. Yet they may be put forward as a further contribution to a broad and still fertile subject of inquiry, viz., the interconnection between public and private international law and the definition of the influence which international law asserts within the sphere of municipal law and before municipal courts. These conclusions may be summarized as follows:

(1) When the conflict rule of the forum refers the court to a foreign law (*lex causae*), the court will not apply the latter if and in so far as it expresses or results from an international delinquency.

(2) Such refusal is independent of the views or interests of the State of the forum, but will be determined solely by the rules of international law.

(3) It follows that if the foreign *lex causae* is inconsistent with a rule of customary international law or with treaty obligations operating in relation to a third State, the forum, though it is not directly affected, may in an appropriate case disregard the *lex causae*.

(4) Since it is international law itself which in the event of an

compensation in lieu thereof) lost through force, coercion or duress as a result of Nazi persecution in Germany, is to relieve American courts from any restraint upon the exercise of their jurisdiction to pass upon the validity of the acts of Nazi officials.'

international delinquency supersedes the *lex causae*, the refusal to recognize or give effect to an international delinquency arises as a matter not of right but of duty.

(5) The question whether an international delinquency has been committed is to be answered according to the generally accepted principles of international law, but a municipal court will not answer it affirmatively except where both the law and the facts are clearly established.

(6) The decision will not be influenced by the attitude which either the forum or the *lex causae* adopts towards conflicts between their respective municipal legal systems and international law, or by the fact that a foreign act of state is involved.

(7) The refusal to give effect to an international wrong should be viewed as a consequence of the fact that no court is permitted or compelled to recognize any other limits of a foreign State's territorial, personal or substantive jurisdiction than international law defines.

(8) The resulting extension of the sphere within which international law asserts itself before municipal courts should be welcomed.

# XI

# JUDICIARY AND EXECUTIVE IN FOREIGN AFFAIRS*

AFTER more than three hundred years the relationship between the Law and the Executive is still a theme which, as recent events confirm,[1] continues to be of the greatest practical importance and theoretical interest and which in the future may well lead to vital issues. Yet there exists a particular aspect of that wide topic which in this country, as opposed to the United States of America,[2] has been somewhat neglected by those interested in first principles, viz. the relationship between the Law and the Executive in foreign affairs. In many respects that relationship has developed in a rather haphazard way, in a spirit of subconsciousness and inarticulateness. It is, however, of deep and increasing significance and the following observations are designed to suggest to more competent experts the necessity for further investigation and for a solution based on principle rather than casuistry.

Two basic propositions may serve as starting-points. It is an established rule of constitutional law that it is the King's prerogative to act as the representative of the nation in the conduct of foreign affairs.[3] This does not mean that the King also determines what the nation's foreign policy should be; on the

---

* From *Grot. Soc.* (1945), 143.

[1] See, e.g., *Liversidge* v. *Anderson*, [1942] A. C. 206, and *Duncan* v. *Cammell Laird and Co. Ltd.*, [1942] A. C. 624, and the lively discussion provoked by these decisions: Sir William Holdsworth, 58 *L.Q.R.* (1942),1; Allen, ibidem, pp. 232, 462; Goodhart, ibidem, pp. 243, 436; Keeton, 5 *Mod. L.R.*,(1942) 162; Note, 56 *Harv. L.R.* (1943), 806.

[2] The most important publication seems to be Jaffe, *Judicial Aspects of Foreign Relations* (1933)—an interesting book in which there will be found a complete list of previous American literature. In this connection it will therefore be sufficient to refer to P. Quincy Wright, *The Control of American Foreign Relations* (1922); Finkelstein, 'Judicial Self-limitation', 37 *Harv. L.R.* (1924), 338; Weston, 'Political Questions', 38 *Harv. L.R.* (1925), 296; and the most recent study by C. G. Post, *The Supreme Court and Political Questions* (1936).

[3] See, e.g., Blackstone (8th edition), i.252 seq.; Halsbury (–Hailsham), vi.503; Ridges' *Constitutional Law of England* (6th ed.), p. 299; Wade and Phillips, *Constitutional Law* (2nd ed.), p. 226.

contrary, the exercise of the prerogative is dependent on the advice of responsible Ministers, and hence in effect subject to parliamentary control. Yet it is the Crown, and the Crown only, which in law is capable of performing such acts as are indicative of this country's attitude in foreign affairs, and although even the highest judicial authorities are wont to speak of H.M. Government as performing acts of foreign policy,[1] such loose references, justifiably deprecated by Slesser L.J.,[2] cannot displace the true constitutional position.

On the other hand, it is an equally firmly rooted ingredient of the English legal system that 'the King is subject not to men, but to God and the law'. This doctrine of the supremacy of the law denotes, *inter alia*, the overriding power of the courts to secure and control the observance of statute and common law in all spheres except those clearly reserved to the King's prerogative or delegated by Parliament to other agencies. In a negative sense it means that the King cannot alter the law. Consequently, while the existence of the King's prerogative in foreign affairs is undeniable, its extent may be inquired into when the occasion arises.

However axiomatic these propositions may be, the difficulties begin immediately the conduct of foreign affairs is treated from the point of view of the Executive's powers. The conduct of foreign affairs often leads to a change in the law. Thus the recognition of a foreigner as ambassador has the effect of rendering him and his property immune from legal process. Or the recognition of a state of war between foreign Powers may impose upon subjects certain duties arising from the King's policy of neutrality. In these and similar connections it has never been doubted that, though the King cannot alter the law and therefor, e.g., cannot by treaty grant a licence to commit trespass,[3] his policy may have the incidental effect of creating rights and duties which did not exist prior to the expression of his will. It was in connection with the treaty-making power of the Crown and, in particular, with the cession of British territory that the Crown's incapacity of making a change in the law has given

---

[1] See, e.g., *The Arantzazu Mendi*, [1939] A. C. 256, and many other decisions. The Foreign Office nearly always speaks of recognition by His Majesty's Government and so forth. See Lauterpacht, *B.T.I.L.* (1939), 125.

[2] *The Arantzazu Mendi*, [1939] P. 37, 42.

[3] *Walker v. Baird*, [1892] A. C. 491.

rise to intensive discussion. The King can cede territory, because this is clearly an aspect of his conduct of foreign affairs. But if he does cede territory, the inhabitants are deprived of their British nationality.[1] Is this not a change in the law which the King cannot effect and which should therefore result in a denial of his power to cede territory altogether? There exists, it is true, a practice, now almost a binding constitutional convention,[2] whereby such treaties require the approval of Parliament. But Sir William Holdsworth[3] is probably right in suggesting that, according to the better opinion, the Crown can cede territory without the consent of Parliament. As to the general question under what circumstances an alteration of the rights of the subjects is an alteration which the Crown cannot effect by treaty because it amounts to an alteration of the law and, on the other hand, under what circumstances an alteration of the rights of the subject is merely the incidental effect of a treaty so that the Crown is able to make the treaty, Sir William Holdsworth[4] has suggested that the object of the treaty must be regarded as the test:

> If the object of the treaty is the doing of an act which the Crown has power to do, e.g., the recognition of the status of a foreign sovereign or a public ship or a cession of territory, the fact that it will have the effect of altering the rights of the subject will not preclude the Crown from making it. But if . . . its object is to alter the rights of the subject, it cannot take effect without the consent of the Parliament, because in this case it amounts to an alteration of the law.

If, then, object is to be made the test, we are probably entitled to apply to royal impulses what Viscount Simon L.C. said of human impulses, viz. that their analysis 'soon leads us into the quagmire of mixed motives'.[5] The crucial question would be: What was the predominant purpose or object in making the treaty? Was it made in order that the subjects' rights be altered or in order to do an act which the Crown had power to do? It may be felt that such questions raise issues of so wide a character

---

[1] *Doe d. Thomas* v. *Acklam* (1824), 2 B. & C. 779; *Doe d. Auchmuty* v. *Mulcaster* (1826), 5 B. & C. 771.

[2] McNair, *The Law of Treaties* (1938), pp. 24 sqq.

[3] *The Treaty-Making Power of the Crown*, 58 *L.Q.R.* (1942), 175 sqq. In the same sense, Lord Caldecote, 7 *Cambridge L.J.* (1941), 310, 322.

[4] op. cit., p. 183.

[5] *Crofter Hand Woven Harris Tweed Co. Ltd.* v. *Veitch*, [1942] A. C. 435, 445 where a valuable discussion of the terms 'object', 'purpose', 'motive', 'intention' will be found.

that a judge may find it difficult to deal with them and that therefore he should be supplied with a test which is less ambiguous and uncertain. For these reasons the only safe test is perhaps the purely formal one: if on its face the act of the Executive contains provisions purporting to alter the law, parliamentary sanction is required, but if on its face it is only concerned with the conduct of foreign affairs, it falls within the ambit of the royal prerogative.

When we now turn to the reverse side of the picture and consider the attitude which the Judiciary has adopted or should adopt towards foreign affairs, a fact of considerable importance stands out: the courts cannot *make* foreign policy. If it be assumed that a court held Eire to be no longer a part of the British Empire,[1] this would not mean that such was the view of the King and his Government. It would not bind the nation. There would be no *res judicata* except, on the ordinary principles, as between the parties. No third person, whether British or foreign, whether an individual or State, would acquire any rights or duties. Nor is there any evidence that any such decision could have the effect of incurring State responsibility within the meaning and practice of international law, because such responsibility does not exist except in case of a denial of justice.[2] The opinion would be a matter of interest to the world and to international lawyers, but it would not commit this country. It will be remembered that at a time when the British Government again and again refused to recognize General Franco's forces as belligerents, when the *de jure* recognition of the insurgent Government would have been contrary to established principles of international law, when the Agents exchanged between this country and Nationalist Spain were expressly denied diplomatic status, when the British Government consistently and expressly refused recognition of the sovereignty of the Franco administration,[3] the House of Lords gave a decision which in effect recognized Nationalist Spain as a foreign sovereign power.[4] There are good grounds for believing[5] that the

---

[1] The opposite was decided in *Murray* v. *Parkes*, [1942] 2 K. B. 123.

[2] Oppenheim (–Lauterpacht), *International Law* (5th ed.), i. pp. 289 and others.

[3] See Lauterpacht, 'Recognition of Insurgents as a *de facto* Government', 3 *Mod. L.R.* (1939) 1, at p. 4.

[4] *The Arantzazu Mendi*, [1939] A. C. 256.

[5] Lauterpacht, op. cit., pp. 8 sqq.

House of Lords thus went considerably further than the Executive ever was prepared to go. Yet the discrepancy neither disturbed the peace of the world nor caused any responsibility of, or inconvenience to, the Executive.

*Prima facie*, therefore, there is no reason why in matters relating to foreign affairs, the courts should not abide by the rule that nothing they decide will amount to the making of policy and why in matters international they should not guard their independence as jealously as in matters municipal. Yet it is a fact, and a really fascinating one, that in international affairs Anglo-American courts have been inclined to surrender a good deal of their independence, to be guided by and even to submit to the Executive and to refrain from that judicial freedom which otherwise is so proud a feature of the English legal system. It seems to have been in the early nineteenth century, i.e. under the shadow of great political turmoil,[1] that the doctrine originated which in 1828 Shadwell J. expressed in the following words which, perhaps fortunately for him, Lord Coke did not live to read and which may now make some of us tremble[2]: 'It appears to me that sound policy requires that the Courts of the King should act in unison with the Government of the King.' The impact of this idea has made itself felt in many individual connections to which reference will have to be made, but it also underlies such general statements as that of McNair[3] who speaks of the 'axiom in international relations that a sovereign cannot speak with two voices', or that of the New York Court of Appeals[4]: 'We should do nothing to thwart the policy which the United States has adopted.' To Lord Sumner, it is true, Shadwell J.'s dictum seemed 'to be rather a maxim of policy than a rule of law',[5] but this cautious warning has gone unheeded and it was entirely in line with the general tendency

---

[1] The Declaration of Independence was still a recent event, the Napoleonic Wars and their aftermath was a vivid memory, the struggle of the South American Colonies for independence from Spain was still proceeding.

[2] *Taylor* v. *Barclay*, 2 Sim. 213, 221. In its context the sentence quoted above is, of course, less ominous than it sounds.

[3] *B.Y.I.L.* (1921–2), p. 65, and see Lord Atkin's dictum quoted below, p. 402, n. 7. See also Bankes L.J. in *The Gagara*, [1919] P. 95, at p. 104.

[4] *Russian Republic* v. *Cibrario* 235 N. Y. 255, 263 (1923); *A.D.* (1923–4), No. 17, recently expressly approved in *United States* v. *Pink*, 315 U. S. 202 (1942), 240 per Mr. Justice Frankfurter.

[5] *Duff Development Co. Ltd.* v. *Government of Kelantan*, [1924] A. C. 797, 826.

when in a recent case eminent Counsel (Sir Stafford Cripps)
argued that in matters touching upon international relations

it is a rule of law in this country that the decision or statement of the
executive Government as to a particular state of facts is not merely conclusive, but also essential, and .. that it was undesirable that the courts
should come to a decision which might embarrass the executive with regard
to matters of state in which this country is or might be concerned.

It sounded therefore like a revolt when Sir Wilfred Greene (as
he then was) retorted[1]:

I do not myself find the fear of the embarrassment of the executive a very
attractive basis upon which to build a rule of English law.

It is submitted with great respect and equal diffidence that the
tendency underlying the dicta of Lord Sumner and Lord
Greene should be welcomed and encouraged as signs of a
possible, though still remote re-orientation, to the limits and
extents of which much searching thought will have to be
devoted. As a preliminary contribution a more detailed yet
incomplete survey of the present situation may perhaps be of
some assistance.

(1) While, as has been shown, the King is subject to English
common and statute law, English municipal courts refuse to
regard any breaches of international law committed by the
Executive as justiciable, and for this reason it is perhaps permissible to formulate that in the eyes of the common law the
King is not subject to international law. Thus the courts have
declared themselves incompetent in cases of state succession.
There is a long line of authorities[2] in which it has been laid
down that, if the Crown or its delegate acquires territory by
cession, a plaintiff cannot be heard in a municipal court to
assert the continuance of rights granted by the preceding sovereign and accepted by the successor according to the terms of
the treaty. As Lord Halsbury said in one of the leading cases,[3]

it is no answer to say that, by the ordinary principles of international law,
private property is respected by the sovereign which accepts the cession and
assumes the duties and legal obligations of the former sovereign with respect

---

[1] *Kawasaki Kisen Kabushiki Kaisha of Kobe* v. *Bantham Steamship Co. Ltd.*, [1939] 2
K. B. 544, 552.
[2] Halsbury (–Hailsham), xxvi.255, and the latest case, *Secretary of State* v.
*Sardor Rustam Khan*, [1941] A. C. 356.
[3] *Cook* v. *Sprigg*, [1899] A. C. 572, 578.

to such private property within the ceded territory. All that can be properly meant by such a proposition is that according to the well-understood rules of international law a change of sovereignty by cession ought not to affect private property, but no municipal tribunal has authority to enforce such an obligation.

A similar idea pervades those cases where a foreigner is injured outside Great Britain by an act of State committed by an officer of the Crown and adopted by it.[1] Here, again, the courts decline jurisdiction and, in effect, refer the plaintiff to diplomatic representations.

There was no *a priori* reason for the refusal of adjudication in such and similar cases, as is shown by the fact that the courts in the United States[2] under the leadership of Chief Justice Marshall did assume jurisdiction, e.g., as to the effects of State succession.[3] The explanation of the English attitude cannot be found in the maxim that the King can do no wrong, for in all cases the action was brought against an official whose liability under common law principles would not be open to doubt. It can therefore only be concluded that the courts recoiled from the possibility of having to find the Executive guilty of a breach of international law and thus to embarrass its standing in international affairs. There may perhaps be some who will be more strongly attracted by the forceful words of John Marshall spoken more than 100 years ago[4]:

> The modern usage of nations which has become law would be violated; that sense of justice and of right which is acknowledged and felt by the whole civilized world would be outraged, if private property should be generally confiscated and private rights annulled. The people change their allegiance; their relationship with their ancient sovereign is dissolved; but their relations to each other and their rights of property remain undisturbed. If this be the modern rule even in cases of conquest, who can doubt its application to the case of an amicable cession of territory.

---

[1] *Buron* v. *Denman* (1848), 2 Exch. 167.

[2] Hyde, *International Law*, i.235 sqq. and the cases mentioned p. 236, n. 1.

[3] See Note 16 *L.Q.R.* (1900), 1.

[4] *United States* v. *Percheman*, (1833) 7 Peters 51, 86. The discussion in the text is of course not intended to suggest that the courts ought to have assumed jurisdiction over all types of claims arising out of a State's activities in the field of foreign relations. In *Nabob of the Carnatic* v. *East India Co.* (1791) 1 Ves. Jr. 370 an attempt was made to enforce in the courts a claim for an account arising out of a transaction which the Court held to be a treaty between Sovereigns. The claim failed on the ground that the rights were not mercantile in their nature, but political. The justification of this principle is not open to doubt.

(2) A second and most important example of 'judicial self-limitation'[1] is to be found in the manner in which the courts usually deal with so-called 'facts of state'.[2] These are matters on which the courts seek and accept guidance by the Executive. Thus they apply to the Executive when they desire to know whether a state of war exists between this and any other country,[3] whether certain territory is recognized to be within the boundaries of a particular State,[4] who is recognized as the head or government of an independent State,[5] whether a party to an action enjoys diplomatic privilege so as to be entitled to immunity.[6] This practice[7] is of comparatively recent origin and is in many respects still in an immature stage. In particular its legal character and its ambit require elucidation.

It is frequently said that facts of the type indicated above are capable of being ascertained by means of what is known as

---

[1] See Finkelstein, quoted above, p. 391, n. 2; Dickinson, 40 *Rec.* (1932), 309, 350 sqq.

[2] Moore, *Acts of State in English Law*, pp. 33–9.

[3] This is undoubted, but there does not appear to be any decision where this has actually been done. The cases referred to by Halsbury (–Hailsham), xxvi.247, nn. d, e, and f, proceed on the principle that the Crown determines the existence of peace or war, but do not preclude the Court from ascertaining the fact by a method other than application to the Executive.

[4] *Foster* v. *Globe Venture Syndicate Ltd.*, [1900] 1 Ch. 811; *The Fagerness*, [1927] P. 311; *Re Cooper*, 143 U. S. 472 (1892).

[5] *Mighell* v. *Sultan of Johore*, [1894] Q. B. 149; *The Gagara*, [1919] P. 95; *The Annette*, [1919] P. 105; *Luther* v. *Sagor and Co.*, [1921] 3 K. B. 532; *Duff Development Co. Ltd.* v. *Government of Kelantan*, [1924] A. C. 797.

[6] *Engelke* v. *Musmann*, [1928] A. C. 433.

[7] In the present state of library facilities it has not been possible to make a comprehensive and reliable survey of the practice prevailing in Continental countries. It would seem that it is by no means uniform: see Lauterpacht, *The Function of Law in the International Community* (1933), p. 389. In particular in pre-Nazi Germany, the courts used to make independent enquiry into the question whether a particular person was entitled to diplomatic immunity. See Court of Appeal, Darmstadt, 20 December 1926, *JW* (1927), 2324, with note by Meurer and *JW* (1928), 76, 77, notes by Josef and Wehberg (also *Annual Digest* (1925–6), No. 244): in conformity with views expressed by the German Foreign Office it was held that a communication by the Foreign Office relating to the extraterritoriality of a member of a foreign embassy was not binding upon the courts. In the same sense, Reichswirtschaftsgericht, 31 December 1928 *JW* (1929), 970, with note by Strupp. Both Courts took the view that the secretary of an ambassador whose appointment is not confirmed or is objected to by Germany is not entitled to immunity—a proposition which, as Wehberg and Strupp point out, seems to be irreconcilable with established principles.

judicial knowledge.[1] This would mean that, if the court knows them, the question of evidence would not arise and the court could act on its own knowledge. On the other hand, if the court does not know them, the proper course is to apply to the Executive for information, and if it is given, it will have to be acted upon according to the best evidence rule, but if no information is given, the court would be free to hear evidence in the usual way. In no event would the court be precluded from amplifying or testing its knowledge by its own investigations. This view which may perhaps be described as the 'rule of best evidence' is supported by a considerable body of authority. But it seems as if the practice is slowly acquiring a radically different complexion and as if a rule has come or is about to be established, which has no trace of the doctrine of best evidence and may be described as the 'rule of obligatory certification'. It would mean that in all cases involving facts of state the court must apply to the Executive, irrespective of what its own knowledge is, and that it must accept the Executive's answer not only as conclusive but also as exhaustive and therefore as precluding any independent investigation by the court.

In 1808 the question of the status of Corfu arose which, being one of the islands forming the Ionian Republic, was occupied by the Russians whose prize commission had condemned a ship. Was the sentence valid? Evidence as to the status of Corfu was received and Lord Ellenborough held the sentence invalid on the ground that 'the Russians must be considered as visitors in Corfu and not as sovereigns'.[2] A few years later the court was called upon to decide whether the plaintiffs, Hamburg merchants, who claimed an insurable interest in a policy of insurance, were enemies so as to make trade with them illegal and their interest incapable of protection.[3] The Court did not apply to the Executive for information. It looked at the Orders in Council made at various times and deduced from them that at the material time trade with Hamburg was in some measure legitimate, that 'the Orders breathe something pacific'[4] and that on their true construction it was proper to regard the

---

[1] Taylor, *On Evidence* (12th ed.), sections 17–21; Phipson, *The Law of Evidence* (8th ed., 1942), at p. 18; Halsbury (–Hailsham), xxvi.256; xiii.619, 620.

[2] *Donaldson* v. *Thompson* (1808), 1 Camp. 429.

[3] *Hagedorn* v. *Bell* (1813), 1 M. and S. 450.

[4] ibidem, at p. 465, per Grose J.

inhabitants of Hamburg as neutral with respect to commerce. A similar method was adopted in three decisions relating to the status of Port au Prince in St. Domingo.[1] Yet when in 1943 the question arose whether a Dutch company was an enemy at common law (there being no doubt as to its enemy character under the Trading with the Enemy Act, 1939), Lord Wright expressed disapproval of the lower courts' omission to inquire of the Foreign Office whether Holland was under effective subjugation by the Germans.[2] In 1801 Sir William Scott[3] had to deal with a ship which, while sailing as an Englishman's property, was captured and carried into the Barbary States and was there sold to a Spanish merchant who sold it to the defendant, a British merchant. The original owner's claim for possession failed. Sir William Scott said[4]:

> This ship appears to have been taken by the Algerines, and it is argued that the Algerines are to be considered in this act as pirates and that no legal conversion of property can be derived from their piratical seizure. Certain it is that the African States were so considered many years ago, but they have long acquired the character of established governments with whom we have regular treaties, acknowledging and confirming to them the relations of legal states. . . . Although their notions of justice, to be observed between nations, differ from those which we entertain, we do not, on that account, venture to call in question their public acts.

Now compare this case with *Luther* v. *Sagor and Co.*[5] The plaintiff's timber had been confiscated by the Soviet Government in Russia and sold to the defendants by the Russian Commercial Delegation in London. Roche J. held that the timber could be recovered by the plaintiffs notwithstanding the fact that, as the Foreign Office had stated, His Majesty's Government assented to the claim of the Delegation to represent in this country a State Government of Russia and, for the purpose of carrying out certain negotiations, had granted immunity to M. Krassin, the authorized representative of the Soviet Government. The status of Russia, therefore, did not substantially differ from that of the African states in 1801, yet since the British Government had 'never officially recognized the Soviet Government in any

---

[1] *The Manilla* (1808), I Edw. Adm. R. 1 (Sir William Scott); *The Pelican* (1809), ibidem, Appendix D (Sir William Grant); *Blackburn* v. *Thompson* (1812), 15 East 81 (Lord Ellenborough and others).

[2] *Sovfracht* v. *Van Udens*, [1943] A. C. 203, 229.

[3] *The Helena*, 4 Rob. Adm. 3.    [4] At p. 5.    [5] [1921] 1 K. B. 456.

way', Roche J. gave judgment in favour of the plaintiffs. Or remember the case of *The Annette*[1] where it was stated that, though His Majesty's Government had not formally recognized the Provisional Government of Northern Russia, both Governments were co-operating in certain respects and had exchanged Commissioners, and where Hill J. said[2]: 'I must be satisfied before I can recognize the Provisional Government of Northern Russia as a sovereign State, for the purposes of this case, that the British Government so recognize it. I am not satisfied.' There is a further decision of Sir William Scott in *The Foltina*[3] which makes interesting reading. Shortly, the point in issue was whether in 1811 when *The Foltina* was seized, Heligoland formed part of the dominions of the Crown of Great Britain. Without reference to the Executive, the Court gave an affirmative answer. On the other hand, the Court of Appeal held in 1927[4] that it was bound by a statement of the Attorney-General, made on behalf of the Home Secretary, that a certain spot in the Bristol Channel was not within the limits to which the territorial sovereignty of His Majesty extended.

In these circumstances it becomes possible to assert with some confidence that the device of applying to the Executive for information was entirely unknown during the first quarter of the nineteenth century.[5] In fact the first report of a case where any enquiry was addressed by the Court to the Executive is dated 1828,[6] and the second seems to be the decision of Sir Robert

---

[1] [1919] P. 105.    [2] At p. 111.

[3] (1814), 1 Dods. 450. On the point of substantive law the decision is no longer authoritative: Oppenheim (–Lauterpacht) (6th ed.), ii.338.

[4] *The Fagerness*, [1927] P. 311.

[5] Sir William Holdsworth, 41 *Col. L.R.* (1941), 1313, 1322, says that the principle 'was beginning to be recognized in the courts of law and equity during the latter part of the eighteenth century'. It is submitted with very great respect that this statement is not borne out by the evidence adduced by Sir William. The earliest cases where the idea is expressed with some, though by no means complete, certainty, are *City of Berne* v. *Bank of England* (1805) 9 Ves. 347, and *Dolder* v. *Lord Huntingfield* (1805) 11 Ves. 282, and some other decisions of that period on which see Bushe-Fox, *B.Y.I.L.* (1931), p. 63. They relate to the peculiar position of the non-recognized Government (see below, p. 409, n. 1) and are in no way conclusive on the point discussed in the text, since no application to the Executive was made. Moreover, Lord Eldon's mind was obviously not settled on the point: see his doubts in *Dolder* v. *Bank of England* (1805) 10 Ves. Jr. 352, 354, and there is perhaps some force in the observation of Jaffe (op. cit., p. 127) that Lord Eldon's statements bear 'the accent of a judge who is also an adviser to the King, and his servant'.

[6] *Taylor* v. *Barclay* (1828), 2 Sim. 213, 220.

Phillimore in *The Charkeih*.[1] In order to decide whether ships owned by the Khedive of Egypt were entitled to immunity, the learned judge had regard to four matters, viz. the general history of the Government of Egypt, the public law of the Ottoman Empire, the European treaties concerning the relations between Egypt and the Ottoman Empire, and lastly 'the answer which the Foreign Office has furnished to an inquiry which I thought it my duty to make'. This answer was that 'the Khedive has not been and is not now recognized by Her Majesty as reigning sovereign of the State of Egypt', but that he 'is recognized . . . the hereditary ruler of the province of Egypt under the supremacy of the Sultan of Egypt'. But this answer did not deter Sir Robert Phillimore from investigating whether the status of the Khedive was such as to make his property immune from legal process, and after a careful review of all relevant facts, he gave an answer in the negative. This method was strongly disapproved by Lord Esher in *Mighell* v. *Sultan of Johore*[2] where he said[3] that the answer given by the Foreign Office was conclusive and precluded any further inquiry.

The conclusiveness of the Executive's certificate is now established beyond doubt.[4] But the conflict between the best-evidence-rule and the rule of obligatory certification still remains. Lord Sumner, it is true, emphatically expressed himself in favour of the former doctrine,[5] and it is very remarkable that recently a Divisional Court felt itself entitled to investigate the status of Eire and to hold, without guidance by the Executive, that it formed part of the British Empire.[6] On the other hand, Lord Atkin has said[7] of an inquiry of the Government

that not only is this the correct procedure but it is the *only procedure by which* the Court can inform itself of the material fact whether the party sought to be impleaded, or whose property is sought to be affected, is a foreign sovereign state. This, I think, is made clear by the opinions in this House in the *Kelantan* case. With great respect, I do not accept the opinion, implied in the

---

[1] (1873), 4 A. and E. 59.     [2] [1894] 1 Q.B. 149.
[3] At p. 158, but see Jaffe, op. cit., p. 210.
[4] *Duff Development Co. Ltd.* v. *Government of Kelantan*, [1924] A. C. 797; *The Arantzazu Mendi*, [1939] A. C. 256, and many other cases.
[5] *Duff's* case, [1924] A. C. 797, 824, and see *The Abodi Mendi*, [1939] P. 178, 192, where Scott L.J. said that the status of the two Spanish Governments was 'common knowledge'.
[6] *Murray* v. *Parkes*, [1942] 2 K. B. 123.
[7] *The Arantzazu Mendi*, [1939] A. C. 256, 264 (italics supplied).

decision of Lord Sumner in that case that recourse to His Majesty's Government is only one way in which the judge can ascertain the relevant fact. The reason is, I think, obvious. Our State cannot speak with two voices on such a matter, the judiciary saying one thing, the executive another. Our Sovereign has to decide whom he will recognize as a fellow sovereign in the family fo states, and the relations of the foreign state with ours in the matter of state immunities must flow from that decision alone.

Although, perhaps, some may still prefer the doctrine which was propounded by Lord Sumner and which, as has been shown, falls into line with the practice originally adopted in the early nineteenth century, there is probably no substantial reason to question the soundness of Lord Atkin's view.[1] It is much more important however, to define clearly the extent to which the Executive has power of giving binding information to the Court: the principle seems to be that the certificate is binding upon the courts if it concerns facts the creation or recognition of which falls within the limits of the Crown's prerogative of conducting foreign affairs.[2]

It would be wrong to say that *all* facts having international aspects are withdrawn from judicial decision. Thus it has been held that the time when a particular foreign Government comes into existence is a matter for the Court to determine, at least in the absence of determination by the Executive[3]; that neither questions of a purely geographical nature[4] nor such matters as the date of specific events occurring during a war[5] are 'political' ones; that even if in the view of the Foreign Office two foreign nations are at peace, the Court is entitled to

[1] It fails, however, to provide for cases where the Executive does not give the information requested by the Court. In *Duff's* case, [1924] A. C. 797, 825, Lord Sumner said that, if the Crown declines to answer, the Court would be entitled to accept secondary evidence in default of the best.

[2] This definition is substantially supported by Wade and Phillips, *Constitutional Law* (2nd ed.), p. 235 and Holdsworth, 'Act of State', 41 *Col. L.R.* (1941), 1313, 1331.

[3] *White Child and Beney Ltd.* v. *Simmons* (1922), 127 L. T. 571 (C. A.). In its reply the Foreign Office had given much useful information but refused to 'express any opinion as to how far or over what area the power of the Soviet Government was effective, the questions being also questions of fact for the courts to determine on the evidence laid before them'. In the Court of first instance Roche J. felt neither qualified nor entitled, still less bound, to answer the question, notwithstanding the hint clearly given to him.

[4] See Lord Sumner in *Duff Development Co. Ltd.* v. *Government of Kelantan*, [1924] A. C. 797, 826, 827.

[5] *Commonwealth Shipping Representative* v. *P. and O. Branch Service*, [1923] A. C. 191, 197, per Viscount Cave, L.C.

hold that within the meaning of a particular charterparty a state of war exists between them[1]; that for the purposes of section 8 of the Foreign Enlistment Act, 1870, two foreign nations may be at 'war' prior to a formal declaration of war and prior to the publication of a declaration of neutrality by the British Government[2]; and that the Court is apparently at liberty to determine not only the existence of a blockade,[3] but also its effectiveness.[4] On the other hand, cases where courts have declined independent decision are exemplified, not only by those English decisions which have been mentioned above, but also by numerous American authorities of considerable interest.[5] While they do not contribute much to the elucidation of the underlying principle, they do suggest a note of warning. A perusal of the reports shows that frequently the courts have been inclined not only to ask, but to press the Executive for information. They have equally often spoken of their reluctance to decide the question for themselves, and they have done this even in the face of an intimation by the Executive that the question may be one for the Court to decide.[6] While it is certain that the practice of applying to the Executive is in many respects a useful device, it should not be overlooked that it may sometimes be more embarrassing to the Executive than an independent decision of the courts which does not commit the Government and may be, therefore, often less prejudicial than judges are inclined to think. The Judiciary, as we have seen, cannot determine policy or political facts. The Executive which can determine them may not wish to do so. Particularly in those cases where the Executive has not taken any positive action in

---

[1] *Kawasaki Kisen Kabushiki Kaisha of Kobe* v. *Bantham Steamship Co. Ltd.*, [1939] 2 K. B. 544 (C. A.). The attitude of the British Government may similarly be immaterial in a case concerning a contract governed by foreign law.

[2] *United States* v. *Pelly* (1899) W. N. 11.

[3] *Spanish Government* v. *North of England Steamship Co. Ltd.* (1938), 54 T. L. R. 852, 855.

[4] *W. J. Tatem and Co.* v. *Gamboa*, [1938] 3 All E. R. 135.

[5] For references, see the writers mentioned above p. 391, n. 2.

[6] See above, p. 403, n. 3. In *Luther* v. *Sagor and Co.*, [1921] 1 K. B. 456, 461, the Foreign Office disclaimed any intention of deciding 'difficult and, it may be, very special questions of law upon which it may become necessary for the courts to pronounce'. A similar intimation in the letter written by the Foreign Office in *The Arantzazu Mendi*, [1939] A. C. 256, at p. 258 (more fully [1938] 3 All E. R. 333, 336) and in *Banco de Bilbao* v. *Rey*, [1938] 2 K. B. 176. On this point, and on some other matters discussed in the text, see Lauterpacht, *B.Y.I.L.* (1939), pp. 125, 127.

the political field, the danger of the existing practice lies in compelling an unwilling or temporizing Executive to disclose its views or intentions.[1] The Judiciary should therefore be conscious of the seriousness of the decision to label a question as a political one and thus induce a statement by the Executive.

The other consequence to which the legal basis of the practice leads is that *only* facts of a certain character are capable of being determined by the Executive. The law applicable to such facts must be found by the courts. Were this not so, one of the fundamental principles of English law would be disregarded. Thus the mere fact that a person is entitled to immunity or the property of such a person is impleaded, does not necessarily mean that the Court will set aside the proceedings; it is for the Court to determine the extent and effect of immunity. It will therefore decide whether a counter-claim may be brought against the sovereign plaintiff[2] or whether the impleaded ship is in the control of a foreign sovereign State or is a public ship.[3] It is however, significant to observe that in the United States a further extension of the Executive's powers is in course of being brought about by recent developments. According to the practice of the Supreme Court a foreign Government may assert the public status of a ship and assert her immunity either through diplomatic channels or as a claimant in the courts. In the latter case the foreign Government must prove its allegation that the ship is a public one. In the former case, however, if the claim is recognized and allowed by the Executive, it is the duty of the courts to release the vessel upon appropriate suggestion by the

[1] The reader may be interested to know that when in 1887 the authors of the German Civil Code produced a complete Code of Private International Law, Bismarck prevented its publication and eventually the Code contained only a few specific rules, the intention being that the rest should be developed by the courts. The reason probably was that the German Government was afraid lest its views on foreign policy might be discernible from the tenor of the proposed legislation, while judicial decisions could not be said to commit the Government. See German Supreme Court, 12 October 1903, *RGZ* 55, 345, 353, and Niemeyer, *Das internationale Privatrecht des Bürgerlichen Gesetzbuches*, pp. 4, 5.

[2] *South African Republic* v. *La Compagnie Franco-Belge*, [1897] 2 Ch. 487; [1898] 1 Ch. 190.

[3] See, e.g., *The Cristina*, [1938] A. C. 485. The assertion of a foreign recognized Sovereign is not sufficient: ibidem, at p. 506, per Lord Wright, at pp. 516, 517, per Lord Maugham; *Haile Selassie* v. *Cable and Wireless Ltd.* (*No. 1*), [1938] Ch. 839; but see *The Parlement Belge*, [1880] 5 P. D. 197, 219; *Luther* v. *Sagor and Co.*, [1921] 3 K. B. 532, 557, per Scrutton L.J.

Attorney-General which is conclusive and obviates any proof of the status of the ship.[1] There is no evidence that English courts will ever delegate such functions to the Executive. The court's privilege to decide legal questions is well exemplified by another American decision[2]: If the Nationalist Government of Spain claims from the Federal Reserve Bank the return of silver sold to it by the Republican Government by a contract which is alleged to be *ultra vires* under Spanish law, this is not a ('political') question of fact, but a question of law and the defendants cannot rely on a statement of the Secretary of the Treasury (Mr. Morgenthau) to the effect that the sale was valid. Similarly it should not be open to doubt that the Executive cannot create new categories of persons entitled to immunity. Thus, even if a (foreign or British) corporation which is owned by a foreign Government were to be recognized by the Executive as an agency or a department of the foreign Government, the courts, it is submitted, could not treat it as immune, unless such immunity were sanctioned by the accepted principles of the law of nations.[3] Finally, it has been held by Mr Justice Russell (as he then was) that an English Court is both entitled and bound to construe a statute enacted for the purpose of giving effect to a treaty such as the Treaty of Versailles[4]; on this point the powers of an English judge seem to be much wider than those of his French colleague,[5] nor does he appear to be fettered by such rules of construction as that adopted by the Supreme Court of the United States according to which the construction of a treaty by the Political Department of the Government,

---

[1] *The Navemar*, 303 U. S. 68 (1938); *Annual Digest* (1938–40), No. 68.

[2] *Banco de España* v. *Federal Reserve Bank*, (1940) 114 F. (2d) 438; *Annual Digest* (1938–40), No. 6 (United States Circuit Court of Appeals).

[3] On state-owned foreign corporations see the two recent decisions of the Supreme Court of New York (Appellate Division) containing a full review of the present situation: *Hannes* v. *Kingdom of Roumania Monopolis Institute, A.D.* (1938–40), 72; *Ulen and Co.* v. *Bank Gospoderstwa Krajowego*, ibidem, No. 74.

[4] *Stoeck* v. *Public Trustee*, [1921] 2 Ch. 68, 71.

[5] The practice of the French Cour de Cassation is that the courts are precluded from interpreting treaties unless 'cette interprétation se rapporte à des interêts privés dont le règlement est soumis à leur appréciation et non lorsqu'elle soulève des questions d'ordre public international'. See Cass. Crim. 23 February 1912, Clunet (1913), 182; 22 March 1923, Clunet (1923), 847, and many other decisions mentioned by Maury, 57 *Rec.* (1936), 443 sqq., or Mestre, 38 *Rec.* (1931), 240.

while not conclusive upon a court, should nevertheless be given 'much weight'.[1]

The principle that it is the function of the court to apply the law to the facts stated by the Executive, also provides guidance for the solution of the difficult question of what attitude the court should adopt towards communications made by the Executive. It has been said that a statement made by the Executive is not open to criticism since this would be disrespectful to the Crown itself. This is true, but by no means exhaustive. The real problem is whether and to what extent the statement is open, not to criticism, but to construction in the ordinary and usual sense of the word. In this connection, too, we are greatly indebted to Lord Sumner for a clear exposition of the various aspects of this problem.[2] The answer supplied by the Executive may be 'temporary if not temporizing', and in such or similar circumstances the court has to collect the true meaning of the communication for itself, and its construction becomes 'a matter for argument before and for decision by the courts'. Moreover, the court may have to consider 'whether the statements as to sovereignty made in the communication and the expressions 'sovereign' or 'independent' sovereign used in the legal rule mean the same thing'. It is submitted with great respect that these are sound and wise directions which should have exercised stronger influence than has been accorded to them in practice. There are many cases where, it is believed, the courts have unnecessarily restricted their powers of inter-

---

[1] *Charlton* v. *Kelly*, 229 U. S. 447, 468 (1917); *Sullivan* v. *Kidd*, 254 U. S. 433, 442 (1920). In this connection the reader should remember the interesting attitude adopted by the American Judiciary towards the Behring Sea Dispute. An Act of 1868 had forbidden the killing of 'otter, mink . . . or other fur-bearing animal within the limits of Alaska territory or in the waters thereof'. The Executive claimed jurisdiction beyond the three miles limit in the Behring Sea, but an Act of 1889 merely declared that the earlier statute should 'include and apply to all the dominions of the United States in the waters of the Behring Sea', thus leaving open the question of the extent of these waters. The courts held that they were bound by the political decision and they therefore so construed the statute as to condemn Canadian vessels found sixty miles from shore: *U.S.* v. *La Ninfa*, 49 Fed. 575; and see *In re Cooper*, 143 U. S. 472, 502, 505 (1892). After the conclusion of the arbitration proceedings on which see Moore, *International Arbitration*, sections 756–960, and *Digest* i.890–929, the opposite view was adopted: *La Ninfa* v. *U.S.*, 75 Fed. 513. On the foregoing see P. Quincy Wright, *The Control of American Foreign Relations* (1922), pp. 170–5.

[2] *Duff Development Co. Ltd.* v. *Government of Kelantan*, [1924] A. C. 797, 825–8.

pretation,[1] but it may suffice to refer to the decision in the *Arantzazu Mendi*[2] where the House of Lords held that the *de facto* recognition which, it decided, had been granted to the Nationalist Government of Spain, necessitated the conclusion that its property was entitled to immunity as against the *de jure* government—a *non sequitur* which Professor Lauterpacht has convincingly exposed.[3] The courts have shown a tendency to be almost hypnotized by the presence or absence of the words 'recognition', 'sovereign' and so forth, and since the practice of the courts is less flexible or capable of alteration than that of the Executive, it may be well to consider whether statements by the Executive should not be so framed as to describe a situation rather than to state results. This may enable and compel the court in proper cases to deduce for itself whether the facts described amount to 'recognition,' 'sovereignty', etc. within the meaning, not of diplomatic language, but of international law.

(3) The third connection in which the Judiciary's dependence on the Executive in foreign affairs has become apparent, is that rules of substantive law have been developed which cannot be explained otherwise than by the desire of disembarrassing the Executive.

It has been shown that information supplied by the Executive to the courts is conclusive only in so far as it relates to facts of a certain type. Even if the Executive were to make an express statement of law, this would not be binding upon the courts, and as an illustration of this proposition we instanced the hypothetical case of the Executive granting immunity to a corporation, and submitted that in the absence of an established rule of the law of nations no such grant would bind the Court. Notwithstanding its incapacity to create or impose rules of law, however, the attitude of the Executive has frequently influenced the formation of rules of law. The most important example of this aspect of the 'political question' is to be found in the law relating to the position of the non-recognized State or Government. The basic idea seems to be that without recognition the court cannot in any way take notice of the existence of the

---

[1] The most important of these cases are *Duff's* case (see the preceding note) on which Jaffe, op. cit., pp. 210, 211, made valuable observations, and *Luther* v. *Sagor and Co.*, [1921] 1 K. B. 456; 3 K. B. 532 (C. A.).    [2] [1939] A. C. 256.
[3] 3 *Mod. L.R.* (1939), 1; on that case see also Briggs, *A.J.* (1939), 689.

unrecognized State or Government, and this appears to have been the reason by virtue of which the courts have come to hold that the unrecognized Government cannot sue[1]; that the unrecognized Government and its property is probably not entitled to immunity[2]; that the court will grant no relief to a person who relies on a contract made with an unrecognized Government and thus founds his case on the allegation 'that there was that existing as an independent Government acknowledged by this country, which in fact was not so'[3]; that a person who takes a ship out of the lawful control of an unrecognized Government may yet be rendering meritorious service entitling him to salvage money[4]; that the law of an unrecognized Government and its acts of state are to be disregarded and cannot be given effect in this country.[5]

It may perhaps be useful to select the last proposition for closer examination.[6] It has produced manifold results: Russian companies, dissolved by Soviet law, have been treated as subsisting[7]; property confiscated in Russia by the Soviet Government and transferred to a purchaser has been held to be still vested in the original owner[8]; French,[9] Belgian,[10] Italian,[11] and

---

[1] *City of Berne* v. *Bank of England* (1804), 9 Ves. Jr. 347; *Dolder* v. *Bank of England* (1805), 10 Ves. Jr. 352; *Dolder* v. *Lord Huntingfield* (1805), 11 Ves. Jr. 283 (see also above, p. 401, n. 5); *Guaranty Trust Co. of New York* v. *United States*, 304 U. S. 126 (1938) per Mr. Justice Stone.

[2] *The Annette*, [1919] P. 105; in the opposite sense, however, the New York Court of Appeals in *Wulfsohn* v. *R.S.F.S.R.*, 234 Y. N. 372 (1923); *Annual Digest* (1923–4), No. 16.

[3] *Taylor* v. *Barclay* (1828), 2 Sim. 213, 221, per Shadwell J.; *Jones* v. *García del Rio* (1823), Turner and Russell, 297.

[4] This seems to follow from *The Lomonosoff*, [1921] P. 97.

[5] *Luther* v. *Sagor and Co.*, [1921] 1 K. B. 456.

[6] The other propositions are in varying degree open to criticism. A full discussion of the problems of the non-recognized power would exceed the ambit of this paper. See generally Borchard, 31 *Yale L.J.* (1922), 543; *A.J.I.L.* (1932), 261; Dickinson, 22 *Mich. L.R.* (1924), 29, 118; *A.J.I.L.* (1925), 263; (1931), 214; Quincy Wright, ibid. (1923), 742; Philip Marshall Brown, *Annuaire de l'Institut de droit international* (1934), p. 302.

[7] *Petrogradsky M.K. Bank* v. *National City Bank*, 253 N. Y. 23 (1930); *Annual Digest* (1929–30), No. 20 (New York Court of Appeals).

[8] *Luther* v. *Sagor and Co.*, [1921] 1 K. B. 456. In the same sense, Tribunal Civil de la Seine, 12 December 1923, Clunet (1924), 133.

[9] See Grouber and Tager, Clunet (1924), 8; Trib. Civ. de la Seine, 2 December 1931, Clunet (1932), 438, refusing retroactive effect to recognition.

[10] Trib. Civ. Bruxelles, 16 June 1928, Clunet (1928), 1253; 5 June 1925, Clunet (1929), 196; 20 December 1930, Clunet (1932), 1086; Liège, 21 March 1929, Clunet (1929), 1158.    [11] Genoa, 19 March 1923, Clunet (1923), 1021.

Egyptian[1] Courts have applied the non-existing Czarist law in deciding the status of Russian refugees; in a 'fantastic'[2] decision an American Court treated the Kerensky régime as the existing Russian Government a decade after its extinction[3]; an American Court has also denied the validity of the appointment of an administratrix by a Mexican Court on the ground that the Mexican Government for the time being in power was not recognized by the United States.[4]

The English case in which a problem of this type, viz. the validity of the transfer of the title to property confiscated in Russia, arose, is *Luther* v. *Sagor and Co.*[5] where Roche J. started from the premiss that the validity of the Russian legislative act depended 'upon whether the power from which it purports to emanate is what it apparently claims to be, a sovereign power'.[6] He then stated the rule that 'if a foreign Government or its sovereignty is not recognized by the Government of this country, the courts of this country either cannot, or at least need not, or ought not, to take notice of or recognize such foreign Government or its sovereignty',[7] and thus arrived at the conclusion that Soviet law was at the time ineffective in England.

It will be observed that the ratio decidendi lies in the familiar dogma that the Court is not 'to take notice' of a non-recognized Government. Why this should be so has not been explained by the learned judge, but a French writer is probably right in suggesting that the refusal of judicial recognition of which he emphatically approves, was due to the intention of, and, indeed, the necessity for, supporting the policy of the Executive.[8] If, so he says in effect, Soviet law is denied recognition by the courts, this will result in the Soviet Government pressing harder for recognition and making the concessions demanded by the British Government. This writer, therefore, candidly welcomes the court making itself an instrument of foreign policy and assum-

---

[1] Court of Appeal of the Mixed Tribunal at Alexandria, 10 March 1931, Clunet (1934), 1020.

[2] *United States* v. *Pink* (1942), 315 U.S 203, at p. 236, per Mr. Justice Frankfurter.

[3] *Lehigh Valley Railroad Co.* v. *State of Russia*, 21 F. (2d), 396.

[4] *Pelzer* v. *United Dredging Co.* reported by Dickinson, 22 *Mich. L.R.* (1923), 29, 30, n. 5.

[5] [1921] 1 K. B. 456.        [6] At p. 473.        [7] At p. 474.

[8] Noël–Henry, *Les Gouvernements de fait devant les Juges* (1927), p. 139, and passim.

ing a function which is not germane to it and of which English Courts usually fight shy.[1] Does this justification not disclose a somewhat naive distortion of the realities of political life? Does it not involve taking a bird's-eye view of the motives and facts determining the relations between great powers? It is believed that where recognition is felt to be in fact redundant by the foreign power, the attitude of the British Judiciary will not make it necessary or desirable, and, conversely, that where a foreign non-recognized Government feels recognition to be necessary or desirable, judicial recognition in England will not make its efforts redundant. Moreover, the soundness of that doctrine in law is open to grave doubts. If it were a question of enforcing the law of an unrecognized State, much could be said in favour of judicial restraint, although even in such a case some continental courts have had no hesitation in giving effect to that law.[2] But in *Luther* v. *Sagor and Co.*[3] and similar Anglo-American cases the Court had to deal with the law prevailing in a recognized State controlled by an unrecognized Government. Established rules of private international law had led it to apply the law of Russia, which means the law of Russia as existing at the material time. In fact this was the law enforced by the Soviet Government and observed in the territories controlled by it.[4] Since in applying Russian law an English Court 'must consider itself sitting in' Russia, the only material question was, What law would a Russian judge apply? To deny that, because of the British Government not recognizing the Soviet Government, a Soviet judge is administering 'law', would only be justified if it were a principle of English private international law that rules prevailing and enforced in a foreign country are 'law' only if that country has a government declaring them to be law. No such principle exists. Even if a foreign country is temporarily without a government, it may

---

[1] This is proved by the attitude towards public policy adopted in such cases as *Janson* v. *Driefontain Consolidated Mines Ltd.*, [1902] A. C. 484 or *Re Schiff*, [1921] 1 Ch. 149. See generally the statement of Parke B. in *Egerton* v. *Brownlow* (1853), 4 H. L. C. 1, at p. 123, which, according to Lord Wright in *Fender* v. *Mildmay*, [1938] A. C. 1, 42, expresses the view of the law which has prevailed.

[2] German Supreme Court, 29 June 1920, *RGStr.* 55, 81; 16 October 1925, *JW* (1926), 1986.

[3] [1921] 1 K. B. 456.

[4] The inquiry addressed to the Foreign Office ought to have dealt with these points rather than with the international standing of the Soviet Government.

yet have a 'law'. Hence it should be clear that if the English Court is merely prevented from taking notice of the—existing—Soviet *Government*, it is open to it to apply the *law* which a Russian judge would apply. While the recognition of a foreign Government does not in itself assure the application of the foreign country's laws,[1] the non-recognition of a foreign Government does not necessarily exclude the application of the foreign law. At a time when Switzerland did not recognize the Soviet Government, the essential point was neatly stated by the Swiss Federal Tribunal[2]:

> Non-recognition of the Soviet Government has merely this consequence that in the relations of international law this government has no standing to represent Russia in Switzerland either in public or private matters. But this does not hinder Russian law from existing and producing effect.

For these reasons it is submitted that the doctrine of *Luther* v. *Sagor and Co.*[3] is due to the Court having taken an exaggerated view of its dependence on the Executive's policy and is, indeed, unsound in law.

(4) Similar, though considerably more dangerous, exaggerations are to be observed in connection with the fourth and last aspect of the political question, viz. the rapidly progressing introduction of a new head of public policy allowing overriding weight to the ideas pervading the foreign policy adopted by the Executive. The impact of these developments has not yet been felt in this country, but in view of the great influence exercised by the Supreme Court of the United States one of its recent decisions should quickly be recognized as a serious warning rather than as an authority if real harm is to be prevented.

---

[1] See below, pp. 420 sqq.

[2] 10 December 1924, Clunet (1925), 488 (translation by Jaffe, op. cit., p. 182). Similarly German and Austrian Courts: see Melchior, *Grundlagen des deutschen internationalen Privatrechts* (1932), p. 85; Freund, Clunet (1924), 5; (1925), 331. In the *Petrogradsky* case (above, p. 409, n. 7) Chief Justice Cardozo said that in the absence of recognition the decrees of the Soviet Republic were 'exhibitions of power. They are not pronouncements of authority.' The wisdom of this statement may be doubtful. M. Wolff, *Internationales Privatrecht* (1933), p. 54, distinguishes between legislation and law and says that in the absence of recognition Soviet decrees have the force of law, though they are not 'legislation', since there may exist 'law' that is not enacted by a State. In the result we respectfully agree, but we prefer to derive it from a less academic argument and to avoid being led into the depths of jurisprudence and, in particular, of Kelsen's theories.

[3] *ubi supra.*

It is incontrovertible that certain fundamental decisions made by a nation in regard to its foreign policy may and, indeed, should be given by the courts the force of public policy. Peace,[1] neutrality,[2] war[3] are the chief examples of facts which in the eyes of the law are matters of public policy, although the English Court's traditional reluctance in urging 'that "unruly horse" from its measured gait'[4] has even in these connections been pronounced.[5] Thus it was clearly right when in the famous case of *The Appam*[6] the Supreme Court of the United States felt it to be its primary duty to uphold the United States' policy of neutrality: a British ship seized by the Germans in 1916 was conducted by a prize crew into Baltimore harbour to be laid up there until the end of the war; the British owners' claim for possession succeeded on the ground that to allow the vessel to remain in Baltimore in charge of a prize crew would have been irreconcilable with American neutrality.

But there is a far cry between this case and the recent decision in *United States* v. *Pink*.[7] On 19 November 1933 the United States recognized the Union of Soviet Socialist Republics as the *de jure* Government of Russia, and on the same day the President accepted from M. Litvinov an assignment of all amounts 'admitted to be due or that may be found to be due (to the Russian Government) as the successor of prior Governments of

---

[1] Thus it is established that it is illegal for British subjects to make contracts contemplating action hostile to a friendly State: *De Wütz* v. *Hendricks* (1824), 2 Bing. 316; Anson, *Law of Contracts* (18th ed., 1937), p. 225. And see *Foster* v. *Driscoll*, [1929] 1 K. B. 470

[2] *The Appam*, 243 U. S. 124 (1917).

[3] Cf. the common law rules relating to trading with the enemy, and the general position of an enemy. See also *Lorentzen* v. *Lydden and Co. Ltd.*, [1942] 2 K. B. 202. The approval of the decision on the ground of public policy expressed 5 *Mod. L.R.* (1942) 262, cannot be maintained. There was no necessity for recognizing the title of the curator, since the Custodian of Enemy Property could have instituted the proceedings. Public policy did not demand that effect should be given to the powers of the Norwegian curator so that proceedings could be instituted by the curator rather than the Custodian.

[4] Language of Simonds J., in *Re Caborne*, [1943] Ch. 224, 228.

[5] See *Janson's* and *Schiff's* case, above, p. 411, n. 1.

[6] 243 U. S. 124 (1917); but see *Re Grazebrook, Ex parte Chavasse* (1865), 4 De G. J. and Sm. 655: it is lawful for a neutral trader to transport munitions of war to a belligerent country. And see *The Helen* (1865) L. R. 1 A. and E.1.

[7] 315 U. S. 203 (1942), discussed by Borchard and Jessup, ibidem, pp. 275, 282, and W. Herzfeld, *Nationalization of Foreign Corporations—Effect upon Local Assets* (Contemporary Law Pamphlets, Series 9, No. 1, New York, 1943), particularly pp. 20 sqq.

Russia or otherwise from American nationals including corporations, companies, partnerships or associations . . .'. This
assignment was 'preparatory to a final settlement of the claims
and counterclaims between' the two countries. In the present
case the United States as assignee of the Russian Government
claimed from the Superintendent of Insurance of the State of
New York certain moneys which had belonged to the New York
branch of a Russian insurance company and which, after payment of all domestic creditors, remained in the defendant's
hands for distribution among foreign creditors of that company
which had been nationalized by the well known Soviet legislation. The Supreme Court held by a majority (Chief Justice
Stone and Mr. Justice Roberts dissenting) that the Russian
legislation in question claimed extraterritorial effect and should
be given extraterritorial effect in New York. The actual ratio
decidendi is probably to be found in the view that the Litvinov
assignment was not a treaty requiring the approval of the
Senate, but an 'international compact' which is within the
exclusive competency of the President and yet has the force of a
'law of the land', and that it was not repugnant to the due
process and just compensation clause of the Fifth Amendment
of the Constitution.[1] But although this restrictive interpretation
of the decision is not impossible, it obviously has a much wider
impact of considerable interest for English lawyers. The Court
accepted the premiss that 'the United States acquired under
the Litvinov assignment only such rights as Russia had'.[2] It
would seem to follow that the United States could succeed only
if it were held that Russian legislation purporting to confiscate
the American assets of Russian Companies effectively vested
them in the State of Russia. Prior to the recognition of the Soviet
Government in 1933 American Courts had steadfastly refused to
give such effect to Soviet legislation of a confiscatory nature,[3]
but *United States* v. *Pink* must be understood as involving a
reversal of that rule as from the date of recognition. Notwithstanding the length of the opinion delivered by Mr. Justice
Douglas its reasoning on this point is somewhat obscure, but it can
probably be summarized as follows: The President is the sole
organ of the Federal Government in the field of international

---

[1] See 58 *L.Q.R.* (1942), 451.    [2] At p. 217, per Mr. Justice Douglas.
[3] At p. 226, per Mr. Justice Douglas.

relations. He has the sole power to determine the policy which is to govern the question of recognition. The Litvinov assignment was 'part and parcel of the new policy of recognition'. Therefore the powers of the President in the conduct of foreign relations included the power to determine the public policy of the United States with respect to the Russian nationalization decrees. 'Unless such a power exists, the power of recognition might be thwarted or seriously diluted.' The opinion delivered by Mr. Justice Frankfurter is in similar vein, but still more outspoken.[1]

This part of the decision is of very great importance to English law. The legal position of the King in foreign affairs is not very different from that of the President of the United States. Suppose the Crown, without the consent of Parliament, enters into a treaty with Russia similar to the Litvinov assignment. Would this compel the English courts to recognize the confiscation of property situate in England by the Soviet Government, notwithstanding the fact that English Courts have always[2] refused to allow a foreign State to confiscate English property? The seriousness of this question is emphasized when it is remembered that the fact of the treaty being part and parcel of a new policy of recognition cannot be of decisive significance. Neither logically nor in fact is there any difference between the new grant of recognition and the continuation of an existing recognition or, in other words, the omission to withdraw recognition. On this basis it is not difficult to visualize other far-reaching consequences. It is a rule of English law, in the last resort derived from public policy, that no foreign State can

---

[1] It is in parts so destructive as to make it very difficult to know how Mr. Justice Frankfurter would deal with many problems that may arise. Thus he said that 'to use such concepts as "situs", "jurisdiction", and "comity" for the solution of controversies international in nature, even though they are presented to the courts in the form of a private litigation, is to invoke a narrow and inadmissible frame of reference' (p. 324). Or, 'when courts deal with such essentially political phenomena as the taking over of Russian businesses by the Russian Government by resorting to the forms and phrases of conventional corporation law, they inevitably fall into a dialectic quagmire'.

[2] Dicey (–Keith), *Conflict of Laws* (5th ed.), p. 610, n. k, and *In re Russian Bank for Foreign Trade*, [1933] Ch. 745, 767; *Bohm* v. *Czerny*, The Times Newspaper, 26 July 1940. The only exception is *Lorentzen* v. *Lydden and Co. Ltd.*, [1942] 2 K. B. 202, which cannot be regarded as conclusive. See Mann, 5 *Mod. L.R.* (1942), 262.

recover taxes by proceedings in the English Courts.[1] Assume one of the Allied Governments at present in London assigns claims for taxes which it has assessed upon its nationals resident in England, to the Crown, not by a private law transaction, but as an ingredient of some arrangement arising out of foreign relations. Could the Crown recover in the courts? Would the courts uphold the argument that the transaction, having been carried out by prerogative power in the course of conducting foreign policy, has the effect of overriding established rules of common law?

It is submitted with some confidence that such results, though in line with the spirit of *United States* v. *Pink*, would be irreconcilable with the tradition of English legal thought. They would involve a return to Baconian ideas[2] and the obsolete doctrine of *Bates'* case[3] where, before the Revolution, it was held that by virtue of its prerogative power over foreign relations and trade the Crown could regulate them by closing ports and otherwise and could, therefore, *a fortiori*, impose duties on imports. The King, by the exercise of his prerogative powers, cannot change the law. As a maxim of public policy the supremacy of the law therefore has greater force than the consummation of the prerogative power over foreign affairs. Consonance 'with the sturdy conduct of our foreign relations'[4] is not a head of public policy disabling the Court to apply the law. The desire to act in unison with, and to avoid thwarting the policy of, the King is not an overriding principle of public policy in the narrower sense of the word.

Yet, as the preceding survey confirms, that desire is at the bottom of the prevailing tendencies. It is a factor of public policy in that wider sense in which 'every rule of law, either

---

[1] *Municipal Council of Sydney* v. *Bull*, [1909] 1 K. B. 7; *In re Visser, Queen of Holland* v. *Drukker*, [1928] Ch. 877.

[2] See Bacon's Essay '*Of Judicature*': . . . 'Therefore it is a happy thing in a State when . . . judges do often consult with the King and State . . . when there is some consideration of state intervenient in matters of law; for many times the things deduced to judgment may be 'meum' and 'tuum', when the reason and consequence thereof may trench to point of estate: I call matter of estate not only the parts of Sovereignty but whatsoever introduceth any great alteration or dangerous precedent; or concerneth manifestly any great portion of people.'

[3] (1606–10), 2 St. Tr. 371.

[4] *United States* v. *Pink*, 315 U. S. 203 (1942), at p. 238, per Mr. Justice Frankfurter.

common law or equity which has been laid down by the courts in that course of judicial legislation which has evolved the law of this country, has been based on consideration of public interest or policy'.[1] Foreign policy has thus become a source of law-making.

But, although it is neither possible nor expedient to suggest a complete reversal of past developments, there are, as has been shown, many gaps discernible which have to be filled, and many new situations may arise for which guidance will be required. There therefore remains the problem whether the basic rule is to be extended or restricted.

The answer would perhaps be less difficult if the rational explanation of the relatively recent developments which have been described were not so vague. The only real attempt at justification has been made by the Supreme Court of the United States. The Court said[2] that the reason for the Judiciary's deference to the Executive in foreign affairs is that 'it makes better international relations, conforms to diplomatic usage in other matters, accords the Executive Department the respect due to it and tends to promote harmony of action and uniformity of decision'.[3] This is periphrasis rather than reasoning, and is on the same level as an equally sweeping statement which has likewise been relied upon,[4] viz. that divergence of decision would 'imperil the amicable relations between Governments and vex the peace of nations'.[5] Such maxims are treacherous ground which will deter those who are conscious of the vital issues involved. In the first place they lead to uncertainty of decision and, if certainty is to remain a paramount object, reticence will be indicated. Secondly, a great and inviolable constitutional principle makes for restraint: the Executive can make policy, but cannot make law; the Judiciary can make

---

[1] *Fender* v. *Mildmay*, [1938] A. C. 38 per Lord Wright.

[2] *Ex parte Muir*, 254 U. S. 522, 533 (1921). The case concerns the conclusiveness of information supplied by the Executive, but the dictum quoted in the text is applicable to all aspects of the 'political question'.

[3] The force of the first ground may be doubtful; the second is difficult to understand; of the third Lord Sumner said that it 'hardly constitutes the whole legal basis' (*Duff Development Co. Ltd.* v. *Government of Kelantan*, [1924] A. C. 797, 827); the fourth is a *petitio principii*.

[4] *United States* v. *Pink*, op. cit., at p. 233, per Mr. Justice Douglas.

[5] *Oetjen* v. *Central Leather Co.*, 246 U. S. 297 (1917), at p. 304. On the dictum quoted in the text see below, p. 452.

law, but cannot make policy. Thirdly, it should be realized that it is undesirable to make the Judiciary 'a mere weathercock of foreign policy'[1] and that the judicial spirit of decision is an asset which is not only to be preserved and strengthened but also should and can be expanded so as to pervade international relations; even national courts should as far as possible resist the tendency of replacing it by the idea of political expediency. Fourthly, the desire of disembarrassing the Executive is apt to misfire and to result in real embarrassment; such effects have been mentioned in connection with cases where an unwilling Executive is compelled by the courts to commit itself; or if an unrecognized government is prevented from suing its agent to recover funds which are alleged to have been misappropriated by him, and the fraudulent agent is thereby enabled to keep the fruits of his crime,[2] the result is so extreme that the Executive may well feel embarrassed by the Court's clumsy attempt of conforming with its policy.[3]

In these circumstances no hard-and-fast rule can be laid down. The matter is one of judicial attitude of mind, of outlook, and mode of thinking. But, it is suggested, guidance may be found in the manner in which the Judiciary has approached the problem of public policy in the sphere of private law, i.e. a problem which has always been treated as one of political expediency.[4] Deference to the foreign policy of the Executive should be a rule of judicial decision 'only in clear cases in which the harm to the public is substantially incontestable and does not depend upon the idiosyncratic inferences of a few judicial minds'[5]; it should rest 'on tangible grounds, not on mere generalizations.'[6] If the courts have regard to realities as

---

[1] Jaffe, op. cit., p. 149.

[2] These were the facts in *Russian Republic* v. *Cibrario* (1923) 235 N. Y. 255; Annual Digest, 1923–4, No. 17.

[3] Attention should be drawn to the words of Philip Marshall Brown who, referring to 'l'obsession', 'le désir de ne pas créer d'embarras au pouvoir exécutif', has emphasized that 'l'administration de la justice, en ces circonstances, a été subordonnée à des considérations politiques et l'indépendance judiciaire s'en est trouvée sérieusement compromise.... Cette attitude de déférence de la part des autorités à l'égard du département politique de l'Etat a abouti à des anomalies surprenantes et à des dénis de justice. See *Annuaire de droit international* (1934), 302 sqq., 305, 306.

[4] See Parke B. in *Egerton* v. *Brownlow* (1853), 4 H.L.C.1. 123.

[5] *Fender* v. *Mildmay*, [1938] A. C. 1, 12, per Lord Atkin.

[6] Ibidem, at p. 42, per Lord Wright.

proved by experience, history and facts rather than to imaginary possibilities, if they act upon evidence rather than 'horrid suspicions to which high-minded men are sometimes prone'[1], they should find it less perplexing, though by no means easy, to delimit the boundaries within which the policy of the Executive should be allowed to influence the law. Mere possibility of embarrassment should not be sufficient. It is the empirically proved likelihood of actual harm to the common weal that should be required to impose upon the Court the duty of deciding in conformity with the policy of the Executive.[2]

[1] Ibidem, at p. 16, per Lord Atkin. The alleged danger of a *casus belli* which has sometimes been referred to (*The Arantzazu Mendi*, [1939] A. C. 256, 265, per Lord Atkin; *Luther* v. *Sagor and Co.*, [1921] 3 K. B. 532, 559, per Scrutton L.J.; Stephen, *History of the Criminal Law of England*, ii.36 is a good example and belongs to that group of objections which Alderson B. has described as ridiculous: *Egerton* v. *Brownlow* (1853) 4 H. L. C. 1, and see *Fender* v. *Mildmay*, [1938] A. C. 1, 16, per Lord Atkin.

[2] The forceful dissenting opinion of Chief Justice Stone in *United States* v. *Pink*, ubi supra, is an outstanding illustration of the principle advanced in the text. He said, *inter alia*: 'In no case in which there was occasion to decide the question (of enforcing confiscatory legislation) has recognition been thought to have subordinated the law of the forum, with respect to property situated within its territorial jurisdiction, to that of the recognized State. One could as well argue that by the Soviet Government's recognition of our own Government which accompanied the transactions now under consideration, it has undertaken to apply in Russia the New York law applicable to Russian property in New York. . . . It is not for this Court to adopt policy, the making of which has been by the Constitution committed to other branches of the government. It is not its function to suppy a policy where none has been declared or defined and none can be inferred.'

# XII

# THE SACROSANCTITY OF THE FOREIGN ACT OF STATE*

## I

### THE PROBLEM

THE expression 'act of State' usually denotes 'an executive or administrative exercise of sovereign power by an independent State or potentate, or by its or his duly authorized agents or officers'.[1] The expression, however, is not a term of art, and it obviously may, and is in fact often intended to, include legislative and judicial acts such as a statute, decree or order, or a judgment of a superior court.[2] It is in this extended sense that the expression will be employed in the following observations.

If such acts of State as emanate from a foreign country come to be considered in the courts of this country, the question often arises whether and to what extent the court is permitted, and consequently bound, to inquire into their validity, legality or propriety. This is a problem of considerable importance: A Joint Resolution of the Congress of the United States, a statute of the State of New York or a decree of the President of the United States is alleged to be invalid under the American Constitution; property confiscated in a foreign country is claimed by the original owner who contends that according to the law of that foreign country the confiscation is invalid or ought not to have been ordered; the grant or revocation of a concession or naturalization by a Minister or other agent of a foreign State is said to have been *ultra vires* or to be based on

---

* From 59 *L.Q.R.* (1943), 42, 155.

[1] Halsbury (–Hailsham) xxvi.246.

[2] Halsbury (–Hailsham), op. cit., n. (*a*) with further references, and see Evidence Act, 1851, section 7: 'Proclamations, treaties, and acts of state'. See, however, Wade, *B.Y.I.L.* (1934), 103, who after a full discussion of the definition of the term restricts it to 'an act of the executive as a matter of policy performed in its relations with another State, including the relations with the subjects of that State, unless they are temporarily within the allegiance of the Crown'.

facts which, in truth, did not exist; the appointment of a guardian of a lunatic by a foreign court is said to be void on the ground that the ward was not in fact a lunatic. Has the court power to listen to such pleas? There are other connections in which the court may be called upon to pass judgment on a foreign act of State. Thus the judge may be asked to grant an injunction excluding its effects in this country or even abroad, or to treat it as a tort and to order a defendant concerned in it to pay damages, or to consider it as irreconcilable with English public policy and therefore to refuse recognition of it.

It is perhaps convenient at the outset to submit that the solution of these problems is not to be found in any such principles of British constitutional law or public international law nor in any such wide maxims of jurisprudence as have often been relied upon for the purpose (below Section II), but in established rules of private international law; that these rules determine the recognition of the foreign act of State (below Section III); that, while foreign judgments are on a special and distinct footing, other foreign acts of State may be questioned here if and to such extent as they are open to judicial review in the country by the law of which they are governed (below Section IV); that in a proper case an English Court may interfere with them by an injunction or treat them as tortious acts or invoke English public policy against them (below Section V).

The views which have thus been summarized and will require a good deal of elaboration, are, however, at variance with a widely accepted doctrine which asserts that foreign acts of State are entitled to some kind of sacrosanctity or immunity. It will be apparent to every international lawyer that this doctrine, if it exists, is bound to have far-reaching consequences. In fact its very generality and vagueness involves obvious dangers. What is required is the specialization of the principle, its adaptation to and harmonization with established rules of international law. This is the task to which the following observations are devoted. It may be added, with the greatest respect, that they are conceived in the spirit of Lord Esher, who could not but 'detest the attempt to fetter the law by maxims. They are almost invariably misleading; they are for the most part so large and general in their language that they always include something which is not really intended to be included in them'.[1] And as Lord Wright recently remarked,[2] 'these general formulae are found in experience often to distract the court's mind from the actual exigencies of the case, and to induce the court to quote them as offering a ready-made solution. It is not safe to act upon them, however, unless, and to the extent that, they received definition and limitation from judicial determination.'

## II

### THE BACKGROUND OF THE DOCTRINE OF SACROSANCTITY

The rational basis of the doctrine of sacrosanctity of a foreign act of State is to be found in a variety of sources some of which require investigation before a detailed discussion of the numerous implications of the suggested rule is attempted.

(1) It is impossible to speak of an act of State unless the authority performing it enjoys the status of a sovereign Government. An act of State can only be done by or on behalf of a Government which is recognized either *de facto* or *de jure*; the acts of usurpers are in general legally non-existent.[3] It is, however, well established that recognition has retroactive effect.[4] Consequently, what prior to recognition were the legally irrelevant acts of a usurper are as from the recognition acts of State. To that extent it is permissible to say that they are validated. It is, however, obvious that what is meant is validity in the sense of international law: the acts have become acts of State. This is the type of validity to which Lord Cave referred when he said in *Russian Commercial and Industrial Bank v. Comptoir d'Escompte de Mulhouse*[5] that, the Soviet Government having

---

[1] *Yarmouth v. France* (1887) 19 Q. B. D. 647, 653.

[2] *Lissenden v. Bosch Ltd.*, [1940] A. C. 412, 435.

[3] *Luther v. Sagor & Co.*, [1921] 1 K. B. 456, decision of Roche J. approved of on this point by the Court of Appeal: [1921] 3 K. B. 532.

[4] The doctrine is founded on *Williams v. Bruffy*, 96 U. S. 176 (1877) and has been reaffirmed in numerous American and English cases which will be referred to below.

[5] [1925] A. C. 112, 123, approving *Luther v. Sagor & Co.*, [1921] 3 K. B. 532.

been recognized by Great Britain, its decrees must be treated by the courts of this country as binding so far as the jurisdiction of the Russian Government extends. Such statements of which there are many to be found in the books do not mean that the acts are necessarily valid within the meaning of the foreign municipal law or of the public policy rules of the forum. If validity in the latter sense was meant, it would follow that the acts of a subsequently recognized Government were protected to a higher degree than those of a Government which was recognized at all material times. The distinction between validity in the international sense and validity in the sense of municipal law was in fact clearly recognized by a Divisional Court in *Re Amand (No. 1)*[1] where the constitutional validity of a Dutch decree issued by Queen Wilhelmina's Government in London was in question. Relying on certain *dicta* which seem to imply the sacrosanctity of the foreign act of State, counsel for the Dutch Government contended that the mere fact of Queen Wilhelmina's Government being recognized as the lawful Government of Holland precluded the Court from investigating the constitutional validity of the decree. The Court, however, held that 'that Government did not thereby (i.e. by recognition) acquire any powers over Netherlands subjects not otherwise possessed by it according to Netherlands law. . . . An Act of Parliament of the United Kingdom proves itself and its validity cannot be challenged. This is not so with a legislative act of a foreign power. Evidence is required to prove what is a question of fact, namely, the foreign law.' Yet the failure to draw that distinction and to investigate the context and real meaning of the *dicta* asserting the sacrosanctity of the foreign act of State led the Supreme Court of New York to deduce from the mere fact of recognition that a decree of Queen Wilhelmina's Government had to be treated as conclusively valid under Dutch law,[2] and also resulted in the acceptance of a similar doctrine by another Divisional Court in *Re Amand (No. 2)*.[3]

---

[1] [1941] 2 K. B. 239, at pp. 252, 253 (Lord Caldecote L.C.J., Humphreys and Singleton JJ.).

[2] *Anderson v. N. V. Transandine Handelmaatschappij* (1941) 28 N. Y. Supp. (2d) 547.

[3] [1942] 1 K. B. 445.

(2) The doctrine of act of State is a well-known ingredient of British constitutional law.

It has two aspects, one of which is clearly referred to by Lord Sumner when he said in *Johnstone* v. *Pedlar*[1] that 'municipal courts do not take it upon themselves to review the dealings of State with State or Sovereign with Sovereign. They do not control the acts of a foreign State done within its own territory, in the exercise of sovereign power, so as to criticize their legality or to require their justification.' It is more particularly expressed in the rule that 'the transactions of independent States with each other are governed by other laws than those which municipal courts administer; such courts have neither the means of deciding what is right, nor the power of enforcing decisions which they make. Hence the courts of this country ... have no jurisdiction to adjudge upon acts committed by one sovereign State towards another in the exercise of its sovereign power, such as the making and performance of treaties, the seizure or annexation of lands or goods in right of conquest, or the declaration of war or of blockade, or upon any rights or liabilities supposed to be acquired in consequence of such acts.'[2] The formulation of this statement makes it apparent that its authors desire it to be of a general character, and they in fact expressly put a foreign act of State on the same level as a British one.[3] Yet there is not a single case to be found in the books where that principle of British constitutional law has been extended to foreign acts of State; all the relevant cases deal with acts of State of the British Crown,[4] and there is in

---

[1] [1921] 2 A. C. 262, 290.

[2] Halsbury (–Hailsham), op. cit., pp. 248, 249. For recent applications of the principle see *Hoani Te Heuheu Tukino* v. *Aotea District Maori Land Board*, [1941] A. C. 308 and *Secretary of State for India* v. *Sardar Rustam Khan*, [1941] A. C. 356.

[3] See Halsbury (-Hailsham) op. cit., p. 248 ('Effects of Acts of State. In General'); p. 253 ('Of Foreign Governments').

[4] *Blad's Case* (1673) 3 Swan. 603 is not really an exception. Lord Nottingham granted an injunction staying an action at law, because in the circumstances he thought it 'monstrous and absurd' to send the case to trial at law 'where either the court must pretend to judge of the validity of the (Danish) King's letter patent in Denmark or of the exposition and meaning of the articles of peace' and where a common jury would have to try 'whether the English have a right to trade in Iceland'. The decision is merely an example of the use formerly made by the Lord Chancellor of his powers of injunction, and of the very understandable reluctance of early lawyers to have important questions of international and foreign law tried by juries. Nor is *Dobree* v. *Napier* (1836), 2 Bing. N. C. 781 an exception. The de-

fact no reason why the restrictions which, inspired by some idea of the separation of powers, the British Courts have imposed upon themselves, should necessarily apply to foreign acts of State. On the Continent it has sometimes been asserted that the municipal principle of the separation of powers also pervades such cases as involve a conflict of laws, but this idea was strikingly disposed of by the Belgian Cour de Cassation.[1] The plaintiff, a painter, had exhibited one of his pictures at the Dutch section of the International Exhibition in Brussels in 1897. At the request of the defendant, the representative of the Dutch Government, the picture was subsequently withdrawn without the plaintiff's consent. In an ensuing action for damages the defendant relied, *inter alia*, on the fact that the act the subject-matter of the proceedings had emanated from an independent sovereign Government. The Court adopted the argument of the Attorney-General:

Le pouvoir judiciare est compétent pour apprécier les causes préjudiciables d'un acte qui est le fait d'une autorité étrangère destituée de tout pouvoir en Belgique et, par conséquent, non assujettie aux principes de notre droit public, notamment pas à celui de la séparation des pouvoirs. Les tribunaux ont tout compétence à l'effet d'apprécier les conséquences d'un acte administratif par rapport aux intérêts civils de la partie lésée.

The other limb of the 'act of State' doctrine is represented by the rule[2] that an agent of the British Crown cannot resist an action for damages suffered by a British subject or a resident friendly alien through an official act on the ground that the act was an act of State, the reason being that such injured person cannot obtain redress through diplomatic channels while this 'privilege' is open to foreigners.[3] Dicey (–Keith) suggests[4] that 'as regards the act of State authorized by foreign Governments

---

cision lays down that a foreign judgment *in rem* condemning a vessel and vesting it in the Queen of Portugal is binding here and that therefore the defendant, acting as the Queen's agent, cannot be made liable for her act; see the following observations, sub-paragraph (3).

[1] 23 May 1898, Clunet (1899), 618.

[2] Halsbury (–Hailsham), op. cit., pp. 250, 251.

[3] This reasoning is not very convincing. On the unsatisfactory character of a rule which, involving a denial of jurisdiction, refers the injured party to diplomatic representations, see Lord Maugham in *The Cristina*, [1938] A. C. 485, 515.

[4] pp. 215, 216; see also Pitt Cobbett's *Cases on International Law* (5th ed.), i. 80, 81.

the courts in England would doubtless apply the same principle', and instances[1] the topical case of a German soldier who, in the course of an invasion, destroys property in England; if after the war he comes to England and is sued for damages, the court is said to be without jurisdiction. The same would no doubt apply to a German airman raiding this country whom Hallett J. recently had no hesitation in describing as a trespasser.[2] It is, however, believed that the defence of 'act of State' is of too special a character to contain anything germane to the problem and the facts under discussion and is incapable of the extension contended for. The result suggested by Dicey (–Keith) is probably correct, but ought to be based on the lawfulness of an act committed in the course of legitimate warfare[3] or on the ground to be discussed presently.

(3) The principle according to which no sovereign State is subject to the jurisdiction of the courts of another State has become a deeply rooted and universally accepted maxim of international law. Yet it has never been possible to reach unanimity on its explanation, and although the principle of the sovereignty, independence or equality of States or similar postulates have often been invoked,[4] no final answer has been given to the question which, from a legal point of view, many regard as fundamental: Is the privilege attached to the person of the defendant potentate, State, minister, and so forth or to the nature of the act which gives rise to the proceedings? In other words, does the privilege exist *ratione personae* or *ratione materiae*?

It is the established practice of the courts in Italy, Belgium, and Egypt and the tendency of some decisions in other coun-

---

[1] p. 218, Illustration 11. The practice of the American Courts as evidenced by *McLeod's Case*, 25 Wend. 483 (1841) and such later cases as *Horn* v. *Mitchell*, 232 Fed. 819 (1916) (Circuit Court of Appeals, 1st) is against Dicey's view. As to diplomatic opinion on the problems of *McLeod's Case* see Oppenheim (–Lauterpacht) i.663.

[2] *Cushing* v. *Walker & Son*, [1941] 2 All E. R. 693, 700.

[3] Oppenheim (–Lauterpacht) (5th ed.) ii.268 sqq.

[4] Whether there is any real distinction between these formulae may perhaps be doubted. The principle of mutual independence is most frequently resorted to: see, e.g. *The Parlement Belge* (1880) 5 P. D. 197, 241, per Brett L.J.; French Cour de Cassation, 22 January 1849, S. 1849.1.81; 10 January 1891, Clunet (1891), 137; 23 January 1933, Clunet (1934), 96. Oppenheim (–Lauterpacht) i.221 sqq. relies on the principle of equality. For other explanations see Lord Wright in *The Cristina*, [1938] A. C. 485, 502.

tries[1] to hold that immunity is granted to the defendant in respect of acts of sovereignty to the exclusion of acts done *jure gestionis*. On this basis it has been possible for the Belgian Professor Charles De Visscher[2] to propound the theory that it is the official act which is entitled to immunity and that therefore, such an act is both necessary and sufficient to deprive the courts of a country of jurisdiction over proceedings which involve inquiry into it. The sacrosanctity of foreign acts of State is inherent in this theory and it also produces this consequence, among others,[3] that even after the termination of his status an ambassador or other official of a foreign State cannot be made liable for acts of State committed in the exercise of his functions.[4]

There cannot be any doubt that in this country, as in most others, the opposite view prevails in practice and theory, and that, accordingly, it is the personal position of the defendant, not the nature of the act the subject-matter of the proceedings, that is of decisive importance.[5] Nevertheless, even in English

---

[1] The latest and most comprehensive collection of material is probably supplied by Van Praag, *Revue de droit international et de législation comparée* (1934), 652; (1935), 100; see also Brookfield, 20 *J. Comparative Legislation* (1938), 1; Fox, *A.J.I.L.* (1941), 632.

[2] *Revue de droit international et de législation comparée* (1922), 300. De Visscher is one of the few continental writers who discusses the *dicta* in the English and American cases based on *Underhill* v. *Hernandez*, 168 U. S. 250 (1897), and for the reason mentioned in the text he approves them.

[3] Thus, according to de Visscher, the question of express or implied submission cannot arise; jurisdiction exists over such immovables as are not used as extra-territorial property, while on the other hand in respect of an official act a State cannot submit to jurisdiction either by instituting proceedings (which would explain the impossibility of applying to the courts of another country for the purpose of enforcing revenue or penal laws) or by defending proceedings without claiming immunity. In this connection de Visscher refers to the interesting decision of the Cour de Bordeaux, 4 December 1917, *Revue internationale de droit maritime*, xxxi.45: a vessel which had been requisitioned by the Greek Government was purchased and armed by the Italian Government. The Greek Government, finding it in a French port, claims possession. The Court declines jurisdiction on this among other grounds that there was a conflict between Governments claiming rights of sovereignty and it was therefore 'relevant du droit international public'. The Court was 'incompétent ratione materiae'.

[4] On this point see below, p. 430, n. 1.

[5] This idea underlies all the authorities on the subject and it may suffice to refer to the statement in Dicey (–Keith), p. 194. The privilege can be waived; see Dicey (–Keith) p. 199, or Oppenheim (–Lauterpacht) i.223, provided the submission is voluntary and unmistakable, or, as the French Cour de Cassation said (Cass. Req., 23 January 1933, Clunet (1933), 96) 'certaine et régulière'; it is, however, noteworthy that there is apparently no English case which decides whether waiver is

law there is perhaps a certain inclination in some cases to attribute immunity to the nature of the act. It is discernible in the speeches of the three Law Lords who have confessed to being uncertain whether the exemption from jurisdiction of ships owned or controlled by a foreign Sovereign should not be confined to such ships as are destined to public uses as opposed to mere trading purposes.[1] And it is perhaps indicated in the important decision of the House of Lords in *Duke of Brunswick* v. *King of Hanover*.[2] The appellant, the formerly reigning Duke of Brunswick who, by an instrument executed in 1833 by King William IV and confirmed by the German Diet, had been put under guardianship, claimed against the respondent, the reigning King of Hanover who was his then guardian and, being a British peer, happened to be in England, that the instrument of 1833 be declared null and void and that the respondent be accountable to him. The appellant failed. The House of Lords expressly disclaimed any intention of dealing with the question of whether the respondent was entitled to personal immunity or whether the fact of his presence in England and of his being a British peer deprived him of the privilege. The House preferred to put its decision on the ground that, in the words of Lord Cottenham L.C.,[3] a foreign Sovereign 'cannot be made responsible here for an act done in his sovereign character in his own country; whether it be an act right or wrong, whether according to the constitution of that country or not, the courts of this country cannot sit in judgment upon an act of a Sovereign, effected by virtue of his sovereign authority abroad'. And again later: 'It is true the bill states that the instrument was contrary to the laws of Hanover and Brunswick, but notwithstanding that it is so stated, still if it is a sovereign act, then whether it be according to law or not

---

permissible where the proceedings involve inquiry into an act of sovereignty. Real property which is not in itself in a privileged position (e.g. a legation building) is also entitled to immunity according to Sir Cecil Hurst, *Recueil* (1926 ii), 144, 180 sqq.; Foster, *Recueil* 65 (1938), p. 87, while Oppenheim (–Lauterpacht), p. 222, n. 4, and Brookfield, op. cit. p. 4, take the opposite view. As to property generally and ships in particular, see *The Cristina*, [1938] A. C. 485, commented upon 2 *Mod. L. R.* (1938), 57.

[1] Lords Thankerton, Macmillan and Maugham in *The Cristina*, [1938] A. C. 485, at pp. 496, 498, 519. Lord Atkin did not commit himself, but Lord Wright consented to the traditional practice granting immunity.

[2] (1848) 2 H. L. C. 1.      [3] pp. 17, 21, 22.

according to law, we cannot inquire into it. . . . No court in this country can entertain questions to bring Sovereigns to account for their acts done in their sovereign capacity abroad.' Lords Lyndhurst, Brougham, and Campbell expressed themselves in a similar vein, the latter adding that the Lord Chancellor 'would not grant an injunction against the French Republic marching an army across the Rhine or the Alps'.[1] These quotations will be sufficient to make the reader doubt whether the House of Lords in fact succeeded in disregarding the personal status of the respondent. If the question of the amenability of a foreign Sovereign was to be left open, Lord Cottenham should not have spoken of a foreign Sovereign being made 'responsible' or brought 'to account', nor should Lord Campbell have referred to an injunction 'against the French Republic'. It is therefore not quite clear whether the House intended to establish an immunity of the foreign act of State, so that the result would have been the same if the respondent had not been a foreign Sovereign, but a solicitor appointed by him as guardian and transitorily resident here. Yet it will appear later that Lord Cottenham's formulations have exercised great influence upon the emergence of a limited doctrine of immunity *ratione materiae*.

It originated from a quite different set of problems. It is generally held that the exemption of a sovereign from jurisdiction ceases upon the termination of his sovereign status[2]; similarly the immunity of an ambassador or other diplomatic officer ends after the presentation of his letters of recall and the expiration of such further period as is reasonably necessary for the winding up of his official business and his private affairs.[3]

---

[1] p. 27.

[2] At least in so far as acts done in a private capacity are concerned: see *Munden* v. *Duke of Brunswick* (1847) 10 Q. B. 656, where the Court said (p. 662) that the annuity deed sued upon was not 'an act of State'. It is, however, not clear whether the result would have been different if it had been an act of State. See Dicey (–Keith), p. 194, n. (*i*).

[3] *Magdalena Steamship Co.* v. *Martin* (1859) E. & E. 94; *Musurus Bey* v. *Gadban*, [1894] 1 Q.B. 533; see Sir Cecil Hurst, *Recueil* (1926 ii), 144, 237 sqq. Cf. Trib. Civ. Seine, 11 February 1892, Clunet (1892), 429; Trib. Correctionnel de la Seine, 18 February 1899, Clunet (1899), 369; Van Praag, *Revue de droit international et de législation comparée* (1923), pp. 436, 453, n. 54, mentions an isolated Dutch decision dated 14 February 1918, according to which immunity of a diplomat continues even after the termination of his functions.

Upon the loss of his status a sovereign or a diplomat thus becomes amenable to jurisdiction not only in respect of subsequent transactions, but also in respect of private or commercial affairs, done during the term of his office. It is, however, said that public or State acts done by the defendant in the performance of his official functions are to be allowed a separate and distinct immunity which continues after the termination of his status and exempts him from liability for such acts.[1] This rule, which is probably derived from the maxim 'ne impediatur officium' and which constitutes a combination of immunity *ratione personae* and *ratione materiae*, provides the background of the fundamental decision of the Supreme Court of the United States in *Underhill* v. *Hernandez*.[2] In the course of a revolution in Venezuela the plaintiff, an American citizen resident in Bolivar, was during a period of about eight weeks refused a passport and permission to leave the country under orders of the defendant, a general in command of the revolutionary forces occupying Bolivar. Later the defendant came to New York where the plaintiff served him with a writ claiming damages for detention, confinement to his own house, and similar matters. The action was dismissed. Chief Justice Fuller, noticeably influenced by the decision in *Duke of Brunswick* v. *King of Hanover*[3] which had already been referred to by the Circuit Court of Appeals, delivered the judgment of the Supreme Court and prefaced it by the often repeated *dictum*:

Every sovereign State is bound to respect the independence of every other sovereign State and the courts of one country will not sit in judgment on the acts of the Government of another done within its own territory. Redress of grievances by reason of such acts must be obtained through the means open to be availed of by sovereign powers as between themselves.

[1] De Visscher, op. cit., p. 312, n. 2; Strisower, *Recueil* (1923 i) 234; Report by Adatci and De Visscher, *Annuaire de l'Institut de Droit International* (1924), pp. 9, 10. See Cour de Paris, 26 February 1880, D. P. (1886) 1, 393: an action against the former diplomatic agent of Honduras for damages for fraud alleged to have been committed in connection with a prospectus which related to bonds issued by his Government, is based upon an 'acte gouvernemental' and the Court is therefore 'sans compétence pour connaître de cet acte et d'apprécier les conséquences dommageables qu'il avait entraînées'. Article 18 of the Draft convention on Diplomatic Privileges and Immunities prepared by the Harvard Law School's Research in International Law (Suppl. *A.J.I.L.* (1932), 19 sqq., 97 sqq.) proposes that 'a receiving State shall not impose liability on a person for an act done by him in the performance of his functions as a member of a mission or as a member of the administrative personnel'.

[2] 168 U. S. 250 (1897).     [3] (1848) 2 H. L. C. 1.

Later he continued:

> The immunity of individuals from suits brought in foreign tribunals for acts done within their own States, in the exercise of governmental authority, whether as civil officers or as military commanders, must necessarily extend to the agents of Governments ruling by paramount authority as a matter of fact. . . . The acts complained of were the acts of a military commander representing the authority of the revolutionary party as a Government which afterwards succeeded and was recognised by the United States. We think the Circuit Court of Appeals was justified in concluding that the acts of the defendant were acts of the Government of Venezuela and as such are not properly the subject of adjudication in the courts of another Government.

It thus became settled law in the United States that an immunity *ratione materiae* is attached to official acts in the sense that, even in the absence of personal immunity of the defendant, he cannot be personally made liable for and that consequently it is impossible to 'sit in judgment' in respect of them. It was the true and only purport of Chief Justice Fuller's *dictum*, from which many later judges and writers have taken their text, to state and paraphrase that American rule.

On this basis the further question arises whether, by a still wider extension of that principle, the immunity of official acts should not be recognized even in such cases as do not involve a claim against the responsible Government or its official. An affirmative answer would lead to the proposition that official acts of a foreign State, being immune exclusively *ratione materiae*, are exempt from the jurisdiction of a foreign court, independently of the status of the parties to the proceedings, that no foreign court can 'sit in judgment' over them even in cases in which they have to be considered only incidentally, that they cannot be questioned, that their legality, validity, and obligatory character has to be accepted, in short that they are sacrosanct. Such a rule would discard the element of personal immunity which is the idea governing English doctrine on the subject, and should therefore be accepted only with much diffidence. Yet, while it is not really supported by *Duke of Brunswick* v. *King of Hanover*[1] as explained above, it does seem to underlie the maxim propounded by Oppenheim (–Lauterpacht) that 'the courts of one State must not be allowed to question the validity or legality of the official acts of another

[1] (1848) 2 H. L. C. 1.

sovereign State or the officially avowed acts of its agents, at any rate in so far as those acts purport to take effect within the sphere of the latter State's own jurisdiction. If the need to question any such act should arise, it should be done through the diplomatic channel.'[1]

(4) There is a fourth line of thought which, it seems, has led writers to proclaim the sacrosanctity of foreign acts of State. Professor Dickinson,[2] speaking of the 'principe établi du droit anglo-américain d'après lequel une juridiction nationale ne peut, en général, statuer sur la validité d'un acte qu'un gouvernement étranger a accompli dans les limites de sa juridiction', does not base it upon any incapacity of the courts to deal judicially with the question of the validity of foreign official acts, but justifies it, 'parce que leur propre compétence comme tribunaux est nationale et non pas internationale et parce qu'ils n'auraient pas le pouvoir d'imposer le respect de leur décision, à supposer qu'ils aient la présomption d'en formuler une'. It has, however, never been suggested that the jurisdiction of a municipal court depends on its decision being respected and recognized throughout the world; in other words, the misapprehension lest a particular decision may not be recognized in a particular country does not prevent the court from exercising jurisdiction. Professor Dickinson's explanation would appear to be influenced by a line of thought which on more than one occasion has caused confusion and which has perhaps found expression in some of the *dicta* in *Duke of Brunswick* v. *King of Hanover*.[3] The obvious rule which precludes a Court from direct interference with a foreign administration, such as 'an injunction against the French Republic marching an army across the Rhine or the Alps', has sometimes been understood to mean that a foreign act of State, even if it has to be considered merely as an incidental matter, cannot be disregarded or treated as invalid. Probably the first expression of this argument is to be found in discussions which arose out of that *cause célèbre* of the

---

[1] 5th ed., (1937), p. 224; the learned editor does not expressly refer to the basic case of *Underhill* v. *Hernandez*, but relies on later decisions which, in turn, are founded on the *dicta* in that case.

[2] 40 *Recueil* (1932), pp. 309, 365. See also, Hyde, *International Law*, i.392. There is a remarkable dearth of discussion of so far-reaching a principle in legal literature and there are many textbooks which do not even mention it.

[3] (1848) 2 H. L. C. 1.

eighteen-seventies, the case of the Princess Bauffremont. The Princess was married to the Prince Bauffremont, a French subject, from whom she obtained a decree of judicial separation in 1874. In 1875 she was naturalized in the German Duchy of Saxe-Altenburg and thus acquired German nationality; shortly afterwards she married the Rumanian Prince Bibesco. According to French law the naturalization was invalid because of the absence of Prince Bauffremont's consent, and the French Courts held the second marriage invalid.[1] The Prince thereupon attempted to enforce a French decree relating to the custody of the children in the Belgian Courts. Adopting the reasoning of an opinion given by Professor Bluntschli[2] the Tribunal Civil at Charleroi felt itself bound to treat the naturalization in Germany and, consequently, the second marriage, as valid.[3] This view, which overlooked the distinction between the acquisition of a new and the loss of a former nationality, was severely criticized[4] and in fact rejected by the Court of Appeal at Brussels.[5] As Von Bar said,[6] 'the Courts are free to consider and pronounce an opinion upon the exercises of sovereign power by a foreign Government, if the consideration of those

[1] Cass. Civ., 18 March 1878, Clunet (1878), 505. The case seems to have attracted quite unusual interest both in the popular press and in legal literature of all continental countries. See, e.g. Labbé, Clunet (1875), 409; (1877), 5; Holtzendorff, Clunet (1876), 5; Stoeltzel, Clunet (1876), 269, with numerous further references.

[2] *Revue Pratique*, xli.305. It would appear that Bluntschli may claim to be the originator of the doctrine of the sacrosanctity of the foreign act of State.

[3] 3 January 1880, Clunet (1880), 215: 'La naturalisation conférée à la défenderesse par le duché de Saxe-Altenburg est un acte de l'autorité souveraine de ce pays; selon les principes du droit public, aucun pouvoir, en dehors de cette autorité, ne peut ni discuter la validité ni en modifier les effets; le duché de Saxe-Altenburg était seul compétent pour décider si la défenderesse réunissait les conditions pour que sa demande de naturalisation lui fût octroyée. Si cette autorité souveraine n'a pas exigé à cette fin le consentement de son mari, c'est qu'elle a jugé que cette formalité n'était pas nécessaire. Le pouvoir judiciaire, pas plus en France qu'ailleurs, n'a qualité pour contrôler cette procédure émanant de l'autorité d'un pays étranger: l'opinion contraire admettant la révision des actes d'un autre gouvernement consacrerait un système qui violerait tous les principes du droit des gens. Cet acte de naturalisation, qui est à l'abri de toute contestation, a changé la nationalité de la défenderesse et a, en conséquence, modifié son statut personnel qui, de français qu'il était, est devenu allemand.'

[4] See, e.g., Louis Renault, Clunet (1880), 178.

[5] 5 August 1880, Clunet (1880), 508.

[6] *Das Internationale Privat- und Strafrecht* (1889) ii.685; *Private International Law* (translation Gillespie), p. 1121 (1892). For a discussion of l'affaire Bauffremont, see i.212 sqq. of the German and pp. 158 sqq. of the English edition.

acts of a foreign Government only constitutes a preliminary to the decision of a question of private rights which in itself is subject to the competency of the Court of law. In fact in such a case the Court is merely dealing with premises on which its judgment in the private suit is to proceed'. Yet it is remarkable that even in recent days that unwarranted fear of indirect interference with a foreign act of State has reappeared. It is impressively illustrated by a decision of the courts in Amsterdam. The plaintiffs were the owners of tobacco stored in 1923 at Galata. A British Police Force under the command of Sir Charles H. Harington, the G.O.C. of the Allied troops in occupation of Constantinople, removed the tobacco and caused it to be sold by public auction. The goods were shipped by the buyer in a Dutch ship which reached Amsterdam where the plaintiffs claimed possession of the tobacco. The action failed. The Court of first instance[1] held that it had no jurisdiction to question the sovereignty of foreign Governments. 'Were the Court to declare the acts whereby the property of the plaintiff had been seized as unlawful and in view thereof to order the restitution of such goods to the plaintiff, then the Court would undo the acts which had been done; as these acts were done by the said G.O.C. in his capacity of representative of the occupying Powers and thereby had the character of authoritative acts of a sovereign Power, the Court would thereby violate such sovereignty.' The fallacy of this argument, which involved the prohibition not only of direct but also of indirect interference in the sense indicated above, was clearly exposed by the Court of Appeal which affirmed the judgment on different grounds.[2]

---

[1] District Court Amsterdam, 17 April 1925, *Annual Digest* (1925–6), No. 19.

[2] Court of Appeal Amsterdam, 13 March 1928, *Annual Digest* (1927–8), No. 17: 'These questions would by international law be withdrawn from the Dutch Courts if any one of the Powers in occupation of Constantinople had itself been a party to the suit in which the legality of its sovereign acts was questioned, but not in the case under consideration where their legality is questioned in a suit between two private individuals. The District Court was wrong in holding that by pronouncing such acts illegal it would have negatived acts which had been done by the occupying Power; on the contrary, all those acts would remain in force, notwithstanding the decision of the Dutch Court. So it is impossible to consider as a violation of foreign sovereignty the decision of a Dutch Court, that such acts of the occupying Power constituted acts of embezzlement under Turkish law. The Dutch tribunal being an independent organ of the State of the Netherlands, . . . cannot be deemed to engage the international responsibility of that State by a judicial decision pronouncing illegal certain acts of a foreign Government.'

(5) Finally, attention must be drawn to an occasional tendency to say that it is the principle of the sovereignty of an independent State which requires the foreign act of State to be treated as sacrosanct.[1] The conception of sovereignty and its history is a controversial topic,[2] but at the present day it can hardly be doubted that if under its own law a foreign Government is not omnipotent but is bound by constitutional or statutory restrictions, its internal supremacy is limited or divided. It cannot therefore be infringed by an English court ascertaining those limits to the same extent as the courts of the foreign country could do. A finding that those limits were exceeded involves the conclusion that to that extent (internal) sovereignty in the sense of absolute power does not exist, and, consequently, cannot entail a lack of respect due to a foreign Sovereign. To say, however, that the mere fact of questioning the (internal) omnipotence or absolute supremacy of a foreign Government and its organs is in itself an act of disrespect, would be a statement from which a Bodin or Hobbes might perhaps not have recoiled, but which in modern times would seem a little extravagant. On the other hand, it is, of course, understandable that a judge will be reluctant to question and perhaps condemn a foreign act of State. But this is a somewhat political consideration which, in the last resort, will often weigh heavily with him but which should not be allowed to be twisted into a denial of his powers and thus deter him from exercising them in a proper case in accordance with the principles presently to be developed.

When all is said it is probably the idea of international comity which has influenced not only Professor Dickinson, but also many others who, in a variety of ways and connections, have expressed themselves in favour of the sacrosanctity of foreign acts of State. However great the historical influence of that idea may have been, in these days it will not be gainsaid that it is insufficient to support a doctrine of so palpable a width and comprehensiveness as that of the sacrosanctity of foreign acts of State.

---

[1] See below, Sections IV and V, *passim*.
[2] Oppenheim (–Lauterpacht), pp. 114 sqq. with further references.

## III

### RECOGNITION OF THE FOREIGN ACT OF STATE

The statement that English courts cannot question the validity or legality of foreign acts of State is usually qualified by the proviso that such acts must purport to take effect within the jurisdiction of the State from which they emanate. Put into positive form the rule would be that English Courts must recognize the validity and legality of official acts of a foreign State acting within its jurisdiction.

From the point of view of public international law a State has jurisdiction over the persons and property within its territory and over its nationals everywhere.[1] On the other hand, according to the established principle of private international law, the application of foreign law does not by any means co-incide with the conception of 'jurisdiction' as developed by public international law. In connection, e.g., with movables and immovables, it is true, the territorial test is adopted, but the chief distinctions are that all questions of status are decided neither by territorial presence nor by allegiance but by domicile, and that contractual obligations are not subject to the law of the *situs* of the obligations but to the proper law of the contract. Private international law has also evolved definite rules relating to the effect of at least one foreign act of State other than legislation, viz., foreign judgments. Briefly, they are recognized and treated as binding in this country if, in the case of judgments *in rem* relating to movable or immovable property, they are pronounced by a competent court of the country where the property is situate, and in the case of judgments *in rem* relating to personal status, they are pronounced by a competent court of the place of domicile. To this extent it is perhaps permissible to say that 'a foreign judgment is merely a specific application of foreign law',[2] but the recognition of a foreign judgment *in personam* is influenced by public rather than by private international law inasmuch as it depends on

---

[1] See Oppenheim (–Lauterpacht), p. 266, or Dicey (–Keith), p. 20.
[2] Cheshire, *Private International Law* (2nd ed.), p. 580. See Nussbaum, *Col. L.R.* (1941), 221, 234.

the territorial test of 'presence and submission'[1] and, perhaps on the fact of the defendant being a subject of the country in which the judgment is given.[2]

It will thus be obvious how difficult it is to suggest a general principle determining the recognition of a foreign act of State in this country. Is guidance to be found in the rules of public international law assigning to a country jurisdiction over all persons and things within its territorial limits and its citizens everywhere, or in the principles governing those acts of State which are known as foreign judgments and which are subject to ideas of partly public partly private international law, or in the principles of private international law applicable to the legal relationship in question?

The second of these solutions, though incapable of providing a general rule, will have to be adopted where the foreign act of State may properly be described as a 'judgment'. Unfortunately, however, it is impossible to elaborate this suggestion, as the term 'judgment' within the meaning of the rule has not yet been authoritatively defined. According to Dicey (–Keith)[3] it 'means a judgment, decree or order of the nature of a judgment (by whatever name it be called) which is pronounced or given by a foreign court' and 'implies the exercise by a court of investigation and decision in a manner akin to English judicial proceedings', while 'a mere executive order will presumably be denied rank as a judgment'.[4] This definition leaves many questions unanswered. It does not explain, for instance, under what circumstances the deciding authority may be described as a 'court'; whether the decision must dispose of a dispute or whether a decision rendered in non-contentious proceedings is a judgment[5]; whether the rules relating to foreign

---

[1] Dicey (–Keith), pp. 30, 32, 403; Cheshire, op. cit., p. 594.

[2] The authorities are collected and discussed by Dicey (–Keith), pp. 405 sqq. and Cheshire, op. cit., p. 602; Dicey (–Keith) justifies the rule by the argument that 'a subject is bound to obey the commands of his Sovereign and therefore the judgments of his sovereign courts'. But Dr. Cheshire convincingly replies that, whatever the importance of allegiance in public international law may be, it is not a reason which on any principle recognized by private international law can justify the exercise of jurisdiction.

[3] p. 391.      [4] p. 393.

[5] Cf. the definition of a judgment in the international sense adopted by the German Supreme Court: 'decisions of a court which dispose of a dispute between parties on the basis of ordinary or summary proceedings in the course of which both

judgments are applicable to foreign decisions in a case which in this country would not be decided by, or require, a judgment, or, conversely, which in this country would require a judgment but is not decided by what the foreign law regards as a judgment.[1] In the present state of the authorities and of research it is impossible to venture an answer to these questions, and for the purpose of the following discussion it is sufficient to express the warning that if and when an appropriate definition of the term 'foreign judgment' is evolved, it may be found to include acts of State which *prima facie* do not appear to be judgments.

Reverting, then, to the search for a general principle applicable to the recognition of foreign acts of State other than legislation or judgments, it is suggested that it is private international law which provides the solution and that, accordingly, the foreign act of State ought to be recognized and allowed effects in this country if it is done subject to or is recognized by that legal system which governs the legal relationship concerned.[2] Support for this view which alone is consistent with established conceptions may be found in the numerous cases where the official act is recognized not (as public international law would require) on the ground that it is effected in the country in which a person resides or of which he is a citizen, but on the ground that it is effected by the authority of the country of the person's domicile. Thus the extent of control which the foreign guardian of a child[3] or the foreign curator of a lunatic[4] is allowed to exercise over movable property in

---

parties are given an opportunity of being heard' (30 June 1886, *RGZ* 16, 427; 28 March 1931, *Juristische Wochenschrift* (1932), 588, 590).

[1] These questions are treated by Melchior, *Grundlagen des deutschen internationalen Privatrechts*, pp. 313 sqq. His observations, though confined to German law, are particularly valuable. If in a German notarial contract the covenantor submits to immediate execution the notary may give a certificate of execution whereupon the deed is enforceable as if it were a judgment. Is it in this country enforceable as a foreign judgment?

[2] In this sense Frankenstein, *Internationales Privatrecht* (1926) i.341 sqq.; Melchior, op. cit., pp. 309 sqq; Neumeyer, *Internationales Verwaltungsrecht* (4 vols., 1910–36) propounds the thesis of the independence of international administrative law. There is at least in this country no evidence to support it.

[3] If the guardian is appointed under the law of the country where the child is domiciled, he seems to have full control (*Mackie* v. *Darling* (1871) L. R. 12 Eq. 712), but appointment by the court of the ward's residence or nationality is insufficient (*Re Chatard's Settlement*, [1899] 1 Ch. 712).

[4] Unless an English Committee has been appointed, the foreign curator appointed by the court of the lunatic's domicile is entitled to the lunatic's property in England,

England, or the recognition of a foreign *legitimatio per rescriptum principis*[1] or adoption order[2] depends on domicile. Similarly the effect of a foreign act of State interfering with contractual obligations[3] and of a foreign order of discharge in bankruptcy[4] is determined by the proper law of the contract. On the other hand, the significance of the *lex situs* rather than the proper law of the contract in connection with the attachment[5] and confiscation[6] of debts is necessitated by the consideration that it is only the *lex situs* which can claim such practical effectiveness as justifies recognition in law, and therefore does not really constitute an exception to the guiding principle suggested above.

The existence of that principle is not only not contradicted but is confirmed by those cases[7] in which there is to be found a statement of the maxim that the court cannot question the binding character of foreign acts of State. They arose out of circumstances which for all legally relevant purposes were identical. In the course of a revolution the leaders of the revolutionary forces or their agents requisitioned, commandeered,

---

while in the case of a curator appointed by the court of the lunatic's residence the English Court has a discretion to allow or disallow the recovery of English property: *Didisheim* v. *London and Westminster Bank*, [1900] 2 Ch. 15 (appointment by court in Belgium where lunatic was domiciled, though not resident); *New York Security Co.* v. *Keyser*, [1901] 1 Ch. 666 (lunatic was British subject domiciled here, but resident in New York).

[1] *Re Luck*, [1940] Ch. 864.    [2] See 56 *L.Q.R.* (1941), 122–5.

[3] *Kleinwort Sons & Co.* v. *Ungarische Baumwolle Industrie A.G.*, [1939] 2 K.B. 678, particularly pp. 698, 699, per du Parcq L.J.

[4] Dicey (–Keith), pp. 503 sqq, 678 sqq., or Cheshire, op. cit., p. 490, and the authorities referred to. In many cases importance is attached to the law of the country where the debt 'arises' or is in fact to be paid. What is meant by these confusing formulations which also occur in other connections (see below, note 5), is the proper law of the contract. See particularly Dicey (–Keith), p. 507.

[5] Although *Swiss Bank Corporation* v. *Boehmische Industrialbank*, [1923] 1 K.B. 673 deals with the effect of an English garnishee order upon the debt due by an English bank to a foreign creditor, the principle laid down in the decision probably can be extended to a foreign garnishee order. In the same sense Cheshire (2nd ed.), p. 455.

[6] As to the materiality of the *lex situs* in connection with the confiscations of debts, see Dicey (–Keith), p. 610, n. (*k*).

[7] *Oetjen* v. *Central Leather Co.* 246 U.S. 297 (1917); *Ricaud* v. *American Metal Co. Ltd.* 246 U.S. 304 (1917); *United States* v. *Belmont*, 301 U.S. 324 (1937); *Terrazas* v. *Holmes*, 275 S.W. 392 (1925); *Annual Digest* (1925 and 1926), No. 43 (Supreme Court of Texas); *Luther* v. *Sagor & Co.*, [1921] 3 K.B. 532; *Princess Paley Olga* v. *Weisz*, [1929] 1 K.B. 718.

seized, or confiscated goods which they found in the territory controlled by them. Subsequently these goods reached another country's territory where the original owner brought an action to recover possession. At the time of the action the Government which had originated in revolution was recognized *de jure* or *de facto* by the Government of the judge's country and the defence was that ownership of the goods had been validly acquired from the lawful Government. In all cases the actions were dismissed. In all Anglo-American and in some other cases the courts stated that they felt themselves precluded from inquiring into the validity of the foreign act of State. It is very doubtful for what precise reason these statements were made. Without anticipating the explanation which will be offered below[1] it may, however, be said negatively that there is no evidence of an intention to assert the rule that the mere existence of a foreign act of State compelled the court to recognize and give effect to it. Nor, it is true, is any reason given why the foreign act of State was considered material at all. Yet the reason is obvious. It is a generally accepted principle of private international law that the transfer of tangible property is subject to the *lex rei sitae*,[2] and this is so whether the transfer is effected by private conveyance, the effect of a statute of limitations, finding, order of the court or confiscation. It is for this reason, not on account of the alleged maxim, that in those confiscation cases the official act of the State in whose territory the property was situate was considered as legally relevant or, in other words, was recognized.

These observations on the recognition of a foreign act of State cannot be concluded without a few words about the effect of a non-recognized foreign act of State. Usually it has no effects in law.[3] Sometimes, however, it may become material as a fact. This may be so if an official act interferes with a legal relationship which is not subject to the law of the country effecting the act. Thus the performance of an English contract may become impossible owing to a supervenient act of State at

---

[1] Section IV, (2) below.

[2] No evidence need be adduced in support of this undoubted rule. It may suffice to refer to Dicey (–Keith), pp. 608 sqq.

[3] Dicey (–Keith), 'Rule 109', p. 458, dealing with foreign judgments.

the place of performance.[1] If a foreign Admiralty Court gives judgment *in rem* against a British ship which is sold under the judgment to a *bona fide* purchaser, he acquires a good title notwithstanding the fact that the judgment has been obtained by fraud and is therefore invalid.[2] If bonds are issued for the purpose of exploiting a concession granted by a foreign Government and the concession is revoked, the trustees holding the capital paid in respect of the bonds have to repay it, it being immaterial whether or not the revocation of the concession is lawful.[3] In these and similar cases[4] the foreign act of State is

---

[1] See *Ralli Bros* v. *Compañia Naviera Sota y Aznar*, [1920] 2 K. B. 287 (as explained in *B.Y.I.L.* (1937), 97, 110 sqq.), which deals with foreign legislation. See now the observations of du Parcq L.J. in *Kleinwort & Sons* v. *Ungarische Baumwolle Industrie A.G.*, [1939] 2 K. B. 678, 698.

[2] *Castrique* v. *Imrie* (1870) L. R. 4 H. L. 414, 433, per Blackburn J.; Dicey (–Keith), pp. 459, 460, 608 sqq.

[3] *National Bolivian Navigation Co.* v. *Wilson*, (1880) L. R. 5 A. C. 176. According to the headnote the House held that the foreign Government's right to cancel the concession 'could not be questioned in legal proceedings in this country'. A perusal of the opinions delivered shows that this summary is misleading. Lord Cairns (pp. 184, 185), Lord Hatherley (p. 190), Lord Penzance (p. 196) and Lord O'Hagan (p. 200) treated the revocation as a fact and regarded it as irrelevant whether it was lawful or unlawful. Lords Selborne and Blackburn, at pp. 204, 209, merely added that the foreign Government had substantial reasons for the revocation.

[4] If under an English contract goods are sold in England and the buyer undertakes to pay the price to the seller's German agent in Germany and as a result of criminal proceedings in Germany the buyer is convicted of an offence against the German currency regulations and the money paid to the agent is confiscated, the seller may rely on the invalidity of the payment and recover the price; the German decision must be accepted as a fact: unreported decision of Tucker J. in *Amalgamated Dental Co. Ltd.* v. *Schindler* (June 1941). If under a foreign judgment which orders the payment of a debt subject to English law but which is invalid in the eyes of English law, the creditor has issued execution abroad and obtained satisfaction, the debtor who subsequently finds the creditor in England probably cannot sue him for the return of the money, since the foreign judgment, even if invalid, is sufficient justification for the creditor retaining the money. See the tendency indicated by *Minna Craig Steamship Co.* v. *Schroeder & Co.*, [1913] 2 K. B. 1. This problem is often discussed on the Continent and usually answered in favour of the creditor: Berlin Court of Appeal, 27 September 1907, *Rechtsprechung der Oberlandesgerichte*, 18, 55; M. Wolff, *Internationales Privatrecht*, p. 82; Frankenstein, pp. 352 sqq., whose observations on the foreign act of State as a fact merit close attention. See, generally, Bartin, *Le Jugement étranger considéré comme un fait*, Clunet (1924), 857. Where the defendant is under a duty to indemnify the plaintiff in respect of a liability under a foreign judgment given against the latter, the defendant must accept the judgment as a fact: see German Court of Appeal at Zweibrücken, 12 December 1900, *Zeitschrift für Internationales Recht*, xi.297, and Frankenstein, op. cit., p. 355 (consignee must indemnify forwarding agent in respect of judgment obtained by carrier). If a foreign concession is sold and then revoked, the vendor

merely an incidental fact. Consequently neither the question of its recognition nor that of its validity can arise.

## IV

### THE VALIDITY OF FOREIGN LEGISLATIVE AND ADMINISTRATIVE ACTS

If, according to the principles maintained by English courts, a foreign act of State appears to be material to the matter to be dealt with or, in other words, is recognizable here, an issue may be raised as to its validity under the law of the country in which it was carried out. The maxim for which Oppenheim (–Lauterpacht) and others[1] contend, would suggest that that validity cannot be questioned, but must be accepted as unimpeachable. Such a rule would involve an enormous extension of immunity *ratione materiae*. Whether it is necessitated or justified by the principle of sovereignty as interpreted by the law of nations, depends on the evidence which will have to be collected and considered. If it should exist, however, it is irreconcilable with another much more firmly established rule which, it is submitted, ought to prevail. It has been shown that generally the only reason why a foreign act of State is recognized here is that the legal relationship in question is subject to its law. If, therefore, that law has to be applied, the court sitting here must apply it in its entirety and 'must consider itself sitting in'[2] the country whose law it applies. If that law permits an inquiry into the validity of the act of State or into the propriety of the proceedings from which it results, or into its merits, there is no reason why an English judge should refuse to avail himself of that permission; if it does not give such permission, an English judge will not arrogate it. The task of the court which has to deal with a foreign act of State is therefore not essentially different from that imposed upon it when dealing with private transactions which are subject to a foreign law.

The question of the validity of a foreign act of State has

probably cannot allege the invalidity of the revocation: French Cour de Cassation, 6 January 1841, S. 1841.1.24 treating the revocation as a 'fait accompli' and disregarding its merits.

[1] See above, p. 431.

[2] See the formula of Sir H. Jenner in *Collier* v. *Rivaz* (1841) 2 Curt. 855, 859, 863.

repeatedly come before the courts in connection with foreign judgments, and it is here that guidance may be found to a definition of the conception of 'validity or legality' which, it is said, cannot be inquired into. When an English judge has to deal with a foreign judgment, he is entitled, and sometimes compelled, in addition to the question of recognition, i.e., of competency of jurisdiction in the international sense,[1] to distinguish three questions. Firstly, he will require to be satisfied that the foreign court was a 'proper court', that is to say, had according to its own constitution jurisdiction or power to decide the issue submitted to it.[2] It is remarkable that this question is examined entirely *in abstracto*. An English judge does not ask himself whether in the particular circumstances of the case the foreign court ought to have exercised jurisdiction; he is merely interested in the general question of whether or not the foreign court was the competent tribunal for a decision on the type of dispute before it.[3] Secondly, if the foreign court was a proper court, the English judge will require evidence on the formal validity of its judgment. This point is not usually emphasized in textbooks, but is well established by the prevailing practice, and is in fact obvious. The question is not merely whether the document or record set up in this country is sufficient proof of the foreign judgment, but it is whether such formalities as the foreign law may prescribe for a promulgation of decisions have been observed. Thirdly, however, a foreign judgment rendered by a proper court of competent jurisdiction in the prescribed manner is not in any way impeachable on its merits; to this extent its validity cannot be questioned. Consequently an English judge will not inquire into the propriety of the proceedings or into the legal justification of the decision[4]; he is 'bound to receive it without inquiry as to its conformity with the laws of the country where it was pronounced'.[5] Thus it has even been held that the decision of a French 'tribunal commercial' which can only deal with cases against

---

[1] See above, p. 436.

[2] Dicey (–Keith), pp. 391 sqq., 444, with references to the authorities.

[3] *Pemberton* v. *Hughes*, [1899] 1 Ch. 781.

[4] This applies even if it appears on the face of the judgment that it is based on an erroneous application of English law: *Castrique* v. *Imrie*, (1870) L. R. 4 H. L. 414; *Godard* v. *Gray*, (1870) L. R. 6 Q. B. 139.

[5] *Doglioni* v. *Crispin*, (1866) L. R. 1 H. L. 301, 315, per Lord Cranworth.

'traders' is not open to attack in the English Courts on the ground that the defendant was no 'trader'.[1] Lindley M.R.[2] has gone still further and said that even if in its home country the judgment is void, it must be treated as valid in England provided the court had jurisdiction in the sense of both international and municipal law. He admitted that 'it sounds paradoxical to say that a decree of a foreign court should be regarded here as more efficacious or with more respect than it is entitled to in the country in which it was pronounced. But this paradox disappears when the principle is examined'. This doctrine, which was not expressly followed by Rigby and Vaughan Williams L.JJ., represents the high-water mark of the rule, and it is probably safer to adopt Dicey's proposition[3] that a judgment which under its own law is null and void *ab initio* must be so treated here, while an irregular judgment based on the incorrect use of an existing power, as opposed to the usurpation of a non-existent power, is valid.[4]

It remains to be seen whether and how far these rules relating to foreign judgments have any bearing upon the question whether the validity of other foreign acts of State, such as legislative, executive or administrative measures, may be examined by an English judge.

(1) If foreign acts of State were sacrosanct, one would expect that the validity and, particularly, the constitutionality of *legislation* which, whether passed by parliamentary statute, governmental decree or prerogative order, constitutes the most solemn method of expressing the Sovereign's will, could not be questioned in the courts of another country. On the other hand the somehow analogous rule according to which the competency or power of the foreign court, though not the propriety of its decision in respect of the issue the subject-matter of the judgment, may be inquired into, would suggest

---

[1] *Vanquelin* v. *Bonard* (1863), 15 C. B. (N.S.) 341.
[2] *Pemberton* v. *Hughes*, [1899] 1 Ch. 781, 790, 791.    [3] pp. 445, 446.
[4] Compare *Pemberton* v. *Hughes*, [1899] 1 Ch. 781, where a judgment of a court in Florida being a 'proper court' was held valid notwithstanding the fact that owing to the failure to serve a subpœna within the prescribed time it was perhaps void by the law of Florida, and *Papadopoulos* v. *Papadopoulos*, [1930] P. 55, where the judgment of a Cypriot Court was held void on the ground that under the law of Cyprus the court had no jurisdiction in the case and therefore was not a 'proper court'.

the conclusion that the question of legislation being *ultra vires* could be ventilated by an English Court even in those numerous cases where the courts of the foreign country are precluded from so doing but that, e.g., the question of a statute having been passed by the required majority of Parliament could not in any case be mooted. While the former rule would deny to an English judge the right to examine the constitutional validity of a Joint Resolution of Congress of the United States of America notwithstanding it being open to American Courts, the latter would permit him to assert the constitutional invalidity of a French statute although a French Court could not even query it. Neither proposition has much to commend it. The sound method is to put a judge who has to apply foreign law in the position of his foreign opposite number and therefore to allow him to inquire into the validity of foreign legislation within the limits set by the foreign law. There are countries where the privilege of examining the constitutional validity of legislation is reserved to special courts whose decisions are binding on all courts of ordinary jurisdiction; in such cases the English judge cannot, of course, assume the task of that special court, but must treat the statute in the same way as the regular judge of the foreign country would do. On the other hand, the fact that the *lex fori* precludes the judge from examining the constitutional validity of his own country's legislation does not put him under a disability to do so in a case where foreign law applies; where such a rule exists, e.g. in this country or in France, it has its foundation in the municipal constitutional law of the country, but cannot be described as having a procedural character so as to impose itself even where foreign law is applicable.[1]

This view is in accordance with the teaching of those few continental authors who have dwelt on the problem,[2] but it

---

[1] For the same reason it is impossible to allow inquiry into the validity of foreign legislation if, and to such extent as, it is permissible according to the *lex fori*. The opposite seems to be indicated by Dr. McNair *L.Q.R.* (1941), 69, 70, who, however, very rightly draws attention to the fact that the validity of Russian decrees was to some extent examined in *Russian Commercial and Industrial Bank* v. *Comptoir d'Escompte de Mulhouse*, [1925] A. C. 112, 125, per Lord Cave; *Princess Paley Olga* v. *Weisz*, [1929] 1 K. B. 718, 731, per Sankey L.J., p. 735, per Russell L.J., and counsel's argument on p. 720.

[2] Zitelmann, *Internationales Privatrecht* (1897), i.286; Niboyet, *Revue de droit international et de législation comparée* (1928), pp. 753 sqq., 769, 770; Fedozzi, 27

must be admitted that it is not in harmony with the tendency of recent decisions both in New York[1] and in this country. The first English case dealing with the point is the important, though not properly reported, decision of Lewis J. in *Banco de Bilbao* v. *Rey*.[2] The learned judge had to deal with a point which disappeared when the case reached the Court of Appeal.[3] The issue was the validity of a power of attorney granted by the Board of the plaintiff bank, and this depended on the question whether the constitution of the Board which had been appointed by the Provisional Government of the Basque territory, was justified by the law of that territory or by the law of Spain. The learned judge prefaced his inquiry into the former point by the statement that, as the parties had agreed, the Basque territory was not a sovereign State and that 'therefore . . . with regard to the Decrees and Orders of the Basque Government, if they are found to be unconstitutional or for any reason invalid, the courts of this country are entitled to say so

---

*Recueil* (1929), 145, 221 sqq.; Melchoir, op. cit., p. 87; Neumeyer, op. cit., 221 sqq., 226; Maury, 57 *Recueil* (1936), 329, 396; Raape, *Deutsche Internationales Privatrecht* (1938), p. 80. See Bartin, *Principes*, i.301, and see also German Supreme Court, 8 October 1918, *RGStr*. 52, 308, which examines the validity of an Austrian decree prohibiting the export of certain goods.

[1] In *Eastern States Petroleum Co.* v. *Asiatic Petroleum Corporation*, 28 F. Supp. 279 (1940), the plaintiffs claimed from the defendants oil which had been confiscated in Mexico by a presidential decree and sold to the defendants. A District Court in New York declined to review the constitutional validity of the decree on the ground that 'a foreign sovereign power must in the Courts of the United States be assumed to be acting lawfully, the meaning of "sovereign" being that the decree of the sovereign makes law'. In *Banco de Espana* v. *Federal Reserve Bank of New York* 114 F. (2d) 438 (1940); *Annual Digest* (1938–40), No. 6, the Circuit Court of Appeals (2d), affirming a New York District Court 28 F. Supp. 958 (1940), rejected the plaintiff bank's claim for the return of silver which it had lent to the Republican Government of Spain and which, acting under an allegedly invalid decree, the latter had sold to the defendants. The Court held that it could not decide whether the governmental decree was constitutionally valid in Spain or consistent with the provisions of a Spanish statute. In *Anderson* v. *N.V. Transandine Handelmaatschappij*, 29 N. Y. Supp. (2d) 547 (1941) the Supreme Court of New York refused to investigate the validity of a decree of Queen Wilhelmina's Government in London by which certain American property of Dutch nationals was vested in the Queen; this decision was affirmed on other grounds by the New York Court of Appeals: 289 N. Y. 9, 43 N.E. 2d 502 (1942). These tendencies are approved in a note 41 *Col. L.R.* (1941), 1072, 1081, 1082, and by Nussbaum, 50 *Yale L.J.* (1941), 1018, 1030, who relies on not very convincing grounds of convenience rather than on legal principle.

[2] It is reported only in Clunet (1938), 602, with note by Elkin. The defendant's solicitors, Messrs. John Bailey & Co., have very kindly supplied the author with a transcript of the decision and he desires to record his thanks to them.

[3] [1938] 2 K. B. 176.

and not to treat them as the enactments of a sovereign State recognized by H.M. Government'. In the result it was held that the Basque Decree under which the Board had been appointed was invalid. Lewis J. proceeded to refer to a Decree issued by the Central Government of Spain which was said to justify the reconstitution of the plaintiff bank's Board and the validity of which was challenged by the defendants. He found, however, that no direct action had been taken by the Government of Spain in pursuance of that Decree and therefore was not really called upon to comment on its validity. Yet in the course of his judgment he pointed out that counsel for the defendants 'conceded that he felt great difficulty in attacking these Orders and Decrees in view of the fact that they were Orders and Decrees of a sovereign State recognized by H.M. Government, and, in my opinion, no judge in this country in one of His Majesty's Courts can in the circumstances criticize or hold as invalid any such Decrees and Orders'.[1] Later in his judgment Lewis J. appeared to throw doubt on the validity of the Spanish Government's Decree, but interrupted himself by insisting that 'this Decree, under whatever power it was made, was a Decree of the Spanish Government and in the opinion which I have formed is not open to criticism in an English Court'. No authority was cited in support of these *dicta*, which are difficult to follow when it is remembered that in the course of his judgment Lewis J. seemed to reject the plaintiff bank's argument that by the Spanish Constitution the only tribunal authorized to deal with the point was the 'Tribunal of Constitutional Guarantees', and apparently reached the view that at least the voidness of regional legislation on the ground of unconstitutionality and perhaps also the voidness on the ground of incompetence in case of conflicts of legislative jurisdiction could be tested by the ordinary courts in Spain.[2] The problem

[1] In this very important connection the transcript contains a mistake which, however, can easily be rectified. In the transcript the words quoted in the text continue as follows: '. . . . of the Basque Government, but, said Sir Patrick Hastings, any such Decrees and Orders are not so sacrosanct'. It is clear that the sentence should read: '. . . . of the Spanish Government, but, said Sir Patrick Hastings, any such Decrees and Orders as are issued by the Basque Government are not so sacrosanct'. On the impact of the principle of sovereignty see above, p. 435.

[2] See also *The Cristina*, [1938] A. C. 485, 509, where Lord Wright referred to but refrained from discussing the question whether it was 'competent for the Court to debate whether the decree was validly made under Spanish law'. The decision of

referred to in this decision again came before the courts in the two cases of *Re Amand,* both of which arose out of an application for a writ of *habeas corpus* and turned on the question of the validity of an Order of the Dutch Government in London in pursuance of which the applicant, a Dutch subject, had been called up for service in the Dutch Army in England. In the first case the Court (Lord Caldecote L.C.J., Humphreys and Singleton JJ.) seems to have thought that the argument presented to it was that the certificate of a foreign Government as to the validity of the act was binding on the Court and excluded any further evidence. The Court rejected this plea, examined the evidence and in the result decided in favour of the validity of the Order.[1] In the second case,[2] however, another Divisional Court (Wrottesley, Croom-Johnson and Cassels JJ.) fully appreciated that the respondents' argument really was that the validity of the Dutch legislation could not be challenged. The Court accepted the existence of the principle, but hesitatingly refused to apply it to the case in point. Wrottesley J. relied on the ground that, in accordance with the wording of Warrington L.J.'s *dictum* in *Luther* v. *Sagor & Co.*[3] the principle of sacrosanctity only applied where the foreign Government legislates with regard to persons or property inside its territory, but does not apply where the foreign legislation expressly deals with a person living in England.[4] On the other hand Croom-Johnson and Cassels JJ. seem to have been impressed by the fact that the applicant could not apply for redress in the Dutch Courts.[5] It would appear, however, that in both cases there was evidence before the Court to the effect that a Dutch Court would have been entitled to examine the

---

Lewis J. indicates a further problem of particular difficulty, viz. the attitude which an English judge should adopt towards legislation in a Federal State. Lewis J. admitted that he could review the validity of regional legislation. But what is the position, if there are two jurisdictions of State Courts and Federal Courts and the one permits while the other excludes judicial review? It is believed that in such a case a judge must find his 'opposite number' and follow the practice adopted by that foreign judge who would have taken seisin of the matter, if it had to be decided abroad; if there are concurrent jurisdictions, the law of that jurisdiction ought to prevail which is more favourable to the plaintiffs and which, therefore, he would have invoked had the case been fought abroad. See Melchior, op. cit., p. 100.

[1] [1941] 2 K. B. 239.       [2] [1942] 1 K. B. 445.
[3] [1921] 3 K. B. 532, 548. The *dictum* is quoted below, p. 461.
[4] p. 449.       [5] Ibid., at pp. 452, 454.

validity of the decree[1] and it is submitted that for this reason the English Court was entitled as well as bound to examine the validity of the Dutch decree.

(2) It is in connection with such foreign acts of State as are neither legislative measures nor judgments that peculiar problems of great practical significance arise.

There is, it is true, no reason of principle why these administrative or executive measures should be entitled to an immunity higher than that accorded to foreign legislation or foreign judgments. It should, therefore, be clear that an English Court is entitled to inquire not only into the formal validity of such acts but also into the question of whether they are within the competency or power of those who have effected them, or whether they are *ultra vires*. Had the foreign Government or its agent power to appoint a curator for the lunatic, to naturalize an alien citizen, to grant the alleged permission, licence or concession, or to incorporate a company by registration? It is believed that it is perfectly in order to raise these questions and that the answers must be supplied by the 'proper law' applicable to the particular matter under review.[2]

The very serious problem, however, arises whether foreign acts of State which are recognizable here, formally valid and effected by the competent authority within its power, are impeachable on their merits, whether their factual or legal basis may be questioned by an English judge or whether the propriety of the decision must be accepted without criticism. Is the person for whom a curator is appointed in fact a lunatic? Had the alien whose naturalization was decreed complied with the requirements of five years' residence? Was the authority right in assuming that the prerequisite of the grant of a concession actually existed? Were the Articles of Association on the strength of which the company was registered, duly subscribed?

On the analogy of the treatment of foreign judgments in

---

[1] This important detail does not appear from the reports, but the author was present in Court while the pertinent part of the evidence was led, and feels able to vouch for the statement in the text.

[2] See *Ginsberg v. Canadian Pacific Steamship Co. Ltd.*, [1940] 66 Ll. L. R. 206, 223, where Atkinson J. felt no difficulty in holding that the German Reich Ministry of Economics had no power to revoke a licence previously granted; see also *The Kabalo*, [1940] 67 Ll. L. R. 572.

English law it is tempting to conclude that the merits of the decision of foreign authorities are not impeachable here. It is submitted, however, that this would be too hard-and-fast a rule. In connection with foreign judgments special considerations apply which result from the fact that both parties have had an opportunity of stating their respective cases and that there is *res judicata*. Decisions other than strictly judicial ones are not always treated in the same way, and it will frequently be found that even in the foreign country from which they emanate they are subject to review by courts of ordinary jurisdiction. If so, an English judge ought to have similar powers. In order to achieve this it is necessary again to revert to fundamental principles and thus to suggest the rule that a judicial review of the merits or the propriety of foreign acts of State other than legislation and judgments is permissible in this country, if and to such extent as it is conceded to a judge of the country from which the act of State emanates.

The treatment of this problem in comparative law is not uniform. There are a few decisions of the French Cour de Cassation which give the impression that the judges of fact have examined the validity of a naturalization in a foreign country.[1] In another decision[2] the Cour de Cassation held that the plaintiff could maintain an action for damages on the ground that the defendant had committed a trespass on land in Egypt by depositing mud there, notwithstanding the fact that the act was done under orders of the Egyptian Government and that the action therefore was to involve an examination of these orders. The Italian practice nearly exclusively relating to naturalization in a foreign country is not firmly established.[3] In Germany the validity of a naturalization in the United States was examined on the ground that an American Court would exercise such a right,[4] while it was said of a French decree appointing a conseil judiciaire for a 'prodigal' that the

---

[1] Cass. Civ., 26 February 1890, Clunet (1890), 117 (affaire Adam): 'attendu . . . que l'arrêt attaqué constate que l'ensemble de ces actes satisfait aux conditions de validité prescrites par la loi argentine'. Cass. Req., 13 February 1922, Clunet (1922), 412 and 996 (affaire Dreyfus–Gonzalès).

[2] Cass. Req. 1 March 1875, Clunet (1876), 274.

[3] Fedozzi, 27 *Recueil* (1929), 145, 199, nn. 2 and 3. As to Holland see District Court of Amsterdam, 22 December 1936, *Annual Digest* (1935–7), No. 126, and as to Egypt see Court of Appeal of the Mixed Tribunal, 23 March 1937, ibid., No. 128.

[4] Supreme Court, 4 March 1915, *JW* (1915), 583.

German judge could not possibly 'subject the legality of an order made by the foreign judge to a re-examination; for the German judge the fact must suffice that there exists a duly made order of the competent foreign authority'.[1] The problem is discussed at length by Fedozzi[2] and by Neumeyer,[3] both of whom maintain that a court may satisfy itself of the foreign act of State conforming to the factual and legal requirements of the foreign law.[4] The former author holds that the right to inquire into the validity and propriety of a foreign act of State within the limits allowed by the foreign law follows from the nature and content of the rule of the forum referring to foreign law, while Neumeyer would appear to give that right even where it is excluded by the foreign law. Both authors deny that there is evidence of a custom among nations to attribute the force of *res judicata* to foreign acts of State, or that the inquiry would amount to an illicit interference with the sovereignty of a foreign State such as is feared by a number of authors.[5]

It is believed that it is in this systematic connection that some famous Anglo-American decisions ought to find their proper place. All of them may be described as 'confiscation cases' and deal with the situation which we already had occasion to indicate. In *Ricaud* v. *American Metal Co. Ltd.*[6] the Supreme Court of the United States was seized with an action against the Collector of Customs in Texas who held the goods which had been confiscated in Mexico but were claimed by the plaintiffs in bond. Dealing with the question of jurisdiction the Court repeated Chief Justice Fuller's *dictum* in *Underhill* v. *Hernandez*[7] and continued[8]:

---

[1] Supreme Court, 24 October 1912, *RGZ* 80, 262, 265. See also Supreme Court, 13 August 1936, *RGStr.* 70, 286; *Annual Digest* (1935–7), No. 165 (relating to extradition proceedings).

[2] L'efficacité extraterritoriale des lois et des actes de droit public, 27 *Recueil* (1929), 145, 199.

[3] *Internationales Verwaltungsrecht* (1936), iv.335 sqq., 342 sqq.

[4] In the same sense apparently Van Praag in his book *Jurisdiction et droit international public* (1915), which unfortunately does not seem to be available in this country. See also Travers, *Droit pénal international* (1921), iii.84 sqq.

[5] Droz, Clunet (1907), 23, and some Italian writers quoted by Fedozzi, op. cit., p. 199. Frankenstein, *Internationales Privatrecht*, i.350, would also appear to exclude the right of inquiry; he seems to regard it as an essential attribute of the recognition itself that the act of State has the character of *res judicata*.

[6] 246 U. S. 304 (1917).

[7] 168 U. S. 250, 253 (1897), quoted above, pp. 430, 431.

[8] p. 309; italic ours.

This last rule, however, does not deprive the courts of jurisdiction once acquired over a case. It requires only that when it is made to appear that the foreign Government has acted in a given way on the subject-matter of the litigation, *the details of such action or the merit of the result cannot be questioned but must be accepted by our Courts as a rule for their decision*. . . . It results that the title to the property in this case must be determined by the result of the action taken by the military authorities of Mexico and that giving effect to this rule is an exercise of jurisdiction. . . .

Proceeding to deal with the question whether the act of the Mexican authorities had the effect of divesting the plaintiff's title the Court referred to the simultaneous decision in *Oetjen* v. *Central Leather Co.*[1] and added that the fact of the title having been in an American citizen not resident in Mexico[2]

does not affect the rule of law that the act within its own boundaries of one sovereign State *cannot become the subject of re-examination and modification* in the Courts of another. Such action . . . becomes . . . a rule of decision for the Courts of this country. Whatever rights such an American citizen may have, can be asserted only through the Courts of Mexico or through the political departments of our Government.

The decision in *Oetjen* v. *Central Leather Co.*[3] relates to similar facts and contains similar statements. Again, Chief Justice Fuller's *dictum* in *Underhill* v. *Hernandez*[4] is repeated, the Court adding that[5] "to permit the validity of the acts of one sovereign State to be re-examined and perhaps condemned by the courts of another would very certainly "imperil the amicable relations between the Governments and vex the peace of nations"". These decisions[6] were followed by the Court of Appeal in this country. *Princess Paley Olga* v. *Weisz*[7,8] related to a claim to

---

[1] 246 U. S. 297 (1917).     [2] p. 130; italics ours.

[3] See above, n. 1.     [4] See above, pp. 430, 431.

[5] p. 304. See also p. 303: 'Such action is not subject to re-examination and modification by the Courts of this country.' The *dictum* quoted in the text was relied upon by the Federal Supreme Court of Argentina, 16 July 1937, *Annual Digest* (1935–7), No. 100.

[6] They were followed in *U.S.* v. *Belmont*, 301 U. S. 324 (1937).

[7] [1929] 1 K. B. 718.

[8] The famous case of *Luther* v. *Sagor & Co.*, [1921] 3 K. B. 532 which Professor Lauterpacht has justly described as 'much overworked' (3 *Mod. L.R.* (1939), 1, 8) is usually quoted in this connection but is not really relevant. It involved three questions: What was the effect of the recognition of the Soviet Government as a *de facto* Government upon the past acts of that Government? Was there sufficient evidence to establish the identity of the recognized Russian Government with the Government which had confiscated and sold the plaintiff's goods? Was the Russian decree of confiscation contrary to public policy as understood in England? The

goods which the defendants had purchased from the Soviet Government who had confiscated them. The defendant in the first place pleaded that 'the plaintiff could not be heard in His Majesty's Courts to dispute the validity of the appropriation of the articles in question by the Russian Government',[1] and in the alternative relied upon two decrees issued by the Soviet authorities. MacKinnon J. (as he then was) upheld the alternative defences, and to this extent the Court of Appeal agreed with him. The Court of Appeal, however, also thought that the principal defence, rejected in the court of first instance, ought to succeed. Scrutton L.J. thought[2] that MacKinnon J. ought to have considered 'what would happen if they [the Russian Government] claimed not by law but by title of force', and held that the American cases as well as *Luther* v. *Sagor & Co.*[3] necessitated the result that no inquiry into the Russian Government's title was possible. Again, Sankey L.J.[4] referred to the American cases and in particular to Chief Justice Fuller's *dictum* in *Underhill* v. *Hernandez*[5] as repeated in *Oetjen's* case[6] and said that the plaintiff was 'dispossessed of this property by an act of State behind which our courts will not go',[7] and he therefore upheld all three defences. Finally, Russell L.J.[8] also held that the 'act of State point' ought to succeed; he did not deal with the earlier authorities but confined himself to the statement that 'this Court will not inquire into the legality of acts done by a foreign Government against its own subjects in respect of property situate in its own territory'.

Thus the circle is closed. While the actual decision in *Underhill* v. *Hernandez*[9] to a very limited degree extended immunity *ratione personae* to immunity *ratione materiae*, Chief

American cases were referred to by Bankes, Warrington, and Scrutton L.JJ. in connection with the first question (see above, p. 423) and by Warrington L.J. also in connection with the third question (see below, p. 461). In a subordinate sentence Scrutton L.J. added (p. 557) that the defendants showed a title 'which by the comity of nations cannot be questioned in the Courts'. He seems to have deduced this remark from what he considered to be a rule of law, viz. that an English Court cannot investigate the truth of a statement made by a recognized sovereign State. But this rule which relates to the proof of foreign law does not in fact exist: see, e.g. *The Cristina*, [1938] A. C. 485, at p. 506, per Lord Wright, at pp. 516, 517, per Lord Maugham; *Haile Selassie* v. *Cable & Wireless Ltd.* (No. 1), [1938] Ch. 839 (C. A.).

[1] p. 719.  [2] p. 724.  [3] [1921] 3 K. B. 532.  [4] pp. 728 sqq.
[5] 168 U. S. 250 (1897).  [6] 246 U. S. 297 (1917).  [7] p. 730.  [8] p. 736.
[9] 168 U. S. 250 (1897).

Justice Fuller's *dictum* led to formulations which create the impression that Anglo-American law had unrestrictedly accepted the idea of immunity *ratione materiae*. Yet these formulae must be subject to considerable qualifications. It must be emphasized that, as Van Praag[1] has rightly pointed out, the invalidity of the act of State was not in issue in any of the American decisions; the observations of the Supreme Court of the United States on that point were therefore merely *dicta*.[2] While they do not preclude an inquiry into the formal validity of an act of State or into the power and competency of the authority responsible for it, they were probably intended as a denial of the power of an American Court to investigate the merits of this foreign act of State.[3] For the reasons indicated above even this restrictive interpretation of the American authorities cannot be regarded as entirely satisfactory inasmuch as it prevents a re-examination of the merits of an act of State where the proper law permits it. In this country, however, it is still more difficult to suggest a method of avoiding the net spread by those authorities, since in *Princess Paley Olga* v. *Weisz*[4] the Court of Appeal expressly rejected the plaintiff's argument that 'where a State purports to act upon a municipal law it cannot be said that its act is exempt from inquiry as an act of State', and asserted the doctrine that an act of State must be treated as obligatory whatever the competency of the responsible official and the propriety of the decisions. The only limitation which can be read into the judgment of the Court of Appeal is that it seems to be confined to acts of a foreign Government itself; although there is no logical reason why the same should not apply to the acts of subordinate officials acting as agents of the Government, it is perhaps possible to exempt such acts from the rule laid down by the Court of Appeal.

---

[1] *Revue de droit international et de législation comparée* (1923), 436, 450 sqq. Van Praag, who apart from De Visscher (above, p. 427, n. 2) is apparently the only continental writer dealing with the Anglo-American cases, severely criticizes their doctrine. He maintains that a court must have power to inquire into questions 'qui n'ont aucune connexité avec la politique de l'Etat étranger'.

[2] See the tendency clearly indicated by *Shapleigh* v. *Mier*, 299 U. S. 468 (1937).

[3] See the Court's reference to the 'details of such action or the merit of the result' and to the prohibition of subjecting it to 're-examination and modification'. This is what is probably meant by the statement that the act becomes 'a rule of decision'.

[4] [1929] 1 K. B. 718, at p. 720.

In conclusion two final matters must be pointed out. No judicial review of any kind is permissible where a foreign act of State is relevant merely as a fact in the sense mentioned above.[1] On the other hand, where the act of State is open to review by the courts of this country, its mere existence may provide evidence of its validity, although it would perhaps be an unwarranted generalization of a rule prevailing in regard to foreign judgments[2] to say that a foreign act of State is presumed to be valid. This principle is supported by the decision in *Carr* v. *Fracis Times & Co.*[3] The question before the House of Lords was whether the seizure of arms within the territorial waters of Muscat under the authority of the Sultan of Muscat was an unlawful act so as to justify an action for tort in England. A court in Muscat had found the seizure lawful and the Sultan had confirmed that view. Yet the Court of Appeal held that there was no justification for the seizure. The House of Lords reversed the decision. Notwithstanding some generalizations by Lord Halsbury[4] the true foundation of the decision was clearly indicated by Lords Lindley and Macnaghten[5] who, in the words of the former, thought that the view taken by the Court of Appeal 'of the finding of the Muscat Court and its approval by the Sultan ignores its value as evidence of the law of Muscat'.

# V

## OTHER ASPECTS OF THE DOCTRINE: INJUNCTIONS. TORT LIABILITY. PUBLIC POLICY.

Owing to its very general, indeterminate, and blurred character the doctrine of the sacrosanctity of the foreign act of

---

[1] pp. 440, 441.   [2] Dicey (–Keith) Rule 111, p. 461.   [3] [1902] A. C. 176.
[4] pp. 179, 180: 'The broad and simple proposition is that the Sultan was authorized to declare that the thing done was lawful, and the thing done was an act of State. It is not an act as between person and person, it is an act of State which the Sultan says authoritatively is lawful; and I cannot doubt that under such circumstances the act done is an act which is done with complete authority and cannot be made the subject of an action here. . . . We are concluded by the determination of these documents that that is the decision of the Sultan of Muscat deciding on an act of State and that therefore it is not open to any tribunal to inquire further into the matter. . . .'
[5] pp. 183, 185.

State is bound to produce quite unexpected ramifications. While it would be futile to speculate on future developments, some matters are clearly discernible on which that fertile but dangerous doctrine has impressed its mark.

(1) It has already been pointed out that according to an established principle of international law to which English Courts will no doubt adhere, a judge is precluded from giving a decision which in effect involves the exercise of the functions of a foreign administration or amounts to direct encroachment upon it. Thus English Courts will not presume to undo an act of State done in a foreign country; indeed, there are many reasons why it is obvious that, even if the courts had any intention thus to interfere with a foreign administration, they do not possess the necessary power.[1] On the other hand, as has also been shown above, they do have the power to undo, or interfere with, a foreign act of State within the limits of their own jurisdiction by examining and, if so advised, negativing the validity of the act; to this extent they may be said indirectly to encroach upon the foreign act of State by excluding its effects upon persons or matters subject to their jurisdiction. The further question, however, arises whether they are also entitled actively to interfere with the act of State by the grant of an injunction intended to operate both here and abroad.

The decision in *Gladstone* v. *Ottoman Bank*[2] might be understood to suggest a negative answer. The plaintiff, who had obtained an exclusive concession from the Sultan of the Ottoman Empire to operate the bank of issue of that country, applied to the court for an injunction restraining the defendants from exploiting a similar concession which, it was alleged, had been granted to them in breach of the plaintiff's concession. Sir William Page Wood refused the injunction on the ground that 'those who depend upon the grant of a foreign sovereign cannot obtain the aid of this Court against the act of the foreign sovereign in making a second grant inconsistent with the first. It is the act of a foreign sovereign power which

---

[1] Neumeyer, *Internationales Verwaltungsrecht*, iv.157. The formula of Dicey (–Keith), p. 25, is much narrower: 'English Courts will not enforce a right otherwise duly acquired under the law of a foreign country . . . where the enforcement of such right involves interference with the authority of a foreign State within the limits of its territory'.

[2] (1863) 1 H. & M. 505.

overrides everything. . . . [It is] impossible to hold that this Court has jurisdiction to interfere with any step which the Ottoman Government may take in this matter according to its own sole will and discretion.'[1] Sir William Page Wood, however, also referred to the fact that if by a statute passed by the British Parliament the plaintiff had been deprived of a benefit conferred upon him by an earlier enactment, he could not complain. This suggests that the ratio decidendi was not so much the lack of jurisdiction as the fact that the plaintiff had no cause of action, and if this were the correct interpretation, the decision would have only little bearing upon the principle which the sentence quoted above would seem to affirm. Such an interpretation is probably also the sounder, as otherwise it would be difficult to reconcile the decision with that of the Court of Appeal in *Ellerman Lines* v. *Read*.[2] The defendant, a British subject, entered into an English contract with the plaintiffs. He breaks it and fraudulently obtains a judgment against the plaintiffs in the Turkish Courts. The plaintiffs apply for a declaration that the Turkish judgment is void, and for an injunction restraining the defendant from enforcing it. The defendant does not deny that an English Court has jurisdiction to restrain proceedings in a foreign court as vexatious or oppressive, but suggests that the foreign judgment, once obtained, is 'sacrosanct'.[3] The Court of Appeal, however, makes the declaration and grants an injunction. Atkin L.J. (as he then was) clearly states that the 'principle upon which an English Court acts in granting injunctions is not that it seeks to assume jurisdiction over the foreign court or that it arrogates to itself some superiority which entitles it to dictate to the foreign court, or that it seeks to criticize the foreign court or its procedure; the English Court has regard to the personal attitude of the person who has obtained the foreign judgment'.[4] The decision no doubt goes very far inasmuch as it restrained the defendant from enforcing the Turkish judgment in Great Britain as well as anywhere in the world, including Turkey, and thus directly interfered with the foreign act of State; it clearly supports, however, the much more modest suggestion that the danger of what has been called indirect interference with such an act, does not

[1] pp. 512, 513.    [2] [1928] 2 K. B. 144.
[3] p. 154.    [4] p. 155.

deprive English Courts of jurisdiction, and to that extent disposes of the doctrine of the sacrosanctity of a foreign act of State, there being no basic distinction between a foreign judgment and another act of State, such as a concession.

(2) Even if a foreign act of State is proved to be invalid or unauthorized and therefore wrongful, it will usually be impossible to institute proceedings in this country against its authors for the purpose of recovering damages, for even if a tort was committed according to the *lex loci delicti commissi*, the rules of personal immunity will usually deprive the court of jurisdiction.[1] The foreign act of State may, however, have been committed in conjunction with or at the instigation of persons who are not entitled to immunity and who are made liable as joint tortfeasors. Is it open to such defendants to rely on immunity *ratione materiae* or on some similar doctrine of sacrosanctity? It is submitted that, here again, the solution should not be sought in wide maxims, but in established rules of private international law. If a tort was committed according to the *lex loci delicti commissi*, there is no reason why an English Court should not so hold. This may compel it to 'criticize' the foreign act of State, and perhaps to impute immoral motives or objects, lawlessness or dishonesty to foreign officials who are not before the court. A judge may dislike, and will therefore be reluctant to arrive at such conclusions, but he should be permitted to do so, provided he strictly observes the conflict rules relating to tortious liability and therefore carefully examines where the act complained of was committed and whether it is a tort under the local law. Yet there is high American authority for the opposite view and thus for a further extension of the doctrine of sacrosanctity. In *American Banana Co.* v. *United Fruit*[2] the plaintiffs claimed damages from the defendants, likewise an American company, on the grounds that the Government of Costa Rica had seized the plaintiffs' banana plantation and done so at the instigation of the defendants. It would probably have been possible to dismiss the action on the ground that the tort, if any, was committed in Costa Rica and that under the law of that country no wrongful act had been done. Mr. Justice Holmes, however, who delivered the opinion of the Supreme Court of the United

---

[1] Above, p. 426.     [2] 213 U. S. 347 (1908).

States, put the result on a very broad basis. He referred to *Underhill* v. *Hernandez*[1] which, he thought, excluded any complaint in respect of the seizure, and added[2]:

> The fundamental reason why persuading a sovereign power to do this or that cannot be a tort is not that the sovereign cannot be joined as a defendant or because it must be assumed to be acting lawfully. . . . The fundamental reason is that it is a contradiction in terms to say that within its jurisdiction it is unlawful to persuade a sovereign power to bring about a result that it declares by its conduct to be desirable and proper. It does not, and a foreign court cannot, admit that the influences were improper or the results bad. It makes the persuasion lawful by its own act. The very meaning of sovereignty is that the decree of the sovereign makes law.

In *Starke* v. *Howe Sound Co.*[3] the plaintiffs specifically alleged that the defendants had bribed certain Mexican authorities and thus caused them to seize and condemn the plaintiffs' goods situate in Mexico. The Appellate Division of the Supreme Court of New York dismissed the action for damages. It declined jurisdiction because it thought that it could not 'pass upon and determine the validity, propriety or legality' of the act of a sovereign State done in the exercise of its sovereign power. In *McCarthy* v. *Reichsbank*[4] the plaintiff sued the German Central Bank for conversion alleged to have been committed by the seizure of property in Germany; it is fair to assume that the defendants were acting within the powers given to them by German law and that, therefore, there was no tort according to the local law. The Appellate Division of the Supreme Court of New York, however, asserted that it was 'powerless to review the acts of another Government in dealing with its citizens within its territory or to call such actions into question, and it is legally immaterial that such acts are unjust morally'.

It is, however, noteworthy that Dicey,[5] while not dealing

---

[1] 213 U. S. 347 (1897).

[2] p. 358. On Mr. Justice Holmes' reasoning, see above, p. 435.

[3] 5 N. Y. Supp. (2d) 551 (1933); *Annual Digest* (1933-4), No. 9.

[4] 20 N. Y. Supp. (2d) 450 (1940). See also the New York Court of Appeals in *Lamont* v. *Travellers Insurance Co.*, 281 N. Y. 362 (1940); *Annual Digest* (1938-40), No. 73. The plaintiff, as the International Committee of Bankers in Mexico for the distribution among holders of bonds issued by the Mexican Government, apparently claimed a declaration that the defendants received certain moneys as trustees for the bondholders, not as agents of the Mexican Government. In the course of its judgment the Court said: 'A State Court cannot grant redress against the agent of a foreign Government for a wrong inflicted within the territory of the foreign Government with the sanction or command of the sovereign.'

[5] (–Keith), pp. 448, 450, 452, 454.

with the question of tortious liability, does not hesitate to treat a foreign judgment as invalid if it is obtained by fraud on the part of the court pronouncing it, as where a court gives judgment for the plaintiff because the judges are bribed by some person (other than the plaintiff) who wishes judgment to be given against the defendant, or because the defendant declines to bribe them. This view, which certainly deserves support, is perhaps not quite in accord with the American disinclination to 'criticize' a foreign act of State.

(3) If it were true that an English Court cannot 'sit in judgment' or question the validity of a foreign act of State it might follow that not only the validity of the act under its own municipal law but also its extraterritorial validity was exempt from inquiry. More particularly, it might mean that it was not open to an English Court to reject the recognition of a foreign act of State on the ground of it being contrary to English public policy.

Unless English law is prepared to forgo any control over the application of foreign law by the weapon of public policy, it is difficult to ascertain the precise limits of the suggested principle. There are, it is true, few instances in which public policy has ever been resorted to for the purpose of excluding the application of foreign law, but there are some,[1] and all textbooks are agreed on the existence of the rule.[2] It underlies the numerous cases which decide that foreign penal laws will not be enforced here[3] or that a foreign penal status will not be recognized here.[4] It finds expression in the cases in which it has been held that foreign judgments are unenforceable here if they have been obtained by fraud or are contrary to public policy as understood in this country or to natural justice.[5] What applies to foreign legislation and to foreign judgments ought to apply equally to other activities of a foreign State, even if activities of the foreign Government itself are concerned.

---

[1] See e.g. *Kaufmann* v. *Gerson*, [1904] 1 K. B. 591; *Rousillon* v. *Rousillon* (1880) 14 Ch. D. 351; *Re Luck*, [1940] Ch. 864, 907, 908, per Scott L.J.; *Société des Hôtels Réunis* v. *Hawker* (1913) 29 T. L. R. 878; *Hope* v. *Hope* (1857) 8 D. M. G. 731; *Re Fitzgerald*, [1904] 1 Ch. 573; *Re Macartney*, [1921] 1 Ch. 522.

[2] Dicey (–Keith) p. 25; Cheshire, pp. 136 sqq.; Westlake (7th ed.), pp. 307, 308 (dealing with contracts only).

[3] Dicey (–Keith), Rule 54, pp. 213 sqq.

[4] Dicey (–Keith), Rule 136, pp. 531 sqq.

[5] Dicey (–Keith), Rules 105 and 107, pp. 448 sqq.; 456 sqq.

Yet Chief Justice Fuller's dictum in *Underhill* v. *Hernandez*[1] has, in this connection too, led to judicial statements which are dangerously sweeping. This is most impressively shown by Warrington L.J.'s judgment in *Luther* v. *Sagor & Co.*,[2] one of the 'confiscation' cases. Dealing with the question[3] 'whether the Court has any power to question the validity of the proceedings under which the property in the goods has *prima facie* been transferred to the defendants', the learned Lord Justice said that it was well settled 'that the validity of the acts of an independent sovereign Government in relation to property and persons within its jurisdiction cannot be questioned in the courts of this country'. He quoted the decision in *Oetjen* v. *Central Leather Co.*[4] and thought that the principle enunciated in such cases as *Kaufmann* v. *Gerson*[5] was inapplicable, as the appellants were not seeking to enforce a contract inconsistent with some essential principle of justice or morality, but were 'resisting an endeavour on the part of the respondents to induce the Court to ignore and override legislative and executive acts of the Government of Russia and its agents affecting the title to property in that country'. This distinction between the enforcement of a foreign contract in England and the transfer of title to goods lying in a foreign country was also the ground on which Bankes L.J. chiefly relied, but he added that[6] 'even if it was open to the courts of this country to consider the morality or justice of the decree of 20 June 1918, I do not see how the courts could treat this particular decree otherwise than as the expression by the *de facto* Government of a civilized country of a policy which it considered to be in the best interest of that country'. Scrutton L.J. took a different line and preferred to state positively that confiscation without compensation was not contrary to English public policy,[7] but also observed that it appeared[8]

a serious breach of international comity, if a State is recognized as a sovereign independent State, to postulate that its legislation is contrary to essential principles of justice and morality. Such an allegation might well, with a susceptible foreign Government, become a *casus belli*, and should in my view be the action of the Sovereign through his Ministers, and not of the

---

[1] 168 U. S. 250 (1897).
[2] [1921] 3 K. B. 532; for criticism of the decision in so far as it relates to public policy, see Fachiri, *B.Y.I.L.* (1931), pp. 95 sqq.
[3] p. 548.   [4] 246 U. S. 297 (1917).   [5] *Ubi supra.*
[6] p. 546.   [7] p. 559.   [8] pp. 558, 559.

judges in reference to a State which their State has recognized. . . . I do not feel able to come to the conclusion that the legislation of a State recognized by any Sovereign as an independent sovereign State is so contrary to moral principle that the judges ought not to recognize it.

The views thus adopted by the Court of Appeal were not followed in New York[1] nor are they in harmony with the practice of the French Cour de Cassation[2] which so recently as in 1939 was most strikingly illustrated by a decision dealing with the Spanish Government's confiscation of goods situate in Spain.[3] The Montpellier Court of Appeal had taken the familiar view that the confiscation of the goods was 'un acte accompli dans sa souveraineté par le Gouvernement espagnol' and that, therefore, 'le juge français n'ayant point qualité pour en apprécier la légalité, ne saurait s'opposer à la livraison d'un connaissement régulier, des marchandises expédiées en exécution de cet acte'. The Cour de Cassation retorts that 'les tribunaux français ne sauraient reconnaître aucune dépossession d'un droit de propriété, en dehors du consentement du propriétaire sans une juste et préalable indemnité'. The Court pointed out that the Spanish decree of 8 August 1936, by which the goods had been confiscated, did not provide for compensation, and even regarded it as immaterial that by decrees of the Spanish Government passed after the arrival of the goods in France compensation was promised with retroactive effect. 'Le caractère rétroactif d'une telle disposition ne saurait, au regard de la législation française, produire effet à l'encontre de droit acquis, notamment en ce qui concerne des marchandises antérieurement débarquées sur le territoire français.'

Thus the Supreme Courts of New York and France not only proceeded to examine the applicability of their respective rules of public policy, but applied them in fact and stigmatized the foreign act of State as immoral. This is not the place to discuss

---

[1] *Vladikavkazsky Railway Co.* v. *New York Trust Co.* 263 N. Y. 369 (1934), *Annual Digest* (1933 and 1934), No. 27; *Dougherty* v. *Equitable Life Assurance Society*, 266 N. Y. 71 (1934), *Annual Digest* (1933 and 1934), No. 28.

[2] The Court recognized the dissolution of Russian companies by the Soviet legislation: Cass. Req., 29 July 1929, Clunet (1930), 680; see also Cour de Bordeaux, 2 January 1928, Clunet (1929), 115; Cour de Paris, 13 June 1928, Clunet (1928), 119; Cass. Rew., 4 July 1933, Clunet (1934), 662. But it refused to give effect to the confiscation of Russian property even if situate within Russia: Cass. Req., 5 March 1928, Clunet (1928), 674, relying on Art. 545, Code Civil.

[3] Cass. Civ., 14 March 1939, Clunet (1939), 615.

the question whether the rules of public policy as understood in England ought to have led to a rejection of the Russian legislation; probably the result reached by the Court of Appeal is sound.[1] The remarkable fact is that comparative law does not by any means provide definite support for the restriction which Bankes and Warrington L.JJ. felt was imposed upon them, or for Scrutton L.J.'s misapprehension that to prevent a *casus belli* the Court had to pursue a policy of appeasement rather than of morality. The student of the history of wars need not be reminded that such decisions as *Rousillon* v. *Rousillon*[2] or *Attorney-General* v. *Scott*[3] did not, and would not now, disturb the peace of the world, nor is there any evidence that the application of the public policy rules of the forum, so often resorted to by the French courts, has ever been regarded as an international delinquency for which the government of the forum could be made responsible.[4]

If, for one reason or another, an English Court were precluded from opposing its principles of justice and morality to foreign acts of State, logic might necessitate the conclusion that foreign confiscatory legislation must also be allowed extra-

[1] The decisive reason is perhaps less the distinction between the enforcement of rights and the acquisition of title to property, than the fact that the transfer of property by confiscation is a transaction entirely executed and completed in the foreign country to the law of which it is subject, and in no way connected with the law of the forum. This formula which corresponds to the principle propounded by M. Wolff, *Internationales Privatrecht*, p. 8; Neumeyer, *Internationales Verwaltungsrecht* iv.251 sqq., and, probably, Cheshire, p. 150, is applicable to other cases which do not involve the transfer of property but with regard to which public policy should also be inapplicable. See the decision of the Court of Appeals of New York in *Dougherty's Case, ubi supra*. The plaintiffs, American subjects, claimed payment of insurance policies taken out by them in Russia subject to Russian law. The action failed on the ground that 'it cannot be against the public policy of this State to hold nationals to the contracts which they have made in their own country to be performed there according to the laws of that country'. Similarly, Court of Appeals of New York in *Salimoff* v. *Standard Oil Co. of New York*, 262 N. Y. 220 (1933), *Annual Digest* (1933 and 1934), No. 8: oil belonging to the plaintiffs was confiscated by the Russian Government and sold by them to the defendants. The action for damages for conversion failed. Russian confiscatory legislation was generally recognized in Germany: Berlin District Court, 1 November 1928, Clunet (1929), 184.

[2] (1880) 14 Ch. D. 351.    [3] (1886) 11 P. D. 128.

[4] On State responsibility for judicial acts see Oppenheim (–Lauterpacht), i.289 sqq.; Wheaton (–Keith), *International Law* (1929), i.424, 428; Strupp, 47 *Recueil* (1934), 562; *Draft Convention on Responsibility of States for Injuries to Aliens*, Special Supplement to *A.J.I.L.* (1929), 133 sqq., 176, 177, 186. Applying internal rules of public policy to an English contract which contemplated smuggling of alcohol to the United States during the period of prohibition, Lawrence L.J.

territorial effect so as to comprise property situate in this country. English Courts have shrunk from arriving at so extraordinary a result.[1] It would appear, however, that the Supreme Court of the United States felt itself compelled to carry the statements in *Underhill* v. *Hernandez*[2] and *Oetjen* v. *Central Leather Co.*[3] to the full length of attributing extraterritorial effect to the Russian confiscatory legislation. In *U.S.* v. *Belmont*[4] the United States Government claimed moneys deposited with the defendant bank in New York which the Russian Government claimed to have acquired by confiscation and which it had assigned to the plaintiff Government. The Court held that the claim disclosed a cause of action and rejected the contention that the confiscation was inconsistent with the Fifth Amendment prohibiting expropriation without just compensation, on the ground that the American Constitution had no extraterritorial effect. As Professor Borchard,[5] who severely criticizes the decision, pointedly remarks, 'this seems strange. The Constitution was invoked to protect private property deposited in New York, not in Soviet Russia.'

The Supreme Court of the United States has also held[6] that even if the confiscated property belonged to an American citizen, the validity of the foreign legislation had to be admitted. Yet it is perhaps a principle of international law that no State

relied on the ground that the recognition of the contract 'by our courts would furnish a just cause for complaint to the United States Government against our Government (of which the partners are subjects), and would be contrary to our obligation of international comity as now understood and recognized and therefore would offend against our notions of public morality': *Foster* v. *Driscoll*, [1929] 1 K. B. 470, 510.

[1] *Re Russian Bank for Foreign Trade*, [1933] 1 Ch. 745, 765; *Bohm* v. *Czerny*, The Times Newspaper, 26 July 1940; but see *Lorentzen* v. *Lydden & Co. Ltd.*, [1942] 2 K. B. 202, commented upon 5 *Mod. L.R.* (1942), 262. Similarly Rumanian Supreme Court 13 February 1929, *Annual Digest* (1929 and 1930), No. 28; 5 December 1932, Clunet (1935), 718, and Annual Digest (1933 and 1934), No. 34; and Swedish Supreme Court, 18 December 1929, 26 June 1931, and 26 March 1932, *Annual Digest* (1929 and 1930), No. 61; 1931 and 1932, Nos. 70, 71.

[2] 168 U. S. 250 (1897).     [3] 246 U. S. 297 (1917).

[4] 301 U. S. 324 (1936). The decision is in many respects somewhat obscure, but it has recently been followed and extended in *U.S.* v. *Pink*, 62 Sup. Ct. 552; 315 U. S. 203 (1942); see Borchard and Jessup, ibid., pp. 275, 282.

[5] *A.J.I.L.* (1937), 675. See, however, *Russian Volunteer Fleet* v. *U.S.*, 282 U. S. 481 (1931): a Russian corporation can rely on the Fifth Amendment, 'although the property of our citizens may be confiscated in the alien's country'.

[6] *Ricaud* v. *American Metal*, 246 U. S. 304 (1917). But see Russell L.J.'s formula in *Princess Paley Olga* v. *Weisz*, [1929] 1 K. B. 718, 736.

may confiscate a foreigner's property unless compensation is paid.[1] A State violating this rule is said to commit an international delinquency. It is, of course, possible that, although the Government of the forum may be entitled to treat an act of State as unlawful according to international law, a court may yet have to regard it as sacrosanct and valid. There may be some, however, to whom such a result will appear paradoxical.[2]

[1] Oppenheim (–Lauterpacht), i.283–5, 547 (whose observations are not free from ambiguity) with further references. See the discussion between Fachiri and Fischer-Williams, *B.Y.I.L.* (1925), p. 159: (1927), p. 1; (1929), p. 32, and M. Wolff, *Internationales Privatrecht*, p. 8.

[2] Keith, Preface to Dicey, *Conflict of Laws* (5th ed.), p. xii.

# XIII

## THE LEGAL CONSEQUENCES OF
### *SABBATINO* *

In *Banco Nacional de Cuba* v. *Sabbatino*[1] the Supreme Court of
the United States held, in effect, that a United States citizen
whose sugar had been confiscated in Cuba could not recover
it from another United States citizen who had it in his possession in the United States.[2] This decision created a sensation all
over the world such as few decisions of any court have produced. Jubilation on the other side of the Iron Curtain was as
emphatic as the grief and consternation among the majority of
lawyers in the West. The latter's feelings had been foreshadowed by Mr. Justice White who, in a dissent of exceptional
forcefulness, confessed to being 'dismayed' by and 'disappointed' at a decision which carried 'a backward looking
doctrine . . . a disconcerting step further'.[3] Within little more
than six months the Congress heeded such and similar criticism
by severely curtailing the effect of the decision.[4] It did so in
the face of vigorous opposition by the executive branch[5] whose

---

* From 51 *Virginia L.R.* (1965), 604.

[1] 376 U. S. 398 (1964).

[2] The case was argued and decided as if the facts were as stated in the text. In
fact, the sugar had never reached the United States, but the action concerned the
proceeds of sale, and the owner of the sugar was not at any time a United States
citizen but a Cuban corporation 'whose capital stock was owned principally by
United States residents.' 376 U. S., at p. 401. The Cuban Government, therefore,
had confiscated the property of a corporation which, *prima facie*, had Cuban nationality. The question whether for purposes of international law the nationality of
the shareholders could change the nationality of the corporation was not discussed
by the Court. It is one of the most remarkable features of the decision that it fails
to lay any foundation for the assumption which it makes and thus appears to
decide a hypothetical case.

[3] 376 U. S., at p. 439 (dissenting opinion).

[4] See Foreign Assistance Act, 1964, Pub. L. No. 88–633, 88th Congr., 2d Sess.
§ 301 (7 October 1964). For a discussion of the act, see below, p. 483, n. 2.

[5] See *Hearings on S. 2659, S. 2660 and H. R. 11380 before the Senate Committee
on Foreign Relations*, 88th Cong., 2d Sess. 618–19 (1964), reprinted in 3 *International
Legal Materials* (1964), 1077–8.

argument as *amicus curiae* had no doubt been largely responsible for the view taken by the majority of the Court.

These are strong reactions. It is their very pungency that imposes a special duty upon the academic lawyer, albeit a non-American lawyer, to assess the strictly legal effect of the Supreme Court's ruling and to analyse the present status of the doctrine of the sacrosanctity of a (foreign) act of State. This is a task which is rendered particularly urgent by reason of the enormous influence the decision is likely to have in many countries. Yet the reasoning put forward by Mr. Justice Harlan on behalf of the majority of the Court is in many respects singularly perplexing. Hence, where clear lines of demarcation are being looked for, and, perhaps, required, it is possible only to offer diffident explanations and vague forecasts.

# I

For the purpose of determining the legal significance in the United States of the Cuban confiscation, all three Courts[1] and all the parties assumed the sacrosanctity of a foreign act of State as the correct and unquestionable starting point. Mr. Chief Justice Fuller's often-quoted dictum once again served as a statement of principle:

Every sovereign State is bound to respect the independence of every other sovereign State, and the courts of one country will not sit in judgment on the acts of the Government of another done within its own territory. Redress of grievances by reason of such acts must be obtained through the means open to be availed of by sovereign powers as between themselves.[2]

However, the position of the original owner of the sugar, which was accepted by the courts below, was that the principle did not cover foreign acts of State done in violation of international law, that in the present case the taking of a United States citizen's property was a violation of international law, and that therefore a title allegedly acquired in Cuba should not be recognized in the United States.

The most significant part of this argument is its first limb.

---

[1] 376 U. S. 398; 307 F. 2d 845 (2d Cir. 1962); 193 F. Supp. 375 (S. D. N. Y. 1961).
[2] *Underhill* v. *Hernandez*, 168 U. S. 250, 252 (1897).

The supremacy of international law is, or should be, the touchstone of any legal system which cherishes its attachment to the fundamental order of mankind and refuses to accept as law what is contrary to the elementary demands of righteousness and morality. In other words, it should be intolerable for any judge to be compelled to apply a law which is, and is known to be, contrary to international law and therefore a wrong. The technical method by which the judge avoids the denial of his judicial function is of no consequence. Against a foreign State's acts he may invoke public policy (*ordre public*), as the French Courts do,[1] or he may adopt a philosophical approach and deny legal quality to acts constituting an 'absolute wrong,' as the tribunals of the Federal Republic of Germany do or are likely to do,[2] or he may make international law the specific test and reject such acts as are not supported by it. In recent times a growing number of tribunals[3] and learned writers,[4] adopting these or other techniques, have rejected positivistic devotion to the sacrosanctity of the foreign act of

---

[1] See Judgment of Cour de Cassation (Ch. civ.), 14 March 1939, 66 *Journal du Droit International*, [Clunet] (1939), 615; Judgment of Cour de Cassation (Ch. req.), 5 March 1928, [1928] *Journal du Droit International* [Clunet] 674.

[2] The problem of international law which arose in *Sabbatino* has never been decided by the German Supreme Court, but in view of many of its decisions dealing with wrongs committed by the Nazis and the relationship between public international law and the federal constitution, it may be expected that the forecast made in the text will prove correct. See Mann, 'Völkerrechtswidrige Enteignungen vor nationalen Gerichten', *Neue Juristische Wochenschrift* (1961), 705, followed in Erman–Arndt, *Handkommentar zum Bürgerlichen Gesetzbuch* (3d ed. 1962), Art. 30, n. 5. See also Dahm, *Festschrift für Herbert Kraus* (1964), 75. The decision in *N. V. Verenigde Deli-Maatschappijen* v. *Deutsch-Indonesische Tabak-Handelsgesellschaft, m.b.H.*, *Hanseatisches Oberlandesgericht Bremen*, 21 August 1959 (*Indonesian Tobacco Case*), 28 Int. L.R. 16, is probably irreconcilable with the prevailing tendencies of German legal thought. Compare Bodenheimer, 'Significant Developments in German Legal Philosophy Since 1945', 3 *A.J.C.L.* (1954), 379.

[3] See *Anglo-Iranian Oil Co.* v. *Soc. S.u.p.o.r.*, Tribunale di Roma, 13 September 1954, 78 *Foro italiano* (1955), 256, [1955] Int. L.R. 23; *Anglo-Iranian Oil Co.* v. *S.u.p.o.r.*, Tribunale di Venezia, 11 March 1953, 76 *Foro italiano* (1953), 719, Int. L.R. (1955), 19; *Anglo-Iranian Oil Co.* v. *Idemitsu Kosan Kabushiki Kaisha*, Int. L.R. (1953), 305 (Tokyo High Court). These decisions state that if a violation of public international law had occurred, the former owner's claims would have succeeded.

[4] It is neither necessary nor possible to give a complete list, but Domke, 'Foreign Nationalizations: Some Aspects of Contemporary International Law', 55 *A.J.I.L.* (1961), 585, 612–13, gives a fairly extensive list of writers who are in accord with the position taken in 'International Delinquencies Before Municipal Courts', above, p. 366.

State, or to the maxim of *lex loci actus*. In regard to both foreign acts of State in general and confiscations in particular, they have acknowledged the primacy of international law.

Although it may surprise some readers and although prevailing impressions are likely to tend in the opposite direction, the Supreme Court of the United States seems to have accepted in *Sabbatino* the suggestion that a foreign act of State ceases to be sacrosanct when it is contrary to international law. If this were correct, the decision could be welcomed as a most noteworthy contribution to a progressive development of the law, and as an outstanding affirmation of the pervading impact of international law.

The kernel of Mr. Justice Harlan's judgment is expressed in the statement that

we decide only that the Judicial Branch will not examine the validity of a taking of property within its own territory by a foreign sovereign government, extant and recognized by this country at the time of suit, in the absence of a treaty or other unambiguous agreement regarding controlling legal principles, even if the complaint alleges that the taking violates customary international law.[1]

In the present context, the operative words are: 'in the absence of a treaty or other unambiguous agreement regarding controlling legal principles.' Where there is agreement of this kind, there exists a rule of international law. 'Unambiguous agreement regarding controlling legal principles' is the same thing as a rule of international law. Without altering the sense of the phrase or doing violence to its language, the latter expression could be substituted for the words used, so that the sentence would read: 'in the absence of a treaty or other rule of international law'. It is true that the subsequent phrase 'even if the complaint alleges that the taking violates customary international law' might speak against the construction just suggested, for those words seem to introduce a contrast (where identity is believed to exist) between 'other unambiguous agreement regarding controlling legal principles' and 'customary international law'. But too much should not be read into the phrase beginning with 'even if'. It is, in any event, an unfortunate phrase in that the mere allegation in the complaint

---

[1] 376 U. S., at p. 428.

is surely irrelevant. Nor is it likely that 'unambiguous agreement' should be read as being *ejusdem generis* with 'treaty'. If this were so, the phrase would have been otiose, since it would add nothing to the term 'treaty'. These points may be marginal and insufficient to eliminate doubt about a crucial aspect of the opinion. However, the interpretation suggested above is strengthened if proper weight is given to a sentence which precedes the summary of the decision and which the dissenting opinion of Mr. Justice White rightly treats as a key sentence:

> It should be apparent that the greater the degree of codification or consensus concerning a particular area of international law, the more appropriate it is for the judiciary to render decisions regarding it, since the courts can then focus on the application of an agreed principle to circumstances of fact rather than on the sensitive task of establishing a principle not inconsistent with the national interest or with international justice.[1]

The 'consensus' permitting and requiring 'the application of an agreed principle to circumstances of fact' establishes and represents a rule of international law and is the same thing as the 'other unambiguous agreement regarding controlling legal principles' referred to a few sentences later. Without 'consensus' there can be no rule of customary international law; 'unambiguous agreement' creates and maintains such a rule. What Mr. Justice Harlan is saying may be reformulated as follows: where there is 'consensus' or 'unambiguous agreement' concerning 'a particular area of international law' or 'controlling legal principles'—where, in other words, there are to be found, in the language of Lord Macmillan, 'the hallmarks of general assent and reciprocity'[2]—a rule of international law is in existence and displaces the doctrine of the sacrosanctity of the foreign act of State.

This conclusion is supported by the fact that it avoids any differentiation between the legal quality of a treaty and a rule of customary international law. No such differentiation is usual or possible. A legal duty imposed by treaty is neither higher nor more effective than a duty arising under customary international law. To treat the breach of a treaty obligation as overriding, yet to disregard the breach of a rule of customary international law, would involve an incongruity incapable of

---

[1] ibid.
[2] *Compañia Naviera Vascongado* v. *Steamship Cristina (the Cristina)*, [1938] A. C. 485.

rational explanation and pregant with injustice. Moreover, no such distinction can exist in the mind of anyone who is aware of the great difficulties and controversies frequently surrounding the question of whether a breach of a treaty obligation has occurred. An example can be taken from the law relating to confiscations. By the Round Table Conference Treaties of 1949,[1] Indonesia gave the most explicit guarantees for the security of Dutch property in Indonesia. Nevertheless, in 1958 Indonesia enacted legislation confiscating Dutch tobacco plantations.[2] The breach of treaty was justified by Indonesia with a variety of arguments unlikely to be acceptable but which involved numerous and difficult problems of fact and law. It cannot have been in Mr. Justice Harlan's mind that they could be more readily solved than problems arising in the application of a rule of customary international law. In short, there is no justification for treating the breach of a treaty obligation as a necessarily or usually clearer and easier case than the breach of a rule of customary law.

Finally, there are numerous cases of treaties which incorporate obligations arising from customary international law. Thus, many modern treaties, of which a treaty between the Netherlands and Tunisia is, perhaps, the latest example, contain words such as these:

> In the event that one Party expropriates or nationalizes property, rights, or interests belonging to persons, physical or juridical, nationals of the other Party, or acts against them in any degree of dispossession, it shall provide payment of an effective and adequate indemnity, *in conformity with international law*.[3]

If the Netherlands takes Tunisian property without paying compensation, i.e. confiscates it, can it reasonably be suggested

---

[1] Round Table Conference Agreements Between Netherlands and Indonesia, 27 December 1949, 69 U. N. T. S. 3, 230–58.

[2] For the text in English, see 6 *Nederlands Tijdschrift voor Internationaal Recht* (1959), 291.

[3] Netherlands–Tunisia Agreement for Encouragement of Capital Investments, 23 May 1963, [1963] Tractatenblad van het Koninkrijk der Nederlanden No. 106, reprinted in 4 *Int. Legal Materials* (1965), 159. (Emphasis added.) Treaties in similar terms were concluded in 1962 between Switzerland and several African States such as Senegal, Tunisia, The Ivory Coast, and Niger. Curiously enough, the Attorney-General of the United States, Mr. Katzenbach, seems to think that the standard of compensation referred to in the text is 'modified' rather than affirmed by the italicized words. Ibid. at p. 581.

that the reference to payment of compensation 'in conformity with international law' creates rather than presupposes an obligation ?

In these circumstances it would seem possible to arrive at the conclusion, tentative and precarious though it may be, that a foreign act of State, even a foreign confiscation, will not be regarded by the courts of the United States as sacrosanct, if it is contrary to conventional or customary international law. Or, to paraphrase Mr. Justice Harlan's dictum, given a treaty or other unambiguous agreement regarding controlling legal principles, the judicial branch will examine the validity of a taking of property by a foreign sovereign Government within its own territory,[1] and will, in suitable cases, hold it invalid.

On this basis, Mr. Justice Harlan may be said to reject that theory which would confine the remedy for a breach of international law to diplomatic protests and, where access is possible, to proceedings for damages in international tribunals. Such a view[2] rests upon the untenable notion that there is in all cases only one remedy to deal with a wrong. The Supreme Court, happily, refused to accept it.

Before leaving the first limb of the respondents' argument, it is convenient to summarize certain other conditions which, according to Mr. Justice Harlan himself, may exclude or at least may affect the operation of the traditional act of State doctrine. In the first place, it is by no means certain whether, and to what extent, the doctrine will apply to acts of State other than takings of property. It is possible that the validity of the requisition of a vessel by a foreign Government[3] or of a revocation of citizenship[4] will not in the future be covered by the doctrine at all, although it will not be easy to find a logical explanation for the distinction. Secondly, there is much to be said for the view that there is now no objection to a court investigating the validity of an act done by a former, as opposed

---

[1] It would seem that Falk, 'The Complexity of Sabbatino', 58 *A.J.I.L.* (1964), 935, 941–2, agrees with this conclusion.

[2] Propagated in particular by Baade, 'Indonesian Nationalization Measures Before Foreign Courts—A Reply', 54 *A.J.I.L.* (1960), 801; Baade, 'The Validity of Foreign Confiscations: An Addendum', 56 *A.J.I.L.* (1962), 504.

[3] *Union Shipping & Trading Co.* v. *United States*, 127 F. 2d 771 (2d Cir. 1942); *The Claveresk*, 264 Fed. 276 (2d Cir. 1920).

[4] *United States ex rel. Steinvorth* v. *Watkins*, 159 F. 2d. 50 (2d Cir. 1947).

to an operating, Government. This would permit the burial of so disastrous a case as *Bernstein* v. *Van Heyghen Frères, S.A.*,[1] where in 1947 the Second Circuit felt compelled to treat as valid an act of a most heinous character allegedly done in 1938 by the Nazi Government. Yet the exception is again unconvincing, for it is difficult to see why an act done in 1963 by the Government of Sir Alec Douglas-Home should be capable of being questioned, as the Court's formulation would seem to suggest, merely by reason of the fact that in 1964, Mr Harold Wilson's Government came to power in Britain. Thirdly, the act of State done by an unrecognized government is not sacrosanct. This is probably in harmony with traditional learning. Fourthly, it has been suggested that Mr. Justice Harlan's words must be understood to mean that the validity of a foreign act of State may be questioned where the implications of the issue involved are of little importance to American foreign relations.[2] Mr. Justice Harlan did mention the point. Whether he intended it to be part of his *ratio decidendi* is open to considerable doubt. That it lacks attraction is certain, for it would be an invidious and unrealistic task for the judiciary to undertake a weighing process in order to ascertain whether a given issue is at the time, or will become at some future date, unimportant to the foreign relations of the United States. This is a matter of such relativity that it should not be made the basis for a far-reaching limitation upon a legal principle.

# II

The second limb of the argument against the operation of the act of State doctrine involved the proposition that, assuming the violation of a rule of international law to constitute an exception and thus to restore normal jurisdiction to the courts,

---

[1] 163 F. 2d 246 (2d Cir.), *cert. denied*, 332 U. S. 772 (1947). This decision, although inspired by so great a lawyer and so liberal a man as Judge Learned Hand, remains a permanent monument to misguided positivism. Those interested in jurisprudence and the judicial process should devote much more attention to this judgment which many regard as a miscarriage of justice. The subsequent well-known history appears in *Bernstein* v. *N. V. Nederlandsche-Amerikaansche Stoomvaart-Maatschappij*, 210 F. 2d 375 (2d Cir. 1954).

[2] See Falk, above, p. 472, n. 1, at 942.

the Cuban confiscations did violate a rule of international law and were therefore not protected by the act of State doctrine.

It was by its answer to this suggestion that the majority of the Supreme Court inflicted an alarming blow upon international law and one of its principles. It is difficult to believe that the judicial and the executive branches have as yet fully appreciated the consequences of the three hundred words or so which the Court devoted to matters of crucial importance to our civilization, which tend to endanger some of the work done during the last three hundred years and the echo of which may still be audible in another three hundred years.

The Court made the momentous pronouncement that the Cuban confiscations did not violate a rule of international law.

The Court held that there were 'few if any issues in international law today on which opinion seems to be so *divided* as the limitations on a state's power to expropriate the property of aliens', that there was '*disagreement* as to relevant international law standards', and that, consequently, there was no such '*consensus*' as made and maintained customary international law.[1] It is quite true that the Court chose formulations which avoided the blunt statement that there existed no such rule of international law as was contended for. But this is what the Court in effect said by speaking in a circuitous manner of lack of consensus, of disagreement, of divergencies. Where there is no consensus there is no rule of international law. A rule of international law presupposes consensus. The synonymity is complete. That the absence of consensus is, in the context, tantamount to the denial of a rule of international law would not have to be explained, were it not for a statement made by the executive branch: 'The decision in the *Sabbatino* case was not a victory for Castro. The Court did not recognize the validity under international law of the Cuban Government's decree.'[2] Perhaps this is a mere play on words: The Supreme Court certainly did not 'recognize' the Cuban decree. On the other hand, the Supreme Court did not hold it to be contrary to international law. It is a necessary implication that what is

---

[1] 376 U. S., at pp. 428, 430. (Emphasis added.)

[2] *Hearings on S. 2659*, above, p. 466, n. 5, at p. 619; 3 *Int. Legal Materials*, at p. 1078.

not invalid, must be valid, what is not illegal is legal. Nor can the Court's denial of a rule of international law be explained away by the following sentence in a footnote of the opinion: 'We do not, of course, mean to say that there is no international standard in this area; we conclude only that the matter is not meet for adjudication by domestic tribunals.'[1] The statements in the text of the opinion are so plain and so strong and constitute so essential a part of the Court's reasoning that the footnote, whatever its meaning may be, unfortunately cannot take the shine out of the text.

Several causes combined to produce this result:

*First,* the Court's conclusion that there was no consensus extended to both the rule that the taking of alien property must be accompanied by the provision of prompt, adequate, and effective compensation (upon which the District Court had relied) and the rule that the taking must not be discriminatory (which the Court of Appeals invoked).[2] The Supreme Court, however, made no attempt to differentiate between the character and status of these two entirely different rules.

The former, it is true, has in recent years been exposed to a certain amount of frequently ill-considered criticism. However, no such criticism has at any time or by anyone been directed against the necessity for compensation. To put it in another way, the legality of theft has not been advocated and, therefore, no question of principle or of liability has been raised. Rather, it has been suggested that compensation does not have to be 'prompt, adequate, and effective'. To some extent the controversy has been verbal: should, for instance, 'just' or 'reasonable' compensation be sufficient? Should resort be had to the principles of unjust enrichment[3] or restitution?[4] The difference of views thus relates to quantum and methods of discharge only. Much could be said about the lack of historical appreciation and of realism which characterizes it, for the form of words

---

[1] 376 U. S., at p. 428, n. 26.

[2] See 207 F. 2d 845, 865–8 (2d Cir. 1962); 193 F. Supp. 375, 383–6 (S. D. N. Y. 1961).

[3] For an affirmative answer see, e.g., Friedmann, *The Changing Structure of International Law* (1964), pp. 206–10, who, incidentally, wrongly treats *Lena Goldfields* as an 'international case'. See id., at p. 207.

[4] See Wortley, *Expropriation in Public International Law* (1959), pp. 72–92, who puts it in the forefront of his argument.

used to describe the amount of compensation traditionally required has a long history and is to this day firmly entrenched in almost universal legal practice.[1] At the same time that form of words has been given a fairly well understood, restricted meaning. Thus it does not indicate an intention to require the payment of the whole amount in one lump sum or of every penny of loss which can be proved to have been suffered.

The rule against discrimination, on the other hand, involves a principle which does not seem to have been challenged in any country or at any time. It is certainly not always easy to define the circumstances in which lack of equality amounts to unlawful discrimination under international law. But given an inequality which is discriminatory in law, which is arbitrary or constitutes an abuse, no one has attempted to defend it.[2] It is one of the most noteworthy features of the decision in *Sabbatino* that it draws no distinction between two different principles and fails to state whether the Cuban confiscations were discriminatory and, if so, whether they were lawful. The opinion is, on this point, almost unbelievably summary.

*Second*, the Court's result is predicated upon the failure to examine in any but the most cursory manner the material supporting either of the rules mentioned above. The Court ignored numerous decisions of great persuasiveness.[3] As to diplomatic practice, one English and two United States diplomatic Notes were the only examples mentioned by the Court. References to writers of authority were limited to an admittedly weighty article by Lord McNair,[4] and neither Oppenheim[5] nor

---

[1] See Mann, 'Outlines of a History of Expropriation', 75 *L.Q.R.* (1959), 188.

[2] Not even Professor Falk. See Falk, above, p. 472, n. 1, at p. 944. In particular, see *In re Claim by Helbert Wagg & Co.*, [1956] 1 Ch. 323, 346; Jennings, 'The Sabbatino Controversy', 20 *Record of N.Y.C.B.A.* (1965), 81, 85, who rightly lays stress on the point made in the text. Professor Jennings' thoughtful, though short, paper contains other points of great interest.

[3] See, e.g., cases cited above, p. 468, n. 3. It would have been appropriate to refer to a pronouncement by Max Huber, one of the greatest international lawyers, who wrote in 1924: 'qu'il peut être considéré comme acquis qu'en droit international un étranger ne peut être privé de sa propriété sans juste indemnité.' *Affaire des biens Britanniques au Maroc Espagnol*, 2 U. N. Rep. Int'l Arb. Awards 615, 647 (1935).

[4] McNair, 'The Seizure of Property and Enterprises in Indonesia', 6 *Nederlands Tijdschrift voor Internationaal Recht* (1959), 218.

[5] Oppenheim, *International Law* (8th ed., Lauterpacht, 1955), i. § 115aa-ab.

authors writing in languages other than English were cited.[1] The Harvard Draft of 1961[2] was not considered in the Court's opinion, nor was Dr. Garcia Amador's Report to the International Law Commission.[3] The most astonishing fact is that not a single treaty, whether multilateral or bilateral, was mentioned. The post-war treaties of Friendship, Commerce, and Navigation which the United States has concluded with some eighteen States and which, by virtue of the most-favoured-nations clause in treaties with other States, have the widest impact are disregarded, although all of them contain clauses similar to the following, taken from the treaty with Iran:

> Such property shall not be taken except for a public purpose, nor shall it be taken without the prompt payment of just compensation. Such compensation shall be in an effectively realizable form and shall represent the full equivalent of the property taken. . . .[4]

Nor is there, finally, any reference to any of the numerous similar treaties which other States have concluded and which cover a very large part of the world.[5]

*Third,* these omissions may, at least to some extent, stem from a failure to give thought to the problem of sources of

---

[1] See, e.g., Guggenheim, *Traité de droit international public* (1953), i.331; Verdross, *Völkerrecht* (5th ed., 1964), 366; Verzijl, 'Festgabe für Makarov', 19 *Zeitschrift für Ausländisches Öffentliches Recht und Völkerrecht* (1958), 531.

[2] Harvard Draft Convention, 'Responsibility of States for Injuries to the Economic Interests of Aliens', 55 *A.J.I.L.* (1961), 545, 555–4.

[3] *Yearbook of the International Law Commission* (1959), ii.1.

[4] Treaty of Amity, Economic Relations, and Consular Rights with Iran, 15 August 1955, [1957] 1 U. S. T. & O. I. A. 900, 903, T. I. A. S., No. 3853. For the most recent analysis of these treaties see Benton, 'The Protection of Property Rights in Commercial Treaties of the United States', 25 *Zeitschrift für Ausländisches Öffentliches Recht und Völkerrecht* (1965), 50.

[5] Professor Jennings lists fifty treaties by 'developing States', see Jennings, above, p. 476, n. 2, at pp. 89–91, but there are many more made between or with States which may not necessarily come within the scope of that somewhat vague term. For example, Germany signed such agreements with Greece and Turkey, the former of which is in force. See Berger, 1 *Aussenwirtschaftsdienst* (1965). Moreover, there is, for instance, the Anglo–Japanese Treaty of Commerce, Establishment and Navigation, 14 November, 1962, Art. 14, Cmd. No. 1874, and the El Salvador–Japan Commercial Treaty of 19 July 1963, Art. IV, 4 *Int. Legal Materials* (1965) 481. It appears that since Professor Jennings wrote, Germany concluded four additional treaties for the Reciprocal Promotion and Protection of Investments with Kenya, Tanzania, Colombia, and Ecuador. The texts conform to Germany's Model Convention and include the usual provision for the protection of property. See Berger, op. cit., above, at p. 251. The German–Indian Agreement which Professor Jennings listed is now published in 4 *Int. Legal Materials* (1965), 491.

international law. Article 38 of the Statute of the International
Court of Justice, which enumerates the sources in a convenient
form and in a manner acceptable to the strongest positivist,
does not seem to have influenced the Court's search for evidence. There is, however, an even more fundamental and
puzzling point. The Court does not make it clear whether, in
its view, there never was a rule of international law bearing
upon the issue, or whether a rule that was at one time in force
has ceased to be effective.[1] Was there never a consensus, or has
a former consensus come to an end? In either case, the question remains: What is the consensus which creates a rule of
international law or the absence of which terminates it? Or, in
other words, what is the extent of consensus which is required
for a rule of international law? What is the strength or the
quality of 'disagreement' which jeopardizes a rule of international law?

These are grave questions to which Mr. Justice Harlan's
opinion gives no answer of any kind. If it permits an inference,
it is to the effect that any disagreement, any divergence is
sufficient to preclude or destroy the existence of a rule of
international law—that international law rests on the destructive foundation of the lowest common denominator. This
impression derives from the fact that the Court treated as
compelling evidence the alleged refusal of 'Communist countries' to recognize an obligation to pay compensation—a refusal
which, as will appear, has little probative force. Moreover, the
Court attached significance to the view of 'certain representatives'[2] of new States who have 'questioned' whether such
States are bound by rules to which they have not expressly
consented—a view which cannot seriously be maintained by a
State that claims to have joined the family of nations and, in
particular, the United Nations Organization whose Charter[3]
imposes the duty to observe international law, not the duty to
be bound by such parts of international law as the emergent
State considers convenient. Again, the Court thought that
there was 'an even more basic divergence' between capital-

---

[1] See 376 U. S., at pp. 429–30.

[2] ibid. To the very few such representatives quoted by the Court, one could now
add Sinha, 'Perspective of the Newly Independent States on the Binding Quality
of International Law', 14 *I.C.L.Q.* (1965), 121.

[3] U.N. Charter Preamble, Art. 1 and passim.

importing and capital-exporting States. It completely over-looked the widespread net of treaties made in the post-war period and protecting investments and capital imports—treaties of a special kind which the United States itself has propagated, but which are not peculiar to the United States, and which make it quite impossible to suggest that capital-importing States feel, or are entitled to feel, free to take alien property without compensation.[1]

However this may be, the problems remain whether the Court was right to demand, apparently, identity of views and universality of practice before it accepted the existence of a rule of international law, or whether, given the existence of a rule of international law, deviation from the rule constitutes not a breach of the law and therefore a wrong but disagree-ment with the law and therefore a lawful act. This is not the place to pursue in all its implications one of the basic problems of international law to which great scholars have devoted much searching thought. It must suffice to recall a simple truth that is unlikely to be doubted except by the most determined disrupters of our legal order and its ideals. The idea of uniform and universal consent has no place in international law. What one looks for is a reasonable level of agreement. A process of selection and weighing-up has to be gone through. The Supreme Court failed to do anything of the kind and thus arrived at the conclusion that the presence of dissenters, however few in number or light in weight, could destroy the law. This is a wholly unacceptable approach. The minimum that is re-quired is an investigation into the question of the legal justi-fication and persuasiveness of the dissent. The dissenter's *ipse dixit* is insufficient.

*Fourth,* and last, it is not at all certain whether Mr. Justice Harlan was justified in suggesting that there exists such dis-agreement as prevents the existence of a rule of international law. It is not true that 'Communist countries, although they have in fact provided a degree of compensation after diplo-matic affairs, commonly recognize no obligation on the part of the taking country'.[2] The true position is that, although Com-munist countries commonly recognize the obligation to pay compensation, they actually provide a fraction only, and this

---

[1] See above, p. 477, n. 5.     [2] 376 U. S., at p. 429.

only after diplomatic efforts. Almost all recent confiscators
have framed their legislation so as to contemplate the payment
of compensation. Accordingly, they have accepted the principle
that it is their duty to pay it. In this sense the practice of States
from which international law is derived is unbroken and uniform. If and in so far as compensation is provided for, it is
impossible to suggest that the legislator knows 'no obligation'.
What would be the point of providing for it if 'no obligation'
were accepted? What these confiscators have failed to do is to
pay compensation, to implement the promise made and the
obligation assumed by their own legislation, to comply with
the duty they recognized. The situation, therefore, is entirely
different from that commonly assumed to exist. It may be that
the provision for compensation is no more than lip-service paid
to the confiscators' international obligations or window-
dressing designed to proclaim compliance with, and thus to
conceal the breach of, international law. But there is no reason
why other States should not take the text of the confiscators'
legislation at face value and should impute to them the intention to deny the international rule, when they merely intend
to break it. In the past, courts have always been faced with the
problem whether there had occurred such actual failure to
make payment of compensation as to constitute a breach of
international law. The existence of the duty to pay and, consequently, the rule of international law, was not usually in
doubt at all, and could not be in doubt because of its affirmation by the confiscator.

The true character of the problem appeared for the first time
when Mexico embarked upon a policy of confiscation in 1938.
The Mexican legislation provided for compensation,[1] but there
was no evidence of a genuine intention to pay it. In 1943 the
validity of the Mexican legislation had to be decided in an
action brought in the French Courts by the El Aguila company
to recover oil sold by Mexico and lying in France.[2] The action
failed. The Court seems to have held that, since Mexican law
contemplated the payment of compensation, it was not confiscatory despite the absence of any actual payment.

---

[1] See Gordon, *The Expropriation of Foreign-Owned Property in Mexico* (1941), 127;
Wortley, 'The Mexican Oil Dispute 1938–1946', 43 *Grot. Soc.* (1959), 15, 26–6.

[2] For an incomplete report, see [1941–5] Sirey Table Quinquennale, Etranger
1 (Fr.).

The second stage in the evolution of the problem was the far-reaching policy of nationalization adopted after the second world war by Czechoslovakia, Poland, Yugoslavia, Hungary, Roumania, and Bulgaria. Subject to certain exceptions, the legislation of all these countries provided for the payment of compensation,[1] although nothing was ever paid save a small measure of compensation which creditor nations succeeded in procuring by negotiating global agreements[2]—in no case more than a moderate dividend, similar to that paid by a recalcitrant debtor or a bankrupt. Contemporaneous Estonian legislation was regarded as confiscatory both in England and in Canada, although it provided for compensation of 25 per cent, which was never paid.[3] The Swiss Federal Tribunal was called upon to determine the validity of the Czechoslovakian legislation and found that it was silent 'about the details which relate to the compensation in the present case, in particular the names of the shareholders entitled to it, the extent, manner and date of payment'.[4] In these circumstances the Court concluded that there was 'no doubt that in the present case we are dealing not with expropriation subject to adequate compensation, but with acquisition without compensation (confiscation)',[5] and that this was ineffective in Switzerland. A similar result was reached by the Court of Appeal at Bologna[6] and by the Austrian Supreme Court, which held that the Hungarian statute contained nothing but a vague promise insufficient to deprive the legislation of its confiscatory nature.[7]

---

[1] See Makarov, *Festgabe für Erich Kaufman* (1950), 249; Bindschedler, 'La Protection de la Propriété Privée en Droit International Public', 90 (1956 ii) *Recueil des Cours* 179, 253; Doman, 'Postwar Nationalization of Foreign Property in Europe', 48 *Col. L.R.* (1948), 1125.

[2] They have been collected and discussed by Foighel, *Nationalization: A Study in the Protection of Alien Property in International Law* (1957), and White, *The Nationalisation of Foreign Property* (1961), although both writers exaggerate their significance.

[3] See *Laane* v. *Estonian State S.S. Line*, [1949] Can. Sup. Ct. 530, [1949] 2 D. L. R. 641, [1948] Ann. Dig. 176 (No. 50); *A/S Tallinna Laevauhisus* v. *Estonian State S.S. Line*, 80 Ll. L. L. R. 99, 111 (C. A. 1947).

[4] *Vereinigte Carborundum- und Elektrikwerke* v. *Eidgenössisches Amt für geistiges Eigentum, Bundesgericht,* 25 September 1956, 81 (I.) *Entscheidungen des Schweizerischen Bundesgerichtes* 196, 199, [1956] Int. L. R. 24, 26.

[5] Id., at p. 25.

[6] Svit Impresa Nazionale e Bata s.p.a.c. Soc. B.S.F. Stiftung, Cipera e Bata, Appello Bologna, 28 April 1956, 40 *Rivista di Diritto Internazionale* (1957), 264.

[7] *Revue Critique de Droit International Privé* (1956), 259.

A third group of cases involving the problem arose out of the taking of the Persian assets of the Anglo-Iranian Oil Company. Persian legislation contained a provision of the utmost vagueness, indicating an intention to pay some measure of compensation.[1] It was the mere existence of this provision which, unfortunately, led Italian and Japanese Courts to hold that the taking was reconcilable with the requirements of public international law.[2]

In 1952 Guatemala confiscated the property of the United Fruit Company and provided for compensation, but the United States protested the inadequacy of the compensation.[3] The Indonesian legislation expropriating Dutch property mentioned above provided that 'the owners . . . will be given compensation, the amount of which will be determined by a Committee whose members are appointed by the Government'.[4] An appeal against the decision of the Committee could be taken to the Supreme Court, but 'the payment of compensation . . . will be further regulated in a separate act'.[5] Such an act was passed a little later; it dealt with procedural questions, but remained silent about the questions of substance. This was sufficient to lead a German Court to conclude that no breach of international law had occurred: the statutory provisions had to be treated as consistent with the demands of international law, unless the former owner could prove that 'no reasonable compensation is to be paid'.[6]

The latest development in this area was the confiscation of United States property by Cuba in 1960. The Cuban legislation[7] contemplated the payment of compensation, though the terms were clearly inadequate, delayed, and ineffective. Again, it is difficult to suggest that Cuba recognized 'no obligation' to pay compensation. It recognized but failed to perform it.

---

[1] See Cmd. No. 8425.
[2] See cases cited, above, p. 468, n. 3.
[3] See Fenwick, 'Jurisdictional Questions Involved in the Guatemalan Revolution', 48 *A.J.I.L.* (1954), 597.
[4] 6 *Nederlands Tijdschrift voor Internationaal Recht* (1959), 291.
[5] Id., at p. 292.
[6] *N. V. Verenigde Deli-Maatschappijen* v. *Deutsch-Indoniesisiche Tabak-Handelsgesellschaft, m.b.H., Hanseatisches Oberlandesgericht Bremen*, 21 August 1959, 28 Int. L. R. (1963), 16, 36.
[7] See 376 U. S. at p. 401, n. 3.

Perhaps Cuba's attitude was such as to compel the conclusion that its recognition was a mere pretence or sham, but even so one cannot impute to Cuba the intention to deny rather than to avoid its international obligations.

Notwithstanding this impressive body of evidence and the other criticism which may be directed against its reasoning, the opinion of the majority of the Supreme Court has apparently sanctioned the view (which, a short time ago, one would have been tempted to describe as subversive) that modern international law imposes no duty to pay compensation for the taking of alien property, even if it occurs in circumstances of gross arbitrariness. It is a remarkable fact that this conclusion is the very antithesis of the doctrine which the executive branch has embraced for many decades. Even after *Sabbatino* had been decided 'the State Department has taken the position that the decree was not valid under international law'.[1] Foreign confiscators will not be slow to exploit this divergence of judicial and executive practice. The inviolability of confiscations has superseded the inviolability of property.[2]


# III

The Supreme Court's refusal to allow an exception to the act of State doctrine was expressly and repeatedly stated to be limited to confiscations. It was in no way explained why 'in this realm of its application'[3] the doctrine should have a different or special meaning. Nor is it possible to see how any

---

[1] 'Hearings on S. 2659', above, p. 466, n. 5, at p. 619, 3 *Int. Legal Materials*, 1078.

[2] For the reasons developed in the preceding section of the text, it is very doubtful whether section 301 of the Foreign Assistance Act, 1964, Pub. L. No. 88–633, 88th Cong., 2d Sess. (7 October 1964) is so formulated as to give effect to the obvious intention to eliminate the doctrine of *Sabbatino*. It provides that the courts shall apply 'the principles of international law in a case in which a claim . . . is asserted . . . based upon . . . a confiscation . . . by an act . . in violation of the principles of international law, including the principles of compensation and the other standards set out in this subsection.' Ibid. No such standards are in fact set out. According to the Supreme Court, the principles of international law, though twice referred to in the subsection, in fact do not exist. It would be desirable if in the future the legislature declared and defined these principles, for instance, in the sense in which United States treaties have done so. See authorities cited, above, p. 477, n. 4. See generally 65 *Col. L.R.* (1965), 530.

[3] 376 U.S., at p. 437.

such differentiation could be justified.[1] The likelihood of the *Sabbatino* case's having repercussions upon the scope of the act of State doctrine as a whole is increased by the fact that the Court discussed 'the foundations on which we deem the act of State doctrine to rest',[2] and, in doing so, adduced arguments claiming general validity.

On the one hand, the Court admitted that the doctrine was not 'compelled either by the inherent nature of sovereign authority . . . or by some principle of international law'.[3] This conclusion is in conformity with a resolution passed by the International Law Association in 1962[4] and, in view of the state of international practice, is hardly open to doubt. But it should have meant the doom of the doctrine of the sacrosanctity of the foreign act of State and brought about the success of the respondents on the ground that the doctrine was not part of the law at all and that, therefore, there was no room for pursuing the problem of an alleged exception to it. For in the past—in particular, in *Underhill* v. *Hernandez*[5]—the rule was derived from the respect which each State owes to the independence of other States. Accordingly, the doctrine as developed in the United States had its roots in the idea of an immunity *ratione materiae*.[6] If, as the Supreme Court now tells us, international law knows no such principle, then the rule would appear to have no *raison d'être*. It may perhaps be added that the rule, even if conceived as an emanation of international law, may in any event cease to have effect where the act of State involves a violation of international law, for in respect of property, for instance, immunity is unlikely to protect a foreign sovereign whose title to the property was unlawfully acquired. *Ex injuria jus non oritur*.[7] By analogy, the act of State doctrine as a doctrine

---

[1] It is one of the criticisms to be made of the writings of Professor Falk on this point that he fails to support the distinctions he draws by reasoned arguments as opposed to assertions. See, e.g., Falk, *The Role of Domestic Courts in the International Legal Order* (1964).

[2] 376 U. S., at p. 421.    [3] ibid.

[4] *Int. Law Assn. Report of the 50th Conference in Brussels* (1963), xiv. The resolution was passed by an overwhelming majority—105 votes to 9, with 6 abstentions. Ibid., at p. 131.

[5] 168 U. S. 250 (1897).

[6] See above, p. 426.

[7] See *The Navemar*, 24 F. Supp. 495 (E. D. N. Y. 1938). But see *Compañia Naviera Vascongado* v. *Steamship Cristina*, [1938] A. C. 485.

of international law may be rendered inapplicable where a breach of international law has occurred.

On the other hand, Mr. Justice Harlan stated that, although 'the text of the Constitution does not require the act of State doctrine', it does

have 'constitutional' underpinnings. It arises out of the basic relationships between branches of government in a system of separation of powers. It concerns the competency of dissimilar institutions to make and implement particular kinds of decisions in the area of international relations. The doctrine as formulated in past decisions expresses the strong sense of the Judicial Branch that its engagement in the task of passing on the validity of foreign acts of State may hinder rather than further this country's pursuit of goals both for itself and for the community of nations as a whole in the international sphere.[1]

These observations were amplified by a long discussion designed to establish the 'wisdom' of the rule,[2] culminating in the somewhat unexpected suggestion that 'both the national interest and progress toward the goal of establishing the rule of law among nations' require the doctrine's unqualified applition.[3] That the rule of law is invoked to support the sacrosanctity of uncompensated takings of property would appear to be one of the most paradoxical lines of reasoning that has ever found its way into a judicial decision. Whether considerations of legal wisdom or folly form part of a judgment's *ratio decidendi* is a question of minor significance. It is much more important that the doctrine undergoes a complete change when it is said to have its basis in constitutional practice, for this is what is presumably meant by the reference to '"contitutional" underpinnings' as opposed to the text of the Constitution.

Such a development was foreshadowed by Mr. Justice Douglas' opinion in *United States* v. *Pink*.[4] One of the questions to be decided in that case was whether New York could distribute the New York assets of a former Russian corporation to the corporation's foreign creditors, though the Litvinov Assignment, made in the course of recognizing the Soviet Union, provided for their assignment to the United States. The majority of the Court gave a negative answer on the ground that

---

[1] 376 U. S., at p. 423.     [2] Id., at pp. 430–7.
[3] Id., at p. 437.     [4] 315 U. S. 203 (1942).

State laws and policies could not be allowed to embarrass or thwart, but had to yield before, the exercise of federal powers in the field of international relations. Such considerations, Mr. Justice Douglas interjected, 'also explain the rule expressed in *Underhill* v. *Hernandez* . . . that "the courts of one country will not sit in judgment on the acts of the government of another done within its own territory".'[1] This *obiter dictum* may have been out of place, for *United States* v. *Pink* was concerned with a conflict between State action and Federal action, and the latter's predominant effect on matters of foreign policy was not proved by pointing to the case of a conflict between the actions of two sovereign States. Nevertheless, it was Mr. Justice Douglas who for the first time placed the act of State doctrine on constitutional underpinnings. This step received support from Judge Learned Hand's decision in *Bernstein* v. *Van Heyghen Frères, S.A.*,[2] which introduced the wholly logical but equally novel idea that, given the background of constitutional practice, the Federal Government had the capacity of *releasing* the Judiciary from the restraint imposed by the act of State doctrine, the analogy to practice in matters of immunity *ratione personae* was thus again emphasized. When, finally, *Sabbatino* reached the Supreme Court, the brief submitted by the United States as *amicus curiae* drew the conclusion in the following sentence:

> The short of it is that it is essential, from the standpoint of conducting foreign relations, that the position to be taken by the United States regarding the legality of the acts of a foreign Government within its jurisdiction should be determined by the Executive, not by individual State and Federal judges.[3]

The Supreme Court then put the seal on the development by stating explicitly that the doctrine is a consequence of the Executive's power over foreign affairs. It is the wish not to embarrass the United States rather than the foreign State that has become the rationale of the act of State doctrine. The latter ensures the sacrosanctity, not of the foreign, but of the domestic act of State inherent in the Executive's foreign policy.

---

[1] Ibid., at p. 233.

[2] 163 F. 2d 246 (2d Cir.), *cert. denied*, 332 U. S. 772 (1947).

[3] Brief for the United States as Amicus Curiae, p. 30, reprinted in 2 *Int. Legal Materials* (1963), 1012, 1019.

This conclusion, it may be suggested, involves so radical a departure, and places the doctrine so clearly in the area of American constitutional law and practice, that at the present juncture of the discussion a foreign observer should tactfully withdraw from the American scene and disqualify himself. Yet he asks to be permitted to offer a few comments which arise from the premise that the act of State doctrine has changed its character and status and is now a principle of American constitutional law.[1]

In the first place, as regards the scope of the doctrine, there is, as has already been observed, no warrant for the view that the transformed doctrine applies only to confiscations. It is likely to extend to all acts of State, whether they are legislative (as in the *Sabbatino* case), executive, or judicial acts. The reason is that, if the constitutional practice of the United States requires the exercise of judicial restraint where there is 'a highly complex and volatile area' or there are 'issues which are politically sensitive,'[2] such practice must be comprehensive in character to accomplish its purpose. The consequences may well be remarkable. Thus, suppose that in the course of anti-trust proceedings instituted by the British Government, an English Court orders E. I. du Pont de Nemours & Company to assign certain United States patents to Imperial Chemical Industries. Du Pont may have granted licences in respect of such patents to X who now applies to a federal court for an injunction against du Pont and alleges that the English order is contrary to international law and ineffective in the United States.[3] The United States Government has made representations to the British Government and is engaged in delicate negotiations. Should the court exercise restraint and thus enable du Pont to comply with the English order? Or suppose a court in the United States is concerned with a statute enacted in Malta making void all marriages of Roman Catholic Maltese con-

---

[1] It might perhaps be added here that the act of State doctrine as now formulated in the United States does not seem to have a counterpart in any other country, not even in countries with a federal constitution, such as Germany.

[2] *Hearings on S. 2659*, above, p. 466, n. 5, at p. 619; 2 *Int. Legal Materials*, p. 1078.

[3] On similar facts the English Court of Appeal held that the foreign decree need not be followed. See *British Nylon Spinners Ltd.* v. *Imperial Chemical Industries Ltd.*, [1953] Ch. 19 (C. A.)

tracted otherwise than by Canon law. Would the court have to give effect to the Maltese statute and hold a marriage contracted by Roman Catholic Maltese in an English register office void on the ground that to treat it as 'an intolerable injustice', as an English judge did,[1] would be an embarrassment to the Executive?

There arises, secondly, the problem of delineating the circumstances in which judicial restraint is to be exercised. The only answer which at present can be given with a reasonable degree of confidence is that it is not (or not yet) the Executive, but the court that decides. On what grounds is the court's decision to be based? At this point the court will be faced with a fundamental difficulty.

Some of Mr. Justice Harlan's observations, in this respect closely following the brief for the United States,[2] give the impression that the test of embarrassment to the executive branch may be met by the mere fact that a judicial finding would 'give offence' to, or 'might be regarded as a serious insult' by, the foreign country or cause it to 'resent'[3] the decision. This would mean that even if there is 'concensus' in regard to the foreign country's international obligations, judical restraint might have to be exercised. It is, however, unlikely that Mr. Justice Harlan's opinion is to be construed in this sense. The statements of principle on which the opinion rests, and to which attention has been drawn,[4] leave no doubt about

---

[1] See *Lepre* v. *Lepre*, [1965] p. 52.

[2] See Brief for the United States as Amicus Curiae, p. 29, reprinted in 2 *Int. Legal Materials* (1963), 1012, 1019.

[3] 376 U. S., at p. 432. This point would perhaps carry more weight if the resentment even of law-abiding, peaceful, and friendly nations had in the past more conspicuously figured as an influence in shaping decisions in the United States. It is well known that the point is completely ignored for purposes of anti-trust, including shipping cases. It is also beginning to be ignored in connection with tax cases. Recently, in *United States* v. *First National City Bank*, 379 U. S. 378 (1965), the Supreme Court reached the result that, irrespective of Uruguayan law, a United States Court had 'authority' to order a United States corporation to freeze a Uruguayan corporation's property in Uruguay. Ibid., at p. 384. The United States Government even argued that a Federal Court officer 'could be sent to Montevideo to make demand upon the . . . [defendant's] branch in the name of the United States.' Id., at p. 395 (Harlan J., dissenting). It would be difficult to imagine a more serious breach of the rules of international jurisdiction, as in his powerful dissent Mr. Justice Harlan himself pointed out. Ibid., at pp. 396–7 and n. 17.

[4] See text accompanying pp. 467, n. 1 to p. 470, n. 1, above.

the overriding effect of 'consensus': consensus confers jurisdiction.

If, then, it is within the judicial function to ascertain the existence of consensus, the court may negative it and thus deny that there is the rule of international rule contended for. In such a case the court will give its reasons. They may or may not be in line with the attitude of the Executive. If they are not, then the judicial decision, by the very fact of the restraint, will be bound to undermine the policy and purposes of the Executive. Or, in other words, the reasoned refusal to adjudicate is tantamount to the assertion by the Judiciary that there exists no consensus or no rule of international law and that, accordingly, any claim by the Executive to the contrary is unfounded. Thus judicial restraint, although born of the desire not to embarrass the Executive, will be embarrassing to it, for it implies the absence of that consensus which, *ex hypothesi*, the Executive asserts. In such circumstances, exemplified by the *Sabbatino* case itself, restraint is unable to achieve the very purpose it is intended to fulfil.

It is a puzzling feature of *Sabbatino* and of the discussion relating to it that this defect of the theory of judicial restraint has not been appreciated. It is an even more serious oddity that the Executive does not seem to regret the enormous loss of prestige it has suffered as a result of the judicial 'restraint' practised in the *Sabbatino* case. For years it has proclaimed the violation of international law which in its view Cuba committed. It has now been told that no such violation has occurred. Yet this result, which so plainly strengthened Cuba's case, is hailed by the Executive as an instance of the wisdom of judicial restraint. It does not seem to be understood that this phrase would be accurate only if, in the area of foreign relations, the Executive could and would effectively suppress judicial decision or at least judicial reasoning altogether. The elimination of the judicial process has not gone that far. It can only be hoped that executive power will not ever reach such extremes and that sooner or later the present tendencies of limiting the justiciability of international disputes will disappear. Mr. Justice Harlan, it is true, thought that his interpretation of the judicial process was serving both national and international purposes as well as 'this country's pursuit of goals both for itself and for the community of nations as a whole in the international sphere'.[1] But this is no more than a guess, an assessment of imponderables from which one is entitled respectfully to dissent on the ground that it is contrary to all human experience and to the ideals of our age. The judicial process is the most potent weapon in the struggle for the primacy of law. Nor is there any justification for Mr. Justice Harlan's sentiment of self-deprecation which made him speak of 'the sanguine presupposition that the decisions of the courts of the world's major capital exporting country and principal exponent of the free enterprise system could be accepted as disinterested expressions of sound legal principle by those adhering to widely different ideologies'.[2] How could international law have grown and flourished if the great judges of the nineteenth century, in the United States and elsewhere, had taken a similarly restricted view of their duty to propound the law and to blaze a trail?[3] For a member of the world's most august tribunal so to underestimate the weight and influence of the Supreme Court's opinions is an unusual occurrence. It is, regrettably, in line with another dictum which some will regard as plainly cynical, which may strike others as 'realism' at its height, but which most, it is hoped, will treat as contrary to all available evidence:

When articulating principles of international law in its relations with other states, the Executive Branch speaks not only as an interpreter of generally accepted and traditional rules, as would the courts, but also as an

---

[1] 376 U. S., at p. 423.

[2] Id., at pp. 434–5. See generally Lauterpacht, 'Decisions of Municipal Courts as a Source of International Law', *B.Y.I.L.* (1929), p. 65.

[3] The history of the development of international law by national courts lends little support to Professor Friedmann's allegation about 'overwhelming nationalistic ways of national courts in matters of international law': Friedmann, 'Act of State: Sabbatino in the Courts and in Congress', 3 *Colum. J. Transnational L.* (1965), 103, 105, though on rare occasions such tendencies may have made themselves felt. Professor Friedmann has also seen fit to suggest that the result in *Sabbatino* could give cause for complaint 'only' to those who assume 'a complete identification of international law with national interest'; that such complaints 'do not stem from a disinterested passion for international law'; and that the Supreme Court has 'shown itself to be a defender of judicial integrity against the pressure of nationalist considerations'. Ibid., at pp. 105, 106. The truth is that those to whom Professor Friedmann, certain of his own disinterested approach, imputes unworthy motives refuse to regard the embarrassment of the Executive Branch, i.e., a national interest, as a standard superior to that provided by international law.

*advocate* of standards it believes desirable for the community of nations and protective of national concerns.[1]

The common understanding was and is that in the leading countries the executive speaks as the interpreter of the nation's appreciation of international law and that, for this reason, its pronouncements contribute to an important source of law rather than a brief.

After *Republic of Mexico* v. *Hoffman*[2] which, it will be remembered, related to the cognate problems of sovereign immunity and allowed the executive an excessive power over the judicial branch,[3] Professor Jessup (as he then was) raised the question: 'Has the Supreme Court abdicated one of its functions?'[4] It seems that an affirmative answer has now been given.

[1] 376 U. S., at pp. 432–3. (Emphasis added.)

[2] 324 U. S. 30 (1945).

[3] Mr. Chief Justice Stone stated that 'it is therefore not for the courts to deny an immunity which our Government has seen fit to allow, or to allow an immunity on new grounds which the Government has not seen fit to recognize'. 324 U. S., at p. 35. Professor Briggs has called this statement 'objectionable': Briggs, *The Law of Nations* (2d ed. 1952), 450.

[4] Jessup, 'Has the Supreme Court Abdicated One of Its Functions?', 40 *A.J.I.L.* (1946), 168.

# XIV

## PREROGATIVE RIGHTS OF FOREIGN STATES AND THE CONFLICT OF LAWS*

### I

THE student of comparative law who has had occasion to glance at Continental, particularly French, decisions and writings on the conflict of laws may have come across the statement that the public law of a foreign country will not be applied by the forum or that certain foreign laws of a public-law character have a strictly territorial effect and are therefore inapplicable in the forum; penal, fiscal, or what are called 'political', but also monetary laws are being contemplated by such formulations.[1] Our imaginary student, if he has a critical mind, will no doubt ask himself what such statements can possibly mean. He cannot have found it easy to discover the answer. It is, of course, obvious that, normally, we do not apply foreign law in England, whether it be public or private law, and we do not expect English law to be applied abroad: the English provision according to which an association of persons cannot qualify as a legal entity and, especially, as a company with limited liability, except as a result of registration by a Registrar of Companies, does not expect to be applied when a company is formed in Utopia; conversely, a Utopian law enjoining the Registrar not to register a company with a capital below a certain amount will not be applied in England. It may be that the maxim, so confidently proclaimed, has a less platitudinous meaning and indicates the idea that, where under the conflict rule of the forum, foreign law would be applicable and such foreign law is public law, it will not be applied by the forum. So understood the maxim would make better sense (although the conception of public law could not readily be defined), but

---

* From 40 *Transactions of the Grotius Society* (1955), 25.

[1] For a recent discussion of the question see Niederer, *Einführung in die allgemeinen Lehren des Internationalen Privatrechts* (Zurich, 1954), pp. 307 sqq.

it would almost certainly be wrong, because there is no evidence that such relevant foreign law as is public law is in fact being disregarded in any Continental country, nor is there any good reason why it should be disregarded.[1]

It would be surprising if in England, where the distinction between public and private law is not accepted, foreign public law were treated differently from foreign private law. No maxim such as that propounded from time to time on the Continent has ever made its appearance here. Nevertheless, in a more specific form even English judges have expressed ideas which, if divorced from their context, are as liable to confuse as their Continental counterparts. Thus Lord Mansfield[2] is the author of the dictum that 'no country ever takes notice of the revenue laws of another'—a dictum which if taken literally would mean that an English Court would have to hold a foreign contract valid, although by virtue of the provisions in the customs laws of the *lex causae* it is invalid. Again it has been said by Buller J.[3] that 'it is a general principle that the penal laws of one country cannot be taken notice of in another'; but it has never been doubted that an English contract the performance of which would be a criminal offence under the law of the country where it is to be performed, is discharged.[4] Notwithstanding Lord Mansfield's and Buller J.'s dicta, the practice of the English Courts is not opposed to taking notice of the fiscal or penal laws of other countries.

Although, then, general statements such as those to which reference has been made are inaccurate and misleading, they

---

[1] See Cass. Civ., 22 November 1898, Clunet (1899), 136: a French exporter, having sent goods to Italy, instructs an Italian firm to attend to the customs clearance in Italy. As a result of false declarations, the Italian firm is fined and ordered to pay surcharges in Italy. It obtains a judgment of the Italian Courts for its outlays. The enforcement of the judgment in France is allowed on the ground that the claim rests on contract. In very similar circumstances the opposite view was taken by Cass. Civ., 3 July 1928, Clunet (1929), 385, on grounds which to the foreign observer are hardly convincing: 'L'administration française ne peut poursuivre devant les tribunaux étrangers le recouvrement des taxes qui lui sont dues sur le territoire français et ... les administrations étrangères ne peuvent poursuivre devant les tribunaux français le recouvrement des impôts qui leur sont dûs sur leur territoire; que s'agissant dans l'espèce du recouvrement d'une taxe instituée par le Gouvernement allemand ces règles doivent recevoir leur application'.

[2] *Holman* v. *Johnson* (1775), 1 Cowp. 341, 343.

[3] *Folliott* v. *Ogden* (1789), 3 T. R. 726, at p. 733.

[4] *Ralli Bros* v. *Compañia Naviera Sota y Aznar*, [1920] 2 K. B. 287.

contain, as so frequently occurs, a kernel of truth. That foreign law, applicable under the conflict rule of the forum, should not be *applied* by the forum on account of its character is a suggestion unsupported by authority and unsupportable by doctrine— public policy apart. On the other hand, it cannot be denied that, public policy again apart, there are foreign laws of a certain type which in a very special sense are incapable of *enforcement* in England.

The distinction between the application and the enforcement of foreign laws has frequently been developed and in this country been emphasized by Sir Arnold McNair.[1] It is a fruitful one, provided the term 'enforcement' is understood in a narrow sense. Every law that is being applied may be said to be enforced. The peculiar enforcement envisaged in the following observations presupposes that it is a foreign State or one of its instrumentalities that asserts before an English Court the public authority conferred upon it by its own law.

In a very broad and preliminary manner it may be said that the enforcement, in this sense, of foreign public law in England, as opposed to its application, is excluded by established legal principles. If a contract subject to Indian law provides for annual payments to be made without deduction of Indian Income Tax and if Indian law includes a section similar to section 506 of the English Income Tax Act, 1952, an English Court will undoubtedly apply Indian law and hold the contract void. But if, under the authority of its tax legislation, the Republic of India should come to an English Court to recover taxes due to it under its legislation, then Indian law would be unenforceable, because an English Court will not constitute itself the tax-collecting agency of a foreign State.[2]

This follows from legal principles of wide impact the elucidation of which is a matter of some interest. For this purpose it will be necessary to ascertain in the first place the origin and legal foundation (below, Section II), thereafter the content and scope of the rule (below, Section III), and against this background, finally, to attempt its correct formulation (below, Section IV).

---

[1] *The Legal Effects of War* (3rd ed., 1948) p. 359.
[2] *Government of India* v. *Taylor*, [1955] A. C. 491.

## II

The claims made by foreign States, which the courts have most frequently held to be unenforceable, are those founded upon the claimant State's penal and revenue legislation. In fact this principle is sanctioned by a judicial practice which appears to be both universal and uniform.[1] However, the reasons on which it rests are frequently stated in somewhat elusive terms.

When discussing a foreign State's inability to recover *taxes* due to it by legal proceedings in England, Sir Raymond Evershed M.R. expressed the view[2] that the origin of the rule 'may well have had to do with questions of freedom of trade and the direct application to that problem of customs duties

---

[1] The international enforcement of *penal* claims in the strict sense does not seem to have been attempted in Continental countries, the unenforceability of such claims being beyond any doubt; as to Great Britain see, in particular, *Huntington* v. *Attrill*, [1893] A. C. 150, and as to the United States of America see the discussion by Beale, *Conflict of Laws*, pp. 1635 sqq. and, in particular, *Huntington* v. *Attrill*, 146 U. S. 657 (1892). The material on the enforcement of *revenue* claims is infinitely richer. Their unenforceability is established in England: *Government of India* v. *Taylor*, [1955] A. C. 491, with references to the earlier authorities. See also the following dicta not all of which were referred to: *Cotton* v. *The King*, [1914] A. C. 176, at p. 195, per Lord Moulton; *Indian & General Investment Trust Ltd.* v. *Borax Consolidated Ltd.*, [1920] 1 K. B. 539, at p. 550 per Sankey J.; and *Re Cohen* [1950] 2 All E. R. 37, at p. 39, per Sir Raymond Evershed M.R.; and see the discussion by Michael Mann, 3 *I.C.L.Q.* (1954), 465; in Austria: Supreme Court, 16 February 1892, Clunet (1893), 930; 22 September 1897, Clunet (1898), 777; 29 October 1935, Clunet (1937), 126; in Germany: see Nussbaum, *Internationales Privatrecht* (1932), with references to the decisions; in Sweden: Supreme Court, 31 December 1924, *A.D.* (1923–4), No. 148; Michaeli, *Internationales Privatrecht*, p. 79, with references; in Denmark; 23 October 1924, *A.D.* (1923–4), No. 147; in Belgium: Cass., 18 February 1929, Pasicrisie 1929–1–96; Trib. Civ. Charleroi, 8 January 1930, Clunet (1930), 1097, also *A.D.* (1929–30), No. 63; in Italy: Court of Appeal of Genoa, 14 January 1932, Clunet (1932), 1146; in Egypt: cf. Mixed Court of Appeal, 4 February 1936, Clunet (1937), 337. In France the position is generally held to be the same, although there is no decision which is quite in point; see, however, Cass. Civ., 3 July 1928, Clunet (1929), 385, referred to above, p. 493, n. 1; Trib. Civ. Seine, 24 February 1949, S. 1949, 2.101 with note by Niboyet. In the United States of America, no truly international case ever seems to have come up for decision and the decision of interstate cases is influenced by the full faith and credit clause of the Constitution; see, generally, Beale, *Conflict of Laws*, pp. 1635 sqq.; Albrecht, 'The Enforcement of Taxation under International Law', *B.Y.I.L.* (1953), 454, at pp. 463, 464. The Belgian decision of 8 January 1930 and the Austrian decision of 29 October 1935 hold that a claim for the payment of social insurance contributions is a revenue claim.

[2] *Re Delhi Electric Supply & Traction Co. Ltd.*, [1954] Ch. 131, at p. 151.

imposed by foreign countries', but he did not investigate the justification for the rule which he accepted 'on general principles of both justice and convenience' and on account of its existence for at least two hundred years or thereabouts.[1] Jenkins L.J. was not much more specific when he stated[2] that the existence of the rule was 'called for by cogent considerations of convenience, international comity and public policy', and when he added[3] that the reason for the rule was indicated by the formula that 'the law of England does not accord extraterritorial validity to the revenue legislation of foreign States'.

Yet the unenforceability of *penal* claims has most attractively been explained in a decision of the Judicial Committee of the Privy Council which must be treated as the foundation of the whole of this branch of the law.[4] In an opinion characterized by its carefully chosen language and the precision of its reasoning, Lord Watson spoke of an 'international rule'[5] requiring the unenforceability of foreign penal laws and, in a pregnant phrase, referred[6] to those actions which include 'penal actions' and which '*by the law of nations are exclusively assigned to their domestic forum*'.

What, then, are the actions which public international law commits exclusively to their domestic forum? They are, it is submitted, such actions as are based upon the *jus imperii* of a State. The reason is that the exercise of a State's imperium ends at the State's frontiers. The emphasis lies on the word 'exercise'. It would certainly not be true to say that the rights which a State derives from its imperium have no extraterritorial existence; on the contrary, their existence is recognized within the framework of the appropriate rules of the conflict of laws. But their exercise is inherently limited to the State's territory. Hence their exercise by judicial enforceability is similarly limited. As Lord Watson put it with reference to penal actions, crimes 'are local in this sense, that they are only cognizable and punishable in the country where they are committed. Accordingly, no proceeding, even in the scope of a civil suit, which has for its object the enforcement by the State, whether directly or indirectly, of punishment imposed for such breaches by the *lex*

---

[1] p. 145.       [2] ibid., p. 164.       [3] ibid., p. 165.
[4] *Huntington* v. *Attrill*, [1893] A. C. 150.
[5] pp. 155, 157.       [6] p. 156.

*fori*, ought to be admitted in the courts of any other country.'[1] Or, as the Permanent Court of International Justice put the same point in more general language, 'the first and foremost restriction imposed by international law upon a State is that, failing the existence of a permissive rule to the contrary, it may not *exercise* its power *in any form* in the territory of another State'.[2]

Although the point is perhaps of minor importance, it may be preferable to approach the problem primarily from the point of view of the limitations of the claimant State's powers rather than to stress, as Oppenheim[3] does, that 'to assist States in the performance of acts of sovereignty in foreign countries' would be in derogation of the territorial supremacy of the forum. In advocating the enforceability of foreign revenue claims, a learned writer has suggested[4] that this would not be contrary to public international law, because public international law is not concerned with the result, viz., the fact of recovery by judgment and payment, but only with the legality of the method, and judicial proceedings are legal. No such argument can be maintained if regard is had to the territorial limits of the exercise of the claimant State's imperium. These limits constitute a bar irrespective of whether the claimant State sends its officials to England to take its debtor's property or whether by legislative measures it transfers English property to itself or whether, for the purpose of enforcing its rights, it invokes the jurisdiction of the English Courts and thus asserts a title denied to it by public international law.

There are several reasons which make it attractive to derive the courts' attitude towards the class of actions under discussion from the rule of public international law according to which the exercise of a State's imperium is territorially limited.

In the first place, the explanation is general rather than specific: it not only justifies the prevailing practice in penal and revenue actions, but also facilitates the decision in numerous other types of cases which may appear heterogeneous, but in truth involve the same fundamental principle.

---

[1] Ibid.

[2] Case of the *S.S. Lotus* (Series A), No. 10, pp. 18, 19 (italics supplied).

[3] *International Law* (8th ed., 1954, by Lauterpacht), section 144b.

[4] Edgar Herzfeld, 'Probleme des Internationalen Steuerrechts', *Vierteljahresschrift für Steuer- und Finanzrecht* (1932) vi.422 sqq., 441 (relating to revenue claims).

Secondly, it is dogmatically satisfactory to be confronted with a further branch of municipal law within which public international law asserts itself, and it is theoretically interesting once again to tread on the borderline between public and private international law. It is hardly necessary to add that public international law, particularly where it has developed so firmly established principles as that operating in the present context, affords a safer guide to decision than public policy, convenience, or similar conceptions.

Thirdly, the suggested explanation is likely to produce results which will appeal to the legal mind and the legal conscience. This is not a problem which could be solved by weighing the justice or injustice of the claim made in particular cases, by considerations such as whether the defendant has deservedly been fined in the foreign State and whether the fine is reasonable or excessive, whether the tax liability in question is one accepted by civilized nations, whether there was 'fiscal evasion by itinerant taxpayers'[1] or moral justification for non-payment. If, then, the solution can only be found by a strictly legal approach, private law fails to provide the requisite categories. Normally the rules of the conflict of laws tell us whether a foreign court or authority has jurisdiction in a particular case and what law is to be applied. How should an English court determine whether the foreign country has jurisdiction to fine, or assess a tax in respect of, a person who may never have been resident in the foreign country? It would, as Sir Raymond Evershed M.R. has pointed out, indeed be an 'arresting'[2] thought if the ordinary courts were called upon to investigate these and similar questions. If this were desirable, it would be open to States to include appropriate provisions in the numerous extradition or taxation treaties which have been and are being concluded. The fact that there do not seem to be any treaties contemplating the judicial enforcement of foreign penal claims, that there are only relatively few treaties[3] providing for

---

[1] Albrecht, 'The Enforcement of Taxation under International Law', *B.Y.I.L.* (1953), pp. 454 sqq., at p. 462. It is a matter of speculation whether the author's criticism of the customary rule would have been so severe if he had fully appreciated its true ratio.

[2] *Re Delhi Electric Supply & Traction Co. Ltd.*, [1954] 2 All E. R. 1452, at p. 1456 B; the passage in [1954] Ch. 131, at pp. 145, 146, is quite different.

[3] See Albrecht, *ubi supra*, pp. 468 sqq.; see, in particular, on mutual collection,

the enforcement of foreign revenue claims and that the United Kingdom, for instance, does not appear to have concluded any such treaty is almost conclusive evidence of the continued existence of the rule of customary international law. Further evidence is provided by the absence of any diplomatic protest against any of the numerous judicial decisions refusing the enforcement of foreign penal and revenue claims. The existing practice of the courts, therefore, is in harmony with the prevailing rule of international law. This is one of the principal reasons for supporting it. It may well be that in course of time, the customary international law on the subject will change.[1] Thus it is conceivable that the customary rule may be influenced by the fact that we have come to think of matters essentially rather than matters exclusively within a State's domestic jurisdiction. On the other hand, the customary rule may be affected by treaty provisions which may come to be introduced. In view, however, of the firmly established practice and the deeply rooted and universally accepted conviction of the international unenforceability of claims *jure imperii*, any qualification of the customary rule will presuppose the clearest possible expression of the international legislators' intention.

# III

To describe the class of claims which a State is precluded from enforcing internationally by the phrase 'claims *jure imperii*' would not be without advantage. It is a term which has a long history[2] with which international lawyers are conversant, and which, notwithstanding inevitable doubts, has a well-established legal meaning. It is better than the American ex-

---

the Double Taxation Treaty between France and the United States of America Art. 12 (Clunet (1950), 395). See also the discussion by Niboyet, *Traité de Droit International Privé Français* (1949), vi.126 sqq. It is remarkable that at p. 129, Niboyet accepts the orthodox view in terms which are almost identical with those used by Sir Raymond Evershed M.R. in *Re Delhi Electric Supply & Traction Co. Ltd.*, [1954] Ch. 131, at p. 145: '*un état ne peut, en effet, ni directement ni indirectement se transformer en pourvoyeur du fisc d'un pays étranger. La souveraineté s'y oppose*'.

[1] See Permanent Court of International Justice in *Case of Nationality Decrees in Tunis and Morocco* (Series 13), No. 4, at pp. 23, 24.

[2] Particularly in the law of immunity (see, e.g., the comparative survey by Lauterpacht, *B.Y.I.L.* (1951), pp. 250 sqq.) and in the law of state contracts (see above, pp. 197 sqq.

pression 'governmental claims'[1] which is so insipid that it could include claims *jure gestionis*, and also the unfortunate word 'political' which, following French precedents, the editors of Dicey seek to introduce into English private international law.[2] It is perhaps also more telling than the reference to claims founded upon 'the public law' of a foreign State which is used by Oppenheim's *International Law*,[3] but which in English law has no accepted meaning. However, the terminological problem is wholly unimportant. No special virtue, therefore, is claimed for the description 'prerogative rights', which may have no other advantage than that no gloss as yet has been put upon it, though it was judicially used almost 100 years ago.[4]

It would be of considerably greater value if it were possible to suggest an accurate and comprehensive definition of the rights which come within the scope of these descriptions. But at no stage of the historical development and in no country have lawyers succeeded in satisfactorily determining what is meant by 'public law' or 'matters *jure imperii*' or, as the phrase went in the early seventeenth century, by 'government',[5] and what comes under the heading of 'private law' or 'matters *jure gestionis*', or 'property'.[5] Yet the inability of the human mind and vocabulary to explain and contain all cases by an all-embracing form of words does not disprove the reality of a distinction which, with respect, must be considered as indispensable, though, in another connection, Professor Lauterpacht[6]

---

[1] Leflar, 'Extrastate Enforcement of Penal and Governmental Claims', 46 *Harv. L.R.* (1932), 193.

[2] *Conflict of Laws* (6th ed., 1949), p. 152. Schmitthoff, *The English Conflict of Laws* (3rd ed., 1954), p. 56, speaks of 'foreign rights of a substantially political character'. In France the phrase is used for instance by Arminjon, *Précis de Droit International Privé* (3rd ed., 1947), pp. 281 sqq. Sometimes French lawyers speak of a '*droit régalien*'.

[3] (8th ed. 1954, by Lauterpacht), section 144b.

[4] *Emperor of Austria* v. *Day* (1861) 3 De G.F. & J.217, at p. 251, per Turner L.J.; see also Jenkins L.J. in *Re Maldonado*, [1954] P. 223, 246.

[5] See Keir and Lawson, *Cases on Constitutional Law* (4th ed., 1954), pp. 57, 63, 64, 69, 171, quoting among others, Bacon: 'it is a true and received division of law into *jus publicum* and *jus privatum*, the one being the sinews of property and the other of government'. On the development of the distinction between public and private law see J. W. Jones, *Historical Introduction to the Theory of Law* (1940), pp. 139 sqq.

[6] *B.Y.I.L.* (1951), p. 240.

has recently described it as 'impracticable and productive of uncertainty'. There are many distinctions which are real and which lawyers must, and do, make practicable, though they escape precise, comprehensive, and uniform definition: the distinction between law and fact or that between substance and procedure are familiar examples. That inability, therefore, should not lead us to discard such distinctions. It merely makes us realize our failings, renders it unwise to attempt to master what has confounded so many and necessitates resort to legal experience and specific decisions rather than generalization.

Where the foreign State pursues a right that by its nature[1] could equally well belong to an individual, no question of a prerogative claim arises and the State's access to the courts is unrestricted. Thus a State whose property is in the defendant's possession can recover it by an action in detinue.[2] A State which has a contractual claim against the defendant is at liberty to recover the money due to it.[3] If a State's ship has been damaged in a collision, an action for damages undoubtedly lies.[4] On the other hand, a foreign State cannot enforce in England such rights as are founded upon its peculiar powers of prerogative. Claims for the payment of penalties, for the recovery of customs duties or the satisfaction of tax liabilities are, of course, the most firmly established examples of this principle. It is also free from doubt that if works of art cannot be exported from Italy without a special licence, the State of Italy cannot come to the English Courts to recover a painting wrongfully exported from Italy.[5] Conversely, a foreign State cannot apply to an English Court to restrain an English merchant from importing goods into the territory of the plaintiff State in viola-

---

[1] The suggestion that it is the nature of the transaction that determines whether it is *jure imperii* or *jure gestionis* was made almost simultaneously by Charles de Visscher, *Revue de Droit international et de législation comparée* (1922), p. 300 and by André Weiss, 1 *Recueil* (1923), 525, who were for a time judges of the International Court of Justice and the Permanent Court of International Justice respectively. It would seem to be an acceptable solution and it must be doubted whether Professor Lauterpacht, *ubi supra*, has succeeded in refuting it. His argument at pp. 225 is perhaps not altogether convincing, and the exceptions listed at pp. 237, 238, are such as to re-introduce the distinction. However, Professor Lauterpacht's views have recently met with approval in America: 63 *Yale L.J.* (1954), 1148.

[2] *Union of Soviet Republics* v. *Belaiew* (1925) 42 T. L. R. 21.

[3] *Haile Selassie* v. *Cable and Wireless*, [1938] Ch. 545, 839.

[4] *The Ardennes*, [1950] 2 All E. R. 517.

[5] *King of Italy* v. *De Medici* (1918), 34 T. L. R. 623.

tion of its import restrictions.[1] Nor can a foreign State or its assignee, by an action in an English Court, recover the property of its nationals which it has requisitioned or vested in itself,[2] at any rate if the property is situate in England and does not include ships.[3] In view of the prerogative character of the claim, it cannot make any difference whether the foreign State's title to property (other than ships) situate in this country is derived from confiscation, expropriation, or requisition: no such action is maintainable here.[4]

It is equally certain that in these matters the court will not allow itself to be misled by appearances: on the contrary, it will investigate whether what the plaintiff asserts is in substance a prerogative right the direct or indirect enforcement of which is being sought.[5] Thus if in truth a prerogative right is being asserted, the Court will reject it, although the claimant is a person other than the foreign State and although the claim sounds in contract or in tort. It was for this reason that a Spanish bank which had deposited with an English bank the securities of the ex-King of Spain was not allowed to recover them where the benefit of the action, notwithstanding its contractual character, would have accrued to the Spanish State which had declared the ex-King guilty of high treason and seized his property.[6] Similarly, when the Nazi Government appointed a so-called trustee in respect of a Jewish owner's business and the trustee was in fact an instrument in the execution of a policy of spoliation pursued by the German Government, he was precluded from claiming the owner's assets in England[7]; and this was held to be so even if the claim appeared to rest on a contract to

---

[1] *Emperor of Austria* v. *Day* (1861) 3 De G. F. & J. 217, at p. 242, per Lord Campbell. *Foster* v. *Driscoll*, [1929] 1 K. B. 470 is a case of application, not of enforcement.

[2] *The El Condado*, 63 (1939) Ll. L. R. 330, also *A.D.* (1938–40), No. 77; *Bank voor Handel en Scheepvaart* v. *Slatford*, [1953] 1 Q. B. 248.

[3] Notwithstanding the decision in *The El Condado, ubi supra*, the position of ships may have to be reviewed in the light of the observations by Sir Arnold McNair, 31 *Grot. Soc.* (1946), 30; *Legal Effects of War* (3rd ed., 1948), pp. 433 sqq.

[4] For a different view see M. Wolff, *Private International Law* (2nd ed., 1950), pp. 527, 528, and see the discussion by Cheshire, *Private International Law* (4th ed., 1952), pp. 138, 139.

[5] This follows from *Huntington* v. *Attrill*, [1893] A. C. 150.

[6] *Banco de Vizcaya* v. *Don Alfonso de Borbon y Austria*, [1935] 1 K. B. 140.

[7] *Frankfurther* v. *W. L. Exner Ltd.*, [1947] Ch. 629.

which the owner was an involuntary party.[1] By parity of reasoning it may be suggested that if a foreign State or its organ or even its assignee obtains an I.O.U. or a foreign judgment for a prerogative claim, such as a tax liability, the debt or judgment cannot be enforced here.[2] Or suppose I give a guarantee to a foreign State to secure a penalty due from my friend; it is submitted that the guarantee would be unenforceable here.[3] And if a foreign ship is subject to a mortgage in respect of a foreign revenue debt and is sold in this country, the foreign State as mortgagee could not participate in the proceeds.[4] A remarkable and, it is respectfully submitted, well-founded decision of the Courts of Eire affords what is perhaps the most vivid illustration of the principle: the liquidator of a Scottish company which had no other creditors than the Inland Revenue Departments of the Crown was held to be precluded from recovering in Eire a debt due from the defendant.[5]

The same guiding ideas are likely to assist in the solution of some difficult questions which have arisen in the law of confiscation. Soviet Russia has confiscated the jewels of Princess Paley Olga. They are situate in Russia and by Russian law title has passed.[6] However, let it be assumed that they remain in the possession of the Princess who succeeds in bringing them to England. If the Russian State brought here an action for conversion, it ought to be dismissed, because its true purpose is to

---

[1] *Novello* v. *Hinrichsens*, [1951] Ch. 595.

[2] Dicey, *Conflict of Laws* (6th ed., 1949), pp. 408, 409, although the rule relating to revenue claims, accepted at p. 154, is there described as 'anachronistic'.

[3] It follows from *Huntington* v. *Attrill*, [1893] A. C. 150, that the Court will apply its own interpretation of the 'international rule'. It will, therefore, be irrelevant that a guarantee for a tax debt is enforceable by proceedings in the ordinary courts.

[4] Cf. *The Eva*, [1921] P. 454, though the decision is not entirely in point.

[5] *Peter Buchanan Ltd.* v. *McVey*, a decision by Kingsmill-Moore J. sitting as a judge of first instance, which is shortly noted at 100 *L.J.* (1950), 497; see also Donaldson, 3 *I.C.L.Q.* (1954), 161 sqq. and, below, p. 504, n. 3 and p. 510, n. 1. A note of the decision of Kingsmill-Moore J. and of the Supreme Court of Eire which affirmed it is now published in England: [1955] A. C. 516. The decisions do not discuss the question whether the result would have been the same if there had been ordinary trade creditors of the Scottish company in addition to the Crown. It is submitted that in such circumstances the liquidator ought to succeed to the extent necessary to satisfy the trade creditors.

[6] This assumption underlies the decision in *Princess Paley Olga* v. *Weisz*, [1929] 1 K. B. 718. But this decision does not deal with the hypothesis discussed in the text.

enforce the plaintiff State's prerogative rights.[1] On the other hand, if the Russian State had obtained possession of the jewels in Russia and they had been stolen from it, then an action against the thief ought to succeed even if the thief was the original owner; the reason is that the Russian State's right had already been completed when it obtained possession, and the action is brought, not in order to implement the confiscation, but to enforce a cause of action arising later than and irrespective of the confiscation.[2] Furthermore, the principle is of importance where companies become subject to confiscatory legislation. Let it be assumed, for instance, that all the shares of a Russian company are bearer shares situate in Russia, that the Government of Russia confiscates them and appoints a new board of directors. The company, represented by its new board, brings an action to recover English property claimed by those who were entitled to represent the company before confiscation. The action should fail, because it is brought to enforce the Russian Government's prerogative rights and for that Government's benefit.[3]

There remain, however, several groups of decided cases which require closer investigation. They give rise to considerable doubt, either because it is uncertain whether the principle, though clearly appreciated by the court, was correctly applied, or because the comprehensive character of the principle was misunderstood or because the principle was ignored:

(1) The case of *Emperor of Austria* v. *Day and Kossuth*[4] falls under the first heading. The defendants had printed in London bank notes which were signed 'In the name of the nation: Kossuth, Louis.'[5] It was the intention of Kossuth, a Hungarian

---

[1] In the same sense Seidl-Hohenveldern, *Internationales Konfiskations und Enteignungsrecht*, p. 39. *Contra* Wolff, *Private International Law* (2nd ed., 1950) pp. 527, 528. Cf. Cheshire, *Private International Law* (4th ed., 1952), p. 135, n. 3.

[2] In the same sense Seidl-Hohenveldern, p. 41.

[3] It is curious that this point has never been decided in England, though it was argued in *Banco de Bilbao* v. *Sancha*, [1938] 2 K. B. 176. The usual situation, of course, is that the company is put into liquidation. In that event section 400 of the Companies Act, 1948, applies. The solution suggested in the text is supported by the decisions referred to above, p. 503, n. 5 and below, p. 510, n. 1, and also by Seidl-Hohenveldern, *Juristische Blätter* (1952), p. 410, and *Betriebsberater* (1953), p. 837, though, unfortunately, not all the decisions relied upon by him are in point. Against him, Hans Lewald, *Juristische Blätter* (1952), p. 238.

[4] (1861), 3 De G. F. & J. 217.

[5] This is an essential aspect of the case. If the notes had been forged, i.e., if they

revolutionary, to introduce them into Hungary upon his restoration to power. The Emperor of Austria claimed, and obtained, an injunction restraining the defendants from continuing the manufacture of these notes. One of the defences put forward was, in effect, that the proceedings were brought to protect the Emperor's political power and prerogatives. Lord Campbell[1] rejected the argument by stating shortly that it was open to a foreign sovereign to institute proceedings 'in respect of property belonging to the foreign sovereign cither in his individual or in his corporate capacity'. Knight Bruce L.J. hardly dealt with this part of the defendant's argument, but Turner L.J. addressed himself to it at length.[2] He accepted as his starting point the proposition that the *jus cudendae monetae* was a prerogative of sovereigns. He then developed his view that 'prerogative rights' of a foreign sovereign could not be enforced in this country, and concluded that in so far as 'this Bill is founded upon the prerogative rights of the plaintiff or upon the political rights of his subjects, my present opinion is against the decree' made by the lower court. However, he continued that the case rested on the ground that the plaintiff's subjects were injured by the threatened introduction of spurious notes. The effect of such introduction was

to endanger, to prejudice and to deteriorate the value of the existing circulating medium and thus to affect directly all the holders of Austrian bank notes and, indirectly if not directly, all the holders of property in the State.

Such damage constituted 'an injury not to the political but to the private rights of the plaintiff's subjects' and could be asserted by the plaintiff in his representative character on behalf of his subjects. It has been suggested with force that the result reached by the court is inconsistent with the premiss from which it started.[3] The court held that the right to issue money was 'a prerogative of sovereigns'. That prerogative may constitute 'property' in a political sense, but it is not property within the accepted legal meaning of the term. And the fact

had purported to be genuine notes, the criticism made in the text would not be justifiable, for it is an international duty to prevent the counterfeiting of a foreign State's currency: Mann, *The Legal Aspect of Money* (2nd ed., 1953), p. 436.

[1] p. 238.    [2] pp. 251 sqq.
[3] Sir W. Harrison Moore, *Act of State* (1906) pp. 148 sqq.; Nussbaum, *Money in the Law, National and International* (1950), pp. 35, 36.

that an injury to a prerogative right of the State may prejudice the State's subjects, though true, does not touch the prerogative right's character or prove its enforceability by the sovereign in England. If the richest inhabitant of the Republic of Andorra does not pay the taxes due from him, the prerogative rights of the Republic and the pockets of its subjects may most seriously be affected, but this does not make a claim for the payment of the taxes enforceable in England. Again, the right to punish criminals is a prerogative right and a criminal's failure to pay a fine may affect 'all the holders of property in the State', yet it does not follow that the penalty can be claimed by proceedings in the English Court. The Emperor of Austria was, *ex hypothesi*, trying to enforce a prerogative right. Indeed, his title to make a claim in his representative character in respect of the damage done to his subjects was itself a prerogative right. The consequence ought to have been to dismiss his claim.

(2) From a practical point of view, a much more serious situation has arisen in regard to the enforcement in England of the exchange restrictions enacted by a foreign country. It is certainly not the view of English law that foreign exchange restrictions cannot be taken notice of or applied here.[1] However, it is another matter whether a foreign State can enforce or execute its exchange restrictions in this country. In *Kahler v. Midland Bank*[2] the plaintiff was the undisputed owner of what in effect were bearer securities. Under a contract governed by Czechoslovakian law he entrusted his Czechoslovakian bank to deposit them with the Midland Bank in London. The plaintiff brought an action for delivery up against the Midland Bank. The defence was that the Midland Bank's bailor was the Czechoslovakian bank which under Czechoslovakian law required, but had not obtained the licence of the Czechoslovakian authorities before it could consent to the delivery of the securities. When the case came before Macnaghten J., he pointed during the argument to the actual securities lying in front of him and exclaimed that he failed to understand how a Czechoslovakian prohibition could be said to preclude an English judge from ordering the securities to be handed over to their rightful owner. He gave judgment for the plaintiff, but it

---

[1] Mann, *The Legal Aspect of Money* (2nd ed., 1953) pp. 360 sqq.
[2] [1950] A. C. 24.

was reversed by the Court of Appeal.[1] A majority of the House of Lords consisting of Lord Simonds, Lord Normand, and Lord Radcliffe (Lord Reid and Lord McDermott dissenting) dismissed the appeal and thus burdened succeeding generations of lawyers with the task of discovering how to reach a less unsatisfactory result in similar cases. Perhaps one of the most effective means leading to this end is provided by the suggestion that the attention of the House of Lords does not seem to have been drawn to the fact that in substance the Midland Bank were asserting the prerogative rights of the Czechoslovakian Government, or to put it another way, that through the Midland Bank the Czechoslovakian Government was indirectly enforcing and executing its exchange control regulations. This is a suggestion which is strengthened by the absence of any report of the argument addressed to the House. It is quite true that the House was apparently invited to hold that the defence involved the enforcement of Czechoslovakian revenue, penal, or confiscatory laws. It is also true that this contention was expressly rejected.[2] At any rate in so far as it was based on the allegedly penal or fiscal character of the Czechoslovakian legislation, it was, with respect, rightly rejected, though that legislation's confiscatory nature might well have required more detailed consideration.[3] However, the House was not invited to hold that penal, fiscal, and confiscatory laws were merely aspects, examples, illustrations of foreign laws which, though recognizable or applicable, are unenforceable here; that the true principle is that what in substance is a foreign prerogative right cannot even indirectly be enforced here; and that, once the generality of this principle is accepted, it imperatively demanded the failure of the defence based on the Czechoslovakian Government's attempt to control English property for no other reason than that under its own law it had the prerogative right of controlling it. One must again ask the question: if the Midland Bank had inadvertently handed the securities to the plaintiff, would the Czechoslovakian bank, acting under the direction of the Czechsolovakian

---

[1] [1948] 1 All E. R. 811.
[2] At p. 27, per Lord Simonds; at p. 36, per Lord Normand; at pp. 46, 47, per Lord Reid; at p. 57, per Lord Radcliffe; and see *Zivnostenska Banka* v. *Frankman*, [1950] A. C. 57, at p. 72, per Lord Simonds.
[3] Mann, op. cit., pp. 374–7, and the literature there referred to.

authorities, have been allowed to recover them? Unless one ignores the traditional practice of English Courts, the answer must be in the negative. If this is accepted then the indirect enforcement of Czechoslovakian exchange control, which in substance occurred in *Kahler's* case, ought to have been disallowed. That, unfortunately, it was allowed need not, it is submitted, fetter the decision of judges who are made aware of the limits within which prerogative rights in general can be exercised.

(3) The third class of case in which prerogative rights of a foreign State were enforced in this country arose out of the trading with the enemy legislation of foreign States, a field of sovereign activity which doubtless is *jure imperii*. During the first world war the French trading with the enemy legislation led to the appointment of an 'administrateur séquestre' in respect of the property of a German subject resident in France, who was entitled to certain dividends in England. The action brought by the administrateur to recover them succeeded before Petersen J.[1] It is not altogether easy to follow the learned Judge's reasoning as reported,[2] but the report is so inadequate that it is probably permissible to suggest that it can hardly be treated as an authoritative statement of the law.

A more serious problem is involved in a recent decision of Pearson J.[3] An Arab firm carrying on business in what was then Palestine took out an insurance policy with the Yorkshire Insurance Company through the medium of their agents in Haifa. When the State of Israel came into being, the Arab owners went to Egypt with the result that the policy moneys which in the meantime had become payable were, under Israeli law, vested in the Israeli Custodian of Enemy Property. He claimed payment from the insurers in England and so did the owners of the assured firm. Pearson J. held that the Custodian succeeded. The judgment in the course of which no less

---

[1] *Lepage* v. *São Paolo Coffee Estates Company*, [1917] W. N. 216.

[2] The learned judge is reported as having said that the plaintiff was appointed 'for the purposes of dealing with any rights she (i.e. the owner) had in France or the French Colonies', yet he allowed the plaintiff to exercise his authority in England. Moreover, he said that 'as she was in France, the right was also in France'—a dictum which can only be explained by the discredited maxim *mobilia sequuntur personam*.

[3] *Jabbour* v. *Custodian of Absentee's Property of State of Israel*, [1954] 1 All E. R. 145, on which see Thomas, 3 *I.C.L.Q.* (1954), 495.

than 64 authorities were referred to by the learned judge,
though he ignored Lord Watson's opinion in *Huntington* v.
*Attrill*,[1] is extraordinarily elaborate, but may be shortly summarized by the statement that the *situs* of the debt due from
the English Company was, in the circumstances of the case, in
Haifa and therefore subject to the vesting effected by Israeli
legislation. It may well be that, at any rate at first sight, the
strictly legal reasoning of the learned judge leaves little room
for criticism. But even the most enthusiastic lawyers are sometimes called upon to ask whether the result reached in a particular case appeals to, or shocks, their sense of justice. If this
question is put in the present case, the answer is that, contrary
to principle, the learned judge allowed a foreign State to
enforce a prerogative right in England. In fact, he did what
was previously thought to be impossible, for there is no difference between Pearon J.'s judgment in favour of the State of
Israel and a judgment allowing the Soviet State to recover
Princess Paley Olga's jewels which were confiscated while on
Russian territory, but brought by the Princess to England
before the act of confiscation had been completed by reducing
the jewels into the Soviet State's possession. The learned judge,
it is true, was invited to hold that the Israeli legislation was
confiscatory, but he thought[2] that there was no confiscation;
that in substance, there was confiscation ought not to be
doubted, seeing that the Arab owners had lost their legal and
beneficial interest in the moneys and had only a *spes restitutionis*.[3]
However, the question whether or no there was confiscation
does not penetrate to the root of the matter. This lies in the
prerogative character of the State of Israel's claim. Once that
character is appreciated, both the reason for the uneasiness
caused by Pearson J.'s decision and the true yet short legal
answer to the claim made by the State of Israel become apparent.
It also follows that the Supreme Court of Sweden correctly
applied the international rule when it held that an English
limited company could not recover money held to its credit by
a Swedish bank where the shares in the capital of the company

---

[1] [1893] A. C. 150.

[2] p. 157.

[3] This follows from *Re Munster*, [1920] 1 Ch. 268, followed by the House of
Lords in *Bank voor Handel en Scheepvaart* v. *Slatford*, [1954] A. C. 584; see, particularly, at p. 628, per Lord Tucker; at p. 631, per Lord Asquith.

had been vested in the Custodian of Enemy Property in England and the company's board acted under his direction.[1]

Such, then, are the English cases which raise the question whether sufficient weight was given to the principle against the enforcement of foreign prerogative rights. On the other hand, English judicial practice cannot be accused of overrating the impact of that principle. This is proved by the English Courts' approach to the perplexing problem which arises when a foreigner dies intestate without leaving any next-of-kin. Does his estate pass to the State in which it is situate or does it pass to the State which, under the deceased's *lex domicilii*, is the ultimate heir? The answer would be plain if there were a principle of public international law according to which a State succeeds to heirless property 'by the exercise of a paramount right of a sovereign.'[2] In that event the sovereign of the country in which the heirless property is situate would take. It is true that historically the State's right of succession has developed as a matter of *juris regalis* and that even today the State takes in discharge of a public duty and in the public interest.[3] It is also true that the French-German Mixed Arbitral Tribunal,[4] among others, has spoken of the 'principe généralement reconnu que les biens vacants appartiennent à l'Etat sur le territoire duquel ils se trouvent'. Yet it is not at all certain whether it is a 'general principle of law recognized by civilized nations' that the matter is to be treated as one of government rather than property: the treaties which have dealt with it do not adopt uniform solutions[5]; the practice of legislators as

---

[1] 25 September, 1944, *A.D.* (1943-5), No. 16 (*re Hopf Products Ltd.*). See above, p. 503, n. 5 and p. 504, n. 3.

[2] This was the argument for the Crown in *Re Maldonado*, [1954] P. 223.

[3] The State takes simply because there is no other person who could take care of the property and wind up the estate. When the text speaks of 'the State', it is of course intended to include what may fairly be described as its instrumentalities. A charity which does not form part of the State's constitutional organization would not be an instrumentality in this sense.

[4] *Zeppenfeld* v. *Etat Allemand*, M.A.T., *Recueil* vi.243, at p. 248.

[5] For the deceased's personal law see the treaties concluded by Switzerland with France, Greece, Italy, and Portugal (Schnitzer, *Handbuch des Internationalen Privatrechts* (3rd ed., 1905) ii.464); the treaty between Spain and Greece (Goldschmidt, *Filosofía del derecho internacional privado* (Barcelona, 1949) ii.262) and the treaties concluded by Germany with the U.S.S.R. and Estonia (Makarov, *Quellen des Internationalen Privatrechts*, p. 442). For the *lex situs* the treaties between Austria and Poland, Austria and Germany, Poland and Latvia, Poland and Estonia (see

well[1] as municipal tribunals[2] varies; jurists of recognized authority have propounded different views.[3] There is no record of any State having asserted, before an international tribunal or in diplomatic correspondence, the existence of a principle of law in either sense.

If by the law of nations no State can claim exclusive jurisdiction over heirless property, the problem must be solved on the footing of the conflict of laws. There thus arises a question of classification which has led to a few decisions and to an enormous literature and on which only a few words can be added by way of parenthesis. To make the outcome of a case dependent on classification is in many ways unsatisfactory. The question should, therefore, not be answered by investigating the legal nature of the State's right of succession or by inquiring whether the classification ought to be supplied by the *lex fori* or by the deceased's personal law. Rather should the answer be founded upon the reality of the position which the foreign law assigns to the State as opposed to the terms in which it describes that position. This was the course followed by the Anglo-German Mixed Arbitral Tribunal,[4] while very recently the Court of Appeal in England[5] and the Cour de Cassation in Belgium[6] have looked to the classification adopted by the deceased's personal law. The somewhat paradoxical

---

Makarov, op. cit.). The Hague Conference of 1928 (see Makarov, op. cit.) also adopted the *lex situs* and so did the American Restatement, section 309 (though the formulation is not altogether clear). The problem, of course, only arises in relation to movables.

[1] But the *lex situs* was adopted by Art. 31 of the Polish law of 2 August 1926, and by section 13 of the Swedish law of 5 March 1937.

[2] The numerous decisions dealing with the classification in municipal law are not in point. The international implications had to be considered only in a few cases. See, in particular, the cases referred to below, nn. 5, 6, and Cass. Req. 28 June 1952, S. (1852), 1.537, a decision which seems to prefer the *lex situs*, but is not conclusive.

[3] For a long, yet incomplete list see Hennebicq, Clunet (1954), 464 sqq. No textbook on the conflict of laws fails to deal with the question.

[4] *Tannenbaum* v. *Matthies*, M.A.T., *Recueil* v.632, a very remarkable decision.

[5] *Re Maldonado*, [1954] P. 223, on which see the useful notes by Lipstein, *Cambridge L.J.* (April 1954), 22–6, and Cohn, 17 *Mod. L.R.* (1954), 381; see also Gower, ibid., p. 167. It was recently held in New York that where the deceased died domiciled in California, intestate and without leaving next-of-kin, his property passed to the State of New York, not to California: *Matter of Menschefrend* (1954) 283 App. Div. 463.

[6] 28 March 1952, Clunet (1954), 462 sqq.

result of the Belgian decision was that Sweden was allowed to succeed to the Belgian property of a Swedish subject, although by virtue of an express provision in a Swedish statute the Belgian State could not have taken the Swedish property of a Belgian subject.[1]

However, these are merely preliminary and tentative suggestions on a problem which in every respect requires much more exhaustive treatment than can be accorded to it today. Their effect for present purposes is a negative and inconclusive one: the territorial sovereign's right of succession to heirless property is probably not one of those prerogative rights the international enforcement of which is precluded by public international law.

The English tendency not to extend the boundaries of prerogative rights is further illustrated by the fact that there is, in English law, no trace of the somewhat strained interpretations which at times have been put forward in the United States of America. Thus the Restatement suggests that where the law of a country places the burden of maintaining a potential pauper on an individual and to that extent relieves the public burden, no action can be brought to enforce the right so created.[2] It is said that for this reason the mother of an illegitimate child cannot bring an action for support against the natural father or that a parent cannot claim support from his or her child. Whatever may be said about the correctness of the result, there does not appear to be any authority for the view that it rests on the ground mentioned. In the United States of America it was also at one time doubtful whether an action could be brought on what has been called a 'foreign death-statute': if by the law of a particular country the dependants of a human being who has been wrongfully killed, are entitled to a sum of not less than $500 or more than $10,000, the amount depending not on the amount of the damage but on the degree of guilt, then it was thought that this was a prerogative, viz., a penal claim which could not be internationally enforced. However, it seems that, as a result of a forceful opinion delivered by

---

[1] See above, p. 511, n. 1 and Michaeli, *Internationales Privatrecht*, pp. 250, 251.

[2] Section 610, Comment d. There is no discussion on this point in Beale's *Conflict of Laws*.

Cardozo J. on behalf of the Court of Appeals of the State of New York,[1] this doctrine is no longer accepted.

Such and many other instances, both actual and imaginary, show how difficult it frequently is to hold the balance and to establish a satisfactory line of demarcation in these matters. In the last resort, as has been pointed out, this is due to the uncertainty surrounding the distinction between public and private law, between Government and property. It is an inevitable and challenging uncertainty which cannot be resolved except by the slow process of judicial evolution and by academic research on a broad comparative basis.

## IV

The preceding view of the law relating to the enforcement of foreign prerogative rights in England provides significant proof of the wisdom of a pronouncement which Lord Asquith of Bishopstone made not long before his lamentably early death[2]:

Nor, speaking more generally, does English jurisprudence start from a broad principle and decide cases in accordance with its logical implications. It starts with a clean slate, scored over, in course of time, with *ad hoc* decisions. General rules are arrived at inductively, from the collation and comparison of these decisions; they do not pre-exist them.

Over the centuries English Courts have refused to enforce foreign revenue, penal, confiscatory, and similar rights. In this manner the slate was scored over and this process continued to such an extent that these expressions, though in strict logic they denote different categories of laws, were often used interchangeably.[3] There were, it is true, inconsistent decisions which left the slate somewhat scarred. Yet it is permissible

---

[1] *Loucks* v. *Standard Oil Company*, 224 N.Y. 99; 120 N. E. 198 (1918), and literature cited by Nussbaum, *Private International Law*, p. 126.

[2] *Chapman* v. *Chapman*, [1954] A. C. 429, at p. 470.

[3] See in particular, the observations in *Kahler* v. *Midland Bank*, referred to above, p. 507, n. 2. Similarly, Romer J. in *Frankfurther* v. *W. L. Exner Ltd.*, [1947] Ch. 629, at pp. 636, 637, said that 'confiscatory laws of this character, though not strictly penal . . . are regarded here in the same light as penal laws'. In *A/S Tallina Laevausisus* v. *Estonian State Line* (1947), 80 Ll. L. R. 99, at p. 111, Scott L.J. said that 'English law treats as penal foreign legislation providing for compulsory acquisition of assets situate in this country . . . unless that legislation provides for just compensation.' Sir Raymond Evershed M.R. in *Delhi Electric Supply & Traction Co. Ltd.*, [1954] Ch. 131, 151, thought that there was 'a certain affinity' between penalties and revenues and that the distinction might 'obviously be somewhat fine'.

today[1] to try to combine the cases into a 'broad principle' and to treat them merely as illustrations of a single rule which, to return to our starting-point represents the English counterpart of the approach to foreign public law usually adopted on the Continent.

The principle which thus emerges may be summarized by the broad statement that an English Court has no jurisdiction to give effect to a claim, whether made by action or by way of defence, which in substance involves the direct or indirect enforcement of the prerogative right of a foreign State.

More particularly, it seems justifiable to make the following five submissions on the effect and extent of the principle:

First, the rule comes into operation whenever a foreign State asserts a prerogative right, that is to say, a right *regis qua regis*, a '*droit régalien*,' a right *jure imperii*, a right peculiar to the supreme power in the State.

Second, whether a right is a prerogative right in this sense is a question to be answered by public international law, that is to say, by reference to what public international law considers as rights exclusively or at least essentially exercisable within the territorial limits of a State's jurisdiction.

Third, the rule extends to claims which are made in substance to implement the prerogative rights of a foreign State, though in form they are based on the general law of contract, tort, foreign judgments and so forth.

Fourth, the rule applies irrespective of whether in form the right is asserted by the foreign State itself, or by any authority or person acting under its direction.

Fifth, it is sufficient if a prerogative right is asserted for the benefit of the foreign State or its instrumentalities of Government.[2]

---

[1] It is not suggested that the submission made in the text is an original one. Thus Nussbaum, *Private International Law*, p. 125, recognizes the connection of the problem with 'the private law, public law distinction which dominates the civil law' and suggests that 'the unenforceability rule . . . extends to all rights derived from foreign sovereignty'.

[2] Since this paper was read, the decision in *Re Delhi Electric Supply & Traction Co. Ltd.*, [1954] Ch. 131, was affirmed by the House of Lords *sub nomine Government of India* v. *Taylor*, [1955] A. C. 491. It was impossible to discuss the speeches made in the House of Lords in the printed version of this paper. The reader's attention, however, is drawn to the succinct formulation of the principle discussed in this paper, which occurs in the speech of Lord Keith, at p. 299.

# XV

## THE EFFECT OF CHANGES OF SOVEREIGNTY UPON NATIONALITY*

THE important decision of a Divisional Court (Lord Caldecote C.J., Humphreys and Singleton JJ.) in *Murray* v. *Parkes*, [1942] 2 K. B. 123, primarily raises the constitutional problem of Anglo-Irish relations. To comment on that part of the case must be the privilege of the trained constitutional lawyer. The case, however, also involves some narrower aspects, and it is on these that one who is in no way qualified, nor intends, to trespass upon those large issues, may perhaps venture to offer some observations.

The appellant, Michael Murray, was born in 1908 in that part of Ireland which is now known as Eire. He had lived in England since 1934, but was domiciled in Eire. In 1941 he refused to submit himself to medical examination under the National Service (Armed Forces) Act, 1939, on the ground that he was not a British subject but a citizen of Eire. He appeared before a magistrate, was convicted, and his appeal by way of case stated failed. It was agreed that by virtue of Art. 3 (First Schedule) of the Irish Free State Constitution Act, 1922, the appellant was a citizen of the Irish Free State, but the Court held that nothing had occurred that resulted in the loss of his wider British nationality.[1]

(1) After having explained that no enactment had given the Irish Free State the right to secede from the British Commonwealth of Nations, and that, moreover, the Government of Eire had never purported to exercise any such right, Lord Caldecote proceeded to indicate with diffidence that, if the international validity of any secession of Eire depended on recognition by the United Kingdom, he could not find it to have been granted either by the Eire (Confirmation of Agreements) Act, 1938, or by the agreements scheduled thereto. Similarly, Singleton J

---

* From 5 *Mod. L.R.* (1942), 218.

[1] In the same sense Keith, *The Governments of the British Empire* (1935), pp. 121, 122; 17 *J. Comparative Legislation* (1935), pp. 115, 116.

shortly reviewed the legislation of 1938, but failed to find anything to prove that 'the Government which was set up in that part of Ireland which was formerly the Irish Free State, has been recognized by H. M. Government as a sovereign, independent democratic State'. Now the point which is remarkable for present purposes is that the Court, however guarded its language was, even ventured to touch upon the question of whether or not in fact the United Kingdom had recognized Eire as a sovereign independent State. In the words of Lord Finlay in *Duff Development C.* v. *Kelantan Government*,[1] 'it has long been settled that on any question of the status of any foreign power the proper course is that the Court should apply to His Majesty's Government and that in any such matter it is bound to act on the information given to them by the proper department'. It is difficult to understand why resort was not had to this course which would have saved the Court from much embarrassment. In the absence of any discussion of the point it cannot be assumed that the Court intended to depart from that rule and to revert to the method of independent investigation which for the last time was adopted by Sir Robert Phillimore in *The Charkieh*[2] but which has failed to reappear ever since that case was disapproved in *Mighell* v. *Sulton of Johore*.[3]

(2) Assuming, however, that Eire has effected a complete secession from the United Kingdom and the British Empire and is recognized as an independent sovereign state, did the appellant lose his 'wider British nationality'? He contended for an affirmative answer on the ground that secession must have the same consequences in respect of nationality as cession (which is clearly right and was accepted by the Court) and that, according to well-established principles, on the cession of British territory British nationality is lost not only by such persons as are inhabitants of, but also by those domiciled in the ceded territory.

For more than two centuries it had been thought that the principle of permanent allegiance as laid down in *Calvin's* case[4] involved the rule that, just as those born in Scotland before the union of the Crowns of England and Scotland remained aliens because they were born aliens, so persons born before a cession

---

[1] [1924] A. C. 797, 813.        [2] (1873) L. R. 4 A & E. 59.
[3] [1894] 1 Q. B. 149.        [4] (1609) 7 Co. Rep. 1.

of territory remained subjects because they were born subjects, although they might simultaneously owe allegiance to the sovereign to whom such territory had passed.[1] In the early nineteenth century, however, it became well established that the inhabitants of ceded British territory lose British nationality.[2] This rule did not assist the appellant, since Lord Caldecote, as well as Humphreys J. who relied on this ground only, and Singleton J. who advanced it as a subsidiary one, were by the special case bound to hold that at the date of the suggested severance the appellant was ordinarily resident in England and therefore not an 'inhabitant' of the ceded territory.

Did it, then, matter that at the material date the appellant was undeniably domiciled in Eire? Lord Caldecote and Humphreys J. were emphatically of the opinion that the question of domicile is irrelevant to the consideration of an individual's nationality. Speaking generally, this is undoubtedly true, and ever since *Udny* v. *Udny*[3] the distinction between nationality and domicile has become a truism which the humblest student would not dare to overlook. But the case of the cession of territory is a peculiar one, because it is here, and probably here only, that nationality is admittedly determined by a territorial test. If in this case allegiance is determined by a territorial test, there is no *a priori* reason why it should be provided by residence rather than by domicile, and it is *nihil ad rem* to point to the distinction between the two conceptions. There is, however, no authority to be found in the books which would support the materiality of domicile.[4] The real reason why residence rather than domicile is decisive, is probably provided by the principle that a change of nationality should be suffered by those who are within the jurisdiction of the new sovereign, and jurisdiction within the accepted meaning of public international law

---

[1] See Holdsworth, *History of English Law* (1926), ix.84–7; Forsyth, *Leading Cases*, pp. 257 sqq.

[2] *Doe d. Thomas* v. *Acklam* (1824) 2 B. & C. 779; *Doe d. Auchmuty* v. *Mulcaster* (1826) 5 B. & C. 771. The doctrine of these cases, arising out of the American Declaration of Independence, is identical with that prevailing in America: *M'Ilvaine* v. *Coxe's Lessee*, 4 Cranch 209 (1808); *Shanks* v. *Dupont*, 3 Peters 242 (1830); *Inglis* v. *Sailor's Snug Harbour*, 3 Peters 99 (1830).

[3] (1869) L. R. 1 Sc. & Div. 441.

[4] See Dicey (–Keith), *Conflict of Laws* (5th ed.), pp. 159, 173; Westlake, *Private International Law* (7th ed.), p. 377.

extends to residents, not to those who in the peculiar sense of English law are domiciled in the territory.[1]

(3) Another noteworthy point arises from the judgment of Singleton J. He derived from *Doe d. Thomas* v. *Acklam* and *Doe d. Auchmuty* v. *Mulcaster, ubi supra,* the rule that the inhabitants of ceded territory have a right to elect: 'It is clear that cession of territory of itself does not rob a person of his status as a British subject. On cession he still has the right to elect what he will do.'

This statement, by its emphasis on the subjective element, might perhaps be understood as involving the result that, provided the intention of exercising the right of election was expressed in any shape or form, a person residing and continuing to reside in the ceded territory could remain a British subject while a person remaining in England after the cession could become a citizen of the ceded state. It is, however, more likely that Singleton J. did not intend to propound this subjective theory *stricto sensu,* but merely desired to emphasize that a person leaving the ceded or annexed territory after its transfer, may by *such change of residence* elect to remain subject to the former sovereign. Such a qualified 'right of election' is not without support in this country,[2] but in view of the decision in *Isaacson* v. *Durant*[3] it is doubtful whether it is possible to speak of the existence of any doctrine of election at all. The question in that case was whether a person resident in this country and born in Hanover at a time when the Crowns of both England and Hanover were held by William IV, became upon the dissolution of the personal union by the death of William IV a citizen of Hanover and an alien or remained a British subject. The Court decided in the former sense on the ground that the claimant owed allegiance to the King in his capacity as King of Hanover and therefore, after William IV's death, continued to owe allegiance to the succeeding King of Hanover. In the course of the argument counsel contended that 'in all cases

---

[1] See Oppenheim (–Lauterpacht), *International Law* (5th ed.), p. 266.

[2] See Edwards, 'Common Law Naturalisation and Expatriation', 15 *J. Comparative Legislation* (1915), 108, 110. The author of this excellent article says that, while the authorities do not recognize an option in the usual sense, for the exercise of such option as there exists the tendency is to require 'evidence more of deeds than of words'. Similarly, Van Pittius, *Nationality within the British Commonwealth of Nations* (1930), pp. 73 sqq., with a full review of the authorities.

[3] (1886) 17 Q.B.D. 54.

where conflicting duties of allegiance arise, the subject has by general law, law which has been adopted into English law, a right of election of which sovereign he will become a subject'. After a full review of the authorities, Lord Coleridge, delivering the opinion of the Court, rejected this view and said that all the earlier cases rested on the objective fact of residence.

The American authorities on the point are equally inconclusive. *Inglis* v. *Sailor's Snug Harbour*[1] dealt with the question whether a native of New York who remained there after the Declaration of Independence in 1776 (which is the decisive date under American law) and returned to England only in 1783 upon the recognition of American independence, had remained a British subject. The Court recognized the right of election and said that the only difficulty was 'to determine the time when the election should be made'. The Court held that 'every act that could be done to signify the choice that had been made except actually withdrawing from the country was done by Charles Inglis', who had thus retained British nationality. In *Boyd* v. *Thayer*,[2] Chief Justice Fuller *obiter* referred to the inhabitants' 'right of election . . . to retain their former nationality by removal or otherwise as may be provided'. And Halleck says[3]:

> If [the inhabitants] remain in the territory after its transfer, they are deemed to have elected to become its subjects and thus have consented to the transfer of their allegiance to the new sovereignty. If they leave *sine animo revertendi*, they are deemed to have elected to continue aliens to the new sovereignty.

(4) The Anglo-American rules relating to the acquisition and loss of British nationality in the event of changes of sovereignty may not only be expected to be in accord with, but are also a source, or at least evidence,[4] of the rules of international law dealing generally with the effect of such changes upon nationality. It is therefore permissible and necessary to view *Murray* v. *Parkes* against the background of those rules of international law and to ascertain whether it contributes towards their clarification.

---

[1] 3 Peters 99 (1830); see above, p. 517, n. 2, and Moore, *International Law Digest*, iii.289 sqq.
[2] 143 U. S. 135, 162, 163 (1892).
[3] (1st ed.), p. 819; (4th ed.), ii.505, 506.
[4] See Oppenheim (–Lauterpacht), p. 29.

The effect of a change of sovereignty upon nationality has of old engaged the attention of international practice and theory.[1] The modern rule of customary international law may be formulated as follows: The nationality of the predecessor State is lost and that of the successor State is acquired by such inhabitants of the ceded or annexed territory as were subjects of the superseded sovereign. While the exclusion of foreigners is self-evident,[2] the other ingredients of the rule require some comment.

(a) According to the statement of the rule it is immaterial whether the change of sovereignty is brought about by conquest and annexation, cession or secession, and whether it results in extinction or dismemberment of the predecessor state. Hall (Higgins)[3] and others[4] suggest that a distinction must be made between the case of a 'wholly conquered' and that of a 'partially conquered state', and that in the former all subjects become subjects of the successor state, while in the latter only such subjects suffer a change of nationality as 'are identified with the conquered territory at the time when the conquest is definitely effected'. The practical effect of this distinction makes itself felt in so far as non-resident subjects of the extinguished state are concerned. It is obvious that they lose their nationality and *prima facie*, therefore, they become stateless. It is this result

---

[1] See generally Halleck, *International Law* (1st ed.), pp. 816 sqq.; (4th ed.), ii.502 sqq.; Westlake, *International Law* (1904), Part I, pp. 69 sqq.; Keith, *The Theory of State Succession* (1907), pp. 42 sqq.; Phillipson, *Termination of War* (1916), p. 35; Hall (–Higgins), *International Law* (1924), p. 685; Wheaton (–Keith), *International Law* (1929), p. 76; Oppenheim (–Lauterpacht), op. cit., pp. 434, 451; Fauchille, *Droit Public International* (1922), i.856; Audinet, *Répertoire de dr. int.*, i.567 sqq., with very rich documentation: Niboyet, *Manuel de dr. int. pr.* (1928), pp. 253 sqq., and *Traité de dr. int. privé français* (1938), i.135 sqq., 324 sqq.; Von Bar, *The Theory and Practice of Private International Law* (transl. Gillespie 1892), pp. 181 sqq.; Liszt (–Fleischmann), *Völkerrecht* (1925), pp. 151 sqq.; Alfred von Verdross, *Völkerrecht* (1937), p. 241; Pillet, *Traité Pratique de dr. int. privé* (1923), i.259 sqq.

[2] It is expressly asserted by the award dated 12 August 1876, of Mr. Thornton, umpire, in *Masson* v. *Mexico*, Moore, *International Arbitrations*, iii.2542; Roumanian-German Mixed Tribunal, 6 November 1924, *Annual Digest* (1923–4), No. 120 (*Wildermann* v. *Stinnes*), Edwards, op. cit., 110; Oppenheim (–Lauterpacht), p. 434, and many others.

[3] p. 686.

[4] Art. 18 of the Draft Convention on Nationality prepared by the Harvard Law School's Research on International Law (Special Supplement *A.J.I.L.* (April 1929)—hereinafter referred to as Harvard Research); Audinet, op. cit., Nos. 397 and 398; Von Verdross, op. cit.

which those contending for the distinction desire to avoid. But it is a result which is not only supported by the numerous decisions of courts making residence the test,[1] but which is also logically inevitable; for unless there is a treaty between the two States dealing with the question (an eventuality with which we are not here concerned), the successor State has no jurisdiction over persons who are not resident in the territory, and cannot therefore impose its nationality upon them. There is thus no justification for the suggested distinction.

(*b*) Inhabitants change their nationality automatically. In the first place this involves the proposition that in the eyes of international law inhabitants acquire the nationality of the successor state, irrespective of whether or not its municipal law makes them citizens.[2] Secondly, the statement implies that, in the absence of special provisions by treaties, customary international law does not recognize an option to elect.[3] The many cases dealing with the complicated provisions of the treaties made after the last war[4] are therefore of little value for the elucidation of the customary rule of international law. It is, however, doubtful whether the rule requires qualification so as to exempt those inhabitants from the change of nationality who within a reasonable time after the cession or annexation leave the territory. The American and, perhaps, the English practice referred to above would appear to indicate an affirmative answer; moreover, Pothier[5] has said that 'les habitants d'un pays démembré de la France peuvent conserver la qualité et les droits de citoyen en venant s'établir dans une autre province de la domination française'. Yet it seems uncertain whether this view 'has the hallmarks of general assent and reciprocity'[6] so as to express an accepted rule of international conduct, and logically the conclusion[7] seems inevitable that individuals

[1] See below, p. 522, n. 5 and p. 523, n. 3.

[2] See, e.g. Oppenheim (–Lauterpacht), op. cit., pp. 434, 451, or Audinet, op. cit., No. 391, or Halleck, op. cit.; indeed, only Verdross takes the view that the question must be answered by municipal law.

[3] See Art. 18 of the Harvard Research's Draft Convention; Kuncz, 31 *Recueil* (1930), 117; Oppenheim (–Lauterpacht), p. 434.

[4] They are summarized by Gettys, *A.J.I.L.* (1927), 268.

[5] *Traité de Personnes*, tit. iii. section 1.

[6] Language of Lord Macmillan in *The Cristina*, [1938] A. C. 485, 497.

[7] It is drawn by Oppenheim (–Lauterpacht), op. cit., p. 452. But Art. 18 of the Harvard Law School's Draft Convention proposes to generalize the American rule, at least in the case of dismemberment.

who leave the territory after cession or annexation, do so at a time when they have already come under the sway of the successor state so that they have become its subjects and cannot, in the absence of municipal legislation, alter their status by emigration.

(c) The most serious difficulty relates to the definition of the class of persons whose nationality changes.

Continental theory and diplomatic practice has suggested at least four tests.[1] A change of nationality is suffered by those subjects who are (1) born in or natives of the territory (irrespective of residence); (2) born and resident in the territory; (3) either born or resident there; (4) resident in the territory irrespective of birth. The first of these solutions was adopted by the Prussian Courts in the well-known case of Count Platen[2] and has often since been applied.[3] Yet in modern times the decision in Count Platen's case has become discredited[4] and the tendency seems to be to favour the fourth solution according to which the new sovereign's nationality is acquired by residents or inhabitants, or 'domiciliés',[5] a term which, it should be remembered, is very different from the English conception of domicile and merely connotes ordinary residence.[6]

---

[1] See Fauchille, Audinet, or Niboyet, above, p. 520, n. 1.

[2] On which see, e.g., Oppenheim (–Lauterpacht), p. 452, n. 2.

[3] French Cass. Crim., 12 June 1874, Clunet (1875), 191; see also Trib. Civil de la Seine, 12 November 1892, Clunet (1893), 563, and Cass. Req., 3 December 1907, Clunet (1908), 824; Polish Supreme Court, 14 August 1923, *Annual Digest* (1923–4), No. 125; Rumanian-German Mixed Tribunal, 6 November 1924, ibid., No. 120 (*Wildermann* v. *Stinnes*); Egyptian Mixed Court of Appeal, 28 April 1925, *Annual Digest* (1925–6), p. 266, although in another case the Court held that where only part of a State is annexed, non-resident natives do not acquire the new sovereign's nationality, so that Cypriots resident outside Cyprus continued to be Ottoman subjects after Great Britain had annexed Cyprus in 1914; 21 January 1920, *Annual Digest* (1919–20), No. 136. See also Rivier, *Principes de Droit de Gens* (1896), ii.438: 'Les régnicoles du pays conquis deviennent régnicoles de l'Etat conquérant'.

[4] See Schönborn in Strupp's *Wörterbuch des Völkerrechts*, ii.271; but Verdross, op. cit., approves the decision.

[5] German-Yugoslav Mixed Tribinal, 18 September 1922, *Annual Digest* (1923–4), No. 121 (*Peinitsch* v. *German State*); Weiss, *Manuel de. dr. int. pr.*, p. 162; Liszt (–Fleischmann), op. cit., p. 152; Audinet, op. cit., No. 400. In France it has been repeatedly decided that 'domicilés' lose their former nationality even if they are not 'originaires': see, e.g., Cass. Crim., 7 December 1883, D. (1884), i.209; Trib. de la Seine, 8 April 1938, Clunet (1939), 92, which relies on an interesting passage from Pothier.

[6] It is unfortunate that it has sometimes been too literally adapted to the English language: see, e.g. Oppenheim (–Lauterpacht), pp. 434, 451.

Although there are some English[1] and American[2] decisions which seem to attach weight to birth rather than residence in the territory, there cannot be any doubt that it is an established Anglo-American rule that a change of nationality is suffered by 'inhabitants'.[3] A person is regarded as an inhabitant, if he or she is ordinarily resident or permanently settled in the ceded or annexed territory, so that on the one hand a mere traveller or visitor has too fleeting a residence to be regarded as an inhabitant, and, on the other hand, domicile in the strict sense of English law is neither necessary nor sufficient.

In *Murray* v. *Parkes, ubi supra*, the Court disapproved of the contention that the appellant had acquired Irish and lost British nationality merely because he was born and domiciled in Eire. It is for this reason that the decision has significance for international law in general. It strengthens the modern tendency of exempting those who are natives of or who are domiciled in, but not residents of the territory, from the change of nationality.

This problem of international law recently acquired considerable practical importance when Germany invaded Austria. On that occasion it was contended that Austrian subjects who at the material date were not resident in Austria and, of course, did not return there or submit themselves to the new sovereign, did not acquire German nationality, but became stateless. The Home Office, however, did not accept this view, which, it is submitted, may derive support from the implications of the Divisional Court's decision.

[1] *Donegani* v. *Donegani* (1835) 3 Knapp 63, 85, refers to 'natives', but probably the term is used merely as an equivalent of 'inhabitants'. The same applies to *Shanks* v. *Dupont*, 3 Peters 242 (1830).

[2] In *Tobin* v. *Walkinshaw* 1 McAlister 186 (1856) Fed. Case No. 14070 (quoted by the Harvard Research, p. 62) the Court held that a *naturalized* Mexican citizen resident in California at the time of its annexation to the United States was not a 'native' of Mexico and therefore did not acquire American nationality.

[3] *Campbell* v. *Hall* (1774), 20 St. Tr. 323, per Lord Mansfield, and many other cases mentioned by Dicey (–Keith), p. 160, or Edwards, op. cit., p. 110; *Boyd* v. *Thayer* 143 U. S. 135, 162, 163 (1892), per Fuller, C.J.; Halleck, op. cit.; Wheaton (–Keith), p. 76, and many others.

# XVI

## THE EFFECT OF STATE SUCCESSION
## UPON CORPORATIONS*

### I

THE effect of changes of sovereignty upon individuals has for long attracted the attention of lawyers all over the world.

As regards domicile, a clear rule, it is true, has not yet emerged, and it is, indeed, remarkable that no court has been confronted with the issue in all its succinctness. To take a case put by Martin Wolff,[1] a German, born in 1890 at Posen when this town was German, undoubtedly had a German domicile of origin. He left Posen in 1910 and died in 1925 in England without ever having acquired a domicile of choice. Since the end of the first world war his birthplace, now known as Poznan, is in Poland. But Germany continues to exist. Did he in 1920 become and is he, at the date of his death, domiciled in Germany or in Poland? The answer should be in favour of Germany, for domicile does not denote the connection with a particular strip of territory, a town, street, house, or 'spot',[2] but with a 'country', that is to say, 'the whole of a territory subject under one sovereign to one body of law'.[3] It is a legal system to which the domicile of origin refers, and this cannot be said to have changed as a result of the transfer of Poznan to Polish sovereignty.[4]

---

* From 88 *L.Q.R.* (1972) 57.

[1] *Private International Law* (2nd ed., 1950), section 106.

[2] See *Re Craignish*, [1892] 3 Ch. 180, 192, per Chitty J.: 'A man may be domiciled in a country without having a fixed habitation in some particular spot in that country.'

[3] Dicey and Morris, *Conflict of Laws* (8th ed., 1967), p. 9.

[4] There is no difference of substance between the terms 'country' and 'legal system' in this connection: see *Whitworth Street Estates Ltd.* v. *Miller*, [1970] A. C. 583, at p. 603, per Lord Reid, at p. 614, per Lord Wilberforce. In this paper, therefore, they are used interchangeably. The point discussed in the text has not been decided in any English case. It does not appear to have been considered in *Re O'Keefe*, [1940] Ch. 124, where it might have provided something in the nature of an analogy. Dicey and Morris, p. 80, seem to take a view opposed to that

On the other hand, in so far as the nationality of individuals is concerned, the law is much more richly documented and more clearly established. It is widely accepted as a rule of international law that the successor State has the right and, possibly, the duty to confer its nationality on such of the predecessor State's nationals as are 'inhabitants'[1] of the transferred territory.[2] At the same time there exists, particularly in the Anglo-American countries, strong support for the view that the inhabitants have 'the right to elect' which they can exercise by departure from the territory.[3] Modern law is hostile to the compulsory imposition of nationality, and 'liberal sentiment and the influence of the principle of self-determination'[4] underline such customary right of option as the earlier law began to develop.[5] It follows from the principle as formulated that nationals of the predecessor State who were not inhabitants of the transferred territory do not acquire the successor State's nationality, though they probably enjoy a similar right to elect

expressed in the text. Martin Wolff (above, p. 524, n. 1) assumes that the *de cujus* in 1910 acquired, but in 1925 abandoned, an English domicile, and argues in favour of the solution adopted in the text on the ground that it was a German domicile that was lost on acquisition of an English domicile of choice. But the solution should be the same if no domicile of choice was ever acquired. See, on the problem, Rosenne, *B.Y.I.L.* (1950), p. 281.

[1] The definition of this term raises many problems on which see, for instance, the paper above, p. 514.

[2] For a detailed discussion, see, in particular, O'Connell, *State Succession* (1967), pp. 497 et seq. and Brownlie, *Principles of International Law*, p. 318. On the problems of nationality discussed in the text, see, generally, Jellinek, *Der automatische Erwerb und Verlust der Staatsangehörigkeit durch völkerrechtliche Vorgänge* (1951); Makarov, *Allgemeine Lehren des Staatsangehörigkeitsrechts* (2nd ed., 1962), pp. 97, 98; Paul Weis, *Nationality and Statelessness in International Law* (1956), pp. 139 et seq., among many other publications.

[3] See, in particular, *Murray v. Parkes*, [1942] 2 K.B. 123, at p. 136, per Singleton J.; J. Mervyn Jones, *British Nationality Law and Practice* (1947), pp. 40 et seq. As to France, see Batiffol, *Droit International Privé* (5th ed., 1970), section 74.

[4] Brownlie (above, n. 2), p. 450. And see, for instance, Sir Gerald Fitzmaurice, 73 *Recueil* (1948 ii), 255, at p. 284: 'On the other hand, the idea of a forcible imposition of nationality on persons who do not want it, in consequence of a transfer of territory is repugnant.'

[5] See above, p. 514. In 1942 it did not seem possible to advocate the enlightened view now supported in the text. Since then human rights have become an acknowledged part of international law, and freedom from the compulsory imposition of nationality may well be one of those absolute and unqualified rights which exist *erga omnes* and are the concern of all States. See, on such rights, paras. 33 and 34 of the judgment in the *Case Concerning Barcelona Traction*, I.C.J. Reports (1970), 32, paragraphs which are likely to cause some surprise, as numerous other paragraphs of that judgment are bound to do.

in its favour by returning or by making an appropriate declaration.[1] The conflicting conceptions are the territoriality of the operation of the successor State's law and the freedom of choice in withdrawing from or submitting to it.

It is possible that such themes will recur when one comes to consider the effect of changes of sovereignty upon the fate of corporations.

## II

As regards corporations, in English law their domicile is determined by the law of the country of incorporation.[2] It also seems that a corporation is considered to have British nationality if it is incorporated in Britain.[3] Such, in fact, is the practice throughout the Anglo-American world.[4] Continental systems substitute the law of the country in which the corporation has its centre of management and control, its actual administrative seat or its real *siège administratif*,[5] for the law of incorporation as adopted in England. The mere registered office or *siège statutaire*, i.e. the seat provided for in the corporation's constitution, is without significance to the conflict of laws.

Whether it is the Anglo-American or the Continental test that applies, it will be necessary to define the law referred to by the conflict rule: is this the law of a country or of a 'spot' such as a town or a building?

An answer in the former sense is, it is believed, in conformity with the general practice of the conflict of laws, which invariably subjects a matter or relationship to a legal system as prevailing

---

[1] See, in particular, *United States, ex rel. Schwarzkopf* v. *Uhl*, 137 F. 2d 898, (1943), also *A.D.* (1943–5), No. 54; *United States* v. *Watkins*, 167 F. 2d 279, (1948), also *A.D.* (1948), No. 51.

[2] Dicey and Morris (above, p. 524, n. 3), p. 481, with references.

[3] *Janson* v. *Driefontein Consolidated Mines*, [1902] A. C. 484, 505, per Lord Lindley; *Att.-Gen.* v. *Jewish Colonisation Association*, [1901] 1 K. B. 123, 135, per Collins L.J.; *Kuenigl* v. *Donnersmarck*, [1955] 1 Q.B. 515, 536. It is frequently said that in the eyes of English law the nationality of a corporation is determined by the law of its incorporation. This is a wrong formulation. The question whether a corporation is the national of a foreign State surely can only be decided by the law of such State, not by English law. See Mann, 'Zum Problem der Staatsangehörigkeit der juristischen Person' in *Festschrift für Martin Wolff* (1952), p. 271.

[4] See Ehrenzweig, *Conflict of Laws* (1962), section 145; Leflar, *American Conflict of Laws* (1968), p. 27, both with further references.

[5] The terminology is frequently misleading. *Siège social* is sometimes used, but on other occasions is meant to indicate the statutory seat.

in a *country* even though, for the sake of convenience, reference is often made to a *place*. When we speak of the *lex loci delicti*, we mean the law of the country within which the tort is committed.[1] Or when Continental lawyers subject a corporation to the law of the *siège*,[2] they mean the law of the country in which the *siège* is situate; nothing can be read into the abbreviated form of words they use. In England Lord Wilberforce, for instance, thought that questions relating to the constitution of a foreign corporation were 'to be decided according to the law prevailing at the place where the [corporation] was incorporated',[3] and relied upon Dicey and Morris[4] who, curiously enough, support the formulation, though elsewhere they use the accurate phrase.[5] In fact the reference to State, country, or legal system is supported by the greater measure of judicial authority. Perhaps it will suffice to mention a particularly succinct statement of the law by Romer L.J.[6] to the effect 'that the status and powers of a foreign corporation which is still in being are ascertained and determined by reference to the law of the country in which it has its domicile..., namely, the country in which it is incorporated. That being so, we would surely look also to the country of the company's incorporation to discover what incidents had been attached by its laws to the body which it had created.'

## III

In normal circumstances the contrast between the law of a country and the law prevailing at a particular place in a country is unlikely to be noticed. It comes to the fore when the effects of a change of sovereignty fall to be considered, for in that event a choice has to be made between two different

---

[1] Dicey and Morris, p. 11, where other examples will be found.

[2] Batiffol, *Droit International Privé* (5th ed., 1970), sections 196, 197; Kegel (Soergel), (10th ed., 1971), n. 150 before Art. 7.

[3] *Carl Zeiss Stiftung* v. *Rayner & Keeler Ltd.*, [1967] A. C. 853 at p. 972.

[4] Rule 73 (2). [5] Rules 70, 71, 73 (1).

[6] *Metliss* v. *National Bank of Greece*, [1975] 2 Q. B. 33, at p. 48. There are many similar statements. In particular, the often-quoted dictum by Lord Wright in *Lazard Brothers & Co.* v. *Midland Bank Ltd.*, [1933] A. C. 289, 297, is fully in line with the submission in the text, because it expressly refers to the creative and destroying power of 'the foreign State'. See also Lord Tucker in *Metliss's* case in the House of Lords, [1958] A. C. 508, at p. 528.

methods of approach. Is it the closeness of the factual or territorial connection that is the test? If the answer is in the affirmative and if the territory in question has suffered a change of sovereignty, a corporation established in it will share its fate. Or does one search for the legal system under which the corporation was created, lives, and operates? If so, it would be open to the corporation by the appropriate corporate measures to retain its ties with such legal system even if, factually, its principal activity or administration or its status as an 'inhabitant' has become subject to a new sovereign.

The most usual and at the same time the least difficult situation arises where the corporation remains within the transferred territory, where no attempt at moving it is made, where, therefore, no competition between two or more legal systems occurs and where the sole problem concerns the identification of the companies affected by the transfer.

It is the most usual state of affairs, because the majority of corporations in fact have such limited objects as to render an inquiry into the problems of State succession superfluous. If the corporation carries on the local electricity works or some similar undertaking and the locality comes under the sway of a new sovereign, there will hardly ever be any need or opportunity for doubting that the corporation has changed its allegiance, legal structure, and organization. As a matter of fact no one is likely to seek to extract it from the new régime and to maintain its connection with the predecessor State. The question whether this could be done will not be put to the test, and in the absence of challenge the lawyer cannot gain any useful experience or derive any legal conclusions from the fact that on numerous occasions in the past corporations have become (or allowed themselves to become) subject to the successor State's legal order.

It is, accordingly, the lack of any attempt to retransfer the corporation and the lack of any controversy that necessitates confining certain remarks of Clauson J. in *Bohemian Union Bank* v. *Administrator of Austrian Property*[1] to what one may describe as the normal case, and protects them against generalization. The case was concerned with the status of the Bohemian Union Bank under the Treaty of St. Germain: was it a person who upon the

---

[1] [1927] 2 Ch. 175.

coming into force of the Treaty 'acquired *ipso facto* in accordance with its provisions the nationality of' Czechoslovakia and thus ceased to be a national of the former Austrian Empire within the meaning of Art. 249 (b) of the Treaty? The elaborate judgment which rested upon the interpretation of the Treaty resulted in the Bank being (rightly) held to be a Czechoslovakian national. But in the introductory part of the judgment the learned judge stated that the Bank was 'clothed according to the Austrian law then prevalent in Prague with the status of a corporation. Its principal place of business, or what is sometimes spoken of as its seat,[1] was in Prague. It was carrying on business in Prague. It derived its position as a corporation and, accordingly, as a legal entity, from the law of the Austrian Empire, which operated in Prague as part of the Austrian Empire.'[2] Later Clauson J. held it to be free from 'any doubt that a company which owed its corporate existence to the law prevailing in Prague, which had its principal place of business and seat in Prague, would become a national of Czechoslovakia'.[3]

The accuracy of these observations cannot be challenged, though they leave open the question as to the essential characteristic that caused the Bohemian Union Bank to become a Czechoslovakian national. Is it the fact that its existence was due 'to the law prevailing in Prague?' It is submitted that this point lacks precision. The legal system to which one has to look is that of a country, in this case the Austro-Hungarian Empire which was continued by the Republic of Austria.[4] Not every corporation created under the law 'prevailing in Prague' can have been affected by the change: a corporation so created may yet have the closest connection with, say, Vienna.

Is it possible, then, to regard the existence of a 'principal place of business and seat in Prague' as decisive? This fact, taken by itself, again cannot provide the test, for a corporation

---

[1] It is clear that the learned judge meant the centre of management and control rather than the registered office.

[2] p. 179.

[3] p. 181. For a similar German formulation see Kegel (Soergel), n. 174, before Art. 7.

[4] The question of the identity of Austria with the Austro-Hungarian monarchy is very controversial. The view followed in the text is probably the better one. See, generally, O'Connell, *State Succession* (1967), i.4, n. 4, or Marek, *Identity and Continuity of States* (1954), pp. 199 et seq.

formed under English law, but having its principal place of business in Prague would be most unlikely to be caught.

It is submitted that a combination of three circumstances is required to bring about a change of domicile and nationality. These are the creation of the corporation under the law of the predecessor State, the presence of the corporation itself in the transferred territory and the continuation of its presence after the transfer. Presence, for this purpose, does not signify the availability of assets such as branches, factories, or buildings or the existence of the corporate home or registered office in the transferred territory if the head office is elsewhere. It means corporate presence in the sense of the existence of both the registered office, the corporate home, and the head office, the *siège administratif*, the centre of corporate control. It is in such circumstances that it is reasonable to regard the corporation as an 'inhabitant' who has elected to remain.

There was no occasion for exploring these conditions in Clauson J.'s case, but they are not inconsistent with his decision or with the facts underlying it and are supported by the principle which attributes primarily territorial scope to changes of sovereignty.

## IV

Now let it be supposed that the Bohemian Union Bank, in accordance with Austrian law, had taken steps to establish itself in Vienna after Czechoslovakia had become independent. Which, in the absence of any problem of recognition as well as of any complexity arising from confiscatory measures and ignored throughout this paper, is the legal system that according to the English conflict of laws governs, first, the validity and, secondly, the consequences of such establishment? In discussing these two questions it will be as well to bear in mind two further matters which must be kept apart: Does the Bohemian Union Bank exist at all in Vienna or rather in the rump State Austria? Has the Bohemian Union Bank ceased to exist in Prague?

Logically the answers need not necessarily be the same in every respect, but it is submitted that all these questions should be answered by the law of Austria. Or, to put it more generally, by the law of the parent State under which the corporation was created and which governs its status as well as its attributes.

This is in line with the approach that has already been suggested. A corporation is not created by, nor does it live under, the law of a place or 'spot'. It is not the law of its registered office, its statutory seat, even its *siège administratif* in the sense of centre of gravity that governs it. Rather it is the legal system of a country, a law district, a political unit. The corporation exists in the whole of such country. It is the creature of its law, whatever theory of legal personality one may prefer. It has not sprung from a piece of territory. The fact that, as a result of the territorial division of that country, certain activities, certain assets, certain of its members and directors have come under the sway of the new sovereign does not necessarily involve the subjection of the corporation's legal personality as a whole to that new sovereign. It is only an election, the corporation's own decision to be and remain subject to the new sovereign that brings about the severance of its relationship with the legal system which created and governs it, and the acceptance of the personal law defined by the new sovereign. No other view ought to be taken by anyone who denies the new sovereign's right to impose its nationality on unwilling inhabitants.

The last remark points to the reason of legal policy which is believed to render the control of the *lex societatis* preferable. That reason lies in the power of self-determination which the *lex societatis* grants or at least facilitates. The effect of the law of the seat is automatic and absolute and, subject to any right granted by the successor State, usually unalterable. The powers of the shareholders should be given the opportunity of asserting themselves in accordance with the law under which they were granted. This is the predecessor State's law. It is the removal of the protection by this law which should not be compulsorily imposed. If, in the territory subsequently transferred, two individuals have entered into a contract it is, naturally, governed by the law of the predecessor State. The later transfer of the territory does not change the proper law.[1] Similarly, the transfer of the territory should not, in the absence of voluntary acceptance, change the *lex societatis* which, in the last resort, is also derived from the will of the founders.

---

[1] In England there is very little material on this question. The Continental material is referred to by Mann, *The Legal Aspect of Money* (3rd ed., 1971), p. 255. In addition see Kegel, n. 275, before Art. 7.

Such an approach is believed to be in harmony with the fundamental test applied by Anglo-American law to corporations: that test is not, as in the Continental countries, the 'territorial' one of the centre of administration, but the much more metaphysical one of incorporation. Neither domicile nor nationality, as determined by the country of incorporation, can in Anglo-American law be (voluntarily) changed.[1] It is, therefore, perhaps a little contradictory, if, in the event of a change of sovereignty, English law were wholly to abandon the ideas underlying the normal test adopted by it.

It follows that the law of the predecessor State decides whether, in what circumstances or conditions and with what attributes a corporation undoubtedly created under the law of the predecessor State, continues to exist in such State.

Thus it is for Austrian law to say whether the Bohemian Union Bank, formed in Austria under Austrian law, is after the splitting-up of the Austrian Empire in existence in Austria and identical with the original body corporate, whether its establishment or continuation requires any corporate act (such as a resolution transferring the seat), and what conditions such act has to comply with to be valid under the law of Austria.

If it is right to look to the predecessor State's law for the answers to those questions, this implies that in respect of the same matters the law of the successor State is irrelevant. It may well be that the law of the successor State denies the existence of a corporation in the predecessor State or its identity with the original corporation or the validity of the transfer of the seat. Such a denial, if disregarded by the law of the predecessor State, should be disregarded in England. Nor should it be material to ask whether, by the application of its law to so much of the corporation as it finds within its confines, the successor State has purported to change the character and status of the corporation. It may have passed a law rendering its own Companies Act applicable to the corporation. The result may have been that the corporation's capital was expressed in a different currency, that it was given a new Board, that its corporate powers were restricted and so forth. If, within a period of time which in the circumstances appears reasonable, the corporation establishes itself in the predecessor State in

[1] Dicey and Morris, p. 482.

pursuance of the latter's law and in reliance upon the legal system under which it was incorporated, it continues to be the same identity as existed before the split, and changes purported to be effected by the successor State have a strictly territorial scope. An individual who elects to leave the successor State's territory has been its national, but resumes his old nationality upon departure. Unless one resigns oneself to the 'repugnant' thought of imposing a legal change upon corporations (and the individuals behind them), the law ought to provide them with similar remedies.

Consequently in Czechoslovakia there may be a Bohemian Union Bank in existence and it may be regarded as the original and only one. The law of England will in certain events readily recognize Czechoslovakian law in both respects. Yet where the corporation has withdrawn from Czechoslovakia, where, therefore, the law originally applicable to it continues to apply to it and where such law differs from that of Czechoslovakia, then its solution alone ought, in principle, to be accepted by English law. If there is in England property belonging to the original Bohemian Union Bank, English law should treat it as belonging to the entity which the law of Austria considers as the original Bank.

This does not mean that the Prague Bank will not be recognized. English property acquired by it after the split belongs to it. It only means that the Prague Bank, notwithstanding the identity of name, is not the original Bohemian Union Bank created by and living under the law of Austria.

It is against the background of these submissions of principle that it is proposed to test them in the light of the law in Continental countries (below, Section 1) and in the United States of America (below, Section 2) and then to consider English legal practice as at present developed (below, Section 3). Such a review will lead to the somewhat paradoxical conclusion that, although on the Continent the normal test is that of the *siège*, in the event of territorial changes, Continental courts (rightly) allow the law of the country of incorporation to prevail, while in England and the United States, where a corporation is normally subject to the law of the country of incorporation, the courts (wrongly) seem to prefer the test of the *siège* and thus are opposed to the approach advocated above.

In considering the three groups of cases it will be appropriate to have regard also to decisions which, in the strict sense, involve the setting-up in part of the territory, not of a new State, but of a rival government only. Although in the latter event no change of sovereignty occurs, the legal effects of both types of circumstances are so similar as to permit analogous treatment.

(1) The case which came before the German Supreme Court was the following.[1] The plaintiff company, known as the Lothringer Portland-Cementwerke A.G., was created in 1905 with its seat at Strasbourg, then part of Germany. All its works and two branches were situate in Lorraine which, by virtue of the Treaty of Versailles put into force early in 1920, became French with effect from 11 November 1918, and where the company came under the administration of a custodian. On 7 January 1920, the sole director of the company who was then in Germany called an extraordinary general meeting which passed a resolution for the transfer of the company's seat to Karlsruhe where shortly afterwards the company was entered in the commercial register. The question was whether the company so constituted was a member of the defendant, a German company formed for the purpose of distributing cement, of which the original Strasbourg company had been a member. The court of first instance dismissed the action on the ground that the plaintiff lacked legal personality. The Court of Appeal reversed and its judgment was affirmed by the Supreme Court. The latter held[2]

that the sequestration and liquidation ordered in respect of the Lothringer Portland Cement-Werke A.G. did not touch the company's property situate in Germany and as regards the administration of the company had only the effect of excluding its powers in respect of property situate in the annexed territory without affecting its existence or that of the company.

---

[1] *RGZ* 107, 94 (29 June 1923). No really different practice was followed by one of the highest authorities of pre-Hitlerian Germany, namely, the First Senate of the Court of Appeal in Berlin. In relation to a company formed at Kattowitz in the then German part of Silesia, but moved to Beuthen in Germany after Kattowitz had become part of Poland, the Court attached decisive importance to the question whether the relevant law of the old and the new seat was the same. Since Poland had not changed German company law, a transfer in pursuance of a law applicable both in Germany and Poland was lawful and effective: 7 February 1924, *JFG* 2, 252; 15 April 1926, *JW* (1962), 1351; see also 28 April, 1927, *JFG* 4, 184. The Court of Appeal's test does not help where the successor State has changed the law or imposed prohibitions.

[2] p. 98.

The Court added that normally the transfer of a corporation to a foreign country involved its dissolution, but this was not so in the case of the resolution of 7 January 1920,[1]

for although this involved a transfer of the seat 'to a foreign country' as intended by the shareholders, such 'foreign country' was the very law district in accordance with whose law the company had been formed, and the shareholders' intention aimed at preserving the company's German nationality.

For reasons which have been developed in some detail this decision which, more recently was followed by the Federal Supreme Court[2] is believed to merit approval. It looks at the matter, however, from the point of view of the predecessor State and has nothing to say about the attitude which a third State such as the United Kingdom should or would adopt. The latter is faced with the existence of two companies, one called Lothringer Portland-Cementwerke A.G. at Karlsruhe, the other called Société Anonyme des Ciments Portland de Lorraine at Strasbourg, and has to decide which of them is entitled to property in England on or before 11 November 1918.

The French decision concerned the Caisse Centrale de Réassurance des Mutuelles Agricoles. This corporation was created in 1907 at Algiers which was then French, where French law applied and where it had its *siège social* as well as its *siège administratif*, though it carried on business in Algeria as well as in other African countries. On 1 July 1962, Algeria became independent. In November 1963 the directors transferred the seat of the corporation to Paris and this was duly confirmed by an extraordinary general meeting held in Paris in 1964, but probably ineffective under Algerian law. Caisse Centrale thus constituted in Paris brought proceedings to recover assets held in France by the French defendant for 'the corporation'. In May 1967 the Court of Appeal in Paris decided in favour of the Caisse Centrale in Paris.[3] In 1971 the Cour de Cassation

---

[1] p. 98.

[2] *BGHZ* 25, 134 (139). The decision is regrettably based on the untenable assumption that the Sudeten territory in 1938 became lawfully part of Germany. Consequently, the corporation in question was considered to be subject to German law. It was on this (erroneous) footing that the principle mentioned in the text was (rightly) applied.

[3] Clunet (1967) 874 or, in English, 41 Int. L.R. 369. The company was confiscated in Algeria, but the facts relating to this aspect are omitted in the text, for they are immaterial to the problem here discussed. It is, however, odd that the French

affirmed the judgment.[1] The ratio decidendi was formulated as follows:

si, en principe, la nationalité d'une société se détermine par la situation de son siège social, pareil critère cesse d'avoir application lorsque, le territoire sur lequel est établi ce siège social, étant passé sous une souveraineté étrangère, les personnes qui ont le controle de la société et les organes sociaux investis conformément au pacte social ont décidé de transférer dans le pays auquel elle se rattachait le siège de la société afin qu'elle conserve sa nationalité et continue d'être soumise à la loi qui la régissait.

It is this principle which, after substitution of 'domicile' for nationality and 'incorporation' for seat, should be adopted in England. But it was in 1968 rejected by the Commercial Division of the Court of Annaba in Algeria[2] in a case relating to the same Caisse Centrale. In the course of its remarkably elaborate judgment the Algerian Court relied on what one may describe as the 'territorial' theory, i.e. on the view that the status of a corporation is governed by the law of the place where the *siège social* is located, and this was 'the legal system applicable to the territory of Algeria'. Such, indeed, is the solution advocated by Professor Loussouarn in the course of his comments upon the French decision of 1967 to which he attributed a 'caractère insolite' and a 'caractère hérétique'.[3] More recently Professors Loussouarn and Bredin[4] have criticized the French practice in more cautious language:

Une telle position nous semble fort discutable, car elle méconnait que le changement de nationalité des sociétés pose essentiellement un problème de conflit de lois, et qu'en ce domaine il est traditionellement admis par une jurisprudence constante, que conforte l'article 3 de la loi du 24 juillet 1966, qu'il y a lieu de se référer au siège social.

The last few words are illuminating. It is suggested with respect that it is misleading to refer to the '*siège social*'. The most that a

Court does not consider the confiscation point. It may have made the result inevitable, irrespective of the transfer of the seat, for an action by the Algerian company is likely to have involved the inadmissible assertion of a prerogative right: see Mann, *I.C.L.Q.* (1962), 488 et seq. An earlier decision of the Court of Appeal in Paris (21 October 1965, 2 *Gaz. Pal.* (1965), 353, and summarized in Clunet (1966), 360) does not seem to have involved the case of a transfer, but merely decided that a company whose '*siège*' remained in Algeria acquired Algerian nationality. This is entirely in line with the present writer's submissions.

[1] 30 March 1971, *Rev. Crit.* (1971), 451, with note by Lagarde.
[2] 41 Int. L.R. 384.    [3] Clunet (1967), 882, 883.
[4] *Droit Commercial du Commerce International* (1969), p. 309.

Continental lawyer can say is that the status of a corporation is subject 'à la loi du *pays* dans lequel se trouve le siège social', to the law of the *country* in which the seat is situate. Once the principle is so formulated it becomes clear that in case of a change of sovereignty it does not solve the question whether it is the law of the predecessor State or the law of the successor State that applies either as a matter of legal necessity or as a matter of election. Nor is it correct to say, as Professors Loussouarn and Bredin do,[1] that under the pretext of respect for the intention of the shareholders[2] the doctrine of the French Courts 'en remettant en cause une des rares règles que l'on pouvait considérer comme acquises, risque de déclencher une nouvelle crise de la nationalité des sociétés'. There is no reason to think that the French decisions intended to state a rule applicable in any case other than that of the change of sovereignty, a very special and, fortunately, rare case.

The problem, however, to which the French case does give rise is one of fact. According to the Algerian decision the transfer of the company's seat to Paris took place at the end of 1966 and was ratified by an extraordinary general meeting in 1967. According to the French decision, as mentioned above, the two events occurred, respectively, in November 1963 and June 1964. Whatever the explanation of this discrepancy may be, there is room for the impression that certainly in 1966–7, but perhaps also in 1963–4, an election in favour of Algerian law had, at least impliedly, been made and that, for this reason, a transfer to France otherwise than in pursuance of Algerian law was no longer permitted. It is, however, impossible to come to a final conclusion on the point, as the available factual material is insufficient and there may have been good grounds which account for the delay.

In any event neither the French nor the Algerian Courts have dealt with the status in France or Algeria of a foreign, i.e. a

---

[1] Ibid. Perhaps this is a convenient place to mention that according to Art. 3 of the Companies Act, 1966, 'les sociétés dont le siège social est situé en territoire français sont soumises à la loi française'. Apart from the fact that the term '*siège social*' is perhaps not entirely free from ambiguity, the provision does not seem to have any bearing upon the problem of the effect of a change of sovereignty.

[2] The learned authors recognize that the theory of the Paris Court of Appeal respects the intention of the founders, but regard this as irrelevant on the ground that such a view 's'inspire d'une conception contractuelle de la société qui est, dans une large mesure dépassée'. *Sed quaere.*

third country's corporation which, as a result of State succession, has seemingly come to exist in two countries. It can only be suggested that the doctrine of the Court of Appeal in Paris tends to subject that corporation to the law of the predecessor State and, accordingly, to render it entitled to the original corporation's French property.

(2) The last-mentioned problem has, however, arisen in the United States of America, where the approach unfortunately was different from that of the German and French Courts and where a reappraisal in the light of the preceding observations may be merited.

In *N. V. Suikerfabriek Wono-Aseh* v. *Chase National Bank*[1] the facts were as follows. The plaintiff company was created in and under the law of the Netherlands East Indies which were then part of the Netherlands. As a result of exchange control regulations the plaintiff company's United States assets were brought under the control of a bank in the Netherlands East Indies, the Escomptobank N.V., which in turn held them subject to the control of the Government. In August 1949 the State of Indonesia became the sovereign of the territory of the Netherlands East Indies. In August 1950 the plaintiff corporation, relying on a Dutch decree of April 1940, removed itself to Surinam which was part of the Netherlands and where it was recognized as a Surinam corporation by the Governor-General. The Indonesian Government had not consented to the transfer and opposed the company's claim to the American assets. That claim failed. The principal ground upon which the United States District Court based its decision[2] was that the decree of April 1940 was inconsistent with Indonesian law and therefore did not continue in force in Indonesia, for 'were the law of April 26, 1940, construed as permitting this, it would be effective in depriving the Republic of Indonesia, without its consent, of the control it had already exercised over the assets and the continuation of which it apparently deems necessary to the welfare of its national economy'. In other words, the court applied Indonesian and disregarded Dutch law.

---

[1] 111 F. Supp. 833 (1953), also in 82 Int. L.R. (1953).

[2] The Court also held that the decree of 1940 was applicable only in war-time. This is, of course, a point of Dutch law which is of no significance in the present context.

The Court's preference for Indonesian law seems to have been exclusively based on the fact that the plaintiff company had its principal place of business and its corporate home in the territory which later became Indonesia. No reason is given for the conclusion that the law of the country of incorporation, namely the Netherlands, no longer applied to the company and, therefore, could not assert itself. It is not intended to deny that in Indonesia the decree of April 1940 no longer applied. But this is material only if it is assumed that the plaintiff company, a Netherlands corporation, had legal existence only in Indonesia so as to be subject only to Indonesian law. It is this assumption which it is intended to challenge and which is, it is believed, both unproven and contrary to the accepted rule of the conflict of laws relating to the status of corporations.

(3) The English law, however, is in line with that of the United States.

*Banco de Bilbao* v. *Sancha*[1] was concerned with a corporation constituted under the law of Spain with its corporate home at Bilbao. The essential aspects of the bank's history during the period of the Spanish civil war may be summarized as follows. A new board of directors, set up in January 1937, was in control of the bank of Bilbao in June 1937, when the insurgent forces under General Franco were threatening the town. On 15 June 1937 the new board left the Bilbao offices and removed the bank's records to Republican territory. By a variety of laws enacted in Republican Spain between August and December 1937 the 'domicile' of Bilbao companies such as the Banco de Bilbao was transferred to Republican Spain, the acts of the directors there established were validated and the meetings held and other corporate acts done in Bilbao after June 1937 were declared null and void. On 19 June 1937, on the other hand, the Basque territory of which Bilbao forms part was occupied by the insurgent forces under General Franco. In December 1937 General Franco's Government issued decrees and allowed meetings to be held in Bilbao with a view to ensuring the appointment of a Board of Directors and nullifying the effect of the legislation of the Republic of Spain which has been referred to. By the action instituted in the English Courts the Banco de Bilbao, as established in Republican Spain,

[1] [1938] 2 K. B. 176.

attempted to obtain control of the bank's London branch. That attempt failed and the action was dismissed. In order to assess the principle established by the case it should, in the present context, be assumed that, from the point of view of recognition, the Republican and the Franco Government were legally on the same level and that it made no difference whether the Court proceeded as if there existed two Spanish States or whether there existed a single Spanish State consisting of two areas, each under its own government.[1]

The plaintiff bank's argument was to the effect that its '*siège social*' was 'at Barcelona ever since the *de jure* government made a law decreeing that the head office of the company should be at Barcelona'. Further, 'the law that now applies to this bank is not the law of the '*siège social*' but the law of the country under which it was incorporated. The company must be regarded as being subject not to the laws in operation at Bilbao, but to the laws of Spain.'[2] The material point of law was thus clearly put before the Court. It is, however, far from clear whether and to what extent it was supported by evidence on the law of the predecessor State, namely, the Republic of Spain.

What is clear, however, is that, speaking again through Clauson L.J. (as he had by then become), the Court of Appeal held the law of the Republic of Spain to be immaterial. It will be helpful to set forth the reasoning[3]:

> The question what body of directors have the legal right of representing the Banco de Bilbao, a commercial entity organized under the laws prevailing in Bilbao and having its corporate home in Bilbao, must depend in the first place on the articles under which it is constituted. The interpretation of those articles and the operations of them, having regard to the general law, must be governed by the lex loci contractus (see per Lord Wrenbury in *Russian Commercial and Industrial Bank* v. *Comptoir d'Escompte de Mulhouse*, [1925] A. C. 112, 149), i.e. by the law from time to time prevailing at the place where the corporate home (*domicilio social*) was set up. . . . The question accordingly resolves itself into this. What is the Government whose laws govern in such a matter the Banco de Bilbao? The answer would seem necessarily to be: the laws of the government of the territory in which Bilbao is situate.

It is submitted with great respect that the whole of this reasoning lacks persuasiveness. First, the Banco de Bilbao cannot be said to be subject to 'the laws prevailing in Bilbao' merely

---

[1] On this point see below, p. 548.    [2] p. 186.    [3] pp. 194, 195.

because it had its corporate home there. Surely, before the territorial change, you can form a company in Madrid (or in London) and give it a corporate home in Bilbao (or Birmingham), yet have its constitution governed by the law of Spain (or England). Further, it is by no means impossible to form a company outside Spain, give it a corporate home in Bilbao and thereby subject it to the law of Spain. Secondly, it is at least inaccurate to say that the question what body of directors has the right of representing the company must depend on the company's articles. In truth it depends on the law of the country governing the company, i.e. the *lex societatis*, in the present case Spain, and on the articles to the extent only to which such law allows them to operate. In other words, the articles are a secondary source of authority. Thirdly, it is contrary to principle to suggest that the articles 'must be governed by the *lex loci contractus*'. The status of a corporation, including its existence, operation, and dissolution, is determined by the law of the country of its incorporation[1] which may differ from the place where the contract is made. Fourthly, even if, albeit incorrectly, such law is described as the *lex loci contractus* rather than the *lex societatis*, it is by no means identical with 'the law from time to time prevailing at the *place* where the corporate home (*domicilio social*) was set up'. That law is a legal system, the law of a *country* rather than a place. Fifthly, the suggestion that Lord Wrenbury believed the *lex loci contractus* to be applicable to a corporation is plainly due to a misunderstanding. Lord Wrenbury, whose observations are altogether unlikely to attract a modern lawyer concerned with the status of foreign corporations, raised the question whether a foreign 'association' was 'not to be treated here as an association or partnership of natural persons whose relations *inter se* are to be found in the articles of association of the company and are to be ascertained no doubt with reference to the *lex loci contractus*'. That a body which is not a corporation, but an association or partnership of natural persons, may be governed by the *lex loci contractus*, i.e. the law of the country (as opposed to the place) where the contract was concluded, is a much more acceptable proposition, though we would now refer to the proper law of the partnership agreement and though the point is in any case without materi-

---

[1] See above, p. 527, n. 6.

ality to the status of a corporation, in private international law. These criticisms are of varying weight, but in their totality they show that Clauson L.J.'s reasoning and, in particular, his insistence upon the control of the law of the corporate home rather than the law of the country of incorporation is unacceptable and ought not to be followed. The theory of the Court of Appeal is, moreover, opposed to basic tenets of the conflict of laws, which, if repetition be permitted, require the application of the law of a country rather than a 'spot'. In any case a corporation, like an individual, should be entitled to remove itself from the successor State's territory in accordance with the *lex societatis* applicable to it.

## V

Up to this point it has been assumed that, as regards their respective status in public international law, both the predecessor State and the successor State are equal, that they are both recognized *de jure* by the government of the forum as well as by each other and that, therefore, there is no room for the question whether the results should be in any way different on account of the inferiority of the successor State's status. It is now proposed to consider three cases of such inferiority; this may arise either because the successor State is not recognized at all (below, Section 1), or because it has received *de facto* recognition from Britain, though not from the parent State (below, Section 2), or because Britain has recognized it *de jure*, though again the parent State has withheld recognition (below, Section 3). These three cases are material only where, as at present in Britain, the law of the place governs in which the corporation's seat is situate, for if, in accordance with the Continental doctrine, the transfer of the seat is subject to the law of the predecessor State, there is in any event no room for the problem and the status of the successor State is necessarily without interest.

(1) The successor State may not have received any degree of recognition either from Britain or from the predecessor State which continues to be recognized both *de jure* and *de facto* in respect of the whole of its territory. In such event the successor State is simply a usurper and its acts carry no legal authority, so that a corporation with its corporate home within its territory

continues to remain exclusively subject of the law of the predecessor State. If this permits a transfer of the corporate seat, it will be internationally valid.

It is not open to doubt that such will be the result in the Anglo-American world where absence of recognition deprives the acts of the alleged 'State' of any validity.[1] But the law should be the same everywhere, for, although on the Continent recognition of a State is frequently said not to be a prerequisite of the application of its law, there is probably no decision to this effect and on proper analysis the proposition should appear to be untenable. This is an entirely different case from that of an unrecognized government in an undivided State with which Continental practice seems to have been concerned, which has led to generalized formulations,[2] and which admittedly has, as a rule, been solved on the Continent much more satisfactorily than in the Anglo-American countries.[3] In the present context it must suffice to describe it as unthinkable that if the Mafia sets up a government in Sicily, proclaims the independent Republic of Sicily but fails to obtain recognition from Italy, a Continental court would apply a Sicilian law prohibiting the transfer of the corporate seat of Italian corporations from Sicily to the mainland of Italy.

The example of the 'German Democratic Republic' at a time when it was nowhere recognized in the Western world shows that judicial practice (outside England) is in full conformity with these submissions. The Federal Republic of Germany regarded and perhaps still regards itself and has everywhere (except in English Courts) been regarded as identical with or representing the continuing State of Germany.[4] On

---

[1] The acceptance of this rule underlies the decision of the House of Lords in *Carl Zeiss Stiftung* v. *Rayner & Keeler Ltd.*, [1967] 1 A. C. 853, and is, of course, expressed by the Court of Appeal in the same same case [1965] Ch. 596, whose decision was reversed on entirely different grounds. See below, p. 549, n. 3. As to the United States of America, see such cases as *The Maret*, 145 F. 2d 431 (1944) and numerous other cases mentioned by O'Connell, *International Law* (2nd ed., 1970), i.172 et seq.

[2] As to France, see Batiffol, *Droit International Privé* (5th ed., 1970), section 256; as to Germany Kegel (Soergel), n. 101 before Art. 7. It is possible that in both these countries the problem deserves elaborate discussion with reference to the many different factual situations that have arisen.

[3] A. E. Anton, *Private International Law* (1967), p. 255; Greig, 83 *L.Q.R.* (1967), 96; above, pp. 411, 412, and others.

[4] See below, pp. 679 et seq. with numerous references.

this footing the courts of the Federal Republic have treated the territory occupied by the 'German Democratic Republic' as part of Germany rather than a foreign country, held the conflict of laws to be inapplicable and allowed hundreds of corporations, originally created under German law, to move to the West in accordance with the law administered by the Federal Republic, but in opposition to the law of the 'German Democratic Republic'. A prominent example is the case of *Ihagee Kamerawerk A.G.* which led to conflicting decisions of the Federal Supreme Court[1] and of the East German Supreme Court.[2] An even more conspicuous, though very special,[3] case is that of the *Carl Zeiss Stiftung* which was created in 1889 in Jena, but by West German decrees of 1949 and 1954 and a statute of 1967 was moved to the Federal Republic. Not only the United States courts,[4] but also many Continental courts have tested the removal in the light of the law of Germany as laid down by the courts of the Federal Republic[5] and disregarded the decisions of the Supreme Court of the 'German Democratic Republic'.[6] In the absence of recognition of the

---

[1] 30 January 1969, *Gewerblicher Rechtsschutz und Urheberrecht (GRUR)* (1969), 487.

[2] 20 December 1963, *IzRspr.* (1964–5), No. 72.

[3] The peculiarity arises from the fact that a Foundation is not under the control of individuals and therefore differs, in particular, from a company controlled by shareholders. In certain cases a Foundation is subject to control by the 'competent authority' under section 87 of the Civil Code.

[4] *Carl Zeiss Stiftung* v. *VEB Carl Zeiss*, 433 F. 2d 686 (1970), affirming the decision of Mansfield J., 293 F. Supp. 892 (1968), more fully reported 160 *USPQ* 97. All quotations are from the latter report.

[5] The principal but by no means the only decision is that of the Federal Supreme Court, 15 November 1960, *IzRspr.* (1960–1), No. 52. This is the decision which in *Carl Zeiss Stiftung* v. *Rayner & Keeler, ubi supra,* Cross J. (as he then was) had described as 'perverse', by which Lord Reid (at p. 923) was 'not impressed' and which to Lord Upjohn's mind (p. 949) was 'quite unconvincing'. On the other hand, Mansfield J. (above, n. 4) at p. 130 characterized it as 'restrained, objective, reasonably logical and dispassionate'. Lord Reid's main complaint seems to have been that the Federal Supreme Court did not apply the principles of private international law. Yet he appreciated (p. 922) that in that Court's view Germany 'is still one country'. Could the Republic of Spain be expected to apply the Nationalist Government's law as introduced in the Basque territory? Does not the United Kingdom refuse to recognize the law of the Smith régime in Rhodesia? (See *Madzimbamuto* v. *Lardner-Burke,* [1969] A. C. 645; *Adams* v. *Adams,* [1970] 3 All E. R. 572). What would be the view of the United Kingdom if a third country, having recognized the Smith régime, should not only apply the present Rhodesian law, but also criticize the United Kingdom and its courts for their failure to do so?

[6] 6 April 1954, *IzRspr.* (1964–5), No. 50; 23 March 1961, *IzRspr.* (1960–1), No. 136. Of these decisions it was said by Lord Reid (*ubi supra*), p. 924) that, while they

'German Democratic Republic' this is believed to be clearly right.

A similar situation arising from Chinese affairs fell to be considered by an American Court. The Bank of China, established as the Central Bank in 1912 in Shanghai, had a deposit account with the Wells Fargo Bank and Union Trust in San Francisco. The Chinese Nationalist Government, recognized by the United States as the only Government of China, moved the bank to Taipeh in Formosa where it functions under the control of the Nationalist Government and whence it directs its affairs in various parts of the world. But the People's Government of China, established on the mainland, yet lacking any degree of recognition by the United States, also operates a Bank of China in Peiping. Both banks claim to be, and are operated as if they were, the original Bank of China formed in 1912. Both claimed the deposit and so Goodman J., sitting in the United States District Court in California, was confronted with the question: Which Bank of China is legally entitled to the deposit? The learned judge rejected a 'strictly pragmatic approach' involving a division of the deposit between the two banks in the degree that each now exercises the functions of the Bank of China. He also rejected the suggestion that he might award the deposit to the bank being the closest counterpart of the corporation created in 1912. Rather it was held that since the Nationalist Government was deemed by the United States to be best able to further the common interests of China and the United States, it should be treated 'as legally entitled to exercise the controlling corporate authority of the Bank of China in respect to the deposit in suit'.[1] The result demands approval, though it might have been preferable to derive it from the rule that, as a result of the incidence of recognition, in a court of the

---

contained Communist 'embellishments', 'going behind this ornamentation' he could find 'a judicial approach and a reasonable result'. In New York Mansfield J. said (p. 129) that they were 'so completely lacking in any objectivity of approach and so thoroughly saturated with a combination of Communist propaganda, diatribes against the "capitalist oriented" decisions of the West German Courts, and absence of judicial restraint that any logical analysis is obfuscated by their obvious political mission.' A further opinion, largely inconsistent with the above decisions, was rendered by the East German Supreme Court on 19 November 1970, i.e. a few weeks before the beginning of further *Zeiss* litigation in England, and is not yet published.

[1] *Bank of China* v. *Wells Fargo Bank*, 104 F.Supp. 59 (1952), at p. 66.

United States the law of China as applicable to a Chinese corporation is laid down by Nationalist China.

(2) The successor State may be recognized *de facto* by Britain, while the predecessor State, itself recognized *de jure*, may withhold any recognition from it. Suppose Sicily has proclaimed its independence and Britain recognizes it *de facto*, while Italy continues to regard it as part of her sovereignty. Could a corporation formed under the law of Italy with its seat at Palermo transfer itself to Rome in accordance with Italian, but in defiance of Sicilian law, so that it could claim English assets of 'the corporation', that is to say, assets belonging to it before the split?[1] A negative answer would at first sight probably be vouchsafed by those who look to the law at the place of the actual seat, for they would regard the corporation as Sicilian, whatever its connection with the Italian legal system may have been before the alleged change of sovereignty and by English law the acts of a government recognized *de facto* cannot be impugned by a rival government, even though it may be the predecessor.[2]

Yet the question arises whether even on the footing of this 'territorial' view an exception ought not to be made in the case in which the predecessor State and government is recognized *de jure* by Britain in respect of the whole territory, continues to exercise sovereign control *de jure* and *de facto* over a large part of its territory and itself does not recognize the successor State or government established in another part of the country. It is submitted that in such a case of a conflict between rivals recognized, respectively, *de jure* and *de facto*, much is to be said in favour of Britain applying the law of the predecessor State. It must in the first place be remembered that the recognition *de facto* of a State and government which is in control of only part of a State's territory may be not only an affront to the *de jure* Government, but also contrary to public international law; as Lord McNair has put it with his usual caution, the attempt made during the Spanish civil war to recognize a *de*

---

[1] To avoid misunderstanding it should again be stated that it cannot be open to doubt that each of the two corporations is under its own law (and, therefore, everywhere) lawfully in possession of whatever property it holds or has acquired, and, if dispossessed, can recover it. The problem only relates to pre-split property held in a third country.

[2] The principal authority is *Luther* v. *Sagor*, [1921] 3 K. B. 532.

*facto* government which is in control of part of the State's territory only was 'an innovation' and must 'be followed in the future with the greatest circumspection'.[1] Indeed, the truth of the matter is that during the Spanish civil war that attempt may not even have occurred, for to recognize insurgents as a government exercising *de facto* administrative control over the territory occupied by them (and not more than this happened before February 1938[2]) is by no means the same thing as the *de facto* recognition of a new State or of a new government of the whole of the original State.[3] Secondly, even if such a type of recognition is possible in law, it should not have the effect of depriving the lawful sovereign of his right and function to exercise supreme legislative, administrative and judicial authority on behalf of the nation. If, therefore, a corporation created by him and under his law and existing in the territory controlled by him is recognized by him to have a certain identity, this should prevail everywhere, notwithstanding the fact that in some part of the national territory a government recognized merely *de facto* claims the same corporation as being under its control. This is one of the cases in which *de jure* recognition should have a substantially higher status and effect than mere *de facto* recognition.[4] The validity of the internal law of a State recognized *de jure* cannot easily be denied merely on the ground that part of the State's territory is under the provisional control of another State or that if the single State were under the control of a *de facto* government its acts could claim international validity. When the Soviet Government, for instance, assumed, and was recognized *de facto* to have assumed, control of the whole of Russia it would clearly have been difficult to deny, as a matter of legal necessity, validity to its acts.

---

[1] *The Legal Effects of War* (4th ed., 1966), pp. 402, 403.

[2] When *Banco de Bilbao's* case was argued in the Court of Appeal.

[3] See on the points alluded to in the text, Sir Hersch Lauterpacht, *Recognition in International Law* (1947), pp. 284, 285, 294, 343, 365. Contrary to Sir Hersch's impression the communication from the Foreign Office in the case of *Banco de Bilbao* does not seem to have referred expressly to the insurgent character of General Franco's Government. Yet it was remarkable in that it referred only to administrative control and was limited to conditions in the Basque territory.

[4] *Luther* v. *Sagor, ubi supra*, dealt with a factual situation which is different from that discussed in the text and consequently required a different answer in law. The Soviet Government was the only government in control of the whole country. Moreover, there was no conflict between its legislative and executive acts and the legislation of a rival *de jure* government.

But no such reasons of policy prevail, when there does exist a conflict, not yet finally resolved,[1] between the parent State, recognized *de jure* and in effective control of large parts of the State's territory, and the successor State, recognized only provisionally and only in respect of the territories under its control. If, as is readily admitted, the acts of a *de facto* State or government cannot be impugned in an English court, the same applies to the *de jure* State or government. Each of them recognizes the existence within its territory of the corporaton and claims control over it. Faced with such a conflict the English Court ought to allow the law of the *de jure* State to prevail, particularly if it happens to be also the law under which the corporation was created and which constitutes its personal law.

It must, however, be conceded that such reasoning is contrary to the decision of the Court of Appeal, as delivered by Clauson L.J. in *Banco de Bilbao* v. *Sancha*.[2] The facts have already been referred to and it will be remembered that the case was decided as if the Basque territory under General Franco had been recognized both by Britain and by Spain as a separate State or as a part of Spain controlled by the Nationalist Government, or to put it differently, without regard to the fact that the Republic of Spain had not granted any recognition to General Franco, his Government or the State believed to be created in the territory controlled by him. The ratio can be summarized as follows: As the British Government 'recognize the insurgent Government of General Franco as the government *de facto* of the area in which Bilbao is situate', the Court must 'treat the acts of a rival government claiming jurisdiction over the same area, even if the latter government be recognized by His Majesty's Government as the *de jure* government of the area, as a mere nullity and as matters which cannot be taken into account in any way in any of His Majesty's courts'.[3] This passage, it is true, was approved by the House of Lords[4] and, therefore, states the English law. Yet it does not purport to

---

[1] Sir Hersch Lauterpacht, op. cit., pp. 94, 95, 279, 290–3, has emphasized that so long as the civil war lasts it is contrary to international law to recognize insurgents as a *de jure* government. If they can be recognized as a *de facto* government, they must not be put on exactly the same level as a *de jure* government.

[2] [1938] 2 K. B. 176.        [3] p. 196.

[4] *Carl Zeiss Stiftung* v. *Rayner & Keeler Ltd.*, [1967] A. C. 853, at p. 905, per Lord Reid.

suggest that General Franco led the Government of Spain. In fact it may require reconsideration by the House of Lords in the light of the preceding observations. In assessing the weight to be attributed today to the English decisions which not only deal with the Spanish civil war, but also include a remarkable case, once again decided by Clauson J., on the effect of the Abyssinian war,[1] it will unfortunately not be possible to disregard the very special attitudes of mind which prevailed in England in 1937 and 1938, but which should not rule all subsequent generations.

(3) There is, finally, the most difficult and at the same time the most singular of all cases: both the parent State and the successor State, each in respect of its own territory, is recognized *de jure* by Britain, but the two States in question do not recognize each other and, in particular, the parent State withholds recognition from the successor State. If, in such circumstances, a corporation with its corporate seat in the successor State, moves to the parent State in accordance with the latter's law, will it be entitled to English assets to the exclusion of the corporation which in the successor State continues to exist?

This question does not seem to have arisen anywhere, but is liable to arise in England in regard to corporations which were created in territories now controlled by the 'German Democratic Republic' and have since 1949 purported to transfer their seat to the Federal Republic of Germany. England recognizes the Federal Republic as the *de jure* sovereign of the territories under its control. While it had not granted any measure of recognition to the 'German Democratic Republic', its courts, as opposed to its government,[2] treated the latter as the subordinate organ of the Soviet Union, the '*de jure* sovereign',[3] with the result that in practice it had the status of a fully recognized State.

---

[1] *Bank of Ethiopia* v. *National Bank of Egypt*, [1937] Ch. 513, a case which, it is believed, cannot survive the criticism by Sir Hersch Lauterpacht, op. cit., pp. 284–7 and by Lord McNair, op. cit., pp. 396–8. The decision relates to the law of belligerent occupation and is, therefore, outside the scope of the present discussion.

[2] The material which became available before the beginning of 1967 is collected below, pp. 673–4, but much additional evidence has come into existence since then.

[3] *Carl Zeiss Stiftung* v. *Rayner & Keeler, ubi supra*, at p. 905 and passim. No trace of this doctrine, widely regarded as a little surprising and described by Professor

The peculiarities of the relationship between predecessor and successor State should be without effect in the State of the forum, which, in substance, has granted *de jure* recognition to both. They cannot in the forum lead to a result different from that in the normal case which was discussed in Section IV above and in which there exists *de jure* recognition throughout. The laws of logic and justice deny to the forum the right to limit the powers of the predecessor State and its law merely because this attributes international inferiority to the successor State. Moreover, it must be remembered that of the two corporations which exist in the predecessor and in the successor State respectively and which *prima facie* enjoy complete equality of status only one has the additional characteristic relevant in the present context; only the corporation existing in the predecessor State is, in the eyes of an English Court, German, governed by the law of Germany and subject to German sovereignty. It is this feature which, it is believed, confers upon the West German corporation legal identity with the original one.

Such reasoning, it is true, appears to be contrary to the *Banco de Bilbao's* case. But for the reasons which have been developed that case lacks persuasiveness. While lower courts have to follow it, the House of Lords will, it is hoped, reconsider the approval which in 1967 it bestowed upon it.[1]

# VI

Is the fundamental approach suggested in this paper affected by any rule of international law?

The answer is that customary international law is silent. In

---

Jennings (121 *Recueil* (1967 ii), 361) as 'bold if unconvincing', has made its appearance in any foreign country, including the United States of America. It may be taken as certain that, when the British Government described the Government of the Soviet Union 'as *de jure* entitled to exercise *governing* authority' in East Germany, nothing was further from its mind than the idea that the Soviet Union was the *de jure* sovereign or that its governing authority was not very severely circumscribed. But the House of Lords refused to obtain enlightenment from the Government with the result that it developed a wholly unique doctrine. Professor O'Connell, *International Law* (1970), i.170, rightly says that the House 'resorted to a legal system . . . which . . . is neither international law nor the law of the country concerned', but he is less than fair to the Foreign Office when he continues that the legal system applied was 'an invention of the Foreign Office'.

[1] Above, p. 548, n. 4.

the absence of a complete survey of the innumerable treaties which have regulated the consequences of State succession, there is, however, room for the impression that conventional international law rejects the idea of the immutable subjection of a corporation to the law of the territory in which it has its corporate or administrative seat.

While the Treaty of Versailles does not include any special provision,[1] the Treaty of Peace with Italy of 10 February 1947[2] provides that 'companies incorporated under Italian law and having *siège social*[3] in the ceded territory, which wish to remove *siège social* to Italy' shall be permitted to take their property with them, 'provided that more than 50 per cent of the capital of the company is owned by persons usually resident outside the ceded territory or by persons who opt for Italian nationality under the present Treaty and who move to Italy, and provided also that the greater part of the activity of the company is carried on outside the ceded territory'.[4] The conditions thus laid down appear to be more restrictive than the legal principle developed in the present paper would require. But in practice the distinction is likely to disappear, for the company cannot, in practice, be moved except if it is controlled by non-residents, nor will it in fact be moved, unless its activities outside the transferred territory justify or necessitate such a step.

The somewhat cursory search which has been made failed to produce any further texts other than the treaties made between France and its former African colonies. All or most of them include the following provision[5]:

De même, les sociétés ayant leur siège social sur le territoire de la République centralafricaine dont la majorité du capital appertient à des Français et dont plus de la moitié des administrateurs ou gérants sont de

[1] See on this question German Supreme Court, 29 June 1923, *RGZ* 107, 97.

[2] Cmd. 7481.

[3] One wonders what this term, when used in a treaty, may mean. Probably the centre of administration rather than the registered office. This is an interesting example of a *renvoi* by a treaty to the municipal law of unspecified countries.

[4] Annex XIV, para. 12.

[5] The text is taken from Art. 11 (3) of the Establishment Convention between France and the Central African Republic of 13 August 1960, *Rev. Crit.* (1961), 215. Similar provisions are to be found, for instance, in the Convention between France and Chad of 11 August 1960, and between France and Congo of 15 August 1960, ibid., at pp. 220 and 217 respectively, and in the Convention between France and Malagasy of 27 June 1960, Clunet (1960), 1138.

nationalité française pourront, sur déclaration faite au registre du commerce, conserver leur statut actuel en ce qui concerne les règles régissant leur constitution, leur fonctionnement, leur liquidation et, d'une manière générale, les rapports entre associés ou actionnaires.

It is possible, though by no means certain, that if the '*statut actuel*' permits a removal of the corporation from the territory of the Central African Republic such right is preserved. In that event it would be interesting to note that the transfer of the capital would depend upon the French nationality of the majority of both shareholders and directors, but that no activity outside the ceded territory would be required.

Whatever the details of the right of removal may be, such treaties as have been found do support the conclusion that, like physical persons, corporations which normally would become 'inhabitants' of the successor State are entitled to elect in favour of a transfer of their corporate entity. In broad terms such is the principle which this paper has endeavoured to put forward.

# XVII

## INTERNATIONAL CORPORATIONS AND NATIONAL LAW*

### I

THE term 'international company' may have at least three different meanings.

(1) A company which, plainly, is a national company may have an international business and may, for this reason, conveniently be referred to as an international company.

This may occur in the case of General Motors, or Shell, simply because these companies do export business, have foreign agents, branches, subsidiaries, or are contractually committed to the sharing of profits with foreign companies, as happens, for instance, in the case of Shell and Royal Dutch. In these cases the description 'international company' is a misnomer: it is due to a confusion between an international company and an international business. Shell is an English company, Royal Dutch is a Dutch company. This would be so even if, as a result of the unification or harmonization of company law, the English and Dutch company law should become identical. The fact that in two or more countries the law is the same does not render the corporation formed under such unified law an international one. The English Companies Act has been adopted in many countries. Yet a company incorporated in a particular country under a law which is common to other countries belongs to that country and none other.

(2) There are companies created under national law, but described as international, because their formation is agreed, or at least contemplated, in a treaty concluded by States. Such companies owe their conception, though not their birth, to treaties concluded between States and in law are national in character.

Two clear examples come from Commonwealth practice. On

* From *British Yearbook of International Law* (1967), 145.

4 August 1947[1] the United Kingdom, Australia, and New Zealand entered into a treaty providing for the formation of British Commonwealth Airlines Ltd. as a jointly-owned Australian company operating Trans-Pacific Air Services. Similarly, on 15 September 1949[2] the same three Governments entered into a treaty according to which Tasman Empire Airways Ltd. was to operate air services across the Tasman sea between Australia and New Zealand. Notwithstanding their origin, these are clearly national companies and the treaty has now no other significance than that it may, in remote circumstances, throw light on the interpretation of the Articles of Association.

Perhaps the most interesting example of this type of corporation is the company which is referred to in Article 84 of the treaty concluded between France and Germany on 27 October 1956[3] and which is concerned with co-ordinating sales of coal produced in the Saar and in Lorraine. It is known as Saarlor and is, it appears, registered with identical Articles of Association both in France and in Germany, with seats in both centres, but (*si venia sit verbo*) 'split down the middle' in that, as a result of the treaty provisions, the company is to be treated as two companies, one in each of the two countries, 'as if each of the two seats owned the moiety of the capital, the assets, the liabilities and the reserves of the company and the moiety of the turnover and of the profits, and distributed the moiety of its dividends and other payments to shareholders'.[4] On proper legal analysis there would appear to exist two companies with different seats and nationalities, but with identical Articles and tied to each other by the provisions of the treaty requiring complete equalization between them.[5] This can be achieved

---

[1] U.N.T.S., xxviii.41; ibid., liii.241; Professor Paul de Visscher, 102 *Recueil des cours* (1961 i), p. 494, expresses unjustifiable doubt as to the Australian nationality of the company mentioned in the text.

[2] U.N.T.S., liii.235.

[3] For text, see *Bundesgesetzblatt* (1956 ii), pp. 1634, 1791.

[4] Art. 84, paragraph 6.

[5] In this sense the helpful contribution by Professor Bärmann, 'Supranationale Aktiengesellschaften', *Archiv für die zivilistische Praxis* (1957), p. 156, particularly pp. 167 et seq., 211 (double seat, double nationality), pp. 170–1 (the *jus cogens* of each country must be observed). Beitzke, *Mitteilungen der Deutschen Gesellschaft für Völkerrecht* (1968), ix.77, says correctly that 'the company' has French nationality in France and German nationality in Germany, but proceeds to reject the view that there exist two corporations, and suggests that there exist 'only two legal bodies which relate to the same substratum and do not destroy the unity of the legal

by contract (as it has been achieved in the case of Royal Dutch–Shell or in the case of Unilever N.V. and Unilever Ltd.) and there is, therefore, nothing remarkable in Saarlor's legal structure. The French–German treaty, it is true, contains some detailed provisions which have been incorporated into French and German law and, therefore, have much stronger force than purely contractual arrangements. But, subject to this point, the legal structure of Saarlor does not fundamentally differ from that of well-known national companies operating internationally.

Much more difficult questions arise in the case of certain companies which, in pursuance of a treaty and adopting the Articles of Association laid down in the treaty, were recently formed in Switzerland, Germany, and Belgium respectively under Swiss, German, and Belgian law,[1] but subject to a provision in the treaty of the following type[2]:

> The Company shall be governed by the present Convention, by the Statute and, residuarily, by the law of the State in which its Headquarters are situated, in so far as the present Convention or the Statute do not derogate therefrom.

It is submitted, though not without diffidence, that such a company is a national rather than an international corporation.[3]

---

person'. Seidl-Hohenveldern, *Das Recht der Internationalen Organisationen* (1967), No. 338, seems to agree with the text, but is not entirely clear. It may be explained here that the German word 'Rechtsfähigkeit' has no precise equivalent in the English language. It indicates the existence of a person, as opposed to the capacity to act which the existing person enjoys. Jenks, *English Civil Law* (4th ed., 1947), i.1, clearly sees the point and suggests that 'legal capacity' covers both apects, viz. what he calls passive and active personality. Such terminology is cumbersome and misleading. In the above quotation the word 'legal bodies' was used, but in future the word personality will usually be employed to indicate what Jenks understands by passive capacity.

[1] Treaty between Germany, Austria, Belgium, Denmark, Spain, France, Italy, Luxembourg, Norway, Netherlands, Portugal, Sweden, Yugoslavia relating to 'Eurofima' (European Company for Financing Railway Material), 20 October 1955, *Bundesgesetzblatt* (1956 ii), p. 907; Treaty between France and Germany relating to Navigation on the Moselle, 22 December 1956, ibid., p. 1837; Convention on the Constitution of a European Company for the Chemical Processing of Irradiated Fuels (Eurochemic), 20 December 1957, ibid. (1959 ii), p. 621.

[2] Art. 2 of the last-mentioned treaty.

[3] In the same sense Beitzke, op. cit. (above, p. 554, n. 5), p. 91. Hahn, 'International and Supranational Public Authorities', *Law and Contemporary Problems* (1961), xxvi.651, 653, 657; Scheuner, *Jahrbuch* (1966) (Ministerpräsident des Landes Nordrhein-Westfalen, Landesamt für Forschung), p. 576, but see also p. 580; Sereni, 96 *Recueil des cours* (1959 i), pp. 171–2, and perhaps also Friedmann, *The Changing Structure of International Law* (1964), p. 183, though his reasoning is far

Though the company is primarily subject to the Convention, though its Statutes cannot be freely amended and though it is in many respects immune from control by the local sovereign,[1] it is his law that brings the company into existence and retains some measure of authority and supervision over it. Thus a change of the local company law in fields not covered by the Convention or the Statute would have its effect upon the company. In such circumstances it does not seem possible to suggest that the company is so completely outside any municipal law as to be a truly international corporation.[2]

Contrariwise, Switzerland does not enjoy any power of regulation in respect of the Bank for International Settlements and in its case it is, therefore, very arguable that it should be treated as an international corporation. The provision of fundamental importance is contained in Article 1 of the International Convention respecting the Bank for International Settlements signed at The Hague on 20 January 1930 between Germany, Belgium, France, the United Kingdom, Italy, Japan, and Switzerland[3]:

> Switzerland undertakes to grant to the Bank for International Settlements, without delay, the following constituent charter having force of law: not to abrogate this charter, not to amend or add to it, and not to sanction amendments to the Statutes of the Bank referred to in paragraph 4 of the charter otherwise than in agreement with the other signatory Governments.

Moreover, by virtue of the charter the Bank's 'constitution, operations and activities are defined and governed by the annexed Statutes' which are declared to 'be valid and operative notwithstanding any inconsistency therewith in the provisions of any present of future Swiss law'. Although the Bank has been

---

from clear; he describes Eurofima as a Swiss company governed by Swiss law, yet as 'essentially an international company' and says of Eurochemic that it 'goes one step further than Eurofima in the direction of a genuinely international company'. See also Seidl-Hohenveldern, op. cit. (above, p. 554, n. 5), Nos. 339–41, who seems to attribute to the corporations mentioned in the text a mixed national and international character. For a different view see Paul de Visscher, op. cit. (above, p. 554, n. 1), p. 497.

[1] On immunity see Arts. 7 and 8 and on the amendment see Arts. 14 and 15 of the last of the treaties mentioned, p. 555, n. 1.

[2] For a case in which it was doubtful whether a corporation was Albanian or Italian, see the remarks on the status of the National Bank of Albania in Professor Sauser-Hall's award in the case of *Gold looted by Germany from Rome in* 1943, Int. L.R. (1953), p. 441, at pp. 446 et seq.

[3] Cmd. 3766.

treated as subject to the jurisdiction of the Swiss Courts,[1] it is immune from Swiss legislation. Accordingly, much can be urged in support of the conclusion that in substance Switzerland has no control over the Bank, its status or operations at all. If this is correct, the Bank would appear to be an international corporation.[2]

(3) The third category comprises those corporations which are not only contemplated, but also created by the treaty itself, which are organized and live under public international law alone, which are international persons and which, in regard to their status, owe nothing to any national system of law, however much they may participate in activities proceeding under national law. One of the most important and earliest examples is the International Bank for Reconstruction and Development.[3] It was created in Bretton Woods by Articles of Agreement which are not so very different from Articles of Association of a private company as these are generally known. It is an institution which has offices in Washington, yet is completely free of the law of the United States of America. It is an international person which the United States allows to operate in its territory and which, in fact, operates on the level of both international and national law. Thus it enters into treaties with States and also into contracts with the printers who print its stationery. The number of such truly international corporations of a commercial or quasi-commercial character is

---

[1] *BGE* 62, ii.140. The problem of immunity from jurisdiction was, surprisingly, not raised in this case. That problem is nowhere referred to in any of the constituent texts. If the Bank were entitled to immunity the very serious consequence would have to be faced that it could not be sued anywhere. Such a result cannot readily be accepted. Nor is the submission of the Bank to the jurisdiction of the Swiss Courts irreconcilable with its status as an international corporation.

[2] This is the conclusion of Seidl-Hohenveldern, op. cit. (above p. 554, n. 5), No. 337, and Paul de Visscher, op. cit. (above, p. 554, n. 1), p. 500, but the majority of writers regard the Bank as a Swiss corporation; Beitzke, *Die Rechtsstellung der Bank für Internationalen Zahlungsausgleich* (1932), and in his recent paper (above, p. 554, n. 5), p. 82; Gutzwiller, *Mitteilungen der Deutschen Gesellschaft für Völkerrecht* (1933), p. 116, at pp. 175–6, who refers to Switzerland's official view in the same sense, but treats the point as problematical; Sereni, 96 *Recueil des cours* (1959 i), p. 159; Hudson, *A.J.I.L.* (1930), p. 561; Schwarzenberger, *Die Internationalen Banken* (1932), pp. 15 et seq.; Martin Wolff, *Internationales Privatrecht* (3rd ed., 1954), p. 121, n. 29. Mann, above, p. 186, followed the latter view.

[3] Cmd. 6546. On the Bank see, for instance, Broches, 98 *Recueil des cours*, (1964 iii), p. 301, whose observations on the Bank's status (pp. 323–8) labour an obvious point.

rapidly increasing, particularly in the field of banking. The International Finance Corporation,[1] created in 1955, was followed in 1959 by the Inter-American Development Bank,[2] in 1960 by the European Investment Bank,[3] in 1963 by the International Bank for Economic Cooperation formed by the Soviet bloc,[4] in 1965 by the Asian Development Bank,[5] and in 1967 by the East African Development Bank.[6]

These institutions are in law not fundamentally different from those numerous international organizations which, in the course of the last few decades have taken control of so large a field of world affairs and attracted much attention from legal scholars. Yet they not only show a peculiar affinity to companies in municipal law, but also participate perhaps more than other international organizations in international commercial life on the national level. And it must be expected that their numbers and the scope of their activities will increase. Accordingly, it does not seem inappropriate to single them out for special study in considering their status in municipal law.

## II

It is of the essence of an international corporation that it is created, and lives, under public international law. Accordingly, as in the case of international organizations in general, the constituent treaty, analogies derived from other treaties and from municipal law, international decisions and whatever other sources make up the body of international law as a whole govern its status *inter se*, its corporate structure, its activities on the plane of international law.[7] No problem of the conflict of laws normally confronts an international tribunal, just as a French

---

[1] Cmd. 9502.      [2] U.N.T.S. ccclxxxix.69.
[3] Ibid., cclxxxix.120.      [4] *Int. Legal Materials*, 3 (1964), p. 324.
[5] Ibid., 5 (1966), p. 262 (and see p. 292).
[6] Ibid., 6 (1967), p. 932, particularly p. 1003.
[7] Finn Seyersted, *Objective International Personality of International Organisations* (Copenhagen, 1963), has developed a theory of 'objective international personality' (a phrase used by the International Court of Justice in the case mentioned below, p. 559, n. 2). Such personality is said to be independent of the treaties establishing the international organization. This is unconvincing. Does it not depend upon the acts and intentions of the parties whether they create a limited company or a limited partnership?

Court considering a French company in France is relieved of any conflict problem.[1]

On the one hand, this does not mean that an international corporation is subject to international law in the same sense and to the same extent as a State; to hold an organization to be an international person 'is not the same thing as saying that it is a State which it certainly is not, or that its legal personality and rights and duties are the same as those of a State'.[2] Thus, while an international corporation may well be able to enter into some treaties, it does not follow that it could conclude all kinds of treaties and that the law of treaties applicable to it is necessarily the same as that applicable to States; hence the International Law Commission was wise, contrary to earlier plans, to limit its draft of a Law of Treaties to treaties concluded by States.[3] Or there is the question of responsibility; it is not certain that the rules of State responsibility which have been developed in regard to States can indiscriminately be applied to international organizations in general or international corporations in particular.[4]

On the other hand, the international corporation's dependence upon and submission to public international law does mean that it exists entirely outside the realm of municipal law. No doubt, like the State it may and, indeed, it must enter into contracts governed by municipal law; moreover, rules of municipal law may provide an analogy and lead to the acceptance of a general principle recognized by civilized nations. Those rules may thus throw light upon the structure of the corporation, the interpretation of its constitution or the validity of its acts. Yet municipal law as such, the law of any single State, is without direct relevance to the elucidation of an international corporation's legal position, for, in Dr. Clive Parry's striking phrase, an international corporation 'is everywhere abroad and nowhere at home'.[5] This involves two consequences.

---

[1] A different view seems to be taken by Dr. Jenks, *The Proper Law of International Organisations* (1962), pp. 13–17, but it is difficult to visualize the practical cases he has in mind.

[2] *Reparations for Injuries Suffered in the Service of the United Nations*, I.C.J. Reports (1949), p. 174, at pp. 178–9.

[3] See the Commission's Comment on Art. 1, *A.J.I.L.* (1967), p. 286.

[4] The problem has been much neglected and is in need of thorough investigation.

[5] In Friedmann (ed.), *The Public Corporation* (1954), p. 514.

In the first place, an international corporation cannot have a nationality.[1] It is, by nature and definition, an international, not a national, person. Thus, if a treaty benefits the nationals of a certain State, an international person is excluded from its operation even in case the constitution of the corporation adopts and embodies, by way of reference, the company law of the State in question.[2] This is quite different in the case of a State, for a State is, or may be, its own most prominent national. Even where the wording of the treaty or statute covers all those States which happen to be member States of the international corporation, the latter would not, in the absence of a special context, permitting an interpretation in the opposite sense, be caught, for it is different from its constituent members. Accordingly, if a treaty applied to the nationals of all States in the Americas, the Inter-American Development Bank would, probably, not be included. Nor is a member State bound to treat an international corporation as if it were its own national. The corporation does not possess the nationality of any State and there is no necessity and, indeed, no room for any fiction, though the opposite view is supported by the high authority of Professor Martin Wolff.[3] The consequences of the preceding submission are likely to be particularly serious in the field of copyright where nationality of one of the member States of the Universal Copyright Convention is one of the conditions of protection. It may be a matter for regret that the revised Convention signed in Stockholm in 1967 again seems to have failed to take care of the point.

Secondly, an international corporation does not have, in law, its seat, domicile or residence in a particular State so as to be within its territory in any legally relevant sense[4]: The United

---

[1] In the same sense Jenks, op. cit. (above, p. 559, n. 1), pp. 1, 12. Cf. *Balfour Guthrie & Co. Ltd.* v. *United States*, 90 F. Supp. 831 (1950), also Int. L.R. (1950), p. 323: 'International organizations, such as the United Nations and its agencies, of which the United States is a member, are not alien bodies'.

[2] This is conceivable, but has not yet occurred. If it did occur it would be a case of 'incorporation' or *materiellrechtliche Verweisung* such as the conflict of laws knows well. See, generally, Jenks, op. cit., pp. 7–8.

[3] *Internationales Privatrecht* (3rd ed., 1953), p. 121; in the same sense probably Beitzke on whom see below, pp. 156–7. Cf. Gutzwiller, op. cit. (above, p. 557, n. 2), p. 166. The idea that an international corporation has as many nationalities as there are members would seem to be totally unrealistic and unacceptable.

[4] Probably Jenks, op. cit. (above, p. 559, n. 1), pp. 1, 12, agrees.

Nations Organization is not a resident of New York. The Inter-American Development Bank does not have its seat or domicile in Washington D.C. According to the latter's constitution[1] 'the principal office of the Bank shall be located in Washington', but this does not subject the Bank to the territorial sovereignty or control of the United States of America[2]; the banking laws of the District of Columbia do not reach it. It follows that it is impossible to suggest that the law of the country in which the corporation has its seat is either primarily or subsidiarily applicable to it. Thus if a treaty or statute refers to residents of the United States of America it does not contemplate an international corporation such as the Inter-American Development Bank. It follows also that, in the eyes of English common or statutory law, an international organization established in a certain State cannot, for instance, be an 'enemy' of Britain even though the State in question and all persons, physical and legal, resident in it are enemies. An international corporation is bound to operate in the territory of a sovereign and it needs the consent of the local sovereign, which is usually given by the so-called Headquarters Agreement. Factually, it may well be said to be resident at its principal office. Yet in law it is and operates outside the confines of any State. In certain circumstances obvious dangers may flow from the absence of any territorial residence in the legal sense of the term, but this cannot jeopardize the principle.

Here, as elsewhere, the remedy lies in remembering that an international corporation does not exist except in the eyes of such States as have granted recognition to, and not withdrawn recognition from, it.[3] Recognition may, of course, be granted expressly or impliedly. The most impressive manner of granting it is for the State to become a member. An equally clear method

---

[1] Art. XIV, section 1.

[2] It has, of course, been granted the numerous immunities which have become almost standard practice: Art. XI, sections 3–10.

[3] The necessity for the recognition of an international person is emphasized by few writers: Schwarzenberger, *International Law* (1957), i.129; Bindschedler, *Archiv für Völkerrecht* 9 (1961–2), pp. 387–8; also in Strupp-Schlochauer, *Wörterbuch des Völkerrecht* ii.79; Mosler, 22 *Zeitschrift für ausländisches und öffentliches Recht und Völkerrecht* (1962), p. 32; Seidl-Hohenveldern, op. cit. (above, p. 554, n. 5), Nos. 701–14; Hahn, 71 *Harvard Law Review*, (1958), p. 1048. Against the necessity for recognition, see Sorensen, 101 *Recueil des cours* (1960 iii), pp. 137–9, and Seyersted, op. cit. (above, p. 558, n. 7).

is the grant of immunities[1] or the conclusion of a treaty, while other contractual arrangements do not necessarily involve the recognition of the existence of an international person. In any case, recognition is a matter for the Executive and does not require legislation.[2] The requirement of recognition has not always received that emphasis which it deserves. In particular, one must not be misled by the very special case of the United Nations Organization which, as the International Court of Justice decided, has capacity to bring an international claim even against a non-member State on the ground 'that fifty States, representing the vast majority of the members of the international community, had the power, in conformity with international law, to bring into being an entity possessing objective international personality, and not merely personality recognized by them alone, together with capacity to bring international claims'.[3] It may be that, exceptionally, a similar rule can be applied to such a corporation as the International Bank for Reconstruction and Development, a world organization comprising well over a hundred member States. But if in other instances of much more limited scope recognition were dispensed with, it would mean that a few States, perhaps even unrecognized States, could set up an international corporation and transfer certain functions to it, with the result not only that the rest of the family of nations would have to recognize the corporation, but also that the constituent member States might make it difficult, if not impossible, to hold anyone other than the corporation with its limited resources responsible for damages flowing from the exercise of the transferred functions. Questions of this type need careful consideration before any State which refuses to grant recognition should be bound to accept the international personality of a corporate body. Moreover, it would seem desirable to ensure that without recognition international organizations cannot participate in the law-making process which is peculiar to subjects of inter-

---

[1] In some countries the Executive has power to grant immunity to international bodies, even though the State in question is not a member. This is so, for instance, in the Federal Republic of Germany, where the Federal Government may, by virtue of a statute of 28 February 1964 (*Bundesgesetzblatt* (1964 i), p. 187), grant immunity to any 'public international organization'.

[2] Jenks, *B.Y.I.L.* (1945), xxii.274.

[3] I.C.J. Reports (1949), p. 174, at p. 185.

national law and may affect other members of the family of nations. It is impossible to discern any reason of substance or justice which, in the field of recognition, would support a differentiation between States and international corporations. In this connection, the largely sterile discussion between the constitutive and the declaratory view of recognition is quite immaterial. It is not be doubted that, in relation to the non-recognizing State, the unrecognized State has no legal existence. The same applies to the international corporation the existence of which cannot be imposed upon non-recognizing States. In the realm of international organizations, as in that of State practice, the requirement of recognition is a necessary safeguard. There is no room for the often practised reliance upon the rule according to which a treaty cannot impose burdens upon third parties.[1] We are not concerned with rights and burdens. We are concerned with the question whether a State has accepted the existence of a new international person. This is a question of recognition.[2]

### III

When a municipal judge, arbitrator, or legal adviser comes to assess the status of an international corporation in municipal law, he will notice that sometimes legislators make things commendably easy for the practitioner, while at the same time they tend to mislead the theorist.

In the constitutions of many international corporations there is to be found a provision such as Article VII, section 2, of the Articles of Agreement of the International Bank for Reconstruction and Development concluded at Bretton Woods in 1944:

The Bank shall possess full juridical personality and, in particular, the capacity
  (i)  to contract;
  (ii)  to acquire and dispose of immovable and movable property;
  (iii) to institute legal proceedings.

[1] Seidl-Hohenveldern tends to rely heavily upon this rule: op. cit. (above, p. 554, n. 5), Nos. 321, 701.
[2] It is very remarkable that the problem of the recognition of international institutions in general and international corporations in particular has met with so little attention. Does an international corporation require recognition by other international corporations?

Those States which became members of the Bank took (or may be expected to have taken) appropriate steps with a view to incorporating the Articles of Agreement or at least Article VII, section 2, into their respective legal systems. If, for instance, in the United Kingdom the Court has to decide upon the question of the Bank's legal personality, it applies Article VII, section 2, which has become part of English law.[1] In many countries the whole of the Bank's Articles of Agreement are incorporated into the local law[2] and, therefore, there is no difficulty in resorting to and construing the text if a question arises which is not expressly dealt with, such as the question whether the acts of an Executive Director are within the scope of his powers.

It follows that in order to define the real problem with which the municipal lawyer may be confronted it should be assumed that the international corporation's status falls to be decided in a non-member State and recognition has either been granted to it or is unnecessary under the local law. (In this connection it should be remembered that in the Anglo-American world recognition is probably[3] a prerequisite of any municipal institution, such as a court, taking cognizance of the international corporation and that the existence or absence of recognition is certified by the Secretary of State for Foreign Affairs. On the Continent the courts are allegedly free to apply the law of a State or other international person[4] that lacks recognition. These are questions which cannot be pursued here, but are mentioned only to explain the assumption above referred to.)

[1] S. R. & O. 1946, No. 36. In more recent years the United Kingdom has followed a different legislative technique. Orders in Council made in pursuance of section 1 of the International Organizations (Immunities and Privileges) Act, 1950, may provide that the international organization of which the United Kingdom is a member 'shall also have the legal capacities of a body corporate'. Numerous Orders in Council in fact so provide. But such a provision does not carry the point very far, for it leaves it open under what law the body corporate lives. Its existence as a legal entity is, of course, recognized. See now section 1 of the International Organizations Act, 1968.

[2] In Germany, for instance: *Bundesgesetzblatt* (1952 ii), p. 637.

[3] While the legal position is fairly clear in regard to States, the point has never been decided in regard to international organizations.

[4] On the Continent, likewise, there is no case in which a court in a non-member State had to consider the status of an international corporation. The doctrine that courts may apply the law of a non-recognized body was developed in cases of non-recognized governments, but the position relating to non-recognized States or other international persons is open.

In such a case no part of the corporation's constitution is embodied in the local sovereign's legal system. Accordingly, it becomes necessary to revert to principle.[1]

This leads once more the the realization that there are two entirely different questions to be posed: First, which is the law that governs an international corporation's status? Secondly, what answer does the law so defined give to the substantive question that arises? The former inquiry involves the conflict of laws, the latter calls for the solution of the problem by the legal system that has been found to be applicable.

As regards the conflict question, it is a universal rule that the status of a corporation is determined by the corporation's personal law. There exists a well-known difference in practice about its identity, for the Anglo-American countries define it as the law of incorporation: 'Just as the status of an individual, his birth, his death, his marriage and succession are governed by the law of his domicile, so also the status of a corporation, its creation, its dissolution, its amalgamation, and succession are governed by the law of its incorporation'.[2] In other countries it is the seat that establishes the point of contact, and it is perhaps not entirely implausible that some have found a conceptualist difficulty in ascertaining the *lex societatis* of a corporation which, in a legal sense, has no seat; it is necessary, therefore, to find the point of contact which has the closest analogy with the seat of a municipal corporation. Even in countries adhering to the test of the seat it should not be too hazardous a suggestion that the law governing an international corporation is the law of incorporation, i.e. public international law.[3] As it has been said on a previous occasion in relation to the proper law of an 'internationalized' contract,[4]

... the conflict of laws has in mind the localization of legal relationships and ... therefore, the conflict rule normally refers to a locally defined legal

---

[1] It is possible, though probably very rare, that even in member States the question of principle may arise. This may happen in cases which are not covered by the text of the corporation's constitution.

[2] *National Bank of Greece* v. *Metliss*, [1957] 2 Q.B. 33, 46, per Denning L.J. (as he then was).

[3] The conflict rule is not usually embodied in statutory provisions, so that fundamental reasoning should readily lead to the result. Even where there are statutory provisions it should not be difficult to draw an analogy.

[4] Above, p. 226.

system. But this is no more than a form of words from which no dogma should be derived. When Savigny uses the well-known metaphor of the 'seat of a legal relation', he certainly contemplates territorially defined systems of law. But an all too literal interpretation would not be in harmony with his genius. Von Bar's phrase of the 'nature of the thing', Gierke's formula of the centre of gravity, and especially Westlake's figure of the law with which a contract has the most real connection no longer maintain the ideal of localization and prove that the reference to a legal system which is not territorially defined is fully reconcilable with the traditional doctrine of the conflict of laws. In any event, it must be emphasized, considerations of a conceptualist character cannot be decisive.

The conclusion is inevitable that, as a matter of the conflict of laws, an international corporation is subject to international law.[1]

Like all rules of the conflict of laws this is a rule of municipal law, put forward here primarily as a rule of the English conflict of laws, but probably entitled to acceptance by other systems of private international law. Accordingly, no fault can be found with the frequently proclaimed view[2] that the status of an international corporation in municipal law is determined, not by public international law, but by the municipal law of each State. Unless the treaty is part of the municipal law of the State concerned, it is the conflict rule of such municipal legal system that points to the applicable substantive law. But the point of contact, as defined by that conflict rule, is the legal system under which the body was created or incorporated, i.e. public international law.

The conflict problem has been discussed by few only. The suggestion which would make the 'seat' a point of contact, at any rate when the corporation's constitution fails to supply the answer, has already been described as unacceptable,[3] because it erroneously assumes the existence of a seat in the legal sense. Professor O'Connell[4] seems to favour 'the municipal law of the

---

[1] In the same sense Jenks, op. cit. (above, p. 559, n. 1), pp. 6, 10; Zemanek, *Das Vertragsrecht der Internationalen Organisationen* (1957), p. 30, who, however, does not mention the conflict rule at all, yet says of the treaty creating the corporation that 'it is single and indivisible and creates a person'; Seidl-Hohenveldern, op. cit. (above, p. 554, n. 4), No. 721, who makes the forceful point that there is no ground for refusing recognition of an international organization because it is created, not by and in one single State, but by several States on the footing of public international law.

[2] See, for instance, Dahm, *Völkerrecht* (1960), ii.8; or Beitzke, op. cit. (above, p. 554, n. 4), p. 94.

[3] Above, p. 560.     [4] *International Law*, pp. 107–8.

State in which the organization is acting'. No argument is advanced in support of a theory which would mean that an international corporation may have as many different kinds of status as there are States in which it is acting. This would be contrary to accepted rules of private international law, their function and their rationale: it would lead to multiplying rather than reducing differences of result. A similar comment probably applies to Professor Friedmann, according to whom[1]

... the legal status of an international organization at the present time is based on the multi-national principle, i.e. on the agreement between the treaty-making parties to confer full juridical status within their jurisdiction on the international organization concerned. Legal personality is thus detached from the dependence on the law of any one country, although the implementation of its legal capacity must of necessity be determined *by the laws of the State in whose jurisdiction it has to be exercised.*

In the following sentence the learned author looks to the future, when international status 'will no longer have to be anchored in the national laws of the member States of the organization'.[2] However much these passages may be lacking in precision, they do seem to reject the idea that international organizations are, even on a national level, subject to international law. It is possible that this view is due to the failure to appreciate the effect of the municipal rule of the conflict of laws. Finally, it is proper to mention the latest and particularly well documentated study by Professor Beitzke, which like most others primarily deals with the problem of legal personality.[3] It seems to suggest that the municipal status of an international organization 'becomes material to a municipal system of law only by way of the treaty and its incorporation into such system'.[4] Or,[5]

... as municipal personality can result only from the municipal law of the various States, in the case of a treaty providing for municipal personality this is granted upon an international organization in pursuance of the treaty by the various members of such organization. There are as many grants of personality as there are State members of the organization. There arise parallel personalities all of which relate to the same substratum, the same organization. It would not be accurate to assume, as writers have occasionally done, a common grant of personality by all member States. It is only the treaty that is common; but this is derived from

---

[1] op. cit. (above, p. 555, n. 3), pp. 288–9 (italics supplied).
[2] ibid., p. 218.    [3] op. cit. (above, p. 554, n. 5).
[4] ibid., p. 86.    [5] ibid., p. 94.

public international law and cannot grant personality with direct effect for the municipal legal system. Within the individual systems of law personality is granted only by the individual legal systems. . . . In sum, there does not exist an international or supranational, but a plurinational personality of international organizations and institutions.

This view seems to involve the conclusion that in non-member States an international corporation cannot have any claim to existence at all and that in member States it has the legal position defined by such provisions of the treaty as are adopted by the local law. It is not possible to attempt an explanation of this somewhat surprising theory. The basic criticism to be levelled against it is that it disregards altogether the rule of private international law according to which the status of a corporation is determined by its personal law and that in all the circumstances this can only be public international law which includes, of course, the terms of the treaty. If and in so far as these are part of municipal law, many conflict problems are solved or eliminated, but such adoption does not affect the overriding control of public international law or nationalize what is essentially international. If a Ruritanian Court has to consider the status of a corporation which is incorporated and has its seat in France, it is directed by its private international law to apply French law. Similarly, if the Ruritanian Court has to deal with a corporation created and operating under public international law, the same rule of private international law, applied directly or by way of analogy, demands the application of public international law.

In conclusion, it may be useful to recall Dr. Jenks's attractive summary[1]:

The legal capacity of public international organizations, like that of individual foreign States, derives from public international law; municipal legislation may be necessary to secure effective recognition of this capacity for municipal purposes but the function of such legislation is declaratory and not constitutive; it is compatible with the declaratory function of such legislation that it should prescribe any conditions which may be thought appropriate for the exercise within the jurisdiction of the State concerned of legal personality attributed to the organization in question by an international constituent instrument or by customary international law; but it is as inherently fantastic as it is destructive of any international legal order to regard the existence and extent of legal personality provided for in the constituent instrument of an international organization as being derived

[1] *B.Y.I.L.* (1945), xxii.267, at p. 270.

from, dependent upon, and limited by, the constitution and laws of its individual member States.

## IV

The largely theoretical character of the preceding analysis will strike some readers as unattractive and unhelpful, but the abstract problem has perplexed many and, in view of the very limited judicial material so far available, it would be lacking in respect to formative academic thought if its principal representatives and their preoccupations had not been accorded due attention. Yet it remains much more significant to turn to the more practical aspects of an international corporation's status, which have already emerged or may in future require clarification.

As regards legal personality in particular, a body is a legal person if it exists as such, distinct and separate from its founders and members, independent of all persons or institutions other than its own organs. There is, so it should be added, no justification for speaking of the extent of legal personality, of complete or partial personality. A person that exists has personality and it would be tautologous to describe it as having full personality. Less than 'full' personality is not known to the modern law.[1]

A body existing in and under public international law as a legal person, as a body corporate, is (or should be) recognized and treated as such universally. In particular, for the reasons which have been developed it is (or should be) accepted as an international person by the legal systems of both member and non-member States.

Whether or not a body exists as a legal person is a question which in many countries depends on the presence or absence of recognition but, subject to local practice on this point, depends on public international law, that is to say, usually, on the interpretation of the treaty of establishment.[2] The problem

---

[1] It is, of course, possible to have less than full capacity in the sense of active capacity (see above, p. 554, n. 5). The distinction has been blurred by a large number of writers, particularly in Germany.

[2] Resort may of course be had to other sources of international law. Seidl-Hohenveldern, op. cit. (above, p. 554, n. 5), No. 722, suggests that it might be justifiable to apply the principles of law common to the municipal law of member

has long been familiar to international lawyers and its solution has been much assisted by the decision of the International Court of Justice in the case of *Reparation for Injuries Suffered in the Service of the United Nations*[1]; but, it should be emphasized again, that this related to a very special case and does not therefore lend itself to generalization, and that its reasoning has been much criticized.[2] The answer depends on a close investigation of the terms of the international organization's constitution.[3] Such terms as provide for legal personality in member States will be equally important in non-member States, for, to take an example, a corporation formed in France under French law and with a view to activities in France is a corporation elsewhere notwithstanding the absence of any provision to this effect in French law or in the corporation's constitution. The curious idea that an international corporation cannot have any existence in the eyes of municipal law except as a result of special and express municipal legislation (rather than the conflict rule) is reminiscent of what more than a hundred years ago happened in the conflict of laws relating to corporations of foreign nationality. In 1839 it was believed in the United States of America[4]

. . . that a corporation can have no legal existence out of the boundaries of the sovereignty by which it is created. It exists only in contemplation of law, and by force of the law, and where that law ceases to operate, and is no longer obligatory, the corporation can have no existence.

And ten years later, in a similar vein, the Belgian Cour de Cassation treated a French corporation as non-existent.[5] Surely such

---

States. Where there are such principles, the suggestion may well be in line with the demands of a reasonably developed commercial law of nations; see above, p. 140. But elsewhere the familiar and established sources of international law must prevail.

[1] I.C.J. Reports (1949), p. 174. That the observations of the Court do not necessarily apply to international organizations other than the United Nations is rightly emphasized by Paul de Visscher, 102 *Recueil des cours* (1961 i), 483.

[2] Particularly by Professor Verzijl, *The Jurisprudence of the World Court* (1966), ii.42, who describes it as 'rather flimsy and lacking in coherence from the doctrinal point of view'. For other criticism, see Schwarzenberger, op. cit., i.129; Zemanek, op. cit. (above, p. 566, n. 1), p. 27.

[3] For a short, but helpful statement, see Bowett, *The Law of International Institutions* (1963), p. 275. Or see Dahm, op. cit. (above, p. 566, n. 2), pp. 6 et seq. with further references.

[4] *Bank of Augusta* v. *Earle*, 13 Peters 519 (1839).

[5] See Batiffol, *Droit international privé* (4th ed., 1967), section 201.

absurd scruples no longer trouble the modern private international lawyer, irrespective of whether the corporation is national or international in origin.

It is, accordingly, by no means surprising to notice that practitioners do not seem to have experienced any difficulty. Much of the evidence comes from Italy where already in 1930 the Corte di Cassazione decided[1] that the International Institute of Agriculture, in view of the terms of the treaty setting it up, was 'an international legal person'. More recently a most interesting case came before the Tribunal of Florence.[2] The defendant was the Headquarters of Allied Forces, Southern Europe, established under the North Atlantic Treaty. In the course of the judgment the Court said that

... under our legal system an Italian Court may apply the rules of international law which regulate the legal status of the Allied Headquarters even without the enactment of specific laws ratifying and bringing into force the relevant convention. One of the rules of our private international law ... can be applied to the case before the Court. Article 17, paragraph 1, enacts that the status and the legal capacity of persons are regulated by the law of the State to which they belong. With that provision in mind the solution of our problem appears simpler.

On the basis of this reasoning, which is entirely in conformity with the submissions in this article, and interpreting the terms of the relevant treaties, the Court reached the conclusion that the North Atlantic Treaty Organization had created the Headquarters as a subject of international law having juridical personality. A similar case occurred in Belgium, where the United Nations brought an action against a former U.N.R.R.A. officer. In his defence he denied the legal personality of the plaintiff. The Tribunal Civil of Brussels pointed out that the treaties setting up the United Nations and U.N.R.R.A. had been ratified by Belgium and continued[3]:

---

[1] 26 February 1931, 23 *Rivista di diritto internazionale* (1931), 386, also *Annual Digest* (1929–30), p. 413.

[2] 2 January 1954, *Rivista di diritto internazionale* (1955), p. 354, also Int. L.R. (1955), p. 758, at p. 761. The decision of the United Chambers of the Corte di Cassazione, 14 June 1954, *Giurisprudenza italiana* (1954 i), p. 904, also Int. L.R. (1955), p. 754, is less clear on the point now under discussion. It finds that the North Atlantic Treaty Organization is an autonomous subject of international law, but it seems to rely on the Italian law which brought the treaty into operation in Italy.

[3] 27 March 1952, *Pasicrisie belge* (1953 iii), p. 65, also Int. L.R. (1952), p. 490.

Since these public international establishments have been recognized by Belgium, they have legal personality in Belgium.

The most authoritative decision, also relating to U.N.R.R.A., was rendered by the Dutch *Hoge Raad*.[1] The Court of Appeal at Utrecht had held that 'U.N.R.R.A. had been called into existence as a separate body capable of entering into legal relationships. As a result it must also be considered a legal person under Dutch law and as such competent to act as a party to legal proceedings.' Under Dutch law an appeal to the supreme tribunal only lies if a violation of a rule of Dutch law is alleged. In the present case the *Hoge Raad* declared the appeal inadmissible, because 'the question whether such a body must be recognized as a legal entity in an action in Holland did not depend on any provision of Netherlands law'.

## V

Public international law (which includes, of course, the constituent treaty) also governs the international corporation's corporate status.

(1) This rule applies, in the first place, to the question whether the member States are in any way responsible for the corporation's liabilities and, if so, whether their liability is limited or unlimited. The existence of a body corporate does not necessarily relieve member States of such responsibility. The corporation may be the agent of its members. In France a partnership enjoys legal personality. In England an unlimited company is a body corporate. Yet in both cases members are, or may be, liable to the corporation's creditors.

The answer is not always as clear as in the case of the East African Development Bank, for Article 4 (9) of its Charter provides that 'no member shall be liable, by reason of its membership in the Bank, for obligations of the Bank'. There is a similar provision in Article II, section 4, of the Articles of Agreement of the International Finance Corporation. But in the case of the International Bank for Reconstruction and Development,[2] and in that of the Inter-American Development Bank,[3] 'liability on shares shall be limited to the unpaid

---

[1] *Annual Digest* (1949), p. 337.      [2] Art. II, section 6.
[3] Art. II, section 3 (d), and Art. IV, section 45.

portion' of the issue price of the shares, there being no express statement as to whether, to the extent of any unpaid portion, a creditor of the Bank may claim directly against the member. As a matter of substantive law the answer will depend on the construction of the treaty and on such general principles as the company law of civilized nations may have developed.

(2) A similar problem arises as a result of the provision, included in most Charters of international banking institutions, that shares 'shall be transferable only to the Bank'[1] and that, when a State ceases to be a member, the Bank may and, indeed, shall arrange for the repurchase of its shares.[2] In other words, the Bank, so it seems, may purchase its own shares and thus bring about a reduction of its capital without any reference to its creditors—a situation which in the municipal company law of many civilized nations is considered as wholly illegal and involving the direct liability, towards the corporation's creditors, of the shareholder who is repaid. The point is, however, not free from doubt, for under the heading of 'suspension of operations and settlement of obligations' one finds a provision to the effect[3] that 'no distribution shall be made to members on account of their subscriptions to the capital stock of the Bank until', *inter alia*, 'all liabilities to creditors have been discharged or provided for'. But this qualification may apply only in case of the suspension of operations and, accordingly, may not cover the ordinary case of a transfer of a share to the Bank or of its repurchase by the Bank.

(3) A further illustration of the problems likely to arise is to be found in the fact that none of the Charters at present available makes adequate provision for the case of the corporation's insolvency—a contingency which States apparently prefer to ignore, but which, in the interest of creditors, should not be treated as entirely academic. Are all securities granted to creditors effective even if their creation precedes the suspension of operations only by a few days? Would a liquidator or receiver appointed by a court at the instance of a bondholder have in law rights and powers in respect of the affairs of the

---

[1] See, for instance, Articles of Agreement of the International Bank for Reconstruction and Development, Art. II, section 10.

[2] See, for instance, ibid., Art. VI, section 4 (b).

[3] Art. VI, section 5 (e).

corporation and would he be subject to the *lex loci* or to public international law?

In most cases the Charter refers, somewhat euphemistically, to 'termination of operations'. This occurs as a result, not of the creditor's initiative, but of a resolution of the governing body. If such a resolution is passed, it is true, 'the Bank shall forthwith cease all activities except those incident to the conservation, preservation and realization of its assets and settlement of its obligations',[1] and, as has already been pointed out, assets shall not be distributed to members before the discharge of all debts. Nothing is said, however, about the power of those in control. Apparently the governing organ continues to function. No liquidator is appointed. Nor is anything said about the order of priority in which debts are to be paid. Can arrears of salaries or current salaries be paid notwithstanding the cessation of all activities?

If one disregards the problem of immunity which may, or may not, prevent the appointment of a liquidator or receiver by a municipal court,[2] the type of problem here contemplated should, it is submitted, be subject to the *lex loci* of the tribunal. The questions are incidental to the procedure to be followed by a liquidator or receiver who derives his powers from, and is appointed by virtue of, the *lex fori*. The personal law of the corporation is to a corresponding extent superseded by the local law. This is contrary to the view of Dr. Jenks who would apply the corporation's 'personal law, which is international in character'. The reason is said to be that 'special considerations apply to an international body corporate which, *ex hypothesi*, was created as such to place it outside the control of any one State'.[3] This is correct, but the argument is not in point, because we are dealing with a case in which a municipal tribunal in fact has made an order which can, of course, have effect only within its own territory. It is, therefore, not very helpful to base an argument upon the suggestion that the local tribunal ought not to have made an order.

(4) Finally, a few words should be devoted to the case in which two or more international corporations are merged or

---

[1] See, for instance, Agreement relating to the Inter-American Development Bank, Art. **X**, section 2.

[2] See below, pp. 583 et seq.    [3] Jenks, op. cit. (above, p. 559, n. 1), p. 202.

amalgamated into a single corporate body. This could occur by virtue of a treaty between the corporations, which would have to be authorized by a (probably unanimous) resolution of the member States and which one would expect to make provision for the fate of the assets and liabilities of the amalgamated bodies. Suppose these own buildings and are entered as proprietors in the local land registers. Is the registrar entitled, merely by virtue of the treaty of amalgamation, to register the new corporation as proprietor? Or suppose one of the old corporations has issued bonds which are introduced at a Stock Exchange and held by private individuals. Can the bond-holders claim against the new corporation or can they prevent a transfer of assets except upon terms giving them adequate security? Does it matter, for these purposes, whether the bonds are subject to the municipal law of a given State or to public international law? Such questions, admittedly, will not often arise, but they are far from unrealistic, because even if the constitutions of existing international corporations seem to contain sufficient safeguards they are liable to be altered; moreover, none of them deals specifically with the contingency of a merger.

From the point of view of municipal law, such problems as relate to status should, it is submitted, be answered by the corporation's personal law, i.e. public international law.[1] If, under the treaty, the new corporation is the universal successor to the predecessor corporations, the mere production of the treaty should be sufficient to permit the registration of the new corporation in the land register; if, on the other hand, the new corporation is no more than an assignee or transferee of property, an instrument of transfer conforming to the requirements of the local law would appear to be required. Or, to take another example, if the treaty provides for universal succession, the new corporation would, in international law, be subject to all liabilities and municipal law should recognize such succession. On the other hand, to take over all assets without taking over all liabilities or for less than full consideration would plainly disentitle the treaty to be recognized in either

[1] On the principles of the conflicts of laws, see the decisions of the House of Lords in *Metliss* v. *National Bank of Greece*, [1958] A. C. 509, and *Adams* v. *National Bank of Greece*, [1961] A. C. 255, which give much guidance on the problem of characterization which underlies the discussion in the text.

international or national law. In such a case *ordre public* would override all obstacles, including the rules of immunity, and permit and, indeed, compel the appointment of a liquidator or receiver in accordance with such provisions as national laws may include.

## VI

As a result of the conflict rule which prevails in the municipal laws of the world, the legal existence, or personality, of an international corporation as well as its corporate status, as we have seen, is, and is bound to be, subject to public international law, irrespective of the context in which it falls to be considered. It does not matter whether, for instance, the personality of the corporation becomes an issue in connection with the corporation's *locus standi* in an international court or as a result of some act or transaction performed on the level of municipal law. The origin of the corporation, the source of the law governing its status, is always the same.

In other fields, however, a further problem of some complication remains to be solved. Take the case of a fraud committed by an official of the corporation. If it occurs in the course of negotiations about a loan to a State, i.e. within the realm of public international law alone, the imputability of the official's tortious act to the corporation depends on the rules about international or 'State' responsibility. Such cases are outside the scope of the present article. Now suppose that the fraud is committed when the official negotiates a lease of premises intended to be used by the corporation's branch office and that the corporation's capacity to commit a (municipal) tort is in issue. According to the conflict rule of the forum such a question may be subject, not to the personal law governing the wrong-doer's status, but to the *lex loci delicti commissi*. In such a case the conflict rule does not refer to public international law and its constituent sources such as treaties. Again suppose that the international corporation grants the loan to a private company whose government guarantees it, that the loan is governed by a municipal system of law, but that the guarantee is subject to international law. Here municipal liability for the official's fraud depends not only on the place, but also on the sphere of the tort, and the first task is to ascertain whether the issue arises on the international or the municipal level. In the latter case the conflict rule of the forum determines the branch of law applicable to the question of capacity. In the following discussion it will be assumed that the issue arises on the level of municipal law.

The capacity to act is a quality which is different not only from the (antecedent) problem of the corporation's existence or personality, but also from the (subsequent) problem of the authority of the corporation's particular organ that is acting. Capacity is the ability or power of a corporation in law to perform the act in issue. The question of whether an act is *intra* or *ultra vires* the corporation has numerous aspects and implications only some of which will be referred to.

(1) As a matter of the conflict of laws, it is a general rule that capacity, being an ingredient of a person's status, is governed by the personal law. In the case of international corporations, as has been shown, this is public international law. The only doubt is whether the exception frequently admitted or advocated in favour of the *lex loci actus* or similar system such as, perhaps, the law with which the contract is most closely connected,[1] should apply in the case of international corporations. Suppose that the International Bank for Reconstruction and Development has, under international law, the capacity to enter into a certain contract, but it is made by its Geneva branch under Swiss law with a Swiss merchant. Had the corporation been created under the law of, or were it to have its seat or residence, in, a given country, the conflict rule might refer the question of capacity to Swiss law rather than the *lex societatis*. Should such an exception be allowed to prevail in the case of international corporations? It is submitted that the answer should be in the negative. The exception is intended to protect the trader who may reasonably have believed in the capacity of the person he is contracting with. International corporations are still so limited in number, their transactions within a municipal system of law are so unusual, their very character is still so obscure that the burden of inquiry which the rule imposes and the exception qualifies does not appear unreasonable. International corporations, moreover, administer public funds and are themselves entitled to protection. It would be much too

---

[1] Dicey and Morris, *Conflict of Laws* (8th ed., 1967), p. 744.

facile a view that everyone should expect them to enjoy the powers with which national corporations are known to be endowed.[1]

(2) The nature and extent of an international corporation's powers are often expressly defined in the constitution. Thus the power to contract, to acquire and dispose of property and to institute legal proceedings is expressly conferred not only by the Articles of Agreement of the International Bank for Reconstruction and Development,[2] but by many other treaties.[3] Yet this enumeration is misleading, because the powers so enumerated are both too wide and too narrow. Is the Bank, for instance, meant to enter into all contracts of any kind or to acquire any property? Can it accept bills of exchange or issue letters of credit or build a concert hall? Can it buy a hotel or a painting by Picasso and does it matter whether the hotel is intended as an investment or a vacation home for members of the staff, or whether the painting is a speculation or an ornament for the board room? Does the power to institute proceedings extend to an action against a member State?[4] On the other hand, it is obvious that the Bank must have additional powers to those enumerated, such as the power to lease or inherit property or defend proceedings. And although more will have to be said about this, it does seem unlikely that the Bank has no power to commit a tort such as a libel or a fraud.

The powers enumerated in the constitution of an international organization, no less than those enumerated in the constitution of a federal State, are clearly only an illustration, a guide. It is the totality of the constitution, of its terms, intentions, purposes and functions that has to be looked at to ascertain the corporation's capacity. In the case of the Bank this is made clear by the provision[5] that it 'shall be guided in all its decisions by the purposes set forth above'. In other cases one finds the provision[6] that 'the resources and facilities of the

---

[1] Cf. Hahn, 62 *Columbia R.L.* (1962), p. 915.     [2] Above, p. 563.

[3] Agreement relating to the Inter-American Development Bank, Art. XI, section 2; Agreement relating to East African Development Bank, Art. 43 (for these Agreements, see above, p. 558).

[4] An affirmative answer was given by the decision in *Balfour Guthrie & Co. Ltd.* v. *United States*, 90 F. Supp. 831 (1950), also Int. L.R. (1950), p. 323.

[5] Art. I, paragraph 2.

[6] Inter-American Development Bank (see above, p. 558, n. 2), Art. III, section 1; East African Development Bank (see above, p. 558, n. 6), Art. 8.

Bank shall be used exclusively to implement the purpose and functions enumerated in Article 1 of this Agreement'. The functional approach to the definition of an international corporation's capacity which the constitutions thus enjoin, is in line with the tendencies which dominate the law of international organizations in general since in two fundamental decisions the International Court of Justice took 'the purposes and functions as specified or implied in its constitutional documents and developed in practice'[1] as a yardstick. Yet this represents, not a solution, but a starting-point only. In a given case the decision is liable to be fraught with uncertainty and difficulty. Where the commercial activities of an international corporation are concerned, it will, therefore, be particularly appropriate and helpful to remember the analogies which private law provides. The doctrine that a corporation's powers are determined by its constitution is firmly developed in Anglo-American law; in France it is known as the *principe de spécialité* and in Germany it has recently come into prominence in a limited field.[2] In private law, it is true, fine distinctions are being drawn between corporations of public and private law, corporations sole and aggregate, statutory and charter companies, commercial and non-commercial entities and so forth. In the case of international corporations a broader view will have to be taken and the common element[3] will have to be discovered and applied, though the analogy provided by the law of public law corporations will have to be given special weight on account of the employment, in both cases, of public funds.

(3) As regards liability for tort, in particular, the functional approach is again likely to afford some guidance. The experience of municipal law seems to teach us that if a tort is incidental to some act that is *intra vires* it is itself *intra vires* the company.[4]

---

[1] *Reparations for Injuries Suffered in the Service of the United Nations*, I.C.J. Reports (1949), p. 149, at p. 180; *Certain Expenses of the United Nations*, ibid., 1962, p. 168. For a useful survey, see Brownlie, *Principles of Public International Law* (1966), p. 526.

[2] For a comparative survey, see W. Kunkel, *Rechtsvergleichendes Handwörterbuch*, iv.578–81. The *principe de spécialité* was invoked as early as 1931 by Gutzwiller, op. cit. (above, p. 557, n. 2), pp. 126–7. As to Germany, in particular, see, for instance, Enneccerus-Nipperdey, *Allgemeiner Teil* (1959), section 105, and the fundamental decision of the Federal Supreme Court, 28 February 1956, *BGHZ* 20, 119.

[3] See, generally, Zemanek, op. cit. (above, p. 566, n. 1), p. 29.

[4] See, for instance, Gower, *Modern Company Law* (2nd ed., 1957), p. 91, or Winfield, *On Tort* (7th ed., 1963), pp. 80–3.

Accordingly, if an Executive Director of the International Bank for Reconstruction and Development, in granting a loan in conformity with the Articles of Agreement, defrauds a borrower, the Bank would seem to be liable. Suppose, however, that the tort is incidental to an act that is *ultra vires:* The Executive Director commits a libel while communicating a commercial letter of credit purported to be opened by the Bank in favour of a private person. Since the issue of such a letter of credit is outside the powers of the Bank, it probably cannot be liable for the Director's tort.

(4) The legal effects of an act which is *ultra vires* the international corporation can only be assessed by the application of rules developed in municipal law. Such an act, though not illegal,[1] is void and incapable of being ratified or of becoming valid by estoppel, laches, or acquiescence.

In private law an act that is outside the corporation's capacity could be validated by retrospective legislation. Are the members of an international corporation to be put on the same level as the municipal legislator and, therefore, entitled to change the corporation's constitution? Or are they merely in the position of members of a municipal company who are themselves subject to the law and unable to alter it? It is suggested that the former question requires an answer in the affirmative, but the resolution must be unanimous, for *ex hypothesi* the act is not within the purposes of the corporation, a new purpose would have to be introduced into the constitution and, if the resolution is to be *intra vires*, this cannot be done by a majority decision. But in the event of unanimity there is no reasonable ground which would prevent the members of the corporation from acting as legislators.

(5) The question whether a particular act is within or beyond the capacity of the international corporation is to be decided by the tribunal before which the point arises. The answer will invariably depend on the interpretation of the corporation's constitution in the light of all the relevant circumstances.

A certificate issued by the executive organs of the corporation will not be conclusive and, one would expect, will be inadmis-

---

[1] On illegality, see E. Lauterpacht, 'The Legal Effect of Illegal Acts of International Organizations', in *Cambridge Essays in International Law* (Essays in Honour of Lord McNair), p. 88.

sible as evidence in legal proceedings. There is nowhere any provision supporting the legality of the issue and utilization of such a certificate.

Since the Bretton Woods Agreements of 1944 it has (unfortunately) become fashionable to provide that questions of interpretation arising between the international corporation and its members or between members are decided by the highest organ of the corporation 'whose decision shall be final'. The nature and extent of such 'finality' is in many respects not free from doubt, but it is submitted that in proceedings with a private person the tribunal is both entitled and bound to disregard the allegedly 'final' decision and to reach a result on the footing of its own investigation of a purely legal character. This should be so even where the private party before the tribunal belongs to a State which is a member of the corporation and thus bound by the terms of its constitution. The Article providing for the 'finality' of decisions on legal points extrajudicially arrived at should be narrowly construed. When it refers to 'members', it should be understood to mean the member States only to the exclusion of their nationals. It would be intolerable if, in the absence of a compelling text and a formulation of unquestionable clarity, private persons and municipal tribunals were, in a justiciable matter, subjected to the 'finality' of a decision which is not supported by reasons, which is not rendered by lawyers after due process of law, and which may be derived from political or other reasons far removed from legal appreciation.

## VII

The acts of a corporation, whether national or international, are necessarily performed by individuals whose ultimate source of authority is the corporation's constitution. Whether, in the case of an international corporation, a particular act can be performed by the holder of a particular office is a question of law to be decided by the constitution or any rule of international law that may be applicable; whether a particular person is the holder of a particular office is, normally, a question of fact.

Among the numerous problems to which the acts of the agent

of an international corporation may give rise, the scope of his authority is in practice probably the most important. According to the constitution of the Inter-American Development Bank, 'the President of the Bank shall be the legal representative of the Bank'. He conducts its 'ordinary business' under the direction of the Board of Executive Directors who shall also appoint, and confer authority and functions upon, the Executive Vice-President and may appoint other Vice-Presidents.[1] Since there is no public register recording the status of each Vice-President, it is obvious that, while the President can automatically perform all acts that are *intra vires* the corporation, a Vice-President will in each case have to prove his authority.

To what extent is an international corporation bound by the acts, done on the level of municipal law, of an official?

This is a question which, it is submitted, depends not on the law of the country where the act is performed or whose law governs the transaction in issue, but on the constitution of the corporation, that is to say, on public international law. The analogy of the conflict of laws would seem to support the suggestion. Once again there is no need for the protection of those who enter into business with so rare a body as an international corporation. Its character is still so unusual, its occurrence is still so infrequent that private individuals contracting with it may fairly be put on inquiry.

If, then, the authority of an official is primarily determined by the treaty establishing the corporation, third parties dealing with the corporation must be treated as having knowledge of the terms of the treaty. Thus, in the case of the Inter-American Development Bank it must be clear to everyone that a member of the Board of Governors has no executive authority or function and that, in the absence of special circumstances such as estoppel, his acts cannot bind the corporation.

On the other hand, much can be said in favour of the proposition that a third person is not expected to make inquiries beyond the text of the treaty. Thus the Board of Governors and the Board of Executive Directors of the Inter-American Development Bank 'may adopt such rules and regulations as may be necessary or appropriate to conduct the business of the

---

[1] Art. VIII, section 5.

Bank'.[1] If such rules and regulations should purport to preclude the President from entering into a particular transaction, this is unlikely to affect a third person who has no actual or constructive knowledge of the restriction; as a Governor will have notice and may have to be considered a representative of his State,[2] a member State probably cannot help being saddled with notice. Nor is it the third party's business to inquire whether there was the quorum required by Article VIII, section 3 (f) for the meetings of the Board of Executive Directors, at which a resolution was passed.

In short, it is submitted that if an international corporation transacts business with a private person its liability for the acts of its officials is determined by its constitution supplemented by those general principles of law which in similar situations are applicable to municipal corporations. Accordingly, where the international corporation's liability falls to be considered in a municipal tribunal, the guiding analogy is, not that of the responsibility of States for the acts of its officials, but the corporation law of the civilized world. This does not mean that, in adopting and following the comparative method, the law of State responsibility should be ignored; on the contrary, it may, on some aspects, provide assistance. But it does not necessarily or even primarily govern. Thus, it is plain[3] that in resisting an international claim a State cannot rely upon its municipal law, including its constitution, as a defence. An international corporation, sued in a municipal tribunal, may, within the limits referred to, invoke its constitution to assert the defence that the impugned acts were *ultra vires* its officials.

# VIII

The last problem which requires clarification relates to the international corporation's immunities and privileges. These are by no means the same in both member States and non-member States.

(1) As concerns the former, the text of the treaty creating

---

[1] Art. VIII, section 2 (g).

[2] Art. VIII, section 5 (d) would seem to support this conclusion. It provides an *argumentum a contrario*.

[3] See, for instance, Brownlie, op. cit. (above, p. 579, n. 1), p. 369.

the corporation invariably defines the extent of the immunities. If any doubt arises it has to be resolved primarily by construing the provisions of the treaty. They are usually incorporated into the municipal law of member States[1] and since the Bretton Woods Agreements[2] have become almost standardized. They extend to immunity from judicial proceedings, immunity of assets, inviolability of archives, immunity of assets from restrictions, privileges for communications, immunities from taxation, personal immunities of officers and staff.

This is not the place to write a commentary upon these provisions which, in many respects, are identical with those applicable to numerous other international organizations.[3] But in view of the references to proceedings brought in municipal courts against international corporations, which more than once were made in the course of the preceding observations, it is perhaps helpful to dwell upon the scope of the immunity from judicial proceedings envisaged by the standard clause.

Such immunity exists only in those member States in which the Bank has neither an office nor an agent authorized to accept service of process nor issued or guaranteed securities.[4] To put it affirmatively, the Bank may be sued in the courts of any member State in which it has an office or an agent authorized to accept service of processs or issued or guaranteed securities.[5]

---

[1] In the United Kingdom the statutory basis is now to be found in the International Organizations Act, 1968. By virtue of section 1 (1) it applies to any international organization declared by Order in Council to be one of which the United Kingdom or one or more sovereign powers are members. According to section 1 (2) the Order in Council may provide for the immunities set forth in Part I of Schedule 1. These differ, both in wording and scope, from those usually included in the treaty; in particular immunity of assets is not mentioned at all. Where a conflict arises the provisions of the Order in Council will, in the United Kingdom, have precedence.

[2] These were incorporated into the law of the United Kingdom by the Bretton Woods Agreements Order, S. R. & O. 1946, No. 36.

[3] See, generally, Jenks, *International Immunities* (1961).

[4] Where are securities issued or guaranteed? This may be a peculiarly elusive problem. It should not be solved by investigating the narrow question of the *locus contractus* in municipal law, but the liberal approach of public international law, assisted by comparative research, should prevail. Thus it is suggested that the place of issue is not only the place where the bond, duly signed by the borrower, is delivered to the lender or his agent, but also the place where a prospectus is published or where the bonds are introduced at a Stock Exchange.

[5] The question whether proceedings may be brought even in respect of acts which arise *jure imperii* is probably otiose, for in so far as international corporations act *jure imperii* (for instance, by entering into a treaty) municipal courts are in any

The immunity is, accordingly, very limited indeed.[1] Its restricted scope is underscored by the fact that after final judgment has been pronounced against the Bank its property becomes subject to seizure, attachment or execution. This would clearly include the appointment of a liquidator or receiver. Whether a court is entitled, pending judgment, to grant interlocutory relief by appointing a provisional liquidator or receiver is less certain. Such an appointment would involve measures which are probably intended to be comprised in the prohibited 'seizure' of property and, moreover, 'final judgment' seems to mean a judgment finally disposing of the cause of action, though subject to appeal. It would seem likely, therefore, that such interlocutory relief cannot be granted.

The text of the standard clauses does not refer to arbitration proceedings brought against the international corporation and thus confirms the view[2] that an international person cannot, by virtue of its immunity, avoid arbitration proceedings; moreover an award pronounced against it can be turned into a final judgment by a tribunal in any member State in which the corporation could be sued. Similarly, it is at least doubtful whether the standard clauses refer to criminal proceedings against the corporation or whether its criminal liability is a *casus omissus*. 'Actions . . . brought against the Bank' is a phrase that would seem to contemplate primarily civil proceedings. Yet it is difficult to believe that it was intended to render an international corporation subject to prosecutions. It is an *a fortiori* argument that should lead to the exclusion of criminal 'actions'.

This leads to the comment that, where the international corporation's constitution enumerates its immunities and privileges, the list is exhaustive and customary international law

---

event unlikely to have jurisdiction, so that there is no room for the problem of immunity.

[1] In *Lutcher S.A.* v. *Inter-American Development Bank*, 382 F. 2d 454 (1967), also 6 *Int. Legal Materials* (1967), p. 683, the defendant Bank tried to extend the immunity by the argument that the provision referred to in the text applied only to suits by bondholders and other like creditors and the beneficiaries of its guarantees. The Court of Appeals for the District of Columbia had no difficulty in rejecting so untenable an argument and also indicated that the provision did not merely describe available venues.

[2] See above, p. 275.

cannot be invoked to extend it. The texts usually state expressly that the corporation shall have the immunities and privileges 'set forth in this Article'. Such words, it is submitted, exclude all other immunities.

(2) There remains the much more difficult and important problem of the international corporation's immunities in such States as are non-members of, but have recognized, the corporation.

(a) Can these immunities be wider than those envisaged by the corporation's constitution for operation 'in the territories of such member'? In other words, does the constitution define the maximum of the immunities to which the corporation is entitled anywhere? Suppose the corporation has an office in a non-member State. Can it be said that it is not entitled to immunity from judicial proceedings, because if the office were in a member State it would not be so entitled? Or the corporation has issued securities in a non-member State. Is it subject to the jurisdiction of the courts in such State on the grounds that it would be subject if the issue had taken place in a member State?

The point is by no means free from doubt, but it is submitted that in non-member States immunity depends upon the general body of international law and it is irrelevant that 'in the territories of each member' the immunity is more restricted. There are good reasons why in a member State the corporation's privileges are limited, for the corporation and the totality of its members know each member, its legal system and standards. Hence it may well concede greater subjection to the law and jurisdiction of member States than would be acceptable elsewhere.

(b) Nor can it be suggested that the immunities recognized in the international corporation's constitution must be regarded as the minimum and cannot, therefore, be exceeded. If customary international law allows a lesser scope to the doctrine of immunity, the international corporation does not acquire additional immunities by reason of the fact that in a member State it would enjoy them. According to customary international law as understood in some countries an international corporation whose primary function is the promotion of the investment of public and private capital for development purposes[1] is probably not entitled to immunity at all. It does not become so entitled by reason only of its status in member States.

(c) The constitution of an international organization is, accordingly, no more than a piece of evidence, one of the many sources of customary international law. Broadly, the immunities and privileges of an international corporation in non-member States must be derived from the general body of customary international law. The real question is whether and to what extent, in regard to immunities and privileges, international corporations are to be equiparated to States.

No judicial decision has as yet pronounced upon this question. Legal literature is frequently unhelpful in that no clear distinction is drawn between the law in member and non-member States; the number of authors who discuss the latter only is very small. Nor is it always clear whether the discussion relates only to immunity from suit or extends to a wider, and perhaps even to the whole, range of immunities. Professor Sorensen, referring to immunity from suit and execution only, supports the conclusion, derived from Article 105 of the United Nations Charter and the General Convention on the Privileges and Immunities of the United Nations,[2] that 'une règle coutumière est sur le point de s'établir'.[3] Dr. Lalive gives the impression that the approach should be a functional one and that from this point of view the general immunities of an international organization are 'une necessité inéluctable'.[4] Similarly, Professor Reuter asserts that international organizations 'have the right to obtain from the national law of each State the legal status appropriate to the proper exercise of their functions inside each country'.[5] On the other hand, Dr. Brownlie seems to suggest[6] that it is general opinion that 'there is as yet no customary rule supporting international immunities'.

The problem becomes even more elusive when it is realized that what applies, probably, to the United Nations and its Agencies and, possibly, to the general body of international

---

[1] Inter-American Development Bank, Art. 1, section 2.
[2] U.N.T.S., i.15; see also ibid., xxxiii.261.
[3] 101 *Recueil des cours* (1960 iii), p. 173.    [4] ibid., 84 (1953 iii), p. 300.
[5] *International Institutions* (London, 1958), p. 232.
[6] *Principles of Public International Law*, p. 423.

organizations does not necessarily apply to international corporations. For there is no doubt that their functions could almost always be performed with equal efficiency by corporations formed under municipal law and having the member States as its shareholders. It is, for instance, difficult to see why the Inter-American Development Bank could not have been created in the form of such a corporation, though it would have been less convenient and might have necessitated special arrangements with the host State about taxation and similar matters. But these are considerations which in a non-member State will carry very much less weight.

In such a State the international corporation of the type contemplated in this paper has no function requiring its immunity. Its status should not be different from that of a national corporation with States as shareholders. In countries in which the law confers immunity only upon international entities in respect of their acts done *jure imperii* the result should not be in doubt. In other countries it should be borne in mind that there is no existing rule of international law requiring immunity; that as a matter of legal policy there is, in view of the nature and functions of an international corporation, no need for any—and certainly no justification for a general— immunity; and that none of the old maxims which have given birth to a largely obsolete doctrine apply in the case of international corporations. Thus, there is no room for the maxim *par in parem non habet jurisdictionem*, for an international corporation is not on a par with a State. Nor can it be suggested that the dignity or independence of an international corporation is such as to permit the doctrine to be invoked.

Even if the immunity of an international corporation could be justified in a limited field, for instance, in regard to legal proceedings, it would not in any event lend itself to generalization. If the Inter-American Development Bank made investments in the United Kingdom there would be no rational ground for suggesting that it should be exempt from taxation or exchange control.[1]

---

[1] This presupposes that no Order in Council under the Act mentioned above, p. 584, n. 1, has been made. It may be expected that in most cases the much-extended power to make an Order in Council will be exercised. Accordingly the problem discussed in the text is, in the United Kingdom, unlikely to arise except

It is submitted, therefore, that in non-member States and in the absence of special treaty arrangements or legislation, an international corporation should not be entitled to any immunities or privileges.

## IX

The principal submissions developed in this paper may be summarized as follows:

(1) An international corporation in the true sense of the word is a body corporate created by treaty.

(2) Though the status of an international corporation so defined is not in every respect the same as that of a State, it is, in general, subject only to international law. Accordingly,

(a) it has no nationality;

(b) it has no seat, domicile, or residence in the sense of municipal law, but

(c) as an international person it will, in general, require recognition in the same way as a State.

(3) The status of an international corporation in municipal law, at any rate in non-member States, is determined, in accordance with the general rule of the conflict of laws, by the personal law; this can only be public international law.

(4) Accordingly, even in a municipal court public international law answers the question whether the body corporate exists as a legal person.

(5) Furthermore, public international law determines the international corporation's corporate status, that is to say, such questions as whether and to what extent the member States are responsible for the corporation's liabilities, whether the corporation may purchase its own shares, what the effects of insolvency or amalgamation are.

(6) Again, public international law determines, even in a municipal court, the question of the international corporation's capacity, i.e. the question whether an act is or is not *ultra vires* the corporation.

in respect of international corporations which have only international organizations as members, or in respect of immunities which Schedule 1, Part I, of the Act does not sanction, such as the immunity of assets and the immunity from exchange control.

(7) Finally, even in a municipal court, public international law determines the authority of the officials acting on behalf of the international corporation.

(8) While in member States the immunities and privileges of an international corporation will almost invariably be defined by the terms of the treaty creating it, in non-member States the international corporation does not, in the absence of special treaties or legislation, enjoy any such immunities or privileges at all.

# XVIII

## THE 'INTERPRETATION' OF THE CONSTITUTIONS OF INTERNATIONAL FINANCIAL ORGANIZATIONS*

ARTICLE XVIII of the Articles of Agreement of the International Monetary Fund, as amended in 1969, reads as follows:

*Interpretation*:

(a) Any question of interpretation of the provisions of this Agreement arising between any member and the Fund or between any members of the Fund shall be submitted to the Executive Directors for their decision. If the question particularly affects any member not entitled to appoint an executive director it shall be entitled to representation in accordance with Article XII, section 3 (*j*).

(b) In any case where the Executive Directors have given a decision under (*a*) above, any member may require, within three months from the date of the decision, that the question be referred to the Board of Governors, whose decision shall be final. Any question referred to the Board of Governors shall be considered by a Committee on Interpretation of the Board of Governors. Each Committee member shall have one vote. The Board of Governors shall establish the membership, procedures, and voting majorities of the Committee. A decision of the Committee shall be the decision of the Board of Governors unless the Board by an eighty-five per cent majority of the total voting power decides otherwise. Pending the result of the reference to the Board the Fund may, so far as it deems necessary, act on the basis of the decision of the Executive Directors.

(c) Whenever a disagreement arises between the Fund and a member which has withdrawn, or between the Fund and any member during liquidation of the Fund, such disagreement shall be submitted to arbitration by a tribunal of three arbitrators, one appointed by the Fund, another by the member or withdrawing member and an umpire who, unless the parties otherwise agree, shall be appointed by the President of the International Court of Justice or such other authority as may have been prescribed by regulation adopted by the Fund. The umpire shall have full power to settle all questions of procedure in any case where the parties are in disagreement with respect thereto.

A similar provision was, in 1944, included in the Articles of Agreement of the Bank for Reconstruction and Development,[1]

* From *British Year Book of International Law* (1968–9), 1.
[1] Article IX.

and has, since then, found its way into the constitutions of other international organizations, such as the International Finance Corporation,[1] the Inter-American Development Bank,[2] and the Asian Development Bank.[3] It is, therefore, not without general interest to determine the scope and effect of the interpretative procedure which governs the life of such international organizations. This will be done with a view to Article XVIII of the Fund's Articles of Agreement, for the material relating to the Fund's practice and the publications of its legal advisers about the subject are very much richer than in the case of any of the other institutions. The conclusions reached in regard to Article XVIII, however, will not necessarily apply in the case of the other institutions which have followed the Bretton Woods pattern for, in so far as construction depends on other provisions of their respective charters, these may be different, so that in some respects there may be variations of result, albeit of a minor character.

I

Whenever 'any question of interpretation of the provisions' of the Agreement arises between members and the Fund or between members, is submitted by the member or the Fund to the Executive Directors 'for their decision', and is decided by them, the procedure laid down by Article XVIII operates. Unless the question arises only within the Fund, it does not matter whether or not the decision is described as one rendered in pursuance of Article XVIII. Nor does it matter whether the member, the Fund, or the Executive Directors have Article XVIII in mind at the time when the question arises, is submitted or is decided. By giving to the decision some different label, Article XVIII cannot be avoided, even if this were intended by the Executive Directors. Conversely, by classifying

---

[1] Cmd. 9502. Article VIII.      [2] Article XIII.

[3] Article 60; 5 *Int. Legal Materials* (1966), p. 262. Article 53 of the Charter of the East African Development Bank (ibid., 6 (1967), p. 1025) provides that 'any question of interpretation or application' shall be submitted to the Directors 'for decision'. But in the event of a disagreement, including disagreement in respect of a decision under Article 53, the matter shall be decided by arbitrators whose decision 'shall be final and binding on the parties' (Article 54).

a decision as coming within Article XVIII, a ruling cannot be given the character which it does not possess, and which in truth takes it outside the scope of Article XVIII.

These submissions which, it is believed, are fully supported by the plain text of Article XVIII, seem to be opposed to the practice of the Fund. It appears that there exist only ten interpretations which purport to be made under Article XVIII. In addition, 'a considerable number of interpretations have been necessary, in order to enable the Fund to function efficiently'. The overwhelming proportion of these interpretations have been adopted outside Article XVIII.[1] Moreover, so we are told, 'it must not be thought that there is any essential difference between interpretations under Article XVIII and those not adopted under that provision, apart from the more formal and authoritative character of the former'.[2] Yet there exists in the Fund 'the practice of making most of its interpretations outside Article XVIII' and it is 'not easy' to say why this practice has developed.[3] This is particularly mysterious if it is realized that, in many cases, a decision purportedly made outside Article XVIII takes exactly the same form as an interpretation under Article XVIII. One example may suffice to prove this point. Thus, there is a decision made in 1948 outside Article XVIII, according to which[4]

... dealings in paper money and coins are deemed to be 'other exchange transactions' within the meaning of Article IV, section 3, whether or not the importation and exportation of such money and coins to and from the country of origin are subject to restrictions. The dealings are in consequence subject to the provisions of that Section. Members shall not permit transactions in such paper money and coins within their territories in a manner or to an extent which will negate the par values agreed with the Fund. Where the transactions in fact have such an effect the Fund will be obliged to intervene.

Compare this, for instance, with an interpretation, admittedly made under Article XVIII, of Article VI, section 1[5]:

---

[1] Gold, *Interpretation by the Fund* (International Monetary Fund Pamphlet Series, No. 11, 1968), p. 14. The forerunners of this publication, namely articles published by Mr. Gold in the *I.C.L.Q.* (1954), p. 256 and (1967), p. 289, have been superseded by the pamphlet, and will not hereinafter be referred to.

[2] Gold, ibid., p. 15.       [3] Gold, ibid., p. 15.

[4] *Selected Decisions of the Executive Directors* (Third Issue), International Monetary Fund (January 1965), p. 16.

[5] Ibid., p. 54.

The Executive Directors of the International Monetary Fund interpret the Articles of Agreement to mean that authority to use the resources of the Fund is limited to use in accordance with its purposes to give temporary assistance in financing balance of payments deficits on current account for monetary stabilisation operations.

Both 'interpretations' evidently deal with different points, but they are so similar in character, structure, and language that it would be difficult to say which is, and which is not, an interpretation under Article XVIII. For the reasons which have been given, there cannot be any interpretation which fulfils the conditions contemplated by Article XVIII, yet falls outside it.

It is an entirely different matter that the Fund has developed 'a large number of principles and policies which are contained in many thousands of documents' and which 'are continuously adjusted to changing circumstances, are known to the Executive Directors and to the staff and to a lesser extent to the members. They constitute the internal law of the Fund, which would be applied in interpretative decisions.'[1] The point is that such 'principles and policies' are not interpretative decisions—not because they are made 'outside Article XVIII', but because their nature is such as to render Article XVIII necessarily inapplicable.

## II

The words 'question of interpretation of the provisions' of the Agreement do not touch three areas of considerable importance.

In the first place, a question of interpretation frequently arises against the background of a possibly disputed set of facts. In such a case it is important to remember that Article XVIII is concerned only with the abstract question of interpreting the Agreement, namely a question of law. It does not confer upon the Directors or the Governors jurisdiction to decide facts. Thus, it is a matter of interpretation what the conceptions of 'competitive exchange alterations'[2] or 'fundamental disequilibrium'[3] mean, or, indeed, whether, in a admitted set of facts, the requirements of the definition are fulfilled; but whether or not facts exist which are said to create 'competitive exchange

---

[1] Hexner, 'Interpretation by Public International Organizations of their Basic Documents', *A.J.I.L.* (1959), p. 341, at p. 350.
[2] Article IV, section 4.      [3] Article IV, section 5 (a).

alterations' or 'fundamental disequilibrium' is a question outside the scope of Article XVIII altogether.[1]

Secondly, a question of general international law arising independently of mere interpretation does not fall to be decided under Article XVIII. Thus, members 'may exercise such controls as are necessary to regulate international capital movements'.[2] Suppose that, in a particular case, it is alleged that either the introduction or the management of the control of capital transfers constitutes an *abus de droit*. This is not a matter which, in its factual or legal aspects, can be considered or judged by any organ of the Fund except, possibly, in a purely advisory manner. This does not mean that if, in the interpretative process itself, a rule of public international law falls to be considered this may not be applied or observed. On the contrary, any rule of public international law relating to the interpretation of documents would apply, and the question arising under Article XVIII must be interpreted against the background of public international law.

Thirdly, even where, in the strict sense of the term, mere 'interpretation of the provisions' of the Articles of Agreement is concerned, the interpretative jurisdiction conferred by Article XVIII is limited in scope, for it must never involve what may fairly be described as an amendment of the Articles of Agreement. Perhaps it would be desirable if the exercise of 'interpretative powers were less circumscribed, but on many occasions the interpretative process is likely to come up against Article XVII, which subjects the amendment of the Agreement to a special procedure.[3]

## III

The next, and much more important, question is whether the interpretative procedure contemplated by Article XVIII is

---

[1] A different view, perhaps, is taken by Wengler, *Völkerrecht* (1964), i.754, who admits that the words 'do not cover a dispute about a legally relevant fact'. But he adds that the Articles are 'probably to be so understood that they comprise even such disputes'. No reason is given nor, it is submitted, can any supporting reason be found.

[2] Article VI, section 3.

[3] This point is well made by T. Treves, *Il Controllo dei cambi nel diritto internazionale privato* (1967), p. 218, who says that interpretation is concerned with one of several possible meanings, but can never be made *praeter* or *contra legem*.

judicial in character. If the answer were in the affirmative, it would hardly be open to doubt, for instance, that a member directly interested in a particular question would have the right to be heard, not only to be represented among the Executive Directors, as Article XVIII (*a*) provides. Moreover, the rule *nemo judex in re sua*, well recognized in public international law,[1] might perhaps preclude a Governor whose country is a party to the dispute, and whose vote might be decisive, from participating in the decision on the question of interpretation. Or, if the procedure is judicial, it would have to be judicially exercised, and this would demand the application of legal rules and the exclusion of 'considerations of policies or expediency which are permissible for the administrator but which must be altogether excluded by the judge'.[2]

While some deny the judicial character of the decision under Article XVIII,[3] others assert it, albeit without giving reasons.[4] It is submitted that the latter view should be rejected and the interpretative procedure under Article XVIII should be treated as administrative.[5]

The reason can be put on the narrow ground of a comparison between Article XV and Article XVIII. The former[6] sets forth

---

[1] See the advisory opinion of the Permanent Court of International Justice relating to *Interpretation of the Treaty of Lausanne* (Iraq Boundary) (Series B), No. 12 (1925).

[2] *United Engineering Workers' Union* v. *Devanayagam*, [1968] A. C. 356, at 387, per Lord Devlin and Lord Guest—a case to which it will be necessary to revert.

[3] In 'this sense Fawcett (a former General Counsel to the Fund), *R.T.B.I.L.* 1960, pp. 325 et seq.; Wengler, *Völkerrecht* (1964), i.751.

[4] Broches, 98 *Recueil des cours* (1959 iii), p. 313, though he also says that there exist 'both judicial and legislative elements'. But, in effect, he denies the former by stating that the Directors may decide 'according to their own discretion'; this is wholly contrary to the judicial process. Seidl-Hohenveldern, *Das Recht der Internationalen Organisationen* (1967), No. 1312. And see the same author in 'International Arbitration' (*Liber Amicorum for Martin Domke*), p. 324. Alexandrowicz, *World Economic Agencies* (1962), p. 188, n. 1, says: 'The Executive Directors (having exclusive jurisdiction) would act in a quasi-judicial way.' This remark is in more than one respect inaccurate.

[5] Hexner, op. cit. (above, p. 594, n. 1), at p. 367, approaches the problem, but does not answer it. In *Das Verfassungs- und Rechtssystem des Internationalen Währungsfonds* (1960), p. 76, he suggests that all interpretative decisions are 'in a substantial sense legislative acts'.

[6] Article XV: *Withdrawal from Membership. Section* 1. Right of Members to Withdraw.—Any member may withdraw from the Fund at any time by transmitting a notice in writing to the Fund at its principal office. Withdrawal shall become effective on the date such notice is received.

the penalties which the Agreement has devised to enforce its provisions, i.e. ineligibility to use the resources of the Fund and, eventually, expulsion, politely called 'compulsory withdrawal'. In both cases, under regulations to be adopted, Article XV, section 2 (c) requires that 'the member shall be informed in reasonable time of the complaint against it and given an adequate opportunity for stating its case, both orally and in writing'. Where penalties of any kind are to be considered, this would seem to be a minimum requirement imposed by generally accepted principles of law. No such requirement is made by Article XVIII, which merely gives a member the right for 'a representative to attend' a meeting of the Executive Directors. There is, therefore, at least a strong *prima facie* case for suggesting that, in the absence of an essential element in the judicial process, Article XVIII cannot envisage judicial procedure at all.

The same conclusion is reached by a more broadly based line of reasoning. The problem of the definition of the judicial process has arisen on many occasions in municipal law. Whether there exists so wide a measure of agreement as to establish a practice of States, or a principle of law recognized by civilized nations, is a question which merits exhaustive comparative research. No attempt can at present be made to suggest an answer. But a possible, and perhaps probable, result of an

*Section 2.* Compulsory withdrawal.—(*a*) If a member fails to fulfil any of its obligations under this Agreement, the Fund may declare the member ineligible to use the resources of the Fund. Nothing in this section shall be deemed to limit the provisions of Article IV, section 6, Article V, section 5, or Article VI, section 1.

(*b*) If, after the expiration of a reasonable period the member persists in its failure to fulfil any of its obligations under this Agreement, or a difference between a member and the Fund under Article IV, section 6, continues, that member may be required to withdraw from membership in the Fund by a decision of the Board of Governors carried by a majority of the governors representing a majority of the total voting power.

(*c*) Regulations shall be adopted to ensure that before action is taken against any member under (*a*) or (*b*) above, the member shall be informed in reasonable time of the complaint against it and given an adequate opportunity for stating its case, both orally and in writing.

*Section 3.* Settlement of accounts with members withdrawing.—When a member withdraws from the Fund, normal transactions of the Fund in its currency shall cease and settlement of all accounts between it and the Fund shall be made with reasonable despatch by agreement between it and the Fund. If agreement is not reached promptly, the provisions of Schedule D shall apply to the settlement of accounts.

inquiry can be indicated by surveying the experience which the practice of the British Commonwealth of Nations has evolved. This is material since, as is well known, the Anglo-American influence at Bretton Woods was considerable, and Anglo-American law is, therefore, a valuable tool in interpreting the Articles of Agreement.

It must at once be admitted that what in the British Commonwealth has become the recognized, though rather less than profound, definition of the judicial process is of no significance in the present context. Lord Simonds[1] on behalf of the Judicial Committee of the Privy Council and, following him, Lord Dilhorne[2] have said that it 'is as good a test as any other of analogy to ask whether the subject matter of the assumed justiciable issue makes it desirable that the judges should have the same qualifications as those which distinguish the judges of the superior or other courts'. This does not help in interpreting Article XVIII, because, *ex hypothesi*, both the Executive Directors and the Governors are bankers rather than judges and cannot, therefore, have judicial qualifications. But the cases have also spoken of a variety of more specific characteristics which are expressive of the judicial process. Most, or at least some, of these attributes were recently listed and discussed by Lord Devlin and Lord Guest in an opinion which, though a dissenting one, dissents less on the law than on the application of the law to the particular case at hand, namely, the nature of a Labour Tribunal created in Ceylon, and which, for present purposes, therefore, may be said to have great value. The remarkable fact is that few of the characteristics of judicial office mentioned in that opinion are to be found in, or required by, Article XVIII. Thus, Article XVIII does not presuppose a controversy about rights. It is not necessarily concerned with existing rights rather than those rights which it may be thought members ought to have in the future, and which, in municipal law, may be the subject-matter of arbitration. It says nothing about the manner of exercising the power conferred by Article XVIII; this may be of an entirely political or administrative or discretionary character, but it is in no sense

---

[1] *Labour Relations Board of Saskatchewan* v. *John East Iron Works*, [1949] A. C. 134, at pp. 148–9.
[2] *United Engineering Workers' Union* v. *Devanayagam*, [1968] A. C. 356, at p. 367.

such as is usually associated with a judge. This is made particularly plain by the fact that, in the last resort, the decisions are subject to the weighted votes which Governors enjoy; a system such as the weighted voting system is wholly alien to the judicial process.

Professor Hexner[1] is, no doubt, justified in suggesting that 'it would be far-fetched to imply from the absence of "judicial redress" and the unavoidable balancing of interests which is inherent in the interpretative machinery of the Fund that the rule of law, especially the principles of good faith and reasonableness, was not intended to apply in the rendering of interpretative decisions'. Yet, there is a far cry between the observance of good faith and reasonableness, characteristic of all relationships arising under public international law, and a judicial procedure.

It is, finally, not without significance that very many 'decisions' of the Executive Directors are couched in terms and expressed in a form which is alien to the judicial pronouncement. The Executive Directors tend to paraphrase the text of the Articles of Agreement without adding much or anything to them by way of interpretation. Frequently, therefore, they are tautologous in character. They do not even purport to speak the language of a decision-maker. Perhaps it will be helpful to look at a case which, on account of its great importance, was entitled to, but, in fact, did not receive, a clear interpretative decision.[2] In November 1953 the Executive Directors took the view that, contrary to its obligations under Article VIII, section 5 (a), Czechoslovakia had failed to furnish the Fund with information about its official holdings of gold and foreign exchange, total exports and imports of merchandise, balance of payments and other matters there referred to. Moreover, the Fund took the view that Czechoslovakia had failed to consult it as to the further retention of exchange restrictions as required by Article XIV, section 4. The Czechoslovak Government's defence was that reasons of national security precluded it from furnishing the information or entering into the consultation contemplated by the Articles of Agreement and that, therefore,

---

[1] op. cit. (above, p. 594, n. 1), p. 367.
[2] On the case discussed in the text see ibid., pp. 362, 363, and Gold, op. cit. (above, p. 593, n. 1), pp. 11–14.

it had not committed any failure to fulfil its obligations, which justified the Fund in declaring Czechoslovakia ineligible to use the Fund's resources or to require it to withdraw from membership. On 11 August 1954 the Executive Directors issued an 'interpretative decision' which the Board of Governors confirmed on 28 September 1954, and which read as follows[1]:

> Action may be taken by the Fund to require a member to withdraw when the following conditions have been met:
>
> (1) The member has been declared ineligible to use the resources of the Fund pursuant to Article XV, section 2 (a);
>
> (2) A reasonable time has passed since the member was declared ineligible to use the resources of the Fund pursuant to Article XV, section 2 (a), whether or not a fixed period of time had been prescribed in connection with such action, and the member persists in failing to fulfil its obligations;
>
> (3) The member has been informed in reasonable time of the complaint against it and given adequate opportunity to state, both orally and in writing, any fact or legal argument relevant to the issue before the Fund.

It will be observed that this interpretation simply repeats what Article XV, section 2 (a) states, and wholly ignores the point raised by Czechoslovakia in defence. The point may have been good or bad, but no judge could or would have ignored it.

Another example of a slightly different nature is the often quoted interpretation of Article VIII, section 2 (b), which the Executive Directors rendered in June 1949 and which states 'the meaning and effect of this provision' to be as follows[2]:

> (1) Parties entering into exchange contracts involving the currency of any member of the Fund and contrary to exchange control regulations of that member which are maintained or imposed consistently with the Fund Agreement will not receive the assistance of the judicial or administrative authorities of other members in obtaining the performance of such contracts. That is to say, the obligations of such contracts will not be implemented by the judicial or administrative authorities of member countries, for example by decreeing performance of the contracts or by awarding damages for their non-performance.
>
> (2) By accepting the Fund Agreement members have undertaken to make the principle mentioned above effectively part of their national law. This applies to all members, whether or not they have availed themselves of the transitional arrangements of Article XIV, section 2.
>
> An obvious result of the foregoing undertaking is that if a party to an exchange contract of the kind referred to in Article VIII, section 2 (b) seeks to enforce such a contract, the tribunal of the member country before which

---

[1] *Selected Decisions of the Executive Directors* (1965), p. 99.
[2] Ibid., p. 73.

the proceedings are brought will not, on the ground that they are contrary to the public policy (*ordre public*) of the forum, refuse recognition of the exchange control regulations of the other member which are maintained or imposed consistently with the Fund Agreement. It also follows that such contracts will be treated as unenforceable notwithstanding that under the private international law of the forum, the law under which the foreign exchange control regulations are maintained or imposed is not the law which governs the exchange contract or its performance.

The Fund will be pleased to lend its assistance in connection with any problem which may arise in relation to the foregoing interpretation or any other aspect of Article VIII, section 2 (*b*). In addition, the Fund is prepared to advise whether particular exchange control regulations are maintained or imposed consistently with the Fund Agreement.

Without going through this decision word for word, it will be obvious to any legal mind that nothing is said in this 'interpretation' which is new or goes beyond a paraphrase of Article VIII, section 2 (*b*), or, indeed, decides a single one of the innumerable and difficult questions of interpretation to which this Article gives rise. The only statement which could possibly be said to have interpretative effect is that if a State has accepted the Articles of Agreement, it cannot, except in case of inconsistency, refuse recognition to the exchange control regulations of other members on the ground that they are contrary to public policy. Even if so platitudinous an observation is treated as a decision on interpretation, the remaining sentences do not lend themselves to similarly benevolent construction.

In short, these interpretative statements are guide-lines issued by an administrative authority; they do not bear the hall-mark or carry the authority of a judicial pronouncement.

## IV

The next, and by far the most important, problem raised by Article XVIII is: What is meant by the provision that the Board of Governors' 'decision shall be final'?

Professor Hexner has no doubt about the answer. While 'any member may request at any time reconsideration (*ex nunc*) of an interpretative decision'[1] and while, therefore, a final decision is not final in the sense of being permanent, interpretation is 'binding' upon the Fund and its members: depending upon

---

[1] op. cit. (above, p. 594, n. 1), p. 353.

the constitutional law, an interpretative decision may even have direct binding force upon the municipal authorities, or may render it necessary to adapt municipal law in accordance with Article XX, section 2 (*a*). The present General Counsel to the Fund, Mr. Joseph Gold, writing in his personal capacity, but with the full force of his authority, experience, and legal acumen, is hardly less definite. On the one hand, he states categorically that interpretative decisions under Article XVIII are unquestionably 'binding on member Governments'.[1] Whether such interpretations 'have binding effects on forums in member countries' is a question on which 'there is very little authority'; but, after a long discussion, he answers it in the affirmative. He goes so far as to suggest that 'there can be little doubt that an international tribunal would regard itself as concluded by an interpretation under Article XVIII'.[2] On the other hand, Mr. Gold states elsewhere[3] that finality may 'mean only that no appeal lies from the Board of Governors to some other body, whether within or outside the Fund', and that the Articles of Agreement do not preclude the reversal by the Executive Directors or the Board of Governors of past interpretations. He also seems to admit[4] that an interpretative decision is subject to clarification and reinterpretation, and probably also to reversal or variation.[5]

It is not intended to suggest that the conclusions reached by these two experts are altogether wrong. The suggestion is that the point requires some elaboration and clarification which will throw a different light upon it.

In assessing the meaning of 'finality' it is material to appreciate the fact of paramount importance that the text of Article

---

[1] Gold, op. cit. (above, p. 593, n. 1), p. 32.    [2] Ibid., p. 47.
[3] Ibid., p. 29.    [4] Ibid., pp. 26–31.
[5] Very little discussion of the point is to be found in the books. Learned authors who deal with it do so by stating a conclusion rather than submitting any argument. Thus Professor O'Connell, *International Law* (1965), ii.1107, simply states that members are bound by the interpretation. Professor Seidl-Hohenveldern, *Das Recht der Internationalen Organisationen* (1967), No. 1614, reports that the Governors claim 'the right to authentic interpretations'. These, so he continues, are often disguised amendments of the Articles of Agreement. Aufricht, *The International Monetary Fund* (1964), p. 13, suggests in very guarded language that an interpretation under Article XVIII 'may render not only the Fund Agreement as such, but the Fund Agreement as interpreted by the Executive Directors (and/or the Board of Governors) directly binding on member Governments and, where applicable, on private individuals within the jurisdiction of member countries'.

XVIII makes no reference whatever to the decision's being binding or conclusive, although municipal law is very familiar with the juxtaposition of the words 'final and conclusive'. If it is suggested that a word such as 'binding' is to be implied, it would be difficult to appreciate the rules of construction which permit or require the proposed implication into the text of the Articles of Agreement. If it is suggested, on the other hand, that even without the implication of any terms, 'finality' as such and standing alone means conclusiveness or binding force, either upon member States or upon municipal authorities, or upon international tribunals, then this would require much further analysis. Nor is it possible to agree with Professor Hexner, who suggests that the word 'decision' in itself implies conclusiveness.[1] This surely goes far beyond the usual and natural meaning of the term.

The *prima facie* meaning of 'finality' is that which Mr. Gold at least considers possible, and which has already been referred to, namely, the exclusion of an appeal or reference from the Board of Governors to some other body. The Articles of Agreement know of no such procedure. The possibility of obtaining advisory opinions of the International Court of Justice arose only under the Charter of the United Nations, promulgated in 1945, and an Agreement made in 1947 between the United Nations and the Fund, and cannot, therefore, throw light upon the construction of a treaty adopted at Bretton Woods in 1944. If, then, there is no procedure by which a decision of the Governors can be questioned, can 'finality' be read as excluding what, *ex hypothesi*, does not exist? In other words, are we not back at the point where the argument turns on the alternative between words being regarded as redundant or given some meaning?

It is suggested that 'finality' does have a definite meaning and function, though it is different from that envisaged by Mr. Gold. It is the inability of the Governors to revoke, whether *ex tunc* or *ex nunc*, the particular answer to the particular question arising between the particular entities which submit it for decision. It is the particular question arising in the particular case that is finally disposed of by a decision which cannot be rescinded and, in this limited sense, is binding. This does not

---

[1] *Das Verfassungs- und Rechtssystem des Internationalen Währungsfonds* (1960), p. 74.

mean that it is impossible to qualify, reformulate or add to a decision once taken. All it means is that the process of clarification cannot lead to the original decision's being reversed or varied. But the decision of the Governors does not constitute an irreversible precedent for other—future—cases.

Finality, so understood, makes good sense, for it avoids the almost absurd consequence that a decision of the Governors could immediately be challenged by a member, possibly the same member, bringing the point once more before the Executive Directors. In particular, this could be done by the Fund itself, which, it will be noted, cannot appeal from the Executive Directors to the Governors, and which, if it is upheld by the former but overruled by the latter, might be tempted to start again. Were it not for the 'finality' of decision it would be possible not only to reconsider the original 'question of interpretation', but also to revoke the original decision. Such results cannot reasonably have been intended. This conclusion is supported by the fact that the decision of the Executive Directors (as opposed to that of the Governors) is not stated to be final.[1] Initially, no member may require the matter to be referred to the Governors. Under the amended text, such a reference must and can only be made within three months from the Executive Directors' decision. If such reference is not made, it is open to a member or to the Fund to bring the point again before the Executive Directors and, on appeal, the Governors may reverse or vary it, and their decision is final. The contrast provided by the finality of the Governors' decision and the transient character of the Executive Directors' decision is striking.

That 'finality' denotes preclusion of rescission is a view strongly supported by the judicial practice in at least one country whose legal system may provide a helpful analogy. A learned writer recently summarized it in words which, for present purposes, should be sufficient[2]:

> The only practical effects of a finality clause appear to be to take away a right of appeal where one already exists . . . and to preclude a body from rescinding one of its own valid decisions.

[1] Wengler, *Völkerrecht* (1964), i.766, realizes that the Executive Directors' decision is not stated to be final. Yet he suggests that it should be clothed with the same finality as the Governor's decision.

[2] S. A. de Smith, *Judicial Review of Administrative Acts* (2nd ed., 1968), p. 345.

## V

If the preceding analysis of 'finality' is accepted, the question remains whether, and in what sense, a decision of the Governors can be said to be 'binding'.

(1) The first point to note is that no question of 'finality' or 'binding effect' can arise in regard to a 'decision' by the Executive Directors. Such a decision, in contrast to a decision by the Governors, is not stated to be 'final'. It is true that, according to the 1969 amendment of Article XVIII, a member's time for appeal[1] or for having the question referred to the Governors is three months from the date of the Executive Directors' decision; but the failure to make an appeal probably cannot, in the absence of appropriate words, preclude a member from reopening the question by making a fresh application to the Executive Directors. Their decision, therefore, cannot in any case have a binding force.[2]

(2) The next point to note is that the Governors do not possess any exclusive right of decision. There may, it is true, be few other bodies which may be called upon to render an interpretative decision, and these can operate only on rare occasions. Yet, this should not detract from the legal significance of the fact that the jurisdiction to render a decision may arise in a variety of circumstances and be vested in a large number of different bodies, as will appear from the more detailed discussion below.

(3) In its most striking form, the problem of the binding force arises where the decision involves the 'obligations' of members, and where the failure to fulfil them under Article XV (2) may lead to ineligibility to use the Fund's resources and eventually to withdrawal. The existence of a failure to fulfil obligations depends on the terms of the Articles of Agreement and their interpretation. It is a question which demands an objective answer. It is, moreover, a question which may receive an objective answer from a truly judicial body, namely, the arbitration tribunal constituted under Article XVIII if 'a

---

[1] See the wording of Article XIII, section 2 (*b*) (viii).

[2] Aufricht, op. cit. (above, p. 602, n. 5), p. 12, states that 'the decision of the Executive Directors is final, unless a member requires that it be reviewed by the Board of Governors'. For the reasons given in the text this is unacceptable. On the points made in the text see Treves (above, p. 595, n. 3), pp. 216–19.

disagreement arises between the Fund and a member which has withdrawn', i.e. lawfully withdrawn. A member which asserts that it has fulfilled its obligation and which is eventually held to have done so cannot be compulsorily withdrawn. Its expulsion is unlawful.

The Governors' decision under Article XVIII may have a bearing upon the existence or non-existence of a failure to fulfil obligations. It cannot, however, alter or increase the member's obligations. If it purported to do so, it would be *ultra vires*. Indeed, only an interpretation which is correct is effective so as to become a permissible step in assessing the obligation of members. An incorrect interpretation cannot be 'binding' so as to preclude a review of the question of the fulfilment of obligations, either by the Fund or the Governors, or, still less, the arbitration tribunal. For these reasons the arbitration tribunal is entitled and may be bound to review the existence or non-existence of obligations and, consequently, the correctness of interpretative decisions. Hence, in the context of Article XV, the Fund and the Governors must always have a similar right and a similar duty.

(4) Next, what is the effect of interpretative decisions in the tribunals or before the authorities of a Fund member?

Municipal courts and authorities are organs of the State, and, as a matter of public international law, bound by such international duties as are imposed upon the State. In the case of the Articles of Agreement, this point is emphasized by Article XX, section 2 (*a*), according to which each member is bound to take 'all the steps necessary to enable it to carry out all of its obligations under this Agreement'. It is clear, therefore, that the duties of the State and its organs do not exceed the scope of what can truly be described as the 'obligations under this Agreement'. It follows that if and in so far as the interpretative decision is inconsistent with the Articles of Agreement, and therefore incapable of imposing duties upon a member, the member as well as its organs have no obligation to follow it.[1] No doubt they will consider and examine it. Indeed, they will give great weight to it, and experience has shown that, in certain countries where the general law permits it, the courts have gone very far in having regard to interpretative decisions,

---

[1] Nussbaum, *Money in the Law* (1950), p. 529, agrees.

and even to views expressed by the Legal Department of the Fund.[1] One should not, however, read too much into incidental remarks which a court makes, or could—but did not—make. Nor should one attach any significance to the mere reference by a court to the Executive Directors' or even the Governors' interpretation. Such a reference cannot fairly be said to support the 'implication' that the court considered itself bound. And a lower court's decision which on appeal is reversed can only rarely claim any right to survival at all. Still less should it be suggested that a court which refrains from mentioning any Fund's interpretation, but whose decision happens to be in line with it, disregarded it because the court felt it 'unnecessary' to raise the question of its binding force.[2] Such reasoning, it is submitted, is artificial and unconvincing. In the United States, it is true, the Federal Communications Commission treated an interpretative decision as binding,[3] and a decision of the Court of Appeal of Louisiana (4th Circuit)[4] even adds an *obiter dictum* to the effect that an interpretative decision of the Fund is 'binding on all its members'. But these are hardly observations which may claim to originate from close analysis or to carry such authority as to add much to the discussion.[5] They cannot affect the conclusion that the theory of the binding force of the Executive Directors' or even the Governors' interpretation rests on so insecure a foundation that it should be abandoned. They cannot alter the fact that the Governors' decision, even if it were capable of being binding at all, cannot possibly bind except to the extent to which, on investigation, it appears to conform to and express the members' obligations embodied in the Articles of Agreement.

The point can be put slightly differently. It is the Agreement itself which alone is binding. There is nothing in the Agreement which confers upon the Governors the exclusive right of decision. On the contrary, the correctness of the interpretative decision will, if necessary, be decided by the arbitration tribunal. Admittedly, a member and the Fund's organs which

---

[1] See Gold, op. cit. (above, p. 593, n. 1), p. 46.
[2] See Gold, op. cit., p. 41.    [3] Ibid., p. 33.
[4] *Theye y Ajuria* v. *Pan American Life Insurance Company*, 154 So. 2d 450 (1963), reversed 161 So. 2d 70 (1964).
[5] The view put forward in the text seems to be in line, for instance, with Seidl-Hohenveldern, *Österreichische Zeitschrift für öffentliches Recht* (1957), pp. 90 et seq.

ignore the interpretative decision run the risk that the arbitration tribunal will disagree with them and find a failure to fulfil an obligation. This is a risk which the member and its organs must take, but they also take the risk inherent in the opposite attitude: they may follow an interpretative decision; in the case of some other member which fails to observe it or in some other circumstances the arbitration tribunal is called upon to consider it and expresses disapproval; in following the original interpretative decision the member would have committed a breach of obligation.

(5) The remaining question is: what attitude should the international tribunal adopt? This may arise when the International Court of Justice is asked for an advisory opinion, or when a dispute between two States who are members of the Fund comes before an international tribunal of their own choice, and the effect of a decision under Article XVIII is in issue.

It is difficult to see the basis for the view, so unhesitatingly expressed by Mr. Gold,[1] that the international tribunal would be precluded from independent investigation of the problem of interpretation. All that has been urged in the course of the preceding observations tends to establish that there is no such basis, and that, in particular, it cannot be derived from the words 'whose decision shall be final' which are applicable to Governors' decisions only. Even if all the preceding submissions proved to be wrong, the contention now under consideration according to which international tribunals, including those set up under Article XVIII (c), are bound 'by an interpretation under Article XVIII' (i.e. apparently also Executive Directors' decisions) cannot meet with approval, for it overlooks an additional point of some importance.

There is much evidence to support the submission that, according to the practice of numerous States, the 'finality' of a non-judicial decision hardly ever precludes it from being reviewed by a competent judicial body. If the interpretative decision as an administrative act were to bind the Fund and its members, this could only be so pending a decision of an international tribunal.

In England and the British Commonwealth of Nations it has been the law for centuries that, notwithstanding a 'finality'

[1] op. cit. (above, p. 593, n. 1), p. 47.

clause in any enactment, the courts, by virtue of the prerogative writs, can review the legality of any Act other than the
judgment of a superior court.[1] The law in the United States of
America seems to be similar[2] and is illustrated by such land-
mark cases as *Estep* v. *United States*[3] where Mr.
Justice Douglas on behalf of the majority of the Court said[4]:

> The provision making the claim of the local Boards 'final' means to us
> that Congress chose not to give administrative action under this Act the
> customary scope of judicial review which obtains under other statutes. It
> means that the courts are not to weigh the evidence to determine whether
> the classifications made by the local Boards are justified. The decisions of the
> local Boards made in conformity with the regulations are final, though they
> may be erroneous. The question of jurisdiction of the local Board is reached
> only if there is no basis in fact for the classification which it gave the regis-
> tration.

Finally, the same rule prevails, for instance, in France, where it
is well established that even express words do not preclude
judicial review of legality.[5]

It is, therefore, no exaggeration to suggest that, on full inquiry
which cannot be made in the present context, it may well appear
to be a general principle of law that a competent tribunal is not
precluded from reviewing the legality of a decision said to be
'final'.

Such a conclusion is in no way contradicted and may, on the
contrary, be supported by a dictum of the International Court
of Justice which said of a tribunal 'established, not as an
advisory organ or a mere subordinate committee of the General
Assembly of the United Nations, but as an independent and
truly judicial body pronouncing final judgments without appeal

---

[1] For present purposes, it must be sufficient to refer to S. A. de Smith, *Judicial
Review of Administrative Acts* (2nd ed., 1968), pp. 340 et seq., and such cases as *R.* v.
*Medical Appeal Tribunal*, [1957] 1 Q.B. 574, where a decision of the Medical Appeal
Tribunal under the National Insurance (Industrial Injuries) Act, 1946, described
in the Act as 'final' was liable to be set aside if it disclosed an error of law, and
*Anisminic Ltd.* v. *The Foreign Compensation Commission*, [1969] 2 A. C. 147, the
most recent decision of the House of Lords.

[2] See generally, L. L. Jaffé, 'The Right to Judicial Review', 71 *Harvard Law
Review* (1958), pp. 401, 769, 786–90. And see Bernard Schwartz, *An Introduction to
American Administrative Law* (2nd ed., 1962), pp. 175–8 (an administrative decision
'is not final in the sense that courts cannot do anything about it').

[3] 327 U. S. 114 (1945).        [4] Ibid., at p. 122.

[5] Bernard Schwartz, *French Administrative Law and the Common Law World* (1954),
p. 157.

within the limited field of its functions' that, according to a generally recognized principle of law, 'a judgment rendered by such a judicial body is *res judicata* and has binding force between the parties to the dispute'.[1] The idea of binding force and finality outside the realm of judicial decisions clearly did not seem worthy of consideration to the International Court.

# VI

The results of the preceding discussion may be summarized as follows:

(1) Any decision of the Executive Directors or the Governors which fulfils the conditions contemplated by Article XVIII is a decision under Article XVIII, whether or not it is so described or is intended as such.

(2) The powers of interpretation conferred by Article XVIII relate only to 'the interpretation of the provisions of' the Articles of Agreement, and do not extend to a decision on questions of fact or public international law, or permit what, in effect, is an amendment of the Articles.

(3) Neither the Executive Directors nor the Governors acting under Article XVIII do so in a judicial capacity.

(4) An interpretative decision of the Executive Directors, even after expiration of the time limit for a reference to the Governors, is not in any sense final.

(5) An interpretative decision of Governors rendered as a result of a reference by a member (not the Fund) is 'final' in the sense that it cannot be rescinded or varied except by the legislative process under Article XVII.

(6) Neither the Executive Directors nor the Governors have the exclusive right or duty of deciding a question of interpretation

(7) An interpretative decision by the Governors which is erroneous in law is not binding upon members in the sense of affecting their respective obligations.

(8) The question whether or not an interpretative decision by the Governors is or is not legally correct may freely be considered and pronounced upon—

---

[1] *Effect of Awards of Compensation made by the United Nations Administrative Tribunal*, I.C.J. Reports (1954), p. 47, at p. 53.

(a) by any international tribunal having jurisdiction, such as the arbitration tribunal under Article XVII (c), the International Court of Justice in case of a reference for an advisory opinion, or any tribunal appointed by treaty between members:

(b) by any municipal tribunal, provided its decision does not constitute a breach of obligation within the meaning of Article XV (which in the last resort arbitrators under Article XVIII (c) will have to decide).

These conclusions lead to four further implications which need a few explanatory words.

First, the suggestions made in this article are likely to provoke the comment that both in content and tendency they reduce the self-regulating powers of an international organization as represented by its bureaucracy. This is correct, but should, it is believed, be welcomed by all. The treaty setting up the Fund or a similar international organization should be seen as a fundamental law creating a legal order. In other words, it is the law, rather than expediency, which should be treated as the paramount guide. The opportunities of largely discretionary decision should be curtailed in the sphere of international law no less than in that of municipal law.

Secondly, it has been suggested that in the case of the Fund and certain other international organizations, most questions of interpretation involve matters of so technical and specialist a nature that it is difficult or undesirable to submit them to the decision of any body of persons other than experts. It is quite true that technical points are best decided by technicians; the trade arbitrations under the arbitration provisions of trade associations such as the London Metal Exchange are based on this elementary principle. But just as such arbitrators are not qualified to decide questions under the Sale of Goods Act, or questions of construction arising under the contract of the parties or the constitution of the Exchange, so in the case of the Fund technicians are not qualified to decide legal questions. There is, therefore, no justification for concluding that both types of question are most efficiently decided by the same body of persons. On the contrary, it is the duty of the lawyer to draw attention to the distinctiveness of function and, accordingly, of qualification, and to insist that legal questions should be decided by lawyers. Admittedly, the Fund's Articles of Agreement do not draw the distinction. On the other hand, it does not follow that the Articles of Agreement should be interpreted as if it did not exist.

Thirdly, it may be said that the Articles of Agreement should be viewed as a constitution and that, for this reason, they should be interpreted and developed with the breadth and liberality which, in countries such as the United States of America, has been characteristic of constitutional law. One may even quote Lord Radcliffe who, so he tells us,[1] often thought 'that far back in our history a very great mistake was made when people tried to express legislative enactments in the form of precise rules of law. Statutes, whatever the refinements of their drafting, should be ideas of law, not law itself.' Even if this thought could be injected into public international law in general, it should not alter the approach towards the Fund's Articles of Agreement. Constitutional texts or statutes as 'ideas of law' lend themselves to broad and flexible interpretation only where there is a judicial process which continuously functions to supervise and check, to expand and to confine. Where, as in the case of the Fund, such a process is missing, traditional methods of treaty interpretation cannot be dispensed with.

Fourthly, it is not intended to deny that acquiescence by member States may have particularly far-reaching effects in the context of an international organization's internal law.[2] As Mr. Fawcett has aptly said,[3] the very absence of direct judicial control 'creates habits and, indeed, a state of mind in an organization which militate against the use of the judicial process even when it is available'. There develops in various respects what one may describe first as an *esprit de corps*, then as a practice and, finally, as binding custom. Nothing said in this article is intended to deny the potentiality or the formative strength of acquiescence, practice, custom or whatever term one may employ to indicate actual or implied consent by conduct. It will be a matter of evidence, depending on the circumstances of

---

[1] *Not in Feather Beds* (1968), p. 272.

[2] E. Lauterpacht, 'The Legal Effect of Illegal Acts of International Organizations', in *Cambridge Essays in International Law in Honour of Lord McNair*, p. 88, at p. 117.

[3] *B.Y.I.L.* (1960), xxxvi.327.

each case, to decide whether the results to which the strictly legal interpretation of the Fund's Articles of Agreement prima facie leads are displaced by the conduct of members. The decision may be different in the case of different members. This is a circumstance that underlines the necessity for starting from the treaty, its text and its meaning. Thereafter, as a next step, it will be possible to investigate whether and to what extent a secondary rule of practice has emerged. Finally it may be appropriate to ask whether, at least in respect of certain members or even a single member, acquiescence will not operate so as to preclude the reopening of a point of interpretation. Unfortunately, once again, these are questions which it will often be difficult to answer in the absence of a judicial process. No doubt on occasion they may require an answer opposed to some of the suggestions made or implied in this article. At present it can only be said that no attempt to displace them by reference to the Fund's practice or custom of a binding nature has yet been made.

# XIX

## THE INTERPRETATION OF UNIFORM STATUTES*

In the early days of the post-war period it may be predicted with confidence that the coming years will witness the resumption of a great deal of international legislation in the sense of treaties the text of which is being agreed and recommended for general acceptance at international conferences by the representatives of numerous nations and which, if ratified, will by varying constitutional methods be infused into the municipal law of contracting states. The English statute book already contains numerous instances of Acts which result from such international legislation and the counterparts of which are to be found in other countries; only recently a statute of momentous importance was added to the series.[1]

Legislation of this type is undoubtedly to be welcomed as promoting uniformity of law. Yet it should not be overlooked that adoption of international legislation by Parliament is merely a step, however essential, along the road leading to the goal and that, in order to reach it, courts and practitioners alike must make their no less significant contribution. As Scott L.J. has said, 'the maintenance of uniformity in the interpretation of a rule after its international adoption is just as important as the initial removal of divergencies. That we should, in a branch covered by an international convention, preserve uniformity, is an obvious advantage, if it is judicially possible.'[2] Or to quote the terse formulation of an anonymous American writer, 'uniformity of the "judge-made" law is as essential as uniformity of the statute law'.[3]

Uniformity in the application of uniform statutes, however, involves grave problems of interpretation. They are of a peculiar

---

* From 62 *L.Q.R.* (1946), 278.
[1] Bretton Woods Agreements Act, 1945; Bretton Woods Agreements Order in Council, 1946, S. R. & O., 1946, No. 36.
[2] *The Eurymedon*, [1938] P. 41, at p. 61.
[3] 29 *Harv. L.R.* (1915–16), 541.

character and merit more intensive attention than they have received in the past. The following observations are devoted to a review of the prevailing situation in England (I) and in some foreign countries (II) and to suggestions for a solution (III).

## I

The rules of interpretation of an English statute are well settled and familiar to all students. For the purpose of ascertaining the intention of the Legislature the meaning of statutes is primarily to be sought in themselves. The words of the statute must generally be interpreted in their ordinary grammatical sense, and if they are ambiguous, the Legislature's intention must be sought first in the statute itself, then in other legislation and contemporaneous circumstances, and finally in the four rules laid down in *Heydon's Case*[1] which enjoin the judge to have regard to the common law in force before the Act, to the mischief not provided for by the common law, the remedy appointed by Parliament and its true reason. The circumstances attending the passing of the Act such as travaux préparatoires, debates, etc., cannot be inquired into and such principles as *stare decisis* or construction *ejusdem generis* apply to statutory interpretation no less than to the interpretation of deeds.

It is understandable that these and similar rules are *prima facie* followed when international legislation adopted by this country is to be interpreted by the courts. For by the constitutional law of England a treaty which purports to alter the law requires an Act of Parliament before it becomes English law. Consequently it is tempting to argue that a statute adopting a treaty is on the same level as a statute relating, e.g., to copyhold and that the established rules of interpretation apply in both cases. This, indeed, is the view towards which the common lawyer instinctively tends to lean, though a more rational attitude has of late become discernible.

In order to obtain a reliable picture of prevailing tendencies it is necessary to distinguish between the four methods which, it seems, Parliament may employ when it is giving effect to an international Convention.

(1) The statute may omit any reference to the treaty so that

---

[1] (1584) 3 Co. Rep. 7a.

on its face it is in no way connected with the antecedent international discussions. In this case (of which the present writer knows no example) it is clear that for the purpose of the construction of the statute the treaty is as irrelevant as any other kind of travaux préparatoires.

(2) The Act of Parliament may refer to the treaty, yet give independent effect to its provisions, without enacting its terms as such. Thus the British Nationality and Status of Aliens Act, 1933, is described in the title as 'an Act to amend the law relating to the national status of married women so far as is necessary for giving effect to a Convention . . . signed on behalf of His Majesty at The Hague on the 12th April, 1930, and for purposes incidental to the matter aforesaid'. In the text of the statute, however, the Convention is not mentioned. The Maritime Conventions Act, 1911, and the Counterfeit Currency (Convention) Act, 1935, are of a similar type except that in both cases not only the title, but also the preamble, refers to the Convention.[1]

The only decision relating to the construction of a statute which in this manner incorporates a treaty into the law of England seems to be *The Danube II*.[2] The question was whether a claim against the Crown for damage by collision was statute-barred after six months under the Public Authorities Protection Act, 1893, although under section 8 of the Maritime Conventions Act, 1911, claims for the recovery of such damage become barred only at the expiration of two years. The Court of Appeal answered in the affirmative. Lord Sterndale found no inconsistency between the two Acts. Scrutton L.J.[3] expressly relied on the rule laid down by Lord Coke in *Foster's* case[4] and frequently reaffirmed according to which an earlier statute is not impliedly repealed by a subsequent statute except in case of repugnancy; the learned Lord Justice failed to see any repugnancy and he did not discuss the peculiar character and object of the Act of 1911.

(3) A third type is represented by the Merchant Shipping

---

[1] See also the Dangerous Drugs Act, 1925; the Geneva Convention Act, 1937; or the Patents, etc. (International Conventions) Act, 1938.

[2] [1921] P. 183.

[3] At p. 186.

[4] (1614) Rep. 56b, 63a. This case should be compared with the German decision below, p. 627, n. 3.

(International Labour Convention) Act, 1925. It recites that
certain draft Conventions contain 'the provisions set out in
Parts I, II, and III respectively of the First Schedule' and that
'it is expedient that for the purpose of giving effect to the said
draft Conventions such provision should be made as is contained
in this Act'. The statute then sets out the operative provisions.
In this case, therefore, the draft Conventions contained in the
Schedule cannot be a source of law. They are added merely
*informationis causa.*[1]

The Act of 1925 has led to two important decisions in the
House of Lords. Section 1 provides that where by reason of
the wreck or loss of a ship in which a seaman is employed his
service terminates before the date contemplated by his agreement, he shall be entitled, in respect of each day on which he is
in fact unemployed during a period of two months from the date
of the termination of the service, to receive wages at the rate
to which he was entitled at that date. It seems fairly obvious
that it was intended to provide for the case where the contractual period of the seaman's service would have continued
for not less than two months, but where owing to general rules
of law the wreck or loss of the ship results in the immediate
termination of the contract and the seaman, consequently,
suffers hardship by loss of wages from the date of the wreck or
loss until re-employment. The Convention emphasizes this
intention by speaking of an 'indemnity' payable to the seaman.
Yet in *Ellerman Lines* v. *Murray*[2] the House of Lords (Lord
Blanesburgh dissenting) held that, if a ship is wrecked on 27
February 1929, and in the normal course the seaman's service
would have terminated on 3 March 1929, he can recover wages
for the full period of two months from 28 February 1929. Lord
Dunedin with whom Lord Warrington concurred as well as
Lords Tomlin and Macmillan held that the wording of the Act
was plain and unambiguous. The permissibility of referring to

[1] For similar instances see the Anglo-Portuguese Commercial Treaty Acts, 1914
and 1916; the Employment of Women, Young Persons and Children Act, 1920;
the Treaties of Washington Act, 1922; the Arbitration Clauses (Protocol) Act,
1924; the Arbitration (Foreign Awards) Act, 1930; Merchant Shipping (Safety and
Load Line Conventions) Act, 1932. An interesting and difficult point arising from a
divergency between the Arbitration (Foreign Awards) Act, 1930, and the Convention attached to it is mentioned by M. Wolff, *Private International Law* (1945),
p. 261, n. 4; see also Nussbaum, 56 *Harv. L.R.* (1949), 219.

[2] [1931] A. C. 126.

the scheduled Convention was left open by Lord Macmillan,[1] while Lord Tomlin explicitly denied that 'assuming there is any divergency between the draft Convention and the Act, it would be proper to resort to the draft Convention for the purpose of giving to the section a meaning other than that . . . which is its natural meaning'.[2] The result of the decision has been severely criticized.[3] On the question of method it is inconclusive and it is not at all certain whether Sir Arnold McNair is justified in deriving from it the rule that in case of ambiguity resort may be had to the Convention in the Schedule.[4]

The second decision relates to the construction of the word 'wreck' in section 1. In *Barras* v. *Aberdeen Steam Trawling and Fishing Co., Ltd.*,[5] Lords Buckmaster, Warrington, Russell, and Macmillan held (Lord Blanesburgh dissenting) that that word had a well-established meaning in English law[6] and that, therefore, the settled principle applied according to which, where a word of doubtful meaning has received a clear judicial interpretation, a subsequent statute incorporating the same word in a similar context must be construed so that the word is given the meaning which has previously been assigned to it.[7]

This decision necessitates a conclusion of great significance to the type of legislation discussed in the present section. The House of Lords ignores the origin of the Act. It disregards the fact that the statute is passed to give effect to an international

---

[1] At p. 149. Lord Blanesburgh examined the Convention 'merely as a matter of interest' (p. 143).

[2] At p. 147. In the Court of Appeal Scrutton and Greer L.JJ. had stated that ' the words are plain and unambiguous and we are therefore not entitled to look at the preamble or draft Convention . . . for the purpose of giving a special meaning to words which are in themselves plain and unambiguous': [1930] P. 197, 201, 209.

[3] Allen, *Law in the Making* (3rd ed.), p. 423; Eastwood, *The Journal of the Society of Public Teachers of Law* (1935), p. 5; Graham-Harrison, ibid, p. 37; see also Gutteridge, 8 *Tulane L.R.* (1933), 1, at p. 9. Section 7 of the Act of 1925 provides that 'this Act . . . shall be construed as one with the Merchant Shipping Acts, 1894 to 1923'. But this provision cannot supersede the object of the Act of 1925 as stated in its title, preamble, and text.

[4] *B.Y.I.L.* (1932), 120. This suggestion is supported by Scrutton and Greer L.JJ. (above, n. 2) and by Lord Parker in *The Cairnbahn*, [1914] P. 25, at p. 30.

[5] [1933] A. C. 402.    [6] *The Olympic*, [1933] P. 92.

[7] On this principle see Allen, op. cit., at p. 419, and the authorities there referred to. Gutteridge, op. cit., at p. 17, says of the decision of the House of Lords that it introduces an element which was never contemplated by the framers of the Convention.

(draft) agreement, but places it squarely into the framework of English law and treats it as development rather than as a new departure.

(4) It is less easy to draw a definite conclusion from those decisions which relate to the fourth type of uniform legislation. This is characterized by the fact that the Schedule which sets out the Convention and is attached to the statute is itself an operative part of it—a source of law. Sometimes Parliament confines itself to adopting the Convention; it legislates in form, but in substance merely ratifies legislation carried through elsewhere. The most unequivocal example of this type of legislation is to be found in a number of statutes relating to Sea Fisheries.[1] The more widely known Carriage by Air Act, 1932, belongs to the same group. After reciting that 'it is expedient that provision should be made for giving effect to' the Warsaw Convention, the Act lays down in section 1 that the provisions of the Convention 'as set out in the First Schedule to this Act shall . . . have the force of law in the United Kingdom'. The various Treaty of Peace Acts and the Orders in Council made thereunder in 1919 and 1920 probably also belong to this category, although they do not adopt the Treaties of Peace as a whole, but only selected parts. Sometimes, however, Parliament adopts the Convention only subject to certain modifications introduced by the national Legislature and in that case the alterations will have to be clearly ascertained and distinguished, since for purposes of construction they may not be on the same footing as the original text of the treaty. Thus the preamble of the Carriage of Goods by Sea Act, 1924, refers to the international conferences at which the Hague Rules had been agreed and amended and continues that 'it is expedient that the said rules as so amended and as set out with modifications in the Schedule to this Act . . . should . . . be given the force of law'. Apart from the modifications which are national legislation in every sense of the word, the statute, therefore, represents transformed international legislation.

In these circumstances it would not have been difficult to

---

[1] The first of the series is the Fisheries Act, 1843; after reference to a Convention with France in the title and the preamble it provides in section 1 that 'the said Articles shall be binding on all persons and shall have the force of law as fully as if they were herein severally and specially enacted'. For similar statutes see Halsbury, *Statutes sub verbo* 'Fisheries'.

regard the Carriage of Goods by Sea Act, 1924, as a fresh chapter in the evolution of English law. In matters of maritime law, it is true, the pre-eminence of English law and its impact upon foreign legal systems are such as to justify the English Courts' reluctance to depart from well-established principles and to facilitate the assumption of a close connection between English law and the international Convention. Yet the courts have been inclined to go further and to find identity of meaning or continuity of development established where proof might still have been required. Thus, when the House of Lords had to interpret the words 'management of the ship' in Article IV, rule 2 (*a*), of the Schedule[1] Viscount Hailsham L.C. pointed to the long judicial history of these words in England and continued[2]:

> I am unable to find any reason for supposing that the words as used by the Legislature in the Act of 1924 have any different meaning to that which has been judicially assigned to them when used in contracts for the carriage of goods by sea before that date; and I think that the decisions which have already been given are sufficient to determine the meaning to be put upon them in the statute now under discussion.

Lord Sumner expressed himself in similar vein and added the interesting observation[3] that

> of foreign decisions, of course, the Legislature is not deemed to take notice and although the Conference was doubtless well acquainted with the United States cases, it has not yet been held that the Legislature of this country is deemed to know what those whose reports or conventions it affirms have been familiar with.

A very different spirit, however, pervades a slightly later decision of the House of Lords relating to the construction of the words 'reasonable deviation' in Article IV, rule 4, of the Schedule.[4] Lord Atkin emphasized that for the sake of uniformity 'the courts should apply themselves to the consideration only of the words used without any predilection for the former law', though he added the qualification that 'words used in the English language which have already in the particular context received judicial interpretation may be presumed to be used in

---

[1] *Gosse Millard, Ltd.* v. *Canadian Government Merchant Marine Ltd.*, [1929] A. C. 223.
[2] At p. 230.     [3] At p. 237.
[4] *Stag Line Ltd.* v. *Foscolo Mango & Co.*, [1932] A. C. 328.

the sense already judicially imputed to them'.[1] The broadest statement came from Lord Macmillan[2] who did not mention the presumption favoured by Lord Atkin:

It is important to remember that the Act of 1924 was the outcome of an international conference and that the rules in the Schedule have an international currency. As these rules must come under the consideration of foreign courts it is desirable in the interests of uniformity that their interpretation should not be rigidly controlled by domestic precedents of antecedent date but rather that the language of the rules should be construed *on broad principles of general acceptation.*

In cases relating to other than maritime law the absence of a principle guiding the approach to the construction of uniform statutes is no less noticeable. No attempt appears ever to have been made to apply to the Treaties of Peace any of the peculiarly English rules of construction and when it was argued before the House of Lords that according to English conceptions the 'charge' created by the Treaty of Trianon in favour of the Administrator of Austrian Property did not prevent an Austrian creditor from enforcing his debt against his English debtor, Lord Sumner pointed out that no doctrine corresponding to the mortgagor's equity of redemption was contemplated by the framers of the Treaty and that the English doctrine of the legal and equitable estate and the rights arising therefrom could not reasonably be supposed to have been in the minds of the 'parties'.[3] On the other hand the decision of the House of Lords in *Kramer* v. *Attorney-General*[4] discloses perhaps a somewhat narrower conception. The question was whether the appellant who was both a British subject and a German citizen could properly be described as a German national within the meaning of the Treaty of Peace Order so as to subject his property to the charge created in favour of the Administrator of German Property. Although it recognized that reference could be made to the Treaty to ascertain the true construction of the Order, the House gave an affirmative answer on the ground that 'both in the Treaty of Peace and in the Order the expression "German national" means a person who is by German law a subject of

[1] At p. 343.  [2] At p. 350. Italics supplied.
[3] *Josef Inwald A. G.* v. *Pfeiffer* (1928) 44 T. L. R. 352 (H. L.) On this case see Maugham J. (as he then was) in *Administrator of German Property* v. *Knoop*, [1933] Ch. 439, p. 454.
[4] [1923] A. C. 528.

Germany'.[1] If it was the Treaty rather than the Order which had to be construed,[2] then it would have been arguable that neither the German nor the British law of nationality had any claim to predominance, but that for the purpose of the Treaty the nationality should be determined by what is known as the principle of effective nationality.[3]

That the inherent objects of uniform legislation are a paramount guide for its interpretation was emphasized in connection with the Carriage of Goods by Air Act, 1932, both by Greer L.J. and by Greene L.J. (as he then was).[4] The former said[5] that 'if there be any doubt or ambiguity in the language used, the statute should be so interpreted as to carry out the express and implied provisions of the Convention', while the latter stressed the establishment of a uniform international code as one of the main objects of the Convention and regarded it as 'essential to approach it with a proper appreciation of this circumstance in mind'.[6]

This short, but probably incomplete review of the prevailing English practice reveals the lack of a principled approach to the problems involved in the interpretation of uniform legislation. In recent years the courts have shown greater understanding of them, but the impact of the existing precedents is such that on the whole the tendency of applying municipal rules of statutory interpretation is bound to persist. Whether the results reached by the courts were right or wrong, is a matter of indifference to this paper which is concerned exclusively with methods. That these are uncertain and haphazard, is undeniable.

Broadly speaking, the present position may probably be summarized as follows:

---

[1] At p. 537, per Lord Cave L.C.

[2] At p. 533, per Lord Cave. This was clearly possible, since section 1 of the Order provides that the sections of the Treaty set out in the Schedule should have full force and effect as law.

[3] See Article 5 of the Hague Convention concerning certain questions relating to the conflict of nationalities, 1930, in Hudson, *International Legislation* v.359; Pfeiffer, *Das Problem der effektiven Staatsangehörigkeit* (1933); Schwarzenberger, *International Law*, i.151–3, with references to the decisions of international tribunals. In view of Article 305 of the Treaty of Versailles it would have been particularly appropriate for an English Court to have regard to the rule applied by international tribunals.

[4] *Grein* v. *Imperial Airways, Ltd.*, [1937] 1 K. B. 50.

[5] At pp. 66–7.

[6] At p. 76; see Scott L.J., above, p. 614, n. 2.

(1) English Courts tend to regard uniform legislation as a step in the development of English law.

(2) Accordingly they are inclined to apply to such legislation canons of construction developed by English municipal law.

(3) In particular English Courts are likely to construe such legislation in the light of previous English authorities.

## II

The treatment which has been meted out to uniform legislation in foreign countries is fundamentally different.

This is due to a variety of reasons. In the first place, almost everywhere the municipal rules of statutory interpretation are so much more liberal and flexible than in England that at the outset they permit methods of construction which readily conform to the particular requirements of uniform legislation; this is notoriously so on the Continent where precedents have persuasive as opposed to binding authority, where the historical method of interpretation is freely resorted to and where the intention and object of legislation is of far greater weight than its language,[1] and even in the United States the rigidity of the common law has of late been greatly alleviated.[2] Secondly, the constitutional methods of transforming treaties into municipal law are in most countries such that the character of treaties is preserved: they are not usually given the form of statutes in the ordinary sense of the word. Thirdly, many countries have developed specific theories relating to the interpretation of uniform legislation, and these have undoubtedly contributed to an understanding of its problems.

(1) By the law of the Third French Republic the President negotiates and ratifies treaties, but in many cases his ratification is dependent on the prior assent of Parliament which is given in

---

[1] See, e.g., Professor H. A. Smith, 9 *Comparative Legislation and Int. Law* (3rd series) (1927), 153; Gutteridge, op cit., passim; Amos and Walton, *Introduction to French Law* (1935), p. 11.

[2] Thus legislative material is freely used for the purpose of assisting statutory interpretation. See the informative Note 50, *Harv. L.R.* (1936–7), 822, and for a very recent case *Markham* v. *Cabell*, 326 U. S. 404 (1945).

the form of a law duly promulgated.[1] According to the constant formula of the Cour de Cassation, 'les traités diplomatiques régulièrement promulgués en France ont force de loi et doivent, à ce titre, être appliqués par l'autorité judiciaire'.[2] The judicial interpretation of treaties which have been properly promulgated is restricted to cases where the dispute is 'd'ordre privé'[3] and where the bilateral interpretation by a supplemental Convention or an exchange of letters has not intervened.[4]

It is within these limits that the problem of methodology arises. It has been most elaborately treated by E. Bartin[5] whose discussion merits a summary. He poses the question whether Articles 1156 sqq. of the Code Civil which deal with the interpretation of agreements are applicable; if so it would be necessary to ascertain 'l'intention des parties, plus précisément l'intention des négociateurs qui les représentaient'. Bartin's answer is in the negative:—

Le traité s'interprète, pour les juges français, par référence aux dispositions correspondantes de la loi française, qui interviennent alors comme dis-

---

[1] See Article 8 of the Constitutional Act of 16 July 1875, according to which treaties of peace and commerce, treaties involving the finances of the State and treaties 'qui touchent à l'état des personnes et au droit de propriété des Français à l'étranger' require Parliament's assent. It has been the practice to obtain it in many cases in which, according to the text of the Act, it might not have been strictly necessary. See Masters, *International Law in National Courts* (1932), pp. 127 sqq.

[2] This is old practice. See, e.g., Cour de Cassation, 28 November 1834, S. (1834), 1, 822; 10 January 1842, S. (1842), 1, 236; 19 May 1863, 1, 353; 27 July 1877, S. (1877), 1, 485; 15 December 1928, D.H. (1929), 69; 28 February 1930, Clunet (1930), 1030, and many others.

[3] Recent cases have been collected in *Annual Digest* (1931–2), pp. 370–1; see in particular Cass. Crim., 23 February 1912, Clunet (1913), 182; 22 March 1923, Clunet (1923), 847; 9 August 1923, Clunet (1924), 396. While the Conseil d'Etat denies to the courts all power of interpreting treaties, many writers have attacked the distinction made by the Cour de Cassation and favour unrestricted interpretation: see, e.g., Appert, Clunet (1899), 432; Niboyet, S. (1932), 1, 257 (note); Rosenmark, *Académie Diplomatique Internationale* (Séances et Travaux v. (1931), 154, and *Dictionnaire Diplomatique* ii.959. According to Van Houtte, *L'interprétation des traités internationaux, Mélanges Mahaim* (1935), ii.372 sqq., the practice of the Belgian Courts is similar to that of the French Cour de Cassation.

[4] Cass. Civ., 2 February 1936, S. (1936), 1, 257.

[5] *Principes de droit international privé* (1930), pp. 104 sqq. and 31 *Recueil* (1930), 614; see also Duez, *Rev. Gén.* (1925), 429, 441, who formulates the two possibilities as follows—either we assume a reception of the treaty by municipal law, then the judge is entitled to ignore public international law and to apply municipal law pure and simple; or we assume a renvoi from municipal law to public international law, then the judge must apply the latter. As to Belgium, see Muûs, *Revue Générale de droit international et de législation comparée* (1934), 451.

positions complémentaires. . . . Il se rattache alors automatiquement à l'ensemble du droit interne français de telle sorte que ses prescriptions insuffisantes s'éclairent et se complètent naturellement par l'addition nécessaire, qu'y font les juges français, du droit français.

The only exception is made for Conventions 'qui impliquent tant par l'origine que par le charactère de leurs dispositions, une sorte d'unification', *i.e.* for Unions: in interpreting them, the intention of the States who are parties to them is the supreme test.

This distinction, which, indeed, touches the kernel of the problem, has been adopted by Mestre,[1] but is opposed by Maury[2] and Niboyet,[3] who admit a psychological tendency to have recourse to national legislation, but regard it as unsatisfactory from a practical point of view (since it treats divergent national interpretations as normal and legitimate), as theoretically criticizable (since it can be supported only by the dualistic theory of law) and as inconsistent with the actual French practice.

This, however, is meagre and inconclusive. It is still dominated by the decision of the Cour de Cassation in the famous case of the Duke of Richmond.[4] The third Duke was the owner of the Duchy of Aubigny which during the Napoleonic wars was sequestrated. By a secret clause attached to the treaty of 1814 it was provided that 'le séquestre opposé sur le duché d'Aubigny et sur les biens qui en dépendent sera levé, et le duc de Richmond sera remis en possession de ces biens tels qu'ils sont actuellement'. The third Duke had died before 1814 and was succeeded by the fourth Duke who, relying on the wording of the secret clause, claimed the lands to the exclusion of those who according to French rules of private international law would have been entitled to share in the land. In the course of its decision by which the Duke's claim was rejected, the Cour de Cassation said:

Les traités diplomatiques doivent être entendus dans le sens qui les met en harmonie avec le droit civil et public admis chez les peuples qui contractent; que l'interprétation donnée à la clause par l'arrêt attaqué la mettrait en opposition avec toutes les lois, tant du droit civil que du droit public français.

---

[1] 38 *Recueil* (1931), 237, at pp. 299 sqq.; see also Naurois, *Les Traités Internationaux devant les jurisdictions nationales* (1934), pp. 176 sqq.

[2] 57 *Rec.* (1936), 447 sqq.

[3] *Traité de droit international privé français* (1944), iii.375, 382 sqq.; also *Revue Critique* (1935), 1, with a detailed review of the French cases some of which do not seem to be relevant.

[4] Cas. Civ., 24 June 1839, S. (1839) 1, 578.

This formula is not free from ambiguity, but it supports the tendency which Bartin favours and which, in fact, finds expression in one or two other cases.[1] No decision has propounded any definite rule,[2] nor is there any case which relates to the interpretation of such Conventions as established Unions.[3]

(2) The position in pre-Nazi Germany was reversed, inasmuch as theoretical discussion was rare and insignificant, but numerous judicial authorities led to the existence of a firm rule of practice.

According to the constitution of 1919 treaties were concluded by the President of the Reich, but required the consent of the Reichstag if they referred to matters of federal legislation (Art. 45). They were published in the Official Gazette and thus became law.

On numerous occasions German Courts have been called upon to construe treaties which had thus been incorporated into German law. Such treaties usually received what one may describe as a liberal construction.[4] In recent cases relating to treaties other than the Treaty of Versailles, which was put on a distinct footing,[5] the Supreme Court emphasized the guiding principle that[6]

---

[1] See, in particular, Trib. Civil de Bayonne, 8 February 1887, Clunet (1887), 326; Trib. Civil de Bordeaux, 11 July 1892, Clunet (1892), 937 (affirmed on slightly different grounds by Cour de Bordeaux, 21 February 1893, Clunet (1893), 565); cf. Cour de Paris, 3 February 1926, Clunet (1927) 73. Cass. Req., 26 November 1929, Clunet (1930), 159, refers to the intention of the High Contracting States for the purpose of construing the Treaty of St. Germain.

[2] See the article by Niboyet, above, p. 625, n. 3, and Bioux, *La position de la jurisprudence française vis à vis les traités* (Lille, 1933).

[3] But see the decision of 26 November 1929, above, n. 1.

[4] For the older practice see *Fontes Juris Gentium*, A, II, 1, pp. 150 sqq. Representative recent decisions are Supreme Court, 2 February 1931, *RGZ* 131, 250, and A.D. (1931–2), No. 207 (League of Nations); 11 November 1933, *RGZ* 142, 241 International Railway Convention); 18 January 1935, *RGZ* 146, 325 (Trade Mark Convention); 17 September 1935, *RGZ* 149, 83 (Legal Protection Clause in Commercial Treaty). See, generally, the discussion in Frankenstein, *Internationales Privatrecht* i.295, and Melchior, *Grundlagen des internationalen Privatrechts*, pp. 178 sqq., who treats the problem under the heading of classification. In the same sense Nussbaum, *Internationales Privatrecht* (1932), p. 51, who says that terms are to be classified from the point of view of local municipal law.

[5] Supreme Court, 1 July 1926, *RGZ* 114, 188; 27 February 1930, *Die Deutsche Rechtsprechung auf dem Gebiet des internationalen Privatrechts* (1930), No. 159; 14 February 1932, *RGZ* 137, 1, and A.D. (1931–2), No. 206. The Supreme Court explained that the 'objective sense' of a provision was decisive.

[6] 20 May 1922, *RGZ* 104, 352; 8 November 1939, *RGZ* 130, 220; 4 February 1931, *JW* (1932), 243, and A.D. (1931–2), No. 210, and Clunet (1933), 164, 1008,

in the first place such common intention of the contracting parties is decisive as is to be deduced from the text, the object and the history. In this connection the literal interpretation of individual words is not permissible, but the true intention is to be ascertained from the whole of the circumstances. In the case of doubt, however, greater significance will have to be attached to the text of an individual provision than in connection with the interpretation of rules of municipal law by the judge of the country of origin.

Thus in a particularly illuminating case[1] the question arose when a loan was 'created' within the meaning of the German–Swiss Gold Mortgage Convention; according to German law a loan is 'created' at the time of the actual advance of the money, while according to Swiss law the date of the contract is decisive. The Supreme Court held that it was wrong to have resort to the German conception unless and until all possibilities of ascertaining the contracting States' common intention had been exhausted and that for this purpose the court had to allow the parties to procure the evidence of representatives of the two Governments. In view of the decision of the Court of Appeal in *The Danube II*[2] it may be of interest to mention another case[3] which related to the question whether German war-time regulations interrupting the running of the Statutes of Limitations for a period of two years applied to claims under the International Railway Freight Convention which fixed the period at one year from the date of the dispatch of the goods. The Supreme Court answered in the negative on the ground that the Convention intended to bring about substantial uniformity of law and that it would be irreconcilable with the uniform character of the legislation in all participating countries if a contracting State unilaterally altered the provisions of the Convention.

It may be said that this practice[4] is of limited value for com-

---

with note by Philonenko; 20 May 1933, *RGZ* 140, 353; Berlin Court of Appeal, 7 November 1935, *JW* (1936), 338. All these decisions relate to the German–Swiss Gold Mortgage Convention.

[1] See the decision of 4 February 1931, p. 626, n. 6.          [2] [1921] P. 183.

[3] 22 February 1919, *RGZ* 95, 33. In connection with the same Convention the Supreme Court repeatedly emphasized that gaps deliberately left open by the Convention were to be filled by a reference to municipal law: 25 February 1904, *RGZ* 57, 142; 16 November 1907, *RGZ* 67, 171.

[4] It has not always been consistent. Thus in the decision of 14 March 1932, *RGStr.* 66, 165, relating to the German–Polish Convention about frontier traffic the term 'place of the undertaking' was interpreted in the light of German legislation employing the same phrase.

parative law, because it relates to the construction of treaties as such rather than statutes derived from treaties. There is little doubt, however, that that practice would extend to the case in which Germany re-enacts the text of a Convention and gives it statutory form. This happened in the case of the Bills of Exchange Act based on the Geneva Convention of 1930.[1] The paramount rule governing its construction is consonance with the unification intended by the Act; the purely formal view that the statute is a piece of national legislation has generally been rejected; it follows that legal conceptions known to other German legislation and occurring in the statute must be construed not in the sense of German law as such, but in the sense adopted by the community of contracting States[2]; 'were this not so, the agreement achieved by the Convention would be afflicted with a "concealed dissensus"'.[3]

(3) The practice of the United States of America as to the treatment of uniform legislation provides material which is particularly instructive for an English lawyer.

In this connection it is not the practice of the Supreme Court relating to the interpretation of treaties that requires attention. Under Art. VI (2) of the Constitution treaties when ratified by the Senate are the supreme law of the land and it is therefore only natural that they are construed as treaties in the narrow sense of the term; their interpretation has come up for decision in innumerable cases which are important contributions to the development of public international law proper, but have no bearing on the peculiar problem dealt with in this paper. On the other hand there are instances in which Congress has not ratified the treaty as such but has enacted legislation transforming the treaty into statute law. Thus the Carriage of Goods by Sea Act, 1936,[4] adopted the Hague Rules, subject to certain modifications. According to the material available in this

---

[1] Hudson, *International Legislation*, v.516 sqq.

[2] See, generally, Staub–Stranz, *Kommentar zum Wechselgesetz* (1934), pp. 49 sqq.; Ulmer, *Das Recht der Wertpapiere* (1938), p. 174; see also Court of Appeal at Stuttgart, 13 November 1936, *JW* (1937), 548.

[3] Professor Martin Wolff, *Ueber den Verkehrsschutz im neuen Wechselrecht, Festgabe für Wieland* (Basle, 1934), pp. 438, 445 sqq.; also *Internationales Privatrecht* (1933), p. 20, n. 47, and *Private International Law* (1945, section 133. The term 'concealed dissensus' describes what Cheshire and Fifoot, *Law of Contracts* (1945), p. 141, define as mutual mistake.

[4] Published, e.g., in *American Maritime Cases* (1936), 485.

country no authoritative pronouncement has as yet settled the principles governing the interpretation of such statutes.[1]

It is the attitude adopted by American Courts towards Uniform State Laws that should attract the English lawyer's interest. Mr. Lawson[2] has recently given an illuminating description of the movement which began at the end of the last century and has since led to the acceptance in many State jurisdictions of model laws approved by the National Conference of Commissioners on Uniform State Laws; the Uniform Negotiable Instruments Act and the Uniform Warehouse Receipts Act are particularly well-known examples, but there are very many other Acts which have found a large measure of acceptance. Wherever adopted these Acts represent municipal law of the adopting State. It follows that a Michigan Court, for instance, when called upon to construe a Uniform Act adopted in other States, is faced with the same problem as that which confronts an English judge who has to construe an Act of Parliament resulting from international legislation.

In most cases, it is true, the Michigan Court would receive some guidance from a clause which since about 1913[3] has been included in all Uniform Acts and which provides that the Act 'shall be so interpreted and construed as to effectuate its general purpose of making uniform the law of those States which enact it'. Yet in almost every field covered by a Uniform Act there exists a minority of State decisions which, in effect, reject such liberal construction as would promote uniformity of law, but prefer to construe the law strictly in favour of the pre-existing law of the State.[4] It was this tendency which was disapproved, though apparently not entirely eliminated, by the United States

[1] While the paramount object of achieving uniformity has been emphasized as a guide, in several decisions the Act of 1936 has been interpreted in the light of decisions relating to the Harter Act: see a number of cases reported in *American Maritime Cases* between 1939 and 1942.

[2] 26 *J. Comparative Legislation and Int. Law* (3rd series) (1944), 16.

[3] When the Commissioners appointed a Committee on Uniformity of Judicial Decisions: see 38 Reports American Bar Association, p. 980.

[4] As to the Uniform Negotiable Instruments Act, e.g., see Brannan (–Chafee), *The Negotiable Instruments Law Annotated* (4th ed.) (1926), pp. 1, 2. See also Harvey Walker, *Law Making in the United States* (1934), pp. 262 sqq. On the Uniform State Laws generally see the following literature which was unfortunately not available to the present writer: Beutel, 6 *Tulane L.R.* (1931), 1; 9 *Tulane L.R.* (1934), 64; *Univ. Chicago L.R.* (1933), 1, 81. As to a similar movement in Canada see Lawson op. cit.; Willis, *Univ. Toronto L.J.* 5 (1944), 352.

Supreme Court when, speaking through Mr. Justice Hughes, it gave the following authoritative ruling[1]:

> It is said that under the law of Louisiana, as it stood prior to the enactment of the Uniform Warehouse Receipts Act, the Commercial Bank would not have taken title as against the Canal–Louisiana Bank; and it is urged that the new statute is but a step in the development of the law and that decisions under the former State statutes are safe guides to its construction. We do not find it necessary to review these decisions. It is apparent that, if these Uniform Acts are construed in the several States adopting them according to former local views upon analogous subjects, we shall miss the desired uniformity and we shall erect upon the foundation of uniform language separate legal structures as distinct as were the former varying laws. It was to prevent this result that the Uniform Warehouse Receipts Act expressly provides (section 57): 'This Act shall be so interpreted and construed as to effectuate its general purpose to make uniform the law of those States which enact it.' This rule of construction requires that in order to accomplish the beneficial object of unifying, so far as this is possible under our dual system, the commercial law of the country, there should be taken into consideration the fundamental purpose of the Uniform Act and that it should not be regarded merely as an off-shoot of local law.

# III

The preceding discussion proves the existence of considerable distinctions between the English and the foreign approach to the interpretation of uniform laws. They are indeed such as to be capable of jeopardizing the very object which these laws pursue.

The root of the trouble, it is submitted, lies in the fact that English constitutional law requires an Act of Parliament to incorporate treaties into the English legal system. It is, however, neither necessary nor possible to suggest that, in order to open the way to a more satisfactory solution of the problem, this requirement should be dispensed with. It would be a sufficient remedy if it became generally and firmly realized that in the case under discussion legislation by Parliament is, broadly speaking, merely machinery rather than a source of law, that, in other words, Parliament is not the real law-giver, but merely the law-transformer, and that it is only the same form that Parliament employs to discharge inherently different functions. This distinction, it is true, is not universally applicable. It

---

[1] *Commercial National Bank of New Orleans* v. *Louisiana Canal Bank & Trust Co.*, 239 U. S. 520 (1915), at p. 528.

would clearly be excluded where the Act of Parliament omits any reference to the international legislation from which it results (above, Section I (1)), and its admissibility may be doubtful or limited in other cases (see above, Section I (2) and (3)). But where the statute confines itself to enacting a convention scheduled to it, even subject to amendments or modifications (see Section I (4), above), the suggested manner of approach is readily justifiable.

If it is accepted as a premiss, then some important consequences should follow.

In the first place the task of the judge would be unequivocally defined. It would consist in ascertaining the intention of the parties to the convention. The intention of the legislator in Westminster would, on the whole, be irrelevant.

Secondly, the usual rules of statutory interpretation would not bind the judge nor would he be subject to the principle of *stare decisis*.

Thirdly, the judge would not have to apply English municipal rules relating to the interpretation of contracts or deeds, but would be free to apply those rules of interpretation which are undeniably more appropriate to the peculiar task confronting him than the somewhat rigid and very special rules of interpretation which distinguish the English legal system from all others, viz. the rules of interpretation applicable to treaties and evolved by the rich practice of international tribunals and such municipal courts as the Supreme Court of the United States of America.

This would be a result which would be desirable both from a practical and a theoretical point of view. There can be no doubt that it is only in very exceptional cases that a term employed by the authors of a treaty is meant to be 'an off-shoot of local law' (as Mr. Justice Hughes has put it); there is therefore no reason to suppose that the treaty is intended to be 'but a step in the development' of local law and that it could be adequately construed in the light of purely municipal practice. If an international tribunal should have to interpret it (as well it might in the event of one of the signatories being made internationally responsible for a breach of the treaty), it would undoubtedly apply those principles which, over a long period of years, public international law has developed. For a national court to deviate from them is therefore not without dangers. It should not be objected that they are vague and difficult to define or to find— in truth they constitute a body of law which, notwithstanding inevitable uncertainties in some details, may be counted among one of the most firmly established and most richly documented achievements of public international law.[1] Nor would English judges lack experience in the interpretation of treaties. There are numerous cases in the books in which English judges with facility and resourcefulness have undertaken and discharged the task of construing treaties,[2] and in this connection they have not only made themselves free from all fetters which their municipal rules would have imposed upon them, but have also had resort to such auxiliaries as travaux préparatoires or comparative material.[3] Moreover they had proclaimed the necessity for what is known as 'liberal interpretation'[4]—in short they have followed principles which are equally appropriate where the object of interpretation is not a treaty pure and simple, but a treaty in the form of a statute.

The suggested solution would entail the substantial advantage that, for the particular field where uniformity is the very aim, it would assimilate English practice to that prevailing abroad and would thus contribute to the fulfilment of the object of unifying legislation. The danger of divergencies of interpretation, as various international conferences have recognized,[5]

---

[1] See Oppenheim (–Lauterpacht) (5th ed.) i.750 sqq., or the excellent discussion by the Harvard Research on the *Law of Treaties*, Supplement to *A.J.I.L.* (1935) (Part III), pp. 937 sqq. It is one of the undoubted principles of public international law that in the absence of an express or implied reference (renvoi) to national legislation the terms of a treaty are to be construed independently of such legislation; see the Permanent Court of International Justice (Series B), No. 10, p. 19 (Exchange of Greek and Turkish Populations).

[2] McNair, 43 *Recueil* ( 1933), 251, 264 sqq.: *Law of Treaties* (1938), pp. 195 sqq., 222 sqq.

[3] Lauterpacht, 'Les Travaux Préparatoires et l'interprétation des traités', 48 *Recueil* (1934), 713, 734 sqq.; the same, 48 *Harv. L.R.* (1934–5), 549, 563–1.

[4] For a good example see *Bohemian Union Bank* v. *Administrator of Austrian Property*, [1927] 2 Ch. 175, particularly at pp. 195–6 (decision of Clauson J.); see also *Imperial Japanese Government* v. *P. & O. Co.*, [1895] A. C. 644, at p. 657; *Re Arlan* (No. 2), [1896] 1 Q. B. 509, at p. 517, per Lord Russell L.C.J.

[5] On the deliberations of the Conferences for the unification of the law of bills of exchange and cheques and the proposals for an international tribunal, see Arminjon et Carry, *La Lettre de Change* (1938), pp. 444–5. See also *Annuaire de l'Institut de Droit International* (1936), i.246 sqq.; ii.305, where the report of Gidel traces the history of the suggestion for an International Court of Appeal. This suggestion has also

cannot for the present be excluded. But its reduction should be welcomed.

It may well be that the practice of the English Courts is so well settled as to make it unlikely that the adoption of a principle on the lines of that suggested above would be possible, even if it were found to be attractive. If so, it may be worth while considering whether future statutes incorporating a treaty into the law of England should not contain a section to the effect that the courts should construe them according to the principles which an international tribunal would apply.[1] For these are the 'broad principles of general acceptation' the application of which was urged by Lord Macmillan.[2]

been made by André Weiss, Clunet (1925), 5, and by Vallindas in his book on the uniformity of interpretation of conventions relating to private international law which appeared in the Greek language in 1932 and the thesis of which may be gathered from reviews in *Zeitschrift für Ausländisches und internationales Privatrecht* (1933), 170; *Rev. Gén.* (1933), 114; and *Revue de droit international privé* (1932), 727.

[1] cf. Article 11 of the 'Project of a Unified Law of Sale', published by the Institute for the Unification of Private Law in Rome: 'Pour les cas non visés expressément par les dispositions de la présente loi, et lorsque cette dernière n'a pas prévu formellement l'application d'une loi nationale, le tribunal saisi statue d'après les principes généraux dont s'inspire la présente loi.' See the comments by Rabel, *Zeitschrift für ausländisches und internationales Privatrecht* (1935), 1 sqq., 54, and see Rabel. *Das Recht des Warenkaufs*, p. 48.

[2] Above, p. 621, n. 1.

# XX

# THE PRESENT LEGAL STATUS
# OF GERMANY*

## I

THE legal position of Germany, as it has developed since the summer of the year 1945, has so far attracted singularly little attention on the part of jurists.[1] Although it is of a wholly unprecedented character, the only contribution to its clarification which is at present available comes from the pen of Professor Kelsen who, in 1944, published an article showing a remarkable degree of foresight,[2] and in July 1945, made a brilliant analysis of the situation which had then been created for a month or so.[3]

It is unlikely that the difficulty of competing with Professor Kelsen is the only reason for such silence. There is probably a widespread feeling that the present phase in the evolution of Germany's legal status is a temporary one and therefore not in need of further research.

Such an attitude disregards the fact that, however soon they may be displaced by a permanent arrangement, the conditions which have existed for almost two years are bound to give rise to a host of practical problems. Although the underlying facts may disappear, legal acts performed on their basis may have to be scrutinized in years to come. Thus an arrest made in Germany by an official of Military Government in Germany may lead to an application for a writ of habeas corpus which would involve the question whether Germany or the British Zone of Occupation[4] can be said to be part of the dominions

---

* From *International Law Quarterly* (1947), 314, or 33 *Grot. Soc.* (1947), 119, or *Jahrbuch für internationales und ausländisches Öffentliches Recht* (1948), i.27.

[1] The substance of this paper was read on 5 March 1947 before the Grotius Society. Articles which appeared after that date could not be taken into account; this applies in particular to the article by Mr. R. Y. Jennings in *B.Y.I.L.* (1946).

[2] 38 *A.J.I.L.* (1944), 689.      [3] 39 *A.J.I.L.* (1945), 518.

[4] British Military Government frequently speaks of 'Zone of Control'; see particularly Ordinance No. 4 (*Military Government Gazette*, No. 4, p. 5).

of the Crown.[1] A writ of certiorari directed against a decision of a British Military Government Court in Germany may impose upon a Divisional Court in England the duty of ascertaining whether or no the Military Government Court is a British Court. The effect of naturalization purporting to confer German nationality and effected by British Military Government in the British Zone may have to be tested. The validity of the confiscation of British-owned property by Military Government may become an issue in an English Court. The last-mentioned example is perhaps particularly instructive. If a British official in Hamburg wrongfully confiscates the property of a British subject, and an action is brought against the official in an English Court, it would become necessary to decide whether the defendant acted as the agent of a German State or of the British Crown; in the latter event the defence of act of State would not be available[2]; in the former event the defendant could pray in aid the often enunciated, though perhaps assailable, principle that 'every sovereign State is bound to respect the independence of every other sovereign State and the courts of one country will not sit in judgment on the acts of the Government of another done within its own territory'.[3]

Considerable practical importance for both international and municipal law, therefore, attaches to the determination of Germany's present legal status; even the established rule according to which in these matters municipal courts are to a large extent guided by statements provided by the Executive, renders it in no way futile to clarify the issues.

## II

These issues involve an evaluation of Germany's international and constitutional position. In order to avoid confusion it is necessary at the outset to state certain matters with which this paper is not concerned.

When General Eisenhower led his Allied Expeditionary

---

[1] If this cannot be said, the writ cannot issue: *Ex parte Anderson* (1861) 3 E. & E. 487; *Re Ning Yi-Ching* (1939–40) 56 T.L.R. 3.
[2] *Johnstone* v. *Pedlar*, [1921] 2 A. C. 262, and the authorities there referred to.
[3] *Underhill* v. *Hernandez*, 168 U. S. 250 (1897); cf. *Princess Paley Olga* v. *Weisz*, [1929] 1 K. B. 718, and numerous other cases discussed above, pp. 420 et seq.

Force into Germany, he had the double capacity of Supreme Commander of the Allied Forces and of Military Governor.[1] Even now the Commander-in-Chief of the British Zone of Occupation exercises the distinct functions of Commander-in-Chief of the British Army of Occupation and of Military Governor. In so far, however, as the armed forces are concerned, they live under their own law. Their position is governed by the familiar rules of international law applicable to armies stationed in foreign territory.[2] They do not form part of the German administration. They are distinct from Military Government. Consequently they are subject neither to German nor to Military Government law or courts.[3] but exclusively to their own military, naval, or air force law which they took with them. Therefore a Military Court in the British Zone of Occupation is a British Military Court; British naval law lays down the conditions under which a British seaman may be arrested, and so forth.

Military Government, on the other hand, is exercised by (civilian) Military Government Officers. Their position within the framework of German administration will have to be considered in the course of the following observations. If, and to the extent to which, they exercise the functions of Allied administration in Germany, their position is material to this paper. But the internal law under which they are organized and live should be recognized as a separate issue which is in no way dependent upon their external administrative work in Germany. It is submitted that, whatever may be the legal character of administrative functions discharged by a Military Government Officer, e.g. of a confiscation of property effected by him, internally Military Government of each of the Allied nations is

---

[1] See below, p. 637, n. 5.

[2] Oppenheim (–Lauterpacht), *International Law* (5th ed.), section 445.

[3] Art. II. of Ordinance No. 2 gives Military Government Courts jurisdiction 'over all persons in the occupied territory except persons other than civilians who are subject to military, naval, or air force laws'. Military Government Courts have no jurisdiction in matters other than criminal cases. It is quite true that under Art. VII (d) Military Government has the power to transfer to the jurisdiction of Military Government Courts any case or class of cases, but this cannot apply to civil cases. (See Art. II of Ordinance No. 2.) Except with the consent of Military Government no German Court has jurisdiction in cases against any of the United Nations or its nationals: Law No. 2, Art. VI (SHAEF), as amended by British Zone Ordinance No. 29.

an organization which, like the army, lives under its own national law. Thus, the British Military Government Officer who writes a libellous letter about a colleague is subject to English law.[1] And a British Military Government Court which exercises jurisdiction over a British Military Government Officer[2] is, it is suggested, a British Court, though it may have quite a different character when it exercises jurisdiction over a German or a Swiss. A Maritime Court which, during the war, the Dutch Government was allowed to establish in England, was a Dutch Court.[3] If, during the war, the Dutch Government in London had a Dutchman arrested here, his remedy lay in the Dutch Courts and was determined by Dutch law.[4] Similarly, in its internal aspects and relationships the instrumentality of Government set up by the British in Germany is British. No other result would be consistent with sound principle, the requirements of justice and the ideas which British civilian officers in Germany expect to be given effect to.

According to Ordinance No. 5, British civilians in Germany are subject to English criminal law; they cannot be tried for an offence against German law (which term, in this context, includes Military Government Law) except with the express authority of Military Government; and they cannot be arrested or detained by British police officers in Germany except in cases where British military police had the powers of arrest or detention of a member of the British armed forces under British Military Law. It is suggested that these provisions give expression to a general principle.

# III

When the Western Allies entered Germany, General Eisenhower brought with him the fundamental Proclamation No. 1 which reads as follows[5]:

[1] See note in 9 *Mod. L.R.* (1946), 179 on the case of *Szalatny-Stacho* v. *Fink*, [1946] 1 All E. R. 303 (Henn Collins J.); [1947] K. B. 1 (C. A.).

[2] See Ordinance No. 5, *Military Government Gazette*, No. 4, p. 5.

[3] See the Allied Powers (Maritime Courts) Act, 1941, and Viscount Simon, 24 *Comparative Legislation* (3rd series) (1942), 1; 58 *L.Q.R.* (1942) 41.

[4] *Re Amand (No. 2)*, [1942] 1 K. B. 345.

[5] *Military Government Gazette*, Germany, 21st Army Group Area of Control, No. 2, p. 1, Art. I of Proclamation No. 1, issued by Field-Marshal Lord Alexander in Italy read as follows: 'All powers of government and jurisdiction in occupied

Supreme legislative, judicial, and executive authority and powers within the occupied territory are vested in me as Supreme Commander of the Allied Forces and as Military Governor, and the Military Government is established to exercise these powers under my direction.

This Proclamation, like all other enactments of General Eisenhower, remained in force within the British Zone after the dissolution of SHAEF,[1] but is, in fact, superseded by three documents which were issued in Berlin on 5 June 1945, and contain what must now be regarded as the paramount laws of Germany.[2]

The first is a 'Declaration' made by the Supreme Commands of the four Allies 'acting by authority of their respective Governments and in the interests of the United Nations'. It recites Germany's unconditional surrender, the absence of any central Government and the fact that it is necessary 'without prejudice to any subsequent decisions that may be taken respecting Germany to make provision for the cessation of any further hostilities on the part of the German armed forces, for the maintenance of order in Germany and for the administration of the country, and to announce the immediate requirements with which Germany must comply'. It then proceeds as follows:

The Governments of the United Kingdom, the United States of America and the Union of Soviet Socialist Republics, and the Provisional Government of the French Republic, hereby assume supreme authority with respect to Germany, including all the powers possessed by the German Government, the High Command and any State, municipal or local government or authority. The assumption, for the purpose stated above, of the said authority and power does not effect the annexation of Germany.

The Governments of the United Kingdom, the United States of America and the Union of Soviet Socialist Republics and the Provisional Govern-

territories and over the inhabitants and final administrative responsibilities are vested in me, General Officer Commanding the Allied Forces and Military Governor, and in the Allied Military Government of occupied territory established to exercise the powers under my direction'. (See *B.Y.I.L.* (1944), 155.) There is probably little practical difference between these two Proclamations. The question whether and to what extent they are in conformity with the traditional law relating to belligerent occupancy has now only historical interest.

[1] Ordinance No. 4.

[2] Cmd. 6648. The Declaration of Berlin mentioned in the text was amplified by Proclamation No. 2 concerning 'certain additional requirements imposed on Germany' (*Control Council Gazette*, No. 1, p. 8). Under clause 48 any doubt as to the interpretation of the Declaration or regulations issued thereunder will be decided by the Allied Representatives.

ment of the French Republic will hereafter determine the boundaries of Germany or any part thereof and the status of Germany or of any area at present being part of German territory.

The second document is a 'Statement' according to which

supreme authority in Germany will be exercised, on instructions from their Governments, by the British, United States, Soviet, and French Commanders-in-Chief, each in his own zone of occupation, and also jointly, in matters affecting Germany as a whole. The four Commanders-in-Chief will together constitute the Control Council.

The third document is another Statement establishing the four zones of occupation.[1]

The supreme organ of Germany as a whole, therefore, is the Control Council. It consists of the four Commanders-in-Chief as political heads, and its work is being carried on by a quadripartite organization, viz. the permanent Co-ordinating Committee and the Control Staff comprising thirteen functional Directorates or Divisions (Military, Naval, Air, Transport, Political, Economic, Finance, Reparations, Deliveries and Restitution, Internal Affairs and Communications, Legal, Prisoners of War and Displaced Persons, Manpower)[2]; these 'Ministries' have established numerous quadripartite Committees which prepare and assist in the work of the Directorates.

The supreme authority of the Control Council, however, is territorially limited: according to the Statement of Berlin the Commanders-in-Chief exercise 'supreme authority *in* Germany' only. Supreme authority in external matters is reserved

---

[1] Special provisions have been made for the area of 'Greater Berlin' which is being occupied by forces of the four Powers. An Inter-Allied Governing Authority, the Allied Kommandatura, has been established 'to direct jointly its administration'. The Allied Kommandatura, therefore, has only administrative but no legislative powers, except in so far as such powers are being delegated to it by the Control Council. The British Sector of Berlin is not included in the British Zone of Occupation (Ordinance No. 4, Art. III) so that British zonal legislation does not apply to it; it would seem to follow, e.g. that Military Government Courts set up in the British Sector are without legal basis. Since the Kommandatura has no original legislative powers, British (and, similarly, United States and French) zonal legislation does not apply to Berlin and Berlin forms part of the Soviet zone, Soviet zonal legislation would appear to apply to Berlin; in practice, however, the administration of such legislation will be impossible without the consent of the Powers occupying the Sectors.

[2] Statement of Berlin, clause 3; on the work of the Control Council see Anne Whyte, *Quadripartite Rule in Berlin, International Affairs* (1947), xxiii.30.

to the Allied Governments. It was, therefore, fully consistent when the Agreement with Switzerland concerning the liquidation of German property in Switzerland (Cmd. 6884) was made by the Allied Governments who 'claimed title to German property in Switzerland by reason of the capitulation of Germany and the exercise of supreme authority in Germany', or when, in the Treaties of Peace with the five satellite countries, provisions are contained which prima facie affect a third party, i.e. Germany; thus, it has been agreed that Italian property in Germany should no longer be treated as enemy property and should be restored 'in accordance with measures which will be determined by the Powers in occupation in Germany', that Italy waives most of her and her nationals' claims against Germany and German nationals, and that German assets in Italy are to be transferred in such manner 'as may be determined by those of the Powers occupying Germany which are empowered to dispose of the said assets'.[1]

In so far as enactments of the Control Council have not interfered with his discretion, each Commander-in-Chief as Military Governor is supreme within his zone of occupation. His authority undoubtedly includes legislation, and in the British Zone numerous enactments, called Ordinances, have in fact been issued, though this is to some extent different in the United States Zone where usually German authorities, controlled and guided by the Commander-in-Chief, enact legislation and where, consequently, a different conception has become apparent.[2] But while the Control Council's jurisdiction is unlimited, that of the Commanders-in-Chief is restricted not only

---

[1] Cmd. 7022. Art. 77 of the Treaty with Italy, Art. 28 of the Treaty with Roumania, Art. 26 of the Treaty with Bulgaria, Art. 30 of the Treaty with Hungary, Art. 28 of the Treaty with Finland.

[2] But see Ordinance No. 31 relating to the Establishment of a Central Legal Office for the British Zone and Ordinance No. 52 relating to the 'Constitution and Functions of the German Economic Administration for the British Zone' which involves a substantial transfer of authority to a German administrative body. As a Special Correspondent of *The Times*, who is known to possess great experience, said (4 March 1947), 'United States theory is that all power originates with the people. The bizonal agencies are therefore presumed to derive their authority from the consent of the Laender, acting through the Laenderrat, the free and equal association of the three Laender. British Military Government takes the probably more realistic view that the administrations are based on an agreement between two of the occupying Powers and derive their authority clearly and squarely from Military Government.'

*ratione loci*, but also *ratione materiae*: they have no jurisdiction in matters affecting Germany as a whole. Although the State-ment of Berlin provides that the Control Council 'will ensure appropriate uniformity of action by the Commanders-in-Chief in their respective zones of occupation', conflicts are liable to arise. The difficulty results from the ambiguity of the phrase 'matters affecting Germany as a whole', 'questions intéressant l'ensemble de l'Allemagne'. Does it cover only matters which purport and are intended to affect Germany as a whole, or does it extend to matters the incidental effect of which may be felt in Germany as a whole? The new Municipal Code, e.g., introduced in the British Zone by Ordinance No. 21, is a measure which, notwithstanding its great significance, is clearly of a strictly local character. But the British-American Agree-ment for the economic fusion of the United States and United Kingdom Zones[1] is a much more serious matter and has pro-voked some criticism on account of its far-reaching effects upon the other zones of occupation. If the French Commander-in-Chief introduced in his zone the French Civil Code in sub-stitution for the German Civil Code, this would be an unequiv-ocal example of a matter affecting Germany as a whole, although prima facie it would be territorial legislation. Probably the phrase will have to be given a wide interpretation so as to achieve the obviously desired object of uniformity.[2]

## IV

The first question to which the preceding summary of the relevant texts gives rise is whether Germany can be said to be under belligerent occupation within the meaning of Articles 42 to 56 of the Hague Regulations.

Arguing before the Court of Appeal, the Attorney-General, Sir Hartley Shawcross, K.C., said: 'The position is that this country is now in belligerent occupation of Germany, with the Army of Occupation in control.'[3] If this were a considered statement of the strictly legal position and represented the true

---

[1] Cmd. 7001.

[2] The validity of zonal legislation does not seem to be a matter which is with-drawn from the jurisdiction of German Courts, and it is likely to become an issue in proceedings outside Germany.

[3] *R. v. Bottrill, ex parte Kuechenmeister*, [1947] 1 K. B. 41, at p. 45.

view, the consequences would be grave, for there cannot be any doubt that the Allies have not kept, and have not shown the intention to keep, within the limits of the Hague Regulations. This follows not only from the Declaration of Berlin itself by which the Allied Governments rather than the Commanders-in-Chief assumed supreme authority,[1] but also from many subsequent pronouncements and enactments which cannot be supported by traditional law. In the particular case of Germany, it is true, a belligerent occupant would have had rights which prior to the rise of the fascist State were unthinkable, but which may be brought within the letter and spirit of established law. Thus, it may well be said that the repeal of Nazi legislation is permitted by the Hague Regulations, because this is legislation which an occupant is absolutely prevented from respecting.[2] It can also be contended that numerous measures taken for the purpose of demilitarization, changing the political system of Germany and controlling the economic resources of a highly centralized totalitarian State are required for the maintenance and safety of the occupying Powers and the consummation of their victory. Many other enactments, though startling at first sight, can be justified by the object of restoring and ensuring public order and safety. But even if an interpretation of the Hague Regulations, which is both broad and adapted to the peculiar circumstances, renders a large part of Allied policy in Germany consistent with traditional law, there remains enough that cannot be fitted into its frame. The Declaration of Berlin, supplemented by Proclamation No. 2, as well as the Potsdam Agreement which, though it constitutes an agreement between the heads of government of three occupying Powers, must be considered as a basic document of German law, provide for matters which admittedly are requisite not for completing the victory over Germany, but for 'future peace and security'[3]; it is difficult to believe that the desired decentralization of administration in Germany[4] is temporarily necessitated by the interests of military control; to place the City of Koenigsberg and the territories east of the Oder–Neisse line under Soviet and Polish administration respectively[5] far

---

[1] The phrase 'supreme authority' in itself would be inconclusive.
[2] Art. 43.
[3] Declaration of Berlin, Art. 13.     [4] Potsdam Agreement, III, 9.
[5] Ibidem, VI and IX.

exceeds the limits within which a mere belligerent occupant could act; no belligerent occupant could withdraw diplomatic missions[1] or require 'German authorities and all persons in Germany' to hand over all gold, silver, and platinum,[2] or acquire the right to have placed 'at the unrestricted disposal of the Allied Representatives' the entire German shipping and the whole of the German inland transport system.[3] And if one looks at the legislation of the Control Council, one finds Law No. 4 about the reorganization of the German judicial system, or Law No. 16 the marriage law, Law No. 36 about administrative courts or Law No. 38 amending section 204 of the German Code of Civil Procedure, and Law No. 46 about the dissolution of Prussia, all of which contain provisions in no way required for ensuring public order and safety. The establishment of new Länder with new Constitutions in the British and American Zones are prominent examples of zonal legislation which point in the same direction.

The Allies' failure to exercise the qualified rights of a belligerent occupant seems to be undeniable. As such it is not really relevant. For to say that, because there is a breach of the law, the law cannot apply, is not an admissible argument. The material question is why the Allies have an internationally recognizable right to behave otherwise than as belligerent occupants.

It would be unsatisfactory to make the answer dependent upon the existence or non-existence of a state of war. Some publicists would probably be inclined to say that, if the war has ended, Germany cannot, and that, if the war continues, she must needs be under belligerent occupation.[4] The latter proposition would involve a *petitio principii*; the former would overlook the fact that the rules relating to military occupation of enemy territory are minimum rules which extend to 'peaceful occupation' by virtue of an armistice or a treaty of peace.[5]

---

[1] Proclamation No. 2, 7 (c).
[2] Ibidem, clause 15.
[3] Ibidem, clauses 28 and 29.
[4] Cf. 'E', *B.Y.I.L.* (1938), p. 236; Sir Arnold McNair, *Legal Effects of War* (2nd ed.), pp. 342, 343.
[5] Oppenheim–Lauterpacht, *International Law* (6th ed., revised), ii.338, n. 6, and p. 339, n. 2; Feilchenfeld, *The International Economic Law of Belligerent Occupation* (1942), pp. 6, 108 sqq.

Neither unconditional surrender in itself,[1] nor the mere absence of a central government, would prevent those rules from coming into operation—it would obviously lead to questionable results, if by eliminating the occupied country's government, a belligerent could enlarge his powers.[2] Finally, to invoke the conception of reprisals would discredit rather than promote the cause of international law.

Although neither the end of hostilities nor the unconditional surrender nor the disappearance of a central government could, in themselves, have entitled the Allied Governments to adopt an attitude other than that of a belligerent occupant, it is, in the peculiar situation of Germany in 1945, the co-existence of these three facts which provides an internationally recognizable justification for Allied action. The rules relating to belligerent occupation seek to establish a compromise between military necessities and the interests of the inhabitants. They presuppose an interplay between military and civilian authority. They assume the precariousness of the occupant's position which demands such protection as the legitimate needs of the civilian population permit. They are pervaded by the idea that the inhabitants are non-combatants with whose mode of life a belligerent should, and can afford to, interfere as little as possible. They are far removed from the atmosphere of a totalitarian State which forces children no less than the aged into its service. They expect, from both sides, a standard of conduct which becomes impracticable when every single activity of the occupied State expresses a doctrine the eradication of which is the very aim of the war. The unconditional surrender which the Allies had demanded for years had been preceded by the unconditional surrender of all nations allied with Germany except remote Japan, herself on the verge of surrender. It meant that the Allies were free to take all measures necessary to carry out their object. No German Government could have been formed to co-operate with a mere belligerent occupant. If the Allies had assumed only the role of belligerent occupants, they and the United Nations in whose interests they act, could not

---

[1] Feilchenfeld, op. cit., passim.

[2] The decision of Clauson J. in *Bank of Ethiopia* v. *National Bank of Egypt*, [1937] Ch. 513, may be said to indicate a different view, but has singularly failed to arouse the approval of international lawyers and is indeed open to grave criticism. See Sir Arnold McNair, above, p. 643, n. 4.

achieve their war aims, which go far beyond military victory; indeed, they would have failed to fulfil their duty and historic mission. It is the unique character of the circumstances which required and sanctioned a unique solution, a new departure.[1] It is submitted that it is more satisfactory and also in harmony with the spirit of international law as a living law to recognize the existence of a new experiment rather than so to stretch the words of the Hague Regulations that they sanction Allied practice in Germany.

## V

Even if the Allies are not merely belligerent occupants, it cannot possibly be contended that any of the four zones of occupation is in any sense a dominion of the occupying Power, that the United Kingdom exercises jurisdiction in the British Zone, that the Commander-in-Chief as Military Governor of the British Zone is a representative of the British Government acting on its behalf, that he or any officer or authority acting under his direction perform acts for which the United Kingdom bears legal, as opposed to political or parliamentary, responsibility. The true position is that the Commander-in-Chief as Military Governor of his Zone is the Delegate of the four Governments; it is by their authority that he exercises zonal jurisdiction the nature of which will have to be considered below.[2]

The four Governments have assumed 'supreme authority with respect to Germany'. This is the overriding pronouncement of the Declaration of Berlin. It follows that no single Government can claim supreme authority with respect to Germany or any part thereof. Such authority as the Commander-in-Chief of any Zone has is derived not from the Declaration of Berlin, but from the Statement of Berlin which deals with the *exercise* of the supreme authority *assumed* by the four Governments under the Declaration of Berlin. Such

---

[1] Kelsen, 39 *A.J.I.L.* (1945), 518, arrives at the same conclusion and bases it on the absence of a central government and on his theory that Germany is no longer a State and that the war has ended. On the observations in the text see Friedmann, 3 *Mod. L.R.* (1940–1), 177; *Grot. Soc.* (1940), 211, and in other publications.

[2] See p. 654.

authority is being exercised jointly by the four Commanders-in-Chief constituting the Control Council in matters affecting Germany as a whole, and by each of them in his zone of occupation. Although the separation of supreme authority and its exercise cannot be regarded as a new development,[1] the four Governments, having assumed supreme authority with respect to Germany as a whole, would normally exercise it themselves. If they allow the Commanders-in-Chief to exercise it in their respective zones, this involves delegation and, in law, renders the delegate a representative of the delegant, i.e. the four Governments jointly rather than his own Government. None of the four Powers as such is invested with supreme authority or any divisible part of it. Each of them could have acquired or exercised it only if, instead of appointing the Commanders-in-Chief, the Statement of Berlin had so provided. Consequently none of the four Governments could confer supreme authority in its zone on an official other than the Commander-in-Chief for the time being.

This conclusion could be nullified only by attributing wider significance than they merit to those words of the Statement according to which the Commanders-in-Chief exercise their authority 'on instructions from their Governments'. In fact, it could be nullified only by assuming that, having jointly assumed supreme authority, the four Governments have divided it zonally not only for the purpose of its exercise, but also for the purpose of divesting themselves of it and allocating to each of them what belongs to them jointly. It is submitted that there is no warrant for such a view, and that the subjection of the Commander-in-Chief to his Government's instructions is, in law, immaterial to his legal position. The High Commissioner of Palestine is subject to instructions from the British Government. But whatever the true view of the legal status of Palestine[2] may be, it cannot be suggested that the mere power of giving instructions makes Great Britain the Sovereign of Palestine or renders Palestine a part of Great Britain or establishes British jurisdiction in Palestine. The power of giving instructions is not irreconcilable with sovereignty over Palestine

---

[1] See, generally, Lauterpacht, *Private Law Sources and Analogies of International Law*, p. 189.

[2] See Oppenheim–Lauterpacht, *International Law* (5th ed.), i.191, 197 seq.

being vested in others than the mandatory Power. There is no reason in law why the power of giving instructions in the exercise of supreme authority should not be differentiated from the holding of such authority.

## VI

The next question is whether Germany as a whole now so 'belongs' to the four occupant States as to necessitate the inference that they have placed her under their joint sovereignty and established a condominium, a new State the creation of which would entail many intricate problems of State succession.[1]

According to traditional doctrine it would be impossible to give an affirmative answer. The acquisition of territorial sovereignty could be achieved only by one of the five well-defined methods[2] of which subjugation alone would demand consideration. Subjugation would require conquest and annexation. Since the Declaration of Berlin expressly states that 'the assumption, for the purposes stated above, of the said authority and powers does not effect the annexation of Germany', subjugation would clearly have to be negatived.

Yet it is Professor Kelsen's thesis that the four Allies hold Germany under their joint sovereignty. In his view subjugation is possible without annexation which is normally understood as presupposing the conqueror's intention to hold the territory permanently for himself, to acquire both the legal and the beneficial title to the country:

The establishment of territorial sovereignty does not depend on the new sovereign's intention to hold the territory for good. He may have the intention to cede the territory or part of it later on to another State. Such an intention does not prevent the acquisition of sovereignty. . . . If there is a difference at all between formal annexation and placing the territory under the conqueror's sovereignty without the latter's intention to hold it perma-

---

[1] Kelsen, op. cit., p. 522, makes a gallant attempt at dealing with the problem of German nationality. But he does not mention the nationality of those Germans who at the material times were outside Germany and who, therefore, could not be said to have acquired the new German nationality which is implicit in Kelsen's remarks, but would be stateless (see above, p. 514). Nor does Kelsen deal with any of the other problems of State succession.

[2] Oppenheim–Lauterpacht (5th ed.), i, section 211.

nently, it is rather a political than a legal one. The rights and duties of the territorial sovereign are the same in both cases.[1]

It must be admitted that there is no *a priori* reason why the categories of methods of acquiring territorial sovereignty should be considered as closed. International law is not so rigid as to exclude new developments. It may well be, therefore, that there exists a sixth method of acquiring territorial sovereignty, viz. conquest, and an intention to vest only the legal title to the territory in the conqueror who would hold it temporarily, pending further disposition, until he decided to hold it for himself or to retransfer or cede it so that the beneficial title would be in suspense.

A theory on these lines seems to be at the back of Professor Kelsen's mind,[2] but even if it is considered as a possible one, it could not actually apply to the case of Germany. Professor Kelsen is a little dogmatic on this point, and does not attach sufficient weight to the fact that in the last resort the problem must depend on the four Governments' intention as expressed in or to be inferred from the Declaration of Berlin. It is submitted that the text does not support the existence of an intention to acquire sovereignty.

Firstly, one would expect so important a result to have been unequivocally expressed, e.g. by the words that the four Powers assume 'all rights and *title*' over Germany.[3] The suppression of such a statement, even if primarily due to political reasons, cannot be without legal significance.

Secondly, it should be remembered that the first document by which the Big Three gave particulars of their intentions with regard to Germany, i.e. the Communiqué issued after the Crimean Conference in February 1945 contained no hint of such an intention. It declared that it was the Allies' 'inflexible purpose' to destroy German militarism and Nazism, but not to 'destroy the people of Germany', that under agreed plans the forces of three Allies[4] would each occupy a separate zone of Germany, and that these plans provided for 'co-ordinated

---

[1] op. cit., p. 521.

[2] His formulation is not too precise, but the reference to the legal position of Cuba after the Spanish-American war makes his views clear.

[3] See Art. 99 of the Treaty of Versailles.

[4] The French Government did not participate in the Conference.

administration and control'. This indicates something less than the acquisition of territorial sovereignty.

Thirdly, it should be noted that by the Declaration of Berlin supreme authority was assumed by the *Governments* of the four nations, neither by the heads of the Allied States nor by the Allied States as such. In so far as the United Kingdom is concerned this wording is a little remarkable, though, in itself, it is certainly inconclusive. If the United Kingdom had desired to assume joint sovereignty over Germany, it would have been the better and perhaps more usual method for the Government of the United Kingdom to act expressly on behalf of the King as the nation's representative in the conduct of foreign affairs. Perhaps it is possible to find in this language an indication of the intention to assume supreme authority, not for the purpose of acquiring State sovereignty, but for the purpose of establishing governmental control.

Fourthly, by the Declaration of Berlin supreme authority was assumed only for three specified purposes, viz. 'to make provision for the cessation of any further hostilities on the part of the German armed forces, for the maintenance of order in Germany, and for the administration of the country, and to announce the immediate requirements with which Germany must comply'. This was 'without prejudice to any subsequent decisions that may be taken respecting Germany' and, moreover, in another passage, the four Governments state that they 'will hereafter determine the boundaries of Germany or any part thereof and the status of Germany or of any area at present being part of German territory'. These reservations underline the limited and provisional character of Allied intentions, and indicate that, in connection with future decisions, territorial sovereignty may be acquired. If the Allies had already acquired it, those reservations would be superfluous.

Fifthly, the assumption of territorial sovereignty by the Allies would be so retrograde a development that very strong evidence would be required to support it. It is an accepted maxim of international law that belligerent occupancy does not confer or justify the assumption of territorial sovereignty. Even though the Allies are not merely belligerent occupants, they cannot be presumed to revert to a practice which more than a century ago was condemned by international law and discarded in practice.

In Austria, it is true, by virtue of an Inter-Allied Agreement of 4 July 1945, which was in force until 28 June 1946 (Cmd. 6958), an Allied Commission was in operation to *exercise* supreme authority; while its organization was and, for its limited purposes, still is very similar to the German organization, the Allies never *assumed* supreme authority in Austria. But it would not be permissible to put forward an *argumentum e contrario* to the effect that the supreme authority assumed with respect to Germany must mean more than that governmental authority which in Austria was conferred by much less solemn words. The Declaration of Berlin envisages a long-term arrangement, while the Austrian Agreement intended to set up machinery 'which will operate until the establishment of a freely elected Austrian Government recognized by the Four Powers', and was therefore of a strictly temporary character. This difference justifies and explains the difference of formulation.

## VII

If the four Governments have not acquired sovereignty either in their respective zones of occupation or over Germany as a whole, the question arises whether Germany is still a State. On this point it is necessary to make a distinction.

Germany certainly is not a sovereign State in the accepted sense of the law of nations.[1] It is an essential element of the conception of a sovereign State that the country is under the control of its own independent Government. Germany has no Government which is her own, or which is free from control over its internal administration or its foreign relations; even if it were possible to describe the Allied Control Council as a German Government, it would be subject to instructions given by the four Allied Governments.

Moreover, Germany maintains no relations with the world at large. According to the Statement of Berlin, it is true, 'liaison with the other United Nations Governments chiefly

---

[1] Kelsen, op. cit., p. 519, says that Germany is not a State. He does not draw the distinction made in the text, but obviously speaks only of statehood in international law, and, generally, is no doubt influenced to a large extent by his own theory of the State and of sovereignty.

interested will be established through the appointment by such Governments of military missions (which may include civilian members) to the Control Council'.[1] This representation is so limited and one-sided that it is impossible to say that Germany maintains normal foreign relations, particularly since it has also been provided[2] that 'the Allied Representatives will regulate all matters affecting Germany's relations with other countries', 'will give directions concerning the abrogation, bringing into force, revival or application of any treaty, convention or other international agreement, or any part or provision thereof, to which Germany is or has been a party', and 'may require the withdrawal from Germany' of neutral missions. German diplomatic missions have been recalled,[3] and it has been expressly declared that 'in virtue of the unconditional surrender of Germany, and as of the date of such surrender, the diplomatic, consular, commercial and other relations of the German State with other States have ceased to exist'.

*Pace* Professor Kelson who would not accept the distinction,[4] it is submitted, however, that though she is not a State within the meaning of international law, Germany still is a State in the general sense of the term. In this connection it is unnecessary to embark upon a discussion which would lead into the depths of jurisprudence. It will be generally agreed that there exists a State, if a body of people, inhabiting a defined territory, is so organized under supreme civil rule and government as to constitute a coherent body politic.[5] These conditions are fulfilled in the case of Germany, provided the Allied Control Council can fairly be regarded as the Government of Germany.

---

[1] Paragraph 5.

[2] Proclamation No. 2, clauses 5–7. There is no authority for the view that treaties made by a sovereign State automatically lapse, if such State suffers 'une extinction partielle' and becomes a dependent State.

[3] Ibidem.

[4] See above, p. 650, n. 1, and his writing on the State, Sovereignty, etc.

[5] In this connection the use of the word 'sovereign' should be avoided. The German State, if it exists, has of course internal sovereignty. This has no bearing upon the existence or non-existence of external sovereignty which is clearly missing, and without which Germany cannot be a sovereign State in the sense of international law. Kelsen's thesis (op. cit., p. 521) that 'Germany certainly has ceased to exist as a sovereign State and since the territory is not under Germany's own sovereignty, it would be no State's if it were not under the sovereignty of the occupant Powers' is untenable and can only be explained by the fact that he has become a victim of the dangers attending the word 'sovereignty'.

Although the Control Council is not a German Government, it does constitute the Government of Germany, because it is vested with supreme authority in matters affecting Germany as a whole. This governmental authority of the Control Council, it is true, is limited to internal German affairs and is derived from the four Allied Governments which assumed supreme authority and then delegated[1] its exercise in Germany. But this only means that, admittedly and professedly, the Control Council is not a German Government. It is not the root of title, but the actual governmental function and authority that is decisive. Nor can any counter-argument be deduced from that passage of the Declaration of Berlin according to which the Allied Governments will hereafter determine 'the status (statut) of Germany or any area at present being part of German territory'. Whatever the linguistic connection between the word 'State' and the word 'status' may be,[2] the argument that because the determination of Germany's status is reserved she cannot at present be regarded as a State, would be too far-fetched to be attractive.

If the above submissions are accepted, it becomes possible to define the present status of Germany a little more precisely.

From the point of view of international law Germany is a dependent State. The circumstances are so unique, however, that any attempt at further classification is bound to fail. The position of the Allied Governments probably is that they exercise what certain publicists have described as co-imperium.[3] While in the case of a condominium a community of States has

---

[1] This does not preclude the four Allied Governments from exercising supreme authority themselves, if they wish so to do. An example of such exercise of supreme authority is provided by the Agreement for the Prosecution and Punishment of the Major War Criminals of the European Axis which was made on 8 August 1945 by the Governments of the United States of America, France, the United Kingdom, and the U.S.S.R., 'acting in the interests of all the United Nations' and to which the Charter of the International Military Tribunal is annexed (*A.J.I.L.* (*Official Documents*) (1945), 257). The Nürnberg Tribunal quite correctly said in its judgment: 'The making of the Charter was the exercise of the sovereign legislative power by the countries to which the German Reich had unconditionally surrendered; and the undoubted right of these countries to legislate for the occupied territories had been recognized by the civilized world.'

[2] See, e.g. the summary given by Dowdall, 39 *L.Q.R.* (1923), 98.

[3] Verdross, *Völkerrecht*, pp. 128, 132; 30 *Hague Recueil* (1929), 275 sqq., 396. Usually the term 'condominium' is used indiscriminately, but the distinction explained in the text seems logical and attractive. Cf. Art. 81 of the United Nations

sovereignty over a territory belonging to them jointly, a co-imperium exists, if several States jointly exercise jurisdiction or governmental functions and powers in territory belonging to another State; the administration by Austria–Hungary of Bosnia and Herzegovina from 1878 to 1908, while the territory belonged to Turkey, is usually given as an example of such co-imperium.

The German State is not a new State.[1] It is the same State as that which existed immediately prior to the Declaration of Berlin. Its identity was preserved, though its status was impaired and reduced and it suffered what Fauchille would describe as an 'extinction partielle'.[2] Nor does it matter that a new Government has taken power. A change of Government, however revolutionary its origin may be, does not involve the formation of a new State.[3]

From the point of view of municipal law the Control Council performs and, indeed, intends to perform the functions of a German Government. It enacts German legislation. The acts of its executive officers are acts of the German State. Thus, by Law No. 5,[4] the German External Property Commission was established 'as an inter-governmental agency of the Control Council'; the law vests in the Commission, 'all rights, titles, and interests in respect of any property outside Germany' of certain categories of persons (Arts. II and III), and confers powers upon it for the purpose of obtaining control over the property (Art. VII). Or by Law No. 9, the property and assets of I. G. Farbenindustrie have been vested in the Control Council and a Committee has been set up to deal with this property. If the External Property Commission exceeds its

Charter according to which the administering authority exercising trusteeship 'may be one or more States'. 'Co-imperium' as opposed to 'condominium' is a type of fiduciary administration as explained by the Supreme Court of the U.S. in the decisions relating to the Status of Cuba in the treaty of 1898; see 108 U. S. 109, 120. Such fiduciary administration by England occurred, e.g. in the case of Cyprus which from 1878 to 1914 was 'assigned to England in order to be occupied and administered'. The term seems to be an appropriate description of the present German situation.

[1] cf. Oppenheim–Lauterpacht, *International Law* (5th ed.), i.145, n. 1.

[2] *Traité de droit international public*, i.373, 382 sqq.

[3] *The Government of Spain* v. *Chancery Lane Deposit Co., Ltd.; The State of Spain* v. *The Same, B.Y.I.L.* (1944), pp. 195, 196.

[4] *Gazette No. 2*, p. 27, and see the amendment of Art. III by Regulation No. 1 in *Gazette No. 8*, p. 160.

powers (e.g. by misinterpreting the terms 'rights, titles, and interests') or if a creditor of I. G. Farbenindustrie claims against the Control Council,[1] the liability of individual members or of the German State is determined by the general German law.[2] And if the Control Council should engage in international trade, it would be the 'German Government' within the meaning of Article 281 of the Treaty of Versailles and could not claim immunity where this Article is in force.[3]

Further, the Commander-in-Chief in his zone and his zonal authorities and officials are likewise representatives of the Government of Germany. The Commander-in-Chief is not the representative of the occupying State which has appointed him (see above, section V). Nor is he a delegate of the Control Council, because in his zone he does not exercise the (delegated) authority of the Control Council, which is a distinct body exercising authority only in matters affecting Germany as a whole. The Commander-in-Chief, according to the Statement of Berlin, is entrusted with 'supreme authority in Germany . . . in his own zone of occupation'. This formulation is not, as one might think at first sight, contradictory or illogical. It clearly expresses the idea that locally the Commander-in-Chief is the supreme authority in Germany, the supreme representative of the German State, the Government of Germany. If he engages in international trade, Article 281 of the Treaty of Versailles would apply to him.

The position of the German authorities can only be described in general terms. Broadly speaking, they are organs of the German State. The judgment of a German Court whose judges have sworn 'to obey the laws of Germany',[4] is a German judgment. The naturalization granted by a competent German

---

[1] See section 419 of the German Civil Code.

[2] Under SHAEF Law No. 2, as amended (above, p. 636, n. 3), no German Court can, without the consent of Military Government, deal with cases involving money claims 'against the German Government or any legal entity existing under public law'. Actions against the Control Council or the Germans State would be covered by this provision.

[3] Immunity from local jurisdiction may be enjoyed by States which are not sovereign: cf., e.g., *Sullivan* v. *State of São Paolo*, *Annual Digest* (1941–2), No. 50 (C.C.A., 2nd), on the one hand and *The Superintendent, Government Soap Factory* v. *Commissioner of Income Tax*, ibidem, No. 10 (Supreme Court of Ceylon), on the other hand.

[4] This is so where SHAEF Law No. 2 (Art. V) applies.

authority is a valid German naturalization. Yet it cannot be overlooked that as a result of the division of Germany into four zones, not everything done in Germany is being done by the authority of German law. There exists German law in so far as it comprises law enacted prior to June 1945, and Control Council legislation. Zonal legislation, whether enacted by Military Government or German authorities, is not German law, but local law. This is of importance for many questions of private international law which may arise outside Germany, and has led to many difficulties inside Germany. The tax liability of an undertaking carrying on business in more than one zone; the effect of the dissolution of companies or of the confiscation of property in a particular zone upon property situated in other zones; the treatment of criminals who have committed an offence under the law of one zone and are being apprehended in another zone—these are some of the problems with which German practice is being faced.

By and large the views propounded above seem to be in harmony with the attitude adopted by the Foreign Office in *R. v. Bottrill, ex parte Kuechenmeister.*[1] A German national who was being detained here in pursuance of an order made under the Royal Prerogative, applied for a writ of habeas corpus; before the Divisional Court his principal contention was that by virtue of the Declaration of Berlin Germany had ceased to be a State so that, being outside Germany at the relevant date, he became stateless and could, therefore, not be interned as an enemy alien. The Court felt bound[2] by a certificate of the Secretary of State for Foreign Affairs which said, after referring to the Declaration of Berlin, that

in consequence of this declaration Germany still exists as a State and German nationality as a nationality, but the Allied Control Commission

---

[1] [1947] K. B. 41. See also Sir Hartley Shawcross, K.C., M.P., *Hansard* (1947), 1044.

[2] In *The Arantzazu Mendi*, [1939] A. C. 256, 258, the Secretary of State said in his certificate: 'The question whether the Nationalist Government is to be regarded as that of a foreign sovereign State appears to be a question of law to be answered in the light of the preceding statements and having regard to the particular issue or circumstances with respect to which the question is raised.' Whether a country is a sovereign State or merely a State cannot make any difference in this connection and it is therefore not certain whether in *Kuechenmeister's* case the Court was really bound by the certificate on a question of law; see generally above, pp. 385 et seq.

[*sic*] are the agency through which the Government of Germany is carried on.

For the purpose of the proceedings it was unnecessary to certify whether Germany still is a sovereign State in the sense of international law. But the Secretary of State did certify that Germany was a State and that the Control Council was its Government.[1]

## VIII

There remains the question whether a state of war continues to exist between this country and Germany. This is a problem the gravity of which will be obvious to every international lawyer. As we realized during the time when 'non-belligerency' was fashionable, there is no halfway house between war and peace. Whichever decision is made, the dilemma is undeniable: If a state of war exists, the rights and duties of neutrals are in

---

[1] In the same sense an Opinion of the Supreme Finance Court at Munich mentioned by G. A. Zinn, the Minister of Justice of Greater Hesse in his paper, 'Das Staatsrechtliche Problem Deutschlands' (2 *Sueddeutsche Juristen Zeitung* (1947), 4). In the course of the discussion following this lecture, Dr. Paul Abel and Dr. G. Weis were good enough to draw the author's attention to two interesting decisions of the Austrian Supreme Court and the Court of Appeal in Zurich respectively. In the former case, which related to a question of jurisdiction in a matrimonial cause, it was held without extensive discussion that the German State and, consequently, German nationality, continued to exist: 24 January 1946, 68 *Juristische Blaetter* (1946), 142; see also 28 January 1946, ibidem, p. 100. The latter decision gave an affirmative answer to the question whether the Hague Conventions, exempting a German plaintiff from the duty of providing security for costs, were still in force as between Germany and Switzerland: 1 December 1945, *Schweizerische Juristenzeitung* (1946), 89, also *Deutsche Rechts-Zeitschrift* (1947), 31. The elaborate decision merits a short summary. The President of Switzerland had supplied the Court with a certificate to the effect that Germany was still a State and that Switzerland had not denounced the applicability of the Hague Conventions in the case of Germany. In the course of an independent investigation the Court found that Germany had not been annexed, because the Allies had not expressed an intention of annexation. Consequently, the Court said, 'the present situation can only be that of belligerent occupation'. But can it be said that Germany 'has lost her Government and, therefore, her character as a State, i.e., a subject of international law'? The Court argues that a change of the régime does not involve the abolition of the State and concludes that 'the occupying powers exercise the authority of the German State by virtue of public international law. . . . In international law this is a novelty. But international law requires development. . . . The present situation in Germany corresponds most closely to a kind of fiduciary administration of the authority of the German State by the occupying powers.' It is doubtful whether the point before the Court could not have been dealt with on a simpler ground: see above, p. 651. See also District Court at Hamburg, 18 March 1947, *Monatsschrift für Deutsches Recht* (1947), 39.

force. If there is peace, the belligerents' jurisdiction in prize has come to an end.

In *R.* v. *Bottrill, ex parte Kuechenmeister,*[1] the Secretary of State's certificate said that

no treaty of peace or declaration of the Allied Powers having been made terminating the state of war with Germany, His Majesty is still in a state of war with Germany.

It is not known whether the war of which the certificate speaks is the war in the international sense or in the sense of municipal law. Before the Court of Appeal it was argued that, even if the applicant was still a German, he was not an enemy, because the war had ended, and that, therefore, he could not be detained under the Royal Prerogative. The Court held in effect that it was concerned only with municipal law and that in municipal law a state of war unquestionably existed.[2]

Does it exist in international law? Professor Kelsen suggests[3] that 'Germany having ceased to exist as a State, the status of war has been terminated, because such a status can exist only between belligerent States'. It is difficult to say what is meant by 'belligerent States' in this context. Probably it is suggested that Germany is no longer a sovereign State, and that for this reason she has no capacity of waging war. But the doctrine that full sovereign States alone possess the legal qualification to become belligerents is too rigid. It is well known that belligerency does not necessarily presuppose sovereignty,[4] and even if only full sovereign States could *become* belligerents, it would not follow that States which cease to enjoy full sovereignty *cease* to be belligerents.

In the absence of a treaty or declaration of peace or of subjugation there is only one type of termination of war which has to be considered, viz. simple cessation of hostilities,[5] a situation

---

[1] [1947] 1 K. B. 41 (C. A.).

[2] The case of *Kotzias* v. *Tyser,* [1920] 2 K. B. 69, relates to 'war' in the sense of municipal law. The same applies to Lord Macnaghten's dictum in *Janson* v. *Driefontein Consolidated Mines, Ltd.,* [1902] A. C. 484, 497, that the law 'knows nothing of an intermediate state which is neither the one nor the other, neither peace nor war'.

[3] op. cit., p. 519.

[4] Oppenheim (–Lauterpacht) (6th ed., revised), ii, sections 56, 74 sqq.; Wheaton (–Keith), *International Law* (7th ed., 1944), ii.99.

[5] See, generally, Tansill, 38 *L.Q.R.* (1922), 26.

when belligerents drift into a state of peace. This can occur only on rare occasions, because the differences between war and peace are too great to allow an informal change at an undefinable moment.[1] Very strong evidence will have to be available before the termination of war in such a way can be affirmed.

In the case of Germany there is an outstanding fact which makes it difficult to think that the war is continuing. The Government of Germany is composed of the British, United States, Soviet, and French Commanders-in-Chief. Can the United Kingdom really be at war with a State whose Government included Field-Marshal Lord Montgomery and Sir Sholto Douglas, Marshal of the Royal Air Force, and supreme authority over whom has been assumed by this country jointly with its principal Allies?

## IX

The following are the principal conclusions which are submitted:

(1) Germany is not at present under belligerent occupation in the legal sense of the term.

(2) The four Powers have not assumed territorial sovereignty over Germany as a whole or their respective zones of occupation.

(3) The four Governments have jointly assumed governmental sovereignty 'with respect to Germany'. They have reserved to themselves supreme authority over Germany's external affairs, but have delegated the exercise of 'supreme authority in Germany' to the four Commanders-in-Chief.

(4) Although each of the Commanders-in-Chief is the delegate of the four Governments because he exercises their authority rather than that of his own Government, he is subject not to their control, but to the instructions of his own Government. Nor is he subject to the Control Council, whose authority extends only to matters affecting Germany as a whole.

(5) Germany has ceased to be an independent sovereign State in the sense of international law, but continues to be a State.

(6) The Government of Germany consists of the Control

---

[1] See, in particular, Hyde, *International Law* (2nd ed., 1945), iii.2385 sqq.

Council in matters affecting Germany as a whole, and of the four Commanders-in-Chief in their respective zones of occupation. Such Government exercises authority 'in Germany' only.

(7) Since the British Commander-in-Chief represents in his zone the Government of Germany, British administration in the British Zone of Occupation, though subject to the instructions of the British Government and, internally, to English law, constitutes a co-ordinated part of the Government of Germany.

(8) The state of war (in the sense of international law) between this country and Germany (probably) came to an end on 5 June 1945.

# XXI

## GERMANY'S PRESENT LEGAL STATUS REVISITED*

### I

TWENTY years ago, on 5 March 1947, the Grotius Society, one of this Institute's component societies, listened to a lecture on the then legal status of Germany.[1] It was the early fruit, conceived during service in the British delegation to the Allied Control Council in Berlin, of a harvest which in Germany was to assume enormous proportions,[2] but in England, as in most other countries, produced a crop of moderate size only.[3] In fact, outside Germany, the field has been left fallow for a very long time, although today some of the problems are as vivid as ever. Hence the practical interest persists. Even if, by the time of their publication, the following remarks should be overtaken by events, the effort would not be wasted, for Germany provides a pre-eminent illustration and stimulates discussion of a multitude of legal questions of a general character. Nor can the academic writer's responsibility towards his subject be shirked by invoking more recent professional involvement with it.[4] On

---

\* From *International and Comparative Law Quarterly* (1967), 760.

[1] Above, p. 634. In German: *Süddeutsche Juristenzeitung* (1947), 463.

[2] Some of the leading cases will be referred to below. It is almost impossible to collect all the decisions and all the academic writings which have appeared in the course of two decades. It must suffice to mention some of the more recent books which contain ample lists of earlier publications: Walther Freiherr Marschall von Bieberstein, *Zum Problem der völkerrechtlichen Anerkennung der beiden deutschen Regierungen* (1959); Gerhart Scheuer, *Die Rechtslage des geteilten Deutschlands* (1960); Rudolf Schuster, *Deutschlands Staatliche Existenz* (1963); Jens Hacker, *Die Rechtslage der Sowjetischen Besatzungszone* (1965); Dieter Blumenwitz, *Die Grundlagen eines Friedensvertrags mit Deutschland* (1966).

[3] The material is collected by Oppenheim, *International Law* (7th ed., by Lauterpacht, 1952), ii.604, 605. Add: Bathurst and Simpson, *Germany and the North Atlantic Community* (1956). Jennings, 'Government in Commission', *B.Y.I.L.* (1946), xxii.112, appeared after the publication mentioned in n. 1 above, and, therefore, could not be taken into account by it.

[4] The writer acted for the unsuccessful respondents in *Carl Zeiss Stiftung* v. *Rayner & Keeler and Others*, [1967] 1 A. C. 853. In that case the question was what effect

the contrary, it may be argued that this makes his duty even stronger.

In approaching the German problem it is necessary to state four guiding principles which must be carefully observed and which, to some extent, raise very general questions.

(1) It must, in the first place, be emphasized that lawyers have the paramount duty, as far as may humanly be possible, to discuss Germany from a strictly legal point of view. There are few topics in contemporary international affairs which more strongly require the lawyer to eliminate politics and policy and even legal policy from his mind, but which suffer more gravely from political overtones and invite political judgments. Most people are prepared to pass them, because they have political views. Even descriptions depend on political inclinations and preferences: the German Democratic Republic with or without inverted commas, the Soviet Zone of Occupation, and Eastern or Central Germany are terms which unfortunately, imply evaluations. The lawyer's sole salvation lies in resorting to law and evidence. Nor can or should his attitude be dependent upon the question whether, if he were a politician, he would like or dislike the result.

(2) The problem of Germany's legal status is primarily one of public international law. In Germany itself, it is true, the teachings of constitutional law may point the way. Thus the Basic Law of the Federal Republic makes it very clear that it is capable of being extended to German territories not at present under the Federal Republic's control.[1] Such provisions, as the Federal Supreme Court has put it,[2] impose upon the Federal Republic 'the responsibility for Germany as a whole'. Constitutional aspects of this type may be a piece of evidence of the public international law which it is proposed to ascertain, particularly as the Basic Law carries the blessing of the United States of America, France, and Great Britain. Similarly, the courts or the government of a particular State may have ex-

---

an English Court could give (a) to legislation enacted by the 'German Democratic Republic' through its 'Parliament', 'Government', and 'President' and (b) to a decision of the Supreme Court set up by that 'Republic', which differed from a decision of the Supreme Court of the Federal Republic on the very same point of German law arising between the very same parties.

[1] See Arts. 23, 123, 134, 135a, 146 and the Preamble.
[2] *BGHZ* 42, 99, at p. 105 (14 July 1964).

pressed certain views about the German problem, and these may even have found their way into legislative pronouncements. Yet from the point of view of public international law and its tribunals, the practice of one State is inconclusive. It may be expressive of the existing public international law on the point. It may, on the other hand, be so far removed from legal accuracy that it constitutes a violation rather than evidence of international law. In short, the inquiry that is being undertaken is concerned, not with municipal law, but with public international law.

(3) The most fruitful and, indeed, the only decisive sources of public international law relating to Germany are those treaties, declarations, or other international documents that have defined and explained Germany's present legal status, though, of course, other pieces of evidence, such as the views put forward in the speeches or writings of statesmen, should not be ignored. It would be inappropriate to formulate so platitudinous a postulate were it not for the fact that discussions about Germany have occasionally been characterized by a tendency of theorizing and of proclaiming axioms where reasoned interpretations of international documents would alone have been helpful. It is not *a priori* reasoning about the nature of a State, for instance, or about the effects of recognition or non-recognition that will throw light upon the German problem and its peculiarities. There is, therefore, no justification for the frequent *cri de cœur* that the German problem is incapable of being solved in a sense which may claim to be 'correct' in law and that, accordingly, lawyers should cease to discuss it. Such a counsel of despair overlooks both the practical need for a legally acceptable solution and the entirely pragmatic character of the relevant sources.

(4) Yet the public international law relating to Germany's status which is to be found in these sources is not necessarily the same in all countries. Some States may be parties to treaties and may thus have assumed obligations to which others may have refused to adhere. Or the granting of recognition by one State may involve consequences for it which do not affect such States as pursue a policy of withholding recognition.[1] It is

---

[1] Perhaps this is a convenient place to draw attention to the obvious fact that in relation to a State which does not recognize it a State or Government cannot have

possible, therefore, and cannot be described as contrary to law, that in the eyes of one State Germany's status is different from that accepted by another State. In the course of the following observations it will be attempted to define that status in terms of such international sources are as binding upon the Western world and, in particular, Great Britain.

I

Between 1945 and 1949 Germany's legal status was centred around the fundamental fact, established by the Declaration of Berlin of 5 June 1945, and apparently never doubted except perhaps in England in 1966,[1] that neither Germany as a whole nor any part of it[2] had, as a result of the surrender and the occupation, come under the sovereignty of another State, for the Four Governments expressly disclaimed any intention of annexation which in any event would have offended against one of the most firmly accepted principles of public international law.[3, 4]

They confined themselves to assuming 'supreme authority with respect to Germany'. This meant governmental authority, not a condominium, but a coimperium.

The Four Governments exercised it themselves in so far as Germany's external affairs were concerned. Thus, they entered into treaties with a number of neutral countries about German

any existence in law, whatever the factual position may be. In this sense recognition doubtless has constitutive effect. The point is made very clearly in the decision of the Federal Supreme Court, *BGHZ* 31, 374, at p. 383; also 28 *Int. L.R.* 82.

[1] See below, p. 692.

[2] No position is intended to be taken by this phrase in regard to the vexed question of the territories east of the Oder–Neisse line, which are dealt with in sections V and VIII of the Potsdam Agreement, Selected Documents, No. 13 (extracts only).

[3] See, e.g., O'Connell, *International Law*, i.501, 502, and Federal Supreme Court, *RzW* (1966), 367.

[4] For the proposition that German occupied territory did not come under the sovereignty of the occupant, see also Willmer J. (as he then was) in *Reederei und Bergungs A.G.* v. *S.S. Brighton*, [1951] 2 T. L. R. 409; *U.S. Military Government* v. *Ybarbo* (United States Military Government Court of Appeal) (1949), *Annual Digest*, 439; *Schaffner* v. *International Refugee Organization* (United States Military Government Court of Appeal) (1951), Int. L.R. 444; *Acheson* v. *Wohlimuth* (1952), 196 F. 2d 866.

property.[1] The treaty with Spain, in particular, recited that 'the powers and authority of the Government of the German Reich had been assumed by a Representation of the Allied Governments' and repeatedly referred to the Allied Powers as acting 'in the name of the Government of Germany'.[2]

'Supreme authority in Germany', however, was exercised by the Four Governments' respective Commanders-in-Chief, that is to say, through the four of them jointly forming the Allied Control Council in matters affecting Germany as a whole and through each of them individually in their respective zones of occupation.[3]

The Allied Control Council, though not a German Government, was the Government of Germany in matters affecting Germany as a whole, 'questions intéressant l'ensemble de l'Allemagne'. The clearest confirmation of this view was provided by the above-mentioned treaty with Spain which refers to 'whatever German Government succeeds the Allied Control Council for Germany in the government of Germany'.[4] It was open to the Control Council to take care of any matter and thus to make it one affecting Germany as a whole. But the proper interpretation of the Statement of Berlin of 5 June 1945 probably was that, even so long as this had not happened, a matter which *ratione materiae* affected Germany as a whole fell within the exclusive competence of the Control Council.[5] A final definition of such matters was never reached.[6] The suggestion, for instance, that the new Municipal Code introduced in the British Zone was not, but that the substitution in the French

---

[1] Agreement with Switzerland, Cmd. 6884; Agreement with Sweden, Cmd. 7241; Agreement with Spain, Cmd. 7558. On these Agreements see Mann, *B.Y.I.L.* (1946), xxiii.354; *B.Y.I.L.* (1947), xxiv.240; Simpson *B.Y.I.L.* (1958), xxxv.374.

[2] See, in particular, Art. 12.

[3] Statement of Berlin of 5 June 1945, Selected Documents, No. 9.

[4] Art. 15.

[5] For a helpful discussion of this problem, see Günther Jaenicke, *Der Abbau der Kontrollratsgesetzgebung* (1952), p. 23 et seq., who refers to earlier material, but takes a different view.

[6] The Federal Supreme Court had no difficulty in holding that, for such matters as the admissibility of appeals, Control Council legislation had the same quality as legislation of the Reich: *BGHZ* 1, 11; 21, 363. The word 'affecting' must certainly be given the wider of the meanings discussed in *Re Bluston*, [1966] 3 All E. R. 220. It is, of course, a word that has great significance in American constitutional law: see, e.g., *Schechter* v. *U.S.*, 295 U. S., 495 (1935).

Zone of the French for the German Civil Code would have been such a matter, did not come to be tested.

In their respective zones of occupation the Commanders-in-Chief exercised the joint authority of the Four Governments. None of the Governments had any direct and several authority at all. The Commanders-in-Chief were, in Professor Jennings' words, 'the instrumentalities, not of their own Governments, but of the four Allied Governments jointly'.[1] They were the Four Governments' delegates. They had, it is true, to exercise the authority so delegated to them in accordance with their respective Governments' instructions, but this did not make the Commanders-in-Chief their own Governments' agents.[2] If and in so far as a Commander-in-Chief exercised his governmental authority, the effect was limited to his zone. The point is attractively illustrated by a decision of the Federal Supreme Court[3]: in order to facilitate the smuggling of American coffee and cigarettes into West Berlin the Soviet authorities exempted the importers in the East from the payment of customs duty for these goods. In view of the merely zonal effect of the exemption the liability to customs duty arose when intermediaries imported the goods into West Berlin. In order to validate the exemption outside the Soviet Zone, the intervention of the Control Council would have been required.

As the Commanders-in-Chief, whether acting jointly or individually, constituted the Government of Germany, they had to exercise their authority with due regard to the necessities of the occupation and to the interests of the German nation towards whom they had duties which were frequently described as fiduciary in character. As the Supreme Restitution Court for the United States Zone put it,[4] 'the Allied Control Council and the Military Governments of the four zones are not organs solely of the occupying nations, but they

---

[1] *B.Y.I.L.* (1946), xxiii.116.

[2] For a contrary view, see Jaenicke (above, p. 664, n. 5), p. 28.

[3] (1953) N.J.W. 953 (19 March 1953).

[4] Court of Restitution Appeals Reports, I (1951), No. 60, p. 463 (25 January 1951), with references to earlier German material. Such views have frequently been expressed. See, for instance, Federal Supreme Court (Great Senate for Civil Matters), *BGHZ* 6, 208, at p. 209 (11 June 1952): 'The occupation Powers themselves, in so far as within Germany they have assumed legislative authority, exercise German legislative authority in a fiduciary capacity'; *BGHZ* 13, 165, at p. 294 (20 May 1954).

are fiduciary holders of the German sovereign power for the people'.

Because the Four Governments did not acquire sovereignty in Germany and because the four Commanders-in-Chief were the Government of Germany, their legislation was German legislation.[1] Their acts were not subject to such review as according to the law of their respective home countries would have been possible in regard to acts done by them in their national capacity. Thus, the French Conseil d'Etat denied the liability of the French State for acts of the Office for External Commerce set up by the French Commander-in-Chief. He 'must be regarded as exercising a function appertaining to the Government of Germany. He does not in that matter act as a public authority of the French State.'[2] Similarly, a court set up by the Commander-in-Chief, such as a Military Government Court, was a German Court, except in so far as it had jurisdiction over (military or civilian) members of the occupation forces.[3] Thus, a German convicted by a United States Court in the United States Zone was, contrary to the views of the Federal Supreme Court,[4]

---

[1] This also applies to occupation law enacted before 5 June 1945. Curiously enough, this was badly misunderstood in the United States, where it was held that such legislation as Law No. 53 was binding on the U.S. Court 'as an expression of the dominant policy of the United States' and that a violation could not be validated in 1953 by the Government of the Federal Republic: Re Muller, 104 N. Y. Supp. 2d 133 (1951); Re Meyer (1951) 107 Cal. App. 2d 799, 238 P. 2d 597; Callwood v. Virgin Islands National Bank, 121 F. Supp. 2d 379 (1954). About and against these cases, Bavarian Supreme Court (1953) NJW 944 (28 November 1952), and many writers, in particular, Domke, American-German Private International Law (1956), pp. 42, 43.

[2] 29 June 1951, S. (1951), 3.107, or Int. L.R. (1951), 573.

[3] This, it is believed, is the true significance of the decision of the Supreme Court of the United States, in Madson v. Kinsella, 343 U. S. 341 (1952); also Int. L.R. (1952), 602. The problems relating to the (internal) law of the occupation forces were in practice very considerable, but led to little discussion. See, however, above, pp. 636, 637.

[4] See, e.g., Federal Supreme Court, BGHStr. 5, 370 (5 March 1954); also Int. L.R. (1954), 479; JZ (1954), 614 (21 May 1954); also Int. L.R. (1954), 480; Court of Appeal, Hamburg N.J.W. (1954), 1697 (19 August 1954); also Int. L.R. (1954), 482. The German Courts held, therefore, that ne bis in idem did not apply or that a higher penalty for recidivism was not possible, if there was an earlier conviction by a Military Government Court. On the other hand, in a fundamental decision the European Commission for Human Rights at Strasbourg held that the Supreme Restitution Court at Nürnberg was not a German court: Yearbook of the European Convention on Human Rights, ii.256; 25 Int. L.R. 190, on which see Pinto, Les Organisations Européennes (1963), p. 166; Golsong, 110 Recueil des cours (1963 iii), 99 et seq.; Vasak, La Convention Européenne des Droits de l'Homme (Paris 1964),

convicted by a court of Germany and could not, for this reason, apply in the United States for a writ of habeas corpus.[1]

Commanders-in-Chief were at liberty, in the exercise of their supreme governmental authority, to appoint Germans for the purpose of enacting legislation in limited fields as directed or authorized by them. Such delegated legislation of which there are innumerable examples is *a fortiori* German in character and, therefore, is disentitled to the privileges which attached to occupation law *stricto sensu*.[2] But since, under the Statement of Berlin, each Commander-in-Chief himself only had the powers delegated to him by the Four Governments[3] and did not, on behalf of his own Government, have sovereign rights over his zone, there could be no question of any right to transfer his responsibilities or his rights as a whole; in the absence of the Four Governments' consent this would have been *ultra vires* a Commander-in-Chief. *Delegatus delegare non potest.* Moreover, such transfer would have been a matter affecting Germany as a whole. Just as the Congress of the United States 'is not permitted to abdicate or transfer to others the essential legislative function with which it is . . . vested' except to the extent of 'leaving to selected instrumentalities the making of subordinate

---

pp. 100–3. See also *Yearbook* i.167–9. The facts of the case disclosed a disturbing miscarriage of justice. It is regrettable that neither the Federal nor the U.S. Government saw fit to display a measure of generosity.

[1] *Flick* v. *Johnson*, 174 F. 2d 983 (1949), cert. den. 338 U.S. 879 (1949), where the United States Military Tribunal at Nürnberg which had convicted Flick was, however, (wrongly) described as an international tribunal; in truth, it was part of the judicial organization in Germany, though not a German Court.

[2] Occupation law *stricto sensu* was in a different category in that (a) much of it could not be freely amended or rescinded by the German legislator; (b) its reconcilability with the Basic Law could not be judicially discussed; and (c) even if it was contrary to constitutional provisions its validity had to be accepted. These privileges did not attach to what what was sometimes called 'concealed occupation law', i.e., law enacted by Germans, but directed, authorized, or at least tolerated by the occupation authorities. The problem of delimitation arose only where the content of the German legislation was completely prescribed by the occupation authorities. It was solved by reference to the purely formal question of the identity of the authority from which it emanated. See the two great decisions of the Federal Constitutional Court, *BVerfG* 2, 181, at pp. 199 et seq. (18 March 1953); 4, 74, at pp. 89–90; also *NJW* 17 (1955) (21 October 1954). On the problem, see Maier, *Juristenzeitung* (1953), p. 367, among many others. On this problem and, generally, on occupation law, see the material collected by Münch, 22 *ZaöVR* (1962), 729, at pp. 747 et seq.

[3] Above, p. 665.

rules within prescribed limits',[1] or just as 'trustees have no right to shift their duty on other persons, and if they do so, they remain subject to responsibility',[2] while they can, of course, delegate defined ministerial duties, or just as directors of a corporation cannot transfer their discretion as a board, so the Commander-in-Chief could not wash his hands of his zone. Sub-delegation was permitted to him only if, in the words of Cardozo J., the delegated discretion was 'not unconfined and vagrant' but 'canalized within banks that keep it from overflowing'.[3]

The underlying idea of all these complicated arrangements undoubtedly was that Germany as a State, though not as a sovereign State,[4] continued to exist, and that it remained a single, unitary State, though it was governed by five different governmental authorities. This came to be the almost unanimous view both in and outside Germany, both of judicial practice[5] and academic writers.[6]

The Hague Regulations were clearly applicable in Germany during the period up to 5 June 1945.[7] The question whether they were applicable after that date was in Germany answered

---

[1] Chief Justice Hughes in the leading case of *Schechter Poultry Corporation* v. *United States*, 295 U. S. 495 (1935), at pp. 529, 530. See also, among numerous other cases, *U.S.* v. *Shreveport Grain & Elevator Co.*, 287 U. S. 45 (1932).

[2] *Turner* v. *Corney* (1841) 5 Beav. 517, per Lord Langdale. See, generally, Lewin on *Trusts* (16th ed., 1964), pp. 174 et seq., and see p. 180: 'If the trust be of a discretionary character, not only is the trustee answerable for all the mischievous consequences of the delegation, but the exercise of the discretion by the substitute will be void.'

[3] *Panama Ref. Co.* v. *Ryan*, 293 U. S. 388 (1934), at p. 440.

[4] Federal Supreme Court (Great Senate for Civil Matters), *BGHZ* 13, 265, at p. 294 (20 May 1954). It could not be a sovereign State, seeing that it had a government imposed by the Allies and lacked control over its foreign affairs.

[5] *R.* v. *Bottrill, ex parte Kuechenmeister*, [1947] 1 K. B. 41; Supreme Court for the British Zone, *OGHZ* 2, 379; Federal Constitutional Court, *BVerfG* 3, 288, at p. 319 (26 February 1954), and numerous other decisions, some of which relate to the period after September 1949, but comprise the period 1945–9: below, p. 680, n. 4. One of the outstanding landmarks was the very early decision of the Court of Appeal, Zürich (1 December 1945) (1946), *Schweizerische Juristenzeitung*, 89; also *Annual Digest* (1946), 187.

[6] The most comprehensive work which appeared prior to 1949 was Stödter, *Deutschlands Rechtslage* (1948). In the sense of the text, e.g., Oppenheim, op. cit. (8th ed., by Lauterpacht, 1955), i.568. For a collection of non-German material, see Meister, 13 *ZaöVR* (1950–51), 123.

[7] *BGHZ* 5, 124; also Int. L.R. (1952), 621.

in the affirmative, but the reaons for an answer in the opposite sense were compelling.[1]

While in the sense of English municipal law the war ended only on 9 July 1951,[2] there was room for the suggestion that the war in the sense of international law terminated on 5 June 1945, with the result, for instance, that as from that date 'the belligerents' jurisdiction in prize has come to an end'. Yet it is an extraordinary fact that the Crown continued until 1949 to apply for and obtain the condemnation of German vessels. As Lord Merriman said on 10 May 1951, when delivering judgment in *The Hermes*[3]:

> To complete this curious story it only remains to mention that in the course of the argument the ex-Attorney-General[4] admitted for the first time on behalf of the Crown that by virtue of the Declaration relating to the unconditional surrender of Germany dated 5 June 1945, . . . it was impossible to assert that the right to seize German property in prize subsisted after that date, for the simple and sufficient reason . . . that the assumption of the government of Germany by all the Allied Powers upon the unconditional surrender of Germany . . . was quite inconsistent with any right thereafter of one belligerent Ally to seize any of such shipping in prize.

## III

The legal structure created in 1945 became impracticable in the course of 1947, when in numerous respects the Soviet

---

[1] This answer, supported by Oppenheim, *International Law* (7th ed., by Lauterpacht, 1952), ii.602, was in fact given by the United States Military Tribunal at Nuremberg in *Re Altstötter* (Justices Trial), *Annual Digest* (1947), 278, and in *Re Weizsäcker* (Ministries Trial), *Annual Digest* (1949), 344, at pp. 358, 359, and by the Control Commission Court of Criminal Appeal for the British Zone in *Grahame* v. *Director of Prosecutions*, *Annual Digest* (1947), 228, and in *Dalldorf* v. *Director o¹ Prosecutions*, *Annual Digest* (1949), 435. As to German Courts, see Hahn, 14 *ZaöRV* (1951–2), 271, at pp. 283, 284. The leading case is the decision of the Federal Supreme Court, *NJW* 222 (1957); also (in part) Int. L.R. (1956), 795; a divorce decree pronounced by a lawyer who had been appointed by a Soviet officer was recognized, because the appointment came within the provisions of the Hague Regulations. Also Supreme Court, 2 February 1952, *Betriebsberater* (1952), 157; 11 October 1951, *L.M.*, Art. 3, *AHKG* 13.

[2] See the Proclamation printed in *Re Grotrian*, [1955] Ch. 501. See, generally, Mosler and Doehring, *Die Beendigung des Kriegszustands mit Deutschland nach dem zweiten Weltkrieg* (1963).

[3] (1940–57) 1 Ll. P. C. (2nd) 289. The decision is also reported [1951] P. 347 and elsewhere, but the passage quoted in the text, the earlier history of the case and the practice of the Prize Court are fully reported only in *Lloyd's Prize Cases*. Lord Merriman's decision was affirmed by the Privy Council, *sub nom. Schiffahrt-Treuhand G.m.b.H.* v. *H.M. Procurator-General*, [1953] A. C. 232, where the point is very shortly referred to at p. 257. But see Oppenheim (above, n. 1), at p. 602.

[4] Sir Hartley Shawcross, K.C. (as he then was).

Union failed to implement the Potsdam Agreement of 2 August 1945.[1] The most serious breach, among many others,[2] was the refusal to treat Germany 'as a single economic unit'.[3] The legal arrangements of 1945 were finally paralysed when on 20 March 1948, the Soviet Commander-in-Chief walked out of the Allied Control Council which never reassembled and therefore ceased to be an effective Government of Germany. After many months of preparatory work[4] the vacuum was filled by the creation of the Federal Republic of Germany on 21 September 1949, and of the so-called 'German Democratic Republic' on 7 October 1949.

The creation of both republics was, it is submitted, *prima facie* contrary to the arrangements made in 1945 by the Four Governments, unless these could be said to have been repudiated by Soviet violations. The principal reasons are that no Commander-in-Chief could transfer his authority and that there can be no plainer case of a matter affecting Germany as a whole, and thus subject to the joint control of the Four Governments, than the establishment of two republics. It is, however, unnecessary to pursue these obvious points in detail, for by 1955, a clearly defined pattern became discernible.

(1) The Federal Republic at first remained subject to an Occupation Statute which also entered into force on 21 September 1949, and provided for a measure of control by an Allied High Commission consisting of High Commissioners appointed by the three Western Allies.[5] The Occupation Statute came to an end on 5 May 1955 when the five Conventions concluded in Bonn on 26 May 1952, and in Paris on 23 October 1954, took effect.[6] The second of them, viz., the Convention on Relations between the Three Powers and the Federal Republic of Germany, defined the latter's status. The Three Powers declared that the Federal Republic shall have

---

[1] The text can be found, for instance, in Selected Documents, p. 49.

[2] They are referred to in the famous speech made by Mr. James Byrnes at Stuttgart on 6 September 1946; Selected Documents, No. 19. There are, however, numerous other sources.

[3] This particular obligation is laid down in section II (14).

[4] During this period, it will be remembered, there occurred the blockade of Berlin and the Berlin air-lift: Selected Documents, pp. 4, 5.

[5] Cmd. 7677. It was subsequently revised on many occasions, beginning with Cmd. 8252. The text is also printed in 14 $\mathcal{Z}a\ddot{o}VR$ (1951–2), 153.

[6] Cmd. 9368.

'the full authority of a sovereign State over its internal and external affairs'.[1] The Three Powers, however, retained 'the rights and the responsibilities heretofore exercised or held by them relating to Berlin and to Germany as a whole, including the reunification of Germany and a peace settlement',[2] although they undertook to consult with the Federal Republic on these problems.[3]

In due course, the majority of nations[4] recognized the Federal Republic and established diplomatic relations with it. In particular, the Soviet Union did so on 13 September 1955,[5] though the other member States of the Communist *bloc* (except Roumania, which followed the Soviet example early in 1967) have up to the present refused to follow.[6]

The effect of the Soviet recognition was not only retrospective to 1949, but also involved the ratification and validation of the action taken in 1949 by the Western Allies in creating the Federal Republic. Accordingly, the question of the original legality or illegality of this action is no longer useful.

(2) The position in the East is entirely different. The Soviet Union, it is true, transferred to the 'German Democratic Republic' immediately upon its formation 'the function of administration which hitherto belonged to the Soviet Administration', and brought a Soviet Control Commission into being.[7] It allegedly did not exercise control over legislative or administrative activities or over foreign affairs, but its functions were confined to certain duties of a supervisory character.

On 25 March 1954 the Soviet Union established 'the same relations with the German Democratic Republic as with other sovereign States' and henceforth retained only limited rights relating to security.[8] On paper, even the last-mentioned restriction disappeared on 20 September 1955 when Soviet forces in Germany were left with the sole function of controlling traffic to and from Berlin.[9] It is said, however, that in fact many Soviet divisions are stationed in East Germany.

While the countries of the Communist *bloc* recognized the

---

[1] Art. 1 (2).    [2] Art. 2.    [3] Arts. 6 (1) and 7 (4).
[4] By the end of 1961 the number was 92: Jurina, 23 *ZaöVR* (1963), 455.
[5] Selected Documents, pp. 224–6.
[6] See, e.g., Marschall von Bieberstein (above, p. 660, n. 2), p. 193.
[7] Selected Documents, Nos. 37, 40.    [8] ibid., No. 66.
[9] ibid., Nos. 85 and 86.

'German Democratic Republic' from 1949 onwards,[1] neither the United States of America nor France nor Great Britain granted any kind of recognition. Indeed, the policy of non-recognition was not only reaffirmed on many occasions, but, as will appear later,[2] is also likely to have become a treaty obligation, in that the Western Allies agreed to consider the Federal Government 'as the only German Government freely and legitimately constituted and therefore entitled to speak for Germany as the representative of the German people in international affairs'; an agreement in these terms does seem to prohibit the recognition of another German Government. Moreover, the Three Powers agreed with the Federal Republic that they would 'co-operate to achieve, by peaceful means, their common aim of a reunified Germany'.[3] Such an aim, so it may be said, would be stultified by, and therefore probably precludes, the recognition of the 'German Democratic Republic'.[4] The reasons for non-recognition are not in doubt. The creation of the 'German Democratic Republic' in 1949 and the transfer to it of the Soviet Commander-in-Chief's rights and powers was a breach of the Soviet Union's obligations and was invalid under the arrangements of 1945[5] and, therefore, engaged its responsibility in public international law, the release from which was at no time contemplated by the Three Powers. Moreover, the latter expressed grave doubt whether, politically, the 'German

---

[1] Marschall von Bieberstein (above, p. 660, n. 2), p. 174.

[2] Below, p. 683, n. 4.

[3] Art. 7 (2) of the Convention on Relations between the Three Powers and the Federal Republic (Cmd. 9368).

[4] The Federal Republic has frequently claimed that there are additional sources of the Allies' legal obligation to ensure the reunification of Germany and therefore, for instance, to refrain from recognizing the 'German Democratic Republic'. See the material collected by Steinberger, 18 *ZaöVR* (1958), 732; Bräutigam, 20 ibid. (1960), 120, at p. 121. This assertion rests mainly on the terms of the Directive of the Heads of Government of the Four Powers of 23 July 1955 (Selected Documents, No. 80), and the Berlin Declaration of the Foreign Ministers of 29 July 1957 (Selected Documents, No. 109). In both documents there is a reference to reunification being the 'joint responsibility' of the Four Powers who in 1945 assumed supreme command. These and similar statements may be material for purposes of interpretation, but it is doubtful whether any independent legal duty can be founded upon them. They seem to have primarily a political character. It would be in line with normal British policy in the circumstances to grant recognition, as appears from Mr. Morrison's statement in 1951 which, in the *Carl Zeiss* case, Lord Reid, at p. 906, considered relevant. Hence non-recognition by Britain is likely to rest upon special circumstances such as treaty obligation.

[5] Above, p. 667.

Democratic Republic' enjoyed any independence at all.[1] Finally, there may be an argument, strongly put forward in the Federal Republic but probably lacking persuasiveness, that some of the legal prerequisites of recognition are missing.[2] The refusal to recognize the 'German Democratic Republic,' de jure or de facto, has been expressed by the West on many occasions and in many ways. The Federal Republic repeatedly made it clear that it regarded the recognition of the Eastern régime as an unfriendly act.[3] In pursuance of its policy of non-recognition the United Kingdom has stated that it refuses to recognize the purported accession of the 'German Democratic Republic' to the Geneva Convention for the Protection of War Victims[4] or to accept the Soviet notification of the signature of the Nuclear Test Ban Treaty by the East German régime[5]; that it refuses to accept a Note addressed to it[6] or a passport

[1] This is not a legal point, but is one which the Western Powers were entitled to, and did, take. Thus, the British Government's view is that the 'German Democratic Republic' lacks 'the characteristics of an independent State': Hansard (House of Commons), vol. 584, col. 26 (10 March 1958); also E. Lauterpacht 7 I.C.L.Q. (1958), 522.

[2] The following are the principal reasons which are given in support of the suggestion that there is no organization in the East which fulfils the prerequisites of a State: (1) There is no autochthonous people in the East, because the vast majority consider themselves Germans rather than East Germans and would wish to escape to or to join with the Federal Republic were they not prevented by force, such as the Berlin Wall, from doing so. (2) The existence of a State would constitute an unlawful intervention in the affairs of the Federal Republic as representing Germany (see below, p. 683). (3) There can be no State so long as the East has had no opportunity of exercising its inherent and fundamental right of self-determination. (4) A State could not have been created by the Soviet Union, because a belligerent occupant or even the Powers in occupation under the 1945 arrangements would have committed an unquestionable international wrong in doing so (above, p. 663); in this sense, in particular, Münch, in Gibt es Zwei Deutsche Staaten? (1963), p. 30. The Federal Republic has since its inception adopted all or any of these arguments and its pronouncements are collected in the most useful annual reports which are referred to below, p. 681, n. 3. The literature is collected in the works referred above, p. 660, n. 2 and is so vast as to make it invidious to mention individual contributions.

[3] For references, see 21 ZaöVR (1961), 286; 23 ZaöVR (1963), 381; 26 ZaöVR (1966), 152, at p. 154.

[4] E. Lauterpacht, 'U.K. Contemporary Practice', 8 I.C.L.Q. (1959), 159.

[5] Hansard (House of Commons), vol. 684, col. 1 (13 November 1963); also E. Lauterpacht British Practice in International Law (1963), p. 90. The reason given was that 'they do not recognize the Soviet Zone as a State or as an entity possessing national sovereignty or recognize the local authorities as a government'.

[6] Hansard (House of Commons), vol. 597, col. 5 (8 December 1958); also E. Lauterpacht, above, n. 4, at pp. 158, 159.

issued by the so-called German Democratic Republic.[1] As recently as 19 November 1964, the Prime Minister (Mr. Harold Wilson) declared that 'as the British Government do not recognize the East German authorities, we cannot receive official communications from them.'[2]

Being unrecognized, the 'German Democratic Republic' is not a member of any international organization or a party to a treaty which the West has signed. Where, for practical reasons, it became necessary or advisable to associate the 'German Democratic Republic' with a multilateral treaty, special arrangements were made or appropriate reservations were carefully formulated to eliminate any impression of recognition.[3]

The clear conclusion in Western countries is that, in the absence of recognition, the 'German Democratic Republic' does not in law exist. (From a factual point of view this, of course, is a fiction, for in fact the 'German Democratic Republic' undoubtedly is in control, but it is a fiction of a type which is well known to the law and arises whenever the law imposes the sanction of nullity.) At least the 'German Democratic Republic' does not exist as a State, 'as an entity possessing national sovereignty'. Nor does the West recognize even 'the local authorities as a government'.[4] Does the 'German Democratic Republic' perhaps exist as a 'subordinate body which the U.S.S.R. set up to act on its behalf'? That this is so

---

[1] E. Lauterpacht, *British Practice in International Law* (1964), p. 27; see also p. 26.

[2] *Hansard* (House of Commons), vol. 702, col. 89; Lauterpacht, *British Practice in International Law* (1964), p. 139.

[3] These developments require a monograph. All that can be done here is to refer the reader to some material. Berne Convention for the Protection of Literary and Artistic Work: Pinto, Clunet (1959), 307 et seq. Convention for the Protection of Industrial Property: ibid, at pp. 411, 412; Federal Supreme Court, *BGHZ* 31, 344 (18 December 1959); also 28 Int. L.R. 82. International Railway Conventions: Pinto, op. cit., at pp. 415–19; Mosler, 19 *ZaöVR* (1958), 275 et seq., 299, 300. Warsaw Convention of 1929: E. Lauterpacht, 7 *I.C.L.Q.* (1958), 523. Geneva Conventions of 1949: Pinto, op. cit., at pp. 420, 421; E. Lauterpacht, 8 *I.C.L.Q.* (1959), 159. International Labour Office: 23 *ZaöVR* (1963), 302. Atomic weapons: 25 ibid. (1965), 333 et seq. International air traffic: 26 ibid. (1966), 152–4. Nuclear Test Ban Treaty: 26 ibid. (1966), 153; Schwelb, *A.J.I.L.* (1964), 654 et seq.; E. Lauterpacht, *British Practice in International Law* (1963), 90.

[4] Above, p. 673, n. 5. A little earlier the same formula was employed by Secretary of State Dean Rusk: see Schwelb, *A.J.I.L.* (1964), 655. It is noteworthy that the three Western Allies have gone so far as to state that they 'do not recognize the East German régime nor the existence of a State in the Soviet Zone': Selected Documents, No. 87 (28 September 1955); Lauterpacht, *British Practice in International Law* (1964), 276 (26 June 1964).

is the proposition recently enunciated in England.[1] Thus, the question arises whether such an analysis is acceptable to the public international lawyer and, if so, whether it is capable of producing legally useful results.

(a) The Soviet Union, so the argument runs, was and continues to be 'the *de jure* sovereign' or the '*de jure* sovereign governing authority'[2] in the Soviet Zone. Such sovereignty is recognized by Britain. It enabled the Soviet Union to set up the 'German Democratic Republic' as 'a dependent or subordinate organization through which the U.S.S.R. is entitled to exercise indirect rule'.[3] From this it is said to follow that the English Courts 'must regard the acts of the German Democratic Republic, its government organs and officers as acts done with the consent of the U.S.S.R. as the government entitled to exercise governing authority'.[4,5]

[1] By the House of Lords in *Carl Zeiss Stiftung* v. *Rayner & Keeler*, [1967] 1 A. C. 853, and, subsequently, with an essential qualification by the British Government in *Hansard* (House of Commons), vol. 735, col. 203 (7 November 1966). The words quoted in the preceding sentence were used by Lord Reid at p. 906.

[2] Lord Reid, at pp. 905, 906.　　　　[3] Lord Reid, at p. 904.

[4] Lord Reid, at p. 906. The whole of the reasoning by Lord Reid, with whom Lords Hodson, Guest, and Upjohn agreed and whom, in effect, Lord Wilberforce followed, is derived from a single sentence in the Foreign Office Certificate: 'Since that time (i.e. 1945) and up to the present date Her Majesty's Government have recognized the State and Government of the Union of Soviet Socialist Republics as *de jure* entitled to exercise governing authority in respect of the zone.' There cannot at any time or place have been a case in which the interpretations read into and the inferences drawn from a single sentence in a Certificate were so far-reaching and at the same time so diametrically opposed to what may safely be assumed to have been Her Majesty's Government's real intentions. What the Foreign Office intended to say was probably something on the following lines: 'If the Soviet Union (or rather its Commander-in-Chief) had at any time after 1949 exercised or purported to exercise or claimed the supreme authority in its zone which it acquired in 1945 to the extent then defined and never enlarged, Her Majesty's Government would consider it as being *de jure* entitled so to do.' The Certificate, duly interpreted, would continue as follows: 'In 1949, however, the Soviet Union ceased to exercise governmental control over its zone, though it retained its political influence, and set up the "German Democratic Republic" which it treats and which purports to act as a sovereign State. This was beyond the powers of the U.S.S.R. and a breach of its treaty obligations, for which it is held responsible. Her Majesty's Government does not recognize the "German Democratic Republic" as a State, government, local authority or régime. Nor does Her Majesty's Government recognize the U.S.S.R. as the governing authority, because the Soviet Union does not in fact govern in, but has withdrawn from the government of the zone.'

[5] It is hoped that it will not be thought cynical if the question is asked whether between 1949 and 1955 the Soviet Union was and at the present time Czechoslovakia (which does not recognize the Federal Republic) is bound to regard the

It was allegedly Mr. John Foster Dulles who first described the relationship between the 'German Democratic Republic' and the Soviet Union as one of agency[1] and thus resumed Mr. Dean Acheson's earlier characterization of the 'German Democratic Republic' as 'a subservient and controlled government, since its actions will be dictated behind the scenes, not by the people of the Soviet Zone, but by the Communist Party directed from Moscow'.[2] But these are political phrases, and the Soviet Union's undoubted political control over East Germany (as over the whole Communist *bloc*) is without relevance in the present context. If such phrases are to be transposed to the legal realm, then this appears to require no less than three fictions, with the result that, as it has been put in a few pregnant and illuminating words, the picture becomes contrary to 'whatever may be thought to be common knowledge on this point.'[3] Even so, however, the effects of nonrecognition cannot be cured.

First, the Soviet Union is deemed to be entitled to set up the 'German Democratic Republic' as a subordinate organization[4]; in truth, the Soviet Union has no sovereignty but only limited rights in the zone and these do not include the Commander-in Chief's authority to abdicate and to transfer the

acts of the Federal Republic as done with the consent of the Three Western Powers.

[1] Scheuer (above, p. 660, n. 2), at p. 169.

[2] Selected Documents, No. 39 (12 October 1949). Occasionally mere political control has, somewhat rhetorically, been described as tantamount to effective control. Thus, on 6 December 1963, the Permanent Representatives to the United Nations of France, the United Kingdom, and the United States of America declared: 'East Germany is merely an occupied portion of German territory. The so-called "German Democratic Republic" in East Germany is a régime imposed upon and not chosen by the population': see E. Lauterpacht, *British Practice in International Law* (1963), p. 71. At about the same time the Federal Republic stated: 'The Soviet Zone of Occupation is not a State, but a part of Germany where the Soviet Union by military force and with the assistance of the Socialist Union Party which is dependent on it wields in fact power': see Schwelb, *A.J.I.L.* (1964), 642, at p. 657.

[3] These 11 words out of a total of some 37,000 were spoken in the *Zeiss* case by Lord Upjohn, at p. 941. Readers will not fail to ponder over their highly significant implications.

[4] The situation was thus treated as if a sovereign had granted independence to a dependency. This case is twice referred to by Lord Reid, at pp. 905, 906, but it is not clear whether it is his view that in such case a third State such as Britain would have to treat the new State, which, *ex hypothesi*, would be unrecognized, as a State clothed with sovereignty by its parent or at least as an organization of the parent. Neither alternative is likely to meet with support by international lawyers.

whole of his discretionary powers of government to another organization.[1,2] Secondly, the Soviet Union is deemed to have set up the 'German Democratic Republic' to be its subordinate organization; in truth, we know (and the argument is expressly stated to assume) 'that the U.S.S.R. did purport to confer independence on the "German Democratic Republic".'[3] Thirdly, the 'German Democratic Republic' is deemed to act as if it were a subordinate organ of the Soviet Union; in truth (and again the argument is said to assume it), that body 'does purport to act as if it were an independent State',[4] as, indeed, every one of its activities proves.[5]

(b) Where does all this lead? Let it be assumed that acts done by the 'German Democratic Republic' on its own behalf and by reference to its own sovereignty have to be treated as acts of the Soviet Union.[6] The effect is that the 'German Demo-

---

[1] Above, p. 667. Lord Reid, at p. 903, records that it 'was not argued that the matter which I am now considering is one affecting Germany as a whole'. In fact, this was argued. Cf. p. 865. What was expressly disclaimed was any suggestion to the effect that the creation of the Council of Gera as a local authority was a matter affecting Germany as a whole. See n. 2 below.

[2] At this point it is necessary to explain that the point discussed in the text was first formulated, not by the appellants, but by Lord Reid. It was put primarily in the form that the Council of Gera, which had been created by the legislation of the 'German Democratic Republic', was an organ of the U.S.S.R. It was this point which was intended to be met by the 'unduly formalistic' argument discussed by Lord Wilberforce, at p. 959. In fact, it was a point which, had there been evidence of specific delegation, was well known to the law of the German occupation: above, p. 667. On other, less frequent occasions, Lord Reid seemed to suggest that the whole of the 'German Democratic Republic' was a subordinate organization of the U.S.S.R. In the opinions delivered by the House of Lords this view formed the *ratio decidendi*, but the discussion during the argument did not always clearly differentiate.

[3] Lord Reid, at p. 900. He who sets up an (allegedly) independent State and government cannot be said to set up a subordinate organ.

[4] ibid. The third fiction is underlined by the fact that it was immaterial 'to know to what extent the U.S.S.R. in fact exercise their right of control' (Lord Reid, at p. 904). In other words, even if they do not exercise control at all, the 'German Democratic Republic' is their subordinate organization. This was an essential part of the reasoning, for, as Lord Reid says, at pp. 874, 904, the House did not think it necessary to obtain guidance on this point from the Foreign Office.

[5] Lord Reid, at p. 907, and Lord Upjohn, at p. 941, describe the 'German Democratic Republic' as a body set up by the U.S.S.R. to act 'on its behalf'. The inconsistency between this holding and the assumption 'that the U.S.S.R. did purport to confer independence on the "German Democratic Republic"' and that that body 'does purport to act as if it were an independent State' (p. 900, per Lord Reid) will not be missed.

[6] From the point of view of general law of agency this would not seem to be a

cratic Republic' enjoys exactly the same status as a State (and government) recognized *de jure*.[1] This is the point at which fiction must end and control must be taken by the paramount fact that, in the absence of recognition, the 'German Democratic Republic' is not a State and does not exist. It does not help, therefore, to describe it as an agent or subordinate organ of the Soviet Union or rather of its Commander-in-Chief; at the moment when that organ purports to act, not as such, but as an allegedly independent government on its own behalf and in the exercise of its own discretion, it acts as a State. To put it differently, the attribution of the acts of the 'German Democratic Republic', which does, but is not entitled to, act, to the Soviet Union, which does not, though it would be entitled to, act, must stop short at the point where it involves recognition of the German Democratic Republic. Her Majesty's Government 'cannot' accept a Note addressed to it by, or enter into governmental negotiations with, the 'German Democratic Republic'.[2] It would be intolerable if the Note had to be treated as written or authorized by the Soviet Union and, therefore, had to be accepted as if it emanated from a recognized State. As Her Majesty's Immigration Officer cannot, of course, recognize East German passports issued by the 'German Democratic Republic',[3] it would be a little incongruous if Her Majesty's judges, while adhering to their rule about the ineffectiveness of the legislation of unrecognized States,[4] could and, indeed, must look at laws issued by the same body. Whatever the Soviet Union could or might do, the overriding fact is that it is the 'German Democratic Republic' which purports to act as a sovereign. Every piece of legislation, every judicial decision, every executive act shows that it emanates,[5] not from

possible conception. An argument to this effect was addressed to the House (p. 871), but unlike others is not reflected in the opinions delivered.

[1] Lord Wilberforce, at p. 961, attempts to answer this point which is not mentioned in the other opinions. It is possible that the learned Lord merely restated his conclusions.

[2] See above, p. 673, n. 6.      [3] See above, p. 674, n. 1.

[4] It is very important to the proper understanding of the decision in the *Carl Zeiss* case that, for the time being, English Courts strictly follow this rule and that the scope of any exceptions is very doubtful: see below, p. 697, n. 1. If that rule had been abandoned, the point peculiar to the *Carl Zeiss* case would not have arisen.

[5] See the formulation of Roche J. in *Luther* v. *Sagor*, [1921] 1 K. B. 456, 473, which must still be regarded as persuasive.

Germany nor even from the Four Governments, nor from the Soviet Commander-in-Chief, but exclusively from the 'German Democratic Republic', a legally non-existing body purporting to exercise its own sovereignty. This it cannot at present do. If the basic reason of the doctrine of non-recognition is lack of independence of the 'State' in question, it is a paradoxical twist to allow it to produce results which are identical with those prevailing in case of recognition *de jure*, provided only the lack of independence is so complete as to involve subordination; non-recognition is thus deprived of its character of a sanction in the case in which this is most needed.[1] Is not 'a most deplorable result'[2] inherent in, and the very purpose of, the policy of non-recognition?

On 7 November 1966, Her Majesty's Government declared[3]:

> The East German authorities have been set up as a subordinate organization of the Government of the U.S.S.R.; but this in no way involves recognition by Her Majesty's Government of those authorities as a government *de jure* or *de facto*.

It is likely that by these words Her Majesty's Government subtly yet clearly dissociated itself from a legal theory of agency, and at the same time pointed to the reason why.

## IV

If, then, in the eyes of public international law as understood in England the Federal Republic has the full authority of a sovereign State, while the 'German Democratic Republic' does not exist at all, what has become of the Germany which came into being in 1871, survived the revolution of 1918 and the catastrophe of 1933, and continued to exist at least until September 1949? There are two possible answers.

Either Germany ceased to exist in 1949. In such event the Federal Republic would have emerged as a new State. It would have become the (partial) successor to Germany. The law relating to State succession would define its (limited) effect in

---

[1] The formulation of this point owes much to Professor R. Y. Jennings, to whom the author desires to express his gratitude.

[2] This description is used by Lord Upjohn in the *Carl Zeiss* case, at p. 940.

[3] *Hansard* (House of Commons), vol. 735, col. 204. The first part of the statement cannot readily be reconciled with the statements mentioned above, p. 673, n. 5, and p. 674, n. 4.

numerous spheres of State activity. The 'German Democratic Republic' would not even claim to have succeeded to Germany. For its so-called Supreme Court has decided that it is an entirely new organization which is neither identical with nor a successor to Germany, so that not even provinces, municipal authorities, or other administrative agencies are the same as those previously existing.[1] This is said to follow from an 'analysis of class-structure'.[2] Whether in East Germany or in this country it is permissible to disregard such explicit reasons of a decision, to treat them as a 'form of embellishment' or 'ornamentation' and to look 'behind' them for what are believed to be the true reasons[3] is a question which, however fascinating it may be, need not be pursued in the present context.

Or Germany continues to exist, because the Federal Republic is identical with it and thus continues its personality. It would make no practical difference of any kind if, in application of a novel conception, Germany were conceived as an entity distinct from the Federal Republic, but 'represented' by the latter's Government. Logically this is a possible method of ensuring the continuation of Germany's existence, but in its substantive effects it amounts to no more than a conceptualist play with words.

In the Federal Republic it has always and universally been accepted that Germany survived the events of 1949 and still exists as a State.[4] In addition, however, the continuation of Germany by the Federal Republic or the theory of identity, as it has come to be called, whether in its narrow sense or in the

---

[1] *Entscheidungen des Obersten Gerichts der Deutschen Demokratischen Republik in Zivilisachen*, 1, 236 (31 October 1951).

[2] Ibid., at pp. 240, 245.

[3] These are formulations and processes sanctioned by Lord Reid in the *Carl Zeiss* case, at p. 924.

[4] On this point (which, of course, leaves it open whether Germany exists as an entity distinct from or identical with the Federal Republic) see, among numerous other decisions Great Senate for Civil Matters, *BGHZ* 13, 292 (20 May 1954); Federal Supreme Court, *NJW* (1954), 1724 (21 June 1954); Federal Supreme Court, *BGHZ* 3, 308 (30 October 1951); also Int. L.R. (1951), p. 40; *BGHZ* 19, 259 (14 December 1955); 34, 134, at pp. 137, 139 (30 November 1960); *BGStr* 5, 317 (23 February 1954); also Int. L.R. (1954), 43; Federal Constitutional Court, *BVerfG* 2, 266, at pp. 288, 319, 320 (7 May 1953). In the case of *Carl Zeiss Stiftung* Lord Wilberforce, in this respect differing from his colleagues, stated (p. 955): 'The State of Germany remained (and remains) in existence.'

sense of representation, has met with almost general approval in the Federal Republic since before its inception. It dominates German doctrine which has subjected it to numerous variations, refinements, and reformulations.[1] It was officially adopted and proclaimed by the Federal Government as early as on 21 October 1949,[2] and has since been repeated on innumerable occasions by Ministers and officials, orally as well as in diplomatic documents of all kinds in Germany and outside,[3] particularly in the course of the Suez Conference of 1956[4] and of the Ottawa Conference of the Universal Postal Union in 1957.[5] It also forms the basis of many decisions rendered in the Federal Republic, including those of its highest courts.[6] Most

---

[1] See the literature referred to above, p. 660, n. 2, but see, in particular, the early yet fundamental contribution by Professor Scheuner, 'Die staatsrechtliche Kontinuität Deutschlands,' in *Deutsches Verwaltungsblatt* (1950), pp. 481, 514.

[2] Dr. Adenauer, 1. Bundestag, *StenBer* 308. There were many similar statements; some of them are collected by Marschall von Bieberstein (above, p. 660, n. 2), p. 135. Exactly the same statement was made in the course of the last declaration by Chancellor Kiesinger on 13 December 1966: *Europa-Archiv* (1967), D. 18.

[3] The most valuable and convenient source from which references to all the relevant material can be obtained is to be found in the summaries of the Federal Republic's international practice which appear from year to year in *ZaöVR*. For *1949–55*: Böhmer and Walter (1963), 23, 300, at p. 301, where the Federal Government adheres to the theory of identity; at pp. 304–8 the Federal Government's claim to the sole State organization of the German people is asserted. For *1956*: Steinberger (1958), 28, 731 et seq. For *1957*: Bräutigam (1960), 20, 120 et seq. For *1959:* Morvay (1961), 21, 259 et seq., at p. 286, where there is further material about the thesis of Germany's unity to be found. For *1960*: Bleckmann, ibid., at p. 329 et seq, 378, where the continued existence of Germany as an international person is asserted. For *1961*: Jurina, ibid., at p. 405 et seq. with an interesting Memorandum prepared in June 1961 by the German Foreign Office which repeats and develops the thesis and adds that the Basic Law of 1949 merely involved the reorganization of the German State and a change of name; at pp. 456, 457, the 'German Democratic Republic' is described, not as a State, but as 'an arbitrarily separated part of Germany'. For *1962*: Platz and Lörcher (1964), 24, 637, at p. 699: Germany continues to exist. For *1963*: Bothe (1965), 25, 223. The Federal Republic is alone authorized 'to represent Germany abroad': at pp. 327, 328. For *1964*: Buschbeck (1966), 26, 85, at p. 152, with a long list of statements to the effect that Germany continues to be a subject of international law.

[4] In the course of the Conference the Federal Republic made a formal statement to the effect that it continued the personality of the *Reich* and was, therefore, a signatory to the Convention of Constantinople of 29 October 1888. The French Foreign Minister expressly accepted this claim. No State represented at the Conference contradicted. For details, see Steinberger, 18 *ZaöVR* (1957–8), 731.

[5] See the Report by Bräutigam, 20 *ZaöVR* (1959–60), 125, at p. 134.

[6] The Federal Supreme Court adopted the theory of identity in *BGHZ* 3, 313 (30 October 1951) and has adhered to it ever since. See also Federal Finance Court, *BFH* 56, 324 (21 February 1952), and the Federal Constitutional Court, below, p. 682, n. 3. There are innumerable decisions to the same effect.

of these cases, it is true, involve problems of constitutional law, such as the question of the liability for Germany's debts,[1] and rest upon the terms and ideology of the Constitution of 1949.[2] But others are of a more general character. In particular, the Federal Constitutional Court, by the most authoritative pronouncement, established that treaties concluded by Germany continued in force so as to bind the Federal Republic,[3] the reason being that Germany and the Federal Republic were identical, though the latter's jurisdiction, as has invariably been accepted, 'was for the time being confined to part of German territory'. It must be added that on no single occasion has any Western government protested against or otherwise objected to the Federal Republic's claim. This is significant even outside the field of acquiescence or estoppel. It affords a valuable aid to the interpretation of such documents as fall to be considered.

As regards the attitude of the West in general and Britain in particular, we know that the claim to identity which originated in Germany was asserted within a month of the Federal Republic's birth by a Note addressed to the Allied High Com-

---

[1] The question of liability for the internal debts has, not surprisingly, given rise to much discussion. The question was never doubtful in regard to the debts of the *Reich*: the Federal Republic continues Germany and is, therefore, liable for its debts: see, for instance, the Federal Finance Court, above, p. 691, n. 6. On this problem, in general, see Feaux de la Croix, *Die Problematik der Reichsverbindlichkeiten* (1955). The liability for the debts of former organizations such as Prussia or of local authorities, etc., caused greater difficulty. It is in this connection that the idea of 'Funktionsnachfolge', of liability by virtue of functional succession, was developed: *BGHZ* 8, 169 (177); 10, 220; 16, 184; 19, 258. As to such organizations as the railways or the Post Office, see *BGHZ* 8, 174; *NJW* (1954), 1724. The whole problem is discussed in particular by Reinhard, 'Identität und Rechtsnachfolge', *NJW* (1952), 441, whose contribution was fundamental and who developed the idea of rendering continuity of purposes, organization, and property the test. See also Scheuner, 'Die Funktionsnachfolge und das Problem der staatsrechtlichen Kontinuität', *Festschrift für Nawiasky* (1956), pp. 9 et seq. Public international lawyers may find these discussions helpful in solving their own problems. The problem was eventually solved by legislation, i.e., by section 1 of the 'Allgemeine Kriegsfolgengesetz' of 5 November 1957, according to which, in principle, claims against the *Reich* were 'extinguished'. This principle and the exceptions to it were largely influenced by the analogy of the law of bankruptcy: *BVerfG* 15. 126 (14 November 1962).

[2] See, in particular, Arts. 134 and 135a of the Basic Law.

[3] *BVerfG* 6, 309, at pp. 338, 363, 366 (26 March 1957). See also 2, 266, at p. 277 (5 May 1953); 5, 85, at p. 126 (12 August 1956), where the Court said that in creating the Federal Republic it was merely intended 'to reorganize part of the unitary German State'.

mission.[1] The Allied Governments remained silent until 19 September 1950, when in New York they made the following formal statement[2]:

Pending the unification of Germany the Three Governments consider the Government of the Federal Republic as the only German Government freely and legitimately constituted and therefore entitled to speak for Germany as the representative of the German people in international affairs.

This statement was to have the unusual distinction that it was repeated by the Three Governments on no less than three occasions in 1955, 1964, and 1966,[3] and that in 1954 it was incorporated into treaties between the fourteen member States of the North Atlantic Treaty Organization and the Federal Republic,[4] and thus acquired contractual character.

The question thus arises whether and to what extent the

[1] This is reported by Ellinor von Puttkamer, 'Vorgeschichte und Zustandekommen der Pariser Verträge', 17 $Za\"oVR$ (1956–7), 448, at p. 465.

[2] The text has frequently been published: see, for instance, Selected Documents, No. 49.

[3] On 28 September 1955 (Selected Documents, No. 87), and on 26 June 1964 (E. Lauterpacht, *British Practice in International Law* (1964), 276, at p. 277; text also in 26 $Za\"oVR$ (1966), 159). According to a statement issued in Washington in 1964 the President of the United States and the German Federal Chancellor went much further in that they 'reaffirmed that until Germany is reunified only the freely elected and legitimately constituted Government of the Federal Republic of Germany and no one else can speak for the German people': 50 *Department of State Bulletin* (1964), 992, at p. 993 and 26 $Za\"oVR$ (1966), p. 158. On 16 March 1966 the Representatives of France, the United Kingdom, and the United States to the United Nations again reaffirmed the Declaration: 5 *Int. Legal Materials* (1966), 545.

[4] This occurred in the first place by the Final Act of the Nine-Power Conference held in London between 28 September and 3 October 1954 (Cmd. 9289), the decisions of which 'formed part of one general settlement'; the mutual Declarations are set forth in section V (pp. 10 and 11). On the contractual character of these arrangements, see Briggs, *A.J.I.L.* (1955), 148. The next step was a Conference of Ministers held in Paris between 20 and 23 October 1954 (Cmd. 9304), when the Federal Republic became a member of the North Atlantic Treaty Organization and the Council passed a Resolution noting the mutual Declarations of 3 October 1954 (p. 54). On the same occasion, Belgium, Canada, Denmark, France, Greece, Iceland, Italy, Luxembourg, Netherlands, Norway, Portugal, Turkey, the United Kingdom, and the United States of America, signed a Protocol to the North Atlantic Treaty (p. 56) reciting 'that all member governments have associated themselves with the declaration also made on 3 October 1954 by the Governments of the United States, the United Kingdom and the French Republic in connection with the aforesaid declaration of the Federal Republic'. On 14 May 1964 the Council of Ministers of NATO repeated the Declaration: Buschbeck, 26 $Za\"oVR$ (1966), 152, n. 328.

Declaration supports the Federal Republic's claim and what its meaning and effect is.[1] In an English Court this is a matter for determination by the Secretary of State for Foreign Affairs, for it concerns the status, quality, and character of a foreign sovereign and the scope of the recognition granted by Her Majesty's Government.[2] Where tribunals are bound or entitled to determine the point themselves, they will approach it as one involving the interpretation of a treaty[3]; accordingly, they will follow Professor Brierley's direction[4]:

There are no technical rules in international law for the interpretation of treaties; its object can only be to give effect to the intention of the parties as fully and fairly as possible. But lawyers who are trained in the methods of interpretation applied by an English Court should bear in mind that English draftsmanship tends to be more detailed than Continental, and it receives, and perhaps demands, a more literal interpretation. Similarly, diplomatic documents, including treaties, do not as a rule invite the very strict methods of interpretation that an English Court applies, for example, to an Act of Parliament.

The difficulty arises from the fact that the language of the Declaration of New York is unusual and inconclusive and that it would have been easy to express the theory of identity, if this had been desired, in simple and plain terms. Moreover, it is a remarkable and weighty fact that the formula of 1950, while it was frequently repeated with almost monotonous regularity, was never clarified, expanded, or refined. Were the Western Allies reluctant to commit themselves? Did they wish to leave doors open? Or were these thought to have been shut in 1950? Was clarification believed to be unnecessary? The answers are

---

[1] Apart from the fact that the Declaration would seem to preclude the other States which participated in the treaties of 1954 from recognizing any German Government other than the Federal Government. The first part of the Declaration, put into contractual terms, cannot have any other meaning.

[2] In the *Zeiss* case, a different view was taken by the House of Lords on the ground, stated by Lord Wilberforce, at p. 974, that the House was confronted with 'questions of law which it is the function of the courts to determine and which they are in a position to determine on the basis of the certificate previously given, the terms of which are sufficiently clear'. The House did not appreciate that a question of recognition rather than construction was involved.

[3] In the *Carl Zeiss* case the House was told that a question of Britain's treaty obligations was involved. The House did not apply the well-known principles relating to the interpretation of treaties, which, incidentally, are not different from those applicable to any international or diplomatic document.

[4] *The Law of Nations* (6th ed., 1963, by Waldock), p. 325, approved by Judge Jessup, in the *South West African Cases*, [1966] I.C.J. Reports 353.

far from plain. Even if, in such circumstances, one were inclined to submit an international pronouncement of great
weight to a strictly literal interpretation, it could not be so
restrictively construed as to attribute to it only a political con-
notation and to negative any intention to bear upon the legal
status of the Federal Republic.[1] The words clearly indicate an
identifiable legal effect. Nor does the Declaration express
merely a right of political or diplomatic representation.[2] Such
a view ignores that part of the Declaration which renders the
Government of the Federal Republic 'the only German
Government'. It also unduly limits what a government may do
when it is allowed to 'speak'; even treaties may, as we know,
be concluded by word of mouth.[3] For this reason it would also
be wrong to follow Professor Virally in drawing a distinction
between 'speaking' and 'acting'[4]; speaking may constitute
acting.

It thus becomes necessary to inquire a little more deeply.
Among the few *travaux préparatoires* which have been published
and which the public international lawyer considers one of the
foremost aids to interpretation of treaties or instruments
analogous to treaties,[5] one finds an interesting Memorandum
submitted to the Department of State by its Legal Adviser on
13 July 1950, some two months before the date of the Declara-

---

[1] This is the view taken by Professor Virally, *Annuaire Français de Droit International* (1955), p. 31, at pp. 44, 45; similarly, Professor Pinto, Clunet (1959),
313, at pp. 317 et seq. Kunz, 'Identity of States under International Law', *A.J.I.L.*,
(1955), 68, and ibid., at p. 210, denies that the Federal Republic is identical with
the *Reich*, and asserts that it is a new State which is a successor to the *Reich*. But he
examines only a very small part of the documentary material that throws light on
the problem.

[2] This, however, was the view that was taken in the *Carl Zeiss* case by Lord
Hodson, at p. 930, and by Lord Wilberforce, at p. 974, Lords Reid, Guest, and
Upjohn agreeing with the former. It is perhaps convenient at this point to explain
that the whole of the respondents' argument on what was called their 'third point'
proceeded without any interruption, without any question being asked and without any point being put by the House. The appellants were not called upon to reply
to it. Accordingly, it was impossible to know how the House would deal with the
matter, and to present any argument designed to influence judicial reasoning. The
reasons eventually given were not adumbrated during the argument.

[3] See Oppenheim (8th ed., 1955, by Lauterpacht), i.898.

[4] Above, n. 1, at p. 44.

[5] See, e.g., Brierley, op. cit., Judge Jessup (above, p. 684, n. 4), at p. 352, and
Art. 28 of the International Law Commission's Draft Articles on the Law of
Treaties (1966).

tion.[1] It concludes with the statement that in the view of the
Three Powers 'the Government of the Federal Republic is the
one and only legitimate Government qualified to speak for the
German people. The existence of the Eastern German Govern-
ment is not recognized as legitimate.' The Memorandum leaves
no doubt about the fact that the Government of the Federal
Republic 'may be considered as the Government of Germany'.
A very knowledgeable German author[2] suggests that the De-
claration was intended to affirm the identity of Germany and the
Federal Republic. Furthermore, great weight attaches to the
conclusions reached by two exceptionally well-informed
English observers, Messrs. Bathurst and Simpson, who state[3]

that the reunification of Germany remains a fundamental goal of policy. It
would be wholly inconsistent with this to say that the division of Germany
had been accepted as permanent, and therefore premature to regard either
the Federal Republic or East Germany as States distinct from each other.
They must each be regarded as parts of one continuing German State. Of
that German State the NATO Powers regard the Federal Government as
the representative in international affairs, with the obvious though not
always expressed reservations that it can so act only in so far as the territorial limitations on its competence permit. . . .

Finally, there is a piece of evidence which in almost compelling
words explains the effect of the Declaration. It is a letter written
on 23 October 1950 to the Federal Chancellor by the Allied
High Commissioners, Sir Ivone Kirkpatrick, M. André
François-Poncet and Mr. John J. McCloy[4]:

The Three Governments hold that, at the moment when the Federal
Republic assumes responsibility for the conduct of its foreign relations, the
status of the obligations resting upon it in its relations with foreign countries
should be clarified. The Three Governments regard the Federal Government as the only German Government which can speak for Germany and
represent the German people in international affairs pending the reunification of Germany. They consider, therefore, that pending a final peace
settlement and without prejudice to its terms, the Federal Government is the
only Government entitled to assume the rights and fulfil the obligations of
the former German *Reich*.

The last few words, 'the only Government entitled to assume
the rights and fulfil the obligations of the former German

---

[1] The full text of Mr. Raymond's Memorandum is printed in Whiteman, *Digest
of International Law*, ii.795.
[2] Ellinor von Puttkamer (above, p. 683, n. 1), at p. 466.
[3] Above, p. 660, n. 3, at p. 194.    [4] Cmd. 8252, at p. 5.

*Reich*', do seem to indicate that the Federal Republic is, or stands in the shoes of or represents, Germany to the exclusion of all other contenders.

The public international lawyer, however, will not be satisfied with even so pregnant a commentary, but will prefer to assess the meaning of the Declaration in the light of available evidence about its implementation, the States' subsequent conduct being another valuable tool of interpretation that public international law sanctions.[1]

(1) The first and best known piece of evidence arises from the undoubted existence of only one single German nationality.[2] All Germans, including those resident outside its frontiers, are recognized and accepted as such by the Federal Republic; in particular, those who succeed in escaping from the Soviet Zone to the West are Germans, and this is unlikely to be affected by the attempt made in February 1967 to create a separate East German nationality. Such refugees have the constitutionally guaranteed right to establishment in the Federal Republic.[3] Persons naturalized in the Soviet Zone are not recognized as Germans except in so far as the naturalization conforms to German Nationality Acts.[4] The Federal Republic is entitled to protect Germans abroad and is obliged to accept their return or otherwise take care of them; this right has in general not been denied to it,[5] this duty has always been acknowledged by it. There has never been any suggestion that a German lost his German nationality as a result of the creation of the Federal Republic[6]; had there been a succession such a loss would have occurred in numerous instances. All these features point to a state of continuity between Germany and the Federal Republic.

(2) The problem of the effect of treaties concluded by

---

[1] It is rejected by English municipal law, but accepted by public international law; see Art. 27 (3) (b) of the Draft Articles referred to above, p. 685, n. 5. The dangers to which English judges are exposed if, unaided, they undertake to construe international documents are bound to be serious.

[2] Federal Supreme Court, *BGHStr* 5, 317; also *NJW* (1954), 651, and Int. L.R. 43 (23 February 1954), where the existence of only one State is asserted.

[3] Federal Constitutional Court, *BVerfG* 2, 266 (7 May 1953).

[4] See above, n. 2.

[5] Though, in so far as consuls of the Federal Republic are concerned, the United States has taken the position that they are not authorized to act on behalf of German nationals residing in Eastern Germany: *A.J.I.L.* (1963), 410.

[6] It was decided at an early date that German nationality continued to exist after 5 June 1945: *R. v. Bottrill, ex parte Kuechenmeister*, [1947] K. B. 41.

Germany before the war is bedevilled by a certain confusion between two entirely different questions. The first is whether, as a result of the outbreak of war, a treaty came to an end or its operation was interrupted and whether, therefore, in and after 1949 it required reinstatement. In relation to neutral countries this question could not arise and as regards other countries, it was solved by a procedure which made it possible to 'give effect' to the treaties.[1] There is, secondly, the question whether a treaty to which Germany was a party continued to be or, if revived, was binding upon the Federal Republic.

On the latter question which alone is material to the present discussion significant pronouncements were made by courts which had to decide whether the Hague Convention on Civil Procedure of 1905 was still in force. As early as 1 December 1945 the Court of Appeal in Zürich[2] was faced with the problem and at that time had no difficulty in holding that Germany was in existence and, consequently, the Convention in force. In 1952 the Swiss Federal Tribunal was called upon to decide the point.[3] It held that the Federal Republic was intended not to be 'a new West German State, but rather to reorganize the existing German State to the extent permitted by the occupying States. Accordingly ... earlier treaties concluded with Germany continue to be in force in relation to the Federal Republic.' Also in 1952 the District Court at Rotterdam reached the same result again on the ground that the Federal Republic 'was not a new State; it was the continuation of the German State which existed previously and had never ceased to exist'.[4] Shortly afterwards, under the new procedure for the reinstatement of old treaties, the Convention of 1905 was put into force again by an exchange of Notes. This caused the Dutch Supreme Court to state in 1958[5] that the Convention had 'again become operative between the Netherlands and the German Federal Republic, the latter being the continuation under international law of the former German *Reich*'.

---

[1] For details, see Peischke, 'Reactivation of Prewar German Treaties', *A.J.I.L.* (1954), 245; Bathurst and Simpson (above, p. 660, n. 3), at pp. 108, 117.

[2] *Schweizerische Juristenzeitung* (1946), 89; also *Annual Digest* (1946), 187.

[3] *BGE* 78 i.124; also Int. L.R. (1952), 31. In the same sense Court of Appeal in Berlin (West), *IPRspr.* (1954–5), No. 186 (6 February 1955).

[4] *N.J.* (1952), No. 327; also Int. L.R. (1952), 29 (*Gevato* v. *Deutsche Bank*).

[5] *N.J.* (1958), No. 304; also 26 Int. L.R. 577 (*Re Swane*).

The United Kingdom, in particular, exchanged Notes with the Federal Republic as a result of which more than thirty treaties 'concluded between the German *Reich* and the United Kingdom of Great Britain and Northern Ireland are, as from 1 January 1953 again to be applied in relation to the Federal Republic, and the United Kingdom'.[1] It seems to be a widely held impression that the use of the word 'again', as the whole process of reinstatement, was intended to recognize the idea of identity. In fact, no case has become known in which a State refused effect to a treaty on the ground of the Federal Republic not being the contracting party. Nor is any case known in which the Federal Republic denied being bound by a pre-war treaty with Germany. A multitude of treaties is in existence, which had been concluded by Germany before the war and to which the Federal Republic is now a party.

(3) There is, thirdly, the fact that the Federal Republic has accepted liability for the whole of Germany's foreign debts by reason of and with reference to the Declaration of New York. In this connection it does not matter whether it has assumed or 'confirmed' liability.[2] On the other hand, it should be emphasized that the scope and extent of the liability was at no time curtailed on account of part of Germany being outside the Federal Republic's control. It is helpful to dwell for a moment upon these aspects, for if, as appears to be the case, vast sums (in fact, it is understood, more than 5,000m. DM, or about £450m.) were extracted from the Federal Republic in express reliance upon its identity with Germany, it is a little difficult in other respects to refuse recognition of the consequences of such identity.

The question of the Federal Republic's liability for the foreign debts of the *Reich* was raised within four days of the New York Declaration. On 23 September 1950 the three High Commissioners gave Dr. Adenauer 'a detailed report' of the

---

[1] It has not been possible to find the Notes and their English text. The words in the text above are translated from the German version in *Bundesgesetzblatt* (1953), ii.116, 593.

[2] The letter of 23 October 1950 (referred to above, p. 686, n. 4), asked the Federal Republic to 'assume' responsibility. By the reply of 6 March 1951 (below, p. 690, n. 8), the Federal Republic 'confirms' its liability. Bathurst and Simpson (above, p. 660, n. 3), at p. 189, rightly regard the change of words as insignificant.

New York Conference.[1] They stated, *inter alia*, that before 'the modifications decided on in New York could be put into effect, the three Foreign Ministers expected the Federal Republic to assume' certain obligations, in particular 'to acknowledge German pre-war debts. . . . There was no reason whatsoever to assume that the Federal Republic was going to be asked for astronomical sums. It was more a matter of recognizing a principle that had always obtained in international law and which maintained the continuity between a political régime and its successor.'[2] On the following day the American High Commissioner, Mr. McCloy, visited Dr. Adenauer to give 'some additional information on the course of the New York Foreign Ministers' Conference'.[3] Dr. Adenauer reports[4]:

McCloy then commented on the resolution of the New York Foreign Ministers' Conference expressly recognizing the Federal Government as the only legitimate Government in Germany. According to McCloy it followed from this that the Federal Government had the exclusive right to assume the rights and obligations of the former German *Reich*. . . .

Dr. Adenauer 'agreed with the Foreign Ministers' demand for an acknowledgement of earlier foreign debts'.[5] On 23 October 1950 the Allied High Commissioners addressed to Dr. Adenauer a formal communication the essential passage of which has already been quoted[6] and which concluded[7] with the request that

The Three Governments would appreciate receiving a formal assurance from the Federal Government that it regards itself as responsible for the pre-war external debt of the German *Reich*. . . .

Accordingly, on 6 March 1951 Dr. Adenauer's reply stated as follows[8]:

The Federal Republic hereby confirms that it is liable for the pre-war external debt of the German *Reich*, including those debts of other corporate bodies subsequently to be declared liabilities of the *Reich*, as well as for interest and other charges on securities of the Government of Austria to the extent that such interests and charges became due after 12 March 1938, and before 8 May 1945.

The details relating to the discharge of these liabilities were

---

[1] Adenauer, *Memoirs 1945–1953* (English ed. by Weidenfeld and Nicolson, London, 1965), p. 285.
[2] Ibid., at p. 287.      [3] Ibid., at p. 289.
[4] Ibid., at p. 290.      [5] Ibid., at p. 291.      [6] Above, p. 686.
[7] Cmd. 8252, at pp. 5–7.      [8] Ibid., at p. 8; also Cmnd. 626, at p. 156.

embodied in the Agreement on German External Debts concluded in London on 27 February 1953.[1]

Since then the Federal Republic's liability for the foreign obligations of the *Reich* and, consequently, the doctrine of continuity has received further emphasis as a result of the fact that the Federal Republic has entered into treaties with certain States, in particular with the United Kingdom,[2] whereby it undertook to pay substantial sums for the benefit of persons 'who were victims of National-Socialist measures of persecution and who, as a result of such measures, suffered loss of liberty or damage to their health, or, in the case of those who died in consequence of such measures, for the benefit of their dependants'. The evidence provided by these treaties is particularly telling in that the Federal Republic has always proclaimed its refusal to enter into such a treaty with any State, such as Yugoslavia, which does not recognize its identity with Germany.[3] It may well be suggested that the mere conclusion of such a treaty precludes any liberty to challenge the doctrine of identity.

## V

If Germany still exists and survives in the Federal Republic whose Government represents it, and if, in the eyes of the West, the 'German Democratic Republic' does not in law have any existence as a State at all, then the conclusion is inescapable that the territories in fact controlled by the 'German Democratic Republic' are still German and still form part of Germany. In other words the necessary legal consequence, purpose, and meaning of the refusal to recognize the 'German Democratic Republic' is that Germany is still a single, undivided, unitary State. It has not suffered any dismemberment or loss of territory. As Messrs. Bathurst and Simpson said in 1955, West and East Germany 'must be regarded as parts of one continuing German State'.[4] And as the same authors report, the Interpretative Minute of 1955 stated that the arrangements then made rested 'on the premise that the

---

[1] Cmd. 626.     [2] Cmd. 2388 (9 June 1964).
[3] See the statement set forth in the report by Buschbeck, 26 *ZaöVR* (1966), 140, n. 269.
[4] At p. 194.

German State continues to exist'. Nothing has occurred since
that affects this judgment. The point can be tested by asking
who could possibly have acquired sovereignty over the Eastern
territories. Certainly not the 'German Democratic Republic',
for it does not exist as a State. Certainly not the Soviet Union,
for not even the Four Allies jointly annexed Germany in 1945
and neither the Soviet Union nor its Commander-in-Chief,
even if they had been entitled to do so, ever purported to
assume sovereignty. Therefore, no State other than Germany
can lay claim or title to the Eastern territories. So long as the
present Western policy continues, one cannot get away from
the fundamental conclusion that there exists in law a single
German State which is represented by the Federal Republic.

This is contrary to the view held in the East, where the
recognition of the 'German Democratic Republic' inevitably
led to what has become known as the dual-State theory: Germany is now divided into two States.[1]

In these circumstances, it is not easy to assess the significance
of the view, recently expressed in England and already noted,
that the Soviet Union was and still is 'the *de jure* sovereign' or
the '*de jure* governing authority' in the Soviet Zone.[2] The
difficulties are not lessened by further observations such as this:
'Germany is, for the time being at least, divided; the Federal
Republic being sovereign in West Germany, and the U.S.S.R.
having sovereign authority in the Eastern zone.'[3] Or 'the two
parts of Germany are at present under different sovereignties:
they have separate legal systems and are separate jurisdictions'.[4]
And again: 'There are in the two parts of Germany two separate legal systems operating independently of one another, the
East German courts deriving their authority from the sovereignty of the U.S.S.R. and the West German courts from the
sovereignty which lies in the Federal Republic of Germany as
at present constituted.'[5] It also follows that the Federal Supreme

---

[1] On this view, see, in particular, the literature mentioned above, p. 660,
n. 2, with many further references. Such references are also to be found in 20
*ZaöVR* (1960), 124, n. 126. The only author in the West who supports the Soviet
thesis is Pinto, Clunet (1959), 313, at pp. 345–67. He is one of those authors who
reasons *a priori*, but neglects international documents and the attitude of States.

[2] Above, p. 675, n. 2.    [3] Lord Reid, at p. 920.

[4] Lord Reid, at p. 923.

[5] Lord Hodson, at p. 930, who at p. 925 speaks of the U.S.S.R. 'having *de jure*
sovereignty over the so-called German Democratic Republic'.

Court is subjected to criticism when it takes 'the view that Germany is still one country',[1] and when it refuses to accept an East German decision as one 'of a foreign court as to its own law'.[2] The authors of all these phrases are known to observe the highest accuracy of formulation, so that lack of terminological precision must be ruled out as an explanation.[3] If, rejecting any guidance from the Foreign Office, they treat Germany as divided in law, this is only explicable by reference to the legally indefensible assumption that the Soviet Union became the sovereign of East Germany.

# VI

There is, then, on the one hand, the Federal Republic enjoying the full authority of a sovereign State and recognized as being the reorganization of or another name for or identical with or continuing or at least exclusively representing the still existing Germany as a whole, and, on the other hand, the 'German Democratic Republic', unrecognized as a State or government or a mere local authority, lifeless in spite of Soviet influence and in spite of factual control over large territories which still belong to the undivided Germany and have never passed into any other nation's sovereignty. What is the relationship between the Federal Republic and that ill-defined organization in the East?

It is submitted that, notwithstanding certain variations presently to be mentioned, the answer can be found if resort is had to a somewhat analogous situation. In relation to Germany as a whole, now continued by the Federal Republic, the 'German Democratic Republic' is an insurgent régime, just as during the American Civil War the Confederate States were insurgents in relation to the Union. The essential features permitting the analogy are that the East is under the control of a régime opposed to the continuing State of Germany which has not recognized it and which has proclaimed, in conformity with

---

[1] Lord Reid, at p. 922 (italics supplied).

[2] Lord Reid, at p. 924.

[3] The conclusions which were built upon the views mentioned in the text were that an English Court had to apply East German law without regard to the law of Germany as continued by the Federal Republic or as represented by the Federal Government. On this point, see below, p. 699.

its fourteen Western partners, a peaceful policy of reunification. The East does not accept the sovereignty or even the
existence of Germany and in this sense has purported to secede
from Germany which is still the sovereign of all German
territories.[1] The analogy, however, is not complete.

The Federal Republic does not exercise control over nor can
it govern or legislate for the Soviet Zone. Such a right which,
incidentally, has never been claimed or exercised is for international purposes expressly denied to the Federal Republic by
an unpublished Interpretative Minute communicated to it
together with the Declaration of New York in 1950.[2] It stated
that the Declaration was based on the continuing existence of
the German State; that the recognition of the Federal Republic
had a provisional character in that it had effect only pending
the peaceful reunification of Germany; and that, therefore, the
Government of the Federal Republic was not recognized as the
*de jure* government of all Germany. This means that the Federal
Government cannot act in regard to the Soviet Zone, whether
by legislation, by administrative acts, or otherwise. While the
United States could in law exercise its constitutional rights over
the Confederate States during the insurgency, the Federal
Government is without similar powers. It is only in international affairs that the Federal Government has the sole right
of speaking for and representing Germany as a whole, both
West and East. The distinction which the arrangements of
1950 thus draw between national and international affairs will
require some consideration.

As regards the converse side of the picture, namely, the effect
which the legislation of the insurgents has outside the Soviet
Zone, this is in no way determined by the territorially limited
status and powers of the Federal Government. The fact that
the Federal Government cannot so govern in the Soviet Zone

---

[1] It seems that this view was first alluded to by Scheuner, *Deutsches Verwaltungsblatt* (1950), p. 515. It was developed by Marschall von Biberstein (above, p. 660,
n. 2), at pp. 161 et seq. As Lord Reid mentions, at p. 904, in the *Carl Zeiss* case,
*ubi supra*, it was argued that the case was 'analogous to cases where subjects of an
existing sovereign have rebelled and have succeeded in gaining control of a part of
the old sovereign's dominions'. The argument was rejected, because the House
interpreted the Foreign Secretary's Certificate as meaning that the German Democratic Republic derived, and could derive, 'its authority and status from the Government of the U.S.S.R.'. This was probably a misinterpretation (above, p. 675, n. 4).

[2] For the text, see Bathurst and Simpson (above, p. 660, n. 3), at p. 188.

as to exercise there internationally recognized control does not mean that the (insurgent) Government in the Soviet Zone can so govern there as to secure, outside the Soviet Zone, recognition of its governing authority. Or, to put it more succinctly, the inability of the Federal Republic to govern in the East does not, logically or in practical effect, imply the ability of the East to have its legislation recognized in the Federal Republic or in the West in general. These are two entirely different sides of the coin which have not always been distinguished.[1] Normally both sides produce a parallelism of results. In the present case they fail to do so, because the Western family of nations has created a novel and unusual structure. If closely analysed it produces, however, a fairly clear picture to the assembly of which it is now possible to turn.

(1) In 1949 the attitude of the Federal Republic could have been that it refused to give any recognition to the institutions, the law or the acts of the 'German Democratic Republic' or of those acting in its name. Only the old law and the officials appointed by the pre-1949 régime would have been recognized. Such a solution could have been supported by constitutional considerations and would not have been contrary to public international law, for the latter has no bearing upon relations between various parts of a single State. Yet it would have been an unwise, unjust, and unworkable solution. It would have meant, for instance, that a marriage performed by a newly appointed registrar would have been invalid, that a will made in accordance with some new provisions of a Wills Act would not have been recognized, that a power of attorney authenticated by a county court judge appointed by the new régime

---

[1] In particular, in the *Carl Zeiss* case, *ubi supra*, Lord Hodson, at p. 929, and Lord Wilberforce, at p. 974, failed to do so. They believed that the Declaration of New York could be construed by means of the fact that the Federal Government is not the Government of the East. However, the Federal Government's status in Germany in general and in the East in particular is in no way conclusive in regard to the entirely different question of its standing in relation to foreign countries. That the Federal Government does not in law or in fact exercise control in the East does not preclude foreign governments from recognizing, in its relationship with them, the Federal Government as entitled to *represent* Germany, including the East. They might well prefer that their dealings with Germany as a whole will be conducted only through the Federal Republic. Whether this is so or not cannot in logic be decided by the status which the Federal Government does not enjoy inside Germany.

would have been ineffective.¹ Such results are so absurd that the total rejection of East German legal activity could not reasonably be contemplated.

Another solution would have involved the adoption of those principles which the Supreme Court of the United States developed during and after the Civil War,² which now dominate this branch of constitutional (not international) law and have only recently again been illustrated in Southern Rhodesia.³ They mean that where private rights arise within the territory controlled by insurgents and the public policy of the parent State is not infringed, effect may be given to the insurgents' legislative and other acts. The details which have been worked out in the course of a very elaborate judicial practice in the United States need not be pursued here, but it is clear that, however difficult it may be in a given case to draw the line,⁴

---

¹ cf. the remarkable decision in *Re Luks Estate*, 256 N.Y.S. 2d 194 (1965).

² For general statements and numerous references, see Lauterpacht, *Recognition* (1947), p. 146; Wengler, 'Fragen der Faktizität und Legitimität,' in *Festschrift für Lewald* (1953), p. 615. The principal cases are *Texas* v. *White*, 7 Wall. 700 (1868); *Thorington* v. *Smith*, 8 Wall. 1 (1868); *Delmas* v. *Merchants National Insurance*, 14 Wall. 661 (1871); *United States* v. *Insurance Companies*, 22 Wall. 99 (1874); *Williams* v. *Bruffy*, 96 U.S. 176 (1878); *Ford* v. *Surget*, 97 U.S. 604 (1879); *Baldy* v. *Hunter*, 171 U.S. 388 (1898).

³ See *Madzimbamuto* v. *Lardner-Burke*, [1969] A. C. 645.

⁴ The effectiveness of the law of 1952 by which the Council of Gera was set up, and which fell to be considered in the *Carl Zeiss* case, has never been considered in the Federal Republic. It is, however, plain that it is a highly political law designed to intensify Communist organization in the East. It would be a matter for detailed examination whether the principles invoked by the Supreme Court of the United States would permit or require the application of such a law outside the insurgents' territory. The law of 1952 has not been published in any report. It may be helpful to indicate its character by setting forth at least its Preamble:

'The task of ensuring the further democratic and industrial advance of the German Democratic Republic necessitates the linking so far as possible of the executive public authorities with the population and a broader integration of workers in the management of the State.

The system of administrative structure originating from Imperial Germany, consisting of states with their own state governments and large territories, does not assure a solution of the new tasks of our State.

The State of the Old Germany had nothing to do with the management of industry, since the factories, works, and mines as well as the banks belonged to a few large capitalists who profited by the exploitation of the workers. The new, truly democratic State of the German Democratic Republic, which has made an end of exploitation by large capitalists, manages with the authority of the people the industry which has become nationalized property and which serves the interests of the people.

The old German State of large capitalists and landowners, who deliberately

the exception is broad rather than narrow and provides relatively firm guidance.[1] The courts of the Federal Republic, however, have only recently shown a slight tendency to follow this line of approach. So far this seems to have occurred only in connection with the incredibly difficult problem of the effect which in the Federal Republic may be attributed to decrees of divorce pronounced in the Soviet Zone by virtue of a Marriage and Divorce Act of 1955 which radically differs from West German law and incorporates many Communist ideas. Such a decree will not be recognized in the Federal Republic if the respondent spouse is resident there, refused to accept the East German decree and could not have been divorced under West German law.[2] This principle is derived from the idea that while in general East German law is not entitled to recognition in

---

barred the working classes, endeavoured to keep the people out of politics and to exclude them from day-to-day participation in matters of State.

The new socialist State of the German Democratic Republic on the other hand will only become an invincible force if it remains in close touch with the working classes and if it draws the workers into politics and leads the people to a permanent, systematic, active, and decisive participation in the management of the State.

Therefore, the old administrative structure even with the alterations effected after 1945 has now become an obstacle to new advancement. The executive public authorities must, therefore, be so reorganized as to afford the State machinery the possibility of complying inviolably with the will of the workers, as expressed in the laws of the German Democratic Republic, and of carrying out a policy for the working classes based on the initiative of the masses.

The territorial sphere of activity of the local executive public authorities must therefore be regulated in such a way that these Authorities can fully carry out the management of industrial and cultural development. The effective guidance and control of subordinate authorities by superior ones as well as by the people themselves must be assured. Thereby our State, one of the most important instruments for the development of Socialism in our country, will be strengthened.

Having regard to the foregoing the People's Chamber of the German Democratic Republic has passed the following law: . . .'

[1] The remarks made in the *Carl Zeiss* case by Lord Reid and Wilberforce (pp. 907, 954) about the scope of the exception are perhaps in need of some clarification. There is in the first place the question whether the non-recognition of a State or government in public international law involves the non-recognition of such State's or government's legislation; it seems that the House has confirmed the affirmative answer given in such cases as *Luther* v. *Sagor*, [1921] 1 K. B. 456. There was, secondly, the question whether that principle of public international law was subject to any exceptions. Whether and to what extent they exist is an obscure question. If and in so far as they do exist, they seem to be derived from the analogy provided by constitutional law as developed in the United States and referred to in the text. These constitutional principles are much less obscure.

[2] See the three great decisions of 30 November 1960, *BGHZ* 34, 134; 28 March 1962, *BGHZ* 38, 1; 14 July 1964, *BGHZ* 42, 99.

the West, for reasons of justice it will be recognized if and in so far as it does not cause injustice and can be applied without 'violation of the responsibility towards Germany as a whole, which, according to its Basic Law, the Federal Republic as the State representing Germany accepts'.[1] Here one has the possibly fertile germ of a rule of constitutional law which recalls memorable American precedents.

On the whole, however, and perhaps on occasions a little unhappily, judicial practice in the Federal Republic has followed a different route. When suddenly faced with the problem in 1949, the courts followed those who suggested[2] a solution based upon the analogy of conflict rules. Thus, on the basis of private international law, there arose a system of inter-zonal law. It was developed by decisions which by 1961 came to not less than 1,300 and are collected in six substantial volumes.[3] The effect was that much East German law, created after 1949, was recognized and applied in the Federal Republic, subject only to such exceptions as *ordre public* requires.

It must, however, be emphasized that the Federal Republic did not at any time abandon its fundamental assumption that the Soviet Zone formed part of a single and undivided Germany and is German territory.[4] Accordingly, there is, for instance, no room for extradition proceedings, but, in the manner usual in Germany, courts assist each other in the administration of criminal justice[5]; judgments rendered by courts in the Eastern zone are German, not foreign judgments[6]; orders for the

---

[1] The last few words are taken from *BGHZ* 42, 99, at p. 105. See already Federal Constitutional Court, *BVerfG* 4, 171.

[2] They included, in particular, Ernst Wolff, 'Probleme des Interlokalen Privatrechts', *Festschrift für Raape* (1948), p. 181, and Ficker, *Grundfragen des deutschen interlokalen Rechts* (1952). Since then a vast number of academic contributions have discussed the problem. There are, in particular, some very valuable articles by Professor Wengler. These, and much additional material, are referred to by Drobnig, 'Die entsprechende Anwendung des Internationalen Privatrechts auf das Interzonale Recht Deutschlands', *Jahrbuch für Ostrecht* (1961), 31, one of the most recent and most illuminating discussions of the subject. Inter-zonal law, though derived from private international law, has had a fertile influence on its parentage.

[3] They are called 'Interzonale Rechtsprechung,' abbreviated as IzRspr.

[4] See, generally, Wengler, 'Deutschland als Rechtsbegriff,' *Festschrift für Nawiasky* (1956), p. 49, and Federal Supreme Court, *NJW* (1955), 271 (28 October 1954).

[5] *BVerfG* 1, 333; also *NJW* (1952), 1129 (13 June 1952).

[6] Federal Supreme Court, *BGHZ* 20, 3; 134, at pp. 136, 139, where, however, it is also said that for the purposes of section 606 of the Code of Civil Procedure the

custody of children made in the East are German orders enforceable in the West[1]; conflicts are solved, not by private international law, but by inter-zonal law.[2]

(2) When the relationship between the Federal Republic and the Soviet Zone falls to be considered outside the territory of the former, particularly in England, the starting-point should be free from doubt. Germany still exists as an undivided and unitary State. It is represented by the Federal Republic. If, therefore, the British Government wishes to communicate with Germany or if an English Court has to apply German law, it looks to the Federal Republic, its institutions, its organs, its law. It cannot turn to the 'German Democratic Republic', which has no legal existence. The British Government is entirely consistent when it feels unable to accept a Memorandum addressed to it by the 'German Democratic Republic'. Similarly, the courts, when required to apply the law of Germany, cannot directly apply the law at present prevailing in the Eastern zone, for Her Majesty's judges, let it be repeated,[3] surely cannot look at texts which cannot even be tendered to Her Majesty's Government.

If an English Court applies the law of Germany as represented by the Federal Republic, it may find that the latter refers to East German law. Effect must be given to such a reference. It means that in an English Court East German law is applicable if and in so far and in the same sense as it is recognized and applied by the courts of the Federal Republic, this being the State in which Germany as a whole now survives and which, therefore, is alone qualified to determine the nature, meaning, and effect of German law. If and in so far as it recognizes Eastern law as German law, an English Court can and will apply it. In this matter, therefore, the Declaration of New York fills what would otherwise be 'a legal vacuum'[4] in the

Soviet Zone is foreign territory; Federal Supreme Court, *BGHSt* 20, 5 (19 August 1964).

[1] *BGHZ* 21, 306 (14 July 1956).

[2] See, for instance, Kegel, *Internationales Privatrecht* (1964), p. 14; Raape, *Internationales Privatrecht* (1961), p. 152; and many others.

[3] See above, pp. 673, 674 and 678.

[4] Lord Wilberforce in the *Carl Zeiss* case, *ubi supra*, at p. 953. As the opening remarks of Lord Upjohn's opinion make clear (p. 840), the fear of 'a legal vacuum' had considerable influence.

Eastern zone, and protects an English Court against the invidious necessity for implementing Communist legal policy in a
manner inconsistent with German law.[1] One reaches the same
result if one starts from the more familiar situation that arises
from time to time in private international law. Inside a unitary
State with a legal system which, on the whole, is unitary, such
as France, Italy, or Switzerland, there may exist local variations in specific respects. The English judge would apply French,
Italian, or Swiss law. He would apply the law of the region or
locality in question if and to the extent that the law of the
unitary State so requires or permits.

Thus, suppose an English Court has to apply the rules of
intestacy prevailing in the country of the intestate's domicile of
origin. Suppose he was born at Leipzig. So long as the Eastern
zone forms part of Germany, so long as Germany is undivided,
the English Court should take the view that the domicile of
origin was German, not East German.[2] It will apply, therefore,
German law, i.e. the law prevailing in the Federal Republic,
including its 'inter-zonal' law. It may find that the law of the
Federal Republic allows the law prevailing at Leipzig to
govern. In such event the English Court, too, will apply the
Leipzig law. But it will not directly apply Leipzig law without
reference to the law of the sovereign of Leipzig, who continues
to be Germany as represented by the Federal Republic.

Or suppose a husband, now domiciled at Leipzig, obtains
there a decree of divorce from his wife who lives in England. It
is pronounced by a judge appointed, and by virtue of a law

---

[1] In the *Carl Zeiss* case the House of Lords followed a different course. The
fundamental assumption which led to this result was that 'Germany is, for the
time being at least, divided, the Federal Republic being sovereign in West Germany, and the U.S.S.R. having sovereign authority in the Eastern zone' (Lord
Reid, at p. 920). If in accordance with the submissions made in this paper Germany is treated as a single State and if the Federal Republic is identical with or
representing Germany, then it is plainly inevitable to conclude that the law of
the Federal Republic has to be applied in an English Court. It is the express or
implied denial of both or either of those conditions that is at the root of the decision in the *Carl Zeiss* case. It is possible that Münch, Clunet (1962), 7; *JZ*
(1967), 7, advocating the fiction of 'partial occupation,' would differ from the
view put forward in this paper.

[2] There has been much discussion of the question what becomes of the domicile
of origin in the event of a change of sovereignty. See Dicey (7th ed., 1958), p. 87.
The point does not arise in the present connection, because the sovereignty has not
changed.

enacted, by the 'German Democratic Republic'. The decree is valid in England to the extent to which it is recognized in the Federal Republic.

Or suppose that one of the State-owned corporations formed in East Germany brings an action in England. Is it precluded from doing so on the ground that the law creating it was enacted by the 'German Democratic Republic'? An English Court should find the answer in the law of Germany, i.e. in the law applied in the Federal Republic. This is very likely to recognize the creation of the corporation.[1]

In all these and similar cases the Federal Government acts as Germany's international representative. It does not matter, therefore, that it is not the *de jure* government of all Germany.[2]

The proposed solution would avoid results which would or could be not only unjust, but also embarrassing to this country and which may conveniently be exemplified by a reference to a hypothetical case occurring during the American Civil War in which, it will be remembered, the Confederate States were recognized by Britain as belligerents. Suppose that in a case arising in Virginia the English Courts had decided a question of federal law in accordance with the decision of a court set up by the Confederate Government in Virginia, but contrary to a decision of the United States Supreme Court. The Government of the Union would have been unlikely to welcome such an attitude on the part of the English Court. Now suppose that Her Majesty's Government had undertaken by treaty to consider the Government of the Union as the only American Government and to deny any international status to the Government of the Confederacy. If, in such circumstances, effect would have been given to the Virginian decision, a situation comparable to that created by the famous case of the *Alabama* could easily have arisen.

Finally, it should be pointed out that in English municipal

---

[1] For this reason the result reached in *Upright* v. *Mercury Business Machines Co.*, 213 N.Y.S. 2d 417 (1961), also 32 Int. L.R. 65, merits approval.

[2] The broad result of the suggestions made in the text would seem to be satisfactory. In particular, they avoid some of the dangers which troubled the House of Lords in the *Carl Zeiss* case, and to which Lord Upjohn at pp. 940, 941, gave frank and eloquent expression. On the other hand, they would have compelled the House of Lords to follow the decision of the Federal Supreme Court reported *IzRspr.* (1960–1), No. 52, and on this ground to dismiss the appeal.

law the effects of the non-recognition of a State or government may be different and much more far-reaching; it may be that, subject to ill-defined exceptions, an English Court cannot apply the legislation of a non-recognized State or government at all.[1] This question is outside the scope of the present observations, which are exclusively concerned with public international law. They are designed to show the limits within which, in the case of Germany, public international law confines the application of East German law. It is open to a State to draw those limits more narrowly, and it is possible that England has done so.

(3) There remains the question whether the Federal Republic has any power to conclude treaties with effect for the East. In principle, the answer must be in the negative. The Federal Government, it is true, has the sole right to represent Germany as a whole in international affairs, and this, *prima facie*, includes the right to enter into treaties. But the Federal Government is not the Government in the East. It is, therefore, unable to render treaties effective in respect of the East. Hence, it cannot conclude treaties which require implementation in the East. Nor, it appears, has the Federal Republic ever attempted to do so.

It is an entirely different question whether the Federal Republic is entitled to make treaty arrangements which have effect, but do not require any governmental action, in the East. This was the real point that arose in a case decided by the Supreme Court of Oregon.[2] German nationals resident in the East claimed to be entitled to succeed to the estate of an Oregon intestate. Since the Treaty of Friendship, Commerce, and Navigation concluded in 1954 between the United States of America and the Federal Republic was expressed to extend

---

[1] See *Luther* v. *Sagor & Co.*, [1921] 1 K. B. 456; [1921] 3 K. B. 532, as approved by the House of Lords in the case of *Carl Zeiss Stiftung*. Whether, in the case of a non-recognized government (as opposed to the case of a non-recognized State), English municipal law does not go much too far is an open question: see above, pp. 411, 412; Greig, 83 *L.Q.R.* (1967), 96. This problem requires much further thought in the light of the doctrine referred to below, p. 705, n. 1, and of the very special standing and prestige enjoyed by English judges, which may make it more difficult to suggest the adoption of the Continental method of approach. There is also a clear but frequently overlooked distinction between the non-recognition of States and governments. The *Zeiss* case concerned the former.

[2] *Zschernig* v. *Miller*, 412 P. 2d 781 (1966).

only to the territory of the Federal Republic, the right of succession depended on the continuing validity in the East of Article IV of the Treaty of Friendship, Commerce, and Consular Rights concluded in 1923 between the United States and Germany. The Treaty of 1954 provides that it 'shall replace and terminate provisions in force in Articles I through V' of the Treaty of 1923.[1] Does this involve the abrogation of the Treaty of 1923 in regard to East Germany? This was a question of construction to be answered in the light of the New York Declaration of 1950. The Supreme Court of Oregon did not approach the problem in this way. Indeed it did not even refer to the Declaration of 1950. It held the Treaty of 1923 to be applicable to the East, primarily on the ground that this was the conclusion put forward, though left unexplained, by the Department of State. For present purposes, it is sufficient to submit that if, as a matter of construction, the High Contracting Parties intended to abrogate Article IV of the Treaty of 1923 with respect to the East, the Federal Republic was entitled to do so, for the abrogation of the Treaty did not require the exercise of any governmental authority in the East, but could be effected by virtue only of the Federal Government's sole right to Germany's representation in international affairs.

## VII

The foremost impression which the preceding discussions leave in one's mind is astonishment at the fact that after so long a time the important problem of Germany's status in public international law is in so many respects still so obscure. Why have governments almost invariably chosen language which seems to avoid legal precision? Why did governments fail to avail themselves of every opportunity of providing clarification and elaboration? Is it too late to hope for a short document in the nature of an Interpretative Minute to remedy prevailing defects?

In the present situation it is impossible to formulate conclusions with complete confidence, but the following suggestions are likely to summarize the picture as existing in public international law:

[1] Art. XXVIII.

(1) Germany still exists as a State.

(2) Germany is an undivided State comprising the territories controlled in the West by the Federal Republic and in the East by the 'German Democratic Republic'.

(3) (a) The status of the Federal Government as the only German Government and the only spokesman for Germany in international affairs is founded upon arrangements which since at least 1954 have the character of a treaty between the member States of the North Atlantic Treaty Organization.

(b) In Germany the rights, powers, and responsibilities of the Government of the Federal Republic are limited to the territory of the Federal Republic, so that the Federal Republic is not the *de jure* Government of Germany.

(c) For international purposes, it may be strongly suggested, Germany now survives or is identical with or is continued by the Federal Republic, so that the latter is nothing but another name for Germany. But Germany is in any event represented only by the Federal Government.

(4) The Soviet Commander-in-Chief acted *ultra vires* in purporting to transfer his rights, powers, and responsibilities to the 'German Democratic Republic' and the Soviet Union remains responsible for his acts as well as those of the 'German Democratic Republic'.

(5) The 'German Democratic Republic' is not recognized as a State or Government. It is strongly arguable that its recognition would require the consent of France, the United States of America, and the Federal Republic as well as of other member States of the North Atlantic Treaty Organization.

(6) The 'German Democratic Republic' cannot in substance and effect be recognized by deeming it to be a subordinate body of the Soviet Union which, as such, did not at any time have any rights in respect of its zone that were independent of the Four Governments.

(7) Acts performed in the name of the 'German Democratic Republic', such as the issue of a passport, the presentation of a diplomatic note or the enactment of legislation, cannot be rendered effective by deeming them to be performed or sanctioned by the Soviet Commander-in-Chief. Such a fiction would involve the violation of the Federal Government's

right of representation and also put the 'German Democratic Republic' on the same level as a recognized State.

(8) In the event of it being necessary outside Germany to refer to German law the law of Germany as surviving in the Federal Republic applies and decides whether, to what extent and in what sense law prevailing in the Eastern zone is internationally recognizable and applicable. In fact, a large part of the law enacted by the 'German Democratic Republic' is given effect in the Federal Republic and may, therefore, be applied outside Germany.

There remains a final, much less controversial word. The German problem touches upon numerous aspects of public international law. The law of belligerent occupation, the status of a non-recognized State, the effects of non-recognition upon governmental activities, the interpretation of international documents, the doctrine of the identity and continuity of States, the relationship of judiciary and executive in foreign affairs,[1] the notion of 'domicile' as well as some other aspects of the conflict of laws—these are only some of the broad headings which require reconsideration in the light of the German experience. If the present contribution had no other effect than to stimulate research into the manifold questions of general significance which are included within, yet far transcend the framework of the German problem, it would have served its purpose and justified the effort.

[1] This is of peculiar significance to the law of the United Kingdom, where the Judiciary and the Executive must not speak with two voices in international affairs. The reason is that the conduct of foreign relations is the prerogative of the Crown, and it is the Crown which, through its judges, dispenses justice: see Sir Francis Vallat, *International Law and the Practitioner* (Manchester, 1966), p. 55, and, generally, above, p. 391. The responsibility of an English judge who, in international affairs, fails to speak with the Sovereign's voice or even causes the Sovereign to commit a breach of treaty is, accordingly, particularly grave. The technique of applying for a Foreign Office Certificate is designed to guard against such dangers. For the reason given the undoubted independence of the British Judiciary would, in an international court, afford even less of a defence than in the case of the judges in other States. Cf. Lord McNair, *Law of Treaties* (1961), p. 346.

# INDEX